Internet Architecture and Innovation

Internet Architecture and Innovation

Barbara van Schewick

The MIT Press
Cambridge, Massachusetts
London, England

For information about special quantity discounts, email special_sales@mitpress.mit .edu.

Set in Stone Sans and Stone Serif by Toppan Best-set Premedia Limited. Printed and bound in the United States of America.

Library of Congress Cataloging-in-Publication Data

Van Schewick, Barbara.
Internet architecture and innovation / Barbara van Schewick.
  p. cm.
Includes bibliographical references and index.
ISBN 978-0-262-01397-0 (hardcover : alk. paper) 1. Internet. 2. Computer network architectures. 3. Technological innovations. 4. Business—Data processing. I. Title.
TK5105.875.I57V378   2010
004.6'5—dc22

                                                    2009037130

10   9   8   7   6   5   4   3   2

for Steffen, Lukas, and Daniel

Contents

Acknowledgments

Over the years, this work has been supported by many people. I am grateful to all of them. I'm immensely grateful to Dean Larry Kramer for his generous support of this project, and for helpful conversations and advice. Many colleagues kindly shared insights or advice. I am particularly grateful to Dick Craswell, Rob Daines, Paul Goldstein, Hank Greely, Joe Grundfest, Mark Kelman, Mike Klausner, Mark Lemley, Helen Stacey, Al Sykes, and Allen Weiner.

Mike Ananny, Bob Briscoe, Josh Cohen, Larry Lessig, Mark Lemley, and Phil Weiser carefully read the entire manuscript and spent hours discussing it with me. Their thoughts and comments were invaluable. Dick Craswell, Matthew Elliott, Brett Frischmann, Shane Greenstein, Joe Grundfest, Al Sykes, and Jonathan Zittrain read one or more chapters. Their thoughtful comments improved the manuscript greatly.

Over the years, I have had many conversations and discussions which helped shape the arguments in this book. I am particularly grateful to Marvin Ammori, Pio Baake, Jack Balkin, Stefan Bechtold, Scott Bradner, Susan Crawford, Gerry Faulhaber, Ed Felten, Terry Fisher, Mark Gaynor, Sharon Gillett, David Isenberg, Scott Hemphill, Louis Kaplow, Bill Lehr, Robert Pepper, Howard Shelanski, Karen Sollins, Larry Solum, Jim Speta, Kevin Werbach, Tim Wu, and Chris Yoo. I have also had many interesting conversations on Internet architecture and policy with my colleagues in the Trilogy project, in particular with Marcelo Bagnulo Braun, Olivier Bonaventure, Bob Briscoe, Louise Burness, Costas Courcoubetis, Phil Eardley, Alan Ford, Lars Eggert, Robert Hancock, Mark Handley, Toby Moncaster, Arnaud Jacquet, Iljitsch van Beijnum, and Damon Wischik.

My work on the book was supported by a number of students. Mike Ananny, Matthew Elliott, Ronan Flanagan, Shira Liu, Pedro Miranda, Samad Nasserian, Elisabeth Oppenheimer, and Hewan Teshome provided excellent research assistance. Mike Annany, Ingrid Erickson, Jordan Segall, and Kathryne Tafolla Young helped edit earlier versions of some of the chapters. Alexander Harris, Stuart Loh, Jonathan Mayer, Michelle Munoz, David Rizk, Emily Roberts, Robert Sensenbrenner, Roman Swoopes, and Andrew Zahn checked the citations. I am very grateful to all of them.

Special thanks to the amazing librarians at Stanford Law School, who found even the most exotic books and got them on my desk in incredibly short time, and to Sonia Moss for excellent interlibrary loan assistance.

Mary Ann Rundell, my assistant, prepared various versions of the manuscript, maintained the bibliographic database, organized and managed the checking of citations, and worked through various versions of the bibliography to find and correct errors. Her dedication to this project was incredible. I am fortunate to work with her. Many thanks to Stephanie Basso for her help in checking the bibliography.

Dolfin Leung ably converted my drawings into professional figures.

I am grateful to everybody at the MIT Press who helped turn the manuscript into a book. Special thanks to Elizabeth Murry, who acquired the manuscript, to John Covell, my editor, for encouragement and advice, and to Paul Bethge for editing the manuscript.

David Reed generously granted permission to reprint his account of the split between TCP and IP in the early days of the Internet.

This book builds on some of my earlier work. An earlier version of the first two sections of chapter 6 was published as "Towards an Economic Framework for Network Neutrality Regulation," *Journal on Telecommunications and High Technology Law* 5 (2007), no. 2: 329–391. I wrote that paper while I was a Senior Researcher at the Telecommunication Networks Group at the Technische Universität Berlin. I'm grateful to Adam Wolisz for supporting my work on this project and for providing an intellectually stimulating environment in which my thinking on these issues could evolve. During this time, I had many interesting discussions on Internet architecture, innovation, and regulation with Mathias Bohge, Marc Emmelmann, Michael Eyrich, James Gross, Vlado Handziski, Sven Hermann, Andreas Koepke, Martin Kubisch, Günter Schäfer, Lars Westerhoff, Sven Wiethölter, Daniel Willkomm, and Andreas Willig. Matthias Bärwolff, Dick Craswell, Einer Elhauge, Joseph Farrell, and Chris Yoo provided important feedback on the final version of this article that helped me improve the arguments in the book. I would also like to thank the participants of the faculty workshops at the law schools at Emory University, Fordham University, Harvard University, Michigan University, New York University, Stanford University, the University of California at Los Angeles, the University of Illinois, the University of Pennsylvania, the University of Southern

California, the University of Virginia, and the Wharton School's Legal Studies Department, and the participants in the 33rd Research Conference on Communication, Information, and Internet Policy (TPRC 2005), the Berkman Center for Internet and Society Luncheon Series at Harvard Law School, and the Computer Science and Artificial Intelligence Laboratory Speaker Series at the Massachusetts Institute of Technology for helpful questions and comments on the arguments of this article and the topic of this book.

Many of the ideas in this book were first explored in my doctoral dissertation at the Technische Universität Berlin. I'm particularly grateful to my advisors, Bernd Lutterbeck and Larry Lessig. I'm indebted to Bernd Lutterbeck for discussions, comments, and support throughout the years. I would also like to thank the other members of my dissertation committee, Ulrich Heiss and Adam Wolisz, for approaching this project with enthusiasm and an open mind. I did a substantial part of my doctoral research at Stanford Law School's Center for Internet and Society, during my time as a residential fellow there and during a later visit. I'm grateful to Stanford Law School and the Center for Internet and Society for their support during this time. My doctoral work was also financially supported by the German National Academic Foundation and the Gottlieb Daimler- and Karl Benz-Foundation. A number of people offered thoughtful comments on the finished dissertation that helped shape the arguments in the book. They include Mike Ananny, Matthias Bärwolff, Stefan Bechtold, Marjory Blumenthal, Ingrid Erickson, Gerry Faulhaber, Josh Lerner, and Doug Lichtman.

Finally, a few more personal thanks:

I owe a lot to Larry Lessig. I became interested in Internet architecture and innovation after reading his work on the role of code in cyberspace and on the impact of the end-to-end arguments on innovation. He invited me to Stanford when I started to work in this field, and volunteered to be my advisor. Our discussions and his comments have been invaluable to me. He continues to be a great colleague, counselor, and friend.

Over the years, I have had many inspiring conversations with Yochai Benkler, David Clark, Brett Frischmann, Arnold Picot, David Reed, and Phil Weiser that went far beyond the topic of this book. I have learned a lot from them. I am extremely grateful for their support and advice.

Jörg Riecken's advice, enthusiasm, and support were instrumental in the formative stages of this project. I am very grateful for everything he has done. I am indebted to my parents for their love, encouragement, and support over the years. They were always there when I needed them. My children, Lukas and Daniel, have grown up with this project. Many thanks for their patience when I couldn't be around, and for being so much fun to be with when I could. Last, but not least, I would like to thank my husband, Steffen van Schewick, for his love, encouragement, and support throughout this project. A lot of arguments in this book have been developed, clarified, and refined in discussions with him. An environmental planner by training, he learned more about the impact of Internet architecture on innovation than he ever wanted to know. He invested an incredible amount of time and energy to support this work in so many ways that it is impossible to mention them all. Without him, this book would not have been possible.

Introduction

In the thirty years since its inception, the Internet has experienced remarkable growth. What started in the 1970s as an experimental network connecting research and military networks has become a global network linking more than 1.6 billion users worldwide.[1] The Internet's growth has been fueled by an unprecedented amount of innovation. Over the years, network engineers have developed numerous new physical networking technologies (including Wi-Fi and optical networking technologies) over which the Internet can run. The Internet now connects everything from sensors to supercomputers. A constant stream of new applications lets users do new things, or do them more efficiently, making the Internet more attractive and useful to diverse users. As more and more users adopt them, these applications, the content they help produce and make available, and the new economic, social, cultural, and political practices they enable are transforming all areas of society. They change, for example, how firms can organize themselves, make their products, and interact with customers and with other firms. They increase the opportunities available to us, helping us to be more productive in our professional and private lives; to interact with relatives, friends, and strangers; to get to know them, communicate, or work with them; to educate ourselves using a variety of sources; and to participate in social, cultural, and democratic discourse.

The Internet's growing size, its transition from a research network operated by public entities to a commercial network operated by commercial providers who need to make profits, and its transition from a network connecting a small community of users who trust one another to a global network with users who do not know one another and may even intend to harm one another put pressure on the Internet's technical foundations. To deal with the impending shortage of Internet addresses, users and network providers deploy network-address translators that let several devices share the same address. To protect their networks against attacks, organizations put firewalls that block potentially harmful applications at the borders of their private networks. To increase their profits, network providers use technologies that enable them to identify and control the applications and the content passing through their networks.

These changes violate the design principles on which the Internet originally was based. They are hotly contested in technical forums such as the Internet Engineering Task Force, which develops and maintains the core Internet standards. The debate has also reached the political arena: arguing that these changes will destroy the Internet as a platform for innovation, free speech, and economic growth, scholars, public-interest organizations, industry organizations, and companies have asked regulatory agencies and legislative bodies all over the world to step in and restore the beneficial environment for innovation that the architecture of the Internet originally created.[2] In the United States, the debates over open access to broadband cable networks, over network neutrality, and over network management in broadband networks have all been shaped by such arguments.[3]

Independent of attempts to solve problems within the framework provided by the existing Internet, a new generation of networking research projects has begun to contemplate how the Internet of the future should look. Many of these projects start from a clean architectural slate, essentially creating a new Internet architecture from scratch.

In each of these cases, network engineers, legislators, and regulators face the same questions: How important are the design principles that shaped the Internet's original architecture? Are the (proposed) deviations much-needed improvements that reflect changed technical or business requirements, or are we losing the very features that were central to the Internet's success?

For regulators, the situation is even more complicated. Shouldn't a technical issue such as how to best structure the architecture of the Internet be left to network engineers? And if certain architectures foster innovation more than others, why won't the market create them?

This book aims to answer these questions. It examines how changes in the Internet's architecture (that is, its underlying technical structure) affect the economic environment for innovation and evaluates the impact of these changes from the perspective of public policy.

The answers are not obvious. After decades of research on innovation, we understand how changes in laws, in norms, or in prices affect the economic environment for innovation and how they affect innovators' decisions to innovate. We lack a similar understanding of how architecture affects innovation. Just as the architecture of a house describes its basic inner structure, the architecture of a complex system describes the basic inner structure of the system—its components, what they do, and how they interact to provide the system's functionality. That such a technical structure may have economic consequences at all is a relatively recent insight.[4] Most people still think of architectures as technical artifacts that are relevant only to engineers.

Thus, understanding how the Internet's architecture affects innovation requires us to think more generally about how architectures affect innovation. How can the architecture of a complex system influence the economic system in general, or an economic activity such as innovation in particular? Which features of an architecture affect the economic environment for innovation, and how do these features vary across different architectures or design principles?

The answers to these questions are relevant beyond the Internet. Since in most cases a system's functional requirements determine the system's architecture only in part, system architects have considerable latitude to choose different architectures, and this latitude allows them to consider other goals too. This freedom is particularly pronounced in software-intensive systems that are less constrained by the laws of nature than the design of physical products is. In particular, if architectures have economic consequences, system architects can create architectures that prioritize and realize particular economic goals.

These insights open new opportunities for businesses, for law, and for public policy. Businesses may want to engage in "strategic design" by creating architectures that shape the competitive environment in their favor. In the future, being able to design architectures that further a firm's strategic interests or knowing how to evaluate other firms' architectural strategies and react to them may be as important to a firm's success in the marketplace as a firm's ability to engage in more conventional forms of competition.[5]

For law and public policy, the economic impact of architecture seems to be empowering and challenging at the same time. Traditionally, policy makers have used the law to bring about desired economic effects. Architecture may provide an alternative way of influencing economic systems. Apart from using architecture to realize their own economic goals, policy makers may have to constrain the extent to which private actors can use architecture to further their private economic interests. This is particularly relevant to communications policy, a field in which certain architectures may seriously restrict regulators' ability to regulate at a later stage. Moreover, as communications networks continue to permeate more and more sectors of the economy, the negative effects of an architecture that strongly favors a few economic actors may be particularly long-term and severe.

To exploit the effect of architecture on the economic system in practice, to design architectures that further our interests, or to understand what other people's architectures may mean for us we need to understand exactly how an architecture influences the economic system and what features of an architecture we must tweak to create a specific economic effect. This book is a step toward that goal.

Overview of Chapters

Chapter 1 introduces a theoretical framework for understanding how architectures relate to economic systems and, more specifically, for understanding how architectures affect innovation. It explains architectures and design principles as concepts, and it highlights ways in which architectures influence economic systems and are influenced by them. In particular, the relationship between architectures and the economic system can be understood within a broader framework that economists use to explain the evolution of the economy as a whole. In this framework, the economic system evolves as economic actors pursue their own interests within a set of constraints, and as they act to change those constraints. Constraints delimit the options available to economic actors and influence the costs and benefits associated with these options. Well-known constraints include prices, laws, norms, and the natural and technical environments in which economic actors exist. Like these other constraints, an architecture can affect human behavior by imposing constraints on those who interact with the architecture or are exposed to it. Specifically, by imposing constraints on those who design, produce, and use a complex system, the architecture of the system (and the design principles that were used to create it) can influence the economic system in which the system is developed, produced, and used. Different architectures may impose different constraints, which may result in different decisions by economic actors, which in turn may result in different firm and market structures and different levels of economic activity. And by changing existing architectures or creating new ones, economic actors can change the constraints that architectures impose.

Before we can understand how specific architectures constrain economically, we need to understand how they constrain technically. Part II of the book introduces the architecture we will use to study the effect of architecture on innovation—the original architecture that governed the

Internet from its inception to the early 1990s[6]—and the design principles that were used to create that architecture: modularity, layering, and the end-to-end arguments.

While network engineers agree that the end-to-end arguments are among the few architectural principles underlying the architecture of the Internet,[7] other scholars have offered widely differing and often contradicting views on what the end-to-end arguments are, what they say, and how they relate to the architecture of the Internet. For example, some suggest that the end-to-end principle is "an important architectural principle that has governed the Internet since its inception"[8]; others say that "the end-to-end principle simply does not dictate a robustly specified functional design for the network"[9] but "follows from (and is an articulation of) the implicit design principle inherent to the layers model of the TCP/IP protocol [*sic*]"[10]; still others argue that "the Internet was never wholly end-to-end"[11] and that the end-to-end argument "is not an organizing principle; . . . if it is a principle, it is probably not true, and . . . even if it is true, it is probably not useful."[12] In policy debates concerning the architecture of the Internet, opponents of regulation often argue that proponents of certain regulatory interventions (for example, of open-access rules or network-neutrality rules) have stretched the end-to-end principle beyond its original meaning.[13] Even networking engineers often disagree about whether a certain technical solution violates the end-to-end arguments or not. In view of the high level of confusion, I discuss the end-to-end arguments and their relationship to the architecture of the Internet in detail.

My analysis yields an important insight: there is no single version of the end-to-end arguments, but two different ones that embody different rules for architectural design. The first version, which I call *the narrow version*, was presented by Jerome Saltzer, David Reed, and David Clark in the 1981 paper in which the end-to-end arguments were first named and identified as a design principle[14]; the second version, which I call *the broad version*, is the focus of later papers by these authors.[15] The difference between the two versions is not immediately apparent, and Saltzer, Reed, and Clark never explicitly drew attention to the change in definition. There are, however, real differences in scope, content, and validity that make it necessary to distinguish between the two versions. At the same time, the silent coexistence of two different design principles under the same name explains some of the confusion that surrounds the end-to-end arguments.

Chapter 2 describes the design principles that were used to create the original architecture of the Internet and highlights the trade-offs involved in each of them. Chapter 3 describes how these design principles shaped the original architecture of the Internet. Chapter 3 also discusses some of the misconceptions surrounding the end-to-end arguments and their relationship to the architecture of the Internet. For example, scholars have argued that the end-to-end arguments rule out architectures that store state in the network, prohibit the provision of Quality of Service in the network,[16] require the network to be simple, or constrain the design of applications by preferring certain application-management structures over others. Others have argued that the original architecture of the Internet was not based on the end-to-end arguments on the ground that the end-to-end arguments are no different from the layering principle, or on the ground that the original paper describing the end-to-end arguments was published after the original architecture of the Internet was developed, or on the ground that e-mail had a certain management structure.

To evaluate how the Internet's architecture affects innovation, we must understand exactly how architecture constrains economic actors. How do design principles and the architectures they shape influence the costs and benefits associated with a given innovation? How do they affect who can design and build an innovation? Answering these questions is the goal of part III. Each chapter in that part focuses on a particular aspect of the relationship between architecture and innovation and explores it in detail. The resulting insights are then applied to assess how the Internet's original architecture affects innovation. Although both versions of the end-to-end arguments shaped the original architecture of the Internet, only the broad version affects the economic environment for innovation. Therefore, parts III and IV focus on modularity, layering, and the broad version.

Chapter 4 explores how architecture influences the cost of realizing an innovation. It first discusses the effect of architecture on the costs of innovation in the context of modular and integrated architectures. Using the theory of real options, it explores the relationship between the costs of innovation implied by different architectures and the value of experimentation under uncertainty. It shows how the different costs of change in modular and integrated architecture affect the option value of these architectures, and how these differences affect the willingness of component designers to take risks when designing their components.

Chapter 4 also explores how differences between alternative modular architectures influence the option value of comparable modules in these architectures. In particular, the analysis shows how differences in the costs of innovation with respect to a module, the nature of dependencies on that module, and the uncertainty surrounding a module may affect the level of investment and rate of change of that module in alternative architectures. The chapter then uses these general insights about the effect of architecture on the costs of innovation and on the likelihood of innovation to determine how specific design choices in the Internet's original architecture affect these factors. It explores how the decision for or against the broad version of the end-to-end arguments influences the costs of developing applications, and how the decision for or against the use of relaxed layering with a portability layer affects the costs of developing the physical network technologies over which the Internet can run. It also highlights how these architectural choices influence the costs of producing, distributing or deploying innovations.

The final subsection of chapter 4 explores how the Internet's original architecture affects the rate of change at the Internet and transport layers. In recent years, the difficulties associated with evolving the core of the Internet have received much attention in the networking community. My analysis traces these difficulties to the deployment context of the commercial Internet, which has made it much more difficult to change certain parts of the Internet's architecture than a purely technical analysis of the structural dependencies within the architecture would suggest. On a more abstract level, the analysis shows how the deployment requirements implied by a network architecture interact with the economic system in which the network is used to constrain the evolution of the architecture beyond what a real-options analysis would predict.

Chapter 5 focuses on the implications of architectural choices for the organizational structures in which the development and production of the system—and subsequent innovation—can take place. The analysis shows how an architecture affects how a single firm that has designed an architecture can organize the subsequent development and production of components to this architecture, and how the organizational options enabled by an architecture may ultimately influence the structure of the industries surrounding the architecture. Ultimately, these mechanisms determine whether independent economic actors other than the system's architect can develop and produce new components for the system, both initially and later. The chapter then applies these insights to the original architecture of the Internet. In particular, it discusses how that architecture affects who can develop new applications. In a network architecture based on the broad version of the end-to-end arguments, anyone who knows (or is willing to learn) how to program and has access to a computer connected to the Internet can develop new applications. An innovator does not have to be an employee of a firm or get outside funding to realize his or her idea for an application. As a result, the set of potential innovators is much larger and more diverse than in network architectures that deviate from the broad version.

Chapter 6 explores how an architecture may affect the competitive strategies available to makers of complementary components. In particular, it analyzes how differences in a component's ability to monitor and control the execution of neighboring components may affect the strategies available to the maker or the users of the controlling component, and how this influences what benefits makers of complementary components can expect to realize. Although the chapter explores the effect of a component's ability to control other components in the context of the Internet's original architecture, the underlying theoretical framework is general enough to apply to other architectures. The chapter shows how architectural differences between the Internet's original architecture and a hypothetical architecture deviating from the broad version of the end-to-end arguments alter network providers' strategic options. It explores the conditions under which a network provider might have an incentive to discriminate against some applications, and it discusses recent instances of discrimination. This chapter also examines whether differences in market structure or laws may moderate the impact of architectural differences. It shows that network providers may have an incentive to exclude applications even if they face competition from other providers. The final section explores the effect of architectural differences on network providers' pricing strategies, such as their ability to charge users application-specific prices or to charge the providers of applications or content for the right to gain access to the customers of an Internet service provider.

Applications are the transmission belts that transform the general functionality of the Internet—transporting data packets from one computer to another—into something that creates value for users (and, in the process, creates value for society). Part IV of the book analyzes how changes in the architecture of the Internet affect the economic environment for innovation in applications and evaluates the public-policy consequences.

Chapters 4–6 provide a variety of insights into the relationship between architectures and design principles, on the one hand, and the economic system, on the other hand, both on a general level and with respect to the original architecture of the Internet and the design principles that shaped it. Chapter 7 draws on those insights to summarize how increases in the amount of application-specific functionality in the network's core change the economic environment for innovation at the application level. Thus, the chapter provides a framework in which the effects of deviations from the broad version of the end-to-end arguments on application-level innovation can be assessed. It shows that as the amount of application-specific functionality in the network increases, independent application developers' incentives to innovate are reduced. At the same time, the range of potential innovators decreases, while the locus of control over the development and deployment of innovations in applications gradually shifts to the network owner. In addition, the chapter evaluates how such architectural changes affect other characteristics of the economic environment for application-level innovation, including network owners' incentives to innovate at this level and the costs associated with adopting new or improved applications.

Chapter 8 explores the effect of these differences on the amount of application innovation that will occur under different network architectures. In particular, drawing on theories of innovation and the histories of specific applications, chapter 8 examines how differences between decentralized and centralized environments for innovation and the associated differences in the number and types of innovators may affect the amount, the quality, and the character of application-level innovation. In a network architecture based on the broad version of the end-to-end arguments, anyone with access to an end host and with the ability to learn a programming language is a potential innovator. Innovators independently decide on their approaches to innovation; users independently choose which applications they want to use. In contrast, in architectures deviating from the broad version, network providers control which applications can be realized and used. At the same time, the set of potential innovators is smaller and less diverse; in the extreme case, network providers are the only remaining innovators. If there is uncertainty or consumer heterogeneity, a larger and more diverse group of innovators under an end-to-end architecture will produce more and better applications than a few network providers who control which applications are realized and used. If users' needs are heterogeneous, innovators in the end-to-end architecture will also produce more diverse applications that better meet users' needs.

Chapter 9 assesses how the various network architectures relate to the public interest and to network providers' private interests. Whereas earlier chapters focused on how network architectures affect innovation, this chapter looks more broadly at the economic and non-economic consequences of complying with or deviating from the broad version of the end-to-end arguments. The analysis shows that the public's interests in network architecture diverge from the network providers' interests, creating a market failure regarding the evolution of the Internet's architecture.

The concluding chapter summarizes the book's main arguments and discusses the implications of the book's results for public policy and network design.

Overall, the book shows that the Internet's original architecture was based on a design principle that I call *the broad version of the end-to-end arguments*. This design fostered innovation in applications. Today, the Internet's architecture changes in ways that deviate from this principle. These changes reduce the amount and the quality of application innovation at significant costs to society: As a general-purpose technology, the Internet does not create value through its existence alone. It creates value by helping users do what they want to do, or by letting them do so more efficiently. Applications are the tools that let users realize this value. By reducing innovation in applications and limiting users' ability to decide how to use the network, these changes significantly reduce the Internet's usefulness and value for users, and, ultimately, for society as a whole. In addition, reducing innovation in applications limits the Internet's ability to contribute to economic growth. Finally, the Internet's ability to enhance individual freedom, its ability to provide a platform for better democratic participation, and its ability to foster a more critical and self-reflective culture are tightly linked to features resulting from the broad version of the end-to-end arguments. By removing these features, the changes to the architecture also threaten the Internet's ability to realize its social, political, and cultural potential. Though the broad version of the end-to-end arguments also has social costs, they are not large enough to justify sacrificing the social benefits created by the broad version.

While public interests suffer, network providers benefit from the changes. They control the evolution of the network, and it is highly unlikely that they will change course without government intervention.

Navigating the Book

The author of an academic book usually assumes that her readers know the relevant literature, and that she only has to add to it. I do not have this luxury. My argument crosses a number of disciplines and speaks to readers with a wide range of backgrounds. The book is designed to be accessible to all of them. In particular, one does not have to have a background in networking or in economics to understand it. As a result, the book is longer than it would be if it were targeted at readers in a single discipline, and it contains explanations that will be familiar to some

Table I.1
The end-to-end arguments from a technical perspective.

Understanding the End-to-End Arguments	Pages
What are the two versions of the end-to-end arguments?	57–75, 377–379
What are the differences between the two versions, and why should we distinguish between the two?	75–81
What is the trade-off underlying the broad version?	68–75, 355–371
Does the broad version differ from the layering principle?	104–105
Does the broad version prohibit quality of service?	106–107
Does the broad version require the network to be stupid or simple?	107
Do the end-to-end arguments prevent state in the network?	105–106
Does the broad version make it more difficult (or even impossible) to make the network secure?	366–368
How can you deviate from the broad version? What does it mean to make the network more controllable or more opaque?	286–287

The End-to-End Arguments and the Architecture of the Internet	Pages
How have the two versions shaped the Internet's original architecture?	90–103, 110–112, 379–381
Is the Internet Protocol general enough?	142, box 4.3
How do the two versions relate to current developments in the Internet, such as the evolution of applications toward a more distributed structure or the proliferation of middleboxes?	383–387, 371–372
Is the trade-off underlying the broad version still appropriate today?	368–371, 355–356
Should the end-to-end arguments continue to guide the Internet's architecture as a technical design principle?	388–389

readers but not to others. For example, engineers will already know about modularity, the layering principle, and the architecture of the Internet, and lawyers, economists, and management scientists will already know how transaction costs influence the boundary choices of firms. I hope that my headings and introductions will help readers recognize things they already know and help them get to what they do not know.

The book can be read straight through, from cover to cover. But one may also follow some of the more specific conceptual threads that run through the book. The first thread explores the end-to-end arguments from a technical perspective (table I.1). The second thread analyzes the social value of architectures based on the broad version of the end-to-end arguments and the resulting policy implications (table I.2).[17] The third thread explores aspects of the approach to "architecture and economics" (box I.1) advanced by the book. Within the framework described in

Table I.2

The social value of the broad version of the end-to-end arguments.

The End-to-End Arguments and Their Relationship to the Internet's Original Architecture	Pages
What are the two versions of the end-to-end arguments, and why should we distinguish between the two?	57–81, 377–379
How have they shaped the Internet's original architecture?	90–103, 110–112, 373–381

The Effect of the Broad Version on Application Innovation	Pages
How does the broad version affect the cost of developing new applications?	137–148, 383–387
How does the broad version affect who can develop new applications?	204–213
Can innovators with no or little outside funding really produce successful applications?	204–213, 300–308, 334–345
How does it affect independent application developers if network providers can control the applications on their network?	215–281
Do network providers have an incentive to discriminate against or exclude unaffiliated applications?	218–273
Does competition among network providers remove this incentive?	255–264
What pricing strategies can network providers follow in a network where they control the applications?	217–218, 273–280
How does the economic environment for application innovation change if networks deviate from the broad version?	285–295, 383–387
How do differences in the size and diversity of the innovator pool and differences in control over application innovation and deployment affect the overall amount, quality, and type of innovation?	297–351
How important is it if innovators other than the network provider can independently choose their approach to innovation?	345–348
How important is user choice for application innovation?	349–351
How do the architectural differences among network architectures that are based on the broad version or deviate from it, taken together, affect the overall amount, quality, and type of application innovation under these architectures?	351–353

The Social Value of Network Architectures Based on the Broad Version	Pages
What are the social benefits associated with the broad version?	355–365
How important is application innovation?	355–360
How important is user choice?	349–351, 361–363
How does the broad version affect the Internet's ability to realize its political, social and cultural potential?	364–365
What are the social costs associated with the broad version?	365–368
How should we trade off among the social benefits and social costs?	368–371
Do network providers' private interests diverge from the public interest?	371–375

Policy Implications	Pages
What do these insights mean for public policy?	218–221, 264, 272–273, 387–392
Should legislators mandate compliance with the broad version?	388

Box I.1

Architecture and Economics

This book's approach to the study of architecture and innovation is an example of a more general approach to studying the architecture of complex systems, an approach I call *architecture and economics*. The approach understands architecture as one of several constraints on human behavior and uses economic theory (broadly defined) to explore the effect of these constraints. In its narrowest meaning, "architecture and economics" denotes efforts to understand how the architectures of complex systems influence, and are influenced by, the economic systems in which the complex systems are designed, produced, and used. As we saw above, the links between architectures and economic systems have important implications for how businesses compete and how public policy is made. While this book focuses on the effect of architecture on a specific economic activity (innovation), the underlying framework is general and can be used to understand the effect of architecture on a much broader range of human behavior. Viewed from this perspective, "architecture and economics" describes a much broader field of research— efforts that use economic theory to understand how architectures affect specific forms of human behavior, and, more generally, how architectures influence, or are influenced by, economic, social, cultural, or political systems.[a] I use the term in the broader sense.[b]

a. I do not mean to imply that this type of research has not existed so far. Most research in this area, however, focuses on specific architectures or design principles. For example, a large body of literature in management science and engineering explores the economic effect of modular and integrated architectures in the design of physical products. (See note 4 to this chapter for references to this literature.) There is some research in software engineering that examines the economic effect of software architectures (e.g., Sullivan et al. 1999; Boehm and Sullivan 2000; Sullivan et al. 2001; Erdogmus et al. 2002). Representative examples of legal scholarship exploring the effect of the Internet's architecture are Lessig 1998, Lemley and Lessig 1999, Lessig 1999a, Lessig 2001, Wu 2003a, Benkler 2006, Balkin 2008, and Zittrain 2008. There is, however, no established field of research that connects work in this field under a common umbrella, nor is there an accepted framework or methodology for exploring these issues. Among others who have advocated for a more unified approach to the study of the architectures of complex systems are Baldwin and Clark (2006b) (who advocate a "science of design" that would cover questions very similar to the ones outlined in the text) and van Schewick (2004).

b. "Law and Economics" has a similar dual meaning. It is used to describe the study of the relationships between law and the economic system, but it also describes, more broadly, efforts to understand the effect of law on human behavior using economic theory. For an overview of the different schools of thought within this field, see Mercuro and Medema 2006.

Table I.3
Architecture and economics.

Factors Mediating the Effect of Architecture	Pages
How do non-architectural constraints interact with architecture?	
Theory	26–28, 31
Examples	196–197, 218–221, 264, 272–273
How do characteristics of the actors exposed to the architecture affect the impact of architecture?	
Theory	30
Examples	204–213, 298–345
How do actors' relationships with other actors affect the impact of architecture?	
Theory	31
Examples	133, 218–221, 255–264, 212–213
The Effect of the Economic System on Architecture	
How is architecture influenced by economic systems?	
Theory	3, 23–26, 28, 32, 389
Examples	151–163, 371–372, 389–392
The Effect of Architecture on Activities Other Than Innovation	
How can the architecture of a complex system affect the economic, social or political systems in which the complex system is used?	
Theory	28, 361–362
Examples	359–361, 362–365
Architecture and Economics: Implications	
What are the implications of the economic impact of architecture for businesses?	
Theory	3
Examples	371–372, 389–392
What are the implications of the economic impact of architecture for law and policy?	
Theory	3–4
Examples	388

chapter 1, the book focuses on the effect of one constraint (architecture) on one specific activity (innovation), and sets aside consideration of other factors (such as the effect of non-architectural constraints, or the mechanisms by which architectures are influenced by economic systems) that are relevant within the framework. This thread ties together the portions of the book that touch on these other factors (table I.3). In doing so, it complements the detailed analysis (in chapters 4–8) of how architectures—particularly that of the Internet—affect innovation.

I Foundations

1 Architecture and Innovation

Engineers focus on technology; managers, legislators, regulators, and the lawyers and economists who advise them focus on economic systems. This common separation of responsibilities may blind us to the links between the two: the architecture of a complex technical system—the description of its basic building blocks—fundamentally influences and is influenced by the economic system that drives the development, production, and use of the system. Failure to appreciate these links may result in policies or strategies that do not realize the economic potential of technical systems. To understand and exploit these links, engineers need to learn a bit about the economics that support their innovation, while managers, lawyers, economists, regulators, and legislators need to learn something about the technologies they aim to manage. This chapter introduces a theoretical framework for understanding how technical architectures relate to economic systems and, more specifically, for understanding how architectures affect innovation. It explains architectures and design principles as concepts, and it highlights the mechanisms by which architectures influence and are influenced by economic systems.

Architecture

Scholars of Internet policy may already feel familiar with the notion of architecture. Since the publication of Lawrence Lessig's book *Code and Other Laws of Cyberspace*, the idea that the 'architecture' of the Internet regulates behavior in cyberspace in a way that is similar to law has gained widespread popularity.[1] The potential effect of this regulation on civil liberties is often captured in the slogan "Architecture is politics."[2]

In the context of this book, this familiarity is misleading. When texts on Internet policy refer to architecture, they usually mean the software and hardware that make up the Internet.[3] In this terminology, the word

Box 1.1
The Place of Architecture Design in the Product-Development Process

The development of a complex system proceeds from the requirements specification to the design to the implementation (for software systems) or production (for physical systems) of the system.[a] The requirements specification
defines the functional, business, and quality requirements the system must
meet. The design creates a detailed specification—a blueprint—from which
the system can be built: it completely describes the system, including instructions about how to produce it. The implementation or production of the
system results in an executable program, or, in the case of physical products,
a usable product. The architecture of a system is produced as part of the design
phase in an intermediate step between requirements specification and detailed
design.[b]

a. These activities are part of every software-development project or (in the
case of physical products) product-development project. Models of software-
development or product-development processes differ in the amount of over-
lapping, interleaving, and iterating among these activities. For an overview
of different models of the software-development process, see van Vliet 2000,
chapter 3. For an overview of different approaches to product development,
see Ulrich and Eppinger 2000, pp. 13–24, 235–272.
b. The text describes the sequence of activities in a development project that
follows best practices. In reality, some software systems are developed without
formal specification of an architecture. Sometimes an architecture emerges over
time, as the people working on the system come to a better understanding as
to what rationales or design principles have implicitly driven the evolution of
the system and make these explicit in a formal description of the architecture.
The original architecture of the Internet seems to have emerged in this way.

'architecture' refers to implemented technical systems—i.e., the networks,
computers, and programs that constitute the operational Internet. 'Architecture' is synonymous with "the system."

In computer science, and throughout this book, 'architecture' has a very
different meaning: it denotes the fundamental structures of a complex
system as defined during the early stages of product development (box 1.1).
Similar to the way the architecture of a house is different from the house
itself, the architecture of a system is not the final, working system; rather,
it is a description of the system's basic building blocks.

When designers create a complex system, they typically seek to reduce
the problem's complexity by decomposing the system into pieces that
work together to provide the required functionality. The architecture

describes the early design decisions about the decomposition of the system. It contains all the information that is necessary to understand how the chosen collection of components will satisfy the functional, business, and quality requirements. In short, the architecture describes the components of the system, what they do, and how they interact.

More precisely, the architecture is a high-level system description that specifies the components of the system, the externally visible properties of the components, and the relationships among components. The externally visible properties of a component are the features that other components must know about if they are to interact with it. They include the services provided by the component, their performance characteristics, fault handling, use of shared resources and other characteristics.[4,5] Architectures of distributed or parallel systems also describe how software components map to hardware elements,[6] or, in the case of physical products, how components map to the physical elements of products.[7] For example, the architecture of the complex system "personal computer" names the components (e.g., central processing unit, keyboard, monitor), describes what they do (e.g., the central processing unit processes software program instructions; the keyboard lets users give input to the system; the monitor displays the output) and describes how components interact (e.g., peripherals may connect to the rest of the system using the Universal Serial Bus standard). But the architecture does not describe how the keyboard operates internally to record and transfer input, or how the monitor displays information transferred to it by the rest of the system. In other words, the architecture provides an abstract view of a system as a collection of "black boxes," describing how they behave and interact but not how they work. In particular, the architecture ignores questions of implementation such as algorithm design and data representation.

Architecture is a hierarchical concept.[8] Components at the highest level of a system's architecture can be decomposed into a set of interrelated subcomponents that may also have architectures.[9] Decomposition can continue until the lowest level of elementary subsystem is reached. In the case of the personal computer, the monitor can be broken down further into interacting subcomponents (the screen, the case, and so on). Going up the hierarchy, a personal computer may be part of a larger complex system, such as a home network or the Internet.

Design Choices

Many different architectures can usually satisfy a complex system's functional requirements.[10] This is because changes to the structure or behavior of one component can often be offset by changing its interactions with other system pieces so that the system's overall functionality stays the same. This interchangeability is especially important in software engineering, because software architectures are less limited by real-world constraints such as the laws of nature that constrain the design of physical products. Apart from a few technical constraints, software designers are free to shape the architecture according to the desired goals. Thus, although the capability of a system to meet the functional requirements depends on a correct architecture, it does not depend on specific architectural choices.

But a number of other qualities of a system *do* depend on architectural choices. Some of these qualities (e.g., performance, availability, reliability, usability, security) have to do with the operation of the system; others (e.g., modifiability, reusability, testability) have to do with the development or maintenance of the system.[11] For example, modifiability (being able to make changes quickly and cost-effectively) depends on how many components must be modified to implement a change.[12] A system is more modifiable if functions that are likely to change together are concentrated in one or a few components. Since the allocation of functionality to components is an architectural issue, the modifiability of a system is determined by its architecture.

Performance, on the other hand, is only partly affected by architectural decisions. The performance of a software system, for example, depends in part on the amount and the complexity of inter-component communication.[13] The amount and the complexity of interaction among components are, in turn, determined by how functionality is distributed among components during the design of the architecture. Thus, the performance of a software system is attributable in part to architectural choices. At the same time, some non-architectural decisions (e.g., the choice of algorithms and their implementation) also affect the performance of the system.

Qualities that depend on specific architectural choices are very difficult, if not impossible, to realize at later stages of the development process if the architecture does not support them. Thus, choosing an architecture that can support the desired qualities is crucial for meeting the quality goals of a system.[14] In this sense, "Architecture is quality."

Unfortunately, qualities do not exist in isolation. Aspects of the architecture that promote one quality may have a negative effect on another quality.[15] For example, fault tolerance in software systems is usually achieved by replicating critical components. When one version of a component fails, an identical version takes over. Additional components, however, may compromise security by offering additional points of attack. Thus, an architectural solution that increases fault tolerance may reduce security.[16] Owing to the interactions among qualities, it is impossible to maximize all qualities simultaneously—choosing an architecture requires trade-offs, prioritizing some qualities at the expense of others. Deciding which attributes are more important than others is not an architectural choice—this decision depends on the requirements that the system has to meet and must be made by the organization who sets these requirements. Usually, this will be the organization that wants to use or sell the system.[17]

Design Principles

Owing to the complex interactions among architectural requirements of different qualities, it is difficult to translate a set of quality requirements into an appropriate architecture that realizes these requirements. Design principles help us move from qualities to architectures.

A design principle describes known connections between architectural choices[18] and the characteristics of the resulting architecture.[19] It describes the architectural means by which a specific set of trade-offs among conflicting qualities is realized. Like a recipe, a design principle describes how to design an architecture for a system with specific quality characteristics, and, like different versions of a dish, the resulting architectures will differ depending on the design principles that were used to create them.[20] Which design principle (or combination of principles) should be used depends on what qualities are desired.[21] Thus, system architects select the design principles that will give them the combination and the prioritization of features they want to realize.

Design principles are still important after the initial architecture is created because they guide the detailed design that follows.[22] Continuing to use the original design principles is especially critical if an architecture exists for a long time. When a system has to evolve in response to additional requirements or changes in technology, adding new parts to the system without considering the original design principles can disturb the balance among conflicting quality attributes that was struck in the original architecture. Adhering to the original design principles ensures that the system will continue to have the qualities and properties that the architecture originally prioritized.

The Relationship between Architecture and the Economic System

The importance of architecture transcends technical considerations: the architecture of a system is tightly tied to the economic system in which it is developed, produced, and used, and to the incentives of the actors who may engage with it. The relationship between architecture and the economic system can be understood in a broader analytical framework that economists use to understand the evolution of the economy as a whole. The framework has two components: first, a set of actors and the relationships among them; second, the constraints under which the actors operate.

In the American financial sector, for example, the actors—both individuals and organizations (i.e., consumers, banks, regulatory agencies, firms)—are connected through a network of social, political, and economic relationships. Sometimes these actors interact through markets: consumers take out loans from banks or deposit money in savings accounts; buyers and sellers trade shares and stocks in markets like the stock exchange. Actors may also interact through other governance structures, as when banks participate in associations such as the American Bankers Association to better pursue their interests.

According to economic theory, the structure of the economic system (the actors active in the economy, the relationships among them, and the governance structures through which they interact) and the behavior of the actors in the economic system emerge from the choices individuals make as they pursue their own interests within a set of constraints. The panoply of possible constraints might include laws, social norms, the natural and technical environments in which the actors exist and economic constraints such as prices or available assets.[23] Constraints delimit the options available to individuals and organizations, and influence the costs and benefits associated with these options. In the financial sector, for example, laws define the structure, responsibilities, and power of the regulatory agency. They define which entities can become banks, and what commercial activities they are allowed to engage in. By imposing reporting requirements and capital-structure requirements on banks, financial regulations can make their operations more or less costly.

By enabling different actions or imposing different costs and benefits, constraints shape firms and markets and affect economic activity (for an example, see box 1.2).[24]

Thus, economists distinguish between the *framework* provided by the constraints and the *system* of actors and relationships that emerges as a consequence of these constraints. The economic system evolves as a result of the dynamic interactions between economic actors and the constraints they face. On one hand, economic structures and behaviors are shaped by

Box 1.2
The Effect of Constraints in the Financial Sector

From the Great Depression until the 1990s, financial regulations in the United States prevented banks from taking ownership interests in firms and did not let firms have interlocking directorates—that is, directors serving on the boards of competing firms.[a] German law did not impose similar constraints.[b] These differences resulted in very different relationships between banks and firms in the two countries. German firms tended to be funded by banks and elite families, who could influence corporate decision making, while German public financial markets were relatively insignificant.[c] In the United States, where there was a clear separation between banks and firms, publicly traded firms were funded by financial markets. Researchers have argued that the German structure encouraged more risk-taking, because the banks providing the financing had better information than the American public about the firm's plans and more ability to influence those plans.[d] In addition, the combination of restriction on interlocking directorates and prohibition of mergers meant that American firms tended to diversify so they could handle more aspects of a business. In Germany, where interlocking directorates were allowed and there were fewer restrictions on cartels, firms remained smaller and less integrated.[e]

a. The Glass-Steagall Act of 1933 restricted US banks from ownership in non-finance firms. Its core provisions were repealed in 1999 by the Gramm-Leach-Bliley Act (U.S. Senate Committee on Banking 1999). The Clayton Anti-Trust Act of 1914 restricts interlocking directorates in the US, i.e., having a director sit on the board of more than one corporation at a time. This restriction applies only to competing corporations and to firms that have "capital, surplus, and undivided profits" exceeding a jurisdictional "trigger," which was recently raised to about $25 million (Clayton Antitrust Act, U.S. Code 15 (2000), §19; Federal Trade Commission 2008). The prohibition is still in effect. A recent *USA Today* survey showed that some non-competing firms have highly interlocked directorates (Krantz 2002).
b. Fligstein and Freeland 1995, pp. 33–37.
c. Roe 1994, pp. 169–177; Allen and Gale 2001, pp. 71–76; Calomiris 2000, pp. 212–219.
d. Calomiris 2000, pp. 213–219. This argument is heavily contested. For a flavor of the debate, see Edwards and Fischer 1994; Easterbrook 1997; Franks and Mayer 1997; Carney 1997.
e. Fligstein and Freeland 1995, pp. 33–37.

individuals' and organizations' responses to constraints. On the other hand, if economic actors feel that their interests are better served by a different set of constraints, they may work toward changing them through lobbying, voting, and so on. Naturally, some constraints may be easier to change than others.[25]

To complicate matters further, constraints do not operate autonomously; rather, one constraint may influence the effectiveness and the evolution of another. Two constraints operating simultaneously may support or contradict each other, ultimately reinforcing or weakening the other constraint's effect on an actor.[26] For example, laws aligned with social norms may last longer than laws that oppose them; conversely, laws can strengthen or weaken social norms.[27] Constraints imposed by the natural and technical environment may operate analogously: technical systems may effectively displace laws, and changes in technology can undercut a law's effectiveness even if the law's text remains unchanged. Laws can support architectural constraints by criminalizing attempts to circumvent them, or can weaken their effectiveness by prohibiting their use (for some examples, see box 1.3).

Box 1.3
Interactions between Legal and Technical Constraints

Legal and technical constraints may interact in different ways. Technical systems may effectively displace laws. Constraints imposed by a system influence what users can or cannot do with the system. If these constraints disable or discourage behavior that would be necessary in order to exercise certain rights, the system changes the effectiveness of these rights: while using the system, users cannot exercise these rights even if they would be legally entitled to do so. Thus, the system determines which rights are *effectively* available to the users of the system, effectively displacing the law.

For example, "digital rights management systems" control access to and use of copyrighted digital content. A digital rights management system that prohibits *any* copying not only protects the content against illegal copying, it also makes it impossible for a user to make copies that are justified under the fair-use doctrine of copyright law. Thus, although the law stays the same, this system effectively displaces the fair-use doctrine of copyright law. A system with a different set of constraints may disable only illegal copying while enabling copying for fair-use purposes, respecting the fair-use doctrine of copyright law.[a] Thus, the constraints established by these systems effectively displace the law to different degrees.[b]

Box 1.3
(continued)

Changes in technology can reduce a law's effectiveness even if the law's text is not changed. For example, the Internet has changed the effectiveness of copyright law. Before the Internet, only a few intermediaries had the technological means to copy and distribute copyrighted works on a large scale. As a result, copyright could effectively be enforced by finding and holding liable those intermediaries who engaged in illegal copying. In contrast, the Internet lets many different people copy and distribute digital content at almost no cost and with no deterioration in quality. In addition, peer-to-peer file-sharing networks let users engage in mass distribution of illicit copies. Thus, the Internet and peer-to-peer file-sharing networks greatly increase the number of potential copyright violators by eliminating the need for intermediaries in the copying and distribution of copyrighted works. As a result, those enforcing copyright can no longer focus on a limited number of intermediaries but must direct their efforts toward a huge number of individual violators, which makes copyright enforcement considerably more difficult and costly. Thus, although the copyright laws have not changed, copyright owners today are less effectively protected against infringement than they were before the Internet.[c]

Law can support architectural constraints by criminalizing attempts to circumvent them, or can weaken their effectiveness by prohibiting their use. For example, the American Digital Millennium Copyright Act makes it a felony to circumvent copyright-management schemes. By legally protecting copyright-management schemes from circumvention, the law strengthens the constraints imposed by them.[d]

a. On technical solutions for digital rights management systems that may enable copying for fair-use purposes, see Burk and Cohen 2001.

b. See Lessig 1999b, pp. 521–530.

c. See Wu 2003b, pp. 131–136.

d. See Digital Millennium Copyright Act, U.S. Statutes at Large 112 (1998): 2863, §1201(a)(1). For a critical discussion of this provision, see Lessig 1999b, pp. 538–541.

One type of constraint can also be used to change another. In particular, economic actors may try to use legal constraints to change other, non-legal constraints.[28] For example, laws can influence prices by imposing taxes or granting subsidies, or can affect the structure of a market by regulating entry into an industry.[29] Laws can change norms, too: a law may provide financial incentives to ignore a norm, or may weaken a norm by creating tension between the existing norm and the norm of engaging in law-abiding behavior.[30] Laws can affect the technical environment by regulating technical systems, or by encouraging the development of specific technologies by letting public entities participate in standard setting, funding the development of desired technologies, or restricting public procurement to the technologies the state wants to foster.[31]

The relationship between architecture and the economic system can be understood within this analytical framework. Like laws or social norms, architecture shapes human behavior by imposing constraints on those who interact with it. By imposing constraints, the architecture of a complex system affects the economic system for its development, production, and use—that is, the actors who will develop, produce, or use the system, the relationships among them, the governance structures they use to interact with one another, and the behavior of these actors. And by changing existing architectures or creating new ones, economic actors can change the constraints that architecture imposes.

The Relationship between Architecture and Innovation

This book explores the relationship between architecture and the economic system in the context of a specific economic activity: innovation.[32] The word 'innovation' refers to creating or improving goods, services, or methods of production.[33] The book focuses on innovation that can be influenced by architectural features—developing components for a new system, improving existing components or developing new ones, changing an architecture to enable new functionality, or creating new architectures. These innovations drive a system's initial development and its continued evolution.

The literature on innovation often uses the term to describe the innovative activities that firms perform to increase their profits.[34] To appreciate more fully the relationship between architecture and innovation, this book adopts a broader definition, using the word 'innovators' to denote a wide range of actors—including individuals, groups, firms, and other organizations—whose actions and products may be motivated by various economic or non-economic concerns.

The architecture of a system influences economic structures and behaviors regarding the development and evolution of the system, and affects the amount and kind of innovation that might occur. In particular, architectural features influence which actors may develop and change a complex system, the incentives under which they act, and the governance structures through which their activity is organized. Conversely, innovation may change existing architectures or create new ones.

Architecture affects behavior by imposing constraints on the actors who interact with it. Constraints, in turn, influence behavior by defining and limiting available courses of action, and by influencing the costs and benefits associated with specific actions. Actors respond to changes in incentives in observable, predictable ways.[35] By creating incentives and disincentives, or by making some actions available and precluding others, particular architectures may lead to specific firm structures or market structures, or may enable different levels of innovative activity.

Imagine that several potential innovators each have an idea for a new system component and have to decide whether, and how, to build it. Suppose that under Architecture A the only actor able to design and build new components is the system's original architect. As we will see in chapter 5, this may happen if the architecture has been designed using an integrated approach. In this scenario, the potential innovator's sole option is to sell his idea to the system architect. Suppose that under Architectures B and C developers are able to design and implement the innovation themselves, but that the costs of realizing the innovation are higher for all innovators under Architecture C than under Architectures A and B (table 1.1). Owing to these differences among architectures, the potential innovators may make different choices when deciding whether to realize their innovative

Table 1.1
Effects of different architectures.

Aspects influenced by architectural features	Architecture A	Architecture B	Architecture C
Actors able to realize the innovative idea, i.e., design and build a new component	System architect	System architect or potential innovator	System architect or potential innovator
Costs of realizing the innovative idea, i.e., designing and building a new component	Low	Low	Higher

idea. For some innovations, a potential innovator may expect the benefits to outweigh the costs under Architecture B, but not under Architecture C; these innovations will not be realized under Architecture C. Some innovations that may be realized by an independent innovator under Architecture B may not be realized under Architecture A, perhaps because the independent innovator did not enter into negotiations with the system architect or because the negotiations were not successful; if they are realized under Architecture A, they will be realized by the system architect and not by the person with the original idea. As a result, who realizes innovative ideas (the system architect or the developer with an innovative idea) and how many innovative ideas are realized will differ depending on the architecture.

Understanding that architecture may constrain potential innovators is only the first step toward explaining the relationship between architecture and innovation. An economic actor's reaction to a constraint depends on the characteristics of the economic actor, on the other constraints on the actor, and on the actor's existing relationships and anticipated interactions with other actors.

First, architectural constraints take effect through the reactions of those exposed to them—that is, they induce behavior rather than enforce compliance. The economic actors can be individuals or organizations—"groups of individuals, bound together by a common purpose"[36] and founded to achieve certain social, cultural, political, or economic objectives. Certainly organizations consist of individuals, each pursuing his own interest within the framework of constraints imposed on him, but in general this book treats organizations as singular units with resources, cost structures, goals, motivations, and cost-benefit assessment processes that influence how they make decisions. Processes and structures *within* organizations will be discussed only when they are relevant to the effect of architecture on the organization of innovation (chapter 5) and to the reactions of organizations to opportunities for innovation (chapter 8).

Actors may have different resources, cost structures,[37] goals, motivations, and cost-benefit assessment practices; consequently, their perception of costs and benefits is idiosyncratic, and they may react differently to the same architectural constraint.[38] An actor who hopes to profit from selling her innovation may be disinclined to innovate if she is operating within an architecture that reduces her potential sales revenue. In contrast, an actor who innovates to use the innovation himself may remain unaffected by the same architectural change (so long as the architecture lets him use the innovation). Thus, the effect of architecture depends on the characteristics of the actors exposed to it.

Second, architecture is not the only constraint on potential innovators. Laws, social norms, market conditions, and the natural and technical environments also influence innovators' actions.[39] Like architecture, these constraints delimit the available choices and affect the corresponding costs and benefits. Intellectual-property laws, for example, influence the expected benefits of an innovation by conferring a temporary monopoly on the innovator but impose costs on subsequent innovators who want to build on the original innovation. By striking different balances between the interests of the original innovator and those of subsequent innovators, alternative intellectual-property regimes that differ in duration and in scope facilitate different types and amounts of innovative activity.[40] Antitrust laws shape the range of legal strategies available to an innovator once her innovation reaches the product market, thus affecting the benefits an innovator can expect to gain. Social norms that encourage risk-taking and challenging conventions but also tolerate failure may be especially conducive to innovation. The structures and operations of capital and labor markets (both heavily influenced by laws and norms) may affect the ease with which a potential innovator can acquire the financial and human capital necessary to realize his innovation.

Finally, a potential innovator's response to a constraint may be influenced by his extant relationships and anticipated interactions with other actors. For example, if a market has only a few potential or anticipated innovators, each firm will base its level of investment on the level of investment it expects from the others. A firm that has long collaborated with another firm may be able to work with that firm on innovative projects that require constant interaction, because the trust and coordination mechanisms resulting from the long-term relationship may enable it to overcome the coordination problems that usually prevent firms from coordinating closely interdependent activities across firm boundaries.[41]

Thus, the same architecture, operating in environments with different actors and constraints, may enable very different types and levels of innovative activity.[42] For example, consider an architecture that encourages entrepreneurial innovation but requires more capital than entrepreneurs usually are able to invest individually. In this case, we would expect to see more innovation from entrepreneurs in an environment in which funding from venture capitalists is available than in an environment in which similar financial actors do not exist.[43] All this implies that the effect of a specific architecture on innovation cannot be determined without considering the characteristics of the actors exposed to it, the other constraints under which they operate, and the actors' existing or expected relationships.

Just as architectures shape economic behavior, economic behaviors may shape the evolution of architectures.[44] This is most apparent when an innovation involves changing an architecture or building a new one. There is, however, a more general link between economic actors and architectures: architectures are created by economic actors. Functional requirements rarely determine the architecture of a system fully, since there are usually several alternative architectures that meet the functional requirements. Thus, an architect makes many choices not formally prescribed by the functional requirements. Like other decisions, these choices—and, consequently, the evolution of the architectural design—will be influenced by the architect's individual characteristics, by his relationships within the economic system, and by the constraints he faces (laws, norms, economic constraints, and so on). Different constraints, actors, and relationships may therefore result in different architectures. Furthermore, since economic considerations shape actors' decisions, system architects will tend to favor architectures that support their own economic interests. At least in part, then, architectural designs hinge on the choices of economic actors, all of whom pursue their own interests under their particular constraints. Thus, the evolution of architectures is partly endogenous.

In summary, an analytical framework that explains the relationship between architecture and the economic system includes a set of actors, all subject to constraints imposed by system architectures, existing laws, prevailing social norms, the actors' technological and natural environments, and the well-known constraints described in traditional economic theory, such as prices and the resources available to actors. When operating simultaneously, such constraints interact and influence one another in complex ways: they can influence one another's evolution or removal, and they can emerge from purposeful and idiosyncratic actions of a diverse set of economic actors.

Within the framework outlined above, this book focuses on the effects of one constraint (architecture) on one type of economic behavior (innovation). To this end, the book focuses on a particular architecture (the original architecture of the Internet, which governed the Internet from its inception to the early 1990s[45]), abstracting from it the circumstances and motivations that led to its creation. To highlight the impact of the end-to-end arguments (the design principles on which the original architecture of the Internet was based), the original architecture of the Internet will be compared with hypothetical architectures that deviate from the end-to-end arguments in different ways. To focus on the specific effect of architecture, the analysis assumes that while the architecture changes, everything else (i.e., the group of actors exposed to the architecture and the other constraints under which they operate) stays the same.[46]

Understanding architecture as a constraint on economic actors makes it possible to use economic theory to predict how economic actors will react to architectural features. The framework developed so far does not depend on specific models of human behavior; instead, it is compatible with several models, including the rational-actor model, models of bounded rationality, and models used in behavioral economics.[47] Since the appropriateness of a model depends on the situation under analysis, modeling will be discussed more thoroughly in the chapters that follow.

This chapter has outlined the general mechanism through which architecture influences innovative behavior. To predict how a specific architectural structure will affect an innovation, we must understand exactly how architecture constrains economic actors. How do design principles and specific architectural features shape the costs and benefits associated with a certain innovation? How do they affect who can design and build an innovation? Before we can explore these questions, we need to understand the original architecture of the Internet and the design principles that led to it. Those will be the subjects of the next two chapters.

II The End-to-End Arguments and the Original Architecture of the Internet

2   Internet Design Principles

Design principles shape architectures by imposing rules that system architects must follow.[1,2] They may constrain how a system is decomposed into components, how functionality is distributed among these components, or how components may depend on one another. Since different design principles impose different constraints, the technical characteristics of the resulting architectures may differ depending on the design principles that were used to create them. The technical differences among architectures, in turn, may translate into different economic constraints on those who design, produce, and use the resulting systems. Thus, before we can understand how architectures (and the design principles that shaped them) constrain *economically*, we need to understand how they constrain *technically*.

To this end, chapters 2 and 3 introduce the architecture we will use to study the effect of architecture on innovation—the original architecture of the Internet—and the design principles that were used to create it. Though policy debates often focus on the end-to-end arguments, they are not the only design principles on which the Internet's original architecture was based. Before the end-to-end arguments can be applied, other, more fundamental design decisions have to be made. The end-to-end arguments guide how functionality is distributed in a multi-layer network; thus, the layering principle has to be applied first. Layering, in turn, is a special case of modularity. Together, these design principles—modularity, layering, and the end-to-end arguments—shaped the Internet's architecture and its technical and economic characteristics.

This chapter describes the constraints that each of the three design principles imposes on the design of an architecture and highlights the trade-offs that underlie each of these principles. Because of the high level of confusion surrounding the end-to-end arguments, they are analyzed in detail. As will become apparent, some of the confusion can be attributed to the silent coexistence of two different design principles under the same name: the narrow version and the broad version of the end-to-end arguments. While the narrow version only applies to some functions within a system, the broad version applies to the complete functionality of a system. The two versions constrain designers to different degrees, which makes it important to distinguish between them.

Modularity

Architectures differ fundamentally in the degree to which their components are "loosely" or "tightly" coupled. Coupling is a measure of the degree to which components are interdependent. Modularity is a design principle that intentionally makes components highly independent ("loosely coupled").[3] Components of modular designs are called *modules*. When designing a modular architecture, system architects decompose the system in a way that minimizes dependencies among components. The remaining interdependencies and points of interaction between components are addressed and resolved in the course of the architectural design process; the resulting detailed interface specifications are not allowed to change during detailed design.[4] There are degrees of modularity because modular architectures may differ in the degree of coupling between components.[5]

The goal of modularity is to create architectures whose components can be designed independently but still work together. (On other types of modularity, see box 2.1.) To make components independent, and to maintain their independence, modularity employs abstraction, information hiding, and a strict separation of concerns.[6]

A modular approach to design distinguishes between two types of information.[7] information that is relevant to more than one module is completely specified as part of the architectural design process and is not allowed to change during detailed design. This information is available or "visible" to all designers, and is therefore called the architecture's *visible information*. In particular, this includes all the information modules need to work together, such as the information necessary to use a module or to otherwise interact with it. For each module, this information is completely defined in detailed interface specifications that describe all interdependencies or points of interaction between that module and other modules and specify how they will be resolved.[8,9] Thus, a module's visible information provides an external view of the module that lets other designers treat the module as a black box, letting them abstract from the complexity of the module.

Box 2.1
Modularity in Design, Production, and Use

The modularity described in the text is not the only type of modularity. Modularity as described in the text creates a high degree of independence among components with respect to design. In the literature on physical products, the word 'modularity' is sometimes also used to describe approaches that intentionally create a high degree of independence among components with respect to production or use. To distinguish between these different forms of modularity, they are called *modularity in design, modularity in production*, and *modularity in use*. If a product is modular in design, its components can be designed independently. If it is modular in production, its components can be produced independently. If it is modular in use, users of the product can replace or "mix and match" components at a later stage. A specific product can but does not have to exhibit all forms of modularity. Lego blocks are modular in design, production, and use. Personal computers and stereo systems often are, too. Automobiles are modular in production, but not modular in design and mostly not modular in use.[a]

a. See Baldwin and Clark 2000, p. 78. For an overview of the literature on modularity in design, production, or use in assembled hardware products, see Fixson 2001, pp. 23–27.

In contrast, information that affects only one module—the inside of the black box—is hidden from everyone except its designers; it is called the architecture's *hidden information*. This information is not specified during the design of the architecture, but is determined during the detailed design phase; it is free to evolve within the framework provided by the architecture's visible information until the detailed designing ends.

To ensure that a module remains a black box, access to its data and services is restricted to its interface. Designers working on other parts of the system are not allowed to make any assumptions about a module beyond its visible information. These constraints prevent the designers of a module from relying on another module's hidden information when deciding how to develop their own module's hidden information; they are allowed to rely only on the architecture's visible information. Since the design of their own module does not rely on the hidden information of other modules, the designers of a module are not affected by changes in other modules' hidden information, as long as the other modules' visible information stays the same. This means that the detailed designing of different components—i.e., the designing of the components' hidden information—can proceed independently.[10]

For example, personal computers are based on a modular architecture. The interfaces between the peripheral devices (e.g., printers and screens) and the rest of the system are completely specified by the industry's interface standards. These standards describe the physical shape of the plug and the format and meaning of data transferred through the plug. As a result, the designers of a peripheral device have to worry only about their own device. They do not need to know how the computer will treat the data received from their device. As long as their design follows the interface specification, they know the computer will be able to treat their data properly. If the designers of the computer and the designers of peripheral devices abide by the interface specifications, the design of the computer and of particular peripheral devices can proceed independently.

Modularity in design reduces complexity by allowing component designers to treat other modules as black boxes. By shielding the rest of the system from internal changes to a module, modularity increases designers' flexibility regarding the detailed design of their own modules and lets the detailed design of different modules proceed independently. A modular approach to design may also improve the correctness of the system (box 2.2). The positive impact of modularity in design on the modifiability of the resulting system is discussed in chapter 4.

Modularity is not without costs. An architecture's visible information is not allowed to change during detailed design and is difficult to change later.[11] Thus, modularity makes it more difficult to experiment on the architecture's visible information (such as a module's interfaces) in order to facilitate experimentation on the architecture's hidden information (such as a module's internals). In a way, the inflexibility of the visible information is the price for the flexibility with respect to the architecture's hidden information. To prevent this from becoming problematic, a good modular architecture is designed so that parts that may benefit from improvement or variation are enclosed within a module, so that parts that are likely to change together belong to the same module.[12]

In addition, designers' flexibility with respect to an architecture's hidden information is limited by the constraints imposed by the architecture's visible information.[13] Although interfaces free designers from having to coordinate their detailed design decisions with designers of other components, they introduce a new constraint on the designers of affected modules: all subsequent design is bound by the interface specifications.[14] The more detailed the interface, the more severe the constraint.

Box 2.2

How Modularity Affects the Correctness of Software Systems

When decomposing a system while designing a modular architecture, system architects seek to minimize interdependencies among components in order to reduce the number of design decisions that must be coordinated across components. In the language of software engineering, they strive for high cohesion and low coupling[a]: the internal elements of a module should be strongly interconnected, while the connections to other modules should be weak. Such a design has a positive effect on the correctness of the resulting system: Weakly coupled components are easier to understand, easier to build, and easier to test.[b] The strength of coupling between two modules influences the complexity of the corresponding interfaces, because a module's connections to other modules are completely addressed and resolved in that module's interface specifications.[c] If components are weakly coupled, the connections to other modules are weak, so little communication or interaction across modules is necessary; this results in simple interfaces. A module with a simple interface can usually be understood and built independent of the context in which it is used. Highly independent modules usually can be tested separately.

In contrast, highly coupled components work together closely and must be understood as a whole. Strong connections among modules require interfaces to be complex and highly specific to their interactions. Since the effect of complex interfaces is often difficult to grasp, errors in subsequent development are more likely to occur. In addition, when components interact in complex ways, errors introduced by one component may cause other components to fail.[d] Diagnosing problems may be difficult and time-consuming, since testing components independently is often impossible.

All these factors result in a higher correctness of weakly coupled architectures. Empirical studies show that modular systems with low coupling are less error-prone than architectures whose components are highly coupled.[e]

a. Whereas 'cohesion' describes the strength of intra-module connection (i.e., the degree to which a component's sub-elements are related to one another), 'coupling' describes the strength of interconnection between two components. "Highly coupled" components are joined by strong interconnection; "loosely coupled" components are joined by weak interconnections. (See Yourdon and Constantine 1975, pp. 85, 105–108.) Coupling and cohesion were identified as the two most important criteria for judging the quality of modular designs (effective modularity) in "Structured Design," an important 1974 paper by Wayne Stevens, Glenford Myers, and Larry Constantine (reprinted as Stevens, Myers, and Constantine 1999). The underlying theory

Box 2.2
(continued)

---

was set out in detail in Yourdon and Constantine 1975. Since then, low coupling and high cohesion have become widely accepted as characteristics of good or effective modular design. (See Pressman 1997, pp. 357–361; Sommerville 1996, p. 218; van Vliet 2000, pp. 299–303. For empirical studies, see Troy and Zweben 1981; Selby and Basili 1991.) The usefulness of the concepts is not restricted to particular programming languages such as modular programming languages or to particular design paradigms such as functional design. For example, coupling and cohesion have been shown to be useful indicators of the structural quality of object-oriented code and design as well. See Sommerville 1996; Briand et al. 2000; Briand, Devanbu, and Melo 1997; Briand, Lounis, and Wüst 1999.

b. See Stevens, Myers, and Constantine 1999, pp. 232–237, 254; Pressman 1997, pp. 359–361; van Vliet 2000, pp. 301–303.

c. Of course, an architect has considerable freedom as to the exact design of a particular interface for a given degree of coupling between two modules. Although the architect could choose to make the interface highly specific to the interaction in question or specify a very general interface, the level of complexity forced upon the architect depends on the strength of connections between the two components.

d. Stevens, Myers, and Constantine 1999, p. 233; Pressman 1997, pp. 358–359.

e. The high rate of errors in highly coupled systems has been confirmed empirically for conventional systems as well as for object-oriented ones. For example, a study based on a conventionally designed 148,000-source-line system from a production environment found that the routines with the highest ratios of coupling to strength had 7 times as many errors per 1,000 source statements (excluding comments) as the routines with the lowest ratios of coupling to strength had. The study also found that errors in routines with the highest coupling/strength ratios were 21.7 times as costly to fix. (See Selby and Basili 1991.) For an early empirical study of the quality of structured designs supporting this view, see Troy and Zweben 1981. In recent years, researchers have empirically measured the relationship among coupling, cohesion, and error-proneness in object-oriented systems. For example, Briand, Devanbu, and Melo (1997) found that some coupling measures can predict fault-proneness. In a comprehensive empirical evaluation of all object-oriented design measures found in the literature, Briand et al. (2000) found that many measures of coupling and inheritance are strongly related to the probability of fault detection in a class.

Alternative interface specifications may constrain experimentation to different degrees. For example, until the mid 1990s the standards defining the interfaces between peripherals and the rest of the system were specific to certain types of devices: the printer, the monitor, and so forth. This specificity constrained what kind of innovation could occur with respect to a particular interface. Only a device whose communication with the rest of the system could be designed to fit through the interface could connect through it. New or improved devices had to interact with the rest of the system in ways similar to the way the device for which the standard was originally developed interacted with the rest of the system; otherwise a new type of interface had to be developed first. For example, it was possible to connect ink-jet printers, laser printers, and scanners to the printer interface, but it was not possible to connect a completely new type of device. By contrast, the Universal Serial Bus (USB) standard that lets peripherals connect to the rest of the system was explicitly designed in a more general way to ensure that a wide range of devices can be attached to a personal computer (PC). As a result of this design, cameras, MP3 players, mouses, keyboards, joysticks, printers, and portable hard disks all can connect to a PC using the same USB interface. Similarly, architectures whose components are loosely coupled leave more freedom to the designers of individual modules than architectures consisting of tightly coupled modules (box 2.3).[15]

A modular architecture may negatively affect "global performance" (i.e., the overall performance of the system).[16] In a modular architecture that fosters flexibility, the parts of the system that are likely to change together are grouped within one module. This makes it more likely that later changes to the system can be implemented by changing the internals of the module without requiring any changes to the rest of the system. Though this decomposition is optimal with respect to the flexibility of the system, it may not be the most efficient with respect to performance. Among other things, the performance of a software-intensive system depends on the amount of communication between modules.[17] A decomposition that isolates the parts of the system that are likely to change together in order to reduce the costs of changing them in the future may separate parts that cooperate to provide a particular functionality, thereby increasing inter-module communication and decreasing performance.[18]

A modular approach to design thus assumes that the gains from lower complexity, independent component design, higher modifiability, and higher correctness are more important than the negative effect of the

Box 2.3
Coupling and Flexibility

An architecture whose components are loosely coupled leaves more freedom to the designers of individual modules than an architecture that consists of tightly coupled components. In a strongly coupled architecture, the interfaces needed to enable independent component design will be very complex and may be highly specific to the operation of the affected modules.[a] From the point of view of component design, this is not very desirable. The more detailed the interface, the higher the risk that detailed design decisions will be made during architectural design, when a lot of detailed information may not yet be available. In the worst case, the architects may choose highly specific but inefficient (from a performance perspective) interface specifications that may significantly impede component designers' ability to create an efficient component design. In any case, complex interfaces considerably constrain the flexibility of subsequent component design.

In contrast, a system whose components exhibit low coupling and high cohesion strikes a more productive balance between complexity-reducing certainty and creative uncertainty[b]: few design choices have to be made in the interfaces to enable independent component design; all other choices will be left to the discretion of component designers, leaving more room for creative solutions.

a. For an example, see Sullivan et al. 2001, section 5.1.
b. For an example, see ibid., section 5.3.

constraints imposed by the system's visible information and the potential negative effect on global performance.

Integrated Design

A modular approach to design can be contrasted with an integrated approach, such as has traditionally been used in the designing of physical products.[19]

In an integrated approach to design, all design information is common knowledge for the designers. The system is decomposed into components, but interdependencies among components are not resolved during architectural design. Instead, interface specifications are produced during detailed design and can be changed until the detailed designing ends.

In software systems, interdependencies among components usually arise because different components operate on the same data or because they must interact in order to provide a particular functionality.[20] In physical systems, interdependencies may occur if different components share physical space. If parts of the design are interdependent, the corresponding design decisions must be mutually consistent if the system is to work properly.[21] Thus, design decisions that affect interdependent parameters must be coordinated. Independent component design is not possible.

In an integrated approach to design, unresolved interdependencies that cross the boundaries of components may create chains of dependencies between different parts of the system such that each design choice has to be consistent with all the other decisions in the chain. If a design parameter is part of such a chain, changing this parameter may require widespread adaptations in the rest of the system. In addition, a solution that is locally optimal with respect to one component may not be perfect with respect to design parameters in other components. Finding a solution may require difficult trade-offs across several components, which may add considerably to the complexity of the design process.[22] Since design choices in regard to one component are closely linked to decisions in regard to other components, the resulting components are closely coupled.[23] Architectures with closely coupled components are more error-prone than architectures whose components are loosely coupled (box 2.2).

Although it increases the complexity involved in the design process, resolving interdependencies among components in the detailed design stage may enable designers of different components to optimize their designs with respect to each other. Whereas designers of a modular system do not know how other modules implement their functionalities, designers of integrated systems can fine-tune their choices to the exact circumstances in the other component. In this respect, an integrated approach to design tries to simultaneously optimize *all* of a system's parameters. The resulting design may be more efficient or may exhibit better global performance than a modular system that—in order to reduce complexity and increase flexibility—hides information that may have been useful in optimizing its performance. For example, the Apple iMac is based on an integrated approach to physical design. Since all of its design information is common knowledge, designers can tweak components in order to physically interleave and arrange different components in ways that use minimal space.[24] This allows them to combine all the usual components of a personal computer system—central processing unit, monitor, hard drive, screen, camera, speakers, microphone, wireless interfaces—in one sleek case that looks more like a conventional monitor than like an Intel-based personal computer.

In sum, an integrated approach to design trades off potentially higher global performance against increased complexity, the need to coordinate the detailed design of components, and the potentially lower correctness of the system.

Layering

Modularity in design does not impose any restrictions on the interactions between modules; a module can use or be used by any other module (figure 2.1).

Layering is a special form of modularity that—in addition to the usual constraints imposed by a modular approach to design—restricts the allowable interactions between modules.[25] In a layered system, modules are organized in layers that constrain dependencies between modules. A module assigned to a particular layer can use any of the other modules in the same layer or in a lower layer; however, it cannot use a module belonging to a higher layer. Layering thus organizes modules into a partially ordered hierarchy.[26]

Like any modular architecture, a layered architecture completely specifies all the information that components need to interact during the architectural design and makes that information visible to all designers. A

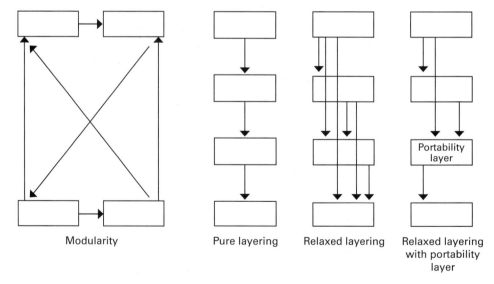

| Modularity | Pure layering | Relaxed layering | Relaxed layering with portability layer |

Figure 2.1
Variants of the layering principle.

layer's visible information defines the services it offers to higher layers and the interfaces through which higher layers invoke those services.[27] The internal implementation of a layer—the way it realizes the services offered to higher layers—is hidden from everyone except that layer's designers. This information is not specified during architectural design and is free to evolve until detailed designing ends.

Different variants of the layering principle constrain dependencies between layers to different degrees.

In the "pure" version of layering, a layer is allowed to use only the layer immediately below it (figure 2.1).[28] As a result, layers interact only with their immediate neighbors: each layer provides services to the layer above and uses the services of the layer below. Since each higher layer adds unique capabilities, a layered system provides increasingly elaborated or specialized services at higher levels. Since each layer is allowed to use the services of the layer immediately below but not those of any other layer, the lower layer hides all the layers below it. Thus, in a system designed according to the pure version, any layer can be seen only by the next higher layer.

In the "relaxed" version of the layering principle, a layer is permitted to use any layer that lies below it (figure 2.1). This is often called *layer bridging.*[29]

As we will see in chapter 3, the architecture of the Internet is based on a variant of the layering principle called *relaxed layering with a portability layer* (figure 2.1).[30] In this version, one of the lower layers is chosen as the portability layer. The layers above the portability layer are allowed to use the services of all layers between them and the portability layer. They are not allowed to use any layers below the portability layer.

For example, the applications, operating system, and hardware of a personal computer are parts of a layered system.[31] The system's hardware—central processing unit, memory, hard disks, monitors, printers, and so on—all resides at the lowest level. Programming hardware is a complicated task that requires detailed knowledge of the inner workings of a device. Therefore, the next higher layer, the operating system, provides *application programming interfaces* (APIs) to applications at the system's highest layer. APIs let the application developers use the system's hardware without having to worry about how it operates or is controlled. In a sense, they know how the hardware *behaves* but not how it *works*. For example, they let application designers create a file, open or read the file, and save the file somewhere without having to worry about how the file system is organized and managed or how to write the data onto a disk. In this context, the operating system constitutes a portability layer.[32] Because applications are not allowed to invoke the services of the computer's physical hardware directly, they must access them through the application programming interfaces provided by the operating system. The operating system operates as a "floor": layers above it cannot access layers below it.

By basing design on increasing levels of abstraction, layering greatly reduces complexity.[33] Owing to the partitioning of fixed, visible information and malleable, hidden information, layers can be designed independently as long as they conform to the architecture's visible information. Since each layer only uses the services of layers below, a layered system can be implemented and tested incrementally. This facilitates implementation and improves the correctness of the final system.

Layering increases the modifiability of the system by shielding lower layers from changes in higher layers, whether or not the change involves visible information. The hardware of the hard disk is not allowed to rely on the operating system or on the applications and thus is not affected by changes to these layers. In addition, as long as the interface to the lower layer stays the same, higher layers are protected from changes in a lower layer. Application designers are not allowed to access specific hardware directly; they must use the operating system's APIs. As a result, changing how the hard disk and the operating system interact does not affect the applications, as long as the API stays the same. Finally, like any modular architecture, a layered architecture shields the rest of the system from changes to the internals of a layer.

Layering may affect performance negatively. First, only a layer's interface is visible to higher layers, while the layer's implementation is hidden. Thus, the interface provides an abstraction of the layer. While a higher layer can implement its services on the basis of knowledge about the interface, sometimes information about details of the implementation may have enabled a more efficient implementation of the higher layer. As a result, the performance may be worse than in a more closely coupled architecture where more information is available.[34] This is a common problem in networking contexts (box 2.4). Second, in a layered architecture, functionalities that operate together may be distributed over different architecture layers. Since communication across components and layers is usually more costly than communication within a component, performance may decrease.[35] This may be ameliorated through prudent implementation.[36]

Box 2.4
How Layering Affects Performance in Communication Networks

By hiding lower-layer information from higher layers, layering may reduce performance. For example, different physical network technologies have different maximum transmission units (MTUs). The maximum transmission unit for a particular physical network technology is the largest size of an Internet Protocol datagram that can be transferred across the network without being broken up into smaller pieces.[a] In the architecture of the Internet, the Internet layer is designed to shield the transport layer from such details of the underlying physical network technologies in order to provide an abstract, technology-independent interface to the services provided by the underlying physical networks. As a result, the designers and implementers of transport protocols only have to pass data packets to the Internet Protocol; they do not have to worry about how the Internet Protocol manages the task of sending the data packets across the different physical networks that make up the Internet and delivering them to the transport-layer protocol at the destination host.

This reduction of complexity, though, may harm performance. If the data packets that the transport protocol passes to the Internet Protocol are too large to be transported across the physical networks on the path from sender to receiver without being broken up into smaller pieces, they must be fragmented and reassembled by the Internet Protocol.[b] This is a complex and time-consuming process. If the transport-layer protocol knew more about the smallest MTU of all the physical networks that a datagram must traverse in the path from sender to receiver, it could adapt the size of data packets passed to the Internet Protocol accordingly. In this case, the datagrams could travel from sender to receiver without time-consuming fragmentation and reassembly.[c] To avoid performance problems of this kind, protocol implementers often relax the strict layering that characterizes the design in the implementation of the protocols and allow information from lower layers such as network MTU to propagate upward.[d]

a. See Peterson and Davie 2007, pp. 239–240.
b. Whereas datagrams may be fragmented at the sending end host and at every router along the way, the Internet Protocol reassembles fragments only at the receiving end host. See Peterson and Davie 2003, p. 245.
c. For an overview of fragmentation and reassembly of IP datagrams by the Internet Protocol, see Peterson and Davie 2003, pp. 242–249.
d. See Comer 2000, p. 192. On the use of upcalls in layered systems generally, see D. D. Clark 1985.

Modularity and Layering in Network Architectures

The design principles described so far can be used in any system. To provide the basis for a discussion of the Internet's architecture, this section introduces the basic concepts that are necessary to understand the issues associated with architectural design in the context of communication networks; it also outlines the constraints imposed by the layering principle in the context of network design.[37]

The goal of a communications network is to make it possible for applications to interact through a network. This is a very complex task. In order to reduce the complexity of the design problem, the functionality required for communicating over a network is commonly decomposed into components and subcomponents by means of modularity and a version of the layering principle that accounts for the distributed nature of communication networks.

At the highest level of a network architecture, designers distinguish two classes of components[38]: the computers or devices that are "on" or "attached to" a network and those that are "in" a network.

Computers "on" the network support users and run application programs; they use the services of the network to communicate with one another. The home computers many people use to surf the Internet, personal digital assistants that send and receive e-mail using the Internet, the Web servers that carry the content provided by Yahoo or the *New York Times*, and the servers through which users access their Gmail accounts are all examples of computers "on" the network.

Computers "in" the network form or implement the network. They establish connectivity among the computers attached to the network.[39] They include the cable modem termination system operated by a cable provider (to which a cable modem is connected to give the user access to the Internet) and the routers that network providers use to forward Internet data from one physical network to another. Viewed from computers in the network, computers on the network are the sources and destinations of data. Data flows travel through computers in the network, but they originate or terminate in computers attached to the network.

Because the communication flows through the network originate or terminate in computers attached to the network, these are also called *endpoints*, *end systems*, or *end hosts*. Computers in the network form its *core*.[40] This terminology denotes a purely functional distinction between users and providers of communication services. It does not imply any topological or administrative relationship.[41] Topologically, an end host may be co-located with routers belonging to the network's core. Administratively, who has ownership or control of the computer in question isn't relevant. A server owned and operated by a network provider is still an end host.

This distinction between devices that use the network and devices that form the network exists in other networks too. End devices such as telephones, fax machines, and modems use the public switched telephone network; the various switches involved in establishing connections from one caller to the other form the core of the network. Electrical devices such as computers, washing machines, and stereo systems use the electricity network; the power transformers used to increase or reduce voltage on the way from the power plant to the customer are devices in the core of the network that work together to supply power to the end devices using the network.

Each computer, whether it belongs to the edge or the core of a computer network, is further subdivided into layers, which are thought of as being arranged in a vertical structure (figure 2.2). Each layer has one or more architectural components called *protocols*. Each protocol provides a well-defined set of services to the layer above, using the services of the layer below.[42] To implement the services provided by the protocol, different instances of the same protocol located on different computers ("protocol peers")[43] cooperate by exchanging messages with one another. Thus, in the networking context, layering operates both horizontally (through the exchange of messages between protocol peers located on different computers) and vertically (through the use of lower-layer protocols) (figure 2.3).

As in any layered approach to design, a protocol that is assigned to a layer can use any of the other protocols in the same layer or in a lower

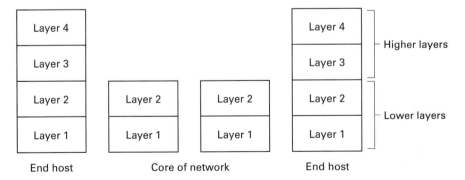

Figure 2.2
Layers, end hosts, and core of the network.

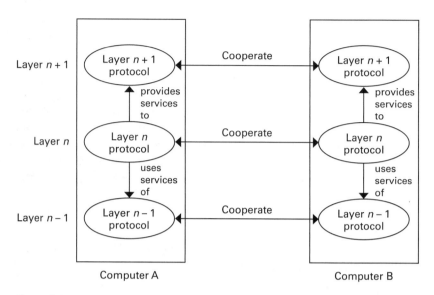

Figure 2.3
Layered protocols.

one, but it cannot use a protocol in a higher layer. In addition, the interaction between protocols is restricted by two additional constraints on the architecture that are specific to layering in the networking context. First, a protocol at a specific layer at a receiver must receive exactly the same object as sent by its protocol peer at the source. Second, a lower-layer protocol is not allowed to make any assumptions about the message passed to it by a higher-layer protocol for delivery to its higher-layer protocol peer. As we will see, these additional constraints maintain the beneficial characteristics of layered architectures in spite of the additional complexity introduced by the need for horizontal communication between protocol peers.

As in any modular or layered system, information necessary to let the components of the system interact is specified during the design of the architecture. Owing to the vertical and horizontal dimensions of layered networking, the visible information of a protocol consists of two different interfaces: a vertical service interface and a horizontal peer interface (figure 2.4). The vertical service interface defines the services that this protocol provides to higher layers. The horizontal peer interface specifies the form and the meaning of messages exchanged between peers and the actions to be taken by the communicating protocol peers upon transmission or receipt of such messages. In other words, the peer interface defines how

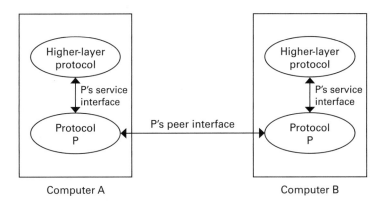

Figure 2.4
The interfaces of a protocol.

the protocol peers communicate and cooperate to realize the services that the protocol provides to higher layers.[44,45] In contrast, how a protocol achieves the functionality implied by this visible information is hidden from all except those implementing a protocol.

To see how vertical and horizontal cooperation between protocols work, consider a slightly modified analogy from the real world. Imagine a researcher, working in the research lab of a big company, who wants to submit travel-reimbursement forms to the company's travel-reimbursement department, which is located in the company's headquarters in another city. At the highest layer, the researcher fills in the form for the reimbursement request, attaches the required documents, and hands them over to the mailroom—the next lower layer—with the name of the receiving administrator within the reimbursement department. Someone in the mailroom puts the form and the supporting documents in an interoffice envelope, adds the internal mail code for the administrator, and hands it over to the next lower layer—the postal service—with postage and the postal address of the receiving location. The postal service puts the interoffice envelope in a postal envelope, adds the address, transports the postal envelope to the company's headquarters, removes the postal envelope, and delivers the interoffice envelope to the mailroom. The mailroom uses the code on the interoffice envelope to identify the recipient, removes the interoffice envelope, and delivers the reimbursement-request form and the documents to the administrator in the reimbursement department. The administrator then processes the reimbursement request according to the company's regulations (figure 2.5).

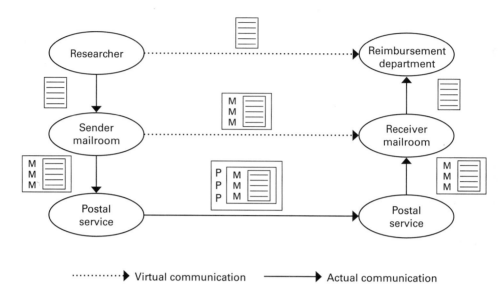

Figure 2.5
Virtual versus actual communication.

In this example, each layer provides a certain service to the next higher layer. The researcher-reimbursement layer provides processing of travel reimbursements. The mailroom layer provides person-to-person delivery within the company. The postal layer provides mailroom-to-mailroom delivery between locations. The way in which a higher layer takes advantage of the services provided by a lower layer and the information that a higher layer must provide to enable the lower layer to fulfill its task are specified by the lower layer's service interface: to deliver a message from one mailroom to the other, for example, the postal service requires the message that the mailroom wants to have delivered to its peer, the appropriate postage, and the address of the receiver.

To realize a layer's service, an entity at that layer cooperates with its peer at the receiving end by exchanging messages.[46] The format of the messages to be exchanged and the actions to be taken by the receiving peer are specified by the protocol's peer interface. At the highest layer, the message consists of the reimbursement-request form and the supporting documents. The company's rules specifying the format of the form, what documentation is required, and what action the reimbursement department will take upon receipt of the message constitute that protocol's peer interface. At the mailroom layer, the message consists of the interoffice envelope containing the higher layer's message[47] plus some control information[48] that tells the receiving mailroom what to do with the envelope, such as the internal postal code that identifies the receiver at the higher layer or additional instructions such as a request for rush service. The internal rules that require the use of interoffice envelopes, define the internal mail code, and specify the format and meaning of additional instructions constitute that layer's peer interface. And so on.

You may have noted that each layer receives exactly the same message that was sent to it by its peer (figure 2.5): the reimbursement department receives the reimbursement-request form and the documentation, the mailroom receives the interoffice envelope. If a lower layer adds information (e.g., to communicate with its own peer), that layer's peer at the receiving end removes that information and only delivers the higher layer's message to the higher-layer protocol at the receiver. This is not an accident; it is the result of the first of the two additional constraints imposed by the version of the layering principle used in network design: that layer n at the destination must receive exactly the same object sent by layer n at the source.[49] This rule requires that a lower-layer protocol may not permanently modify the object passed to it by a higher-layer protocol for delivery to its higher-layer protocol peer.[50] This constraint lets protocol designers think about the horizontal features of protocol design separately from the vertical aspects: if a protocol at a specific layer can be sure that it will receive exactly the message sent to it by its peer at the sending location, how the message gets from one to the other does not make any difference for the interaction between the protocol peers. Although communication between protocol peers at higher layers happens indirectly[51] through the use of lower layers, the protocol's peer interface can be designed as if the two peers communicated directly.[52] Put differently, the lower layers are transparent to the horizontal interactions among communicating protocol components. This greatly reduces the complexity involved in protocol design. The designers of a peer interface can ignore the difficulties associated with getting a message from one protocol peer to another and can instead focus on how to structure the exchange of messages between the peers to realize the additional functionality provided by that protocol. In our example, people thinking about what information is needed to process a reimbursement and under which condition the reimbursement request should be granted do not need to think about how to get the form from the employee requesting the reimbursement to the reimbursement department. Given that the lower layer will deliver exactly the same message that the employee sends, it does not make any difference for the peer interface at the reimbursement layer whether the reimbursement request is delivered in person, by fax, by interoffice mail, or by some other means.

The second constraint specific to layering in the networking context is that a lower-layer protocol cannot make any assumptions about the object (protocol data unit) passed to it by a higher-layer protocol for delivery to its higher-layer protocol peer.[53] Thus, the lower-layer protocol may neither access nor act on the information contained in higher-layer protocol data units. This constraint preserves the central feature of layering: the independence of lower layers from higher layers. To access, interpret, or act upon information contained in higher-layer protocol data units, a lower layer must know the format and the meaning of higher-layer messages. This introduces a dependence on the higher-layer protocol. If the higher-layer protocol changes, the lower-layer protocol will not be able to function correctly without being changed. In the example above, the employee gave the mailroom a message to be delivered and the name of the recipient of the message; the mailroom used the name to look up the recipient's internal mail code in the company directory. Imagine instead that the job of the mailroom was to look at the message provided by the higher layer and infer the recipient itself, using the knowledge that travel reimbursements are processed by the reimbursement department. Now consider what would happen if the responsibility for processing reimbursements were to be transferred to another department. In the original example, the operation of the mailroom layer (to look up the internal mail code for the name given to it by the higher layer) would not be affected by the change. In the variation just discussed, the change at the reimbursement-processing layer would require a change at the mailroom layer, as the existing procedure (deliver reimbursements to the reimbursement department) would deliver the reimbursement request to the wrong department.

The description of the travel-reimbursement example glossed over an important difference between how higher layers and lower layers operate. At the reimbursement layer and at the mailroom layer, a protocol entity at the sending location and a protocol entity at the receiving location exchange messages to realize the service provided by their protocol. In contrast, at the postal layer, the postal-service entities in the sending and receiving locations and additional intermediate entities on the path from origin to destination contribute to the realization of the service. In the postal service, letters are not transported from sender to receiver directly, but through a series of intermediate locations, such as the local mail processing and distribution center, hub and spoke processing centers, and the mail processing and distribution center close to the company's headquarters. At each postal-service location, an entity belonging to the postal layer checks the address on the envelope to determine the next destination on the path and uses the services of yet another layer (let us call it the *transporting layer*) to deliver the envelope to that destination, where the same process is repeated until the envelope arrives at its final destination.

As we will see below, a similar difference in the operation of different layers can often be found in layered networks. Consider a communications path that consists of a series of nodes. Sometimes a higher layer may operate directly between the first and the last node on the path (i.e., end-to-end between the endpoints of the path), while a lower layer may operate hop-by-hop between adjacent nodes along the path (box 2.5, figure 2.8). As we will see, differences in operation between layers that operate hop-by-hop rather than end-to-end have important implications for the inability of lower layers to correctly implement a certain class of functions. This inability, in turn, is an important rationale behind the narrow version of the end-to-end arguments.

The End-to-End Arguments

The end-to-end arguments guide the placement of functionality in a multilayer system. Although the layering principle advises that the functionality of a system should be organized in layers, it does not provide any rules for assigning functions to layers. Thus, when designing a layered system, architects still have to decide how to divide its functionality among layers. In particular, when building a general-purpose system that is intended to support a variety of applications, architects often create a layered structure. The applications reside on top of the general-purpose system, which forms the lower levels of the hierarchy. With this general structure, there are many application requirements that could be implemented at a higher or a lower level, or at several layers in the hierarchy. In particular, functionality that is needed by specific applications could be implemented as part of the application (a higher layer) or could be incorporated in the general-purpose system (which forms the lower layers of the system). With respect to this choice, the end-to-end arguments provide a rationale for moving application-specific functionality upward in a layered system.[54]

In the context of communication networks, the end-to-end arguments have vertical and horizontal dimensions. In layered communication networks, the allocation of functionality among layers affects how functionality is distributed among end hosts and computers in the network's core.[55] Higher layers only have to be implemented on end hosts; they do not have to be implemented on computers in the core of the network. As a result, the decision to place functionality in a higher layer places this functionality at the end host. While lower layers are implemented on all computers, they are the only layers that have to be implemented on computers in the network's core.[56] As a result, their design determines the functionality present in the core of the network.

The end-to-end arguments, which had been implicitly used in system design for years, were first identified, named, and described by Jerome Saltzer, David Reed, and David Clark in 1981.[57] In the networking community, the role of the end-to-end arguments as a fundamental principle governing the design of computer networks is generally acknowledged.[58] The end-to-end arguments are also believed to be among the few architectural principles underlying the design of the Internet.[59] However, there is a great deal of uncertainty about how to apply the end-to-end arguments in specific cases. Often, proponents and opponents of a technical solution refer to the end-to-end principle to justify their view. In view of this widespread disagreement, it is necessary to clarify exactly what is meant by "the end-to-end arguments" before we can test whether a specific technical solution complies with this design principle.

It seems natural to look to Saltzer, Reed, and Clark for an authoritative definition of the principle. Since 1981, when their paper was published, they have revisited the end-to-end principle in several papers. In a joint paper, they evaluated active networking in the context of the end-to-end arguments.[60] In two recent papers, David Clark and Marjory Blumenthal have analyzed the role of the end-to-end arguments in light of the changing requirements of today's Internet.[61] In addition, David Reed and Jerome Saltzer have written short comments referring to the considerations underlying the original paper.[62]

Studying the papers mentioned in the preceding paragraph yields a surprising result: there are two versions of the end-to-end arguments that represent different rules for architectural design.[63] To see this, consider the following two statements of "the end-to-end principle": "A function should only be implemented in a lower layer, if it can be completely and correctly implemented at that layer. Sometimes an incomplete implementation of the function at the lower layer may be useful as a performance enhancement"[64] (first version) and "A function or service should be carried out within a network layer *only if it is needed by all clients of that layer*, and it can be completely implemented in that layer"[65] (second version). The first version paraphrases the end-to-end principle as presented in the original paper (the complete original definition is given below). The second version is directly taken from the paper on active networking and end-to-end arguments. Clearly, the second version establishes much more restrictive requirements for the placement of a function in a lower layer. This insight may be surprising—the authors never explicitly drew attention to the change in definition.[66] In the literature, most texts that refer to "the end-to-end arguments" simply quote either the first or the second version.[67] Whereas technical discusssions often focus on the first version,[68] policy texts and descriptions of the Internet's architecture usually use the second version.[69] Yet nearly all texts refer to the example of reliable file transfer that was used to explain the reasoning behind the end-to-end arguments in the original paper.[70]

Have the end-to-end arguments simply evolved over time?[71] Should we distinguish between the two versions? As the subsequent analysis will show, it is better to distinguish between the two. Both provide a justification for moving functionality upward in a layered system, but there are real differences between the two versions in scope, content, and validity. For example, while the first version (the "narrow" version) applies only to a certain group of functions within a system, the second version (the "broad version") applies to the complete functionality of a system. The terminology ("narrow" vs. "broad") used throughout this book reflects this difference in scope.[72] As we will see, the rules imposed by the broad version are more restrictive than those imposed by the narrow version. Whereas the narrow version is based on an argument about correctness and claims absolute validity, the broad version is the result of a trade-off based on a specific prioritization of values. Designers must follow the narrow version if they want to design a correct system, but they can choose whether to apply the broad version. They should apply the broad version only if the trade-off among values underlying this design principle reflects the combination and the prioritization of values they want to achieve.[73]

Since both versions constrain designers to a different degree, their application may result in different architectures. Some architectures may be compliant with one version but not with the other. Failing to distinguish between the two may lead to incorrect systems, may create confusion, and may lead to unnecessary debates about the correct application of the end-to-end arguments, both in policy debates and in the networking community.

The following analysis explores these questions in more detail. Starting with the narrow version that was presented in the original paper by Saltzer, Reed, and Clark, it sets out the two versions of the end-to-end arguments and outlines the reasoning behind them. It then compares the two versions and highlights the reasons in favor of distinguishing between the two.

The Narrow Version

The Design Principle   The narrow version of the end-to-end arguments was first articulated in the original end-to-end paper by Saltzer, Reed, and Clark, where it was applied to the division of functionality between an application and a communication system[74]:

> The function in question can completely and correctly be implemented only with the knowledge and help of the application standing at the endpoints of the communication system. Therefore, providing that questioned function as a feature of the communication system itself is not possible [i.e., it is not possible to provide a complete and correct implementation of the function within the communication system only]. (Sometimes an incomplete version of the function provided by the communication system may be useful as a performance enhancement.)[75]

Later the principle was applied to the division of responsibility between end systems and the core of the network and generalized to the placement of functionality in higher or lower layers:

> A function should not be implemented in a lower layer, if it cannot be completely and correctly implemented at that layer. Sometimes an incomplete implementation of the function at the lower layer may be useful as a performance enhancement.[76]

In the context of the narrow version, the choice between layers is not always equivalent to the choice between end systems and the core of the network. It is equivalent if the lower layer is implemented in the network and the higher layer operates end-to-end between the end hosts. In this case, placing a function in the higher layer also puts the function at the end host, whereas placing the function in the lower layer puts the function in the network (figure 2.6, case 1). The choice between layers is not equivalent to the choice between end systems and the core of the network if the layers under consideration terminate in the same pair of end systems. In this case, either choice places the function at the end host, but in different layers (figure 2.6, case 2). Thus, the importance of the narrow version goes beyond the division of functionality between end systems and the core of the network.

Analysis   The narrow version of the end-to-end arguments highlights the existence of functions that can be completely and correctly implemented only at the endpoints, i.e., end-to-end between the original source and ultimate destination of data; these are the functions to which the argument

Case 1: Should the function be placed in layer 1, or in layer 2?

Case 2: Should the function be placed in layer 2, or in layer 3?

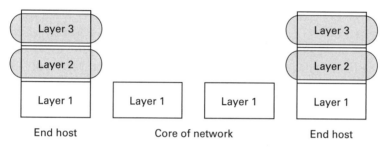

Figure 2.6
The choice between layers is not always equivalent to the choice between end hosts and the core of the network.

applies. Throughout this book, these functions will be called *end-to-end functions*. As we will see, implementing these functions completely and correctly at a lower layer (in the network) is not possible.[77] If designers want to build a correct system—a system that behaves as it is supposed to—these functions must be implemented at a layer where a complete and correct implementation is possible. In general, this will be a higher layer where protocols operate end-to-end between end systems, i.e., between the original source and the ultimate destination of data (at the end hosts). In some cases, it may even be the highest layer—the application itself.

Also implementing a necessarily incomplete version of these functions at a lower layer (in the network) is redundant and usually constitutes an inefficient use of system resources. In some cases, however, an incomplete implementation at the lower layer may be justified to enhance system performance.

The narrow version of the end-to-end arguments, then, provides two design rules for end-to-end functions: first, end-to-end functions must be implemented at a layer where they can be completely and correctly implemented. Second, whether the function should also be implemented at a lower layer must be decided case by case.

But what functions are end-to-end functions to which the narrow version applies, and why can they not be completely and correctly implemented at a lower layer within the network?[78]

In general, a function (e.g., error control to ensure data integrity) cannot be completely and correctly implemented at a lower layer if events falling into the function's responsibility (e.g., corruption of data) can occur outside the scope of control of the lower-layer protocol. In this case, the lower-layer protocol cannot cover all events for which the function is responsible; it is not able to perform the function completely and correctly.

This problem may arise in two cases: in the first case, the lower layer operates hop-by-hop, while the higher layer operates end-to-end, and events falling into the responsibility of the function may occur within the nodes along the path (figure 2.7, threat 1).[79] In this case, the lower layer will not be able to implement the function completely and correctly. In the networking context, the canonical examples of this type of problem are error control to ensure data integrity and encryption to ensure confidentiality.

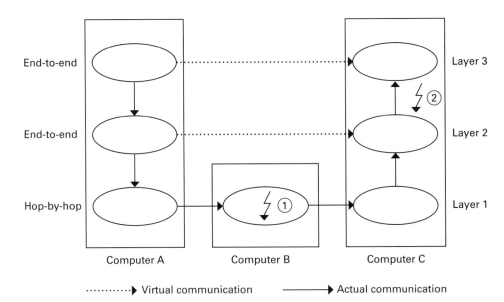

Figure 2.7
Only a higher-layer protocol that operates end-to-end can protect against threat 1. Only a protocol at layer 3 or higher can protect against threat 2.

Consider a communication path that consists of a series of nodes from the origin to the destination. The higher layer operates end-to-end between the origin and the destination, while the lower layer operates hop-by-hop between the nodes along the path (box 2.5).

If error control is performed by a hop-by-hop protocol at each hop along the path, the protocol ensures that the data that leaves the protocol entity

Box 2.5
End-to-End versus Hop-by-Hop Execution of Functionality

Consider a communication path that consists of a series of nodes from the origin to the destination (figure 2.8).[a] A protocol that operates end-to-end between the origin and the destination operates "directly" between these two systems, the endpoints of the path. In such a protocol, the protocol peers at the origin (A) and the destination (B) communicate with each other directly to realize the protocol's functionality.[b] Functionality implemented end-to-end is performed once between the endpoints. A protocol that operates hop-by-hop along this path operates between neighboring computers on the path from the origin to the destination. Functionality implemented in this way is performed locally at each step or "hop" along the path without regard to the protocol's operations at the other hops. At each step, the two protocol peers at neighboring nodes cooperate to execute the function. That is, the protocol entity at the origin (A) does not communicate with its counterpart at the destination to realize the protocol's functionality, but with its peer at the next computer (B) in the path. In the next step, the protocol entity at B communicates with its peer at the next computer (C) in the path, and so on.

a. Whereas the concepts of "end-to-end" and "hop-by-hop" are often presented in the context of communication between end systems, end-to-end versus hop-by-hop is a relative concept that can apply to other sequences of nodes within a network where a source node communicates with a destination node, from which it is separated through a series of nodes. The choice then is whether to implement a function end-to-end between the source and destination or hop-by-hop between the hops along the path. For example, "with respect to the network nodes, flows between switches or routers can be viewed as end-to-end, while links between link repeaters (or bridges) are viewed as hop-by-hop" (Sterbenz and Touch 2001, p. 41). For a more detailed discussion and additional examples, see ibid., pp. 39–41, 345–346.
b. "Direct communication" is a conceptual abstraction. In reality, protocol peers on different computers do not communicate directly; they use the services of lower layers to send messages to their peers.

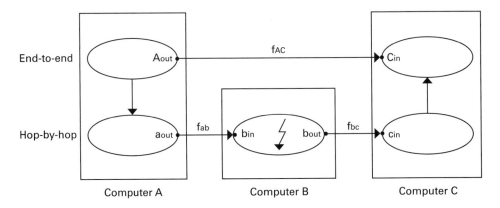

Figure 2.8
End-to-end versus hop-by-hop execution of functionality.

at one node is identical to the data that arrives at this entity's peer at the next node. The protocol does not detect what happens while the data is processed within the node. For example, in figure 2.8, the hop-by-hop protocol would check whether the data that leaves a_{out} is the same as the data that arrives at b_{in} and whether the data that leaves b_{out} is the same as the data that arrives at c_{in}, but it does not test whether the data that arrives at b_{in} is the same as the data that left b_{out}. Thus, if error control is implemented hop-by-hop, data may still get corrupted in the nodes. For example, errors may be introduced within a node while data is transferred from the input to the output buffer, because of errors in the network interface cards or because of memory bit errors.[80]

In contrast, end-to-end error control at the higher layer detects whether the data leaving the higher layer at the first node (at A_{out}) is identical to the data arriving at the higher layer of the last node (at C_{in}). The mechanism identifies all errors that may have been introduced along the path, both between two nodes and within a node. For this reason, error control can be completely and correctly implemented only at a higher layer that operates end-to-end between the data's original source and ultimate destination.[81]

Similarly, if data is encrypted by a protocol in hop-by-hop fashion, the protocol encrypts the data when it leaves the protocol entity at the node. Once the data reaches the protocol peer at the next node, it is decrypted so that this layer or higher layers within the node can process it, and it is not encrypted again until it leaves this layer to be sent out. Thus, while hop-by-hop encryption ensures confidentiality while the data is in transit between two nodes, it does not prevent unauthorized access to data while the data is unencrypted in the nodes along the path. In contrast, if data is encrypted by a higher layer that operates end-to-end between the first and the last node along the path, it is encrypted when it leaves the higher layer at the first node and decrypted when it arrives at the higher layer at the last node. Thus, the data is kept confidential along the entire path.[82]

There is a second case in which a lower layer cannot correctly and completely implement a function (e.g., error control): the case in which both layers terminate in the same pair of computers, but events that the function should cover (e.g., corruption of data) occur before data enters the lower layer or after data leaves the lower layer (figure 2.7, threat 2).[83] In this case, only a function implemented at or above the layer where the event occurs can guarantee the correct execution of the function.

Again, error control and encryption may be afflicted with this problem. Consider two layers that terminate in the same pair of computers. If data may get lost or corrupted after it leaves the lower layer, this layer cannot completely and correctly implement error control. Instead, error control must be performed at or above the layer at which the problem occurs. For example, if the file system introduces errors while storing the data, only an error control performed by the file-transfer application may be able to spot and correct this problem.[84] With respect to encryption, if the end system itself is not secure, unauthorized access may occur after the data leaves the lower layer. Thus, encryption to ensure confidentiality cannot be completely and correctly implemented at this layer. To ensure confidentiality, the data must be encrypted and decrypted at a higher layer—at the lowest trusted layer within the end system.[85]

Error control and encryption are therefore end-to-end functions, and the narrow version of the end-to-end arguments applies to them. Apart from error control and encryption, the original paper mentions delivery guarantees, suppression of duplicate messages, guaranteeing first-in-first-out message delivery, and transaction management as examples of end-to-end functions.

If designers want to build a correct system (one that behaves as required), these end-to-end functions must be implemented at a higher layer at which they can be completely and correctly implemented. Which layer meets this criterion depends on where events occur that have to be covered by the function.[86] In general, the appropriate layer will be a higher layer where protocols operate end-to-end between end systems, i.e., between the original source and ultimate destination of data; in some cases, it may be the highest layer—the application itself.[87]

While an end-to-end function must be implemented at a higher layer to ensure the correct operation of the system, the narrow version of the argument explicitly mentions the possibility of placing an additional implementation of the function at the lower layer.[88] Because the lower layer cannot implement the function completely and correctly, an instantiation at this layer is necessarily incomplete. Although the lower-layer implementation is redundant, it may improve overall performance.[89] Thus, the decision to also implement a necessarily incomplete version of the function at the lower layer is the result of a trade-off.[90] In the words of the original paper, "the amount of effort to put into reliability measures within the data communication system [as an example of a partial low-level implementation] is seen to be an engineering trade-off based on performance, rather than a requirement for correctness."[91]

For example, if some underlying links are very unreliable, performing additional error control hop-by-hop along these links may increase the efficiency with which communication resources are used: as more erroneous data is retransmitted locally over one link instead of end-to-end through the whole network, network load is reduced; so, potentially, is overall delay. However, local error control increases the amount of processing within the network (which may increase delay) and consumes additional bandwidth (because of additional checksums at the lower layer).[92]

Different technologies may justify a different resolution of this trade-off. Consider a computer that accesses the Internet over a wireless link without error control. Because the only error control operates end-to-end between the sending host and the receiving host, packets will have to be retransmitted across the whole network every time a packet is lost. Since wireless networks are very unreliable, there will be many end-to-end retransmissions. Error control on the wireless link would replace these retransmissions across the whole network with retransmissions across the wireless link. The considerable reduction in network traffic may justify the implementation of error control on this link. In contrast, the technology used by a dial-up modem is much more reliable than wireless links, but has far less bandwidth. Because of the modem's reliability, local error control would not drastically reduce the number of end-to-end retransmissions resulting from problems on this link. At the same time, the additional bits needed to implement the error control would consume valuable bandwidth on a link with little to spare. Thus, an additional implementation of error control on the access link may be worth the cost on a wireless access link, but not on the link used by a dial-up modem.[93]

In addition to these general considerations, the original paper mentions two specific costs of performing an end-to-end function at the lower layer that should be considered in the trade-off. First, executing the function is costly for applications that do not need it.[94] Second, the application or higher layers may have more information about their needs than lower layers (the network), and may therefore be able to perform the function more efficiently.[95] These arguments play important parts in the broad version of the argument and will therefore be explained below. They show, however, a bias against partial lower-level implementations of end-to-end functions in the original paper.[96]

The Broad Version

The Design Principle   Whereas the narrow version applies only to functions that cannot be completely and correctly implemented at lower layers (in the network), the broad version provides a general rule for dividing functionality among layers in a multi-layer system and for distributing functions between end systems and the core of the network in multi-layer communication networks. The broad version is emphasized in later texts by the authors of the original paper.[97]

According to the broad version, "specific application-level functions usually cannot, and preferably should not, be built into the lower levels of the system—the core of the network."[98] Instead, "a function or service should be carried out within a network layer only if it is needed by all clients of that layer, and it can be completely implemented in that layer."[99] Lower layers of the system (the network) should provide only general services and functions of broad utility across applications in order to support as many higher-layer applications as possible. Lower-level functions are not optimized to better support specific higher-layer applications. Though this may increase the performance of the particular application, it also constitutes an unnecessary and therefore inefficient feature for applications that do not need this function; it may even rule out the implementation of applications not foreseen at the time of the design.[100]

Thus, according to the broad version, lower layers of the system—the network's core—should provide only general services that can be used by all applications. Application-specific functionality should be concentrated in the higher layers of the system, at the end hosts (figure 2.9). The broad

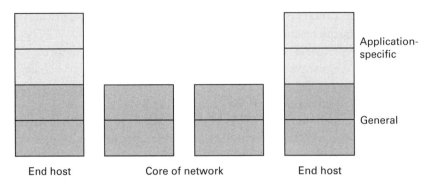

Figure 2.9
Distribution of functionality in a network based on the broad version.

version does not prevent functions from being implemented in the network if they cannot be completely and correctly implemented at the end hosts only.[101]

Analysis On the one hand, applying the broad version of the end-to-end arguments results in an architecture that can accommodate new applications not foreseen at the time of design. Having the designers of applications (who know the needs of their applications) design application-specific functionality may be more efficient than asking designers of lower layers to anticipate the needs of future applications. Finally, an architecture based on the broad version may be more reliable than an architecture that implements application-specific functionality in the core of the network.

On the other hand, the broad version prevents optimizing the performance of current applications if the optimization involves the implementation of application-specific functionality in the core of the network. This reduced performance is the price for the evolvability of the system. The broad version thus represents a trade-off between long-term evolvability, application autonomy, and reliability, on the one hand, and certain types of performance optimization, on the other. Designers should choose the broad version of the end-to-end arguments if the trade-off among qualities underlying the broad version reflects the relative importance of qualities in the system under consideration. In the words of David Reed: "One of the main conclusions of the end-to-end argument is usually to point out the inflexibility or difficulty of evolution of a design to incorporate requirements not known at the time of system design. Non-end-to-end designs usually fail to meet future needs quickly. That's the point. No one would make an end-to-end design if they had a fully specified problem and were searching for the absolute optimum performance where all conditions are known. Yet many of the 'let's rewrite end-to-end' arguments are based on some person's urgency to deliver the maximum performance possible in the shortest possible time, evolvability-be-damned."[102]

Evolvability   A general-purpose system is designed to support various applications that may have different requirements. Implementing functionality in lower layers of a system that is needed by only some applications, or otherwise optimizing the lower layers for the needs of specific applications, will usually improve the performance of these applications.[103] Since the lower layers of the system must be used by all applications, applications with diverging needs will have to bear the impact of the optimization too.[104] Functionality that lets some applications work better may hurt other applications whose needs differ.

Problems caused by application-specific functionality in the network are likely to become more severe if the architecture is intended to last a long time. Though it may be possible to perform a constrained optimization that optimizes the network for a known set of uses, the result is not likely to meet the needs of applications that are unknown and unpredictable at that time.[105] In the best case, a new application must pay the costs of a service it does not need. In the worst case, the functionality contained in the lower layers may prevent the new application from being deployed at all.

Consider two examples. The public switched telephone network was originally designed to transmit human speech. Over time, network providers deployed a number of technologies in the network that optimized the network for the needs of telephony. The telephone network transmits sounds within a certain frequency range (300–3,400 Hz).[106] When sound is transmitted over long cables, the strength of the signal declines rapidly. Higher frequencies lose strength faster than lower frequencies, which reduces the quality of transmission. To ameliorate this, network providers deployed devices called *load coils* on cables longer than 18,000 feet. Load coils boost the strength of the higher frequencies to the same level as the lower frequencies. As a side effect, they effectively cut off frequencies above 3.4 kHz. Since telephony does not use the frequencies above 3.4 kHz, network providers did not view this as problematic. Digital Subscriber Line (DSL), the technology used to transmit digital data over the last mile of the public telephone network, uses the frequencies above 25 kHz. Since load coils cut off signals above 3.4 kHz, they have to be removed before DSL can be used over these lines. Thus, load coils optimized the telephone network for the needs of a specific application (voice telephony), but they are incompatible with another application (high-speed DSL Internet service) that was not foreseen at the time of the optimization.[107]

In the 1990s, various aspects of the Internet's architecture were optimized for the needs of a particular group of applications called *client-server applications*, which were the dominant class of applications at the time.[108] These applications included Web surfing, online shopping, and watching video streams. Client-server applications consist of a client program and a server program, both running on end hosts.[109] The client program and the server program interact in a pattern typical of client-server applications: the client requests a service from the server, and the server delivers the service. Whereas the request for service usually does not use a lot of bandwidth, the delivery of the service is often bandwidth-intensive. For example, when you surf the Web, the browser sends a small amount of data to the server to ask for a specific website. The server returns a large amount of data—the webpage—to the browser. Similarly, the client of a streaming video application such as RealPlayer sends a small amount of data asking for a specific video; the server then sends a large amount of data—the streamed video—to the client.

Given that most of the applications that were known at the time followed this pattern, network providers designed the access links (the links connecting the home to the network provider) of their broadband networks to provide asymmetric bandwidth. Technologies such as ADSL (deployed in telephone networks) and HFC (deployed in cable networks) offer significantly more bandwidth from the provider to the home than from the home to the provider.[110] This lets providers get more downstream bandwidth out of an access link with a certain capacity than if the upstream and downstream bandwidth are given an equal amount of bandwidth. This solution improves the performance of client-server applications by giving them more bandwidth where they need it and less bandwidth where they do not need it. Today, asymmetric bandwidth creates problems for applications that send and receive an equal amount of data; these applications are called *peer-to-peer applications*. Internet-telephony applications (Vonage, Skype), video conferencing software, and file-sharing applications (Napster, Gnutella, BitTorrent) all have these characteristics.[111]

Whereas functionality implemented in the network usually has to be used by all applications, applications can choose the higher-layer protocols they want to use.[112] Thus, following the broad version of the end-to-end arguments and placing application-specific functionality in a higher-layer protocol at the end host restricts the positive as well as the negative effect of application-specific functionality to applications using the protocol.

Since lower layers in a system designed using the broad version provide only very general services and are not optimized for specific higher-level applications, the lower levels can support a wide variety of applications and do not rule out new applications not foreseen at the time of design.

In addition, as we will see in chapter 4, designing a system using the broad version of the end-to-end arguments concentrates functionality that is likely to change in areas of the architecture that are easy to change. Areas of the architecture that are difficult to change contain functionality that is not likely to change over the lifetime of the system.

Application Autonomy   The broad version also supports application autonomy. Application autonomy is the idea that an application or higher layers close to it know best what services they need and should therefore be responsible for meeting these needs.[113] This has two aspects. First, it is very difficult, if not impossible, for lower-layer designers to guess in advance what tailored services potential future applications might require. Thus, it is very likely that some higher layers will always end up having to implement application-specific services themselves. It therefore seems more reasonable (and more efficient, as lower-layer designers would put effort into designing functionality that would ultimately have to be designed again at a higher layer anyway) to let higher layers take care of their specific needs instead of shifting this responsibility to lower layers.[114] Second, the application or higher layers that are more application-specific than lower layers may have more information about their needs than lower layers, and may therefore be able to perform the function in question more efficiently.[115] For example, not all compression algorithms are equally suited to compress certain types of information. Whereas file data such as executable code can only be compressed using lossless compression techniques, the characteristics of video or audio are better suited to the use of lossy compression algorithms.[116] The application, or an application-specific higher layer that knows the type of information it wants to transfer, is in a better position to choose an appropriate compression algorithm than a lower layer that does not have this information.

To fulfill their responsibility, higher layers must be able to use the building blocks provided by lower layers according to their needs.[117] Application autonomy implies a hierarchical relationship between applications and the network: the applications are in control, and the network has a serving role. Lower layers are responsible for providing very general building blocks, which can then be used by the application designer to realize application-specific needs.

In the original Internet, users control end hosts, while network providers control the core of the network. Under these circumstances, by putting applications on end hosts in control, the principle of application autonomy effectively puts control over the use of the network in the hands of the users.[118]

Reliability Finally, using the broad version is likely to increase the reliability of applications and the network.[119] For applications, implementing application-specific functionality in the network introduces additional points of failure in the network that are not under the control of the designer or the user of the application. In contrast, an application that does not depend on the correct implementation and functioning of application-specific services in the network may be more reliable, since all potential points of failure are under the control of the designer or the user of the application.[120]

For the network, concentrating application-specific functionality and services at the end hosts isolates the network from the consequences of erroneous applications[121]: the impact of unexpected malfunctions and failures of application-specific functions is restricted to individual end hosts and data flows and does not affect the network as a whole. In contrast, a failure of application-specific functionality in the network may negatively affect the entire network, not just certain applications. In addition, restricting application-specific functionality to end hosts may reduce the complexity of lower-layer protocols, thereby reducing the complexity of programs that must be implemented on computers in the network's core. Since it is easier to design, implement, and test programs that are less complex, the resulting network is likely to be more reliable.

Lack of Application Awareness and Application Control in the Core of the Network Applying the broad version of the end-to-end arguments results in a network that is not able to distinguish between the different applications running over it, or to control or to positively or negatively affect their execution. This feature is often attributed to the end-to-end arguments directly.[122] As is apparent in the description of both versions above, however, neither version deals explicitly with this question. Thus, those reading either version of the end-to-end arguments and expecting to find a non-discrimination rule will be rightly disappointed. This does not mean that there is no relationship between the end-to-end arguments and non-discrimination, though. The lack of application awareness and application control in the network's core is a direct consequence of the broad version of the end-to-end arguments.[123] This is because it is not possible to design a network architecture that gives the network the ability to distinguish between the applications running over it or to control their execution without violating the broad version of the end-to-end arguments. In order to identify the different applications using the network and to positively or negatively influence their execution, application-specific filtering and control mechanisms must be implemented in the network's core. The implementation of application-specific functionality in protocols in the core of the network directly violates the broad version of the end-to-end arguments that prescribes that application-specific functionality must be concentrated in and be restricted to higher layers at the end host.[124] The filtering and control mechanisms in the network's core may also violate the layering principle if the mechanisms operate at the Internet layer or at a lower layer but access or modify the message[125] (protocol data unit) passed to them by higher-layer protocols.[126] In that case, the mechanisms violate the second constraint imposed by the layering principle in the context of layered communication networks: a lower-layer protocol may not make any assumptions about the protocol data unit passed to it by a higher-layer protocol for delivery to its higher-layer protocol peer, and consequently may neither access nor act on the information contained in higher-layer protocol data units.[127]

The application-blindness of an end-to-end network prevents the network owner from discriminating against applications running on its network. Thus, the broad version of the end-to-end arguments effectively shields independent application developers from strategic behavior by network owners.[128] From the perspective of an independent application developer, this is a benefit resulting from the application of the broad version of the end-to-end arguments. From the point of view of a network owner, this feature constitutes a cost of end-to-end design if the network owner has an incentive to discriminate against independent applications. This question is explored more in chapter 6.

Since the application-blindness of an end-to-end network prevents the network owner from discriminating against applications, an end-to-end network is neutral among applications. The "network neutrality" that results from applying the broad version of the end-to-end arguments is at the core of the current policy debates.[129] Arguing that network neutrality has beneficial effects on innovation, proponents of regulation are asking legislators and regulators worldwide to protect network neutrality by regulating the owners of broadband networks.[130] Opponents of regulation argue that, because network owners do not have an incentive to discriminate against independent applications, network neutrality does not have to be enforced through regulation,[131] or, alternatively,[132] that a network-neutrality regime would reduce network owners' incentives to upgrade their broadband networks in the future.[133]

Costs of the Broad Version of the End-to-End Arguments   The broad version of the end-to-end arguments does not come without costs. First, it may be difficult for inexperienced Internet users to understand and manage complex end hosts. Since all application-specific functionality is concentrated at the end hosts, application software must be installed, configured, upgraded, and maintained by users. For inexperienced users, this may be highly problematic.[134] The problem can be ameliorated, however, by hiding this complexity from the user—for example, users have the option of buying personal computers with pre-installed, pre-configured software. Similarly, software can be upgraded automatically over the Internet.[135] Second, for the network owner, an end-to-end design may complicate network management, security, and pricing. The complications arise mainly from the application-blindness of the network. Network management may be easier if you know what applications are running over the network. For example, data on patterns of use may enable network providers to predict or at least observe changes in the behavior of users, and may facilitate capacity planning in a network.[136] Similarly, a clear overview of the applications using a network at a specific point in time may make it easier to detect security attacks.[137] (How the broad version of the end-to-end arguments affects security is discussed in chapter 9.) Finally, in an application-blind network, it is not possible to price-discriminate between users on the basis of the applications they use. (How differences in application awareness affect the pricing strategies available to a network operator is explored in chapter 6.)

The analysis in the preceding paragraph refers to a network that realizes the broad version of the end-to-end arguments in its pure form. Depending on a network's architectural design, it may be possible to collect some information about the applications running over the network in a way that, although it violates the layering principle, does not destroy the benefits of applying the broad version of the end-to-end arguments. Thus, depending on the architecture, it may be possible to ameliorate the problems with network management and security mentioned above while affecting architectural integrity only slightly. For example, in the architecture of the Internet, the Internet Protocol (IP) header and the transport protocol header contain information that can often be used to infer what application is sending the data (e.g., the IP protocol field and the TCP/UDP/SCTP port numbers).[138] Although these fields were not intended to be interpreted by routers in the network, a packet filter operating at the Internet layer with access to these fields can nevertheless gather this information. Such packet filters are often used by network providers to collect information on user behavior or identify security attacks.[139] Although this violates the layering principle (the packet filter needs information about the format of transport-layer protocol data units, and accesses transport-layer protocol data units[140]), the negative effect of this violation is marginal as long as the packet filter neither modifies nor acts on the data. Since the filter does not modify the higher-layer information or acts upon it, it does not affect the operation of higher-layer protocols. If existing higher-layer protocols are changed, or if new higher-layer protocols are added, the filter may collect useless information, but it does not impede or prevent the operation of these higher-layer protocols. Using such devices constitutes a trade-off between architectural purity on the one hand and network management and security on the other. In contrast, the architectural effect of devices that not only access but also modify or act upon information contained in higher-layer protocol data units is usually quite severe.[141]

Comparison of the Two Versions

The two versions of the end-to-end arguments differ considerably with respect to scope, content, and validity. In other words, they differ with respect to the range of functions to which they apply, the rules for the placement of these functions, and the justifications for these rules.

Scope During the design of a layered architecture, the complete functionality of the system must be assigned to layers. The narrow version applies only to a sub-group of this functionality: end-to-end functions (functions that cannot be completely and correctly implemented in the lower layers of the system). The narrow version does not offer any guidance on functions that do not have these characteristics. In contrast, the broad version guides the design of the system's complete functionality.

Content The two versions of the end-to-end arguments apply different criteria to determine the proper allocation of functionality. The narrow version distinguishes between "complete" and "partial" implementations of end-to-end functions (functions that can only be completely and correctly implemented in higher layers at the end hosts). The design rules provided by the narrow version provide guidance not only with respect to the partitioning of functionality between the network and end hosts but also with respect to the allocation of functionality to different layers in the network or on end hosts. In contrast, the broad version distinguishes between "general" and "application-specific" functions and uses this distinction to allocate functions to the network or end hosts; it does not distinguish further between different layers in the network or on end hosts.

Though the two versions agree that functions that cannot be completely and correctly implemented in the network must be implemented on end hosts, they differ with respect to other functionality (table 2.1).

Table 2.1
Differences in design rules between the narrow version and the broad version.

	Narrow version	Broad version
Case 1: The function can be completely and correctly implemented at the higher layer and at the lower layer and is needed by all clients of the lower layer.	The function can be implemented at the higher or the lower layer.	The function can be implemented at the higher or the lower layer.
Case 2: The function can be completely and correctly implemented at the higher layer and at the lower layer and is not needed by all clients of the lower layer.	The function can be implemented at the higher or the lower layer.	The function should be implemented at the higher layer.
Case 3: The function can only be completely and correctly implemented at the higher layer.	The function must be implemented at the higher layer. An additional implementation of the function at the lower layer is possible for performance reasons; the decision about an additional implementation at the lower layer should be made on a case-by-case basis.	The function should be implemented at the higher layer. No additional implementation of the function at the lower layer for performance reasons.
Case 4: The function can only be completely and correctly implemented at the lower layer.	The function should be implemented at the lower layer.	The function should be implemented at the lower layer.

First, the narrow version does not say anything about functions that can be completely and correctly implemented in lower and higher layers of the system. The decision where to implement these functions is left to the system architects. As a result, a system based solely on the narrow version could implement these functions in lower or higher layers of the system.

In contrast, the broad version only allows implementing functions in lower layers of the system, if they are needed by all clients of the layer and can be completely and correctly implemented at that layer, or if they cannot be correctly implemented at the end hosts. Thus, a system that implements a function in a lower layer of the system that can be completely and correctly implemented in a lower and a higher layer, but is not needed by all clients of the lower layer would violate the broad version but not the narrow version.

Second, according to the narrow version, the designers of the system must decide in each case whether they should implement a necessarily incomplete version of end-to-end functions in lower layers of the system to improve the performance of the system. While the original paper shows a bias against such lower-layer implementations, it presents this choice as an open trade-off that system architects must resolve case by case. The performance improvement resulting from such an additional implementation is an important argument to be considered in this trade-off.

In contrast, the broad version has resolved the trade-off between evolvability and performance on a general basis, and it forbids the implementation of functions (including incomplete lower-level implementations of end-to-end functions) in lower layers of the system unless they are needed by all clients of these layers, owing to their negative effect on the evolvability of the system. The fact that such a design reduces performance has already been factored in the decision to use this design principle. If performance had been more important than evolvability, the system architects would not have chosen to use this design principle. Thus, the broad version entails a strong presumption that the performance gains of implementing application-specific functionality in the lower layers of the system do not outweigh the costs for the evolvability of the system. As a result, the performance gains resulting from such an implementation usually cannot be used to justify a deviation from this rule. Reasons that could justify a deviation from this rule may exist, but they must go beyond those that were already considered in the trade-off. In other words, these reasons must be so important or the circumstances must be so different that they justify reversing the trade-off that originally led to this design rule.[142] For example, as we will see in chapter 9, it may be justifiable to deviate from the broad version to make the Internet more secure.

If designers were allowed to decide whether to deviate from the broad version and implement application-specific functionality in the network case by case, the long-term evolvability of the system would not be adequately protected.[143] A case-by-case analysis biases system designers in favor of deviating from the broad version and quickly reduces the generality of the system. This is because of the problems associated with resolving the trade-off between evolvability and performance case by case. Whereas the benefits of deviating from the broad version (including the reduction in cost and the improvement in performance of certain applications) are immediately apparent, the costs associated with reducing the system's evolvability are difficult to determine because the applications that may suffer from the deviation are not yet known. This makes it impossible to determine whether and to what extent some of these future applications will be harmed. Since the applications are not yet known, their social value cannot be known either; this makes it impossible to determine what the ultimate costs to society will be. As research in behavioral economics has shown, humans tend to assign disproportionately more weight to present benefits (i.e., the performance optimization or cost saving in the present) than to future benefits (i.e., the ability to use unknown applications in the future), which makes it more likely that designers will deviate from the broad version. That the future benefits are uncertain aggravates this bias. Moreover, designers working on a specific problem may lack the architectural knowledge to adequately assess the architectural effect of their solution. For example, when firewalls and network-address translators (which both deviate from the broad version) were first deployed, their negative consequences for the evolvability of the network were not immediately recognized. It took a while to understand why and how they affect different classes of applications. Though the effect of a specific deviation may seem small, the interactions between several deviations quickly erode the evolvability of the system.[144] For example, network-address translators and firewalls together have made it much more difficult to develop certain kinds of applications, and almost impossible to deploy new transport-layer protocols in the Internet, severely constraining the evolvability of the Internet.[145]

Finally, the two versions constrain applications in different ways. As we will see below, the broad version of the end-to-end arguments requires that applications be implemented in higher layers on end hosts. In contrast, the narrow version may require designers to implement certain end-to-end functions in the application itself.

Validity   The two versions are based on different justifications. The narrow version is based on an argument about correctness: if designers want to build a correct system (one that behaves as required), they must follow the first design rule embodied in the narrow version and implement each end-to-end function at a higher layer at the end hosts, where it can be completely and correctly implemented. Whether an additional, necessarily incomplete version of an end-to-end function is implemented at a lower layer does not affect the correctness of the system. The second design rule of the narrow version presents this question as an open trade-off that must be resolved by the system architects case by case.

The broad version is based on different considerations. For all functions other than end-to-end functions (which must be implemented end-to-end for reasons of correctness anyway), the broad version's design rules emerge from a trade-off: they reflect the decision to prioritize long-term system evolvability, application autonomy, and reliability over short-term performance optimizations.[146]

Owing to these differences, both versions offer different amounts of freedom to system architects. Since designers usually want to build a correct system, system architects and subsequent designers must follow the first rule of the narrow version. In contrast, system architects can choose freely whether or not they want to use the broad version. If they do not agree with the trade-off struck by the broad version, they can choose a different design principle and still build a correct system. Once the system architects have chosen the broad version, however, subsequent designers must comply with the rules established by that principle or else the long-term evolvability of the system will suffer.

Rationale for Separation   Even if the authors of the "end-to-end papers" did not intend to propose two different (though related) design principles, it is necessary to distinguish between those two design principles.

Owing to the differences in the content of the rules, both versions constrain the design of an architecture in different ways. Often an architecture is compliant with one version but not with the other. (We will encounter examples in chapter 3.) A clear conceptual separation between the two principles makes it easier for designers to recognize whether none, one, or both of them must or could be applied to solve their particular design problem.

A clear conceptual separation between the two versions would avoid unnecessary arguments about the "correct" application of "the end-to-end argument" and direct attention to the real question: how to resolve the trade-offs associated with the placement of functionality. Over the years, both versions have been adopted by the scientific community as "the end-to-end argument." Whereas general books on network architecture often present the narrow version, texts published by the Internet Engineering Task Force or the Internet Architecture Board and papers on Internet policy usually are based on the broad version. Owing to the different rules embodied in the two versions, two designers can apply "the end-to-end argument" to assess a technical solution and arrive at contradicting results. Thus, contradicting views of compliance with the end-to-end arguments often arise because people use different versions of the end-to-end arguments, not because the same principle is incorrectly applied. In this case, the real issues lie elsewhere. The designers disagree about the proper resolution of the trade-off governing the placement of functionality, and they should argue about the prioritization of values, not about the meaning of the end-to-end arguments.

Failing to recognize the narrow version as a distinct design principle may even lead to incorrect systems. Designers can disagree about resolving a trade-off, but they cannot disagree about the requirements for correctness. Even someone who does not think that application autonomy, reliability, and long-term system evolvability are more important than short-term performance optimizations must comply with the narrow version and implement end-to-end functions end-to-end; otherwise the system will not execute correctly. If the two versions are not separated, there is a danger that designers will not recognize that the requirements for correctness established by the narrow version are independent of the broad version, and that, because they disagree with the trade-off that underlies the broad version, they will not comply with the narrow version.

Because recent developments in the architecture of the Internet differ with respect to the challenges they pose to both arguments, the differences between the two versions may become even more relevant in the future. As will be discussed in the concluding chapter, some architectural solutions contradict one version but comply with the other. In this case, it is important to be aware of the differences between the two versions so as to identify the issues posed by the problem under consideration.

A clear distinction would also resolve some common policy disputes. As was noted above, proponents of network neutrality regulation usually point to the beneficial effect of network neutrality on innovation. Network neutrality, however, does not follow from the *narrow* version of the end-to-end arguments—it is a consequence of applying the *broad* version. The argument in favor of regulation is based on the benefits of applying the broad version of the end-to-end arguments and on the negative consequences of deviating from that version. Opponents of regulation argue that proponents have extended the end-to-end arguments beyond their original meaning, referring to descriptions of the narrow version.[147] Thus, although both sides start from original descriptions of the end-to-end arguments, they arrive at contradicting results. This puzzle might be resolved quickly if the two sides would recognize that they are not using the same argument but rather two different versions of it.

3 The Original Architecture of the Internet

This chapter outlines how the layering principle and the end-to-end arguments shaped the original architecture of the Internet. To situate the discussion, the first section provides an overview of the original architecture of the Internet. (Readers already familiar with the Internet's architecture may skip that section.) The second section discusses the effect of the layering principle and the two versions of the end-to-end arguments on the Internet's original architecture. The final section discusses some common misconceptions about the meaning of the end-to-end arguments and their relationship to the original architecture of the Internet.

Introduction to the Original Architecture of the Internet

The Internet aims to provide universal communication services to applications running on hosts attached to distinct but interconnected networks.[1] A network provides universal communication services if any host can communicate with any other host no matter what network they are attached to.[2]

Many different network technologies can connect computers. For example, wireless networks in homes or at hotspots usually use the IEEE 802.11 family of standards, better known as Wi-Fi technology, to connect computers wirelessly within a local area.[3] Companies or universities often use Ethernet technology to connect the computers that constitute their local network.[4] A network that uses a specific technology to provide connectivity between the computers attached to it is often called a *physical network*.[5] Whereas the technologies and protocols used by a physical network let the network deliver data packets to any computer attached to that network, the differences between the technologies used by different physical networks (such as the different addressing schemes used by various physical network technologies) prevent hosts attached to different

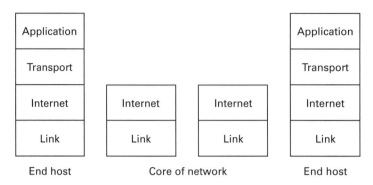

Figure 3.1
Layers in the Internet architecture.

physical networks from communicating with one another. The Internet[6] is designed to solve this: it connects different physical networks using a set of conventions that let computers attached to these networks communicate.[7]

To provide universal communication services across distinct, interconnected networks, the Internet's architecture partitions network functionality into four layers, with one or more protocols implementing the functionality assigned to each layer (figure 3.1).[8] Each layer provides communication services to the next higher layer at a decreasing level of abstraction. To implement these services, each layer uses the services provided by the layer below. The lowest layer is called the *link layer*.[9] Moving upward, it is followed by the *Internet layer*, the *transport layer*, and the *application layer*. The family of protocols used in the global Internet is called the *TCP/IP protocol suite* after its two main protocols, the Transmission Control Protocol (TCP) and the Internet Protocol (IP).

The Link Layer
The link layer contains a wide variety of protocols responsible for transporting data packets to any computer attached to a physical network or for transporting data packets across a point-to-point link.[10] All computers belonging to a particular physical network run the same network protocol. Thus, the collection of protocols at this layer corresponds to the set of physical network or point-to-point technologies that can be attached to the global Internet. The Wi-Fi or Ethernet protocols mentioned above are examples of protocols at this layer.

In the context of the reimbursement-processing example in chapter 2, the link layer consists of the technologies that deliver an envelope from one mail-processing center to the other—airplanes, trains, trucks, bikes, and so on.

The Internet Layer

The Internet layer consists of a single protocol: the Internet Protocol (IP), which transports data packets from one host to another across any set of interconnected networks. The Internet Protocol enables any pair of hosts to exchange data packets, independent of the particular physical network to which they are attached.

The Internet layer is implemented on end hosts at the edge of the network and on special computers called *routers* in the core of the network; it is the highest layer that must be implemented on computers in the core of the network. Layers above the Internet layer only have to be implemented on end hosts; they do not have to be implemented on computers in the core of the network.[11]

To higher layers, IP provides connectionless, unreliable, best-effort delivery of datagrams from end host to end host.[12] Datagrams—data packets in a specific format defined by IP—are the basic unit of data transfer across interconnected networks in a TCP/IP Internet. The delivery is connectionless: instead of establishing a virtual connection through the network from source host to destination host over which all datagrams can travel, each datagram is treated independently from all others and travels separately through the Internet. As a result, two successive packets from one host to another may follow entirely different paths. The service is unreliable in that delivery is not guaranteed. If datagrams are lost, damaged, duplicated, delayed, or delivered out of order, IP does nothing.[13] It merely transmits any datagram arriving at the destination host to the appropriate protocol in the higher layer. Finally, the service model is called *best-effort* because, although IP does its best to deliver datagrams, it does not provide any guarantees regarding delays, bandwidth, or losses.

To implement the aforementioned services, IP specifies an addressing scheme (a way to identify all hosts in the Internet), a method of interconnection between different physical networks, and a set of rules and procedures for moving datagrams from origins to final destinations.[14] IP's addressing scheme can be used to derive unique identifiers—"IP addresses"—for each host and each router in the Internet.[15]

As has already been noted, IP interconnects physical networks through routers in the core of the network. A router links two or more physical networks, receiving datagrams from one network and sending them to another. Typically, a sending host sends a datagram to the nearest router.[16]

If the destination host is attached to one of the physical networks to which the router connects, the router delivers the datagram to the destination end host directly. If not, the router uses the destination address to compute the next router on the path and forwards the datagram to that router. Thus, the datagram travels through the Internet from router to router until it reaches a router that can deliver it directly. At each step, the IP implementation currently holding the datagram uses the service of a physical network at the link layer to move the datagram across that physical network to the next IP implementation on the path.

The postal layer in the reimbursement example in chapter 2 operates in a similar way. At each postal processing center, someone uses the postal address to determine the next stop on the way from the original sender to the ultimate destination. The postal layer then uses the services of the lower layer (trucks, airplanes) to deliver the postal envelope to the next postal location. This process is repeated until the envelope reaches its ultimate destination. Similar to the IP protocol, the basic service of the postal service does not make any guarantees as to the timing of delivery. Envelopes may get lost or damaged or may arrive in a different order (for example, envelopes sent on the same day may arrive on different days, or an envelope sent later may arrive earlier).

The Transport Layer

The Internet Protocol delivers datagrams from one host to another—it does not distinguish between different applications on the same host. Transport-layer protocols deliver data to and from the applications within an end host. They pick up data from the sending application at the end host at the origin and deliver the data to the receiving application at the destination host. In other words, transport-layer protocols are responsible for differentiating among multiple sources or destinations within one host, letting multiple application-level processes[17] on the same end host use the network simultaneously.[18] Transport-layer protocols therefore ensure that application programs on different end hosts can communicate.[19]

Whereas IP is implemented on the routers in the core of the network and on end hosts, transport-layer protocols only have to be implemented on end hosts.[20] The transport-layer protocol implementations on the sending and receiving end hosts exchange messages with each other to implement the protocol's services.

Transport-layer protocols build on the services of the Internet Protocol at the Internet layer to provide additional services that may be useful for particular applications. Thus, the transport layer is the lowest layer implementing application-specific functionality. As we will see below, this division of responsibility follows the broad version of the end-to-end arguments. [21]

The most popular transport-layer protocol, the Transmission Control Protocol (TCP), provides a reliable, connection-oriented byte stream.[22] TCP lets two application-layer processes on different end hosts establish a connection, send and receive data over this connection, and close the connection. The connection lets the application-layer processes send and receive a continuous byte stream (i.e., the sender writes bytes into a TCP connection, which the receiver reads out of the TCP connection). TCP does not interject any boundaries between bytes, but treats the sequence of bytes passed to it by the sender as a continuous stream. TCP ensures that data handed to it by the sending higher-layer process arrives at the receiving higher-layer process without errors or duplicates and in the correct order.

In contrast, the User Datagram Protocol (UDP) provides an unreliable datagram service to application-layer processes, where data may arrive at the next higher layer out of order, duplicated, damaged, or not at all. Unlike TCP, UDP accepts and delivers separate messages, not a continuous data stream.[23]

Similarly, the postal service in the reimbursement example merely delivers mail from one mailroom to the other. It does not deliver mail to specific people within the building. This is the task of the next higher layer, the mailroom layer, which picks up mail from the sender and hands it over to the postal service at the sending location and which receives mail from the postal service at the receiving location and delivers it to the receiver. Thus, the mailroom layer builds on the mailroom-to-mailroom service of the postal layer to provide person-to-person communication services to the highest layer. Like transport-layer protocols, members of the mailroom staff work in the office building at the origin and at the destination, but not in the postal processing centers in between. In our example, there is only one mailroom-layer protocol that provides a service similar to UDP: it accepts and delivers separate pieces of mail. The members of the mailroom staff do not implement additional procedures to ensure that the mail really does arrive at the receiver, or that separate pieces of mail sent between the same two people arrive in the order in which they were sent.

The Application Layer

The application layer contains a range of protocols that let applications communicate with one another. E-mail, the World Wide Web, Internet-telephony applications (e.g., Vonage and Skype), file-sharing applications (e.g., Napster, Kazaa, BitTorrent), and streaming video applications (e.g., Real Player, QuickTime, Windows Media Player) are all examples of applications operating at this layer. An application protocol defines the rules and conventions that govern the interactions among different parts of a distributed application.[24] To communicate with an application on a different end host, both application programs exchange data according to the format and conventions specified in the application protocol.[25] For example, the Web browsers Mozilla Firefox and Internet Explorer are application programs, running on an end host, that communicate with Web servers—application programs running on a different end host—to show users webpages. The browser contacts the server and asks for the desired page; the server then sends a copy of that page back to the browser. Web browsers and Web servers can cooperate in this way because they communicate in accordance with the Hypertext Transfer Protocol (HTTP), which defines the format and the procedure for Web browser-server interactions.

Any distributed application has to define rules governing the interactions among its parts; otherwise, the distributed parts will not be able to communicate or cooperate to accomplish a task. As a result, any designer who builds a distributed application based on the TCP/IP protocol suite specifies an application-layer protocol. For example, the rules that govern the communication among Skype programs operating on different machines form an application-layer protocol. Skype keeps this protocol proprietary, so only Skype implementations produced by Skype can communicate with each other. In contrast, a number of application-level protocols for such popular applications as e-mail and file transfer have been standardized by the Internet Engineering Task Force (IETF), by the World Wide Web Consortium, or by some other standards body to let programs communicate with each other using standardized protocols, no matter who designed them. As a result, an e-mail program produced by one vendor can send e-mail to an e-mail program produced by another vendor if both programs conform to the same application-layer protocol (usually the Simple Mail Transfer Protocol).[26]

The Internet and the Layering Principle

Apart from specifying the division of functionality between layers, the Internet's architecture imposes constraints on the interactions between protocols belonging to different layers and on the number of protocols that may populate a layer.

Whereas lower layers are not allowed to use the services of higher layers, higher layers are allowed to invoke the services of protocols in the same layer or any layer below them, down to the Internet layer. In other words, layers above the Internet layer are not allowed to make direct use of the services of a layer below the Internet layer.[27] Thus, the Internet's architecture realizes relaxed layering with a portability layer at the second-lowest layer, the Internet layer (figure 3.2).[28]

Although the Internet layer is restricted to a single protocol—the Internet Protocol—other layers may host a variety of protocols.[29] As described above, the link layer contains a wide variety of protocols that correspond to the different types of physical networks over which the Internet Protocol can run. Above the Internet layer, each layer is allowed to contain various protocols, which in turn may support multiple protocols at the next higher layer. The resulting structure of protocol dependencies is often likened to an hourglass, with the Internet Protocol as the hourglass's waist (figure 3.2).[30]

This design isolates the transport layer and the application layer from changes below the Internet layer. Owing to the use of the Internet layer as a portability layer, the visibility of the link layer is restricted to the Internet layer.[31] Thus, as long as the service interface provided by the Internet Protocol does not change, the Internet Protocol can take

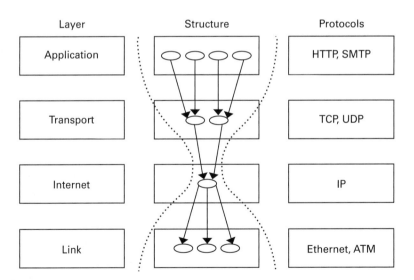

Figure 3.2
Layering in the Internet architecture.

advantage of new physical network infrastructures and new transmission and link technologies without needing changes in the higher layers.

At the same time, since lower layers are not allowed to use the services of higher layers, the Internet layer and the link layer remain unaffected by innovations in the transport and application layers. As a result, the Internet layer divides the protocol stack into two quasi-independent subsystems that can evolve separately.

The Internet and the End-to-End Arguments

The End-to-End Arguments and the Division of Functionality between the Internet Layer and the Transport Layer

During the initial design of the Internet's architecture, end-to-end arguments shaped the division of functionality between the Internet layer and the transport layer. Whereas the narrow version required that functions such as reliable data transfer, duplicate suppression, and reordering be implemented end-to-end between the original source and ultimate destination of data (i.e., end-to-end between end hosts), the broad version influenced the general division of functionality between the two layers. Although the two design principles had not been formally identified, named, and described as design principles when the Internet's original architecture was developed (the relevant papers were published in 1981 and 1998[32]), the Internet's architects implicitly applied and followed the rules that later came to be known as (the two versions of) "the end-to-end arguments."[33]

The Narrow Version   The narrow version of the end-to-end arguments postulates that, since certain functions cannot be completely and correctly implemented in lower layers of the network, they must be implemented end-to-end between the end hosts that are the original source and the ultimate destination of data. As described above, error control, duplicate suppression, and reordering are functions that exhibit this characteristic. Performing these functions hop-by-hop in the Internet layer would not guarantee their correct execution. Consider reliable data transfer. If the Internet Protocol had implemented hop-by-hop error control between hosts and routers and between routers, datagrams would have been transported correctly from host to router, from one router to the next, and from router to host. Datagrams could still be corrupted at the routers themselves (e.g., as a result of memory bit errors in the routers). Only an end-to-end error control covers the entire communication path from source host to destina-

Box 3.1
The Decision to Implement Error Control End-to-End

The decision by the Internet's architects to implement error control end-to-end between the two end hosts involved in the connection constituted a deliberate departure from other network architectures. For example, the Arpanet Host-to-Host Protocol (AHHP) did not use end-to-end acknowledgment and retransmission, but relied on the lower-layer subnet protocols and the host-to-subnet protocols for reliable delivery. As some of the researchers involved in the design of the Internet noted, this design prevented the AHHP from fully guaranteeing reliable delivery (framed in the terminology of the narrow version, they argued that this design does not constitute a complete and correct implementation)—a deficiency the Internet Transmission Control Protocol was designed to correct by performing error control and retransmission end-to-end between the end hosts.[a] Similarly, the X.25 architecture, an alternative network architecture favored by traditional telecommunication carriers, originally did not offer end-to-end error control and retransmission between the computers attached to the network, but instead relied on the communication subnet to deliver data reliably. Researchers involved in the design of the Internet criticized this choice, arguing that the lack of end-to-end integrity checks made it impossible for X.25 networks to guarantee end-to-end reliability (framed in the terminology of the narrow version, they argued that only an end-to-end implementation of the function could completely and correctly implement it).[b] Although the decision by the Internet's architects to implement error control end-to-end seems obvious today, it was controversial at the time.[c]

a. See Garlick, Rom, and Postel 1977, pp. 1–2; Abbate 1999, pp. 127–128.
b. See Bochmann and Goyer 1977, pp. 15–16, 26–29; Cerf and Kirstein 1978, pp. 1397, 1402–1403; Pouzin and Zimmerman 1978, p. 1367; Abbate 1999, p. 158.
c. See Bolt, Beranek and Newman Inc. 1974 (defending Arpanet) or Blackshaw and Cunningham 1980 (defending X.25).

tion host. On the basis of this insight, the Internet's architects decided to implement error control end-to-end between the end hosts (box 3.1).

Functions such as error control and duplicate suppression were originally implemented end-to-end at the Internet layer as part of the Internetwork Transmission Control Protocol, but were later split from the Internet layer and moved to a separate transport-layer protocol called the *Transmission Control Protocol* (TCP).[34] If one assumes that transport-layer protocols

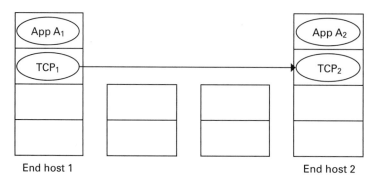

Figure 3.3
TCP operates end-to-end between end host 1 and end host 2.

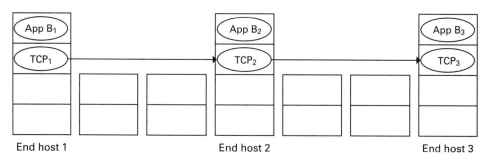

Figure 3.4
TCP operates hop-by-hop between end host 1 and end host 3.

operate end-to-end between the original source and the ultimate destination of data, placing end-to-end functions in a transport-layer protocol such as TCP is compliant with the narrow version (figure 3.3). If this assumption does not hold, end-to-end functions must be implemented at a higher layer that truly operates end-to-end. Ultimately, the appropriate place may be the application itself. For example, if the original source and the ultimate destination of data are connected by a concatenated sequence of transport-layer connections, the transport layer operates hop-by-hop between the original source and the ultimate destination of data (figure 3.4). For example, e-mail or the World Wide Web may exhibit this structure. (For a description of the structure of e-mail, see box 3.6.) As was explained above, however, for end-to-end functions such as reliable data transfer, a concatenation of hop-by-hop functions at the lower layer is not equivalent to a single end-to-end execution of the function at the higher layer.[35]

Box 3.2
Error Control above the Transport Layer in the Current Internet

---

If data may get corrupted after leaving the transport layer, the narrow version requires that error control be performed at a layer above the transport layer, at or above the layer at which data may get corrupted. For example, in their 1984 paper describing the narrow version, Saltzer, Reed, and Clark argue that a file-transfer application must implement end-to-end error control itself in order to eliminate all threats to data integrity that may occur after the data leaves the communication system—for example, when the data is stored on the disk.[a] In spite of this insight, most present-day applications do not implement such functionality themselves but rather use the reliable data-transfer functionality provided by transport-layer protocols such as TCP. On the one hand, implementing integrity checks is difficult and costly. On the other hand, the remaining threats to data integrity in the end system are negligible in regard to the needs of most applications. Thus, for most applications the costs of providing error control in the application outweigh the benefits of doing so.[b] In accordance with the narrow version of the end-to-end arguments, however, it is usually strongly recommended that mission-critical applications that depend on data integrity implement their own integrity checks.[c]

a. See Saltzer, Reed, and Clark 1984, p. 280; Border et al. 2001, section 4.1.3.
b Moors 2002, pp. 1215–1216. The decision where to implement error control is also related to trust (Clark and Blumenthal 2007).
c. See Stone and Partridge 2000, sections 5.4 and 6; Moors 2002, pp. 1215–1216; Border et al. 2001, section 4.1.3.

Placing an end-to-end function in a transport-layer protocol also fails to constitute a complete implementation of the function if events falling within the function's domain occur after the data leaves the transport layer. How likely this is to happen must be judged for each application (box 3.2). If, for a specific application and a specific function, events falling within that function's domain occur after the data leaves the transport layer, the narrow version requires that the functionality be implemented at or above the layer where the event occurs, potentially in the application itself.[36] Although the implementation of the function provided by TCP constitutes only a partial implementation for that application, the application can use TCP's services to guarantee the function's execution across the network and up to the transport layer. Providing reliable data transfer or other end-to-end functions across a communication network is a very complex task that requires sophisticated mechanisms and functionality. Using TCP may thus greatly simplify the end-to-end implementation of the function at the higher layer.[37] Although TCP may not be able to provide a complete implementation of end-to-end functions for all applications, implementing this functionality in a transport-layer protocol lets different applications share this functionality without negatively affecting applications that do not need it. Applications that do not need the functionality and do not want to pay its costs can simply use another transport-layer protocol—one that is more appropriate to their needs. Thus, for applications that must implement an end-to-end function in the application itself to guarantee a function's correct execution, the function's implementation in TCP is a partial implementation that, according to the narrow version, can be justified as a performance enhancement.[38]

Thus, the narrow version shaped the Internet's original architecture by requiring that end-to-end functions such as error control, duplicate suppression, and reordering be implemented end-to-end between the original source and the ultimate destination of data. However, the narrow version does not explain two other, related choices made during the design of the original architecture: the decision to split the original Internetwork Transmission Control Protocol at the Internet layer into two protocols (the Internet Protocol at the Internet layer and the Transmission Control Protocol at the transport layer) and the decision not to implement hop-by-hop error control in the Internet layer.

The researchers working on the Internet's architecture initially proposed an *Internetwork Transmission Control Protocol* for the Internet layer (figure 3.5, left). This protocol combined the hop-by-hop aspects of datagram transfer through the Internet and end-to-end implementation of reliable data transfer, duplicate suppression, and other end-to-end functions. It transferred datagrams hop-by-hop, but it performed error control, duplicate suppression, or packet reordering end-to-end, combining the functionality of today's Internet Protocol and Transmission Control Protocol in a single protocol.[39] Under this proposal, all applications that wanted to use the Internet had to use the services of the Internetwork Transmission Control Protocol, including the parts of the protocol that provided connection-oriented reliable data transfer.[40] This solution complied with the narrow version. As indicated above, the narrow version allows the implementation of functions in a lower layer in the network if the function can be completely and correctly implemented at that layer. Reliable data transfer and duplicate suppression are end-to-end functions that can be completely and correctly implemented only end-to-end between the original source and

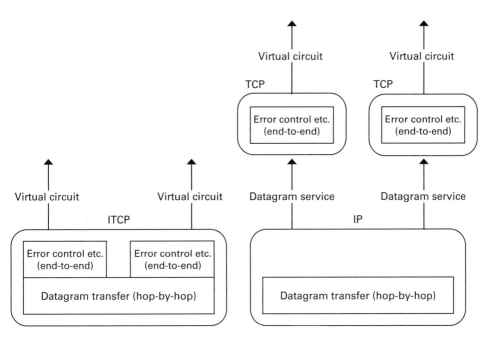

Figure 3.5
Splitting ITCP.

ultimate destination of data. Since the proposed monolithic protocol implemented these functions end-to-end between the sending and receiving end hosts, it implemented them completely and correctly.[41]

Although the Internetwork Transmission Control Protocol complied with the narrow version, the Internet's architects decided to split the protocol into two separate protocols: the Internet Protocol and the Transmission Control Protocol that we know today (figure 3.5, right).[42] In this architecture, end-to-end functions such as reliable data transfer or duplicate transmission are implemented as part of the Transmission Control Protocol at the transport layer. As we saw earlier in this section, this solution also complies with the narrow version.

In addition, the Internet's architects had to decide whether to implement hop-by-hop error control at the Internet layer. Since error control can be completely and correctly implemented only end-to-end, hop-by-hop error control at the lower layer provides only an incomplete implementation of this function. The narrow version explicitly allows (but does not require) such an additional implementation to optimize performance, but leaves this decision for the system architects to make in each individual

Table 3.1
Internet design decisions that only the broad version can explain.

Decision	Does solution comply with narrow version?	Does solution comply with broad version?
One monolithic Internet-layer protocol, combining functionalities of TCP and IP	Yes	No
Split TCP from IP	Yes	Yes
Decision	Does solution comply with narrow version?	Does solution comply with broad version?
Hop-by-hop error control in Internet layer	Yes	No
No hop-by-hop error control in Internet layer	Yes	Yes

case. Although the designers of the Internet's architecture chose not to implement such functionality at the Internet layer, a decision to implement hop-by-hop error control at this layer would have complied with the narrow version.[43]

In neither of the cases discussed above can the narrow version explain why the Internet's architects chose one solution over the other, since all the options under consideration complied with the narrow version. As will be shown in the next subsection, these choices were driven by the broad version of the end-to-end arguments (table 3.1).

The Broad Version   The broad version of the end-to-end arguments argues that application-specific functionality usually cannot—and preferably should not—be implemented in the lower layers of the network, the network's core. Instead, a function should be implemented in a network layer only if it can be completely and correctly implemented at that layer and is used by all clients of that layer. Thus, lower layers, or the core of the network, should provide only general services of broad utility across applications, whereas application-specific functionality should be implemented in higher layers at the end hosts.

Separation of the Internet Layer and the Transport Layer   The initial proposals for an Internetwork Transmission Control Protocol combined the hop-by-hop aspects of datagram transfer through the Internet with the end-to-end implementation of functions such as reliable data transfer and duplicate suppression in a single protocol.[44] In this design, all applications that wanted to use the Internet had to use the Internetwork Transmission Control Protocol, which provided a single service: connection-oriented reliable data transfer (or a "virtual circuit").[45]

Some of the researchers opposed this design. They argued that reliable data transfer and connection orientation are application-specific functions that are needed by some but not all applications, and that implementing these functions in the Internet layer may be inefficient for, and may even hurt, applications that do not need them.[46] The 1998 paper describing the broad version later presented this insight—i.e., that performing application-specific functions in the network may harm or even rule out applications that do not need them—as one important argument for keeping application-specific functions out of the network.[47] Applications have very different requirements regarding reliability, throughput, and delay.[48] For example, e-mail and file transfer require reliability but are less sensitive to delay than some other applications. Real-time transmission of uncompressed voice or video can tolerate a certain amount of data loss, but suffers from increased delay (or variability in delay).[49] Ensuring reliable data transfer by performing end-to-end error control and retransmission usually increases delay (and variability in delay).[50] Thus, researchers working on real-time delivery of voice argued, forcing all applications to use reliable data transfer reduces the performance of applications such as real-time delivery of voice that do not need perfect reliability but suffer from increased delay.[51] Similarly, to provide connection-oriented data transfer, a bi-directional virtual path through the network is established before the actual data transmission starts. Establishing the connection takes time and requires the exchange of several control messages between the sender and the receiver before the actual data transmission can start.[52] Again, the latency of connection set-up and the corresponding signaling overhead may hurt some applications that do not need connections. For example, as researchers working on local-area networks pointed out, when computers communicate with one another they often exchange single packets (not streams of packets) in patterns that differ from the bi-directional point-to-point connections needed by such traditional applications as remote log-in and file sharing.[53] For these types of computer-to-computer communications, setting up a connection to send a single packet creates substantial overhead for a service that the application does not need.

According to the critics, removing all application-specific functions from the Internet layer by splitting the Internetwork Transmission Control Protocol into two protocols and providing only unreliable datagram service in the Internet layer would enable the network to support a broader range of applications. In comparison with virtual circuits, they argued, unreliable datagram service is a more elemental building block out of which a broader range of services can be built.[54] A network offering unreliable datagram service at the Internet layer can support applications that require connection orientation and reliability as well as applications that do not need these functions. For applications that require connection orientation and reliability, transport-layer protocols at the end points can construct a virtual circuit based on an the unreliable datagram service at the Internet layer.[55] Applications that do not require these functions can avoid the associated delay and overhead by choosing a different transport-layer protocol that better meets their needs—for example, one that lets them send individual datagrams without guaranteeing their delivery. In contrast, a network offering a virtual circuit service at the Internet layer cannot efficiently support applications that do not require connection orientation or reliability (i.e., the non-connection-oriented computer-to-computer communications mentioned above) and may even rule out applications (i.e., real-time delivery of voice) that suffer from increased delay. Higher-layer protocols at the end hosts cannot construct an efficient datagram service based on a virtual circuit at the Internet layer, since the delay and the overhead introduced by the Internet layer cannot be removed at a higher layer.

On the basis of these considerations, the Internet's architects decided to split the Internetwork Transmission Control Protocol into two protocols that were allocated to different layers: the Internet Protocol, which offered unreliable datagram service, and the Transmission Control Protocol, which provided connection-oriented reliable data transfer (box 3.3, figure 3.5).[56] Under the new design, which became the Internet's original architecture, the Internet Protocol, the only protocol at the Internet layer, is designed to provide a basic building block of broad utility across applications.[57] Transport-layer protocols can use this building block to construct more elaborated services better suited to specific classes of applications.[58] Thus, the transport layer is the lowest layer that implements application-specific functionality; it is also the lowest layer that only has to be implemented on end hosts (figure 3.6). Although the Internet's architects specified only two transport-layer protocols in the original architecture (the Transmission Control Protocol and the User Datagram Protocol, the latter of which offers unreliable datagram service), they envisaged that more transport-layer protocols would be added over time.

In sum, although the broad version of the end-to-end arguments had not been formally identified and described as a general design principle

Box 3.3

The Decision to Split TCP and IP

The decision to split the initial monolithic protocol into two separate protocols was made at a meeting of the researchers involved in the design of the Internet Transmission Control Protocol on January 30–31, 1978, at the Information Sciences Institute in Marina Del Rey.[a] In an e-mail exchange with Bob Frankston and Vinton Cerf, David Reed (one of the authors of the papers describing the end-to-end arguments) later described the events that led to this decision[b]:

There were a small number of proponents for specifying the Internet protocols as based on datagrams, with the idea of reliable in-order delivery being an "application layer" mechanism. This all came together at the meeting I attended in Marina del Rey. John Schoch, Danny Cohen and I each presented arguments to that effect, from different points of view. John argued based on the PUP architecture, which was an architecture based on datagrams, where streams were one option among many.[c]

Danny argued for the idea that packet speech did not want retransmission, but instead just a sequence-numbered stream of packets, where non-delivery was an option because latency was the key variable and the application could fill gaps. I argued that non-connection based computer-computer protocols, such as those we were developing for interconnected LANs, could be more general, and that end-to-end reliability was ultimately up to the endpoints to assure—for example, there were useful protocols that involved a packet from A to B, handing off of the request from B to C, and a response back from C to A were quite useful, and would be end-to-end reliable at the application level, while gaining little or no benefit from low level "reliability" guarantees. Other protocols, such as multicast, etc. were essentially datagram-oriented. I remember arguing quite strongly that you could support streams on top of datagrams, but by requiring a streams, you'd never get effective or efficient datagram services. Danny equally argued that reliable streams would create latency variability (jitter) where none was necessary. John Schoch argued that PUP was datagram-based, with streams built on top, and that architecture was quite effective. . . .

As I recall, we 3 people, plus Steve Crocker, conspired to argue that we needed a datagram service so we could continue to do research on more general protocols, and in the heat of the argument proposed why not split out the addressing layer from the stream layer, just as we had split the TCP from the functions of the Telnet layer. . . . In the heat of the Marina del Rey meeting, we 3 (sitting next to each other) agreed to push for splitting the TCP packet into two layers, the routing header and the end-to-end stream payload. This resulted in a sidebar meeting in the hall during the next break, where I remember it was Jon [Postel], you [Vinton Cerf], Danny [Cohen], me, Steve [Crocker], and John Schoch, and you [Vinton Cerf] agreed that we should try defining how we'd split the layers, and see if the overhead would be significant. This resulted in 3 protocols, IP, TCP, and UDP (for us datagram nuts). Danny went off being happy that he could define a packet speech protocol layered on UDP, I went off happy that I didn't need to pursue DSP[d] anymore, but could focus on how to use UDP for protocols like TFTP, which we built at MIT shortly thereafter."

Box 3.3

(continued)

---

a. See Postel 1978b, p. 1 (describing the results of the TCP meeting) and Postel 1977b, p. 8 (noting the location of the next meeting). See also Abbate 1999, pp. 129–130.

b. Peter, no date.

c. For a description of the Pup architecture, see Boggs et al. 1980.

d. DSP (which stands for "Data Stream Protocol") was a LAN-centric Inter-networking protocol that David Reed had developed at MIT to allow for both datagram-like and stream-like behavior to coexist (Peter, no date). According to Reed (2009a), "DSP was developed as part of our research work at MIT on protocols for high speed networks to support distributed computing applications. Bob Kahn had insisted that we unify our research with the ongoing TCP project as a condition of funding—because the goal of TCP was to interconnect every kind of transport and every kind of application, he wanted to understand how to make TCP a universal interoperability solution."

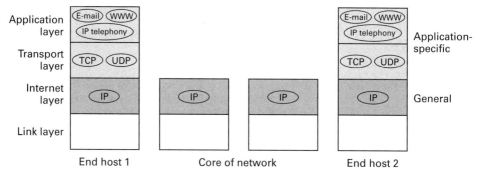

Figure 3.6

Distribution of functionality in the Internet's original architecture.

when the Internet's architects decided to split TCP and IP, they implicitly applied the rules established by the broad version. First, the Internetwork Transmission Control Protocol implemented application-specific functionality in the network, which violates the broad version. The architects rejected this solution. Second, their decision to offer unreliable datagram service at the Internet layer instead of the virtual circuit service provided by the Internetwork Transmission Control Protocol was based on the desire to have a more general service that did not contain application-specific functionality and that, as a result, could support a broader range of applications. Finally, their decision to split TCP and IP placed all application-specific functionality in higher layers at end hosts.

In addition, the choice to offer unreliable datagram service at the Internet layer was motivated by two other design considerations: the designation of the Internet layer as the portability layer and the desire to enable applications to survive partial network failures.

Designating the Internet layer as the portability layer makes it possible to incorporate a wide variety of physical networks into the Internet. As a portability layer, the Internet layer provides an abstract interface independent of the specific characteristics of underlying physical network technologies. To let the Internet Protocol run over a particular physical network, the network only has to be able to transport a packet of reasonable size to any computer attached to it.[59] Though there should be some level of reliability, perfect reliability is not required. Had the service interface provided by the Internet Protocol made stronger assumptions about the services available from underlying networks, some physical network technologies would not have supported all services. To let the Internet Protocol run over such networks, the missing services would have to be implemented in software to simulate their existence for the Internet layer. This would have complicated the incorporation of such networks. Keeping the Internet Protocol's service interface simple made it possible for a wide variety of physical networks to be incorporated in the Internet without requiring much programming in the Internet layer.[60]

Providing a connectionless, unreliable datagram service at the Internet layer, while placing connection-oriented functionality in transport-layer protocols operating end-to-end between end hosts, makes the Internet more robust.[61] Owing to this division of functionality, information about the state of the connection between the two end hosts (such as the number of packets transmitted or the number of packets acknowledged) is concentrated at the end hosts, while computers in the core of the network do not maintain information about the state of ongoing connections. As a result, even if network components or sub-networks fail, no information essential for the continuation of this connection is lost—the transport-layer-protocol entities can continue to use the connection as long as an appropriate communication path through the network remains. Since all the state information regarding the ongoing connection between two end hosts resides at these two hosts, this state is lost only if one or both of the end hosts involved in the connection are destroyed. Since state and communicating entities live and die together, this feature has been called *fate-sharing*.[62] In contrast, a connection-oriented packet-switched network maintains information about specific ongoing connections at packet switches within the network; if one of these packet switches is destroyed, the information about the state of the connections going through this switch is destroyed too, and all connections currently going through this switch fail.

No Hop-by-Hop Error Control in the Internet Layer   The Internet's architects also had to decide whether to implement hop-by-hop error control between hosts and routers, and between the routers along the path.[63] Although performing hop-by-hop error control in the Internet layer increases the performance of applications that need reliability, it also increases delay (box 3.4). Thus, implementing this function in the Internet layer optimizes the network for the needs of some applications (those that require reliability), but makes it more difficult or even impossible to support applications that do not need reliability but are sensitive to delay (e.g., applications that transmit uncompressed speech or other media streams in real time). Thus, implementing hop-by-hop error control in the Internet layer reduces the range of applications that the network can support. On the basis of this argument—one of the main arguments underlying the broad version—

Box 3.4
The Effect of Hop-by-Hop Error Control

Compared to an architecture that only implements error control and retransmission end-to-end, additional hop-by-hop error control and retransmission at a lower layer may reduce the frequency of end-to-end retransmissions initiated by the end-to-end implementation of the same functionality at a higher layer. Since retransmissions from source to destination across the whole network take longer than retransmissions across a single hop, an additional hop-by-hop implementation may reduce overall delay and improve the performance of applications that need reliability.[a]

Hop-by-hop error control, however, increases delay due to the time needed to check integrity and potentially retransmit data at each "hop" along the path. This creates a problem for applications for whom fast transmission is more important than data reliability (e.g., applications that transmit uncompressed speech or other media streams in real time).[b]

a. See Saltzer, Reed, and Clark 1984, p. 281; Moors 2002, p. 1216.
b. Saltzer, Reed, and Clark 1984, p. 282, 284–285; Sterbenz and Touch 2001, p. 373.

the Internet's architects decided not to implement hop-by-hop error control at the Internet layer.[64] Thus, on the basis of the reasoning underlying the broad version, the Internet's architects (implicitly applying the design rule that later was called *the broad version*) decided not to implement an application-specific function in the network.

The End-to-End Arguments and Application Design

Apart from guiding the division of functionality between the Internet and the transport layer, both versions of the end-to-end arguments influence the design of individual applications.

The Narrow Version   As we saw above,[65] the narrow version may require that end-to-end functions be implemented in layers above the transport layer, and ultimately in the application. This is the case if the transport-layer protocols do not operate end-to-end between the original source and the ultimate destination of data, or if events falling into the responsibility of the end-to-end function occur after data leaves the transport layer. In the first case, the function must be implemented at a layer that operates end-to-end between the original source and the ultimate destination of the data. In the second case, it must be implemented at or above the layer at which the event occurs.

The Broad Version   The broad version constrains the design of individual applications by requiring application-specific functionality to be implemented in higher layers at the end hosts, not in the core of the network. Within these boundaries, designers are free to choose any application design they like.

Some Misconceptions about the End-to-End Arguments and Their Relationship to the Architecture of the Internet

This section explores some propositions regarding the meaning of the end-to-end arguments and their relationship to the architecture of the Internet which have been advanced in the literature. These propositions have been used to support arguments against using the end-to-end arguments as Internet design principles or policy guidelines.

The propositions in the first group question the role of the end-to-end arguments in the design of the Internet's original architecture. They are usually used in debates about the relevance of the end-to-end arguments to Internet policy. Scholars argue that—because the end-to-end arguments are no different from the layering principle, or because the original paper describing the end-to-end arguments was published after the original architecture of the Internet was developed, or because e-mail had a certain management structure—the Internet's original architecture was not based on the end-to-end arguments. If the Internet's original architecture was not based on the end-to-end arguments, this line of reasoning continues, the end-to-end arguments cannot and should not have any relevance to Internet policy.

The propositions in the second group are often used to argue against the continuing use of the end-to-end arguments as a principle of design or of policy. According to this stance, the end-to-end arguments constrain the development of the Internet's architecture too much and prevent the network's core from evolving as it should. For example, researchers advancing this argument assert that the end-to-end arguments rule out architectures that store state in the network, prohibit the provision of Quality of Service in the network, require the network to be simple, or constrain the design of applications by preferring certain application-management structures over others. They then go on to argue that, because the end-to-end arguments interfere with the Internet's need for state in the network (or Quality of Service, or a complex network), those arguments no longer should guide the Internet's design.

As we will see, these propositions are based on misconceptions. Though this does not imply that the end-to-end arguments are still the appropriate design principles for the Internet, or that they should guide Internet policy, it does imply that these propositions cannot be used to support the arguments against their use outlined above.

End-to-End Arguments and Layering

Some argue that the broad version of the end-to-end arguments directly flows from the layering principle.[66] This perception is not correct.[67]

The layering principle usually results in a system in which lower layers provide more abstract services than higher layers.[68] Thus, both design principles tend to create systems in which lower layers are more abstract or general than higher layers. The broad version of the end-to-end arguments, however, establishes much more restrictive rules for placing functions in lower layers in the network than the layering principle. A system based on the layering principle must comply with the constraints imposed by that principle—i.e., lower-layer protocols are not allowed to use higher layers, and so on. Beyond these constraints, system architects are free to place functions as they see fit.[69] In contrast, in a system following the broad version, "a function or service should be carried out within a network layer only if it is needed by all clients of that layer, and it can be completely implemented in that layer."[70]

Thus, a layered network architecture that complies with all the constraints imposed by the layering principle, but implements application-specific functions in the network, complies with the layering principle, but violates the broad version of the end-to-end arguments. The Open Systems Interconnection architecture's X.25 protocol suite is an example of such an architecture.[71] It implements error control and error handling at all lower layers up to the transport layer. As we saw above, performing error control in the Internet layer violates the broad version. Thus, this architecture respects the layering principle, but contradicts the broad version of the end-to-end arguments. Similarly, the initial proposals for an Internetwork Transmission Control Protocol that provided reliable connection-oriented data transfer at the Internet layer complied with the layering principle, but violated the broad version.[72]

If applying the layering principle can result in networks that violate the broad version, the broad version cannot flow from, and cannot be an automatic consequence of, the layering principle.

End-to-End Arguments and Fate Sharing

Some researchers assume that the end-to-end arguments require the network architecture to comply with the principle of "fate sharing" (explained above).[73] Thus, they assume that the end-to-end arguments constrain the amount of state in the network. This view can be traced back to "Request for Comments 1958," a document published by the Internet Engineering Task Force that described the architectural principles of the Internet (Carpenter 1996). After quoting the narrow version of the end-to-end arguments from the original paper, the text continues: ". . . this principle has important consequences if we require applications to survive partial network failures. An end-to-end protocol design should not rely on the maintenance of state (i.e. information about the state of the end-to-end communication) inside the network. Such state should be maintained only in the endpoints, in such a way that the state can only be destroyed when the endpoint itself breaks (known as fate-sharing)."[74] Neither version of the end-to-end arguments directly establishes rules for state in the network. Whereas the broad version emphasizes evolvability, the narrow version focuses on correctness. In contrast, fate sharing aims at survivability in case of partial network failures. As the original architecture of the Internet shows, there are situations in which all three principles are usefully applied.

This need not always be the case. As a result, it seems more useful to distinguish clearly between the different rules instead of conflating them in a single design principle.[75]

End-to-End Arguments and Quality of Service

Some researchers assume that the broad version of the end-to-end arguments rules out the provision of Quality of Service in the network.[76] This interpretation of the end-to-end arguments is too strong.[77]

The current version of the Internet Protocol provides the same service to all data packets. The Internet Protocol does its best to deliver a packet to its destination, but does not guarantee a particular bandwidth or a particular delay. If a network provides "Quality of Service," the network offers different types of service. For example, it may guarantee a minimum bandwidth or a maximum delay, or it may give some traffic priority over other traffic without giving absolute guarantees.[78] Providing Quality of Service consists of two tasks: specifying which packets get which level of service quality, and providing packets with the service quality specified. The broad version of the end-to-end arguments constrains the two tasks to different degrees.[79]

Although it is possible to build a service that offers reliable data transfer at a higher layer and operates only on end hosts on the basis of an unreliable datagram service at the Internet layer, it is not possible to build a service that offers guaranteed bandwidth or delay at a higher layer if the Internet layer does not guarantee bandwidth or delay.[80] Thus, providing guaranteed bandwidth or delay is a function that cannot be implemented at the end hosts only. Since the broad version does not prevent functions from being implemented in the network if they cannot be completely and correctly implemented at the end hosts only,[81] it does not prohibit the implementation of functions in the network that are necessary to guarantee bandwidth and delay.

The broad version may constrain which entity determines which packet gets which service quality. The principle of application autonomy described above suggests that applications (or ultimately the users) should determine which type of service they need; this does not imply that they should get this service for free. Imagine that the Internet layer offered different services with different bandwidth and delay characteristics to higher layers at the end hosts. The higher layers would choose the type of service they desired and would communicate that choice to the Internet layer through the Internet layer's service interface (e.g., by setting a type-of-service field). Such an architecture would not require application-specific functionality to be implemented in the network's core beyond what is necessary to implement functions that cannot be implemented by the end hosts alone. Thus, it would not violate the broad version of the end-to-end arguments.

In contrast, a Quality of Service architecture in which the network decides who gets what service quality runs counter to the principle of application autonomy that underlies the broad version. In particular, a Quality of Service architecture in which entities operating at the Internet layer or below make this decision on the basis of information obtained by accessing or modifying messages passed to them by higher-layer protocols, or by mechanisms that implement application-specific functionality in the network's core, would directly violate the layering principle and/or the broad version of the end-to-end arguments. For example, using deep packet inspection to "look into" a data packet and determine to which application it belongs and then slowing down packets that belong to specific applications or classes of applications (e.g., slowing down packets belonging to BitTorrent in particular or to peer-to-peer file-sharing applications in general)[82] would violate the layering principle and the broad version of the end-to-end arguments.[83]

Thus, the broad version of the end-to-end arguments constrains, but does not rule out, the provision of Quality of Service in the network.

End-to-End Arguments and the Stupid Network

Some scholars assume that the end-to-end arguments require the network's core to be "stupid"—that is, to contain only simple functionality.[84] The term "stupid network" was coined by David Isenberg to describe the original Internet (box 3.5). Though Isenberg's arguments in favor of stupid networks are similar to those underlying the broad version of the end-to-end arguments, not all networks based on the broad version are "stupid." The broad version of the end-to-end arguments does not require simplicity; it requires only that network functions be general. The broad version of the end-to-end arguments advises that the network should not contain application-specific functionality and should provide only general services useful for a large variety of applications. The argument does not restrict how the network realizes these services.[85]

End-to-End Arguments and Management Structure of Applications

Some researchers assume that the end-to-end arguments prescribe a specific structure for applications. For example, some researchers assume that distributed applications with application-level intermediaries that are part of

Box 3.5
Stupid Networks

The term "stupid network" was coined by David Isenberg in an article in which he compared the "stupid network" design that characterizes the Internet to the "intelligent network" model, on which conventional telecommunications networks are based.[a] Isenberg's arguments in favor of stupid networks are very similar to those underlying the broad version of the end-to-end arguments: contrary to the telephone network, which is optimized for a single application (telephony), a stupid network is "underspecified" (that is, not optimized in favor of specific applications). This makes it very flexible with respect to new applications.[b] A stupid network only provides "dumb transport," while intelligence is concentrated at the end hosts, under the control of the users. This design shifts control over applications and application-level innovation to users.[c] According to Isenberg, a stupid network is characterized by three features: it has "nothing but dumb transport in the middle, and intelligent user-controlled endpoints,"[d] "the center of the network is based on plentiful infrastructure—cheap bandwidth and switching"—not on scarcity,[e] and "transport is guided by the needs of the data, not the design assumptions of the network."[f]

a. Isenberg 1997.
b. Isenberg 1998, p. 28.
c. Ibid., pp. 28–29.
d. Isenberg 1997, p. 16.
e. Isenberg 1998, p. 26.
f. Isenberg 1997, pp. 16, 18.

---

the application but that are owned and operated by a network or application service provider and that topologically are in the network somehow contradict the end-to-end arguments (figure 3.7). For example, it has been argued that, because e-mail has such a structure (box 3.6), the Internet never was wholly end-to-end.[86] Based on a similar reasoning, some may think that Web-based applications or cloud computing violate the end-to-end arguments.

This view arises from an interpretation of the terms "end hosts" and "in the network" that differs from the interpretation that underlies the end-to-end arguments. Instead of understanding the two categories as indicating a computer's functional relationship to the network as a user or provider of communication services, these researchers interpret them in the context of network topology or in the context of administrative ownership and

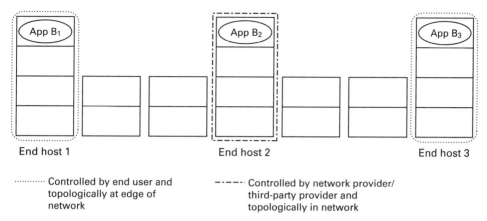

End host 1   End host 2   End host 3

.... Controlled by end user and topologically at edge of network

– – – – Controlled by network provider/ third-party provider and topologically in network

Figure 3.7
Management structure of applications.

Box 3.6
The Structure of E-Mail

In general, the e-mail program running on the sending user's computer transfers the e-mail to an intermediary mail server (i.e., an application program which is typically running on a computer that is topologically in the network and operated by the user's Internet service provider). The intermediary mail server then transfers the e-mail to the receiving user's mail server, typically also running on a computer that is topologically in the network and is operated by the receiver's Internet service provider. Finally, the e-mail program running on the receiving user's computer is used to get the e-mail from the receiver's mail server. Thus, the structure of the overall application consists of one part running on a computer that is topologically at the edge of the network and operated by an end user, two parts running on computers that are topologically in the network and operated by a third party, and one part running on a computer that is topologically at the edge of the network and operated by an end user.[a] Some argue that this structure violates the broad version of the end-to-end arguments, because the two intermediary parts of the application are running on computers topologically in the network and operated by third parties.

a. For a description of the protocols commonly used to send and receive e-mail in the Internet, see Kurose and Ross 2008, pp. 116–130. The topological and management structure for e-mail described above is not the only possible structure. For an overview of possible management structures, see Gaynor 2003, pp. 54–60.

control. Thus, they assume that an "end host" is an end system that is topologically at the edge of the network (i.e., co-located with subscriber end systems) and owned and controlled by an end user; a computer "in the network" is topologically in the network (i.e., co-located with network nodes) and owned and operated by a network provider or by a third-party service provider.[87]

Though differences in location, in ownership, or in control may be relevant from a policy perspective and may also have implications for application innovation,[88] they do not matter for the broad version of the end-to-end arguments. As explained above, the broad version describes how functionality is distributed among layers in a layered network architecture and does not cover topological or administrative relationships.[89] In the context of the broad version, the distinction between end hosts and computers in the core of the network is a purely functional distinction between users and providers of network communication services. End hosts are computers that run applications that use the network; computers in the core of the network provide services to the computers using the network. In the original architecture of the Internet, this distinction maps to the layers in the protocol stack: layers up to the Internet layer are considered to be in the network, layers above the Internet layer are not. Thus, any application implemented in layers above the Internet layer at end hosts is compliant with the broad version of the end-to-end arguments; who controls the different parts of the application and where they are located is not relevant to this design principle.

Similarly, some assume that the broad version of the end-to-end arguments favors peer-to-peer applications over client-server applications. Peer-to-peer applications are often run by "normal" end users on their end systems, whereas the server component of a client-server application is often owned and operated by a network provider or by a third-party service provider and co-located with computers belonging to the network's core.

Again, these differences are not relevant to the broad version. As long as distributed parts of a peer-to-peer application and the client and server components of a client-server application are implemented in layers above the Internet layer at end hosts, the two application architectures are equally compliant with the broad version.

End-to-End Arguments and the History of the Internet

Some claim that the end-to-end arguments cannot have influenced the design of the Internet's original architecture, insofar as the papers that named, identified, and described them as design principles were published in 1981 (narrow version) and 1998 (broad version),[90] after the Internet's original architecture had been created.[91] This view neglects the fact that the design rules and accompanying rationales that later came to be known as the "end-to-end arguments" had been used for many years before the papers formally describing them were published. The 1984 paper (the revised journal version of the 1981 paper that is usually cited when scholars refer to the end-to-end arguments) does not claim to invent a new design principle from scratch; rather, it aims to formally articulate and analyze a design principle that had already been used in a variety of areas.[92] The 1998 paper aims to evaluate whether a new approach to networking ("active networking") complies with the end-to-end arguments (an existing design principle). To do so, it describes the (broad version of the) end-to-end arguments, discussing the trade-offs and the rationale associated with this design principle and its history. Both papers explicitly acknowledge earlier work—by the authors or other researchers—that made an end-to-end argument of the type described in the paper in a specific context and thereby provided the basis for the paper's more general articulation of this design principle.[93] For example, the paper describing the narrow version points to earlier papers making an end-to-end argument in the context of encryption, and to work making an end-to-end argument in the context of reliable file backup. The paper describing the broad version points to the authors' own work on local-area networks and secure operating system kernels, and to research regarding the reduced-instruction-set computer (RISC) architecture, as examples from which the more general principle emerged. Both papers—and other papers by Saltzer, Reed, and Clark— explicitly mention the design of communication networks and the design of the Internet as areas in which end-to-end arguments had been applied.[94] For example, the 1984 paper discusses the decisions on where to place functions such as reliable data transfer, duplicate suppression, or reordering as typical examples of decisions in which end-to-end arguments are applied, and frames the debate over "datagrams, virtual circuits, and connectionless protocols" as a debate about end-to-end arguments.[95] The 1998 paper points to the authors' work on "end-to-end transport protocols in LANs and the Internet Experiment" as work from which the more general design principle emerged, and discusses the decision not to optimize the Internet for "telephony-style virtual circuits" as an example of the application of the (broad version of the) end-to-end arguments that has been validated by history.[96]

In sum, the papers describing the two versions articulate design rules that had been used in various contexts before they were formally recognized as a design principle. The design decisions made during the development of the Internet's original architecture were important (but not the only) examples of earlier applications of the principles from which the general description of the principles emerged. Thus, although the papers formally describing the end-to-end arguments as design principles were published after the Internet-related design decisions ascribed to them were made, the underlying design rules shaped the Internet's original architecture.

As was explained in chapters 2 and 3, the original architecture of the Internet was based on a variant of the layering principle called *relaxed layering with a portability layer* and on the end-to-end arguments. Layering, in turn, is a special form of modularity. There are two versions of the end-to-end arguments, the narrow version and the broad version. Although both versions influenced the Internet's original architecture, only the broad version affects the economic environment for innovation. Therefore, parts III and IV of this book will focus on modularity, relaxed layering with a portability layer, and the broad version.

III Architectural Constraints on Innovation

4 Architecture and the Cost of Innovation

To evaluate how the Internet's architecture affects innovation, we must understand exactly how architecture constrains economic actors. How do design principles and the architectures they shape influence the costs and benefits associated with a given innovation? How do they affect who can design and build an innovation? Answering these questions is the goal of part III. Chapters 4–6 each focus on a particular aspect of the relationship between architecture and innovation and explore it in detail. The resulting insights are then applied to assess how the Internet's original architecture influences innovation.

This chapter examines how architecture affects the costs of realizing innovations (that is, the costs of developing and producing the first complete version of the system that contains the new or improved good or service). This book focuses on innovation that can be influenced by architectural features—developing components for a new system, improving existing components, developing new components for an existing system, changing an architecture to enable new functionality, or creating new architectures. Thus, in the context of this book, innovating involves changing components of a system or its underlying architecture.

Architectures differ in the kinds of changes that are needed to realize a particular innovation: The architecture of a system describes how the system is decomposed into components and how these components cooperate to provide the overall functionality of the system. The distribution of functionality among components affects which components need to be altered to realize the innovation. The nature and strength of dependencies among components determines if these changes require subsequent changes to other parts of the system that depend on the changed functionality. Thus, the architecture of a system affects how many and what kinds of components must be altered to realize a specific innovation, which in turn affects the costs of making these changes (figure 4.1). Changing

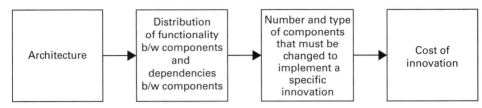

Figure 4.1
How architecture affects the costs of innovation.

many components of an architecture is more difficult and costly than changing only one, even if the total amount of change[1] is the same (box 4.1). And although such costs are decreasing continually, changing a system's hardware components is usually more costly than changing its software components, because of the higher costs associated with prototyping, testing, and manufacturing hardware components.[2]

While an architecture implies what kinds of changes are necessary to realize a particular innovation, the actual costs to an innovator of making these changes may differ among innovators. For example, the costs of having a programmer revise the code for a program may differ depending on whether the revisions are being done by an established firm, by a start-up company, or by a freelance programmer. Each innovator will incur costs—e.g., an established firm and a start-up company may have to hire additional programmers, and a freelance programmer may have to decline another project—but the actual costs may differ because of different salary structures or different amounts of overhead among firms, and their effects may be assessed and felt differently. Similarly, an innovator who owns all the components involved in a change will be able to implement the change at lower costs than an innovator who owns only one of these components (box 4.1). Thus, although the activities causing the costs of change depend on the architecture, the actual costs are relative to the actors and the context in which they are operating.

Because of architectural differences, the number and the kinds of components that need to be changed to realize a particular innovation may differ among architectures. As a result, realizing that innovation may be more costly in one architecture than in another. These differences in cost affect the economic environment for innovation in several ways:

First, the costs of change determine the amount and the kind of investment needed to realize a certain innovation, effectively selecting which economic actor is able to realize the innovation. Innovation that involves prototyping, testing, and ultimately producing physical products requires

Box 4.1

Number of Affected Components and Costs of Change

In general, the costs of changing an architecture rise with the number of architectural components involved in the change.[a] The effort involved in understanding affected components and then designing, implementing, and testing changes rises with the number of components that must be changed; e.g., making five small changes to one component is usually less costly than making one simple alteration in five different components.[b] This is because realizing a change entails more than simply changing code. For example, in large software systems, alterations involving several components must be approved by change control boards, the documentation of affected components must be changed, and the testing of new components and their introduction into the system must be a coordinated across development teams. The higher the number of affected components, the more these development-process costs dominate the economics of a proposed change.

The increase in costs that results from an increase in the number of affected components is particularly large if the various components are owned and maintained by different firms. As we will see in chapter 5, coordinating changes across firm boundaries is considerably more difficult and costly than coordinating changes within a single firm. In addition, one (or more) of the firms involved may use the opportunity to behave strategically in order to improve its (or their) competitive position at the expense of other organizations. For example, a firm may try to "hold up" another (a tactic that will be described in chapter 5).[c]

a. In addition, the costs of change generally rise with the size and complexity of code that must be modified or produced to implement the change. Thus, predicting the real costs of implementing a change requires an estimate of the number of lines of code that are affected. These estimates can then be multiplied by productivity factors derived from empirical studies to yield an estimate of the time required to change the code. These factors vary depending on the kind of programming involved; for example, studies have shown that the productivity of writing new code is higher than that of changing existing code. (See Bosch and Bengtsson 2001, p. 171.) In addition, changing code you have written yourself is easier than changing someone else's code.
b. This is a statement of a general relationship that may not hold in some cases. For example, changing one very complex component may be more difficult than changing several simple ones. Implementing a very simple change across a number of components may be easier than realizing a complex local change. (See Bass, Clements, and Kazman 1998, p. 82.)
c. For an analysis of these and additional factors that may increase the costs of innovation in such a situation, see the discussion in chapter 5 below.

a different type of investment than software innovation. For example, a lone inventor working in a garage may be able to prototype a new piece of hardware but probably is not able to complete the subsequent evaluation, manufacturing, and distribution necessary to commercialize the innovation in the same way a single software programmer may be able to realize and distribute a new piece of code. The effect of the costs of change on the type of economic actors who can realize innovations will be discussed more in the next chapter.

Second, the costs of realizing an innovation establish the minimum benefit that the innovation must provide in order to justify innovating. Different innovators may do their work for different reasons and may evaluate opportunities for innovation in different ways[3]—expressed more formally, they may have different preferences, and act under different decision rules—but we can assume that they will not innovate unless the expected benefits at least equal the expected costs.[4] If the costs of realizing a particular innovation differ between two architectures, the difference between expected benefits and expected costs may lead a particular innovator to innovate in one architecture but not in the other.

Finally, the costs of change implied by an architecture determine whether isolated changes to system components can be made at low costs, allowing innovators to improve pieces of a system without having to change the whole system. As we will see, the ability to experiment at the component level—trying out new functions, novel ways of implementing functions, and new relationships among components—may result in a system that is of higher quality than a system that does not enable this type of experimentation. A system that allows experimentation at the component level will evolve more rapidly than a system that can only be replaced as a whole. The value of being able to experiment at the component level increases with the uncertainty about the best way to innovate, since innovators can take risks on components without compromising the quality of the whole system.

Thus, differences in the costs of innovation among architectures may result in a different *number* of innovations being realized and in different *types of innovators* realizing them.

Costs of Change in Modular and Integrated Architectures

The overall costs of innovation consist of three parts: the costs of realizing an innovation, the costs of production and distribution, and the costs of deployment. The costs of realizing an innovation are the costs of developing and producing the first complete version of the system that contains the new or improved good or service. They are incurred by the innovator and, if the rest of the system has to be changed in order to integrate the new component, by the providers of complementary components.[5] The costs of deployment are the costs of making changes to the operational system that are necessary before the innovation can be used in that system for the first time. This section will focus on how modular and integrated architectures affect the costs of realizing an innovation.

The costs of realizing an innovation can be separated into two categories. First, there are the costs associated with developing and testing the innovation itself; these are the costs of designing and developing the necessary changes to the components directly affected by the innovation. I will call these the *core costs of innovation*. Second, there are the costs associated with developing and testing the changes necessary in the rest of the system in order to enable the new or improved components to function properly. I will call these the *costs of system adaptation*. For example, if Microsoft wants to change an existing application programming interface to its Windows operating system, the core costs of this innovation are the investments it must make in designing and implementing the new version of the application programming interface and the code within the operating system that implements the functionality provided by the application programming interface. If the new version completely replaces the old version of the interface, applications that relied on the old version will not be able to function properly. The costs incurred in changing the applications so that they work with the new version of the interface are the costs of system adaptation.

Architectural Differences and Costs of Innovation

The architectural differences between integrated and modular architectures result in different costs of innovation. In an integrated architecture, it usually isn't possible to make changes to a component that do not trigger subsequent changes in the rest of the system. Owing to the highly interdependent nature of the design, it is very likely that changes in an integrated architecture will affect at least one design parameter that is linked to design choices in other components. Changing such a parameter may start a chain of changes in other components. The cascade of changes resulting from a single change to an interdependent design parameter is often called the *ripple effect*. Because the complexity of the design makes the implications of changes difficult to understand or predict, it is not easy to identify which parts of the system will be affected and exactly how they will be affected. Often various parts of a system have to be redesigned, implemented, and tested; in the worst case, all of a system's components have to be changed.[6]

Suppose the designers of the iMac are thinking of introducing a new screen technology into the next version of the computer. The new screen technology may require more space than its predecessor, and it may produce more heat. Owing to the change in the dimensions of the screen, components that were located adjacent to the screen may no longer fit. Other components may be negatively affected by the heat, and trying to move them elsewhere may require adjustments in the rest of the system.

Thus, even small changes to an integrated architecture usually require changing larger parts of the system. Implementing these changes is difficult, time-consuming, and costly; thus, the costs of system adaptation are high.

Compared to this integrated approach to design, modularity reduces the number of cross-component interdependencies and the level of coupling between components. As a result, a large number of changes can be implemented through autonomous changes—that is, changes that affect only one component and do not require altering the rest of the system.

Owing to the strict partitioning between visible and hidden information, modules can depend only on other modules' visible information. As a result, all changes that do not affect the architecture's existing visible information are autonomous changes that do not affect the rest of the system, resulting in zero costs of system adaptation. Changes in this category include replacing a component with a better implementation without changing its interfaces, adding a new interface to an existing component, and adding a new component.[7] For example, in the modular architecture of the PC, introducing monitors with a new screen technology does not require any changes in the rest of the system as long as the interface between the monitor and the rest of the system stays the same. Similarly, adding a new application programming interface to the Windows operating system without altering the existing application programming interfaces does not require any changes to existing applications, since they can continue to use the existing application programming interfaces.

As we will see later in this chapter, innovations that can be realized through autonomous changes are especially attractive targets for innovative efforts. Since autonomous changes do not incur any costs of system adaptation, the threshold for innovation is considerably lower than for systemic changes, making it more likely that the innovation will be realized. As the next chapter will show, autonomous changes can often be realized independently by actors other than the system architect. They do not require cooperation from the system architect or from other component makers; thus, they free the innovator from the need to convince others of the usefulness of his innovation.[8]

As soon as a change involves altering an architecture's existing visible information, adaptation costs are incurred. These costs depend on the number of system components that directly or indirectly depend on the changed component. This number, in turn, depends on the type and density of interactions among components—i.e., the dependencies and strength of coupling among them—which subsequently depend on the distribution of functionality among components determined by the architecture. For example, the costs of system adaptation associated with changing an existing Windows application programming interface depend on the number of applications that directly or indirectly rely on this interface.

Owing to the costs of system adaptation, innovations that require changes to an architecture's existing visible information are considerably more costly to realize than innovations that can be realized through autonomous changes.[9] Because the costs of system adaptation quickly subsume the benefits of innovation, such innovations must provide considerably higher benefits if they are to be realized. Thus, large costs of system adaptation can quickly neutralize potential gains from innovation, raising the threshold for innovation.

Owing to the different levels of coupling between components, the costs of realizing a specific innovation probably will be greater in an integrated architecture than in a modular architecture. In an integrated architecture, the innovation will almost always require changing large parts of the system. In contrast, in a modular architecture many innovations may be realized through autonomous changes at much lower costs. Owing to these cost differences, it is likely that more innovations will be justified under a modular architecture. For example, the benefits associated with the new screen technology mentioned earlier may be larger than the costs of designing, building, and testing a monitor with the new technology in the modular architecture of the PC, but may not be sufficient to justify a complete redesign of the integrated architecture of the iMac.[10] The difference in costs may also have consequences for the types of innovators that are able to innovate within a certain architecture: smaller firms may be able to muster the resources necessary to improve one component but may not have the resources necessary to develop a complete system.

Options Theory and the Value of Flexibility under Uncertainty

Architectures affect innovation costs by influencing how functionality is distributed among components and how components depend on one another. If innovators can change parts of the architecture at low cost, they are better and more easily able to react to future developments. This flexibility is particularly valuable if there is uncertainty about the best technical approaches to innovation, or about the features that consumers may value. The theory of real options provides a framework for reasoning about the relationship between the costs of innovation implied by an architecture and the value of experimentation under uncertainty. In particular, it lets us understand how architectures can leverage the risks surrounding innovation and shape the potential rewards from innovating.

Innovating on an architecture or its components can be understood as acquiring a real option. Since modular and integrated architectures differ in how much it costs to change them, they also differ in the types of options they provide. Similarly, alternative modular architectures may differ in how much it costs to change a particular module, which may affect the option value of experimenting on that module. These differences in option value, in turn, indicate how much effort innovators will invest in improving that module under the different modular architectures.

Options theory provides a method of analysis that recognizes and quantifies the value of being able to flexibly choose alternative courses of action in the future under conditions of uncertainty. The framework originated in finance, where it is used to value financial options—for example, options on stocks or bonds.[11] Real-options theory extends the framework to options on non-financial (real) assets.[12]

An option is a right, but not an obligation, to take action in the future. For example, a financial option may provide the right to buy a specific stock at a specific price (called the *exercise price*) at some specified time in the future (the *expiration date*). (This is an example of a "European call option.") If the value of the stock is higher on the expiration date than the exercise price, the owner can exercise the option and buy the stock for the exercise price. His payoff will be the difference between the value of the stock at the expiration date and the exercise price. If the value of the stock is lower than the exercise price, the owner does nothing, since he had a right but not an obligation to buy the stock. In this case, his payoff is zero. Thus, the owner of the option can limit his loss in the case of an unfavorable outcome, but can profit from any positive developments.[13]

Thus, an option is a way to deal with uncertainty. It provides an opportunity to delay deciding about an investment whose future value is not known until the uncertainty is resolved. If the future value is negative, the owner of the option does nothing; in this case, his payoff is zero. If the future value is positive, the owner exercises the option. His payoff is the positive future value minus the exercise price. Thus, an option gives its owner the possibility to capture potential future gains while avoiding potential future losses.[14]

The value of an option increases with uncertainty. If uncertainty is high, then very high and very low future values are more likely. Direct investment in the underlying asset would be very risky: there is a chance of high gains, but there also is a chance of high losses. For the owner of an option, the increase in uncertainty has a one-sided effect: there is an increase in the upside potential (the chance of a very high payoff), but there is no increase in potential losses.[15]

Since options can limit risks, it is not surprising that they are valuable. Acquiring an option requires paying a price. The difference between the present value of the option (the equivalent of the future value of the option in terms of wealth today) and its price denotes the net present value, or net option value, of an option. If the net option value is negative, the benefits associated with the ability to limit risks are smaller than the costs of acquiring the option. If the net option value is positive, the benefits are larger than the costs.

Since it is not clear how an option's value will evolve, we need a valuation methodology to determine the present value of the option—a way to translate a range of potential outcomes in the future into a single value in the present. Over the past decades, scholars of finance (including Fischer Black, Myron Scholes, and Robert C. Merton) have developed ways to solve this problem.[16] These methodologies are used to determine the value of options in the financial markets.

Real Options in Modular and Integrated Architectures

The theory of real options extends the theory of financial options to options on real assets.[17] In contrast with financial options, real options are not bought; they arise from investment decisions afflicted with uncertainty that open the opportunity to choose alternative courses of action in the future when the uncertainty is resolved. If the outcome is bad, the firm chooses an action that limits its losses. If the outcome is good, the firm can leverage the situation.

An investment decision can be understood in the context of real-options theory if (1) the decision depends on an uncertain outcome, (2) the decision can be made in a way that opens the opportunity to choose alternative courses of action in the future when the uncertainty is resolved, and (3) these alternative courses of action let the firm either truncate its losses in case of an unfavorable outcome or profit from favorable developments.[18] If these conditions hold, the real option is the opportunity to make the decision in the future, and the firm acquires this option by making the investment decision now. Thus, the "price" of the real option is the cost associated with the current investment. In the real-options framework, the decision about the current investment becomes a decision to acquire an option: although the outcome of the decision depends on characteristics of the investor (for example, a value-maximizing investor who can take on as many projects as he likes would acquire the option by making the investment decision, if the present value of the option exceeds its price, or, in other words, if the net option value is positive),[19] no investor would buy an option if its net option value were negative. Over the past years, a number of methods have been developed that can be used to calculate the value of a real option.[20]

Real options are much harder to detect than financial options. Because real options are hidden in the investments of a firm, the first step of a real-options analysis is to identify and define the real options associated with investment decisions.[21]

A firm's choice to innovate on components of an architecture is such an investment decision. In a sense, when we understand particular types of architectures—e.g., integrated versus modular—in relation to a firm's real options, we may better understand how decisions to innovate in uncertain environments depend on the architecture of the systems being innovated on and the costs associated with doing so. Innovation on existing integrated and modular architectures can thus be understood from a real-options perspective.[22]

First, the decision to innovate is afflicted with uncertainty. It depends on the expected costs and benefits of the innovation. Owing to the inherent complexity of the designs of large systems, it is often impossible to predict how valuable changes to an architecture will be.[23] It may be difficult, for example, to predict which technical approach will provide the best solution to a specific problem (technical uncertainty) and whether and how consumers will value the resulting product (business uncertainty). As a result, the expected value of the innovation is uncertain at the time of the decision. It may be worth more or less than the existing design. Often, the value of the innovation can be determined after it is complete. In particular, this applies to technical uncertainty, insofar as the technical quality of an innovation can be determined once it has been realized.

Although the use of focus groups or customer prototype testing may reduce business uncertainty once an innovation is realized,[24] often only the market can resolve business uncertainty.

Second, innovating on an existing architecture provides the right, but not the obligation, to use or sell the result of the innovative process instead of the existing product. Thus, innovating opens up alternative courses of actions when the uncertainty is resolved.

Third, these alternative courses of action let the firm either truncate its losses in case of an unfavorable outcome or profit from favorable developments. If the result is better than the existing system, the innovator can use the new system and reap the rewards of her innovation. If the result is worse than the existing system, she can continue using or selling the existing product without having to suffer profit losses or produce an inferior product. The innovator can minimize her losses by maintaining the status quo.[25]

Thus, the decision to innovate opens the real option to decide whether or not to use or sell an innovation in the future when its value is known. The cost of acquiring this option is the cost of developing the innovation. An innovator will not innovate if the net option value is negative—that is, if the present value of the innovation is smaller than the cost of acquiring the option.[26] To determine the present value of the innovation, one needs a methodology that translates the uncertain future value of an innovation into a known value today.[27]

Though innovators who innovate on modular or integrated architectures all acquire a real option to use or sell the innovation in the future, they acquire different types of options depending on the architecture. Innovating on an integrated architecture provides an option on a portfolio, whereas innovating on a modular architecture provides a portfolio of options.[28]

In an integrated architecture, it is usually not possible to make changes to a component that do not trigger changes in the rest of the system. As a result, isolated innovation at the level of individual components is rarely feasible. Improving one component requires that large parts of the system be redesigned and tested. Often it is more efficient to redesign an integrated system from scratch than to try to improve the existing system. Thus, innovation on an integrated architecture usually takes place at the system level, providing the option to replace one system with another. Because the new system consists of a fixed set of components, the innovator acquires an option on a portfolio of components.[29]

In contrast, a modular architecture enables innovation at the module level.[30] These changes do not affect the rest of the system as long as the architecture's existing visible information stays the same. As a result, it is possible to improve or change individual components while retaining the rest of the system. For example, it is possible to replace one module with a better version, to add components that offer new functionality using the services of existing modules, or to remove modules that are not used by other modules—all without changing the architecture's existing visible information. Existing modules can be split or merged without any changes to the architecture, or with only minor changes, depending on the system.[31]

Innovating on a specific module provides the option of replacing the existing version of the module with the result of the innovation.[32] If all modules are changed, the innovator acquires corresponding options for all new modules. Instead of getting one option on a complete system (as with an integrated architecture), she acquires as many options as there are modules in the system. As a result, she can choose with respect to each module whether the new version is better than the old one, and can act accordingly. Thus, a modular architecture provides a portfolio of options.[33]

Under very general assumptions (the result has been proved for general probability distributions for any distribution of underlying value, assuming conservation of aggregate value), it can be shown that a "portfolio of options" is more valuable than an "option on a portfolio."[34] This is so because a portfolio of options exploits the lack of correlation in the development of the value of the underlying assets. If the value of the underlying assets is positively correlated, the value of the assets increases and decreases together. If the value of one asset increases, the value of the other assets increases too. Often the value of the underlying assets is not positively correlated. While the value of some assets may rise, the value of others may fall. If one owns an option on a portfolio, one can get the portfolio only as a whole. Even if the option has a positive payoff, increases in the value of some assets may have been neutralized by decreases in the value of other assets. In contrast, the owner of a portfolio of options has separate options on any of the underlying assets. For each of these options, he can exercise the option if the payoff is positive, and can do nothing otherwise. Because his gains will not be diluted by the losses of other assets in the portfolio, he is better off than the owner of the option on a portfolio.

Therefore, from an options perspective, a modular architecture is more valuable than an integrated architecture if the underlying distribution of aggregate value is the same.[35] In general, the results of experiments on different modules will not be correlated.[36] While the value of some components rises, the value of others may fall. In a modular architecture, innovators can use any module innovation that is better than the existing module, and can reject the others. In an integrated architecture, an innovator has to accept or reject a complete system, improvements in some parts of which may be offset by deteriorations in others. As a result, the expected value of the resulting system is higher in the modular architecture.

The difference in option value between modular and integrated architectures also affects how innovators react to the risk of failure associated with uncertainty.[37] In a modular architecture, innovators can experiment on a module without affecting the quality of the whole system. If the innovation fails, they can limit their losses by continuing to use the existing module. Because a modular architecture enables innovators to capture the potentially large benefits associated with risky projects and avoid the downsides, risky projects become very attractive. In an integrated architecture, the failure of a risky approach to one component may compromise the quality of the whole system, owing to the interconnected nature of the design. As a result, innovators in integrated architectures will try to avoid risky approaches so as not to endanger the success of the next generation of the integrated design.

The option to replace an existing module with a better version is not the only option provided by modular architectures. A modular architecture contains a much more complex set of options.[38] In addition to options at the module level, a modular architecture provides options at the system level. For example, with a modular architecture it is possible to first design and produce a minimal system at a lower cost than would be incurred designing and producing a complete system. Instead of requiring innovators to bear all development costs initially, this approach gives them the chance to save a part of the development costs if, for example, demand for the system is too low or the technical challenges become too great. If the system sells well, or if the technical hurdles are overcome, new modules can be added later. If the system does not sell well enough, or if the technical barriers are too great, no more modules are developed. Thus, by developing a minimal system, designers gain the option to proceed with further system design in the future.[39] In the terminology of options theory, a minimal system provides an "option on a portfolio of options."[40] Though it is important to recognize the complex structure of options embedded in modular architectures, it is almost impossible to calculate the value of these more complex options.[41]

The decision to innovate with respect to a specific module, however, depends on the option value of that module, not on the option value of the architecture.

Real Options in Different Modular Architectures

In the preceding subsection we focused on the differences in option value between modular and integrated architectures. In this subsection we will examine more closely the differences among modular architectures and the option values they provide. For a specific module, alternative modular architectures may imply different costs of innovation. Consider the designers of an operating system. Should the functionality needed to communicate with the printer be implemented in hardware, or in software? Because hardware is more difficult and costly to change than software, the core costs of innovation will be much lower if the functionality is implemented in software. Should applications be allowed to interact with the printer directly, or should they only be allowed to interact with the printer through the application programming interfaces provided by the operating system? Relative to the first option, allowing applications to access the printer functionality only through application programming interfaces constrains the dependencies within the system, resulting in lower costs of system adaptation if the printer functionality should change. These architectural decisions affect the option value associated with innovating on a component of a particular architecture by affecting the costs of innovating on a given module. How do these differences affect the amount of effort that innovators will invest in improving the module and the rate of change of the module?

Until now, we have focused on the option to be acquired by developing one innovation on a specific module. Instead of developing one innovation, the innovator could experiment and start several independent, parallel innovative efforts with respect to the same module. As a result, he would acquire the option to replace the existing module with the best of the new versions, if it is better than the existing one. The value of this option depends on the number of approaches pursued by the innovator.[42] If there is uncertainty, increasing the number of experiments will increase the expected quality of the best result. At the same time, innovating on a module is not costless. After a certain number of experiments, the additional benefits may not be worth the costs.[43] Thus, the costs of innovation put an upper limit on the number of approaches that may be pursued to improve a module in a specific architecture.[44] Owing to the differences in the costs of innovation among architectures, different architectures may justify a different number of experiments on a module. By comparing the number of experiments on a module that may be pursued under alternative architectures, one can get an indication of how much innovation will occur on this module in the different architectures.[45]

The following model, which is based on work by Baldwin and Clark (2000), will help us to think more formally about the relationship between the benefits of additional experimentation and the costs of innovation on a module.

Innovating on one module provides the option to replace the existing module if the new module proves to be better. However, by starting *several* innovative efforts on a module, the innovator can replace the existing module with the best of the new ones if it is better than the existing one.[46] To understand the benefits that might accrue from such parallel innovation, we need to know the net option value of being able to select the best module among the module versions created by the different innovative efforts.

The model is based on the following scenario: an innovator starts k innovative efforts on the same module. After the innovations, she chooses the best of the resulting k module versions and compares it with the existing module.[47] If it is better than the existing module, she exercises the option by replacing the existing module and making the necessary adjustments in the rest of the system. If it is worse, she continues to use the existing module.

Thus, the model assumes that the selection of the best of the k alternative module versions can take place at the *module* level once the innovation is realized.[48] It is therefore not necessary to implement any changes in the rest of the system before the best innovation has been chosen and the decision to replace the existing module has been made. As a result, the innovator acquires the option by investing in k independent approaches to innovation. She exercises the option by making the adjustments in the rest of the system.

To simplify this idea, we can assume that there is only one innovator who owns the whole system and, for now, ignore the difficulties associated with coordinating changes across the components of a system. These challenges will be discussed in the next chapter.

The *net option value* of the option consists of the value of the option minus the cost of acquiring and exercising the option. To determine the present value of an option, we must translate uncertain outcomes in the future into a single number in the present. Options theory solves this problem by viewing the time between now and the future as a random experiment leading to a specific outcome. The random experiment begins with acquiring the option and results in a specific payoff. In the terminology of probability theory, the value of the payoff function is a random variable that can be described by a probability distribution.[49] The *present value* of the option equals the *expected value* of this distribution, adjusted for time and risk.[50]

The value of the option to select the best of k versions of a module equals the expected value of the best of k experiment results, as long as the best of the k experiment results is better than the existing module.[51] Following Baldwin and Clark,[52] we assume that a single approach to innovation on one module (module i) can be modeled by a random variable X_i that denotes the outcome of one innovative effort in terms of the increase in consumers' willingness to pay for the improvement in functionality or performance caused by the innovation; in other words, X_i denotes consumers' willingness to pay for the incremental value added by the improved functionality or performance of the module. We assume that X_i can be approximated by a normal distribution with mean μ_i and variance σ_i^2. In a normal distribution, values around the mean are more likely than values far from the mean. Thus, this modeling assumes that, for innovative efforts, values close to the performance of the existing module are more common, and very good or very bad outcomes are rare.[53] The mean, μ_i, represents the existing performance of the module, normalized to zero. The variance, σ_i^2, is a measure of the uncertainty underlying the innovative process with respect to this module.[54] This modeling embodies the assumption that very good or very bad outcomes are more likely if uncertainty is high (figure 4.2).

Given these assumptions and assuming the k approaches are independent,[55] the option value of replacing the existing module i with the best of k designs, $Q_i(k)$, can be described by the equation

$$Q_i(k) = \sigma_i \cdot Q(k),$$

with $Q(k)$ denoting the expected value of the best of k designs, as long as the best of the k designs is better than zero, of a standard normal distribution with mean 0 and variance 1.[56] (See box 4.2.)

The value of $Q_i(k)$ rises with k (that is with the number of experiments), but at a decreasing rate.[57] The value of $Q_i(k)$ also rises with uncertainty.

The cost of acquiring the option is the cost of making k experiments on the module. In the terminology of this book, the costs of making one experiment on the module are the "core costs of innovation" with respect to that module. The costs of acquiring the option increase with the

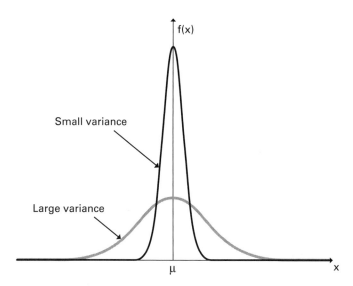

Figure 4.2
Probability density functions $f(x)$ of normal distributions with the same μ but different variance σ^2.

number of experiments and with the core costs of innovation on that module.

The costs of exercising the option are the costs of adjusting the rest of the system to the changes between the existing module and the new module. In the terminology of this book, these are the "costs of system adaptation"; they must be paid if the innovator chooses the best of the k alternative innovations over the existing module. Changes in one module trigger corresponding changes in the rest of the system only if the change affects the visible information of the changed module *and* other modules directly or indirectly depend on this information. The number of modules that have to be changed is the number of modules that directly or indirectly depend on the module's changed visible information. Furthermore, since existing modules will depend on the new module in different ways, the costs of adjusting a particular module may differ among affected modules. Thus, the cost of exercising the option increases with the number of modules that directly or indirectly depend on the module that is the target of the innovation, and increases with the costs of changing the affected modules.

Formally, the net option value of the option to select the best of k designs for module i is the value of the option minus the costs of acquiring

Box 4.2
Calculating the Option Value of Being Able to Select the Best of k Experiments

To calculate the option value, one must first construct a random variable that describes the value of the payoff function of the underlying experiment. In our case, the experiment consists of the following steps: First, an innovator takes k independent approaches to develop an innovation on module i. Each of these approaches can be interpreted as an independent experiment that is modeled by the random variable X_i that describes the result of one innovation on module i. The results are k specific values of X_i that describe the value of the resulting module relative to the value of the existing module. Next, the maximum of these values is selected. This experiment—"choose the best of k independent experiments described by X_i"—can be directly described by another random variable that yields the value of the best experiment. In statistics, this random variable is called *the maximum order statistic of a sample of size k.*[a] The probability distribution of "the maximum order statistic of a sample of size k" describes all potential values of the best of k designs and their associated probabilities. It can be derived from the probability distribution of the random variable X_i using statistical theory.

The value of the option to select the best of k alternative designs of module i, $Q_i(k)$, can be determined by calculating the expected value of the positive value portion of the distribution of "the maximum order statistic of a sample of size k."[b] On the assumption that the k approaches are independent, calculating the value of the option yields

$$Q_i(k) = \sigma_i \cdot Q(k),$$

where $Q(k)$ denotes the expected value of the best of k designs (as long as the value of the best of the k designs is greater than zero) of a standard normal distribution with a mean of 0 and a variance of 1:

$$Q(k) = k \int_0^\infty z[N(z)]^{k-1} n(z)dz$$

where $N(z)$ and $n(z)$ are, respectively, the standard normal distribution and density functions.[c]

a. Lindgren 1962, pp. 268–271.
b. The probability distribution of the maximum order statistic of a sample of size k describes all potential outcomes of the best of the k designs, both positive and negative. Because the innovator will not use the best innovation if it is inferior to the existing module, outcomes lying on the negative-value portion of the distribution (i.e., outcomes that are worse than the existing module, whose performance was normalized to 0) do not influence the option value of the innovation; for these cases, the value of the innovator's payoff function is 0. See Sanchez 1991, p. 30; Baldwin and Clark 2000, pp. 255–256, note 7.
c. See Baldwin and Clark 2000, p. 264, note 17.

and exercising the option:

$$\text{NOV}_i(k) = Q_i(k) - k \cdot C_{\text{Innovation}}(\text{Module}_i) - \Sigma_{j\,\text{"sees"}\,i}\,(C_{\text{Adaptation}}(\text{Module}_j))$$
$$= \sigma_i \cdot Q(k) - k \cdot C_{\text{Innovation}}(\text{Module}_i) - \Sigma_{j\,\text{"sees"}\,i}\,(C_{\text{Adaptation}}(\text{Module}_j)),$$

where module j "sees" module i if it directly or indirectly depends on module i's changed visible information. The net option value varies with k, the number of approaches. The number of approaches $k_{\max}$ that maximizes the net option value depends on the specific characteristics of the module. In particular, it depends on the degree of uncertainty about how best to improve the module as well as on the module's core costs of innovation and costs of system adaptation. The costs of system adaptation, in turn, depend on the visibility of a module, i.e., on the number of modules in the rest of the system that directly or indirectly depend on the module. If no other modules depend on a particular module, it is called a *hidden module*.[58] Innovating on such a module will not incur any costs of system adaptation, so that the costs of exercising the option will be zero.

The net option value formula can be used to predict how differences among modules (e.g., varied costs of innovation among architectures) affect how many innovative approaches innovators will pursue with respect to a specific module. The number of parallel efforts indicates how much innovation will occur on a module.

Exactly how many approaches innovators will pursue depends on the market structures of the design and product markets and on potential innovators' predictions and expectations of the nature of the competition in these markets. It therefore cannot be derived from architecture alone.[59] For example, if the design and product markets for a particular module are controlled by a single actor, he will choose the number of approaches that maximizes the net option value associated with that module. The monopolist will add an approach only if its additional costs—the core costs of innovating on this particular module—are less than the associated increase in expected value of the best approach. More formally, the monopolist will add an additional approach only if the cost of the $(k + 1)$th approach is less than $|Q_i(k + 1) - Q_ik)|$. In this case, the number of approaches is calculated by determining $k_{\max}$, the number of approaches that maximizes the net option value of the module. In contrast, if there is free entry into the design market and the product market is characterized by winner-take-all competition, firms will start additional approaches as long as the net option value of the total number of approaches is positive.[60] In this case, the number of approaches is calculated by determining the largest k for which the net option value is positive.

Table 4.1
Architectural features and likelihood of innovation.

	Parameters that change	Parameters held constant	Effect of change on likelihood of innovation
Observation 1	Core costs of innovation	Visibility, uncertainty, market structure	As the core costs of innovation on a module increase, fewer approaches will be pursued with respect to that module.
Observation 2	Uncertainty	Core costs of innovation, visibility, market structure	As the uncertainty surrounding a module increases, additional approaches on the module become more valuable and more parallel approaches are justified.
Observation 3	Visibility	Core costs of innovation, uncertainty, market structure	As a module's visibility increases, the number of experiments that affect its existing visible information decreases rapidly.
Observation 4	Core costs of innovation, visibility, uncertainty	Market structure	Relative to other modules with the same market structure, hidden modules with high uncertainty and low or medium core costs of innovation justify a particularly large number of parallel approaches.

Even without more information about the specific market structure, we can make the following four observations about how differences among modules may affect the relative likelihood of innovation on these modules (for a summary, see table 4.1).[61] Different modules may incur different core costs of innovation, be more or less visible,[62] be subject to varying degrees of uncertainty, and be developed and sold in markets with different market structures. For the first three observations, assume that out of the four parameters (core costs of innovation, visibility, uncertainty, and market structure) only one parameter changes, and the others stay the same.

First, other things being equal, the higher the core costs of innovation on a module, the fewer the approaches that will be pursued with respect to this module. The higher the number of independent approaches, the higher the option value of the best approach; that is, $Q_i(k) < Q_i(k + 1)$.

Thus, an additional approach always increases the expected value of the best approach.[63] The incremental value of an additional approach is decreasing in k; that is, the incremental value of the $(k + 1)$th approach is smaller than the incremental value of the kth approach; that is,

$$|Q_i(k + 1) - Q_i(k)| < |Q_i(k) - Q_i(k - 1)|.$$

At some stage, the incremental value of an additional approach is lower than the costs of the additional approach.[64] Thus, the number of approaches is limited by the costs of additional experiments, or by the core costs of innovation on that module. Remember the example given at the beginning of this subsection. Implementing a computer's functions for communicating with a printer in hardware rather than in software probably would result in fewer approaches for improving this functionality, owing to the higher core costs of innovation if the functions are implemented in hardware.

Second, other things being equal, the higher the uncertainty surrounding a module, the more valuable it is to add approaches, and the more parallel approaches will be justified. This is because the value of an option increases with uncertainty. If uncertainty is high, very good or very bad outcomes are more likely. Because of the loss-limiting characteristic of options, an innovator profits from the increase in upside potential without being affected by the increase in potential losses.[65] Therefore, the option value of experimenting on a module is highest in modules with a great deal of uncertainty.

Third, other things being equal, as the visibility of a module increases (i.e., as the number of modules that depend on this module increases), the number of experiments that affect its existing visible information will decrease rapidly. For example, an architecture that reduces the visibility of the printer to the rest of the system (e.g., by restricting applications' access to the functionality of the printer to the application programming interfaces of the operating system) will attract a higher number of innovations aimed at improving the printer than an architecture that lets applications access the printer's functionality directly. The system-adaptation costs associated with innovation on a module's visible information increase with the number of modules that depend on this information. Although they are incurred only once, high system-adaptation costs associated with ensuring that changed component behaves correctly with the rest of the system quickly neutralize potential gains from experimentation. As a result, it may not be economically justified to innovate on the existing visible information of highly visible modules.[66] This does not mean that there will be *no* innovation on visible modules. Any module can be a subject of autonomous changes that do not require changes to the rest of the system and therefore do not suffer from the negative effect of high system-adaptation costs. Thus, some experimentation may go into improving the implementation of visible modules without changing their visible information. In addition, adding new interfaces to an existing module without changing its existing interfaces does not require any adaptations in the rest of the system. Existing modules can continue to use the old interfaces, and new modules can take advantage of the added functionality by using the new interfaces. The improved module is thus "backward compatible."[67] In both cases, however, the constraints imposed by the need to adhere to the old visible information may considerably decrease the potential gains from such experiments. As a result, the net option value associated with such changes—and, consequently, the number of approaches that will be justified in view of this net option value—will often be lower than the net option value of (and the number of approaches to) innovation in hidden modules, where innovators can innovate freely without incurring any costs of system adaptation. Thus, although some innovation will take place no matter how visible a module is, visible modules will change much more slowly than hidden modules. In addition, owing to the need for backward compatibility, successive versions of visible modules will exhibit more continuity than successive versions of hidden modules. In essence, the *degree* of innovation will be less among versions; there will be fewer *meaningful* differences among iterations. Thus, the visibility of a module constrains its evolution. Put differently: By influencing the dependencies among modules, an architectural design influences the future evolution of the architecture: by placing certain functionality in hidden modules, architects enable that functionality to evolve more rapidly; by placing certain functionality in modules that are highly visible, architects accept that this functionality will evolve more slowly.

Fourth, relative to other modules developed and sold under the same market structure, hidden modules with high uncertainty and with low or medium core costs of innovation will justify a particularly large number of parallel approaches. The option value of experimenting on a module is highest for modules with a great deal of associated uncertainty. Since no other modules depend on them, changes in hidden modules never require changes in the rest of the system, so the option value is not reduced by system-adaptation costs. Finally, in view of the high value of additional approaches (due to the high uncertainty and the low to medium core costs of innovation), it takes a large number of approaches until the incremental benefit of an additional approach becomes lower than the costs of an additional approach (the decision rule under monopoly in the design and product markets for the module) or until the net option value becomes negative (the decision rule under free entry into the design market and winner-take-all competition in the product market).

Costs of Change in the Original Architecture of the Internet

The general insights about the effects of architecture on the costs of innovation and on the likelihood of innovation in modular and integrated architectures gained above can help us understand how specific design choices in the Internet's original architecture affect these factors. The costs of innovation in the original architecture of the Internet were influenced by two design decisions:[68] using relaxed layering with the Internet layer as a technology-independent portability layer populated by a single protocol, and applying the broad version of the end-to-end arguments. Together, these led to the Internet Protocol's service interface that provides to higher-layer protocols a technology-independent and application-independent interface to the network infrastructure of the Internet. This design isolates applications and transport-layer protocols from the effect of innovation in the network infrastructure, and vice versa.

The following two subsections explain how these design decisions affect the costs of innovation at the application layer and at the link layer; and how the differences in innovation costs between architectures that are or are not based on these design principles affect the amount of innovation happening at these layers. They also highlight the effect of these architectural choices on the costs of production, distribution, and deployment.

By affording or constraining the implementation of functionality in either hardware or software, the architecture of a network influences the costs of producing and distributing an innovation; these costs affect the resources required to commercially exploit the innovation. Since they are borne by the economic actor seeking to produce and distribute the innovation (e.g., the innovator herself, or someone who licenses the idea from her), these costs influence what type of economic actor can commercially exploit an innovation.

Deployment costs consist of the one-time outlays that operators or users of a system must make before they can use an innovation for the first time.[69] These costs are especially noticeable in communication networks. Whereas in stand-alone systems changes can be installed one system at a time, communication networks are distributed systems that consist of computers running protocols that must interoperate to create a functioning network. Before an innovation can be used in the operational network, the new software or hardware components that are needed to let it run must be installed on a potentially large number of computers in the network. A network architecture defines the "what" and the "how" associated with the deployment of an innovation—that is, which components in the operational network will have to be updated or replaced, and whether this can happen incrementally, through individual action, or whether it must be done in one large, coordinated effort that involves a potentially large number of actors. In essence, the scope of changes required for deployment and the associated costs define how difficult it is to adopt the innovation.

In addition, the deployment requirements implied by a network architecture interact with the economic system in which the network is used to constrain the evolution of the architecture.[70] As we will see in the final subsection, the deployment context of the commercial Internet[71] has made it more difficult to change certain parts of the Internet's architecture than a purely technological analysis of the structural dependencies within the architecture would suggest.

The Broad Version of the End-to-End Arguments and Innovation at the Application Layer

Networks that have been designed according to the broad version of the end-to-end arguments differ from other networks in how they distribute application-specific functionality among their layers. In networks that follow the broad version of the end-to-end arguments, applications and all application-specific functionality are concentrated in higher layers at the end hosts. Networks that deviate from these arguments place varying amounts of application-specific functionality in the core of the network. When designers create new applications, the differences in the distribution of functionality among the architectures result in different costs of innovation and deployment.

Adding an application in a non-end-to-end network will often require changing the network's core.[72] Existing application-specific functionality in the network's core may prevent a new application from operating. In this case, the core of the network will have to be changed to enable the new application to function. Usually, this will require changes to the service and peer interfaces of lower-layer protocols. Changing a lower-layer protocol's peer interface means coordinating changes to *all* computers running this protocol, both at end hosts and in the network. And since

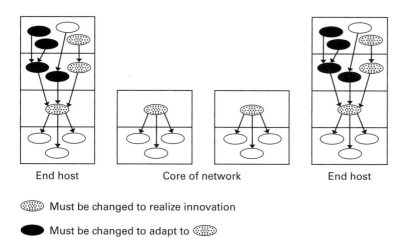

End host   Core of network   End host

🌐 Must be changed to realize innovation

⬤ Must be changed to adapt to 🌐

Figure 4.3
Application innovation in a network deviating from the broad version.

existing higher-layer protocols and applications may have come to depend
on features in the core of the network, altering the network may require
changing them, too. Changes to the core of the network may also be
required if the new application has to implement supporting functionality
in the core of the network—again requiring changes to higher-layer protocols, if they directly or indirectly depended on the changed network
functionality (figure 4.3).

Consider an innovator who wants to develop a new Internet-telephony
application in a network that provides reliable data transfer at the Internet
layer, both hop-by-hop between routers and end-to-end between sending
and receiving end hosts. Such an architecture violates the broad version
of the end-to-end arguments.[73] Ensuring reliable data transfer in the Internet layer creates delays, because lost packets are retransmitted until they
are transmitted successfully. Internet-telephony applications do not need
this functionality, since they do not necessarily require that every one of
their packets be successfully sent and received; their principal uses—people
talking and listening to each other—can tolerate a significant amount of
packet loss without affecting the overall experience. Telephony applications are, however, especially sensitive to delays. If the delay introduced
by the reliability control is too large, the application will not be able to
operate over the network.[74] This functionality may have to be removed to
let the new application work properly. As a result of the changes to the
core of the network, every application that depended on the reliable data

transfer provided by the network will have to be updated, which will incur large costs of system adaptation.

Thus, the core costs of innovation in a network that deviates from the broad version of the end-to-end arguments consist of the costs of designing, implementing, and testing the changes to higher layers at the end hosts and to the core of the network. Whereas higher-layer protocols are usually implemented in software, changes to the core of the network may require experimentation with hardware and software, which increases the costs of innovation. Since the application cannot be tested on the operational network, the innovator usually must have access to a test network.[75] Owing to the need to change not only the end hosts, but also the core of the network, the core costs of innovation associated with new applications are considerably higher in such a network than in a network that is based on the broad version. If the changes to the core of the network require new hardware, it must be manufactured and physically distributed. Thus, the costs of production and distribution associated with the innovation are potentially higher too. In addition, the changes to the core of the network may trigger huge costs of system adaptation.

A new application designed for such a network cannot run unless the core of the network has been changed, but changes to the core of the network usually cannot be made incrementally. They require a coordinated deployment of new hardware or software throughout the network. Since lower-layer protocols usually operate hop-by-hop across a network, adding a new lower-layer protocol requires changing all computers running the protocol. Therefore, to enable the application to run in a particular network, that network must be changed—and to ensure that the application can run across *all* networks attached to the global Internet, *all* networks must be changed.[76] These costs of deployment quickly can become exorbitant.

In an end-to-end network (such as the original Internet) in which network operators and application designers follow the broad version of the end-to-end arguments, designing, implementing, testing, and deploying a new application do not require changing the network's core (figure 4.4). First, since the core does not contain application-specific functionality, and since it provides only general services, it can support a wide variety of applications. As a result, it is unlikely that the core of the network will block a new application or that it will have to be changed to allow an application to be deployed.[77] Second, since the end-to-end arguments prohibit applications from incorporating application-specific functionality in the network, a new application will deliberately concentrate its functionality at higher layers at the end hosts. Third, since lower layers are

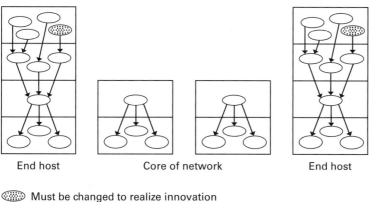

End host   Core of network   End host

 Must be changed to realize innovation

● Must be changed to adapt to

Figure 4.4
Application innovation in a network based on the broad version.

independent of higher layers, an isolated change at a higher layer will never require changes at a lower layer.

Thus, in an end-to-end network, developing a new application consists of writing a program that will run in a higher layer at an end host (figure 4.4). Higher-layer protocols operate end-to-end between end hosts: two specific protocol implementations—one at the source host and one at the destination host—cooperate to implement the protocol's services.[78] As a result, a new application can be tested using the operational network by installing it on two end hosts.

For example, an innovator who wants to develop a new Internet-telephony application in a network based on the original architecture of the Internet writes a software program that can be tested by installing it on two end hosts attached to the Internet. There is no need to change the core of the network: the Internet Protocol was designed to be as general as possible, containing no application-specific functionality (such as reliability controls to which telephony applications are especially sensitive) that might hurt an application's performance or degrade a user's experience (box 4.3).

All this results in very low core costs of innovation and zero costs of system adaptation. Because the innovator can build on the Internet's existing lower-layer infrastructure, she only needs to know how to design and write a distributed application (which requires access to and knowledge of a programming language), to have access to the application programming

Box 4.3
The Generality of the Internet Protocol

Some have argued that the service provided by the Internet layer is not general enough, insofar as the Internet Protocol does not offer Quality of Service.[a] In particular, its best-effort service does not guarantee specific bandwidth or delay. Since it is not possible to construct a transport-layer service that guarantees delay, if the Internet layer does not guarantee delay, the best-effort service may preclude the use of applications that strictly require guaranteed delay. The same argument applies to applications that strictly require guaranteed bandwidth.[b] Viewed from this perspective, the Internet Protocol's best-effort service may not be general enough, insofar as it effectively precludes development of applications in a certain class (those that cannot function properly without guaranteed bandwidth or delay). Though this argument is valid, Skype and other Internet-telephony applications have become quite successful in practice, even though they are forced to use the Internet's best-effort service. In particular, network engineers and application designers have developed techniques that help real-time applications cope with the problems resulting from best-effort service.[c] Thus, so far, the fact that the Internet Protocol does not guarantee bandwidth or delay has not prevented the deployment of real-time applications (such as Internet telephony or video telephony) that may benefit from guaranteed delay. It is possible, though, that this may change if network congestion increases. As we saw in chapter 3, the broad version of the end-to-end arguments does not prevent the introduction of Quality of Service, although it constrains how Quality of Service can be realized.

a. Wu 2003a, pp. 147–149. Technologies that would enable the Internet to offer Quality of Service have been standardized by the Internet Engineering Task Force. As we will see later in this chapter, these technologies have been implemented, but they have not been widely deployed in the operational Internet.
b. Kurose and Ross 2008, p. 199.
c. Kurose and Ross 2008, pp. 608–618.

interfaces to the Internet's lower-layer protocols and knowledge of how to use them, and to have access to an end host connected to the Internet.[79] Insofar as software can be copied and distributed over the Internet at essentially no cost (the exact costs of distribution depend on the costs of operating a server or renting server space from which the software can be downloaded), the innovator has to incur only minor costs to produce and distribute the application.[80] In essence, this type of innovation requires almost no physical capital.[81]

The overall costs of developing an application and making it available to others on an ongoing basis (whether for a fee or not) differ depending on the type of application. For applications that run entirely on users' machines, not on computers provided by the application developers, the costs of renting or operating a server for distributing the software are the only necessary ongoing costs associated with the application, and even these costs can be reduced if the innovator uses an alternative peer-to-peer distribution mechanism such as BitTorrent.[82] Peer-to-peer applications fall in this category: they usually consist of software that users run on their own computers and are largely independent of central servers. When it first came on the market, Skype was entirely based on a peer-to-peer structure. Apart from the servers used to download the software and to authenticate users, the application ran entirely on users' computers. As a result of this structure, adding a new user cost Skype one-tenth of a cent, as *Fortune* reported in 2004.[83] Client-server applications that run entirely on users' computers, not on computers provided by innovators, are another example of applications with this cost structure. For example, the Web server software developed by the Apache Foundation or Microsoft is downloaded by users, who then use the software to run their own Web servers.

In contrast, applications that need servers run by the innovator herself require a higher level of investment. Not only does the innovator incur the one-time costs of acquiring the hardware and software necessary to operate a server; these applications are also more expensive to operate on an ongoing basis, because of the costs of operating the server infrastructure. While an application does not have many users, innovators without additional funding may be able to run a server themselves at relatively low costs. But as the application gets more successful, the costs of operating the server infrastructure (e.g., renting physical space for the servers and paying for electricity, for air conditioning, and for the employees who manage the servers) and connecting it to the Internet become significant. At the same time, operating a server infrastructure is subject to considerable economies of scale. Firms (such as EBay, Amazon, and Google) that operate large data centers that host their servers are able to buy bandwidth, equipment, and software at much lower costs than smaller firms, putting smaller companies at a disadvantage.

Recent developments have drastically reduced the minimum level of investment needed to develop and operate server-based applications.[84] First, in the past, application developers interested in developing server-based applications had to buy the software necessary to operate a server and buy programming tools to program the application-specific part of the server. Today's application developers can rely on a complete stack of open-source software for running servers, consisting of a Linux operating system, Apache Web server software, an open-source database such as MySQL or PostgreSQL, and an open-source application programming and development language such as PHP, Perl, Phyton, or Ruby. All these components are available for free. For the remaining programming tasks, Web-based matching platforms enable innovators to find freelancers from all over the world, which increases access to talented programmers and which potentially lowers costs. Second, following Moore's law, the cost of computer hardware has come down. Third, new hosting services such as those offered by Amazon enable small innovators to benefit (at least some) from the economies of scale realized by the hosting company. Pay-as-you-go offerings that let innovators increase the amount of server space as they need it, while paying only for used resources, reduce the need for up-front investments in server infrastructure when the ultimate demand for the application is not yet known.[85] As we will see in chapter 5, these developments have greatly increased the number and type of innovators who can develop these types of applications.

Finally, since a new application only has to be installed on two end hosts to be used between these hosts, it can be deployed incrementally.[86] The costs of deployment are the costs of installing the application on an end host, and are borne by the user of the application.

Since a non-end-to-end network has application-specific functionality in the network's core, innovators developing a new application that requires changes to the network's core will incur high core costs of innovation and high costs of system adaptation. Furthermore, because the application requires changes in the network, it cannot be run unless the network itself is altered; thus, deployment of the application requires a significant investment by network providers before user demand for the new application is known (table 4.2). In contrast, new applications developed for end-to-end networks have very low core costs of innovation and zero costs of system adaptation, and can be deployed incrementally (table 4.2).[87] Thus, deviating from the broad version of the end-to-end arguments considerably raises the threshold for application-level innovation and the requirements that potential innovators must meet. Owing to the significant differences in innovation costs, a network that uses the broad version of the end-to-end arguments will yield far more new applications, since such programs will more easily meet the threshold required to invest in an innovation. Architectures that deviate from the broad version will produce

Table 4.2
Costs of application-layer innovation.

	Network based on broad version of end-to-end arguments	Network deviating from broad version of end-to-end arguments
Core costs of innovation	Low (developing a software program)	High (developing a software program and developing changes to the network)
Costs of system adaptation	Zero	Potentially high
Deployment	Can be deployed incrementally by users	Changes to the network must be deployed first

far fewer new applications, because, in many cases, the associated costs of innovating will likely not exceed the benefits associated with the new application. In particular, applications targeting niche markets or low-value markets may be profitable under the architecture that is based on the broad version of the end-to-end arguments, but not under the architecture that deviates from that design principle.

The costs of innovating on an existing application depend on the circumstances. If the innovation requires changing the network's core, innovating on an existing application in non-end-to-end networks will cost the same as creating a new application. In this case, the real-options framework developed above would predict that, even if there is uncertainty, no or only few parallel approaches aimed at improving the innovation will be justified (owing to the high core costs of innovation and the high system-adaptation costs), which results in little or no improvement in existing applications (table 4.1, observations 1 and 3).[88]

In contrast, an application in a network based on the broad version, on which no other application depends, is the prototype of a "hidden module" (that is, a module on which no other module depends).[89] Under these circumstances, the architecture lets innovators innovate on existing applications at low costs, without requiring adjustments in the rest of the system. According to real-options analysis, hidden modules with low core costs of innovation may justify a large number of parallel approaches aimed at improving the module (table 4.1, observation 4). The larger the uncertainty, the larger the number of parallel approaches that will be justified. At the same time, being able to experiment at low costs becomes more valuable to innovators as the uncertainty surrounding their applications increases (table 4.1, observation 2). Thus, the real-options framework developed above predicts that, relative to their counterparts in an architecture deviating from the broad version of the end-to-end arguments, applications in end-to-end architectures will evolve much more rapidly, and that the rate of change will increase with uncertainty (box 4.4).

Box 4.4
Factors Influencing an Application's Rate of Change

A specific application's rate of change depends on (among other things) the architecture of the application, the ownership of the architecture's visible information and of the component implementations, the deployment context, the technical or business uncertainty surrounding the application, the structure of the application market, and the demand by consumers for the application. For example, an application-layer protocol (such as HTTP, the protocol governing the interaction between Web browsers and Web servers) that is maintained by a standard-setting organization will change more slowly than a proprietary application protocol such as Skype, since negotiating and coordinating changes among the members of the Internet Engineering Task Force, which maintains the HTTP standard,[a] is more difficult and costly than having Skype (the company) decide on the proper evolution of the Skype protocols internally. The problems associated with distributed ownership of architecture are discussed in chapter 5.

As we will see in the discussion of innovation at the Internet and transport layer later in this chapter, changes that must be deployed by a large number of actors will happen more slowly and will be more incremental than changes that must be deployed by one actor. For example, if the client of a popular client-server application changes, the changes must be deployed by a large number of users before they can be used by all users; at the same time, the application must to continue to function even if not all users have deployed the change yet. These requirements constrain the ways in which traditional client-server applications can evolve. For this reason, new versions of AOL's instant messenger are usually backward compatible; only a few new versions were not. Similarly, new versions of the Skype software are usually backward compatible. In contrast, Web-based applications are impeded neither by distributed ownership nor by deployment requirements, and thus they are able to evolve particularly rapidly. Web-based applications reside on a server run by the application provider; they are accessed by users through their browser. As a result, changes to the application do not require users to make any changes; this eliminates the need to deploy the application to a large number of users. In addition, the application code resides on the server and is under the sole control of the application provider; this eliminates the need to coordinate changes with other parties. As a result, Web-based applications can

Box 4.4
(continued)

---

evolve particularly rapidly. The ability to make, deploy, and reverse changes at low incremental costs makes these applications perfectly suited to a real-options approach to the resolution of technical or business uncertainty. For example, during the early days of Flickr, the Flickr team deployed more than ten new features a day. If the users liked them, the changes stayed; otherwise, the Flickr team restored the original feature (the "fallback option," in real-options terminology).[b] Similarly, Amazon and Google test the effect of changes to their website or search engine in real time on some of their users. If the changes are successful, they are extended to the whole user population; if not, the company continues to use the existing version of the application.[c]

a. Within the Internet Engineering Task Force, the HTTP protocol is maintained by the Hypertext Transfer Protocol Bis (httpbis) Working Group (IETF 2008).
b. Garrett 2005.
c. Helft 2008; Varian 2007; Hansell 2007.

In addition, the two architectures support risk taking with respect to market uncertainty to different degrees. Whereas technological uncertainty is usually resolved during application development, market uncertainty often can be resolved only by the market. Since the incremental costs of making an application available to users in an end-to-end network are low, application developers can test their innovations in the market. Thus, the broad version of the end-to-end arguments enables them to resolve not only technical uncertainty but also market uncertainty at low cost.[90] If the application is successful, the innovator reaps the benefits. If users do not like the application, the application developer can stop offering it, or can change it (again, at low cost) in response to consumer feedback. As we will see in chapter 8, the online payment service PayPal and the photo-sharing platform Flickr emerged in this way. The relatively low incremental cost of failure due to market uncertainty (as opposed to technical uncertainty) will make it easier for application developers to pursue ideas for which market uncertainty is high.

In contrast, in a network deviating from the broad version, applications that require changes to the network's core are very costly to deploy, which reduces network provider's willingness to take risk with respect to market uncertainty. If the application is not successful, the application provider can stop offering it, but the changes to the network will have been made. Thus, the incremental cost of failure due to market uncertainty (as opposed to technical uncertainty) are high. As a result, application developers and network providers will be less willing and able to take on projects for which market uncertainty is high.

Relaxed Layering with a Portability Layer and Innovation at the Link Layer
The Internet's architecture uses relaxed layering with a portability layer at the Internet layer. Compared with an architecture based on relaxed layering without a portability layer, a portability layer constrains the dependencies within the system. These architectural differences result in different costs of innovation at the link layer, and, consequently, different rates of change at this layer under the two architectures.

In both architectures, changing the link layer involves creating new or improved network architectures and protocols for the physical networks underlying the Internet. Innovating at this layer usually includes experiments with hardware and software. Even if the innovation is restricted to software, the innovator must have access to a physical network to experiment with and test the innovation.[91] If the innovation involves new or improved hardware and is to be anything more than an experiment, the corresponding products have to be manufactured and physically distributed. As a result, this type of innovation has higher core costs of innovation than developing a new application in a network based on the broad version of the end-to-end arguments and requires a different type of investment: whereas developing a new application requires programming skills, access to application programming interfaces, and access to an end host, innovation at the link layer requires physical capital for developing the innovation; if the product includes hardware, it also requires that the innovation be produced and distributed.

In the architecture without a portability layer, all higher-layer protocols can potentially use the link-layer protocol. Changing the service interface of protocols at the link layer may require changing all higher-layer protocols that directly or indirectly depend on the changed interface, which will incur huge system-adaptation costs. For example, introducing a new physical network technology such as Wi-Fi may have required changes to transport-layer protocols or applications such as the browser, streaming video, or online gaming (figure 4.5).

In contrast, designating the Internet as a portability layer limits the dependencies within the system: higher-layer protocols can use all protocols down to the Internet layer but are not allowed to use protocols at

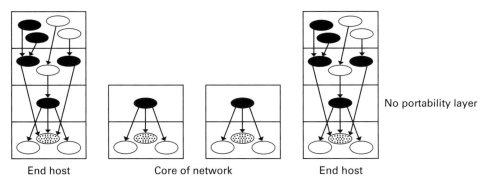

Must be changed to realize innovation

Must be changed to adapt to

Figure 4.5
Link-layer innovation in a network without a portability layer.

layers below the Internet layer (e.g., the link layer). The service interface of the Internet Protocol has been carefully designed to be an abstract interface to the Internet's network infrastructure and not to depend on particular features of any physical network technology. As a result, IP's service interface does not have to change if the underlying network technology changes, as long as the changes to the underlying network technology conform to the IP abstraction.[92] Since higher-layer protocols are only allowed to use the Internet layer, they are not affected by changes to the link layer, as long as IP's service interface stays the same (figure 4.6).[93] Compared with an architecture without a portability layer, this design eliminates the system-adaptation costs associated with changing the link layer. Because this design was used for the architecture of the Internet, introducing Wi-Fi did not require changes to particular applications.

Thus, both architectures have the same core costs of innovation but very different costs of system adaptation (table 4.3). For new physical network technologies, the potentially high costs of changing an architecture without a portability layer considerably increase the threshold for innovation. Instead of simply being larger than the costs of developing the new technology, the expected benefits must also cover the costs of changing a large number of higher-layer protocols. Though the benefits associated with some technologies (e.g., Wi-Fi) may be large enough to justify these changes, the benefits of other technologies may justify their development costs but not the additional investments in adjusting higher-layer protocols.

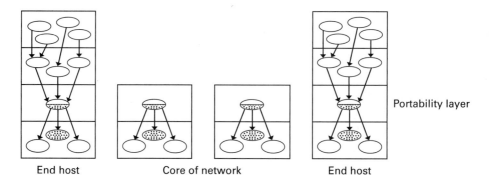

Portability layer

End host   Core of network   End host

 Must be changed to realize innovation

 Must be changed to adapt to

Figure 4.6
Link-layer innovation in a network with a portability layer.

Table 4.3
Costs of network-layer innovation.

	Network based on relaxed layering with portability layer at Internet layer	Network based on relaxed layering without portability layer
Core costs of innovation	Medium to high (may involve hardware and software and require a testbed)	Medium to high (may involve hardware and software and require a testbed)
Costs of system adaptation	Zero	Potentially high
Deployment	Can be deployed one subnet at a time	Depends on network architecture

According to the real-options framework developed above, components with no system-adaptation costs are particularly attractive targets for innovation and change rapidly. Components with the same uncertainty and the same core costs of innovation but higher system-adaptation costs will evolve much more slowly. To avoid these higher costs, subsequent versions of the service interface probably will be backward compatible. (See table 4.1, observations 3 and 4.) Thus, the introduction of a portability layer at the Internet layer drastically increases the likelihood and the rate of innovation at the link layer.

The evolution of the Internet is in line with these predictions. The Internet has been able to incorporate a large number of new physical network technologies (e.g., Wi-Fi, WiMax, new Ethernet technologies, ATM, frame relay, optical network technologies) without changes to the Internet layer.[94]

In the Internet's architecture, a new link-layer protocol or physical network technology can be deployed subnet by subnet (i.e., one physical network at a time). The Internet was designed to interconnect subnets regardless of their physical network technology. In essence, the Internet layer makes different link-layer protocols functionally independent. To connect a new type of subnet to the Internet, all one needs is a router that can connect this type of subnet to a physical network that uses an existing network technology.[95]

Internet Architecture and Innovation at the Internet and Transport Layers
The original architecture of the Internet lets protocols at the network layer and the application layer change rapidly. By restricting dependencies within the system, the broad version of the end-to-end arguments and the relaxed version of the layering principle with a portability layer isolate the rest of the system from changes to network-layer and application-layer protocols. These design choices make it possible to innovate on application-layer protocols (as long as no other application-layer protocols depend on them) and on link-layer protocols (as long as the IP service interface stays the same) without any system-adaptation costs, both when new protocols are added and when existing protocols are innovated upon.

In contrast, the service interfaces of the Internet Protocol and of the transport-layer protocols are used by a large number of higher-layer protocols. Since the Internet Protocol is the only protocol at the Internet layer, and since all network communication goes through this protocol, all higher-layer protocols depend on it directly or indirectly. As all existing applications use one of the transport-layer protocols, transport-layer protocols are less visible than the Internet Protocol, but they are still highly visible.

By placing a large number of dependencies on the service interfaces of the Internet Protocol and the transport-layer protocols, the architecture constrains the evolution of these interfaces (table 4.1, observation 3). Thus, we would expect little or no change in the service interfaces of existing transport-layer protocols (such as TCP and UDP) or in the service interface of the Internet Protocol.

As we saw above, architects may try to avoid the high costs associated with changing the visible information of highly visible modules by realizing their goals in other ways (table 4.1, observation 3 and accompanying text). For example, they may add new components, add new interfaces to existing modules, or make changes to the service interface in ways that are backward compatible. The evolution of the Internet's architecture at the Internet layer and at the transport layer shows the soundness of these predictions (box 4.5).

Architectural features such as the number of dependencies between components facilitate or constrain the evolution of the architecture by influencing the costs of system adaptation. There is, however, another factor that constrains the evolution of a network architecture's visible information: the structure of the economic system in which the network will be used.[96] The economic system in which the network is used consists of the actors who use and operate the network, the relationships among them, and the governance structures through which they interact. By providing the context in which innovations are to be deployed, this economic system may constrain the evolution of certain parts of an architecture more than simply considering the dependencies within an architecture would suggest.

A network's architecture affects which components will have to be changed to deploy an innovation and what the costs and benefits of deployment will be. For example, in an architecture based on the broad version of the end-to-end arguments, deploying a new application requires installing the new application on two end hosts. In contrast, deploying a new application in a network that deviates from the broad version may require changing the end hosts and the network's core. The economic system in which the network is used influences who controls the components that must be altered and what incentives these actors may have to make these changes. For example, in the commercial Internet, end hosts are generally controlled by users whereas the network's core is controlled by many different providers. Thus, in an end-to-end network with a deployment context similar to the commercial Internet, the small costs of deploying an application are borne by users who gain the immediate benefit of being able to use the application. In a non-end-to-end network with the same deployment context, network providers may need to make substantial investments to enable an application to run on their network when it is not clear whether users will value the application enough for the providers to recoup their investments. As we will see in chapter 7, these differences make it much more likely that new and unproven applications or

Box 4.5
Evolution of the Internet Architecture at the Internet Layer and the Transport Layer

At the transport layer, the Internet Engineering Task Force, the organization that develops most of the protocol standards for the TCP/IP protocol suite, has standardized several new transport-layer protocols[a]; the service interfaces of the existing transport-layer protocols, TCP and UDP, have stayed the same.

At the Internet layer, the IETF has standardized several protocols that would augment the Internet layer's functionality with services such as Quality of Service, IP Multicast, and support for mobility.[b] These protocols add to the Internet Protocol's existing service interface but do not change it.

The IETF has also standardized IPv6, a new version of the Internet Protocol.[c] This protocol is intended to replace IPv4, the existing version of the Internet Protocol.[d] At its core, IPv6 introduces a new format for IP addresses that provides a greater number of addresses than the current version. With the current address format, the total number of unique IP addresses on the Internet is limited to 4,294,967,296 (that is, 2^{32}). Owing to the rapid growth of the Internet and the advent of mobile laptop computers, personal digital assistants, mobile phones, and devices that are always connected to the Internet (such as cable or DSL modems), the Internet is expected to run out of IPv4 addresses soon.[e] Since the IP address is used in IP's service and peer interfaces,[f] the replacement requires changing both IP's service interface and its peer interface. Owing to the large number of higher-layer protocols that directly or indirectly depend on IP, this change will result in substantial system-adaptation costs. All applications that directly store or transmit IP addresses will have to be adjusted to accommodate the new address format. Without the increase in IP addresses, the Internet would not be able to continue to operate with a universal address space. Thus, in the case of IPv6 the innovation's expected benefit (enabling the continued operation of the Internet) is large enough to justify the high costs of system adaptation.

In sum, in line with the predictions of the real-options analysis developed above, the designers of transport-layer protocols and the Internet Protocol have generally added new protocols (at the transport layer) or new service interfaces (at the Internet layer) instead of changing the existing service interfaces of TCP, UDP, and IP. In the one case in which the service interface of IP was changed, the improvement is necessary for the Internet's successful operation and growth.

a. The new transport-layer protocols are not yet widely deployed. The problems with deployment are attributable to deviations from the broad version of the end-to-end arguments and will be discussed in the concluding chapter.

Box 4.5
(continued)

---

b. The current version of the Internet Protocol provides a single "best-effort" service, which does not provide any guarantees as to the level of service a data packet receives. In contrast, Quality of Service solutions provide different types of service (for example, some offer guaranteed bandwidth or delay; others give some traffic priority over other traffic without giving absolute guarantees). See Peterson and Davie 2007, pp. 499–525. IP Multicast is a service that simultaneously delivers information to a potentially large number of receivers without creating unnecessary copies of the information. After the sender sends one copy of the data packet into the network, the network takes care of delivering the packet to all receivers, with routers in the network making copies of the packet as needed. See Peterson and Davie 2007, pp. 313–334. Mobile IP allows a mobile end host to move from one network to another without changing its IP address. See Kurose and Ross 2008, pp. 564–569.

c. For short overviews of IPv6 and its history, see Peterson and Davie 2007, pp. 318–329; Kurose and Ross 2008, pp. 360–366

d. Version number 5 was assigned to an experimental protocol, ST-2, that was never standardized. See Kurose and Ross 2008, p. 360.

e. Huston (2008) predicts that the Regional Internet Registries (RIRs), which are responsible for allocating IP addresses within a certain region, will allocate the last unallocated IP address in the year 2011. In the summer of 2007, the RIRs of North America (ARIN) and Latin America and the Caribbean (LACNIC) and the local registry of Japan (JPNIC) issued statements noting the likely exhaustion of unallocated IP addresses in the next few years and strongly recommending transition to IPv6 in their respective geographic areas. See American Registry for Internet Numbers 2007; Latin American and Caribbean Internet Addresses Registry 2007; Asia Pacific Network Information Centre 2007.

f. The transport-layer protocol hands the IP address of the destination to the Internet Protocol through IP's service interface; the IP addresses of the two end hosts that are sending and receiving the datagram are parts of IP's peer interface.

applications serving small, widely dispersed audiences will be deployed in an end-to-end network than in a non-end-to-end network.

To see how a network's deployment context constrains the evolution of its architecture, consider two examples. First, the peer interfaces of the existing transport-layer protocols have evolved much more slowly and incrementally than real-options analysis would predict. Second, many changes involving the Internet Protocol's visible information have been standardized and implemented (as real-options analysis would predict), but they have not yet been widely deployed.

Consider first the evolution of the transport-layer protocols' peer interfaces. By separating the vertical service interface through which higher-layer protocols access a protocol's services from the horizontal peer interface through which the protocol peers cooperate to produce the protocol's service, a layered network architecture makes it possible to change the peer interface without changing the service interface. Recall the real-world analogy introduced in chapter 2: the protocol at the second-highest layer, the mailroom layer, provided person-to-person delivery of documents between company employees. Its service interface required the higher layer to provide the documents to be delivered and the name of the receiver, while its peer interface described the format and meaning of the messages that the mailrooms at the sending and receiving location exchange to implement the mailroom services and actions. In the example, the internal mail code used by the mailroom employees to identify the location of people within the company was part of the mailroom protocol's peer interface. This design lets parts of the peer interface (e.g., the internal mail code) change without changing the mailroom protocol's service interface: Since the service interface asks for the name of the receiver (not her internal mail code), it leaves the job of looking up the internal mail code to the mailroom layer, and the service interface is not affected by the change in the mail code.[97]

The ability to change how the various entities belonging to a protocol communicate and cooperate without affecting the protocol's service interface makes it possible to change a protocol's internal operation without affecting any higher-layer protocols that may use it. The ability to avoid any system-adaptation costs by changing the peer interface in ways that do not affect the service interface is particularly valuable for protocols with highly visible service interfaces (e.g., transport-layer protocols or the Internet Protocol).

Since transport-layer protocols are implemented in higher-layer software at the end host, they have relatively low core costs of innovation. A real-options analysis would suggest that changes without system-adaptation costs (e.g., changes to these protocols' peer interfaces that do not affect the service interface, or changes to the internal implementation of the protocols that do not affect any interface)[98] would attract a significant amount of innovation. As a result, we would expect the peer interface of the transport-layer protocols to evolve much more rapidly than their service interface. (See table 4.1, observations 3 and 4, and accompanying text.)

But although there have been changes to TCP's peer interface, they were all designed to be backward compatible, and they could be deployed incrementally.[99] Thus, the changes to TCP's peer interface were much more incremental than we would expect. Instead of being constrained by characteristics of the architecture alone, the evolution of TCP's peer interface was constrained by the deployment context provided by the economic system that uses the Internet.

Before a new peer interface can be used in the operational Internet, the changes have to be implemented and the new implementations have to be deployed. Higher-layer protocols such as application and transport-layer protocols operate end-to-end between end hosts; in general, protocol implementations using the new versions of the peer interface have to be installed on two end hosts to be used between these two end hosts. Unless the new version of the peer interface is backward compatible, protocol implementations based on different peer interface versions will not cooperate. Thus, in the absence of backward compatibility, it will be necessary to deploy the new version of the protocol on all end hosts using that protocol to ensure that they will be able to communicate.

If a protocol is used by only a small number of end hosts, or if the instances of that protocol that currently run in the network are controlled by a small number of actors, it may be possible to switch all protocol instances in use to the new version simultaneously. In this case, the new version of the peer interface does not have to be backward compatible and can evolve freely from one generation to the next.

However, if there are many different instances of the protocol controlled by a diverse set of actors, it is not likely that all protocol instances will be upgraded at the same time. To ensure that the protocol continues to operate under these circumstances, its designers must let the protocol's different generations co-exist and interoperate.[100] This need for backward compatibility may severely constrain whether and how quickly a protocol evolves. Protocol designers can alleviate the problem by designing peer interfaces that can later be extended. For example, they can require two different protocol instances to negotiate which version should be used, allow the use of options, or reserve fields in the protocol header that can be defined at a later stage.[101] Still, a solution that uses options and allows different protocol instances to negotiate the use of these options may be more cumbersome than a solution that does not need to adhere to the existing specification of the protocol header.[102] This is problematic not only for transport-layer protocols (such as TCP) but also for application-layer protocols (such as HTTP) that are widely deployed and whose instances are under the control of a large, diverse group of actors.

Thus, the context in which a higher-layer protocol is deployed constrains how its peer interface can evolve. If the protocol is used widely and the protocol instances that run in the network are controlled by many different actors, its peer interface will change in ways that are backward compatible, are incrementally deployable, or take advantage of extensibility mechanisms that were designed into the protocol from the start. If the protocol is used by only a small number of end hosts, or if the instances of that protocol that currently run in the network are controlled by a small number of actors, its peer interface can evolve in more radical ways that require a coordinated deployment.

For a second example, consider the changes to the Internet layer standardized by the Internet Engineering Task Force (IETF). The IETF has created a number of protocol standards to augment the existing Internet Protocol, for example by providing Quality of Service, Multicast, or support for mobility. In addition, they also standardized a new version of the Internet Protocol, IPv6. By providing a larger address space than the existing version of the Internet Protocol, the new version of the protocol is designed to prevent the Internet from exhausting its supply of IP addresses (box 4.5). As was noted above, these innovations confirm the predictions made in real-options analysis. Although these protocols were standardized by the IETF and implemented by major vendors of routers and operating systems, they have not yet been widely deployed.

This lack of deployment is attributable to the deployment context provided by the economic system that uses the Internet. The Internet Protocol is deployed on all end hosts and routers in the operational Internet. As a result, adding functionality at the Internet layer or replacing the existing version of the Internet Protocol requires that end hosts and routers be changed. To ensure that the new functionality can be used within a network, it must be deployed on all end hosts and routers on that network. If the functionality is intended to work between *any* two end hosts connected to the Internet, it must be universally deployed on *all* Internet end hosts and routers.[103]

The commercial Internet consists of a large number of providers who operate networks for profit. The original versions of Quality of Service and IP Multicast were not well suited to this multi-network, for-profit deployment context.[104] There was rarely a clear business model that would have let network providers recoup their investments in upgraded infrastructure. The technologies were very complex, and the tools needed to manage them in an operational network were not available. Although data packets often cross multiple network boundaries on their way from the sending to the receiving end hosts, the technologies did not address problems associated with using the technologies across network boundaries.

Thus, while these technologies required a large initial capital investment and significant ongoing costs, their benefits were uncertain. As a result, most network providers did not have an incentive to deploy them. While the technological complexity would still have been an issue with one nationwide, non-profit network, the lack of a business model and the problems associated with inter-domain operation would have been less significant. (For a more detailed discussion of the interaction between architecture and deployment context in the case of multicast, see box 4.6.)

In addition to these technology-specific issues, the structure of the commercial Internet seems to create a more general problem. To make new Internet-layer functionality universally available, all network providers must deploy it in a coordinated way. The need for coordinated group effort creates coordination problems or collective-action problems.[105] Moreover, since network providers have to act together to deploy Internet-layer functionality, deploying such functionality does not create a competitive advantage.[106] This is particularly problematic if there is no clear business model that would let network providers recoup their investments.

There were real problems with the original Quality of Service or IP Multicast proposals that prevented their adoption. Thus, it is not clear to what extent the more fundamental coordination or incentive problems just described helped prevent the deployment of these technologies, or what would have happened if the technologies had better addressed the needs of network providers in the commercial Internet by offering clear benefits for network providers, providing management tools, and tackling issues associated with using the technologies across network boundaries. Some of these shortcomings have been addressed since the protocols were first standardized, so the technologies may still be deployed.

Based on the experience with the deployment (or lack thereof) of Internet-layer technologies, networking researchers have developed two sets of strategies.

Box 4.6

Multicast and the Interaction between Architecture and Deployment Context

Architecture affects which components must be changed in order to deploy an innovation; it also affects the costs and benefits of deployment. The economic system in which the network exists and is used influences who controls the components that must be changed and what incentives these actors may have to make these changes.

Consider multicast, a service that simultaneously delivers information to a potentially large number of receivers without creating unnecessary copies of the information. This service is especially useful for applications used to webcast live events that simultaneously transmit audio or video streams to a potentially large number of viewers, or for video conferencing and online games that transmit data from one participant to all other participants.[a] In the absence of a multicast service, the sender would have to send the same message to every receiver. Multicast lets the sender send only one version of the message, with the multicast service making copies as needed. In comparison with the traditional model, multicast can drastically reduce the number of messages the network has to transmit.[b]

IP multicast realizes the multicast service at the Internet layer. The sender sends the message into the network; the network then takes care of delivering the message to the receivers, routers making copies of it as needed.[c] An alternative architectural solution, application-layer multicast, implements its solution at the application layer, embedding the multicast functionality within a particular application. In this solution, the different instances of the application cooperate to deliver messages to everybody, while minimizing the number of messages.[d]

The two solutions offer different deployment benefits and costs.[e] IP multicast is more efficient than application-layer multicast; for example, application-layer multicast may transfer the same packet over the same link several times, using non-optimal trees to distribute the packet. Thus, the bandwidth savings of application-layer multicast are lower than those of IP multicast. Deploying IP multicast requires changing applications that want to take advantage of IP multicast as well as altering both the service interface and the peer interface of IP at the end hosts; it also requires changing every router on the way from the sender to the receiver. Today, major end-host operating systems and routers are capable of supporting IP multicast. To make IP multicast universally available (i.e., to enable it to be used between any two end hosts attached to the Internet), it would have to be deployed on every router in the Internet.[f] In contrast, to allow a specific group of senders and receivers to use application-layer multicast, only the sending and receiving applications that belong to this group have to support it.

Box 4.6
(continued)

Now consider two different deployment contexts: the commercial Internet and an enterprise network. Consider first the commercial Internet. The bandwidth savings from IP multicast primarily benefit senders who send information to many different receivers.[g] While these benefits accrue to end users, there are no good business and charging models which would enable network providers to transfer at least part of that benefit to themselves. While the end hosts also have to change, the network provider must invest in an upgraded network and incurs considerable operational costs of managing the increased technical complexity with poor tools.[h] Thus, for many network providers, the expected benefits do not justify the expected costs.[i] While application-layer multicast provides comparably lower benefits, it only requires those users who would like to take advantage of it to install the corresponding application, giving them an immediate benefit at a comparatively low cost.[j] With this distribution of deployment costs and benefits, it is not surprising that IP multicast isn't widely deployed in the commercial Internet, while application-layer multicast has been relatively successful.[k]

Now consider an enterprise network. Enterprise networks typically have limited bandwidth. If the company intends to use the network to stream video to its employees (e.g., to distribute enterprise communications or educational offerings), sending the same packet to a large number of employees may overwhelm the network.[l] In this case, the bandwidth savings from introducing IP multicast may justify the costs. Since the company operates both the applications and the network, it benefits from the bandwidth savings. Thus, in this context, the costs and benefits of using IP multicast are aligned in a way that they are not aligned in the commercial Internet. At the same time, some of the operational issues associated with managing multicast (e.g., ensuring the security of the sessions) are easier to tackle within a single, tightly controlled administrative domain.[m] Finally, since the single enterprise controls end hosts and routers on its network, it does not face the coordination difficulties that help prevent deployment in the commercial Internet. In view of the differences between the two deployment contexts, it is not surprising that deployment of IP multicast has been quite successful in enterprise networks, whereas IP multicast has failed to take off in the commercial Internet.[n]

a. Diot et al. 2000, p. 80. It is also useful for sending messages to more than one receiver to synchronize copies of information.
b. In addition, contrary to the traditional unicast model, a multicast sender does not need to know the addresses of the potential receivers (Garber 1999, p. 78).

Box 4.6
(continued)

c. As multicast is not needed by all applications, the provision of multicast in the Internet layer violates the broad version of the end-to-end arguments. According to Reed, Saltzer, and Clark (1998, p. 69, note 1), the authors of the original end-to-end paper, this is one of the rare cases in which the deviation is justified by the cost savings. See also Peterson and Davie 2007, p. 697. For an overview of IP multicast, see Peterson and Davie 2007, pp. 329–343; Kurose and Ross 2008, pp. 408–415.

d. For an overview, see Hosseini et al. 2007.

e. See Hosseini et al. 2007, pp. 60–61; Thaler and Aboba 2008, pp. 20–22.

f. It may be possible to work around this requirement using overlays; see Peterson and Davie 2007, p. 696. This strategy may be difficult to execute, though. For example, MBone, the overlay network that was intended to enable the use of IP multicast until all routers were able to support IP multicast directly, ran into problems as the number of users increased. See Almeroth 2000, p. 14; Thaler and Aboba 2008, p. 21.

g. Diot et al. 2000, p. 80; Thaler and Aboba 2008, p. 20.

h. Diot et al. 2000; Sharma, Perry, and Malpani 2003.

i. Diot et al. 2000, pp. 82–83; Thaler and Aboba 2008, p. 20.

j. Hosseini et al. 2007, pp. 60–61; Thaler and Aboba 2008, p. 20.

k. Hosseini et al. 2007, pp. 60–61; Thaler and Aboba 2008, pp. 20–22.

l. Eubanks 2006, pp. 22–23.

m. Ganjam and Zhang 2005, p. 160; Sarac and Almeroth 2005, p. 85; Hosseini et al. 2007, p. 60.

n. Ganjam and Zhang 2005, p. 163; Sarac and Almeroth 2005, pp. 85, 86; Eubanks 2006, p. 66.

Some advocate changing how Internet-layer protocols are designed to make them more deployable in the commercial Internet. They accept the multi-provider, for-profit nature of the Internet and the fundamental incentive problems that impede the deployment of new Internet-layer technologies. According to them, protocols and other solutions at the Internet layer should be designed in a way that increases their chances of being deployed in this context.[107] This entails exploring business models, developing management tools, and addressing problems associated with the use of Internet-layer protocols across network boundaries.[108] It entails creating solutions that better align adoption costs with their benefits, so that the actor who has to make changes to deploy the innovation also gains the benefits.[109] And it entails designing solutions that can be deployed incrementally (one network at a time) while still providing benefits to those deploying them.[110] These guidelines severely constrain the range of potential solutions that can be considered at the Internet layer. Because these guidelines have been developed to enable networking researchers to innovate more successfully within the deployment context provided by the commercial Internet, they show how the Internet's deployment context constrains the evolution of the Internet layer.

Others suggest solving the deployment problem in a more fundamental way: by changing the architecture to give network providers more incentives to deploy new Internet-layer technologies.[111] They argue that network providers lack incentives to deploy new technologies because the provider who first implements a new Internet-layer technology does not gain a significant competitive advantage. They advocate for introducing mechanisms into the Internet's architecture that let all users attached to the Internet upgrade to a new Internet-layer protocol even if their network provider does not yet offer it. By driving traffic and increasing revenue (through increased settlement charges from interconnection) to the provider offering the new protocol, this solution would reward first movers among network providers and would put pressure on competitors to upgrade. Such an architectural solution would enable several potentially incompatible Internet-layer protocols to coexist until everyone had migrated to the new technology. Proponents of this solution view the coexistence of several potentially incompatible architectures as a transitory occurrence. Some researchers advocate a more radical approach. According to them, the coexistence of several potentially incompatible architectures should become the norm. Instead of providing a mechanism that enables the Internet to transition from one Internet-layer protocol to the next, the infrastructure and the mechanisms necessary to support different coexisting architectures would form the new core of the Internet's architecture, with different coexisting network architectures on top of it.[112]

In the first set of approaches, the deployment context directly constrains the Internet layer's evolution; these approaches accept the constraints resulting from the structure of the commercial Internet and react by constraining the Internet layer's evolution in ways that make it better suited to the deployment context. The approaches in the second set also react to the deployment challenges posed by the commercial Internet. However, instead of accepting the constraints, these approaches (whether they view the coexistence of multiple architectures as a transitory mechanism or a permanent feature of the architecture) aim at changing the constraints by changing the architecture.[113] These two sets of approaches mirror the different ways in which, according to North (2005), organizations and individual actors may react to a given set of constraints. They can play by the "rules of the game" and look for the best strategy given the existing set of constraints (effectively adjusting their behavior to the set of constraints); this is the strategy pursued by the approaches in the first set. Or they can seek to change the "rules of the game" and change the constraints under which they operate; this is the strategy pursued by the approaches in the second set. Though it is too early to judge the merits of these approaches, they show that the economic system in which the Internet exists and is used can significantly influence the evolution of its architecture.

5 Architecture and the Organization of Innovation

This chapter explores how a system's architecture affects the organizational structures in which the development and production of the system, and subsequent innovations, can take place.[1] Product architectures constrain the options for organizing the initial development and production of a system's components, and for organizing subsequent innovation, by enabling or disabling arm's-length relationships. Once an architecture has been created, detailed design can begin. During detailed design, designers must decide how each component will be structured to provide the functionality assigned to it by the architecture; subsequently, each component must be implemented or manufactured according to this specification. Features of the architecture influence whether this work should take place within the boundaries of a single firm or whether independent economic actors can develop various components. This link has important economic implications. First, an architecture created by a single firm affects how that firm can organize the subsequent development and production of components for that architecture. Thus, an architecture influences the organizational options available to individual firms. Second, the constraints imposed by the architecture constrain the potential structure of the industries that develop and produce components for the architecture. Finally, these mechanisms determine whether economic actors other than the system's architect can participate in the development and production of the system's components, both initially and later. Thus, architectural choices have important implications for the range of potential innovators who can innovate with respect to a particular architecture. As we will see in chapter 8, the size and diversity of the innovator pool may, in turn, influence the amount and the type of innovation that can occur with respect to an architecture.

The first section of the chapter explains how exactly an architecture may influence a firm's organizational choices. On the one hand, the architecture of a system provides a framework for dispersing work among design teams, the smallest organizational units involved in the design of the system. As the first subsection shows, the boundaries between components in the architecture determine the boundaries between design teams in the economic system that emerges to develop and produce system components. The second subsection examines how the architecture of a system constrains the feasible organizational structures for the development of the system. The analysis focuses on two types of costs—coordination costs and transaction costs—that economic research has identified as relevant for determining the vertical boundaries of firms. It explains how coordination costs and transaction costs affect firms' boundary choices, and it shows how different product architectures influence these costs. It then uses these insights to examine how modular and integrated product architectures affect the feasible governance structures for innovation at the level of individual components and at the architectural level, both initially and later.

The second section explores what the link between architecture and feasible governance structures in modular and integrated architectures means for the organizational options available to individual firms, the potential structure of the industries for the development and production of system components, and the ability of independent economic actors other than the system's architect to innovate.

The third section applies the insights gained in the preceding sections to the question of how the original architecture of the Internet affects the organization of innovation. It explores the impact of the Internet's original architecture on the organizational options available to individual firms, on the potential structure of the industries for the development and production of system components, and on the ability of economic actors to innovate, particularly in applications.

Architecture and Organization in Modular and Integrated Architectures

There is a close relationship between a product's architecture and the economic structure of the system that emerges to develop and produce the product's components. The architecture of a system constrains the feasible organizational structures for developing and producing the system. First, an architecture provides a framework for dispersing tasks among design teams, the smallest organizational units involved in the design of a product. Second, features of the architecture determine whether the different design teams must be within the same firm or can belong to different, independent firms. Thus, the architecture determines whether independent component development is feasible.

How Architecture Affects Design Teams

Designing a complex system requires a large number of designers. In development projects, the designers involved in the design of a system are organized in several design teams, each of which is responsible for designing one component. Thus, the organizational structure of the project mirrors the technical architecture of the system: components within the architecture correspond to design teams in the development project.[2] This division of labor conforms to the predictions of classic organizational theory,[3] is described by the literature on product and software design,[4] and is widely observed in practice.[5]

According to classic organizational theory, rational organizations assign tasks to organizational units such that overall coordination costs are minimized.[6] In particular, a set of reciprocally interdependent tasks will be allocated to a single group.[7] Two tasks are reciprocally interdependent if they mutually affect each other; they must be executed coherently in order to create a correct overall outcome.[8] If the number of reciprocally interdependent tasks is too large to be managed within a single group, the tasks will be grouped so that task interdependencies within a group are strong and task interdependencies across different groups are weak.[9] This division reflects the insight that coordinating reciprocally interdependent tasks across group boundaries is more difficult than coordinating these tasks within a group.[10] Reciprocally interdependent tasks cannot be performed independently; they require ongoing mutual adjustment. As a result, people performing these tasks must continually communicate and coordinate their decisions. As empirical studies have shown, communication across group boundaries within an organization occurs less frequently than communication within a group.[11] Members of a group communicate personally and frequently on an informal basis ("high bandwidth communication"); the resulting common knowledge base facilitates the communication of new information and the coordination of mutually dependent decisions. Communication across group boundaries tends to be more formalized and is often inhibited by the lack of familiarity with members of other groups and their responsibilities.

The architecture of a system affects the division of responsibility between design teams because decomposing a system into components determines the nature and strength of the interdependencies between the tasks involved in the detailed design of the system.

An architecture implies both a set of tasks and interdependencies between them.[12] An architecture contains an inherent set of design problems which have to be solved to create a workable design. Thus, each design problem implies the task of solving it. If design problems are interdependent, their solutions must be coordinated to ensure a coherent outcome. As a result, an interdependency between design problems implies an interdependency between the corresponding design tasks.

To limit complexity, any product architecture places strongly interconnected design problems within the same component. As a result, interdependencies between design problems inherent in the design of a single component are stronger than those between design problems shared among different components. Whereas the tasks involved in designing a single component are strongly interdependent, there are fewer interdependencies with design choices in different components. Consequently, component boundaries implicitly separate strongly interdependent tasks from less interdependent ones. That, in turn, leads rational organizations, which group tasks so that task interdependencies within a group are strong and task interdependencies across different groups are weak, to use them as boundaries between design teams.

How Architecture Affects Firms' Boundary Choices

Apart from implying the boundaries between the different design teams involved in the design of the system, a system's architecture constrains the number and the types of organizational structures that can feasibly develop the system. In particular, features of the architecture determine whether the various components have to be developed by a single firm or whether they can be developed by independent firms. In the terminology of economics, the product architecture determines a firm's feasible vertical boundaries.

The vertical boundaries of a firm separate the activities it performs itself from those it purchases from independent firms in the market. To define its vertical boundaries, a firm must decide whether to organize transactions internally or across a market. The corresponding decisions are called *make-or-buy decisions*.[13]

Economic theory has long investigated how firms decide whether to internalize certain transactions or to purchase them in the market. Initially, different strands of economic theory focused on different factors— for example, on transaction costs or on capabilities, which were viewed as mutually exclusive explanations for the vertical boundaries of firms. As theoretical and empirical analyses have shown, it is more appropriate to view these theories as complementary approaches that jointly explain the vertical boundaries of firms.[14] According to this view, firms and markets constitute alternative means of economic organization (so-called governance structures), with distinct advantages and disadvantages. To define its vertical boundaries, a firm must decide whether to internalize a transaction and perform the activity itself, or to use the market and purchase it from an independent firm. Owing to the different characteristics of firms and markets, the costs and benefits of organizing the transaction may vary depending on governance structures. Economic theory assumes that firms base this decision on the comparative costs and benefits associated with the transaction under both governance structures.[15] As this chapter will show, product architecture affects the feasibility of different organizational choices by influencing the relative costs of using the market.

The analysis in this chapter focuses on two types of costs that economic research has identified as relevant to a firm's vertical boundary choices: coordination costs and transaction costs (box 5.1). Whereas transaction costs result from the needs to economize on bounded rationality and to safeguard against opportunism, coordination costs arise from the need to ensure consistent treatment of interdependent transactions. According to economic theory, the firm is the superior governance mode for dealing with bounded rationality and opportunism and for ensuring the coordination of interdependent transactions. As a result, economic theory assumes that firms will choose to internalize transactions if transaction costs or coordination costs are high and are not offset by larger benefits of using the market.

Coordination costs and transaction costs are not the only factors affecting the boundary choices of firms. As was noted above, firms base their decision on a joint evaluation of the different costs and benefits associated with the transaction under the different governance structures. Thus, a comparative advantage of internal organization with respect to transaction costs may be offset by a larger comparative advantage of using the market, for example because the market may provide access to superior capabilities or enable firms to take advantage of economies of scale.[16] As a result, an analysis based on coordination-cost and transaction-cost considerations alone is necessarily incomplete and cannot predict the actual choices of specific firms.[17] It does, however, provide an indication of the feasibility of different organizational choices with respect to these costs: If the firm is the superior governance mode with respect to transaction and coordination costs, the analysis of these costs indicates how large countervailing advantages of the market would have to be to eliminate this superiority. If internal organization and arm's-length relationships are equally feasible

Box 5.1
Coordination Costs and Transaction Costs

Whereas transaction costs have long been used to explain the vertical boundaries of firms, coordination costs have only recently been identified as a distinct cost category affecting firms' governance choices.[a]

Historically, the two types of costs have been explored by different strands of economic research.[b] Transaction costs have been analyzed by economics and strategy research, particularly by transaction-cost economics, property-rights theory, and agency theory. Coordination costs have been examined by organizational research such as structure contingencies theories, organizational learning theory, and parts of the literature on product development in engineering science.

Conceptually, transaction-cost reasoning and coordination-cost reasoning are complementary, distinct approaches to the analysis of governance choices. Transaction costs and coordination costs describe different aspects of a relationship between economic actors and represent different concerns influencing the governance choices of firms.

Transaction costs capture the costs involved in the contractual governance of transactions, such as the costs of drafting, negotiating, monitoring, and enforcing contracts in the presence of bounded rationality and opportunism. According to transaction-cost reasoning, governance choices are driven by appropriation concerns. Coordination costs focus on the procedural aspect of the transaction (that is, the coordination of interdependent activities through the day-to-day interactions of the employees involved in executing the transaction); this approach traces firms' boundary choices to the desire to ensure efficient coordination among interdependent activities.

The theoretical differences between the two approaches are also illustrated by the differing roles played by opportunism.[c] Opportunism—which is defined as "self-interest seeking with guile," and which includes lying, cheating, and subtler forms of deceit, such as violating agreements[d]—is one of the main assumptions on which transaction-cost reasoning is based; without it, transaction-cost differences between different governance structures would disappear. In contrast, coordination-cost differences arise even in the absence of opportunism. The magnitude of these differences, however, may be intensified by opportunism. Thus, coordination-cost analysis does not depend on opportunism in the way that transaction-cost theory does.

Since coordination costs and transaction costs arise at different places in the organization, they can be separated empirically.[e] Whereas responsibility for the contractual governance of a relationship is usually located in the purchasing department, the day-to-day communication and decision making that are necessary to coordinate interdependent activities take place among employees involved in the execution of the transaction.

Box 5.1
(continued)

a. The argument that coordination costs are a distinct cost category affecting firms' governance choices that cannot be explained by transaction-cost reasoning and therefore must be studied separately has been advanced by Gulati and Singh (1998), Gulati (1998), Sobrero and Schrader (1998), Sobrero and Roberts (2002), Jacobides (2002), Gulati, Lawrence, and Puranam (2005), and Jaspers and van den Ende (2006).
b. See Sobrero and Schrader 1998, pp. 587–595.
c. See Gulati and Singh 1998, pp. 782–783; Jacobides 2002, pp. 15–18.
d. Williamson 1985, pp. 47–49.
e. See Sobrero and Schrader 1998, p. 586.

from a transaction-cost and coordination-cost perspective, other factors will determine firms' boundary choices. For example, firms and markets differ in their incentive intensity.[18] Whereas firms in an arm's-length transaction directly appropriate the gains of the transaction, the allocation of gains to recipients in an internal transaction is usually less precise and subject to potential manipulation. As a result, in an arm's-length transaction, actions and consequences are often more tightly linked, resulting in higher incentive intensity and, consequently, higher efficiency of market-based transactions. In contrast, internal organization is characterized by lower incentive intensity and added bureaucratic costs. Other things being equal, this shifts firms' preferences toward market-based organization. Firm's governance choices may also be influenced by specific capabilities[19] within the firm or in the market or by the ability to exploit economies of scale.[20] Firms may also base their decisions on such strategic considerations as the desire to maintain or create strategically important capabilities "in house" or the desire to maintain exclusive control over critically important or particularly profitable components.[21]

In the following analysis, we will look at how coordination and transaction costs affect firm's boundary choices and how different product architectures influence these costs. We will focus on a firm's ability to insert an organizational boundary between the definition of the architecture and detailed component design by organizing the detailed design of particular components in an arm's-length relationship (figure 5.1). This interface is particularly relevant to the present book, since detailed component design is an important locus of innovation. If arm's-length relationships across this interface are possible, economic actors other than the system's

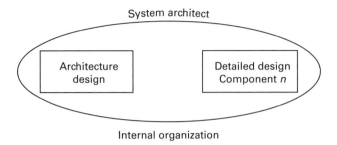

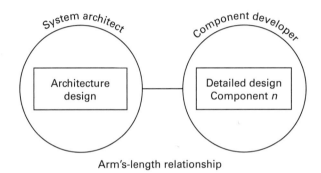

Figure 5.1
Options for organizing detailed design.

architects may be able to develop new or better components, affecting the amount and the type of innovation that may occur.

The analysis assumes that the detailed design and the production of a component are performed by the same firm. In reality, an organizational separation of detailed design and production is quite common. Whether such a separation is feasible can be determined by applying the analysis outlined below to the interface between detailed component design and production.[22]

How Architecture Affects Coordination Costs   Coordination costs are the costs of coordinating interdependent tasks or sets of tasks. Two tasks are interdependent if the execution of one task may affect the execution of the other in a way that influences the correctness of the overall outcome. In this case, their execution must be coordinated to ensure a correct outcome.

Coordination costs have two elements: the costs of communicating relevant information and the costs of ensuring that the task in question is executed coherently.[23]

Coordination-cost reasoning is based on the insight that firms possess distinct characteristics with respect to communication and decision making that enable them to coordinate certain types of interdependent tasks at lower costs within the firm than in arm's-length relationships across firm boundaries.[24] For these tasks, firms will internalize both tasks unless their relative advantage with respect to coordination costs is offset by countervailing advantages of using the market.

The relative advantage of firms over markets depends on the amount of communication and decision making necessary to ensure that the interdependent tasks in question are executed coherently. Thus, the coordination requirements of two particular tasks determine the coordination-cost differences between internal and external organization, which, in turn, influence the feasibility of the different governance choices. Thus, coordination-cost theory links an observable task attribute—the type of task interdependency—to feasible governance choices.[25]

Coordination Advantages of Firms over Markets   Firms may have advantages over markets with respect to communication and decision making. Firms possess certain characteristics that make it easier to transfer information within a firm than across firm boundaries. The effect of these characteristics may differ depending on the type of information that needs to be transferred: whereas the costs of communicating tacit information are usually lower within a firm than across firm boundaries, the two governance structures may be equally efficient in communicating certain types of codified information.

Tacit information is information that is informal, unstructured, uncodified, and stored in people's heads.[26] Since it is closely linked to an individual's specific knowledge and experience, it cannot be written down or shared easily. Instead, transferring tacit information usually requires "rich"[27] interactive communication mechanisms, such as face-to-face communication. Rich communication mechanisms are characterized by their capacity to provide feedback, transmit multiple cues, and use natural language. As a result, they are capable of reducing the inherent ambiguity that makes tacit information difficult to transfer.[28]

In general, the costs of communicating tacit information within a firm are lower than the costs of communicating it across firm boundaries.[29] Rich communication mechanisms are more readily available within a firm. Face-to-face communication is easier to achieve within a firm. Members of a single firm are more likely to be co-located and better able to identify suitable communication partners; membership in the same organization creates a sense of commonality that facilitates establishing new contacts.[30] Should co-location be desired, firms can simply mandate co-location without any of the lengthy and costly negotiations that are common in arm's-length relationships.

In addition, members of the same organization usually develop common languages and communication codes that reduce the potential for misunderstanding and the amount of information needed to explain something; this firm-specific standardization of information further reduces the costs of communicating tacit (and other) information.[31]

Codified information is written down and can be transferred easily. Whether firms can transfer this information internally at lower costs than across firm boundaries depends on the information in question. On the one hand, the existence of firm-specific language and communication codes may lower the costs of communicating within the firm. On the other hand, efforts toward industry-wide standardization of information and advances in information technology are reducing the advantages of firms with respect to codified information. Efforts toward industry-wide standardization of information remove potential ambiguity. By eliminating the need for rich, interactive communication media, they make it easier to transfer this information across firm boundaries.[32]

Electronic information systems reduce the costs of transferring large amounts of complex information. In the beginning, however, this cost reduction was restricted to information transfers within firms, because most firms originally adopted proprietary, non-interoperable systems. In recent years, information systems that provide standardized ways of exchanging and interpreting data across firm boundaries have become increasingly common. The widespread adoption of interoperable information systems such as CAD/CAM and systems that implement the electronic data interchange (EDI) standard increases the range of codified information that can efficiently be communicated across firm boundaries.[33]

Thus, if codified information is standardized or well documented to reduce ambiguity, and if there are suitable mechanisms for transferring the information across firm boundaries, the relative advantage of firms with respect to communication is reduced considerably, if not eliminated.

Firms may also have advantages with respect to decision making. Owing to differences in governance structures, firms can make decisions regarding interdependent problems at greater speed, at lower costs, and potentially with better quality. In comparison with an arm's-length relationship, firms benefit from the existence of command structures and authority systems, from the availability of administrative dispute-resolution mechanisms, and from superior access to information.

In an arm's-length relationship, the two parties remain independent entities. There are no command structures or authority systems that let one party impose a decision on the other. Instead, coordinated decision making is brought about by negotiating and convincing, a lengthy and costly process. This process may be further complicated by the existence of divergent goals among multiple parties. Until the issue is resolved, the parties also bear the indirect costs of maladaptation. In contrast, firms already have or can easily create appropriate command structures and authority systems that enable hierarchical decision making. Within the firm, an employee enters into an employment relationship in which she agrees to work at the direction and discretion of a superior within general bonds. Thus, coordinated decision making within the firm can be mandated.[34]

If the parties in an arm's-length transaction cannot reach an agreement, the dispute probably will be resolved by a court. In contrast, courts usually forbear from dealing with disputes within a firm. As a result, such disputes can be resolved within the firm. The firm has access to flexible administrative dispute-resolution mechanisms, such as managerial fiat or informal mediation, that make it possible to resolve conflicts faster and at lower cost.[35]

When tasks are organized internally, managers within the firm may have access to superior information that provides a better basis for decision making. Whereas an employee is subject to comprehensive disclosure requirements, the parties in an arm's-length transaction are protected by the general contractual non-disclosure clause, which restricts each party's right to demand information unless this right was explicitly specified.[36] In addition, the transfer of relevant information in an arm's-length transaction is often impeded by concerns over information leakage. Since they cannot be sure whether the other firm will protect the confidentiality of the information, firms tend to minimize the amount of information they communicate across firm boundaries.[37] Finally, if interdependent transactions are organized internally, it may be easier to recognize and take account of any complementarities and externalities among transactions.

Linking Task Interdependency to Governance Choices   Based on the differences between firms and markets with respect to communication and decision making, the subsequent analysis develops a framework that links an observable task attribute—the type of interdependency between two tasks—to feasible governance choices.

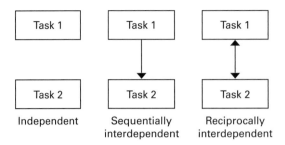

Figure 5.2
Task interdependencies.

Following James Thompson,[38] we can distinguish three types of task interdependency that differ in the amount of communication and in the mechanisms needed to achieve coordination: independence, sequential interdependence, and reciprocal interdependence (figure 5.2). As a result, the type of task interdependency directly influences the coordination costs under the two governance structures (internal organization and arm's-length transaction).

Two tasks are independent if they do not affect each other.[39] They are sequentially interdependent if the output of the first task is an input into the second task, but the reverse is not true. Thus, the execution of the first task influences the range of feasible approaches to the second task.[40] Two tasks are reciprocally interdependent if they mutually affect each other; they must be executed coherently in order to create a correct overall outcome.[41]

In the order introduced above, the three types of task interdependencies place increasingly heavy burdens on communication and on decision making. As the coordination-cost differences between internal and external organization grow, it becomes increasingly infeasible to organize interdependent tasks across firm boundaries in arm's-length relationships.

The execution of two independent tasks does not require any communication or decision making between those performing them. Thus, task independence creates no coordination costs and does not influence the corresponding governance choices.

To ensure the overall coherence of sequentially interdependent tasks, those performing the second task must comply with the constraints imposed by the execution of the first task. Thus, apart from transferring the relevant information or material from the first task to the second, no communication between those performing the tasks is required. Since the hierarchy between the tasks is clear, coordinating sequentially inter-dependent tasks does not require any additional decision making. Instead, the mechanism for ensuring a coherent execution consists of determining whether the execution of the second task complied with the constraints.[42]

Organizing sequentially interdependent tasks within and across firm boundaries is equally feasible if internal organization does not provide any coordination-cost advantages. This is the case if it is equally costly to com-municate the relevant information and to ensure a coherent execution within a firm and across firm boundaries. As was set out above, information can be transferred as efficiently across firm boundaries as within a firm if it is codified, if it is unambiguous, and if efficient transfer mechanisms exist. As will be set out in detail below, the correct execution of a task can be as efficiently monitored in an arm's-length relationship as within a firm if technology is available to measure whether the attributes of the product or service conform to the requirements.

If these two conditions do not hold (i.e., communicating the relevant information or ensuring a coherent execution of the task is less costly within the firm than across firm boundaries), coordinating the tasks inter-nally is less costly than coordinating them across firm boundaries. Unless the relative advantage with respect to coordination costs is offset by coun-tervailing advantages of using the market, a firm will internalize both tasks.

Thus, the effect of sequential interdependence on governance choices depends on the codifiability and transferability of the relevant information as well as on the existence of tests for compliance.

Reciprocally interdependent tasks call for coordination by mutual adjustment.[43] Often the circumstances affecting the execution of each task cannot be predicted in advance, and most of the relevant information will be discovered during the execution of each task. As a result, it is not pos-sible to agree on a coherent approach in advance. Instead, those perform-ing the tasks must communicate on an ongoing basis to let each other assess the effect of potential actions on the other task and identify feasible approaches. They must communicate information as it becomes known (a typical case of tacit information) in order to develop common understand-ings of problems and to design potential solutions. All these tasks require rich communication.[44]

If two tasks are reciprocally interdependent, there may be several pairs of potential actions that are mutually consistent. In this case, each pair of potential actions constitutes a feasible approach; those performing the tasks must decide jointly which pair to adopt. One approach may be optimal with respect to the first task; another may be preferable with respect to the second. As a result, those performing the tasks may disagree on the joint approach that should be adopted. In this case, hierarchical decision making will be necessary to choose the solution that best meets the overall requirements.[45]

As has been described above, it is less costly to communicate tacit information within a firm than across firm boundaries because rich communication is less costly to achieve within a firm. A firm can also reach decisions regarding interdependent problems at greater speed, with lower costs, and potentially with higher quality. As a result, coordinating reciprocally interdependent tasks within a firm is considerably less costly than doing it across firm boundaries. Owing to the high cost, coordinating reciprocally interdependent tasks across an arm's-length relationship is usually not feasible. Unless the relative advantage with respect to coordination costs is offset by countervailing advantages of using the market, a firm will internalize both tasks.[46]

Internal organization is not the only feasible organizational structure for coordinating two reciprocally interdependent tasks. Other governance structures that constitute intermediate forms of economic organization on the spectrum from firms to markets may provide an alternative to internal organization if the coordination costs of using an arm's-length relationship are too high. For example, two firms can choose to establish a common communication framework and to set up procedures for hierarchical decision making and dispute resolution through a joint venture or (less formally) a joint research project.[47] The resulting coordination framework may reduce or eliminate the differences in coordination costs between the intra-firm and inter-firm organization of reciprocally interdependent tasks. The result is a quasi-integrated structure that deviates significantly from the typical governance structure of an arm's-length transaction. Negotiating and implementing such a coordination framework is, however, quite costly. Thus, a firm will choose this solution only if the expected gains outweigh the overall costs, as may be the case if the cooperation provides access to capabilities not available within the firm.[48]

Alternatively, a firm may benefit from past investments in a suitable inter-firm coordination framework—for example, in a repeated relationship. Again, such a framework may significantly lower or even make negligible the differences in coordination costs. For example, Japanese automobile manufacturers maintain long-term relationships with major suppliers that are characterized by frequent face-to-face interaction, co-location of important personnel, and familiarity with the manufacturer's language and procedures. As a result, the costs of coordinating interdependent activities with these suppliers are much lower than in the United States, where most automobile manufacturers deal with their suppliers on a short-term, arm's-length basis.[49]

Thus, though it is not feasible to organize two reciprocally interdependent tasks across an arm's-length relationship (owing to high coordination costs), it may still be feasible to organize them across firm boundaries, using an alternative governance structure.

Empirical Evidence   Several empirical studies have explored particular aspects of the relationship between coordination costs and governance choices. If these studies are interpreted in the light of the framework presented above, the results correspond with the predictions of the framework. For example, coordination costs can explain empirically why semiconductor firms choose to internalize design and production if the tasks involved are reciprocally interdependent, whereas production can be outsourced if the relationship between design and production is characterized by sequential interdependency.[50] A case study of the mortgage banking industry highlights how advances in the industry-wide standardization of mortgage descriptions and the adoption of interoperable information systems eliminated the coordination-cost advantages of internal organization with respect to sequentially interdependent activities, enabling the formation of intermediate markets.[51] According to an empirical study of firms' governance choices for inter-firm alliances, differences in the type of task interdependencies can explain differences in the choice of hierarchical controls in inter-firm alliances.[52]

The Effect of Architecture   From a coordination-cost perspective, product architectures influence the feasibility of various vertical-boundary choices by determining the nature and strength of task interdependencies among component-design teams. As we saw earlier, an interdependency between two design parameters implies an interdependency between the tasks of choosing them. Since component boundaries commonly delineate boundaries between design teams, the design-parameter interdependencies between components determine the task interdependencies between the teams responsible for designing them.

Modular and integrated product architectures differ in the nature and the strength of design-parameter interdependencies between components; the resulting differences in task interdependencies explain why the feasibility of organizational choices varies between modular and integrated architectures.

Though an integrated architecture identifies interfaces between components, interfaces are complex and not well specified.[53] This is because inter-component interdependencies are not resolved during the definition of the architecture, but during detailed design. In fact, "cycling" through parameter interdependencies within and across components to create a globally optimal solution is a crucial part of detailed design. Thus, providing a complete interface specification that resolves all cross-component interdependencies is not possible before the end of detailed design.

An integrated architecture is characterized by complex, unresolved design-parameter interdependencies between components. Since design parameters mutually affect one another without a precedence relationship between them, the corresponding design tasks are reciprocally interdependent across component design teams. As a result, the coordination costs of organizing all detailed component design within a firm are considerably lower than the coordination costs of distributing the design of the different components among independent firms. Unless significant gains are expected from outsourcing the detailed design of specific components or existing inter-firm coordination frameworks can be utilized, the costs of inter-firm coordination are usually prohibitive.

With an integrated architecture, organizing the detailed design of a component in a typical arm's-length relationship will not be feasible; under the conditions outlined above, a "hybrid" governance structure such as the creation of an inter-firm coordination framework, for example in the form of a joint venture or joint research project, or the use of an existing one may constitute a feasible alternative to internalization.[54]

Characteristics of the architecture also affect how subsequent innovation can be organized. In a system based on an integrated architecture, the various components are linked by numerous interdependencies that have been resolved during detailed design. Due to these far-reaching chains of dependencies within the system, it is usually not possible to change parts of a component without triggering changes in the rest of the system. As a result, isolated innovation at the component level is usually not possible.[55] Instead, innovation is a system-level activity that is very similar to designing a new system from scratch. Owing to the reciprocal interdependence between parameters in different components that are revisited in the course of this process, both the redesign of the architecture and the detailed design of the different components consist of reciprocally interdependent tasks that are best organized internally or in a closely integrated alternative governance structure.

In a modular architecture, all cross-component design-parameter interdependencies are resolved during architectural design and documented in detailed interface specifications that are not allowed to change during detailed design. As a result, no unresolved interdependencies between components exist when detailed design starts. Since design decisions within a component are hidden from designers of other components, cross-component interdependencies cannot be reintroduced during detailed design. Design decisions within a component, however, are bound by the visible information defined during architectural design.[56]

Thus, a modular architecture is characterized by two types of design-parameter interdependencies. First, hidden design parameters within a component are sequentially dependent on the visible design parameters contained in the relevant interface specifications. Second, a component's hidden design parameters are independent of the hidden design parameters of any other component.

Consequently, a modular architecture creates two types of task interdependencies (figure 5.3). First, the tasks inherent in the detailed design of each component are sequentially dependent on the tasks required for architectural design. To coordinate these activities, the architecture's visible

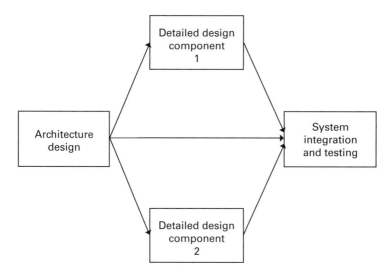

Figure 5.3
Task interdependencies in a mature modular architecture.

information necessary for the design of a particular module must be communicated from the system's architects to the designers of the module. To ensure that the module will function properly within the overall system, the finished component's design must be checked to ensure that it conforms to the relevant interface specifications. Second, the detailed design processes of different components are independent. As a result, there is no need for interaction between the designers of different modules.[57]

Detailed component design can be organized through arm's-length transactions, with different firms responsible for the different components, if (1) the architecture completely captures and resolves all existing cross-component interdependencies, (2) the architecture's visible information is completely specified and well documented to avoid ambiguity, and (3) technology is available to determine whether a module complies with the relevant interface specifications.[58] The first condition ensures that the detailed design of different components is really independent; the second and the third capture the conditions under which the coordination of sequentially interdependent activities is equally efficient within and across firm boundaries. The second condition eliminates the communication advantages of firms; the third removes the advantage of internal organization in monitoring and enforcing performance. If these conditions hold, a module can be traded in an arm's-length transaction, and each module can be designed by a different firm.

Thus, from a coordination-cost perspective, internal organization and arm's-length relationships constitute equally efficient ways of organizing the detailed component design of a modular system, if the three conditions above are met. Owing to the independence between the detailed design processes of different components, the vertical-boundary choices for the different components are independent of each other; as a result, each module can be designed by a different firm. Whether a firm uses this opportunity and outsources the detailed design of some or all components depends on additional factors not related to coordination costs. For example, a firm may wish to keep certain strategically important components in house to maintain exclusive control of critically important or highly profitable components and may choose to outsource others to leverage the benefits of competitive component markets for innovation and pricing.[59]

Thus, a modular architecture does not determine firms' boundary choices for detailed design, nor does it necessarily result in a modular organizational structure with different loosely coupled organizations developing the different components of the system. It merely gives the firm controlling the architecture the ability to choose whether to organize the detailed design of specific components internally or in arm's-length relationships without having to worry about coordination costs.

Finally, the tasks of system integration and testing are sequentially dependent on architecture definition as well as on detailed component design.[60] If the architecture completely captures and resolves all existing cross-component interdependencies and the individual components comply with the interface specifications, no changes to components are required during system integration and testing to ensure that the system functions. In this case, system integration simply involves putting the different components together. Thus, system integrators must know the architecture of the system and must have access to the detailed designs of the components. Apart from that, no interaction among system architects, component designers, and system integrators is required. If the task is not too difficult and does not require technology that isn't available to users, users may be able to perform the task of integrating their own system.[61]

The above analysis of task interdependencies applies only if the architecture completely captures and resolves all existing cross-component interdependencies. Owing to the bounded cognitive abilities of the system's architects, architects working on a new or a relatively young architecture are often unable to capture all dependencies when first defining the architecture. This is a common problem in practice.[62] In this case, resolving unforeseen cross-component interdependencies may require considerable changes in components or in the architecture's visible information during detailed design or during system integration and testing if the system is to function. Thus, if the system's architects have not recognized and resolved all cross-component interdependencies, architectural design, detailed component design, system integration, and testing will be reciprocally interdependent, as will be the detailed design of different components (figure 5.4).[63]

The organization of subsequent innovation in a modular system depends on the type of innovation. Whereas innovation at the component level can proceed independently as long as the architecture's existing visible information is unaffected, innovation at the architectural level requires close coordination. In economic terminology, innovation at the component level constitutes an *autonomous* innovation that can be pursued independently from other innovations. Innovation at the architectural level is *systemic* innovation whose benefits can be realized only in conjunction with related, complementary innovations.[64]

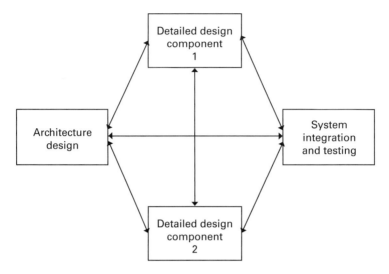

Figure 5.4

Task interdependencies in a modular architecture with unresolved design-parameter interdependencies among components.

As we saw in chapters 2 and 4, changes at the component level that do not affect the architecture's existing visible information (e.g., improving an existing component or adding a new component that uses existing interfaces) do not require any changes in the rest of the system.[65] As a result, innovation of this type can proceed independently.[66] Thus, internal organization and arm's-length relationships are equally feasible organizational arrangements.

This independence has important implications for the locus of control over component-level innovation. Since the architecture of the system remains unaffected, no technical contribution by the system's architects is required to enable this type of innovation. If the architecture captures and resolves all existing cross-component interdependencies and the new or improved component complies with the constraints imposed by the architecture, the component will function smoothly within the overall system. In this case, system integration is reduced to putting the different components together and can potentially be performed by anyone who has access to the necessary technology. As a result, innovators do not have to coordinate their activities with the system's architects or integrators; they do not have to ask for permission to be able to develop an innovation, and, as long as the architecture remains unchanged, the system's architects have no technical way of preventing innovators from acting. Thus, relative to an integrated architecture, a modular architecture shifts control of component-level innovation from the system's architects to component designers.[67] As we will see in chapter 8, this decentralization of control is particularly important if there is uncertainty about the technical or commercial viability of the innovation, since the need to convince another actor decreases the chance that an innovation will be realized.

In contrast, an innovation that involves changing the architecture's visible information (i.e., changes to the interfaces) requires altering different parts of the system. The innovative process consists of two steps. First, those controlling the architecture must agree on the necessary changes and must produce specifications for the refined architecture. This step is similar to the initial design of an architecture. In the new interface specifications, the system's architects must capture and resolve all cross-component interdependencies. Thus, this step consists of reciprocally interconnected tasks and is best organized within a single organization. If the architecture is owned by several firms or is defined in open standards, the economic actors cooperating in the evolution of the architecture will most likely establish an alternative governance structure, perhaps a consortium or a standard-setting body, to coordinate these tasks.[68] Second, module designers must adapt their component design to the new architecture; that is, they must produce a refined detailed design that complies with the new visible information. Owing to the lack of unresolved cross-component interdependencies in a modular architecture, the designers of various modules can perform this task on their own. As with detailed component design in general, the redesign of the various components can be organized equally well internally or in arm's-length relationships, with different firms designing different components.

How Architecture Affects Transaction Costs

An architecture also affects transaction costs. Transaction costs are the costs associated with drafting, negotiating, monitoring, and enforcing contracts in the presence of bounded rationality and opportunism. In addition to the direct costs of managing the relationship, transaction costs include the possible opportunity costs of making inferior governance decisions.[69]

Transaction-cost theory is based on the insight that firms have distinct characteristics that enable them to mitigate problems caused by bounded rationality and opportunistic behavior at lower costs within the firm than in an arm's-length relationship. Thus, if a transaction is afflicted with these problems, the transaction costs associated with internal organization will be lower than the transaction costs of using the market. In this case, and unless the comparative advantage with respect to transaction costs is offset by countervailing advantages of using the market, a firm will internalize the transaction. Whether bounded rationality and opportunism pose problems for a specific transaction can be traced back to specific attributes of the transaction under consideration.

Thus, transaction-cost analysis links attributes of transactions to feasible governance choices. The subsequent analysis does not take account of differences in incentive intensity between internal organization and arm's-length relationships. Though this factor is often included in traditional transaction-cost analysis,[70] I treat the differential incentive intensity of both governance structures separately from transaction-cost considerations, along with other factors that may influence firms' boundary choices.

Behavioral Assumptions: Bounded Rationality and Opportunism   Transaction-cost theory is based on the assumption that human beings are characterized by bounded rationality and opportunism, an assumption that deviates from the behavioral assumptions of neoclassical economics.[71] Bounded rationality defines human beings as "intendedly rational, but only limitedly so."[72] Thus, it refers to the limited information-processing and communication capacities that constrain humans' ability to act rationally.[73] Opportunism, defined as "self-interest seeking with guile," includes lying and cheating as well as subtler forms of deceit, such as violating agreements.[74]

Linking Attributes of Transactions to Governance Choices   Bounded rationality and opportunism pose problems for a transaction if the circumstances of the exchange are uncertain, if it is necessary for one or both of the parties to invest in relationship-specific assets that are less valuable outside of the relationship, or if performance is difficult to measure. If one of these conditions applies, transaction costs will be lower under internal organization. In the absence of uncertainty, asset specificity, and measurement problems, the two governance structures are equally able to manage bounded rationality and opportunism.

Thus, from a transaction-cost perspective, uncertainty, asset specificity, and difficulties in measuring performance are the critical influences on firms' governance choices. This subsection outlines the reasoning that underlies this claim.

The standard way for two parties to organize an arm's-length transaction is to write a contract specifying what is expected from each. In the absence of uncertainty, measurement problems, and asset specificity, the parties can write a complete, enforceable contract that efficiently safeguards against opportunism.[75] Since the circumstances surrounding the exchange are clear, bounded rationality is not a problem: the parties can foresee and resolve all relevant contingencies in advance and write a contract that completely specifies each party's rights and responsibilities. They can do so in unambiguous terms that can be applied by a third party enforcing the contract. And since it is possible to measure performance, both parties, and even a third party, can verify contract compliance. As a result, each party can detect opportunistic behavior by monitoring performance and, should it be necessary, can enforce the agreement by going to court. Finally, since neither party has invested in relationship-specific assets, it is possible for the parties to switch trading partners when the contract is up for renewal if opportunistic behavior has occurred. This acts as an additional deterrent to opportunistic behavior.

As will be described below, firms have access to mechanisms that reduce the incentives for opportunistic behavior and enable them to detect opportunistic actions should they occur. As a result, internal organization is an equally efficient way to safeguard against opportunism.

Thus, in the absence of uncertainty, measurement problems, and asset specificity, internal and external organization are equally feasible from a transaction-cost perspective. Under these circumstances, other considerations—such as the different incentive intensity of firms and markets, the desire to gain access to capabilities that may exist within the firm or in the market, or the desire to exploit economies of scale—will determine firms' boundary choices.[76]

The higher the degree of uncertainty and complexity, the more difficult and costly it is to write a complete contract to organize an arm's-length transaction. Owing to the parties' bounded rationality, contracts will necessarily be incomplete. As a result, the contract may have to be renegotiated should unforeseen circumstances occur. As we saw above, this may be a lengthy and costly process. Since the parties to the transaction may try to exploit any existing incompleteness to their own benefit, reaching agreement on how to adapt the contract may be impeded by opportunistic behavior. Disputes will be resolved by litigation, which further delays adaptation. Thus, in comparison with simple transactions without uncertainty, the transaction costs associated with uncertainty and complexity in an arm's-length transaction not only include higher costs of drafting and negotiating the initial agreement; they also include the costs of communicating new information, renegotiating or litigating agreements, or coordinating activities to adapt to new circumstances. In addition, parties who fail to adapt will incur the opportunity cost of maladaptation.[77]

The problems caused by incomplete contracts are particularly severe if the relationship is supported by specific assets that are less valuable outside the transaction in question.[78] In particular, the party who has invested in specific assets is in danger of being "held up" by its partner: Since the firm cannot costlessly redeploy the specific assets in other ways, its partner has an incentive to appropriate some of the gains from the specialized investment through post-contractual bargaining or threats of termination. This incentive is particularly high when contracts are highly incomplete, so that proving breach of contract is difficult.

Thus, asset specificity may raise the transaction costs of arm's-length market exchange in two ways. First, the chance of "hold-up" may lead to more frequent renegotiations as one party tries to change the terms of contract to his own benefit. Apart from increasing costs, the negotiations are likely to disrupt the execution of the contract, leading to productivity losses. If the party succeeds in changing the contract, the other party will not be able to appropriate the expected gains. Second, the fear of being "held up" in the future may lead a party to underinvest in relationship-specific assets *ex ante*, resulting in productivity losses.

A firm is able to deal with the problems caused by uncertainty and asset specificity at lower costs. As was described above, sequential adaptation to problems as they unfold is easier within a firm because it has command structures and authority systems, can use administrative dispute-resolution mechanisms, and can better access relevant information. As a result, firms can adapt to unforeseen problems and resolve disputes more quickly, at lower cost, and potentially with superior outcomes.[79]

In addition, a firm is better able to deal with opportunistic behavior. For one thing, a firm can reduce the incentives to behave opportunistically.[80] While the interests of two parties in an arm's-length transaction are not necessarily aligned, sociological influences, such as organizational cultures, may create convergent goals between members of the same organization, enhancing the willingness to act in a cooperative way.[81] And a firm can reduce the payoffs from opportunistic behavior by linking long-term rewards such as promotion prospects to cooperative behavior.[82] On the other hand, a firm has access to auditing, monitoring, and control mechanisms that enable it to detect opportunistic behavior should it occur.[83] As we saw above, in an arm's-length transaction access to information is usually quite limited. In addition, though the parties in an arm's-length transaction have the right to test the quality of the transaction's result, a standard contract does not confer the right to monitor how the other party executes the contract within its own organization. In contrast, employees of a firm are subject to extensive information disclosure requirements.[84] Moreover, managers within a firm have access to various monitoring mechanisms that let them closely control how transactions are executed. For example, contrary to parties in an arm's-length transaction, managers can monitor behavior as well as outputs, or can measure the quality of inputs. As a result, behavior is more observable within a firm, making it easier to detect opportunistic actions. Thus, the transaction costs associated with uncertainty and asset specificity are lower under internal organization.

Transaction costs are also influenced by measurement problems. As principal-agent theory has shown, difficulties in measuring performance damage the performance of markets and firms.[85] Under both governance structures, imprecise measurement constrains the incentive intensity of rewards, which limits performance. Incentives are most efficient when rewards are directly linked to performance. Such incentives encourage actors to work harder to meet performance goals. If performance cannot be measured accurately, it cannot be correctly linked to rewards; since the economic actor does not bear the full costs of his or her actions, the rate of productive effort will be lower and shirking more common than if accurate measurement were possible.[86]

Thus, if it is impossible or difficult to measure performance in an arm's-length relationship, it is impossible or difficult to verify whether a party has complied with the agreement. As a result, the party will receive the same compensation whether it shirks or not. Because of this, some economic actors will invest too little effort or diligence when executing such a contract. This problem is particularly profound in an arm's-length relationship if relevant attributes of the object of the transaction cannot be measured: since one party in an arm's-length relationships does not have the right to monitor how the other party executes the contract internally, the two parties cannot use alternative measuring mechanisms to assess performance. As a result, they have to endure the worse performance that results from not being able to accurately measure and reward performance.

Firms can address measurement problems at lower costs than parties in arm's-length relationships. As we saw above, firms have access to superior auditing and monitoring mechanisms that let them closely control how tasks are executed internally. For example, if measuring the quality of the output becomes difficult, managers can use behavioral monitoring to better assess performance.[87] In addition, internal organization may attenuate the incentives for opportunistic behavior.[88]

Thus, in the presence of uncertainty, asset specificity, or measurement problems, the transaction costs associated with internal organization are considerably lower than the transaction costs associated with an arm's-length relationship. As a result, it will rarely be feasible to organize a transaction afflicted with these problems in an arm's length relationship.

While the transaction costs of using an arm's-length relationship to organize a transaction that is subject to uncertainty, asset specificity, or measurement problems will usually be prohibitive, firms may still be able to organize such a transaction across firm boundaries. Firms may be able to reduce the transaction costs associated with executing such transactions by setting up alternative governance structures that better mitigate the problems resulting from bounded rationality or opportunism.[89] For example, to manage uncertainty, firms may agree on specific mechanisms for adaptation and conflict resolution that let them, if adaptation is required, make decisions and resolve disputes faster. To avoid the risk of expropriation *ex post*, firms facing the risk of "hold-up" may invest in contractual safeguards during the initial contract negotiations, or they may make other investments to improve their post-contract bargaining position. To address the risk of shirking, parties can agree on auditing and monitoring methods that help them better measure performance. For example, the parties can replace output measurements with more costly and complicated measurement methods, such as monitoring the behavior of the other party's employees. Although these solutions lower the transaction costs associated with executing the transaction, they require considerable set-up costs, such as drafting and negotiating the original agreement and implementing dispute-resolution or monitoring mechanisms.[90] As a result, a firm will use alternative governance structures only if the benefits of partnering with another firm justify the total transaction costs. Further, firms may be able to organize such transactions across firm boundaries if they benefit from relationship-specific factors that reduce transaction costs. For example, research has shown that trust can considerably reduce transaction costs by reducing the incentives for opportunistic behavior and the perceived need for safeguards.[91] Other firms may benefit from past investments in alternative governance structures.[92]

The Effect of Architecture   From a transaction-cost perspective, product architectures influence how detailed component design can be organized by determining the nature of the tasks that are the object of the transaction. As we saw above, the boundaries among components determine the boundaries among the design teams involved in the detailed design. As a result, the nature of the component specification determines the nature of the tasks design teams are supposed to perform. The nature of the tasks, in turn, determines the attributes of the transaction.

Detailed component design under modular and integrated architectures differs with respect to the existence of uncertainty, asset specificity, and measurement problems.[93]

Under an integrated architecture, detailed component design is characterized by uncertainty, asset specificity, and measurement problems. The object of the transaction (i.e., the design of a component) cannot be specified in advance, since important characteristics of the component (e.g., the exact form of its interfaces) have yet to be determined. In addition, the process necessary to arrive at a suitable design is inherently uncertain: the detailed design of a particular component involves resolving internal design problems and cross-component interdependencies in ways that let the component function within the overall system. In the course of this process, chains of interdependencies through the system must be recognized and resolved. Finding a high-quality solution requires many trade-offs across components, and determining how to best make these trade-offs is an interactive, iterative process. The amount of iteration required depends on contingencies that cannot be planned for. Thus, both the detailed design process and its result are afflicted with considerable uncertainty and cannot be specified in advance. As a result, a contract will be highly incomplete, leaving considerable room for opportunistic behavior.

Detailed component design in an integrated architecture also requires designers to invest in specific assets. To recognize and resolve cross-component interdependencies, designers of a particular component must interact closely with other design teams. If the design of this component is organized in an arm's-length transaction, the other design teams will belong to a different firm. Efficient coordination across firm boundaries requires considerable investment in learning the responsibilities, language, and routines of the other firm.[94] In addition, to be able to assess the effect of their design decisions, designers must acquire knowledge about other components. Thus, to successfully execute the transaction, designers must acquire skills, know-how, and information that are specific to the particular trading partner and system architecture and therefore more valuable inside this relationship than outside it—a typical case of human asset specificity.[95] Thus, an independent firm that designs a component in an integrated architecture faces the risk of "hold-up" by its partner.

Finally, detailed component design in an integrated architecture suffers from measurement problems. Since the parties cannot contractually specify the desired characteristics of a particular detailed component design in advance, they cannot measure performance by simply comparing specifications and results. Though it is possible to determine whether the component design correctly interacts with the rest of the system, it is difficult to assess the quality of the design. If the component has problems interacting with the rest of the system, the many interdependencies among components make it difficult to determine what causes these problems and which party is responsible for them. As a result, it is difficult to measure how well the transaction was executed. At the same time, because organizations rarely have the right to monitor across firm boundaries, it is not possible to determine whether the other party worked hard enough to acquire relevant transaction-specific information and skills and to solve the actual design problems.[96] Thus, under an integrated architecture, it is difficult, if not impossible, to assess the quality of the product and the quality of the service. This results in lower incentive intensity and, potentially, lower performance.

Owing to the uncertainty, the asset specificity, and the measurement problems associated with detailed component design under an integrated architecture, organizing the detailed design of individual components in an arm's-length transaction is not feasible. A firm may nevertheless choose an alternative governance structure if the benefits of using another firm are high enough to justify the total costs.[97]

As we saw above, innovating on an existing integrated architecture is very similar to developing a new system from scratch. As a result, organizing subsequent innovation is subject to the same constraints as initially developing a system.

Under a modular architecture, detailed component design is not subject to uncertainty or measurement difficulty. The degree of asset specificity depends on additional factors.

A modular architecture completely specifies the relevant characteristics of a component, both in terms of expected behavior and in terms of the interfaces governing its interaction with the rest of the system. Module designers must develop a component that complies with these constraints. Since the architecture completely captures and resolves all existing cross-component interdependencies and is not allowed to change during detailed design, the constraints imposed by the architecture are stable and well defined. In addition, module design is independent of the detailed design of other components; this removes another potential source of uncertainty.[98] As a result, it is possible to specify the object of the transaction (i.e., the design for a module) with certainty by referring to the module's architectural specification.

Under a modular architecture, parties can assess minimum contractual performance by checking whether a component's design conforms to the component's interface specifications. A component that does not meet the interface specifications cannot function with the rest of the system. Since the design of each module is independent of the design of other modules, responsibility for a component's inability to correctly interact with the rest of the system can be clearly assigned to the designers of the module under consideration. Determining the quality of the design requires additional knowledge and technology. If metrics exist that summarize the performance of a module and tests are available that can capture these metrics, performance can be measured by using these tests to measure the quality of the design. And since it is possible to measure the quality of the output, it is not necessary to determine the quality of the service. Whereas it is more difficult to monitor the quality of a service across firm boundaries, applying a test to the object of a transaction is equally feasible within and across firm boundaries. Thus, if appropriate metrics and tests are available, a modular architecture does not present any measurement problems. This requirement is usually met after an architecture has existed for some time.[99]

Whether designers must invest in relationship-specific assets depends on the architecture. Since the designers of different modules do not have to interact with one another, they do not have to learn about other firms' rules and procedures, or about the internals of other modules. They only have to acquire knowledge about the architecture and the relevant interface specifications. Whether this knowledge can be used outside of the particular relationship depends on the architecture. If the architecture constitutes a standard (open or proprietary) that is followed by a number of firms, knowledge of the architecture probably will be valuable in other relationships too. If a firm is being "held up," it probably will be able to find an alternative trading partner. Thus, for standards-based architectures, asset specificity is low. Asset specificity is particularly low in the case of an open standard, whose evolution no single firm can control.[100] In contrast, if the architecture is proprietary and the relevant architectural information has been disclosed to the firm in an exclusive relationship, asset specificity is higher. Since the idiosyncratic knowledge is restricted to knowledge about the architecture, asset specificity is still considerably lower than under an integrated architecture.

In sum, whether the detailed design of a particular module can be organized in an arm's-length transaction depends on whether metrics and tests for the performance of that module exist and on the degree of asset specificity. Thus, relative to coordination-cost reasoning, a transaction-cost perspective introduces an additional criterion (asset specificity) that influences the feasibility of arm's-length transactions in modular architectures.

A modular architecture also affects how subsequent innovation can be organized. If the architect envisions a particular function for a module and is able to specify its visible behavior and relevant interfaces, the corresponding detailed design process is very similar to the initial designing of a module.

A modular architecture also allows for component-level innovation that the architect may not have foreseen. For example, as long as the architecture's existing visible information is unaffected, new components with completely new functionalities can be added using the services of existing modules. In this case, an important part of the innovative process is coming up with new and creative ways of enriching the existing system. As a result, the parties cannot specify the object of the transaction in sufficient detail *ex ante* to enforce the contract in court *ex post*. In addition, whether the innovator will actually find a useful new component is highly uncertain, which makes this task difficult to contract upon. Not being able to specify the object of the transaction in advance also creates measurement problems similar to those encountered in an integrated architecture. Moreover, metrics and tests for an object yet unknown will not be available. The degree of asset specificity depends on the factors discussed above. Thus, owing to the high level of uncertainty and the existence of measurement problems, organizing this type of innovation in a typical arm's-length transaction will usually not be feasible.[101]

Nevertheless, internal organization is not the only possible governance structure for this type of innovation. This is because innovation at the component level that does not require changing an architecture's existing visible information can proceed independently. The innovator requires neither permission nor any form of cooperation from the system's architect. Thus, she does not have to reach a contractual agreement with the architect before starting to innovate. Once the innovative process has been successful, a considerable source of uncertainty is reduced. If intellectual-property rights safeguard the innovator against appropriation of her innovation, she can disclose the idea and sell it, or she can contract for the corresponding detailed design in an arm's-length transaction.

Alternatively, she can develop (and produce) the complete component and trade the finished product in an arm's-length transaction.[102]

Implications of the Link between Architecture and Feasible Governance Structures

As this chapter has shown, product architectures constrain how the initial development and production of system components can be organized as well as how subsequent innovation might occur by enabling or disabling arm's-length transactions. The constraints imposed by the architecture have implications for the organizational options available to individual firms, for the potential structure of the industries for the development and production of system components, and for the ability of independent economic actors other than the system's architect to innovate.

Effect on Firms' Organizational Options

From the perspectives of transaction costs and coordination costs, detailed component design under an integrated architecture must take place within a vertically integrated firm or a closely integrated alternative governance structure. Organizing the detailed design of individual components in an arm's-length relationship is not feasible. Since gaining access to other firms' capabilities requires closely integrated alternative governance structures and usually comes at considerable cost, the firm's strategic flexibility with respect to organization is severely limited.

Under a modular architecture, organizing the detailed design of the different components internally and in arm's-length relationships is equally feasible if the architecture completely captures and resolves all existing cross-component interdependencies, if the architecture's visible information is completely specified and well documented to avoid ambiguity, if technology is available to determine the relative quality of a module, and if asset specificity is not too high. If these conditions are met, a modular architecture lets a firm exploit the benefits of using the market by outsourcing the detailed design of one or more components in arm's-length relationships—an important source of strategic flexibility. Whether a firm uses this opportunity depends on additional factors, two of which are the existence of differential capabilities and the desire to maintain exclusive control over critically important or highly profitable components.[103] Thus, a modular architecture enables, but does not determine, organizational choices.[104]

Effect on the Structure of the Industries for the Development and Production of Components

The effect of product architecture goes beyond constraining the organizational options available to individual firms. By enabling or disabling arm's-length relationships, product architectures also constrain the potential structure of the industries that design and produce the components of a system.

If integrated architectures prevail, an industry will be populated by vertically integrated firms, or by closely integrated networks of firms, each of which produces its own proprietary system. In such an industry, competition takes place among different proprietary systems.

Although modular architectures can support the same industry structure, they tend to facilitate vertical disintegration by enabling a firm to outsource the detailed design of one or more components in arm's-length relationships. Moreover, the feasibility of arm's-length relationships is an important prerequisite for forming markets.[105] As a result, a specific modular architecture can provide the basis for a "modular cluster"[106]—that is, a horizontally stratified industry in which firms in different sub-industries design and produce components compatible with the architecture. In a modular cluster, firms in one sub-industry specialize in providing a particular module or set of modules, and markets arise at the interfaces among different sub-industries. In such an industry structure, firms operating in different sub-industries are complementors,[107] whereas firms in the same sub-industry are competitors. Thus, competition shifts from competition between proprietary systems to competition between components within the same architecture.

In addition to independent component developers, a new type of company, a so-called system integrator, might emerge to specialize in assembling components into a complete system.[108] If assembly is not too difficult and does not require technology unavailable to individual consumers, users might put together their own systems.[109]

Although vertically integrated firms that produce and assemble their own components can operate in such an industry, small specialized firms may be at a competitive advantage: they are driven by the high-powered incentives of market-based organization, they can focus on areas where their superior capabilities give them a competitive advantage, and they may be better able to exploit economies of scale or learning economies.[110]

The formation of a sub-industry specializing in a particular module requires that many different firms have the architectural information needed to design compatible components. Without this information, designing a compatible component will not be possible. Firms can learn this information from the original architect or through reverse engineering. Since reverse engineering is usually very difficult and costly, and sometimes illegal,[111] a system's architect can influence the industry's future structure by deciding whether and to what extent to disclose the relevant information. Thus, the architectural and contractual choices made by a system's architect interact with the existing legal framework to shape the economic environment for innovation.[112] By determining the strength of intellectual-property protection for interface specifications, intellectual-property laws can make it more or less difficult for independent third parties to design and produce a system's components if the architect does not voluntarily provide access to the interface information.

The vertical disintegration of an industry into a modular cluster following the emergence of modular architectures has been documented in a variety of industries. For example, this phenomenon has been observed in the stereo-component industry,[113] the disk-drive industry,[114] the computer industry,[115] the mortgage industry,[116] and the microprocessor industry.[117] At some stage, modular architectures might become integrated again, for example, to realize performance gains.[118] When and how architectures evolve toward more modularity or more integration is an area of active research.[119]

Effect on Ability to Innovate

By enabling or disabling arm's-length relationships, modular and integrated architectures also affect how easily actors other than the system's architect can innovate, for example by developing new system components.

Innovation on an integrated architecture must occur within a single vertically integrated firm or within a closely integrated governance structure. Thus, although economic actors other than system architects can participate in such an innovative effort, they must closely integrate and coordinate their activities with other participants. They cannot innovate independently.

In a modular architecture, the ability to innovate depends on the type of innovation.

Innovation at the component level that leaves the architecture's existing visible information unchanged (e.g., improving existing components or adding new components that connect through existing interfaces) can be realized by economic actors other than the system's architect if they have access to the architectural information necessary to design a compatible component. For example, an independent application developer can create a new application for the Windows operating system that uses Windows' existing application programming interfaces if she has access to the architectural specifications of these interfaces.

The ability of independent economic actors to innovate at the component level has important implications for the type of actors who can innovate as well as for the nature of the innovation that can occur.

First, developing a single component does not require a great amount of investment. Whereas small firms may not be able to raise enough capital to develop a complete system, they may be able to raise enough for component-level innovation. In particular, new firms may be able to obtain financial support from venture capitalists.[120] Thus, a modular architecture probably increases the range of potential innovators at the component level.[121]

Second, as we saw above, a modular architecture shifts control over component-level innovation from the system's architect to developers of components. They can innovate independently as long as they abide by the architecture's visible information. As a result, whereas under an integrated architecture the system's architect completely controls a system's evolution, a modular architecture enables decentralized innovation at the component level.[122] As we will see in chapter 8, if there is uncertainty, this increases the chances that potential innovators will be able to realize their innovative ideas, since they do not have to convince any other decision maker.

Innovations requiring changes to the architecture's existing visible information (e.g., changes to the interfaces) occur in two steps. First, those controlling the architecture must agree on the necessary changes and produce the specifications for the refined architecture. Second, module designers must adapt the design of their component so that the component works with the new architecture; that is, they must produce a refined detailed design and, ultimately, a component that complies with the new visible information.

Who can participate in this type of systemic innovation and how difficult it is to realize depends on who owns the architecture and how detailed component design is organized.

A vertically integrated firm that owns the architecture and designs all components itself can mandate the adoption of the new architecture and efficiently coordinate the necessary activities internally. Thus, it can realize such an innovation on its own. Originally, IBM was in this situation.[123] Apple often follows this approach.

If a firm controls the architecture but depends on independent firms to provide compatible components, it can change the architecture on its own, but it must induce independent component providers to produce components to the new specifications. For example, Microsoft owns and can unilaterally change the application programming interfaces of the Windows operating system, but it depends (at least somewhat) on independent software vendors to produce software that takes advantage of new specifications. Getting independent component designers to adopt new interface specifications is not easy.[124] Adapting a component to new interface specifications is an innovation in its own right. In a platform system in which different firms design, produce, and sell the various components, however, incentives to innovate will usually be too low. First, owing to the complementarity between components, innovation in one component has a beneficial effect on the demand for the other components that is not appropriated by the innovator. Because of this externality, it is usually assumed that component providers' incentives to innovate are too low if different firms design, produce, and sell the various components.[125] The same externality affects decisions by producers of complementary components to adopt new interfaces. Second, additional factors may further reduce independent component developers' incentives to innovate—for example, a platform monopolist may vertically integrate into a complementary market in which multiple independent component makers operate.[126] Thus, it is usually assumed that the architect of a system must exert considerable effort to induce independent component designers to adopt new architectural specifications.

If ownership of the architecture is distributed among different firms, or if the architecture is an open standard, firms must cooperate to change the architecture. For example, ownership of the current architecture of the personal computer is distributed among a variety of firms and standards organizations: Microsoft owns the application programming interfaces to its operating systems; Intel owns the interfaces to its processors, and so on. Often, changes in processor interfaces must be complemented by changes in the operating system's application programming interfaces before improvements in the processor can make a difference for the user. Coordinating such architectural changes across firms is much more difficult than coordinating them within a single firm. The distributed ownership of architecture may give rise to serious coordination problems, strategic problems, and collective-action problems. First, as we saw above, the costs of coordinating reciprocally interdependent tasks across firm boundaries are significant, especially those necessary for gaining agreement on new architectural specifications across firm boundaries. Second, strategic behavior by some or all of the firms involved may further complicate the decision making.[127] Finally, there may be collective-action problems if no firm feels responsible for evolving the architecture, even though all firms would benefit from the evolution. (This problem plagued the personal-computer industry in the early 1990s.[128]) To overcome the coordination problem at the architectural level, firms often form separate consortia or standards-setting bodies, which then coordinate and specify architectural changes.[129] As in the other scenarios where firms other than the system's architects develop components, the firms owning the architecture also must motivate unaffiliated component designers to adapt their components to the new specifications. For example, to realize the benefits of changes to processors or operating systems for users, independent software vendors or independent hardware producers must change their products to accord with the new specifications.

The greater the number of parties involved in the design and production of a system, the more difficult it is to realize systemic innovations. Thus, those controlling the architecture face a trade-off between the ability to benefit from third parties' creativity and capabilities and the ease with which systemic innovations can be realized.

In sum, even in a modular architecture, independent economic actors other than the owner of the system's architecture cannot realize a systemic innovation on their own. They may, though, be able to influence the evolution of the architecture by participating in the corresponding innovative efforts—for example, by working with the system's architect or by participating in standard setting. They can also participate in systemic innovation by developing and producing components according to the new specifications if they have access to the necessary architectural information. As was noted above, this activity is an autonomous innovation that can proceed independently.

The link between architecture and organization provides system architects with a number of strategic choices. In particular, they can design their architecture strategically to invite or preclude third-party innovation. If they choose a modular architecture instead of an integrated one, they can allow third-party innovators to innovate on some or all components (though opening the system to third-party innovation makes it more difficult to change the architecture's visible information).[130]

If they have chosen a modular architecture, system architects can influence how easy it is for independent economic actors to innovate by strategically distributing functionality to components. For example, if functions that contribute to a specific feature are distributed across multiple components, innovating on this feature will require systemic innovation. In contrast, if functions are allocated to a single component, innovation will be autonomous. Similarly, by incorporating specific functionality in a larger component, a system's architect makes it impossible to specialize in providing that functionality alone. Instead, firms must provide the complete component. For example, in luxury cars, cell-phone functionality could be integrated with the audio system, or could be allocated to a separate subsystem. A luxury car's audio system is usually developed by the car maker. Owing to the strong degree of integration, the first design would most likely require that the complete audio-and-cell-phone system be developed in house, eliminating the opportunity to involve independent economic actors. In contrast, under the second design, independent economic actors could develop the cell-phone subsystem on their own.[131]

Finally, companies competing within an existing modular cluster can change the nature of the competition by making a modular architecture more integrated. If one competitor starts offering a product based on an integrated architecture, this may force competitors to offer integrated systems too.[132]

Architecture and Organization in the Original Architecture of the Internet

The above insights into the links between architecture and organization in modular and integrated architectures can be used to understand the effect of the Internet's original architecture on firms' organizational options, on potential industry structures for developing and producing components, and on independent actors' ability to innovate.

Effect on Firms' Organizational Options

The Internet is based on a modular architecture. Thus, from the perspective of transaction costs and coordination costs, organizing detailed design (and production) of different components internally and in arm's-length relationships is equally feasible if the architecture completely captures and resolves all existing cross-component interdependencies, the architecture's visible information is completely specified and well documented to avoid ambiguity, technology is available to determine a module's relative quality, and asset specificity is not too high.

The architecture of the Internet meets these requirements.

First, it has a mature, modular structure that captures and resolves all existing cross-component interdependencies in interface specifications.[133]

Second, ownership and maintenance of the Internet architecture's visible information are spread over a number of organizations.[134] For example, the protocols that make up the TCP/IP protocol suite have been standardized by the Internet Engineering Task Force in open standards. The IETF's standard-setting process is open to all participants, and the standards documents are available to all at no cost.[135] The IETF standards for a particular protocol often specify only the services provided by the protocol and the peer interface, i.e., the format and meaning of messages between two components of the particular protocol. To leave sufficient flexibility for protocol implementors, the exact form of the service interface, i.e., the protocol's interface to higher-layer protocols, is not specified by the standard. Instead, the exact form of the service interface is determined by the protocol implementor.[136] For example, since IP, TCP and UDP are implemented in the operating system, the service interface of these protocols is specified by the operating system vendor. Thus, whereas the services and the peer interfaces of these protocols are defined in open standards, the corresponding service interfaces are often part of a proprietary standard maintained by its owner.

Although the ownership and the nature of the standards may differ, the services and interfaces of the Internet's core components are completely specified, well-documented, and publicly available. For example, vendors of operating systems usually publish the specification of the service interfaces to IP, TCP, and UDP so as to enable third-party application programmers to access the services provided by these protocols.

Third, over time, metrics have been developed that make it possible to compare the quality or performance of different implementations of the same component.

Fourth, many of the relevant standards, including those developed by the IETF and the World Wide Web Consortium, are open standards, and their asset specificity is low. In particular, the core protocols at the Internet layer and the transport layer (IP, TCP, and UDP) have been developed by the IETF and are open standards.[137]

Thus, the architecture of the Internet fulfils the conditions under which arm's-length relationships and vertical integration among providers of different components are equally feasible. As a result, firms' governance choices are driven by factors other than transaction costs or coordination costs—for example, strategic considerations or differential capabilities.

Effect on the Structure of the Industries for the Development and Production of Components

The architecture of the Internet forms the basis of a modular cluster, with firms in different sub-industries developing and producing the different components or subsystems.[138] The emergence of a modular cluster has been facilitated by the public availability of the relevant interface specifications that give any interested economic actor the information necessary to design and produce compatible components.

In particular, the design of the Internet layer as a technology-independent and application-independent portability layer populated by a single protocol has enabled the formation of separate, independent sub-industries for providing Internet-infrastructure software and hardware and application software.[139]

Owing to the different types of investment required, the sub-industries have very different costs of entry.[140] Developing Internet-infrastructure components usually requires investments in hardware and software. Products that include hardware and software must be manufactured and physically distributed, requiring a considerable up-front investment in physical capital. In contrast, developing components for the application and the transport layer requires only programming knowledge and access to an end host. The resulting software products can be copied and distributed almost costlessly over the Internet. Thus, entry into the corresponding sub-industries requires almost no physical capital and is considerably less costly. As we will see in the next subsection, this cost structure greatly increases the size and diversity of the pool of innovators in these industries.

Owing to the large number of components making up "the Internet system," no one firm can provide all the necessary components itself. Some firms specialize in one or more separate components; others provide a complete subsystem with a set of adjacent components. For example, Microsoft produces operating systems for end hosts, which include implementations of IP, TCP, and UDP and expose the corresponding service interfaces in so-called application programming interfaces.[141] Thus, Microsoft's operating systems incorporate components belonging to the Internet layer and to the transport layer. Cisco specializes in routers; Cisco's routers contain the various hardware and software components necessary to operate a router, combining components belonging to the link layer and the Internet layer.[142]

Firms of another kind specialize in assembling components into products that are ready to use. For example, Dell assembles the hardware and software components that make up an end host. Other firms may specialize in assembling complete physical subnets. Alternatively, users can assemble their own systems by buying and installing the necessary hardware and software. In addition, users can exchange or add components later.[143]

Effect on Ability to Innovate

The Internet's architecture also affects independent actors' abilities to participate in autonomous and systemic innovation.

Autonomous Innovation As we saw above, an architecture influences independent actors' ability to participate in innovation in two ways. First, it affects whether and when they can innovate independently, without requiring cooperation or permission from the system's architect. Second, by influencing the costs of innovation, it affects which type of actor can participate in innovation.

Owing to its modular structure, the Internet's architecture provides many opportunities for autonomous innovation by independent economic actors. Any innovation that does not affect the architecture's existing visible information can be realized independently. As we saw in chapter 4, because of the use of the design principle of relaxed layering with a portability layer and the broad version of the end-to-end arguments in the design of the Internet's architecture, the architecture enables three specific types of autonomous innovation: developing new application-layer or transport-layer protocols, new link-layer protocols or physical network technology, and new implementations of existing components and subsystems. Innovations belonging to these categories can be deployed incrementally. Owing to architectural differences, the three categories differ considerably in the type of investment required to develop, produce, and distribute the innovation.[144] Thus, by influencing the costs of innovation, the Internet's architecture influences who can engage in these different types of innovations. To see this more clearly, let us focus on how the Internet's architecture affects innovators' ability to develop applications.

The architecture of the Internet influences who can develop applications by allowing application-level innovation to proceed independently and by inducing a particular cost structure: due to the end-to-end design of the Internet, developing components for the application layer requires only access to an end host that is connected to the Internet, programming knowledge, programming tools, and access to the application programming interfaces necessary to let the application send data over the Internet. The resulting software products can be copied and distributed almost cost-lessly over the Internet.[145] Since many of these resources are often already available (e.g., many people have a computer or access to one) or can be acquired at relatively low costs, this cost structure lets a wide range of innovators with diverse motivations and funding models develop new applications.[146]

In particular, an innovator does not have to be an employee of a firm or have outside funding to realize his idea for an application. Because the biggest investment often is the design and programming of the application itself, potential innovators can develop an application in their free time or as a "side project," with the opportunity cost of the time spent the most important cost factor.

Under these conditions, an application does not have to produce a profit in the future to cover the costs of developing it. Instead, a wide range of benefits may be sufficient to cover the development costs. Some innovators develop new applications because they love to program. (This seems to be an important motivation of contributors to open-source projects.[147]) Others develop a new application to meet their own needs[148]; after the fact, they may discover that others may want to use it too. For example, Yahoo grew out of a list of links to research papers in electrical engineering that Jerry Yan and David Phyllo, two graduate students in Stanford University's Electrical Engineering Department, used to keep track of research papers that were relevant to their PhD theses. Yan and Phyllo then began to add other, non-technical categories that were of interest to them in their free time. The list quickly became popular, and Yan and Phyllo spent more and more time on it. In the fall of 1994, the site, which still ran on their student computer workstations attached to Stanford's network, got a million page views per day, which translated to more than 100,000 unique visitors. Recognizing the business potential, Yan and Phyllo decided to turn the website into a business and incorporated Yahoo in March 1995.[149]

Del.icio.us, the online bookmarking service that enables users to share their bookmarks with others, emerged from an application that Joshua Schachter had developed to keep track of his collection of 20,000 bookmarks while he was working at Morgan Stanley as a quantitative analyst. The original version, which Schachter finished in 2001, could be used only by him, but other people could view the website that showed his bookmarks. In 2003, Schachter began working on a version that other people would be able to use. It went online in December 2003, and by the end of 2004 it had 30,000 users. In early 2005, with the user base growing, Schachter decided to leave Morgan Stanley and focus on Del.icio.us full-time.

Innovators may also be driven by a mix of different motivations. For example, throughout the 1970s and the 1980s, most of the programs used to read and send electronic mail were developed by researchers on the ARPANET. Often they started to develop a new program because they were unhappy with the existing programs. Solving their problems involved researching what they enjoyed. And in the days of the ARPANET, people who developed successful applications were highly regarded, so the desire to improve their reputation may have motivated these researchers as well.[150]

The low costs of application innovation under an end-to-end architecture allow innovation based on a variety of funding models. For example, since realizing an application does not require major capital investments, innovators can pursue their idea in their free time. This option is particularly valuable if there is uncertainty about the technical feasibility of, or the user demand for, the application, since innovators can test their ideas risk-free without giving up their day job. For example, Pierre Omidyar developed the online auction website AuctionWeb, which later became eBay, at home over the Labor Day weekend of 1995. At first Omidyar viewed it as a hobby, working on it nights and weekends. Auction Web ran on his personal website, which he operated at home under his existing Internet-service account that cost $30 per month. Throughout 1995, the website attracted thousands of auctions, and more than ten thousand individual bids. When his Internet Service Provider switched Omidyar's account to a commercial account arguing that AuctionWeb's traffic was slowing down their system, Omidyar started charging sellers a small commission for sales enabled through the website. He operated AuctionWeb as a hobby until June 1996, when monthly revenues surpassed $10,000.[151]

Mark Zuckerberg developed the original version of Facebook, an online social network for students at elite universities, over the course of a few months in his dorm room at Harvard College. He launched the site on February 4, 2004. It was an instant success. By the end of February, about three-fourths of Harvard's undergraduates had registered. Over the next few months, Zuckerberg extended the site to 40 other universities. By mid June, 150,000 users had registered. Since Zuckerberg and Dustin Moskovitz (a roommate who had begun to assist him) were working for no pay, their biggest operating costs were the costs of renting server space at $85 per month. They continued to work on Facebook over the summer in a house they had rented in Silicon Valley, and in September 2004 they decided to focus on Facebook full-time. At the time, the site had 250,000 users.[152]

The low level of investment required for developing and operating an application lets small companies and start-ups fund the development themselves or get the necessary funds from small, less formal financing sources. As we saw in the preceding chapter, even applications with servers operated by the innovator can now be financed in this manner.[153] Some innovators use personal funds; others get money from family members, friends, or "angel" investors.[154] Jeff Bezos funded the first six months of Amazon's development himself. His father invested $100,000 in February 1995. In July 1995, when Amazon.com went live, his mother invested $145,553. From summer 1995 to the end of that year, Bezos got $981,000 from 20 private individuals, most of them contributing $30,000.[155] Catarina Fake and Stuart Butterfield, the founders behind Flickr, financed their company Ludicorp using personal funds, money from friends and family members, a loan from the Canadian government, and, later, some angel investment for Flickr.[156]

Others finance the development of applications with income from consulting or from programming jobs, or, at a later stage, with income from existing applications. Evan Williams and Meg Hourihan, the founders behind Blogger, financed their company Pyra Labs for its first year by having one of the three members of the team develop Web applications for Hewlett-Packard.[157] A company called 37signals—a small software company that offers Web-based productivity applications—has used this approach beyond the development of its first product (box 5.2).[158]

By freeing potential innovators from depending on outside funding, an architecture based on the broad version of the end-to-end arguments increases the number of innovative projects that might be realized. Many innovators will not be able to get outside funding, even if they want to, because they are not able to convince others of the viability of their idea. Many innovators whose applications later became very successful could not get venture capital or corporate funding when they first tried.[159] For example, early in 1997 the founders of eBay tried, without success, to sell the company to Times Mirror, a media company that owned the *Los Angeles Times*, the *Baltimore Sun*, and some other newspapers. The decision makers at Times Mirror thought that "strangers would never trade with strangers over the Internet in large numbers," and complained that eBay did not own any assets such as buildings or trucks. In 1997 and 1998, before they decided to commercialize the technology themselves, Sergei Brin and Larry Page tried, without success, to license Google's search technology to existing search engines or portals; they also were unable to get venture capital at the time. In 1996, when the founders of ICQ tried to

Box 5.2
37signals

37signals, a small, privately held software company, financed the development
of its first product—Basecamp, a Web-based project-management application
for individuals and small teams—by doing design work for outside clients.[a]
Over the course of six months, three designers spent about one-third of their
time on designing Basecamp. The programming was done by a computer
science student in Denmark who worked on the project ten hours per week.[b]
After Basecamp went live, in February 2004, the four kept working on it along
with their other projects. The biggest operating expense was the cost of a server
($150 a month). After a year, fees collected from users allowed them to focus
on Basecamp full-time. Since then, 37signals has developed five more applications following the same model. At the time of this writing, the company is
profitable and has no debt. Its revenues have doubled every year since 2004.

a. In 2006, the company took a minority private equity investment from
Bezos Expeditions, a personal investment company of Amazon founder Jeff
Bezos (Fried 2006). The account in the text is based on Fried 2008a, Hammock
2006, Hedlund 2005, Heinemeier Hansson 2008, Livingston 2007, and
Park 2008.
b. He is now a partner in the firm.

---

get funding for their instant-messaging application (the very first instant-
messaging application), venture capitalists were not interested, pointing
out that ICQ had no revenues and no business plan.

In addition, many innovators will not be able to get venture capital
for more general reasons that go beyond disagreements over the viability
of an innovator's specific idea. First, as venture capital funds grow
larger, the venture capitalists managing them may become less interested
in the small investments typically needed for early seed funding.[160] Second,
most projects that a venture capitalist invests in are not successful. Venture
capital funds only work because the gains from a few highly successful
projects more than offset the losses from the majority of projects. This
investment model requires a few projects in a venture capitalist's portfolio
to produce enormous profits. As a result, venture capitalists look for projects that have the potential to realize high returns; they are not interested
in projects that, although economically viable, produce smaller returns.[161]
Finally, there may be periods in which venture-capital funding is not available—for example, during economic downturns or times when less money

flows into venture capital funds. For example, when the initial-public-offering market collapsed in 2000, many venture capitalists drastically reduced their investments in new companies and instead used their remaining funds to save their existing companies. In early 2001, even though Blogger—with 86,000 registered users—had become the most popular weblog publishing tool, its founders were unable to raise any funding after the stock-market bubble burst. In January 2001, Evan Williams, who with Meg Hourihan had founded Pyra Labs (the company that developed Blogger) in 1999, laid off the other members of the team and moved the servers running the Blogger software into his apartment. And in the fall of 2008, venture capitalists began to shift their focus to maintaining their existing venture investments again.[162]

Thus, many application developers will not be able to get finding from venture capitalists or corporate investors. Under an architecture based on the broad version, however, innovator are not dependent on venture capital or corporate funding. Since the funds needed to develop a new application are limited, innovators can finance their innovation themselves or through smaller, less formal funding sources such as family members, friends, or angel investors. More potential sources of funding make it more likely that at least one funder will find the application attractive, increasing the change that the application can be realized. Joe Kraus, a serial entrepreneur who co-founded the search engine and portal Excite in the early 1990s, has put it this way: "A lot more people can raise $100,000 than [can] raise $3,000,000. . . . The sources of funding capable of writing $100,000 checks are a lot more plentiful than those capable of writing $3,000,000 checks."[163] For example, though ICQ and Google were unable to get venture-capital funding at first, they did manage to attract some angel investors.[164]

In addition to enabling potential innovators to pursue projects for which they cannot get outside funding, independence from outside funding increases innovators' organizational options. Some innovators value venture capital for the financial and entrepreneurial support it provides, and for the potential of a very high return, and are willing to cede some control over their start-up ventures to venture capitalists in exchange; other innovators prefer to stay in control of their business, even if this implies lower profits or slower, more organic growth.[165] In a network architecture in which application innovation requires a significant amount of outside funding, innovators do not have this choice.

Innovators' independence from outside funding also has benefits for investors. Since innovators are able to realize an application on their own, potential investors can wait until the uncertainty surrounding an application has been resolved before deciding whether to invest. Through-out the history of the Internet, venture capitalists and corporate investors often withheld investing until after an application had attracted a significant number of users. Although this does not guarantee the ultimate financial success of the investment,[166] it reduces the risk of investing in applications that are not technically viable or attractive to users. For example, in June of 1997, when eBay got its first venture-capital funding from Benchmark Capital, it had more than 45,000 auction listings per day, and in that year it was to earn $4.3 million.[167] In the spring of 1996, when the online book-store Amazon.com got its first venture-capital funding from Kleiner Perkins Caufield and Byer, Amazon had been operating since July of 1995 and was on track to earn $5 million revenue in 1996.[168] In the second half of 1998, when Google got its first angel investments, it was already getting more than 10,000 search queries a day; it passed 500,000 searches in early 1999. At the time of its first venture-capital investment, in June of 1999, Google, still in beta mode, had been included in *PC Magazine*'s list of the Top 100 Web Sites and Search Engines for 1998; its search traffic was growing at a rate of 50 percent per month.[169] When venture capitalists invested in Napster, in Friendster, in MySpace, in Del.icio.us, and in Facebook, the applications already were popular and had large and growing numbers of users. Similarly, although none of them had venture-capital funding, ICQ, Blogger, Flickr, and Bloglines were popular applications with a growing number of users when they were acquired.[170] Venture capitalists and corporate investors could not have pursued this approach to investing if innovators had required significant funding in order to realize and offer these applications.

Network architectures that deviate from the broad version of the end-to-end arguments have a different effect on independent application devel-opers' ability to innovate. As we saw in chapter 4, developing a new application in a non-end-to-end network that implements application-specific functionality in the network may require changing the network's core, which in turn may require changing higher-layer protocols and appli-cations that depend, directly or indirectly, on the changed feature.[171] Thus, in a non-end-to-end network new applications are often *systemic* innova-tions. Unless a single economic actor owns the network infrastructure's visible information, can change it unilaterally, and can change affected higher-layer components (or doesn't care about them), no single economic actor can realize such an innovation alone. Instead, the developer of an application must reach agreement on the necessary changes to the net-work's visible information and must convince the developers of affected components to adapt their components to the new specifications. In addition, higher-layer protocols and applications that relied on the changed network functionality or interfaces must be adapted so they will continue to function over the network, and that requires more coordination.

Thus, an independent economic actor cannot simply develop an application on her own; she must incur considerable coordination costs. In addition, an application developer cannot use the operational network infrastructure to test her application. She needs access to an experimental network in order to implement the necessary changes in the network's core and then test the application in this new environment. If some of the affected functionality is implemented in hardware, the innovator cannot use the network to copy and distribute the innovation. Instead, the new hardware must be manufactured and physically distributed. Thus, developing and (potentially) producing and distributing the innovation is considerably more costly in a non-end-to-end network than in an end-to-end network, and it requires a very different type of investment.

The physical capital required to develop an application will usually prevent non-commercial innovators without additional funding from engaging in this type of innovation. In addition, non-commercial innovators may not have the resources to coordinate development across affected component providers or to reach deployment. Owing to the higher investment required, the level of funds necessary may go beyond what angel investors can provide, forcing innovators to acquire the funds from venture capitalists or corporations. Thus, relative to an end-to-end network, a smaller and significantly different set of innovators may be able to develop applications.

In sum, the architectural differences between architectures based on the broad version of the end-to-end arguments and architectures deviating from it result in two main differences. First, in a network based on the broad version, application developers can innovate independently, without permission or help from the network provider or other component producers. In a non-end-to-end network, application developers usually have to coordinate their innovation with the network provider and, potentially, with other component producers. Second, the set of innovators who can develop applications in an end-to-end network is larger and more diverse. In particular, application developers in an end-to-end network do not necessarily need outside funding. (Some of the benefits associated with this have been discussed above.) How these differences affect the amount and the type of application innovation that will occur under the two architectures will be explored in chapter 8.

We already saw that in the past innovators' ability to realize new applications without (or with only minor) outside funding was important. Throughout the Internet's history, many successful applications, including eBay, Yahoo, Google, and Facebook, were developed by innovators in this category. (Chapter 8 will highlight additional examples.) Many of these innovators were unable to get funding from venture capitalists or corporate investors when they first tried. Everything else except for the network architecture being equal, they could not have realized their applications under a network architecture that required a larger amount of funding to realize the same application.

Thus, innovators with no or little outside funding really can produce successful innovations; this is not just a theoretical possibility. To make this point, the examples above focused on successful applications by innovators in this category. This does not mean that these are the only types of potential innovators. Innovators whose resources go beyond the minimum set of resources required by the architecture can innovate too, and this contributes to the diversity of the innovator pool. A large and diverse set of innovators, in turn, is very important for innovation under uncertainty, as will be shown in chapter 8.

The chapter's focus on successful innovators with no or little outside funding is not meant to imply that innovators from this category will necessarily be successful. This book's overall argument does not require such a claim. As we will see in chapter 8, new technologies are often afflicted with fundamental uncertainty, so no one can identify successful projects in advance. Under these circumstances, exploring a wide range of options is better than exploring only some. Some will succeed, and some will fail, but trying is the only way to find out. Thus, failure is an integral part of the mechanism that produces successful innovation under uncertainty. Failed innovations are consistent with the book's overall argument; they do not invalidate it.

Finally, although this chapter focuses on the minimum requirements for application innovation established by the Internet's architecture, these are not the only factors influencing innovation. As we saw in chapter 1, the ultimate effect of an architecture on innovation at a specific place and time depends not only on the set of architectural and non-architectural constraints, but also on the characteristics of the actors exposed to the architecture and their existing and expected relationships with other actors. For example, Yahoo and Google started at Stanford University, a prestigious and well-connected institution with many formal and informal connections to Silicon Valley and with an infrastructure that encourages and supports student-led and faculty-led entrepreneurship. Mark Zuckerberg's success was incubated in the student social networks of elite universities (Harvard, Yale, Princeton, Stanford) and then developed more maturely only after Zuckerberg moved to Silicon Valley to get access to the capital and human resources available there. Thus, while these innovators were acting independently, using a small set of resources to create worthwhile innovations, they benefited from the organizations, cultures, and networks in which they were embedded. Other innovators with similar personal resources who faced the same architectural constraints, but who were embedded in different organizations, cultures, or networks, may have been less successful in realizing the same innovation.[172] Whereas these differences may matter under an end-to-end architecture, they would not have been relevant under a network architecture that deviates from the broad version and requires a significant amount of outside funding to realize the same application, since none of these actors had the resources necessary to pursue their innovation under that architecture. Thus, the fact that the Internet's architecture enabled independent innovators with no or little outside funding to realize their ideas for an application was a necessary but not necessarily a sufficient condition for their success.

Systemic Innovation Owing to its systemic nature, innovation that requires changes to the Internet architecture's existing visible information—that is, to the specification of services and interfaces of the various components—cannot be performed by an independent economic actor alone. Realizing and deploying such an innovation involves three coordination problems. First, economic actors in affected sub-industries must coordinate their activities to agree on new specifications of the relevant visible information. For example, to change the specifications of the HTTP protocol that governs the interaction between browsers and Web servers, interested parties must cooperate within the Internet Engineering Task Force to adopt new specifications. Second, component providers in the affected sub-industries must adopt the new specifications and must design and produce new components according to the specifications. For example, organizations that develop browsers and servers (for example, Microsoft, Apple, the Mozilla Foundation, the Apache Foundation) must produce new versions of their programs that incorporate the changes. Third, depending on the position of the affected components in the architectural hierarchy, a large number of users and network operators may have to deploy the new components to enable their use in the operational Internet.[173] For example, end users must replace the browsers on their PCs, and content providers (such as the *New York Times*) and providers of other Web-based services (such as Flickr) must replace their servers.

Who can participate in the standard-setting part of these innovative efforts depends on who owns the standard and on how the standard is set. In open standards, any interested party can participate in the standard-setting process. This applies, for example, to the core Internet standards developed and maintained by the Internet Engineering Task Force, and to the Web protocol standards developed by the World Wide Web Consortium. In contrast, industry consortia often limit participation, because of efficiency considerations or for strategic reasons. Finally, a firm that owns a proprietary standard may evolve it independently. For example, Microsoft independently develops the application programming interfaces through which applications access transport-layer protocols such as TCP and UDP.

Once the new specifications are finished, independent economic actors can design and produce components to the new specifications—as long as they have access to the information necessary to design a compatible component. Again, small new firms funded by venture capitalists, and (depending on the component's position in the layered hierarchy) noncommercial innovators, may be able to engage in this activity.

6 Architecture and Competition among Makers of Complementary Components

This chapter focuses on an architectural feature that influences the benefits that component developers can expect from their innovation: the ability of one component to control how other components are executed. By describing how components cooperate to provide the overall functionality of a system, an architecture defines interdependencies between components. As we will see, the nature of these interdependencies at the architectural level affects the economic relationships among the makers of components.

For example, if one component can affect how other components function, the maker of that one component can favor certain versions of the rest of the components. In this case, the architecture tips the balance of power toward the maker of the controlling component, who gains the power to tilt the competitive environment of other components in favor of selected component makers. Thus, by enabling one component to control others, an architecture can affect the range of competitive strategies available to companies.

For-profit innovators usually benefit from an innovation by exploiting it commercially. How much profit they can expect depends on the competitive environment and, if the market is imperfectly competitive, on the economic strategies available to the innovator and the innovator's competitors. Thus, by changing the range of strategies available to component makers (or to those who later use these components), an architecture can influence the benefits that innovators may expect from an innovation.

Suppose that a system's architecture enables the owner of one component to block, or degrade the performance of, complementary components from another innovator. An independent innovator with an idea for a complementary component may anticipate that her new component might be discriminated against. This would lower her profits, and it might render an otherwise profitable innovation unprofitable. Expecting discrimination in the future, she does not innovate today. In contrast, an architecture that provides no opportunity to discriminate against components provides a level playing field. Since innovators will not have to account for a potential profit reduction caused by discrimination, they can expect higher profits than under the "discriminatory" architecture. Thus, more innovations by independent innovators will be profitable under an architecture that precludes discrimination. Conversely, the owner of a controlling component may have a greater incentive to innovate under a discriminatory architecture, since he may be able to realize higher profits by blocking or degrading the performance of complementary components.[1]

Consider the example of Skype. Widespread adoption of Internet-telephony applications reduces network providers' profits from conventional telephone service. If network providers had been able to prevent their users from using Internet-telephony applications in 2002, when Niklas Zennström and Janus Friis were thinking about building an Internet-telephony application based on a peer-to-peer architecture, the innovators might have dropped the idea, fearing that network providers would block their application. But because Internet service providers were not able to detect Internet-telephony applications in 2002,[2] Zennström and Friis did not have to take into account a possible profit reduction due to discrimination or exclusion.

The line of reasoning presented so far assumes that the owner of a controlling component *will* use the discriminatory power conferred by the architecture to discriminate against other components—or, in economic terms, that he will have an incentive to discriminate against them. If the owner of the controlling component has no incentive to use the architecture's discriminatory functionality, component developers will not be affected by the difference in architecture.

This chapter explores the effect of the ability to control components in the context of the Internet's original architecture; the underlying theoretical framework, however, is general enough to apply to other architectures. The first section explains how architectural differences between the original architecture of the Internet and a hypothetical architecture that deviates from the broad version of the end-to-end arguments alter network providers' strategic options. The second section explores the conditions under which a network provider might have an incentive to discriminate against some applications. The third section explores the effect of architectural differences on network providers' pricing strategies.

Architectural Differences—Application Awareness and Application Control

To explore how the broad version of the end-to-end arguments affects network providers' strategic options, I will compare the original end-to-end architecture of the Internet with the architecture of a hypothetical discriminatory network. This discriminatory network has two characteristics. First, it is application-aware: it can distinguish between different applications that are using the network. Moreover, it can determine not only the general type of application (e.g., e-mail or the World Wide Web), but also the specific application (e.g., Firefox versus Internet Explorer) and the content (e.g., the website of the *New York Times* versus that of the *Wall Street Journal*). Second, the network can control the execution of applications. For example, the network provider can discriminate against, or exclude altogether, specific applications or content offerings (e.g., blocking Firefox but not Internet Explorer, or limiting the speed at which content from the *New York Times* website downloads). As we saw in chapter 2, a network with these characteristics violates the broad version of the end-to-end arguments.[3]

Apart from that, the discriminatory network provides the same general functionality as the Internet; it enables computers attached to distinct, interconnected physical networks to communicate. Users will not notice the difference unless the network provider begins to block or slow down the application they are using.

In the original architecture of the Internet, the network is application-blind and unable to control the execution of applications. The Internet protocol receives data packets and transports them to their destination without differentiating between applications. The Internet protocol knows nothing about the application whose data it carries,[4] and the treatment of data packets at the network's routers is independent of the application that sent the data.[5] Thus, as long the network provider respects the layering principle and does not look at the application information within a packet, the network cannot discriminate against applications; it sees only data packets traveling to a particular destination.

For network providers, the ability to control applications creates a set of strategic options that differs from that available under the Internet's original architecture. First, a discriminatory network lets the network provider discriminate against specific applications or exclude them altogether. Second, the owner of a discriminatory network can set different Internet transport prices for different applications (e.g., charge more for an e-mail packet than for a packet of Web content) or exclude applications to price discriminate between customers (e.g., allow the use of video conferencing only for users of its premium Internet service, not for users of its basic service). Third, under a discriminatory network, the owner can set an access charge for providers of complementary products. None of these three options are available in an end-to-end network.

Today's Internet architecture partly follows this latter "discriminatory" design. Whereas the original Internet was application-blind and unable to control the execution of particular applications, technologies such as deep packet inspection now enable Internet service providers and the providers of physical networks to distinguish between, and control, applications that use their networks.[6] However, the Internet does *not* currently enable network providers to set fine-grained, application-specific prices or sophisticated access charges.[7] Thus, today's Internet enables network providers to employ all the discriminatory strategies described in the next section but only some of the pricing strategies described in the final section.

Effect of Ability to Discriminate or Exclude

By enabling a network provider to discriminate against specific applications, a discriminatory network enables a network provider to engage in noncooperative strategic behavior. That is, a network provider may maximize its profits by improving its position relative to potential rivals rather than working with them to maximize overall profits and functionality. This behavior generally increases the profits of one firm while reducing the profits of competing firms.[8] In contrast, in the original end-to-end architecture of the Internet, the Internet layer shields innovators at the transport layer and the application layer from discriminatory or exclusionary actions by actors operating at the Internet layer or the link layer.

Of course, the architectural differences affect independent application developers' decisions to innovate only if a network provider actually makes use (or independent application developers believe it will make use) of the opportunity to discriminate against complementors[9]—in economic terms, if the ability to discriminate is accompanied by an incentive to discriminate.

The effect of the difference in architecture may be moderated by the structure of the market for the controlling component (in our case, the market for Internet services) or by the laws that govern exclusionary and discriminatory conduct by the provider of the controlling component. For example, a network provider may not have an incentive to discriminate if it competes with other Internet service providers. And even if it has an incentive to discriminate, existing rules and regulations may still prevent the network provider from acting on this incentive.[10]

In view of the interaction between architecture, regulations, and market structure, it is not surprising that network providers' deployment of discriminatory technology has triggered a heated debate over whether their ability to discriminate should be regulated. Though the debate has broadened over time (box 6.1), a rule that would prevent network providers from blocking independent applications, content, or portals is central to every regulatory or legislative proposal supporting "network neutrality."[11] Whether network providers have an incentive to use the discriminatory functionality available to them is highly relevant to this debate. Proponents of regulation base their calls for regulatory intervention on the threat of discriminatory or exclusionary behavior by broadband network operators. According to them, regulation is needed to mitigate that threat. If, however, a network operator has no incentive to discriminate against independent portals, content, or applications, regulation is not necessary.[12]

Most commentators believe that the threat of discrimination against independent providers of complementary products can be mitigated by competition in the market for Internet services.[13] They assume that the market will restrict a network operator's ability and incentive to discriminate. Their rationale is that competition has a disciplining effect. For example, if Comcast's Internet-service customers want to access YouTube, but Comcast blocks YouTube, they will switch to another Internet service provider (ISP) that lets them use YouTube. Anticipating this, Comcast, wanting to keep its customers, will not block YouTube. This assumption about how market forces will operate is the basis for two common policy proposals. The first proposal assumes that fostering competition between operators of different physical networks will mitigate a network provider's ability and incentive to discriminate.[14] This proposal would increase competition for Comcast by encouraging entry by other providers of physical networks—for example, by broadband wireless access providers, or by a local electricity company offering broadband service over power lines. The second proposal seeks to restore competition at the ISP level by requiring the owners of broadband networks to allow independent ISPs to offer their services over these networks. This proposal would increase competition for Comcast by giving independent ISPs, such as Earthlink, a right to offer their services over Comcast's network. Depending on the commentator's point of view, this regulatory response is called *open access, multiple access,* or *forced access.*[15]

Box 6.1
What Is Network Neutrality?

Every current network-neutrality proposal includes a rule that would prevent network providers from blocking specific applications or content.[a] But beyond this, proposals for network neutrality differ in several ways. For one, should the rule ban only blocking, or both blocking and discrimination? If the rule does prohibit discrimination, what does it mean to not "discriminate" against an application? Must a network provider treat every packet identically? Or should providers be allowed to treat packets belonging to different classes of applications differently as long as they treat applications with similar requirements alike (e.g., a network provider could treat e-mail packets different from Internet-telephony packets, but could not treat Vonage packets differently from Skype packets)? A proposal's approach to this question determines whether, and in what form, network providers would be able to offer Quality of Service under a network-neutrality regime.[b] Next, if a network-neutrality regime lets network providers offer Quality of Service (or other forms of better transport, such as a higher bandwidth), who should the network providers be allowed to charge for it? There are four potential answers, each supported by at least some proponents of network neutrality: the network provider (1) can offer Quality of Service, but is not allowed to charge anyone for the use of the service (though it can increase the general price for Internet service),[c] (2) can charge its Internet-service customers,[d] (3) can charge its Internet-service customers and/or application and content providers, but is required to offer the service to application and content providers on a non-discriminatory basis,[e] or (4) can charge its Internet-service customers and/or application and content providers. Some proposals would ban any access charges to application and content providers, not just access charges in return for better transport.[f] Finally, proponents of network neutrality disagree over whether a potential non-discrimination rule should be implemented as an *ex ante* rule or as an *ex post* rule, and what agency should be tasked with enforcing it.[g]

a. In some proposals, such a rule takes the form of users' rights to use the (lawful) applications and (legal) content of their choice. Usually there is an exception that allows network providers to block malicious applications and content, such as those involved in denial-of-service attacks.
b. A network that provides "Quality of Service" (QoS) offers different types of service to different data packets. For example, it may guarantee a minimum bandwidth or maximum delay, or it may give some traffic priority over others without giving absolute guarantees. See, e.g., Peterson and Davie 2007, pp. 499–525. For network-neutrality proposals banning QoS, see, e.g., Internet Non-Discrimination Act of 2006 (2006), §4(a)(6); Crawford 2007,

Box 6.1
(continued)

---

pp. 403–404; for network-neutrality proposals allowing QoS, see, e.g., Internet Freedom and Nondiscrimination Act of 2006 (2006), §3(2); Internet Freedom Preservation Act (2007), §12(a)(5); Lessig 2006, p. 10.

c. E.g., Internet Freedom and Nondiscrimination Act of 2006 (2006), §3(2); Network Neutrality Act of 2006 (2006), §4(a)(7); Internet Freedom Preservation Act (2007), §12(a)(5).

d. E.g., Lessig 2006, pp. 8–10. For criticism of this proposal, see Frischmann 2005, pp. 1009–1012.

e. E.g., Lessig 2008b, p. 9. For criticism of this proposal, see Sidak 2006.

f. E.g., Internet Non-Discrimination Act (2006), §4(a)(3); Lee and Wu 2009. For criticism of this proposal, see Hahn and Wallsten (2006) and Hemphill (2008).

g. E.g., Lessig 2008b, pp. 8–9 (favoring a legislative, *ex ante* rule enforced by the FCC); Shelanski 2007, pp. 101–105; Weiser 2008 (both favoring an *ex post* regime enforced by the Federal Communications Commission or by the Federal Trade Commission).

Both the analysis in this chapter and the current policy debates turn on the question of whether, and under what circumstances, a network provider has an incentive to discriminate against, or to exclude, applications or content. After all, if network providers do not have an incentive to use the discriminatory functionality available in the discriminatory architecture, the differences in architecture do not affect the economic environment for innovation. Because the answer may differ depending on the structure of the market for Internet services, the following analysis proceeds in two steps. In the first step, we will suppose that the network provider is a local monopolist.[16] I don't make any assumptions about the size of the network provider's network relative to the nationwide network. Thus, the network provider's network may be much smaller than the nationwide network. In the extreme case, the network provider owns the nationwide network and has a nationwide monopoly on the provision of Internet services. It may also offer products in the market for applications, content, or portals.[17] In the second step, we will suppose that the network provider competes with at least one other provider. To isolate the effect of architecture, we will assume, in both situations, that there are no legal rules preventing discrimination or exclusion.[18] The analysis focuses on the competitive interactions between the "network" and the "applications."

Architecturally, the network consists of the network layer and the Internet layer, while the application domain consists of the transport layer and the application layer.[19] Economically, the network comprises two layers of economic activity: the operation of physical networks and the provision of Internet Protocol (IP) access and transport services. In reality, these activities may (or may not) be provided by different actors with separate economic interests. The resulting competitive interactions between network operators and Internet service providers have featured prominently in the debate over whether independent ISPs should have "open access" to broadband cable networks in the United States.[20] To highlight the effects of architectural differences, the following analysis treats these players as a single economic entity, the "network provider," that provides Internet access and transport services and operates the network infrastructure of a given physical network. The resulting service will be called *Internet service*.

As we will see, a network provider may want to discriminate for one of three reasons: to increase or protect its profits, to control the bandwidth use on its network, or to exclude unwanted content.

The Network Provider Is a Monopolist in the Market for Internet Services
Economic theory predicts that a network operator with a monopoly in the market for Internet services will not generally have an incentive to discriminate against independent applications. According to the "one monopoly rent" theory, a monopolist has no incentive to monopolize the market for a complementary product if the complementary product is used in fixed proportions with the monopoly good and is competitively supplied.[21]

In this case, there is only one final product and therefore only one monopoly profit available in the market. The monopolist can extract the complete monopoly profit through its pricing of the monopoly good, and gains no additional profit from monopolizing the complementary good. (For an example, see box 6.2.)

This line of reasoning suggests that the monopolist need not monopolize the secondary market to extract the entire monopoly rent, and will therefore have no incentive to drive rivals from that market. In the context of the Internet, this would imply that an ISP with a local monopoly in the market for Internet services does not have an incentive to monopolize the market for a particular application, because it can extract the complete monopoly profit simply though the pricing of its Internet service.

Moreover, economists note that the monopolist may benefit from the presence of independent producers in the market for complementary products; if it benefits from their presence, the monopolist will welcome, not

Box 6.2

"One Monopoly Rent" Theory

> To understand the reasoning behind the "one monopoly rent" argument, imagine two complementary products, A and B, that are used in fixed proportions.[a] Consumers are willing to pay amount v for a system consisting of one unit of A and one unit of B. The marginal costs of producing component A and B are c_A and c_B, respectively. Product A is supplied by monopolist M. Under these circumstances, the maximum profit from the sale of a single system will be $v - c_B - c_A$. Monopolizing the market for B would not help the monopolist realize a higher profit.
>
> If the market for product B is perfectly competitive, B will be sold at a price equal to its marginal cost, c_B. Because consumers pay c_B for product B, the monopolist M can charge $v - c_B$ for product A, and will make a profit of $v - c_B - c_A$.
>
> If M has monopolized the market for B, it can sell systems consisting of A and B. Because v is the most consumers are willing to pay for the system, M charges v for the system and again makes a profit of $v - c_B - c_A$. Thus, M cannot increase its profits by extending its monopoly from A to B.
>
> a. For similar examples in the context of tying, see Whinston 2001, p. 70; Gilbert and Katz 2001, pp. 33–34.

exclude, independent producers of complementary products. This argument has been called *internalizing complementary efficiencies*.[22]

If the presence of these independent producers generates additional surplus, the monopolist may be able to capture some of that surplus through its pricing of the primary good. In this case, the monopolist will earn greater profits when its rivals are in the market than when they are not in the market. The monopolist does not want to take sales from its rivals in the secondary market, but derives its profits by charging a higher price for the primary good.[23] Customers may find Internet service more attractive if they can access a broader range of applications and content through this service. Thus, increasing the number of applications and the amount of content available online may enable the network provider to charge a higher price for Internet service.

Whether the presence of independent producers generates additional surplus depends on consumers' preferences, as well as on such things as the intensity of competition and the degree of differentiation in the complementary market (box 6.3).

Box 6.3
Independent Producers as a Source of Surplus

The presence of independent producers of complementary products may benefit the primary-good monopolist. As the intensity of competition increases, prices are driven down to marginal costs. Owing to the complementarity between both products,[a] the monopolist benefits from lower prices in the complementary market. The lower that prices are in the complementary market, the higher the demand (if demand is responsive to price) or the consumer surplus (if demand is inelastic) will be—and, consequently, the higher the profits will be that can be extracted in the primary market.[b]

If the producers of a complementary component are not equally efficient, the monopolist has an incentive to let the most efficient supplier make the sales. This maximizes the consumer surplus available for extraction in the primary market.[c]

Given complementarity between markets and appropriate consumer preferences, an increase in the quality or variety of complementary goods will increase consumers' valuation of the primary good. Consumer surplus rises if a rival with a differentiated complementary product enters the market and some consumers prefer the new product.[d] The value consumers derive from greater variety may differ depending on the type of complementary product. For example, consumers may value a fifth teleconferencing application less than they value a fifth multi-player online game.

Sometimes, innovation and lower prices may be mutually exclusive goals. Behavior by a monopolist that forces independent producers to lower the quality-adjusted price of their products and price closer to marginal cost may improve *ex post* efficiency (the rivals price closer to marginal cost, increasing output and efficiency). However, this may inefficiently destroy their incentives to innovate by reducing or eliminating their returns to innovation.[e]

a. In general, two goods are complements if a decrease in the price of one increases the demand for the other. See Varian 1999, p. 112.
b. See, e.g., Farrell and Katz 2000.
c. See, e.g., Ordover, Sykes, and Willig 1985, p. 117.
d. See, e.g., Whinston 1990, pp. 850–852; Carlton and Waldman 2000, pp. 10–11.
e. For a model demonstrating this effect, see Farrell and Katz 2000.

Whereas the "one monopoly rent" theory argues that exclusionary conduct in the complementary market will not increase the monopolist's profits, the "internalizing complementary efficiencies" theory suggests that such conduct may even reduce its profits.

Economic research shows that this line of reasoning is incomplete. In some cases, the logic underlying the "one monopoly rent" argument breaks down and the monopolist profits from monopolizing the complementary market. In these cases, the monopolist may profit from the presence of independent producers in the complementary market, but the loss of these profits amounts to a cost that may be more than offset by the gains associated with monopolizing the secondary market. In other words, although the monopolist may profit from the presence of independent producers by enjoying higher profits in the primary market, it may profit even more by excluding them from the market. The monopolist will engage in exclusionary conduct only if the associated profits are larger than the associated costs.[24]

In each of the exceptions described below, the network provider faces the same trade-off: the exclusion of rivals in the market for a specific application, content, or portal will increase the network provider's profits. At the same time, the network provider's Internet-service customers may find its Internet service less attractive if they cannot use the excluded application, content, or portal. This will make the network provider's Internet-service offering less profitable. The network provider will have an incentive to discriminate against a particular complementary product only if the gains from excluding it exceed the profits lost in the market for Internet services.

The following analysis sets out the theoretical framework for these exceptions, highlights the conditions under which they apply, and demonstrates that in the context of the Internet, these conditions may be met. In the first set of exceptions, the exclusionary conduct increases the monopolist's current profits. In the second set of exceptions, it preserves the monopolist's current profits.

Exclusionary Conduct Increases Current Profits (Monopoly Extension)
The "one monopoly rent" argument is based on the assumption that the monopolist can extract all potential monopoly profits through sales of its primary good, so monopolizing the second, complementary market does not increase its profits. But research has identified a variety of circumstances in which this assumption does not hold true. Under these circumstances, the monopolist can increase its profits by extending the monopoly to the complementary market.

Four exceptions are particularly relevant in the context of the Internet. In the first exception, rate regulation in the primary market prevents the monopolist from gaining the complete monopoly profit through its pricing of the primary good. In the second exception, the primary good is not necessary for some uses of the complementary good, which makes it impossible for the monopolist to extract all monopoly profits through its pricing of the primary good. In the third exception, the complementary product is a source of outside revenue (such as advertising revenue or sales commissions) that the monopolist cannot extract in the primary market. In the fourth exception, which is a variant of the third, only the monopolist's complementary product is a source of outside revenue, and this revenue is lost when rival producers make the sales. This exception is particularly relevant to Voice over Internet service.

Rate Regulation in the Primary Market   Rate regulation limits the price a monopolist can charge for its product, forcing the monopolist to set a price lower than the monopoly price. If a monopolist is subject to rate regulation in the primary market, this will prevent it from realizing monopoly profits in the primary market. By extending its monopoly to a second, unregulated complementary market, the monopolist gains the ability to recover forgone monopoly profits through sales of the second good.[25]

In the context of the Internet, if regulation restricts the price that a network provider with a local monopoly in the Internet-services market can charge for Internet services, then monopolizing the market for one or more applications may enable the network provider to make up for lost monopoly profits. This may give the network provider an incentive to exclude rivals from that market, or to discriminate against rivals in order to shift sales to its own application product. The profitability of this strategy will depend on several factors, including the extent of product differentiation and the intensity of competition in the application market, the relative efficiency of the different application providers, and the size of the profit margin in the regulated market for IP services.[26] In the United States, network providers are not subject to rate regulation in the market for Internet services, so this exception is not applicable.

Primary Good Not Essential   In this exception, uses of the complementary good that do not require the primary good make it impossible for the monopolist to extract all monopoly profits through its pricing of the primary good. For this exception to apply, three conditions must be met[27]: the monopolized product is not essential for all uses of the complementary good (i.e., some uses of the complementary good do not require the primary

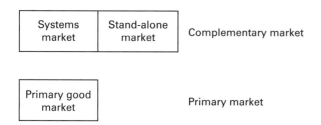

Figure 6.1
The "systems market" and the "stand-alone market."

good), the monopolist can prevent its rivals from selling their version of the complementary good to users of the primary good, and the complementary market is subject to economies of scale or network effects. The first condition explains why the monopolist would want to extend its monopoly to the complementary market in spite of its monopoly in the primary market. The second and third conditions provide the mechanism that enables the monopolist to extend its monopoly to the complementary market.

Suppose there is some use of a complementary good that does not require the primary good. As a result, the complementary market is divided into a "systems market" for uses that require the primary good and a "stand-alone market" for uses that do not require it (figure 6.1). Consumers in the "systems market" desire both the primary and the complementary good, whereas consumers in the "stand-alone market" desire only the complementary good.

Now suppose there are rival producers of the complementary good. The monopolist can extract all monopoly profits in the "systems market" through its pricing of the primary good. But since consumers in the "stand-alone market" do not buy the primary good, the monopolist derives no profit from its rivals' sales in that market. Moreover, the presence of rivals constrains the monopolist's ability to price its version of the complementary good in the "stand-alone market." Thus, the monopolist cannot earn monopoly profits in the "stand-alone market" unless it has a monopoly in that market too. Consequently, the monopolist needs to drive its competitors from the complementary market to be able to charge monopoly profits in the "stand-alone market."[28]

The second and third conditions provide the mechanism that enables the monopolist to extend the monopoly to the complementary market: in the presence of economies of scale or network effects, the monopolist may be able to drive potential rivals from the complementary market by excluding them from the "systems market."

When the second condition is met, the monopolist can deprive rival producers of complementary products of any sales in the "systems market." This behavior does not exclude rivals from the "stand-alone market." Given economies of scale[29] in the complementary market, the remaining sales to customers in the "stand-alone market" may not suffice to reach an economically efficient scale. Thus, rivals excluded from the "systems market" may be forced to exit the "stand-alone market" too.

Similarly, in the presence of network effects (box 6.4) in the complementary market, exclusion from the "systems market" may suffice to drive competitors from the complementary market or into a niche existence.

If the benefits derived from a bigger network are large relative to the benefits of product differentiation in the network good,[30] competition between two incompatible technologies[31, 32] usually will result in domination of the market by a single technology.[33] This is because network effects give rise to strong positive feedback loops in technology adoption. If a technology is subject to network effects and the competing technologies are incompatible, a larger network is more valuable, so more consumers will join that network. The resulting increase in network size will make that network even more valuable, which, in turn, will motivate even more consumers to join it. Once this positive feedback loop sets in, the affected technology will quickly pull ahead of its rivals in market share, and will ultimately dominate the market. This phenomenon is known as "tipping."[34]

Because small initial advantages may quickly get magnified, minute differences (in either perception[35] or reality) may determine who wins the competition for the market. Therefore, establishing an early lead in installed base (i.e., in the total number of customers who already bought the network good) large enough to start the positive feedback loop is an important strategy in network markets.[36] Thus, if a monopolist blocks its rivals from access to its primary-good customers in the "systems market," the monopolist can capture *all* customers who want to buy the complementary product in that market. If the "systems market" is large enough, the monopolist's advantage in that market may enable it to reach a critical mass of the complementary product's customers that is so attractive to other customers that the positive feedback loop sets in. Once this happens, rivals will not be able to catch up.

If the presence of rivals increases consumer surplus, the exclusion of rivals may reduce the monopolist's profits in the "systems market."[37] In this case, monopolizing the complementary market increases the monopolist's profits if the gain from monopolizing the "stand-alone market" is

Box 6.4

Network Effects

Network effects exist if the utility that an individual customer derives from a good depends on, and increases with, the number of other customers who buy that good (or goods compatible with it).[a]

If the benefits of consuming a good directly result from the size of the network,[b] the network effects are "direct."[c] Communication services such as the telephone, e-mail, or instant messaging are examples; the more people who can be reached by using the service, the more valuable the service becomes. Direct network effects exist for some software applications as well. The greater the number of people who use a particular word-processing software, the easier it is to exchange documents. The greater the number of people who own a particular multi-player game, the easier it is to find someone with whom to play it.

Network effects of another kind arise if consumers' demand for the primary good increases with the variety of complementary goods and services.[d] These "indirect" network effects arise from supply-side economies of scale in the complementary market. A larger installed base for the primary product (i.e., a larger number of consumers who have already bought the primary product) allows application developers to spread sunk development costs over a larger potential sales base. Thus, in the presence of economies of scale and free entry into the complementary market, a larger customer base leads to lower costs and greater variety of complementary products. For example, application developers find it more attractive to develop applications for an operating system with a larger number of customers. The higher number of applications available for the operating system with the larger number of customers, in turn, makes this operating system more attractive to customers who consider buying a new operating system. Thus, the value consumers derive from the operating system increases with the number of other users of the operating system. Contrary to direct network effects, consumers do not derive benefits from the larger network as such, but from the increased variety of complementary products that results from the larger network.

a. See the definition by Katz and Shapiro (1985, p. 424). For an analysis of network effects in the context of information goods, see Shapiro and Varian 1999, chapters 7–9. For an analysis of the legal implications of network economic effects, see Lemley and McGowan 1998. For critical voices, see Liebowitz and Margolis 2001; Kolasky 1999.

b. The size of the network is the number of consumers owning compatible units of the network good.

c. See, e.g., Katz and Shapiro 1985, p. 424.

d. See, e.g., Katz and Shapiro 1985, p. 424; Katz and Shapiro 1994, p. 99.

larger than the loss resulting from excluding rivals from the "systems market."[38] Thus, the monopolist has an incentive to exclude its rivals only if the gains in the "stand-alone market" are larger than the losses in the "systems market."

If the complementary market is subject to network effects, two factors make it particularly likely that the gains in the "stand-alone market" are indeed larger than the loss in the "systems market," so that the monopolist will have an incentive to discriminate. First, the potential profits from winning the competition between incompatible technologies are huge. Higher profits from monopolizing the complementary market make it more likely that the benefits of exclusion are larger than the costs. Imagine a competition between incompatible technologies both of which are subject to indirect network effects. If the winning standard is protected by intellectual property, the winner can make money on any primary or complementary product that uses the standard. In view of the potentially large number of complementary products in markets with indirect network effects, licensing fees can lead to substantial profits.[39] For example, in a competition between media-player technologies, a winner with a proprietary standard protected by intellectual property will not only dominate the market for media players, but will also be able to charge licensing fees for every song or video encoded for use with the player. Thus, in markets subject to network effects the benefits of exclusion are particularly high. Second, if the complementary product is subject to network effects, the presence of an independent rival in the complementary market will not necessarily increase the monopolist's profits in the "systems market." If the monopolist's complementary product and the rival's complementary product are not compatible, sales to the rival decrease the size of the user network for the monopolist's complementary product. As a result, the value that users can derive from the monopolist's complementary product (and the profit the monopolist can extract from them in the primary market) is lower than it would be if the rival made no sales.[40] Thus, although the presence of a rival in the complementary market may increase the network provider's profits in the primary market (because customers of the rival product value the ability to use that product), it may also reduce the profits that the network provider can derive from selling its own version of the complementary product. Overall, this lowers the costs of exclusion. Higher benefits and lower costs make it more likely that exclusion will be profitable.

The conditions underlying this model may be met in the Internet context. Consider the market for residential broadband Internet access in the United States.[41] In some areas of the country, the owner of a cable network or a telephone network that provides broadband Internet access through an affiliated broadband Internet access provider may well be a local monopolist.[42] If this network provider offers a complementary product not only to customers of its Internet service but also to customers nationwide, then its primary product, Internet service, will be essential only to its Internet-service customers. The area covered by the network constitutes the "systems market." Customers who live outside that area constitute the "stand-alone market."

This business model is common. For example, where AOL can strike a deal with owners of cable networks, it offers its portal bundled with broadband Internet access. Consumers nationwide can also buy the portal without access; this is known as the "bring your own access" option.[43] Other AOL services, including MapQuest and AOL Moviefone, are also offered to all consumers on the Internet. Microsoft's search engine and Hotmail are available to all, not only to customers of Microsoft's Internet service.[44] Similarly, if a provider of narrowband access has a local monopoly on narrowband access but offers its portal to all Internet users, the narrowband-access service will not be essential for customers accessing the portal via broadband-access services.[45]

In the hypothetical network, the monopolist can prevent rivals' applications, content, or portals from running over its network. As a result, the monopolist's Internet-service customers—the consumers in the "systems market"—are not able to access or use these products. Thus, rivals are deprived of sales in the "systems market."

The markets for software applications, Internet content, and portals are subject to significant economies of scale. Whereas development of these products and services is characterized by large fixed costs, the marginal costs of production and distribution over the Internet are small. Thus, the marginal cost of production[46] is low relative to the average cost of production,[47] resulting in significant economies of scale.[48]

In addition, many software applications are subject to direct or indirect network effects.[49] For example, instant messaging and Internet telephony become more valuable as more and more people can be contacted through them.[50] Viewers of multimedia content are subject to indirect network effects[51]: the larger the catalog of content available in a given format, the more highly users will value viewers that are compatible with that format. At the same time, the larger the installed base of viewers compatible with that format, the more likely it is that a content provider will be willing to incur the costs of coding its content in that particular format.

Given economies of scale or network effects, an Internet service provider may be able to force its rivals from the nationwide market for a particular application, content, or portal by excluding them from access to its Internet-service customers. Whether this exclusion will drive competitors from the nationwide market will depend on the size of economies of scale with respect to the complementary product, on the strength of potential network effects with respect to that product, and on the sizes of the monopolist's network (i.e. the number of its Internet-service customers) and the remaining network (i.e. the number of customers of other Internet-service providers).

If a network provider prevents market rivals for a particular application or for particular content from accessing its Internet-service customers, this reduces the number of applications and the amount of content available to these customers; consequently, these customers may not be willing to pay as much for the Internet service. Thus, a network provider will have an incentive to monopolize the market for a particular type of application, content, or portal only if the profit from additional application, content, or portal sales nationwide more than offsets the reduction in revenues from broadband access.[52] Whether this condition is met is an empirical question.[53]

In some cases, the network provider may not manage to drive its competitors from the complementary market—for example, because the number of its Internet-service customers may be too small, relative to the size of the market for the application or content in question, to deprive its rivals of minimum efficient scale. As we will see, this does not necessarily imply that the network provider will not have an incentive to discriminate: exclusion may still be a profitable strategy, even if the network provider does not manage to monopolize the complementary market.

Complementary Product Source of Outside Revenue   A monopolist in the primary market may also be unable to extract the maximum possible profit through its sales of its primary good if some of the revenue in the complementary market comes from outside sources. For example, a firm might follow the example of the mass media, selling access to its customers to advertisers and other third parties.[54] In the extreme case, consumers get a firm's product or service for free, while all of the firm's revenue comes from outside sources.[55] Google's search engine is an example of this. This exception may apply whether or not the monopolist's primary product is essential for use of the complementary good.

If firms in the complementary market derive some of their revenue from outside sources, a monopolist in the primary market may be unable to maximize profit unless it monopolizes the market for the complementary good too.

Consider first the variant of the exception in which all uses of the complementary good require use of the primary good. For this variant to apply, the monopolist must earn less if it extracts the advertising revenue from its rivals than if it excludes its rivals, monopolizes the complementary market, and captures all outside revenue directly. Exclusion in the market for the complementary good may reduce the value to consumers of the primary good and hence reduce profits in the primary-good market. For exclusion to be profitable overall, the net gains in outside revenue that result from exclusion must be larger than the profit reduction in the primary-good market.

Suppose, for example, that firms in the complementary market offer their product or service for free and make all their revenue from selling access to their customers to advertisers and other third parties.[56] Usually, the primary-good monopolist can use a variety of tactics to "squeeze" revenue from its rivals in the complementary market.[57] Suppose that these tactics are perfectly effective and extract all profits from the complementary market.[58] Even in this case, exclusion can be more profitable than employing these tactics if exclusion increases the total profitability of the complementary market.

If the value of the complementary market is greater when foreclosed, the net gains from exclusion will be larger than the net gains from extraction no matter how well the monopolist is able to extract rents from the complementary market.[59] The crux of this argument is whether and how foreclosure will increase the value of the complementary market. This is where outside revenues are crucial. First, outside revenues may increase with monopolization, insofar as a single provider is able to exert market power and increase prices. Second, the value of access to customers may increase disproportionately with the number of customers being accessed. For example, an advertiser may value access to 100,000 customers at $10,000 (10 cents per customer) but may value access to a million customers at $200,000 (20 cents per customer). Third, the monopolist may have information that allows it to increase the value of access to consumers in the complementary market. Fourth, if all firms in the complementary market incur fixed costs, the reduction in fixed costs resulting from the reduction in the number of firms may increase the overall value of the complementary market. Fifth, employing the tactics used to extract rents without foreclosure may involve higher administrative and negotiation costs than foreclosure.

By monopolizing the complementary market, the primary-good monopolist will also monopolize the side of the market that consists of selling third parties access to the users of the complementary good.[60] Before foreclosure, third parties who wanted to buy access to users of the complementary good had a variety of platforms they could use. After foreclosure, they must go through the monopolist's complementary product. If providers of the complementary product and third parties negotiate advertising fees, the primary-good monopolist probably will be in a stronger bargaining position than suppliers of the complementary good previously were in, and may be able to negotiate a higher price. Alternatively, if advertising prices are determined through an auction, the auction is likely to be more competitive when the third parties all have to bid in the same auction.[61] Finally, if suppliers of the complementary good directly set prices for advertisers, the monopolist may be able to charge higher (per customer) prices directly as a result of the reduced competition than suppliers of the complementary good could previously charge.[62]

For various reasons, third parties may value access to customers disproportionately such that with access to more customers they have a higher value per customer. The value of access to a customer can be thought of as the expected additional profits made from additional sales to that customer less the cost of access to that customer (e.g., delivering an advertisement to that customer). There are then three ways to increase the value of access to a given customer: increase the profit margin on additional sales to that customer, increase the additional sales to that customer, or decrease the cost of accessing that customer. For example, if an advertiser incurs a one-time cost of dealing with a provider of a complementary good (for example, because the advertising prices are negotiated), accessing a large block of customers through a single provider of a complementary good rather than accessing several smaller blocks through several providers will reduce the per-customer costs of accessing customers and will increase the value of accessing a specific customer in the sense defined above. In addition, access to different customers can result in different values through the three components identified above. For example, a customer who buys more items with higher profits margins and is cheaper to access will be more valuable. Ultimately, how buying access to more customers at once affects the value per customer is an empirical question.

Owing to its relationship with consumers in the primary market, the monopolist may have information about its customers that enables it to charge higher prices (per customer) to third parties than other firms in the complementary market.[63] The third parties may value this information, insofar as it allows them to better target the type of consumers in which they are interested.[64]

If fixed costs are high relative to marginal costs, foreclosure will reduce the total costs of servicing customers by eliminating the duplication of the fixed costs. If the primary-good monopolist chooses to extract outside revenue from complementary-market producers without foreclosing the market, the monopolist will have to leave sufficient rents for the producers of the complementary good to cover their costs. Foreclosure can then increase the total rents that can be extracted from the complementary-good market.

Finally, even if the per-customer prices charged to third parties stay the same, the monopolist's profits may be lower if there are rivals in the market, owing to the costs of negotiating and administering the access fees.

Thus, the monopolist will have an incentive to exclude its rivals from the complementary market if the net gains from capturing the outside revenue directly more than offset the reduction in profits that results from the reduction in variety of complementary goods.[65]

The other variant of this exception may apply if the monopolist's primary good is not essential for all uses of the complementary good. This is a special case of the "primary good not essential" exception outlined above. Since the primary-good monopolist cannot extract the outside revenue generated by consumers who use a rival's complementary good without the monopolist's primary good, the monopolist has an incentive to monopolize the market for the complementary good to capture all the outside revenue available in that market. If the complementary good is subject to economies of scale or to network effects, the monopolist may be able to drive its competitors from the "stand-alone market" (the market for uses of the complementary good that do not require the monopolist's primary good) by excluding them from the "systems market" (the market for uses of the complementary good that require the monopolist's primary good).[66] Again, the monopolist will have an incentive to discriminate only if the net gains in the complementary market are larger than the profit reduction in the primary market.

The conditions underlying this exception may be met in the Internet context. In the markets for Internet content, portals, and applications, firms often derive at least some of their revenue from outside sources by selling access to customers to advertisers or to online merchants.[67] For example, the search engine Google makes almost all of its revenue from advertising fees.[68] The portals AOL and Yahoo are at least partly financed by advertising fees or online sales commissions.[69] The social networking site Facebook also is based on this business model.

Consider first the variant of the exception in which the network provider offers the complementary product only to customers of its own Internet service. Since the discriminating functionality in the network enables the monopolist to exclude applications from the network, the monopolist network provider can extract at least some of its rivals' outside revenue. The monopolist can condition the "access" of rivals' complementary products and services on payment of an access fee that captures some or all of the rivals' outside revenue. Some owners of cable networks in the United States use this practice with respect to ISPs. Unaffiliated ISPs who want to offer their service over a cable network have to pay a fixed fee per customer. In addition, the owner of the cable network receives a portion of the outside revenue that the ISP earns per customer.[70]

Thus, the discriminatory technology enables the network provider to choose between two strategies. It can give competing providers of the complementary product access to its network and charge a fee to extract some of their advertising revenue. Under this strategy, the rivals have to keep enough advertising revenue to pay the costs associated with serving the customers of their complementary product. Alternatively, the network provider can exclude all competing providers of the complementary product from its network and sell advertisers access to all of its Internet-service customers who use the complementary product. For example, Comcast could let AOL and Yahoo onto its network, but could require them to pay Comcast at least a portion of their outside revenue, or it could exclude all competing portals from its network, become the only portal available to its Internet-service customers, and directly sell access to its Internet-service customers to all advertisers who would like to advertise to Comcast's Internet-service customers on the portal.

Although a monopolist will be able to capture some or all of its rivals' outside revenue in the complementary market by threatening exclusion, its outside revenue may be higher if it excludes rivals from the complementary market and collects the outside revenue directly.

First, selling access to one large group of customers as a whole may yield substantially more revenue than selling access to subgroups of that group separately. This is obvious if the monopolist network provider manages to monopolize the market in which advertisers buy online access to its Internet-service customers.[71] To do this, however, the network provider would have to exclude from its network all applications, content, and portals that are financed through advertising and are operated by providers not affiliated with the network provider. This may not be a realistic strategy. However, foreclosure of many applications, content offerings, and portals is likely to generate some market power for the network provider and allow it to charge a higher rate per customer even if the network provider cannot completely monopolize the market in which advertisers buy online access to its Internet-service customers. Alternatively, the network provider is likely to gain some market power over advertisers through exclusion from the complementary market if advertisers view "access to customers through the complementary product" as a differentiated product that they cannot get elsewhere. Products in this category may include "yellow pages" (because they provide advertisers with access to customers looking to buy something), portals (because of their reach),[72] websites specializing in a particular type of content such as cars or finance, and websites catering to a specific demographic group (because they provide access to customers with specific interests or characteristics).[73] If the network provider manages to monopolize the customer side of one of these product categories, it may be able to realize higher advertising rates by becoming the sole provider of this type of advertiser access to its Internet-service consumers.[74] Even without monopolizing a specific market in which advertisers buy access to the network provider's Internet customers, selling access to a large block of customers may be more profitable than selling access to subgroups of that block. For example, Google has more users than Yahoo or Microsoft,[75] and is currently able to realize higher revenue per search than either of these companies.[76] The ability to realize higher revenue per search is attributed to two factors. First, there are network effects between the advertiser and the user side of the market. More users make a search engine more attractive for advertisers. Even if an ad is relevant to a user, the probability that a user will click on the ad and buy something on the website is relatively low. As a result, advertisers want to show their ads to a large number of users to have a meaningful number of people actually buy their product.[77] As Google has by far the largest number of users, Google's advertising space is in the greatest demand. The prices for ads shown to users of search engines are determined at auctions where advertisers can bid for the right to have their ads shown. A higher number of advertisers increases competition in these auctions, which increases the prices for ads shown.[78] At the same time, users interested in buying something value the ability to view relevant ads; the more advertisers are willing to show their ads on the search engine, the higher the chance that there will be advertisers whose offerings are relevant to the user.[79] Second, Google's methods of charging for ads and of placing ads result in more revenue per search than, for example, Yahoo's.[80] Google determines where ads will be placed not only on the basis of what price the advertiser is willing to pay, but also on the basis of the likelihood that the ad will be clicked on. This lets relevant ads rise to the top, even if the corresponding advertiser has bid to pay a lower price. As advertisers pay only for ads that are clicked on, and the mechanism shows ads that are more likely to be clicked on, this increases the overall revenue per search. Now suppose that Google was a network provider and could exclude competing providers of search engines from access to its Internet-service customers. Google would make more revenue if it was the only search engine its customers could use (and it sold advertising on its search engine directly) than if some of its Internet-service customers used other search engines, even if the other search engines gave all of the resulting advertising revenue to Google.[81] Owing to the network effects operating between the customer side of the market and the advertiser side, the increase in customers probably would enable Google to realize even higher revenue per search.[82] Furthermore, selling access to a large block of customers as a whole may be more profitable than selling access to subgroups of that block separately, because advertisers value both breadth and depth; they want to reach as many consumers as they can, and they want to reach consumers who have specific needs or characteristics.[83] Content, portal, or application providers with a large number of customers can often meet both needs, so they command higher advertising prices per click. In addition, a large provider of applications or content often has an in-house sales team that sells ad space on the company's online offerings directly to advertisers. Smaller providers of content or applications do not have their own sales teams and often sell their advertising space through advertising networks (intermediaries that aggregate ad space from a large number of content or application providers and sell it to advertisers). Ad space on large websites that is sold directly to publishers can be sold at a much higher rate than ad space sold through advertising networks. For example, the investment firm Piper Jaffray estimated that an ad on a typical portal or a large specialized website could cost at least $8–$10 per 1,000 page views (for example, an ad on MSN may cost $45 to $70 per 1,000 page views, and an add on the website of the *Wall Street Journal*, which reaches a specific and highly valuable audience, may cost $65 to $90 per 1,000 page views), whereas an average collection of sites sold through an advertising network may cost about $1–$2 per 1,000 page views.[84] This means that a website belonging to a larger conglomerate that sells its own advertising space can command much higher advertising revenue per user than an independent website. Imagine a network provider whose website or application belongs to the first category. For example, Yahoo partners with network providers to sell co-branded Internet access services.[85] In addition, Yahoo has many websites, some with very large reach (such as portals) and some targeted at specific customer groups (such as auto and finance sites). This enables Yahoo to sell its advertising space at very high rates.[86] Now imagine that Yahoo's finance offering competes with a new independent website that is not part of a larger conglomerate, does not have its own advertising sales force, and sells its advertising space through an advertising network. Yahoo could realize more advertising revenue if the users of the independent site used Yahoo's website than if they used the independent website, even if the independent website transferred all of its advertising revenue to Yahoo.

Second, the network provider's revenue may be higher if it excludes rivals from the complementary market and collects the outside revenue available in that market directly, because through its billing relationship with customers of its Internet service, a network owner has data about customer demographics. This enables it to charge higher advertising fees or commissions for online sales than many of its rivals in the complementary market.[87]

Third, the network provider may be able to reach higher net gains in outside revenue under foreclosure, if its costs of serving the additional customers after exclusion are lower than the costs incurred previously by its rivals.[88] Without foreclosure, rivals' costs affect the network provider's revenue: the amount of revenue the network provider can extract from applications, content, and portals will be limited, because the providers need to keep enough of their revenue to cover their fixed and variable costs.[89] Many applications, content providers, and portals have high fixed costs and low marginal costs.[90] This makes it more likely that exclusion provides a net gain in outside revenue: owing to the low marginal costs, the network provider's costs of serving additional customers after foreclosure will be small, but the high fixed costs associated with a specific application will be paid only once, not several times.

Finally, owing to the potentially large number of complementary products, negotiating and administering the access charges for unaffiliated content, applications, and portals may be prohibitively expensive. In any event, these transaction costs will further decrease the monopolist's profits if rivals are present in the market.[91]

Thus, if firms in the market for a particular type of application, content, or portal derive some of their revenue from outside sources, a monopolist in Internet services may have an incentive to monopolize that market in order to capture all the outside revenue available in that market directly. This will be true as long as the net gains in the complementary market exceed the reduction in profits in the market for Internet services.

Now consider the second variant of the exception, in which the network provider offers its complementary product not only to its Internet-service customers but also to customers nationwide. In this case, it may have an incentive to exclude its rivals in the complementary market from access to its Internet-service customers in order to drive the rivals from the nationwide market and to capture the advertising revenue in the part of the market that consists of the customers of other network providers who use the complementary product (this is a special case of the "primary good not essential" exception described above). For example, suppose AOL had a monopoly in a particular local market for Internet services. This would not let AOL capture the advertising revenues made by rival portal providers in areas outside AOL's local market. Thus, in this example, AOL would have an incentive to exclude rival portal providers from access to its Internet-service customers, in order to monopolize the nationwide market for portals and capture all the advertising revenue in that market, if the resulting net gains in the complementary market would be larger than the reduction in profits in the market for Internet services. The analysis in this case follows the analysis in the subsection on the "primary good not essential" exception above.

Monopolist's Complementary Product Source of Outside Revenue   In the last exception, only the network provider—not its rivals in the complementary market—can realize higher outside revenues. Thus, letting rivals make the sales and then extracting the outside revenue from them is less profitable to a network provider than making the sales directly.

This exception is a variant of this line of reasoning. The network provider's offering is a source of outside revenue; the rivals' offering does not provide this revenue. Thus, this revenue is lost if rivals make the sales. As a result, the network provider has an incentive to make as many sales as possible directly.

Consider a local phone company that offers broadband Internet service over its network.[92] Vonage, Skype, and other independent companies offer Voice over IP (VoIP) services to customers of this network provider. Since the price of long-distance calls made by means of VoIP tends to be lower than the price of long-distance calls made by means of conventional telephone service, the network provider's customers who use VoIP will place fewer long-distance calls using the network provider's "legacy" telephone service.

To the network provider, conventional long-distance services are a source of outside revenue that is not similarly available to providers of VoIP services. In the United States, local phone companies are paid an "access charge" by long-distance providers for every long-distance call they originate or terminate. Because access charges were traditionally intended to cross-subsidize local telephone service, regulators have mostly set them significantly above the costs of originating or terminating long-distance calls. Thus, for many local phone companies, access charges are an important source of revenue.[93] Independent VoIP providers threaten this revenue. When more of the network provider's customers place their long-distance calls using VoIP, the network provider receives fewer access charges. If independent VoIP providers are excluded from the network and the network provider does not offer a VoIP service itself,[94] customers who want to make long-distance calls will be forced to use the conventional telephone service. Thus, exclusion in the VoIP market protects the network provider's current profits.[95]

It is not surprising that the first publicly documented incident of VoIP blocking in the United States involved a rural telephone company.[96] In February 2005, the VoIP provider Vonage complained to the Federal Communications Commission that its Internet-telephony application was being blocked by Madison River Communications, a rural telephone company based in North Carolina. In March 2005, after a short investigation, Madison River and the FCC entered into a consent decree. Madison River agreed to pay $15,000 to the US Treasury and to stop blocking VoIP applications; the FCC terminated the investigation. Access charges make up a substantial portion of rural phone companies' revenue, so the companies have a high incentive to guard them.

In several countries, monopoly providers of telephony services have blocked international VoIP calls in order to maintain the revenue they accrue from settlement charges. For international calls, carriers in different countries negotiate these charges; a settlement charge is split between the two providers. These charges are often set significantly above costs, especially if one of the providers is a national monopolist in its country.[97] If users in these countries place or receive calls using Internet telephony, the local telephony provider loses the chance to earn revenue from these settlement charges. To prevent this, network providers in Saudi Arabia, the

United Arab Emirates, Mexico, and other countries have blocked Internet-telephony applications altogether.[98]

In the example discussed above, the existence of outside revenue is a result of regulation that requires long-distance providers to pay above-cost access charges to local phone companies. It is more difficult to determine whether local phone companies that are local monopolists in the market for Internet services (this assumption holds throughout the subsection titled "Network Provider Is a Monopolist in the Market for Internet Services") would also have an incentive to block VoIP in the absence of such regulation (box 6.5).

Exclusionary Conduct Preserves Current Profits (Monopoly Preservation)
In the models described above, the monopolist's exclusionary conduct is driven by the desire to extend its monopoly to the complementary market in order to increase its current profits. In this section, the monopolist pursues a different goal: by harming rivals in, or excluding rivals from, the complementary market, it seeks to protect its monopoly in that market or in another market. The exclusionary conduct maintains, rather than increases, the monopolist's current level of profits. In the absence of this conduct, however, the monopolist's profits would shrink or disappear.[99]

Models in this category share the following features: The primary-good monopolist has a monopoly in one market (call it market X) that is threatened by new entry, by the expansion of fringe competitors, or by other developments. For some reason, the presence of rivals in the

Box 6.5
Incentive to Discriminate in the Absence of Regulation

In the absence of regulation, local phone companies would have no incentive to block provision of Internet-telephony, or Voice-over-Internet-Protocol (VoIP), service by independent providers if they could price their Internet service in a way that allowed them to realize the same revenue that they make by offering traditional telephone service. For example, if someone were to stop using the telephone and begin using an independent provider's VoIP service, the network provider could increase that person's Internet-service rate until the additional profit from Internet service equals the profit that the network provider would have realized if the person were still using the telephone (i.e., until the additional profit from Internet service for that customer equaled the lost profit from telephone service for that customer).[a]

Box 6.5
(continued)

Replicating current phone profits via Internet-service rates is not trivial, though. Because some telephone charges are based on use, network providers would not only have to introduce use-based elements into the Internet-service pricing structure (a pricing structure currently based on flat-rate pricing); they would also have to price Internet use differently depending on the application being used—for example, charging a different price for transport of VoIP packets than for transport of e-mail packets. Though this is possible in theory, there are many reasons it may not be feasible in practice—for example, customer resistance to deviations from flat-rate pricing, or the cost of implementing a fine-grained accounting and billing system for Internet use. Thus, simply pricing their Internet services differently may not allow network providers to replicate the profits that they generate from telephone use.

Network providers may be able to reach this goal, however, by excluding independent providers' VoIP applications allowing only their own. This was not an option in the example above, because the outside revenue was lost regardless of who provided the VoIP. But if we assume that there is no outside revenue in the case, then, by excluding independent VoIP providers from access to its Internet-service customers, a network provider who is a local monopolist in the Internet-services market also gains a local monopoly in the market for VoIP services. This monopoly, in turn, will give the network provider more flexibility in pricing VoIP, and may enable it to replicate the revenue formerly realized through traditional phone services. For example, it might offer a higher flat rate for Internet services and VoIP services combined. This idea that a firm with a monopoly in a primary market may have an incentive to exclude competitors from a secondary, complementary market in order to get more pricing flexibility (e.g., to facilitate price discrimination) is well acknowledged in the literature.[b]

In sum, network providers may not be able to replicate their phone revenues simply by pricing their Internet service differently, and thus they may have an incentive to block the VoIP services offered by independent providers even in the absence of regulation of traditional long-distance access charges.

a. The network provider could also try to replicate traditional telephony profits by charging Internet-telephony applications an access charge that is equal to or greater than the potential lost profit. However, for reasons discussed in notes 28 and 95 to this chapter, this alternative may be less attractive than exclusion.
b. See, e.g., Ordover, Sykes, and Willig 1985, pp. 119–121; Farrell and Weiser 2003, pp. 107–109.

complementary market is a part of this threat; stated differently, if the presence of rivals in the complementary market continues, the monopolist's position in market X may be weakened. Exclusionary behavior in the complementary market may be able to deter or destroy the emerging competition. Thus, the monopolist harms or excludes its rivals in the complementary market to preserve the monopoly in market X.

The models differ with respect to the market in which the monopolist's position is threatened; they also differ in how they explain why exclusionary behavior in the complementary market can remove that threat. The following analysis highlights two cases that may be relevant in the context of the Internet.

Monopoly Preservation in the Primary Market   In this class of models, exclusionary behavior in the complementary market maintains a monopoly in the primary market.[100]

In models that fall into this category, the monopolist faces potential competition in the primary market. It can deter entry into the primary market by engaging in exclusionary conduct in the complementary market. By deterring rivals' entry into the primary market, the exclusionary behavior in the complementary market preserves the monopoly in the primary market.

Economists have come up with a number of explanations as to why exclusionary conduct in the complementary market may deter entry into the primary market. One explanation is particularly relevant in the context of the Internet: the exclusionary behavior in the complementary market harms future competitors in the primary market by depriving them of a source of complementary products.[101] As a result, in order to make any sales in the primary market, an entrant to the primary market must also enter the complementary market. If this is significantly more difficult or costly than entering the primary market alone, potential entrants to the primary market may be deterred.

For this strategy to succeed, two conditions must be met. First, the monopolist's exclusionary behavior in the complementary market must deprive a potential entrant into the primary market of a source of complementary products. As a result, the entrant cannot enter only the primary market; it must enter both markets at once. Second, simultaneously entering both markets must be more costly than the sum of the costs of entering each market on its own[102]; otherwise, the exclusionary behavior in the complementary market is not likely to have an adverse effect on entry into the primary market.

Economists have identified four reasons why simultaneous entry into both markets may be significantly more costly than the sum of the costs of entering each market on its own: increased cost of capital, differing economies of scale in the two markets, the uncertainty of innovation, and the existence of indirect network effects.

Increased Cost of Capital   An entrant forced to break into both markets may face an increased cost of capital if it has experience relevant to operating in only one of the markets. If the skills and knowledge necessary to succeed in both markets differ considerably, the increased probability of failure due to inexperience in one of the markets may lead lenders to charge a higher rate for the necessary capital. The risk premium will be even larger if the entrant has to incur huge sunk costs to enter the market, because sunk costs cannot be recovered if the entrant fails.[103]

Differing Economies of Scale   Entering two markets is more difficult than entering one market if the minimum efficient scale in the two markets differs considerably. If it does differ considerably, an entrant must choose between operating on an inefficiently small scale in one market and operating on an unnecessarily large scale in the other. Either strategy may significantly increase an entering firm's operating costs.[104]

Uncertainty of Innovation   In view of the uncertainty associated with the innovative process, the need to innovate successfully in two markets probably will decrease the chance of successful entry. Let us assume that the probability of innovating successfully in one component is k. In this case, the chances of successful innovation in n components are k^n. Unless k is close to 1, k^n is considerably lower than k.[105] Thus, the probability of successful innovation in n components required to enter n markets simultaneously is lower than the probability of successful innovation and successful entry in one component market.

Existence of Indirect Network Effects   If the primary good is subject to indirect network effects[106] and any available complementary goods are offered exclusively with the monopolist's platform, an entrant into the primary market faces a "chicken and egg" problem. Owing to consumers' desire for variety in complementary products, consumers prefer a primary good that already offers a wide array of complementary goods and services. At the same time, owing to economies of scale and sunk costs in the development of complementary products, developers of complementary products prefer to develop products for primary goods that already have a large number of users. Thus, an entrant into the primary market "either has to offer consumers much lower value or has to incur large sunk costs to develop (or subsidize) a wide range of [complementary goods and services] before there is a large user base to purchase them."[107]

The conditions underlying this theory may be met in the Internet context. For exclusion in the complementary market to deter rivals from entering the market for Internet services, the exclusionary behavior in the complementary market must deprive a potential entrant to the Internet-service market of a source of complementary products. By excluding rival producers of Internet portals, content, and applications from its network, the monopolist network provider may be able to drive rivals from the nationwide markets for these products.

To deprive a potential entrant of a source of complementary products, the monopolist not only must drive rival content and application producers from the market; it also must deny access to its own content and applications to consumers outside its network.[108] Otherwise, a rival network provider's customers could simply access the monopolist's content and applications through the rival's Internet service.[109] Hence, for a particular application or content, this strategy and the "primary good not essential" strategy are mutually exclusive.[110]

Thus, this theory is applicable only if an Internet service provider offers proprietary content and applications exclusively to customers of its Internet service[111] and if there are (perhaps owing to the exclusion of rivals) not enough remaining independent applications, content, or portals available that could be used by customers of rival network providers.[112] In this case, a new entrant into the market for Internet services must develop (or subsidize the development of) its own content or applications.

One may wonder whether the second condition mentioned in the preceding paragraph will ever be met in the Internet context. After all, portals, content, and applications are available to anyone using the Internet. But the condition may be met in the market for Internet services for mobile phones, or in emerging national markets in countries outside the United States. For example, there may not be enough independent applications or enough content adapted to the limitations associated with accessing the Internet from a mobile phone.[113] And in a country that recently started adopting the Internet, there may not be enough independent applications or content in the country's national language.

We might also imagine that consumers perceive certain applications and content—for example, search engines or e-mail—as indispensable elements of Internet use. If these applications and this content are available only with the incumbent provider's Internet service, consumers may not consider an entrant's Internet service an adequate alternative unless the entrant offers a similar set of applications and content. In this case, to deter entry into the market for Internet services, the incumbent does not have to drive all existing independent applications, portals, and content from the market. All it has to do is restrict the exclusionary conduct to applications and content that consumers view as essential. Although there will be independent applications and content left that customers of a rival Internet service could use, the entrant will still be forced to enter the market for specific applications and content in order to compete in the primary market.[114]

For exclusion in the complementary market to deter rivals from entering the market for Internet services, the exclusionary conduct must not only deprive a potential entrant into the Internet-service market of a source of complementary products, but simultaneously entering the market for Internet services and the market for content or applications must be more difficult or costly than entering the market for Internet services alone. This requirement is fulfilled too. Simultaneous entry into both markets is more difficult or costly than entry into the Internet-services market if the two markets each exhibit at least one of the four characteristics described above. In the Internet context, all four characteristics are present: entry into both markets requires different capabilities, production in the two markets is subject to differing economies of scale, success in the different markets is uncertain, and, owing to the incumbent's exclusionary conduct, the provision of Internet service is subject to indirect network effects with respect to the individual provider's network.

Developing software applications or interesting content requires capabilities that are very different from the capabilities required to operate a network, and a potential entrant to the market for Internet services may not have both sets of capabilities.[115] In addition, most of the cost of entry into those complementary industries consists of the sunk costs of developing the offering—costs that cannot be recovered in case of failure.[116] Thus, if an entrant to the primary market is required to enter complementary markets as well, the risks associated with entry may be considerably greater than if it only enters the primary market. Taking these risks into account, investors probably will charge higher rates for firms who wish to access both markets simultaneously.

The market for Internet services and the markets for complementary products are subject to very different economies of scale. For example,

McKinsey estimated that assuming an average per-customer revenue of $18.00 to $22.50 in 2005, a broadband PC portal in Germany would need more than 8 million users to break even.[117] In contrast, the economies of scale of building and operating IP networks are much lower.[118]

Although network technology is undergoing rapid change, a new entrant into the market for Internet services does not have to innovate, but can take advantage of existing technology. The development of applications and content is less predictable. If a potential entrant to the market for Internet services has to develop several applications and services in order to compete with the incumbent's Internet service, the uncertainty associated with each development reduces the likelihood of successful entry into the market for Internet services.

Internet service is subject to indirect network effects.[119] The greater the number of applications and content that are available for users, the more valuable Internet service becomes. At the same time, the development of content and applications is subject to economies of scale.[120] Having more users allows developers of applications and developers of content to spread the fixed costs of development over a larger sales base, so that the more users they have, the higher the variety of applications and content and the lower their cost will be (under free entry into these markets).[121]

Technically, any application based on the Internet protocol can run over any network that supports the protocol, as long as the network is connected to the public Internet. As a result, the relevant network for indirect network effects is not an individual provider's network; it is the global Internet. Thus, Internet service providers compete under conditions of compatibility.

By excluding independent applications from its network and offering its own applications exclusively to its own Internet customers, an Internet service provider changes the nature of the competition from competition among compatible networks (in which the benefits resulting from adding a new user—i.e., the increased number of applications resulting from additional users—accrue to anyone connected to the Internet) to competition between incompatible networks (in which the benefits of adding a new user are limited to the customers of the new user's ISP). Thus, by using this strategy, the ISP reintroduces indirect network effects with respect to its own network.[122] Application developers and content developers then have to decide whether to offer their product to the customers of the ISP with the "closed" network or to the customers of ISPs with an "open" strategy. Owing to economies of scale in the production of application and content, the developers will base their decision on the sizes of the different networks.

Because an entrant to the market for Internet services does not have any customers yet, it will have difficulty attracting application developers and content developers to write for its network rather than for that of the incumbent, which already has a large number of customers. Owing to the incumbent's strategy, the entrant will face the "chicken and egg" problem described above: consumers will not subscribe to its Internet service unless it has an attractive array of content and applications, and developers will not produce applications and content for its network without an attractive number of users.[123]

Thus, a monopolist provider of Internet services may be able to deter entry into the Internet-services market by excluding rival producers of applications, content, and portals and offering its own content and applications exclusively to customers of its own Internet service.[124] This strategy may reduce consumers' valuation of the monopolist's Internet service, since excluding rival producers of applications, content, and portals reduces the variety of complementary products available. Thus, in deciding whether to employ such a strategy, the monopolist must trade off the loss in Internet-service fees against the gains in future monopoly profits.

Monopoly Preservation in the Complementary Market   A monopolist may also use its monopoly over the primary good to protect a monopoly in the complementary market against dynamic competition. In this case, the exclusionary conduct in the complementary market preserves the monopoly in that market.[125]

The structure of the model and the underlying reasoning are parallel to the "primary good not essential" case.[126] The monopolist has a monopoly in the primary market; the complementary market is subject to economies of scale or network effects. Some uses of the complementary good do not require the primary good. As a result, the complementary market comprises a "systems market" and a "stand-alone market." By excluding its rivals in the complementary market from the former, the monopolist can force them to exit the latter.

In the "primary good not essential" case, the monopolist uses this mechanism to extend its monopoly to the complementary market. In the case under consideration here, the monopolist uses the same mechanism to protect a legally acquired monopoly against emerging competition in the complementary market.

Such a scenario may be particularly relevant if the complementary market belongs to an R&D-intensive industry in which there is dynamic or "Schumpeterian" competition.[127] Owing to intellectual-property rights, economies of scale, or network effects, R&D-intensive industries are prone to short-run exercises of market power. In other words, competition in these markets often leads to dominating of the market by a single firm. Firms in these industries typically compete "for the market," not "within the market." Though firms with market power (the winners of the competition) are an inherent feature of such industries, their dominance may be temporary. Rapid technological change and pivotal innovations may cause demand for their product to collapse quite suddenly. For example, rivals may come up with a vastly superior product or develop a new product that makes the incumbent's product obsolete. Thus, the primary constraint on incumbents in these industries is dynamic competition—that is, innovation by other firms seeking to replace the existing firm. To avoid being dislodged by rivals, incumbents must innovate.

In the scenario described above, a monopolist could use its market power in the primary market to preserve the legally obtained market power in the complementary market, thereby distorting the dynamic competition for future market power. Instead of innovating to stay ahead of competitors, the monopolist could simply exclude rivals from the systems part of the complementary market, preventing them from ever growing large enough and reaching the scale or network size they must reach to displace the incumbent.

As was explained above, the conditions underlying this model are common in the Internet context. Network providers may be local monopolists in the market for Internet services, but may offer applications, content, or portals to consumers nationwide; these latter markets are usually subject to significant economies of scale—and, potentially, to network effects. In addition, at least some of these markets undergo rapid technological change. Not surprisingly, markets for software applications are the canonical example of R&D-intensive industries subject to dynamic competition.[128]

Now consider a network provider that is a local Internet-services monopolist and has a dominant position in the nationwide market for a particular application. This monopolist has an incentive to exclude rivals from the market for that application to protect itself from dynamic competition.

This theory played an important role in the Federal Communications Commission's evaluation of the merger between AOL and TimeWarner. TimeWarner owned a number of broadband cable networks, while AOL offered its instant-messaging program to consumers nationwide and held a dominant position in that market. The FCC was concerned that the merged firm could use its control over broadband cable networks to disadvantage rivals seeking to overturn AOL's legally acquired monopoly in instant-messaging services. To alleviate this problem, the FCC approved the merger subject to a condition (among others) that required AOL Time-Warner to interoperate with instant-messaging competitors before offering "advanced" instant-messaging services.[129]

Profitability of Discrimination without Monopolization   When thinking about the profitability of exclusionary conduct, researchers commonly focus on the ability of and the incentives for a primary-good monopolist to monopolize the market for selected complementary products. This line of analysis is based on the implicit assumption that discrimination is profitable only if the primary-good monopolist monopolizes the complementary market. But, as will be shown in this section, this focus may be too narrow. A network provider may have an incentive to discriminate against an application even if the network provider fails to drive the application from the market.

Focusing on monopolization leads researchers to underestimate the likelihood of discriminatory behavior by network providers. If discrimination is profitable only if the network provider monopolizes the complementary market, then a network provider will discriminate only when it can expect to drive its competitors from the complementary market. If discrimination is profitable even if the network provider does not manage to monopolize the complementary market, it is much more likely to occur.

The following analysis will cover four of the six exceptions outlined above,[130] and is based on the assumption that depriving rivals of access to the network provider's Internet-service customers will increase sales of the network provider's complementary product. At least some of the network provider's Internet-service customers who, absent exclusion, would have used a rival's complementary product will use the network provider's offering instead. Thus, by excluding rival producers of applications or content from its network, the network provider gains additional sales from its Internet-service customers at the expense of its rivals. If the complementary product is subject to economies of scale or to network effects, and the network provider offers its complementary product to customers nationwide, exclusion from access to the network provider's Internet-service customers may force rivals to operate at an economically less efficient scale or with a smaller network of customers. This puts the rivals at a competitive disadvantage in the rest of the market too, potentially leading to even greater success of the network provider's complementary product in that part of the market.[131]

Will an increase in sales of the network provider's complementary product increase its profits, even if the network provider does not monopolize the complementary market in question? As we will see, the common theme that emerges from the analysis is that, in all the exceptions discussed below, the marginal benefits of serving an additional customer are larger than the marginal costs of serving the customer. As a result, every additional sale results in a net gain for the network provider, whether or not it monopolizes the complementary market.

This alone does not make exclusion a profitable strategy. The network provider has an incentive to exclude its competitors from a specific complementary market only if the net gains from the additional sales in the complementary market are larger than the associated reduction in profits in the Internet-services market.

More Sales at Market Prices   In a perfectly competitive market subject to constant returns to scale, simply increasing the number of sales at the market price will not increase profits. In such an industry, long-run equilibrium prices equal marginal costs, resulting in zero profit per unit sold. As a result, a firm cannot increase its profits by making additional sales at the market price. Instead, it has to gain a monopoly position that enables it to raise prices above marginal costs.

Markets for applications, content, and portals are different. In these markets, exclusionary conduct need not result in a monopoly to increase the network provider's profits; it suffices if exclusion results in a larger number of sales.[132] This is due to the cost structure underlying the production of applications and content; the production of these goods has high fixed costs and low marginal costs. Though the cost of developing the first instance of an application may be significant, the cost of producing additional copies may be small. Because of the need to cover fixed costs, these products are priced significantly above marginal costs.[133] In these circumstances, a firm need not charge monopoly prices to increase its profits; making additional sales at the market price may be sufficient.[134] More sales enable the firm to spread the fixed costs of production over more units, resulting in lower average costs per unit and a higher profit margin at the same price. Put differently, once a firm has made enough sales to cover the fixed costs, any additional sale at the market price only adds to the profits. For example, gross margins of 80 percent or 90 percent are common for computer software,[135] so in these markets any additional sales may lead to a significant increase in profits.

By excluding rival producers of complementary products from its network, a network provider gains additional sales of its own complementary product. If marginal profits are positive, these sales increase the provider's profit even if the rivals are not driven from the complementary market completely. This has important implications for the relevance of the "primary good not essential" exception. As we saw above, a network provider's ability to monopolize a nationwide complementary market by excluding rivals from access to its Internet-service customers will depend on a variety of factors, including the exact size of economies of scale with respect to the complementary product, the strength of potential network effects with respect to that product, and the size of both the monopolist's network and the remaining network.[136]

Ultimately, monopolization may not always be a realistic prospect, but this does not automatically remove the network provider's incentive to discriminate, since monopolization is not necessary to increase the network provider's profits. As long as the exclusion of rivals from its Internet-service customers translates into more sales of its complementary product, and the additional profits are larger than the costs of exclusion, exclusion will be a profitable strategy. And because the conditions underlying the "primary good not essential" exception[137] are often met, exclusion may often be a profitable strategy.

More Outside Revenue   As was explained above,[138] a network provider may have an incentive to monopolize a complementary market if the complementary product garners outside revenue that cannot be extracted in the market for Internet services.

Again, there are two variants of this exception. First, if the network provider offers its complementary product only to its own Internet-service customers, then, as we saw above, its outside revenue may still be higher if it excludes rivals and collects the outside revenue directly than if it tries to capture rivals' outside revenue by threatening exclusion. This increase in profit, however, is not dependent on a monopolization of the market for the complementary product. This is easy to see if the market for the complementary product is subject to network effects between the customer side and the advertiser side of the market, and if demand from advertisers increases faster than the amount of advertising space available. For example, Google collects more advertising revenue per search than its competitors in the search-engine market because of this type of network effect, and because of superior technology—not as the result of a monopoly position in the search-engine market. Similarly, the difference in revenue per customer between websites that belong to a conglomerate that sells its advertising space directly and independent websites that sell their advertising space through advertising networks does not hinge on having a monopoly position in the respective markets for the complementary product.

In addition, through its billing relationship with customers of its Internet service, the network provider has data on customer demographics that may enable it to charge higher per-customer fees than many of its rivals in the market for Internet content, portals, and applications.[139] Again, this ability is not dependent on a monopoly in the complementary market.

If, as in the second variant, the complementary product is offered to customers outside the network provider's network, the provider cannot extract the advertising revenue that rivals realize from customers who do not use the provider's Internet service. The only way to get this advertising revenue is to convince consumers to use the network provider's complementary offering.[140] As we saw above, online advertising rates usually are set per 1,000 page views. Having more customers (and therefore more page views) results in higher advertising revenue even if the advertising rate stays the same. In view of the low marginal costs of serving an additional customer with content, applications, or a portal, the marginal advertising revenue from an additional customer in the complementary market probably will be larger than the marginal cost of serving that customer. Moreover, a larger customer base may enable the network provider to raise its per-customer advertising rate, thereby realizing even higher net gains. More customers make an online offering more attractive. If the number of interested advertisers grows more quickly than the amount of advertising space available, the advertising rate per customer may increase. As we saw above, the search-engine market exhibits such a network effect between the customer side and the advertiser side.[141]

Remember, though, that a network provider will have an incentive to exclude rivals in the complementary market from access to its Internet-service customers only if the increase in advertising profits from the larger number of customers in the complementary product outweighs the reduction in profit in the market for Internet services.

A similar argument applies to the variant of this exception, described above,[142] in which a network provider excludes Internet-telephony providers from access to its Internet-service customers in order to preserve the outside revenue from access charges associated with traditional long-distance calls. This strategy will also be profitable even if the provider does not exclude the Internet-telephony providers from its customers completely. Access charges are per-call charges set by regulators, and can still be charged even if some long-distance customers are lost. Every long-distance call lost to an Internet-telephony provider reduces profits; thus, the more conventional long-distance calls the network provider manages to keep, the higher its profits.

Monopoly Preservation in the Complementary Market In the "monopoly preservation in the complementary market" exception outlined above,[143] the network provider excludes rival producers of a complementary product from access to its Internet-service customers in order to preserve a legally acquired monopoly in the complementary market. This analysis assumes that the monopolist will be able to keep its rivals out of the nationwide market by excluding them from access to its Internet-service customers. Even if the monopolist is not large enough to keep its rivals out of the complementary market completely, exclusion from a part of the market may put them at a competitive disadvantage by making them operate at a less efficient scale or with a smaller network. Relative to a world without exclusion, this may slow the erosion of the network provider's monopoly in the complementary market, extending the length of time that it can charge monopoly profits.[144]

Network Provider Faces Competition in the Market for Internet Services

To this point, we have assumed that the network provider is at least a local monopolist in the market for Internet services. This assumption aligns with standard economic thinking about vertical exclusionary conduct in complementary markets: according to economic theory, an economic actor without monopoly power in the primary market will be incapable of excluding competitors from the complementary market by using vertical practices such as tying, vertical mergers, or exclusive dealing.[145] A monopoly in the primary market is therefore considered an indispensable precondition for successful monopolization of the secondary market.[146]

On this theory, it is not surprising that most of the literature on vertical exclusionary conduct in markets for complementary products focuses on exclusionary conduct by monopolists. After all, the same conduct is not likely to pose any significant anti-competitive threat if the firm faces competition in the primary market.[147] This theory has also shaped economists' evaluation of existing firms' behavior in a complementary market. Allegations of anti-competitive conduct in a secondary market are often countered by evidence that the accused firm does not have monopoly power in the primary market.[148] Alternatively, the analysis of the monopoly case is used as an argument *a maiore ad minus*: if a monopolist in the primary market lacks the ability and incentive to impede competition in the secondary market, it is argued, then a competitive firm's conduct will pose even less of a threat.[149]

Based on this line of reasoning, most commentators believe that the threat of discrimination against independent providers of complementary products can be mitigated by competition in the market for Internet services.[150] Stated differently, it is usually assumed that competition in the market for Internet services will restrict a network operator's ability and incentive to discriminate against independent content, portals, or applications. As we saw above, this assumption is the basis of the proposal to increase facilities-based competition and the proposal to introduce open-access regulation (regulation that would require the owners of broadband networks to allow independent ISPs to offer their services over these networks), both of which seek to mitigate the threat of discrimination by increasing competition in the Internet-services market.

The following analysis shows that the above assumption is not correct. A network provider may have the ability and incentive to exclude rival content, applications, or portals from its network, even if it faces limited competition[151] in the market for Internet services.[152] Apart from increasing the number of cases in which unaffiliated providers of complementary products face a real threat of discrimination, this result also implies that neither facilities-based competition nor open-access regulation is an appropriate tool for mitigating this threat.[153] Three arguments drive this conclusion. First, in the Internet context, the ability to exclude competitors from a complementary market (the market for a particular application, content, or portal) is not dependent on a monopoly position in the primary market (the market for Internet services). Instead, the power to exclude is conferred by network technology. Second, realizing the benefits of exclusion (an increase in profits—or, sometimes, a preservation of current profits) does not require monopolizing the primary market. The absence of a monopoly in the primary market actually increases the network provider's incentive to increase profits through exclusionary conduct in the complementary market, since the provider cannot extract the available monopoly profit by charging higher prices in the primary market. Third, owing to the existence of switching costs or to the network provider's ability to discriminate rather than exclude, the exclusion of rivals will not necessarily cause the network provider's Internet-service customers to switch providers, and that makes the costs of exclusion lower than is commonly assumed. As we will see, these factors confer a degree of market power on the network provider, making competition in the market for Internet services less effective.

The following analysis assumes that the network provider competes with at least one other network provider.[154] In addition, the network provider may offer content or applications. A particular application or particular content may be offered to all consumers or exclusively to the customers of the network provider's own Internet service.

Ability to Exclude In our hypothetical network, as in today's Internet, a network provider can distinguish between different applications and different content running over its network, and can control their execution. This technology lets network provider exclude selected complementary products or slow their execution.

Although the exclusionary power of the technology does not extend beyond the provider's network, exclusion from the provider's Internet-service customers may drive rival producers of a complementary product from the nationwide market for that product if economies of scale or network effects are operating.[155] Whether rivals will be driven from the market is contingent on the size of the economies of scale with respect to the complementary product in question, on the strength of any network effects with respect to that product, and on the numbers of the monopolist's Internet-service customers and the customers of other network providers.[156] Thus, in this context, the ability to drive competitors from the nationwide market for the complementary product depends on the network provider's nationwide market share in the Internet-services market. Again, a monopoly position in this market is not required.

Benefits of Exclusion In a variety of cases, exclusionary conduct will increase, or preserve, a network provider's profits in the complementary market. This effect does not require a monopoly in the market for Internet services, nor, as we saw above, does it require the network provider to gain a monopoly in the complementary market.[157] Instead, the lack of monopoly in the primary market constrains the network provider's ability to extract profits in the Internet-services market, making the opportunity to realize profits in the complementary market even more attractive. As a result, exclusion may be profitable more often than is commonly assumed.

In general, if a network provider excludes rival producers of a complementary product from access to its Internet-service customers, it will increase the sales of its own complementary product.[158] As was explained above, this increase in sales often leads to an increase in profits. In the cases outlined above, the increase in profits results from more sales, not from the ability to charge monopoly profits. Thus, to be profitable, the exclusionary conduct need not drive rivals from the complementary market entirely.

More Sales at Market Prices   In the "more sales at market prices" exception,[159] the increase in profits resulting from the higher number of sales in the complementary market was driven by the specific cost structure of the markets for applications, content, or portals. These markets are characterized by high fixed costs and low marginal costs and this cost structure is not affected by the existence of market power in the market for Internet services.[160]

More Outside Revenue   In the "more outside revenue" exception, the increase in profits resulted from the logic of pricing in the advertising markets.[161] The network provider realized higher outside revenue by selling access to a large group of its Internet-service customers directly instead of letting rival producers of complementary products sell access to smaller groups of customers and then extracting the outside revenue from the rivals. Again, no monopoly is required.

There is evidence that some Internet service providers do, in fact, try to reduce the amount of time their customers spend on content or portal offerings not affiliated with their service. For example, in the AOL–Time Warner merger proceeding, the FCC found that "[t]he record in this proceeding provides some evidence that AOL already seeks to limit its members' access to unaffiliated content on the World Wide Web. For example, AOL requires that content appearing on AOL web sites have only a limited number of hyperlinks to unaffiliated content."[162] This made it more likely that a user who clicked on a link within the AOL portal remained within the AOL portal, where AOL benefited from the advertising revenue or sales commissions generated by this user.

In the variant of this exception,[163] the network provider was interested in excluding VoIP providers from access to its customers because it could charge access charges only for long-distance calls placed using the conventional telephone service, not for those using VoIP. (Access charges are per-call charges set by regulation; they do not depend on a monopoly in the market for Internet services.)

Monopoly Preservation in the Complementary Market   In the "monopoly preservation in the complementary market" exception,[164] the ability to preserve the monopoly depended on the exact size of economies of scale, the strength of potential network effects, and the nationwide number of both the monopolist's Internet-service customers and the customers of other network providers. A monopoly in the market for Internet services was not required.

Costs of Exclusion   Relative to the monopoly case, the existence of other, competing network providers may increase the costs of exclusionary behavior in the complementary market. Owing to the ability to use discrimination instead of exclusion and the existence of switching costs, the costs of exclusion will still be lower than is commonly assumed.[165]

If the network provider is the only supplier of Internet service in a particular geographic area, consumers have no other way to get access to the excluded application or content. Here, the costs of the exclusionary behavior are twofold. First, owing to the reduction in the variety of applications and content, consumers may value the network provider's Internet service less without the exclusion, which may force the network provider to reduce the price of its Internet service.[166] Second, without being able to use the excluded application or content, some consumers may not value the network provider's Internet service enough to pay the lower price.[167] Because the pricing of the service already reflects the reduced value, the number of lost transport customers will probably not be high.

If the provider competes with at least one other network provider, consumers who want access to the excluded application may switch providers. As these consumers do not have to forgo Internet services altogether, the number of lost transport customers will probably be higher than if the excluding network provider faces no competition. Thus, competition increases the costs of exclusionary behavior in the complementary market.[168]

The market for Internet services, however, exhibits a number of characteristics that make competition less effective than is commonly assumed.[169] These factors may limit the costs of exclusionary behavior in spite of competition in the market for Internet services.

First, if the exclusionary conduct drives the producers of the excluded application or content from the market, switching providers will not give consumers access to the excluded product. As a result, fewer consumers will switch as a result of the exclusion.[170]

Second, if all network providers block the same application, there is no provider for consumers to switch to. (For example, in many countries all mobile network providers block Internet-telephony applications to protect their revenue from mobile voice services, leaving customers who would like to use Internet telephony over their wireless Internet connection with no network provider to turn to.)

Third, the network provider may be able to engage in exclusionary conduct without losing too many of its Internet-service customers by using discrimination instead of direct exclusion. For example, it may slow a specific application instead of blocking it.[171] If the network provider blocks a certain complementary product, its Internet-service customers are not able to use the application or to access the blocked content, and they will notice this interference. In contrast, if the network provider merely slows a specific product, its customers may not notice that the network provider is discriminating against specific complementary products, and therefore will see no reason to switch to another provider. If a network provider discriminates against a rival's complementary product by slowing it, the discrimination will work indirectly. Consumers' use of the rival's product will be less satisfactory than their use of the provider's offering, and this will lower their perception of the quality of the rival's product. Because many consumers will not be able to detect the true cause of the lower quality, they may attribute it to poor design. For example, a slow gaming experience might be attributable to bad application programming, insufficient server capacity at the gaming site, or slow Internet transport. The results would look identical to most consumers. Similarly, long waiting times for pages from an online shop could result from bad programming of the underlying databases or from insufficient server speed. Customers may blame the online shop, especially if they do not usually have problems with network speed. With discrimination, consumers can choose the rival's product, but they prefer the network provider's product because they perceive it to be of higher quality. Unlike customers who face direct technical exclusion or tying, customers who face discrimination will not think their choice has been restricted. Thus, by using discrimination, a network provider can exploit customers' incomplete information about the true source of poor performance. That customers' having imperfect information can provide market power to an economic actor who faces competition in the primary market by enabling the actor to impose restrictions in a complementary market that it would not be able to sustain if the primary market was perfectly competitive is well established in the economics literature.[172] Recent behavior by Comcast, the largest provider of broadband over cable in the United States,[173] indicates that network providers do, indeed, use discrimination in the manner just described. Comcast surreptitiously interfered with the operation of BitTorrent, a popular peer-to-peer file-sharing application, on its network. Instead of announcing that it did so, or consistently blocking the use of the application, Comcast sent forged data packets (i.e., packets that look as if they were sent by the other end host) to both end hosts involved in a connection, telling them to sever the connection. As a result, both end hosts terminated the BitTorrent connection. In some cases, this merely delayed a connection; in other cases, it prevented a file from transferring.[174] By using forged packets, Comcast hid its interference with the connection from users. When asked (by a reporter, and later by the Electronic Frontier Foundation) whether Comcast was interfering with BitTorrent, Comcast representatives stated that Comcast "isn't deliberately blocking, degrading, interfering with, or discriminating against particular protocols or kinds of traffic [and] isn't using network management techniques that are designed to disrupt anyone's use of Bit-Torrent (or any other application)."[175] As a result, users, journalists and public-interest organizations had to expend considerable technical effort to understand what Comcast was doing and trace BitTorrent's unusual behavior back to Comcast's intervention. As white papers produced by Sandvine (the equipment vendor Comcast was using) show, Sandvine (and Comcast, by using the equipment in this way) chose this method of interference to prevent customers from noticing it.[176] The use of file-sharing applications is an important driver for broadband adoption, and network providers do not want to lose customers who wish to use file-sharing applications.[177] In sum, if the network provider discriminates against rival products instead of excluding them directly, competition in the market for Internet services does not increase the costs of the exclusionary conduct.

Fourth, even if the network provider's Internet-service customers know that the provider is restricting their access to applications, content, or portals, the cost and time involved in switching Internet services may still prevent many consumers from changing providers.[178]

Switching costs are the costs a customer incurs when switching to a competitor.[179] When deciding whether to switch, customers take these costs into account. A consumer will switch if the present value of switching is larger than the present value of staying with his or her current provider. Switching costs reduce the present value of switching, which reduces customers' willingness to switch (as compared to a world without switching costs). Switching costs make consumers' demand less elastic, enabling a provider to charge a higher price.[180] Similarly, switching costs allow a provider to impose other restrictions that it could not impose in a perfectly competitive market. Whether these costs will prevent a customer from switching depends on the value the customer places on the excluded application and on the magnitude of the switching costs. The higher the switching costs, the fewer customers a network provider loses as a result of its exclusionary conduct.[181]

Switching costs may be substantial in the market for Internet services. Consider first the obvious financial expenses that may be associated with switching providers. A customer who has a long-term contract with a provider will be charged a termination fee.[182] When switching from a broadband-over-cable service to a digital-subscriber-line (DSL) service, a consumer will be charged for installation and will have to buy a DSL modem and other new equipment. If (as is common in the United States) the Internet service is bundled with television and telephony, cancellation of the Internet-service portion of the bundle may result in a loss, or a partial loss, of the bundle discount, and the loss of that discount may then be a significant ongoing financial cost for the consumer.[183]

Further, switching providers may require a customer to invest a significant amount of time and effort. She will have to open an account with the new provider and close her account with her present provider.[184] If she cannot install the access hardware and software herself (which takes time and expertise), she must stay at home for the installation. If she has used other provider-specific offerings available only to her old provider's Internet-service customers (e.g., stock portfolio tracking, instant messaging, or customized news pages), she will have to find alternative offerings and customize them. If she has been using an e-mail address offered by the network provider, she will have to notify various people of her new e-mail address, perhaps have new stationery and business cards printed, update her résumé and her website, and bear the risk of missing e-mail messages sent to the old address.[185] The precise cost of switching e-mail addresses is difficult to measure, but anecdotal evidence indicates that customers view it as substantial. The *New York Times* reported in 2005 that AOL had about 5 million customers who paid $14.95 per month in order to keep using an AOL e-mail address even though they had switched to another broadband-access provider and paid Internet-service fees to the new provider.[186]

In addition, the Internet-service offerings of various providers differ substantially in price, quality, and other characteristics. Therefore, they are not interchangeable. For example, broadband cable networks have different technical characteristics than DSL networks, which differ from broadband offerings provided over fiber networks. Switching in response to the exclusion of a complementary product would require a customer to switch from his most preferred offering to another offering that may meet fewer of his needs.

The trend toward bundling differentiates the market further. Cable customers may not think of the digital or satellite television service offered by phone networks as a perfect substitute for their cable television; on the other hand, customers of a conventional telephony provider may not trust the digital telephony offered by cable companies. Though it is possible to switch only the Internet service and keep the other offerings, this will significantly reduce the bundle discount. The problem is further exacerbated if the network provider offers exclusive content that is valuable to the customer.[187] For example, Deutsche Telekom currently has the exclusive right to transmit games of the Bundesliga, the premier German soccer league, over the Internet.[188] If it offered the streaming of Bundesliga games exclusively to its Internet-service customers, soccer fans would have to value the ability to use the excluded applications at least as much as the opportunity to watch soccer games over the Internet.[189] Thus, product differentiation in the market for Internet services and in the market for bundles of telephony, television, and Internet gives network providers an additional degree of market power over their Internet-service customers.[190]

The exact costs of switching may depend on the circumstances. For example, some customers may use provider-independent e-mail services, such as Hotmail or Gmail; others may not subscribe to a bundle at all. The details of contracts vary too. For example, some customers are not subject to a long-term contract, or a competing provider may wave the installation fee. In countries with open-access regulation where regulation allows independent Internet service providers to offer their services over other providers' networks, customers may be able to switch to another provider that offers its services over the same physical network; that removes the need to buy new equipment.

A particular Internet customer may face any combination of the switching costs discussed above. And every customer has to go through the process of choosing an alternative provider and installing and setting up the access software. These hurdles alone may suffice to deter switching. The cost of searching for and comparing alternative offerings is an important switching cost. Moreover, empirical studies show that the decision to switch depends on the perceived costs of switching, which are not necessarily equivalent to the actual costs. Empirical studies in the UK's market for long-distance telephone service have shown that providers were significantly more likely to retain dissatisfied customers who perceived the switching costs as high than dissatisfied customers who perceived them as low.[191] According to empirical studies in the long-distance and credit-card industries, the perceived costs of switching are significantly increased if the product is perceived as complex, if it has a large number of features, or if it is bundled with other products.[192] Thus, customers in an industry whose services are viewed as complex and are characterized by many features and by bundles, such as Internet services, will perceive switching costs as high.

Finally, research in behavioral economics indicates that even very small costs may prevent customers from switching. Individuals exhibit a "status quo bias"—they are much more likely to keep what they already have than rational-choice theory would predict.[193] For example, this bias is exploited by free trials that automatically convert to a paid subscription at the end of the trial period unless the customer calls or writes to prevent this.[194] If, however, the costs of placing a call or writing a letter are sufficient to prevent people from acting, the significantly higher actual (or perceived) costs of switching Internet service providers may prevent many Internet service customers from switching providers, even if their Internet service provider excludes applications or content they would like to use.

The problem of incomplete customer information is reduced by rules that require network providers to disclose whether, and how, they interfere with applications and content on their networks. But such regulations cannot reduce the perceived or actual switching costs in the market for Internet services and still leave the network provider with substantial market power over its customers—power that enables it to restrict some applications and content without losing too many customers. Similarly, while open access regulations may reduce some of the costs of switching (since customers may not have to switch to another network technology), the costs are still substantial enough to prevent customers from switching in response to exclusion. This suggests that neither disclosure requirements nor open access regulations may be sufficient to mitigate network providers' incentives to discriminate, even if they are competing with at least one other network provider.[195]

Other Incentives to Discriminate or Exclude

Discrimination to Control Bandwidth   Network providers may also have an incentive to block applications so as to control the use of bandwidth on their networks.[196] Networks are designed with certain patterns of use in mind. For example, "last-mile" networks (the networks that connect users' premises to their network provider) usually offer much more bandwidth from the Internet to the home than from the home to the Internet. This design is based on the assumption that users will receive much more data than they send. As we saw in chapter 2, this reflects the demands of client-server applications (such as Web browsing) that were the dominant application class at the time when asymmetric bandwidth was deployed, but creates problems for peer-to-peer applications such as file sharing, video conferencing, Internet telephony, or online gaming, which send and receive equal amounts of data. The design of today's last-mile networks also assumes that users' patterns of Internet use differ enough to enable a number of users to share the connection. The models assume that people don't all use the Internet at the same time, and that even if they do the traffic will be "bursty"—that is, will exhibit uneven patterns. On the basis of these considerations, the link between the cable modem at the end user's home and the provider's cable modem termination system (which communicates with subscribers' cable modems to give them access to the Internet) is shared by a number of users; the exact number is determined by the access provider on the basis of statistical calculations about expected use.[197] If users behave as expected, they will get the predicted bandwidth. If all these users want to use the maximum advertised bandwidth at the same time, they will not be able to get it—a phenomenon known as "oversubscription."

If Internet use increases, or if the patterns of use differ from the expected patterns, the performance of the network may worsen. To restore lost performance, the network provider may have to invest in additional bandwidth capacity in its network, incurring an increase in capital expenses. Higher-than-expected Internet use may also increase a provider's operational costs. If the traffic leaves the provider's network, the provider may have to pay higher interconnection fees to the networks that further transport the traffic.[198]

If use of the Internet increases, or if the patterns of use change, network providers may have an incentive to block or slow certain applications so as to maintain the performance of their network while avoiding the higher costs associated with network upgrades or higher interconnection fees. This incentive may be especially strong if the provider's Internet-service business is based on flat-rate pricing.[199] Because the provider's Internet-service customers pay the same price regardless of the amount of data they send and receive, increased use drives up the provider's costs, but not its revenue.

For example, in 2007 Comcast was shown to interfere with Gnutella, BitTorrent, and other file-sharing applications in a way that slowed or stopped file sharing.[200] Peer-to-peer file-sharing applications challenge traditional assumptions about use: they often send and receive continuous streams of data over longer periods of time (violating the assumption that traffic will be bursty, discontinuous and asymmetric), and they often download or upload data to and from computers on other networks (increasing the network provider's interconnection charges).[201] The Comcast example offers a number of insights. First, it invalidates the common argument that providers would refrain from blocking or excluding applications or content on the notion that more applications and content make the network more attractive. Peer-to-peer file sharing is one of the most popular applications on broadband networks and an important driver for broadband adoption.[202] This did not stop Comcast from blocking these applications; it only motivated Comcast to do so secretly.[203] Second, it demonstrates that discrimination or exclusion may happen even if the network provider does not have a monopoly in the market for Internet services; in many US cities, Comcast competes with the local telephone company that offers DSL. As we saw above, using methods that are difficult to detect reduces the likelihood that customers will switch to another Internet service providers in response to the blocking, since they do not realize that their network provider interferes with the application.

The incident has also fueled the debate over network neutrality in the United States. Many network-neutrality proposals, as well as the Internet Policy Statement adopted by the Federal Communications Commission in 2005,[204] contain an exception for reasonable network management. Proponents of network neutrality claim that singling out specific applications to manage bandwidth on a network is not reasonable network management and should be forbidden under a network-neutrality regime. They do not dispute that network providers may have to engage in traffic management to manage bandwidth on their networks, but they argue that traffic-management techniques should be non-discriminatory.[205] Opponents of network neutrality would like to exempt any practices employed to manage bandwidth on the network, even if the network provider applies them only to a specific application or even a specific application provider.[206] In August 2008, after a complaint and a petition for a declaratory ruling that Comcast's conduct violates the FCC's Internet Policy Statement by public-interest groups and academics (including the author of this book), the FCC ruled that Comcast's conduct did not constitute "reasonable network management" and that it violated the Internet Policy Statement.[207] Comcast has appealed the decision.

Content-Based Discrimination   A network provider may also have an incentive to block, or discriminate against, certain content. For example, providers may have an incentive to block messages harmful to the company's interests. For example, in July 2005, Telus, Canada's second-largest Internet service provider, blocked access to the "Voices for Change" website. At the time, Telus and the Telecommunications Workers Union were involved in a contentious labor dispute, and the "Voices for Change" site, run by a union member,[208] offered online discussion forums for union employees to discuss strategies during the strike. Telus argued that online posts suggesting that striking workers jam Telus's phone lines hurt the company, and that the site's inclusion of pictures of employees crossing picket lines threatened the privacy and safety of these employees. The company restored access to the site after it had obtained "an injunction that prohibited the posting of photos that might intimidate or threaten anyone connected with the dispute."[209] (See box 6.6.)

In April 2006, AOL's e-mail servers temporarily blocked e-mails that contained the URL "dearaol.com."[210] Dearaol.com had been set up by an alliance of nonprofit and public-interest groups organized by MoveOn.org (a liberal advocacy group) and the Electronic Frontier Foundation (an Internet civil-liberties group) in order to protest AOL's plans to adopt CertifiedEmail, a program that would have required high-volume e-mail senders to pay fees in exchange for guaranteed preferred delivery and circumvention of spam filters. The site contained an open letter to AOL and an online petition that users could sign to protest CertifiedEmail. AOL later attributed the blocking to a "software glitch" and removed it within a day.

Network providers may also have an incentive to impose other restrictions on the content transported over their network. For example, in September 2007, Verizon Wireless rejected a request by NARAL Pro-Choice America, an abortion-rights group, to let it send text messages over Verizon Wireless's network using a five-digit code.[211] If Verizon Wireless had granted the request, Verizon Wireless's customers could have sent a short text message to this code to sign up for messages from NARAL; NARAL periodically sends text messages to those who have signed up to inform them about pressing issues or to ask them to take political action. Other wireless providers had complied with NARAL's request, but Verizon Wireless rejected it, arguing that it "does not accept issue-oriented (abortion, war, etc.) programs" and that it would refuse service to "any organization that seeks to promote an agenda or distribute content that, in its discretion, may be seen as controversial or unsavory to any of our users." After the *New York Times* reported the incident in a front-page article, Verizon Wireless reversed its decision, noting that the decision was based on an

Box 6.6
The Telus Incident—A Case of Justified Self-Help?

According to a letter written by a lawyer representing the union member who operated the website Voices for Change, the site contained some content that would have justified an injunction.[a] However, this does not justify the blocking of the site. There are very clear legal procedures (such as getting a court order to get the content removed) for realizing that goal. Every person or entity threatened by online information needs to follow these procedures. A network provider should not have different rights just because it is technically able to engage in some sort of self-help. In fact, the Telus case highlights some of the reasons why network providers should not be allowed to engage in self-help through blocking.

First, in comparison with an injunction, blocking is both over-inclusive and under-inclusive. According to investigations by the OpenNet Initiative at the time of the blocking, by banning access to the IP address of the server on which the website was hosted, Telus not only blocked access to Voices for Change; it also blocked access to 766 other websites hosted on the same server.[b] And blocking Voices for Change affected not only the illegal content but also the many legitimate discussions that were taking place on the site.[c] At the same time, the blocking wasn't an effective way of preventing access to the illegal information; it merely prevented customers of Telus's Internet service (and customers of ISPs who were downstream from Telus) from accessing the site directly. Even Telus's customers were still able to get access through a proxy site or one of the mirror sites that had been set up.

Second, the relevant legal rules assign the right to decide which content is illegal to a court that has no interest in the matter. As the case of Telus shows, an entity whose own interests are at stake may have an incentive to interpret more liberally what should be removed. Telus consistently justified the blocking not just with the threat to employees' safety, but also with the online discussions about jamming Telus's customer service lines that were taking place on the site.[d] These additional concerns related to Telus's business interests featured prominently in other statements by the company.[e] However, neither the settlement with the operator of the website nor the injunction against the Telecommunications Workers Union that Telus obtained in court addressed these business-related concerns. Though there may be other reasons, this suggests that these concerns were not able to withstand judicial scrutiny.

All this suggests that, while there was some illegal content on Voices for Change, blocking the site was not the right method to get it removed.

a. Letter by McGrady, p. 2 (Penmachine 2005b).
b. OpenNet Initiative 2005.
c. Letter by McGrady, p. 2 (Penmachine 2005b).
d. CBC News 2005.
e. See the letters cited in Penmachine 2005a.

"incorrect interpretation of a dusty internal policy" against spam messaging and receiving unwanted messages. Verizon Wireless maintained that it had a right to decide what messages to transmit. Though this incident concerns a service offered over the wireless mobile network, not over the wireless mobile Internet, an analogous motivation could be attributed to Internet service providers.

In August 2007, AT&T deleted some lyrics from a webcast of a Pearl Jam concert at the Lollapalooza festival in Chicago: "George Bush, leave this world alone" and "George Bush, find yourself another home." The webcast was streamed through AT&T's website "The Blue Room," which offers webcasts of live concerts. AT&T, through an agency, hires contractors to monitor the performances. The live webcasts are delayed for a few moments to enable the contractors to censor material that violates AT&T's content policy. AT&T later called the Pearl Jam incident "a mistake." According to an AT&T spokesman, AT&T's "policy is not to edit or censor performances." The contractors are "told only to edit for excessive profanity, not really for the songs, but the banter going on between band members or band members and the audiences, as well as any nudity that can arise" in order to protect younger visitors to the website.[212] Though this is not a direct example of a network provider restricting content on its network (AT&T acted in its role as a content provider at the application layer), it is easy to imagine a virtually identical incident in which a provider enacts a content policy and restricts content that flows through its network.

The last two examples illustrate the two types of problems associated with content policies. First, the content policies themselves may prevent end users from accessing certain content and prevent affected content producers from reaching their audience (as in the Verizon Wireless example). In addition, enforcement of the content policy may result in deliberate or inadvertent misclassifications, resulting in the exclusion of additional content (as in the AT&T example).

A number of states require their network providers to block access to content that the state singles out.[213] Mainly, this includes political content perceived as posing a threat to the current government or to national security, social content perceived to violate local norms and morals, and content describing or providing access to Internet tools that could be used to circumvent restrictions imposed by the state. For example, Bahrain, China, Ethiopia, Libya, Iran, Myanmar, Pakistan, Saudi Arabia, Syria, Thailand, Tunisia, Uzbekistan, and Vietnam all block websites that report on political opposition to the existing government. Many countries in the Middle East, including Iran, Oman, Saudi Arabia, Sudan, Tunisia, and the United Arab Emirates, also filter extensively for content deemed to be religiously, culturally, or socially inappropriate (e.g., content related to pornography, dating, homosexuality, or gaming).

Conclusion on Ability to Discriminate

Although a network provider does not generally have an incentive to discriminate against independent providers of applications or content, the analysis above has highlighted a number of cases in which it may have an incentive to do so in order to increase or preserve its profits, manage bandwidth on its network, or exclude unwanted content. A network provider may have an incentive to discriminate even when it faces competition, not only when it has a local monopoly in the market for Internet services.

Whether the conditions giving rise to such an incentive are present in a real-life situation is a question for empirical inquiry. In most cases, however, the network provider need not gain a monopoly in the complementary market to make exclusion a profitable strategy; thus, the threat of discrimination is more relevant than is commonly assumed.

In most cases, a network provider need not exclude all independent developers of complementary products from its network in order to increase profits. Often it will be profitable to exclude only the complementary products that compete directly with one of the provider's own products.[214] This reduces the costs of exclusion, as the reduction in complementary goods variety is restricted to the products that are actually excluded.

Owing to the specific characteristics of markets for applications and content (such as the cost structure of information goods and—sometimes—the existence of network effects), the exclusion of rivals may lead to gains significantly higher than the gains that can be achieved in traditional markets. As a result, it is more likely that gains from exclusion will exceed associated costs, which makes it more likely that exclusion is a profitable strategy.[215]

Effect on Incentives to Innovate

The preceding subsection highlighted conditions under which a network provider in our hypothetical discriminatory network, and in today's Internet, may have an incentive to exclude independent producers of applications, content, or portals from access to its Internet-service customers. When these conditions are present, independent producers of complementary products face a real threat of discrimination.

The threat of discrimination reduces the amount of application-level innovation by independent producers of complementary products in three ways.

First, when the conditions for profitable exclusion outlined above are present in a particular complementary market, a network provider will discriminate against rivals in that market. As was noted above, discrimination will reduce a rival's profits.[216] A potential innovator bases its decision to innovate on the expected costs and benefits of realizing the innovation; a potential innovator in an affected market will expect lower profits if it anticipates discrimination.

Second, the profitability of exclusion depends on many factors that may not be common knowledge for all participants in a market. As a result, an economic actor with an idea for a complementary product may not know whether a network provider will have an incentive to discriminate against the innovator's final product.[217] As a result, potential innovators face uncertainty about their future competitive environment. This uncertainty may reduce a risk-averse developer's incentive to innovate, even when the factual conditions for profitable exclusion are not present.

Third, the above analysis suggests that independent producers of complementary products need not be concerned that a network provider will exclude their products in order to increase its profits if it does not offer a competing product. (As we saw above, a network provider's incentive to exclude applications or content to manage bandwidth or to exclude unwanted content is independent of whether the network provider offers a similar complementary product.) This seems to imply innovation will be harmed only if the provider is already vertically integrated into a complementary market. But economic theory shows that this is not correct.[218] Even if the provider does not currently offer a competing product, it may be tempted to let the entrant "test the waters" and then—if the entrant begins to achieve success—imitate the entrant and exclude it from the network. Foreseeing this course of events, the independent producer refrains from entering the market. As a result, no one enters the complementary market. (There is a region of forgone invention in which privately and socially beneficial innovations are not realized.)

For the third problem to occur, three conditions must be realized.[219] First, demand in the complementary market must be uncertain. Second, in the presence of demand uncertainty, entry into the complementary market must be attractive for the independent producer but not for the primary-good monopolist (e.g., owing to cost heterogeneity). Third, the

primary-good monopolist must have a selling advantage in the complementary market.

In the context of the Internet, these conditions often are met. First, in
markets for new applications or content there usually is considerable
uncertainty in demand. Second, the literature of economics and business
strategy highlights several reasons why an incumbent network provider
may not have an incentive to enter a complementary market for a new
product in the presence of uncertain demand, whereas an independent
producer may have such an incentive. (For example, start-ups often have
lower entry costs than an incumbent, owing to the different cost structure
of incumbents and new entrants.[220]) Third, the ability to technically
exclude a rival producer of complementary products from its network
provides the network provider with a huge selling advantage in the complementary market. Thus, the number of markets in which independent
developers' incentives to innovate are reduced will be larger than the
exceptions outlined above imply.

In an end-to-end network, technical exclusion is not a strategy available
to network providers. As a result, independent developers of complementary products need not fear discrimination or technical exclusion. Consequently, their incentives to innovate will be higher than in a discriminatory
network.

Whereas the threat of discrimination reduces independent developers'
incentive to innovate at the application level, network providers' incentives to innovate at this level rise as a result of the increase in profit that
discrimination brings. As we will see in chapter 8, under the conditions
present in today's Internet the increase in application-level innovation by
network providers cannot offset the reduction in innovation by independent producers. Thus, the threat of discrimination reduces the amount of
application-level innovation.

These insights have important implications for the current policy debate
regarding the regulation of broadband network providers. The analysis in
this chapter has highlighted a variety of circumstances under which a
network provider may have the ability and an incentive to exclude, or
discriminate against, independent content, portals, or applications. Thus,
there is a real threat that network providers will engage in this kind of
conduct, and that threat bolsters arguments made by proponents of regulation. Contrary to common belief, however, this threat is not necessarily
mitigated by competition in the Internet-services market. Rather, as the
analysis in this section has shown, a network provider may have an incentive to exclude or discriminate even if it faces competition. This finding

suggests that neither increased facilities-based competition nor open-access regulation is an appropriate policy response to that threat. Finally, a network provider may have an incentive to discriminate against unaffiliated applications or content even if they do not compete with one of its own applications—for example, to manage bandwidth on its network, or to exclude unwanted content. This makes it less likely that existing antitrust rules can protect innovators from all discriminatory conduct that may occur.[221]

Effect on Pricing Strategies

The difference in application awareness and application control between a network based on the broad version of the end-to-end arguments and the hypothetical network in my analysis enables the network provider in the latter network to pursue three pricing strategies not available in the former network. First, a network provider in a discriminatory network can charge end users different transport prices for different applications. Second, a provider in a discriminatory network can use its power to exclude applications to price discriminate between Internet-service customers. Third, a provider in a discriminatory network may be able to charge application and content providers to have their applications and content function on its network.

Price Differentiation

In a discriminatory network, the network provider can monitor which applications run. As a result, it can set different individual transport prices for each application.[222] In contrast, an end-to-end network is application-blind; a network provider cannot base transport prices on the application being used, only on observable characteristics such as bandwidth. Thus, in end-to-end networks there will be a single transport price[223] for all applications.

Whereas a provider operating a discriminatory network can set a transport price for each application to maximize transport revenue from that application, a provider in an end-to-end network can only maximize the overall transport revenue from all applications.[224] As a result, the network provider in an end-to-end network may be forced to forgo consumer surplus from use of a single application to capture more consumer surplus from all applications. For this reason, a provider in an end-to-end network can capture less (or, at most, the same) consumer surplus from a particular application than a provider in a discriminatory network.[225]

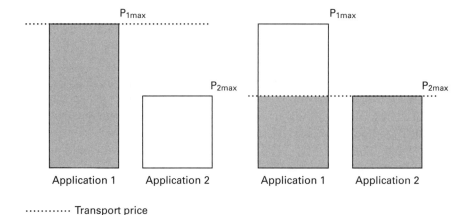

Figure 6.2
Options for setting a uniform transport price.

Consider a network with two applications that have equivalent band-width requirements. The network provider is a monopolist in the Internet-services market. The applications are competitively supplied at a price equal to marginal cost, which is assumed to be zero. Assume that consumers value the first application more than the second (figure 6.2).[226] In this example, the network provider in an end-to-end network has two options. One option is to forgo transport revenue from the second application and choose the highest possible transport price at which consumers are willing to use the first application. Let us call this price p_{1max}. At this price, the network provider captures all consumer surplus from the use of the first application but earns no transport revenue from the second application (figure 6.2, left). Alternatively, the network provider can set the transport price low enough to earn transport revenue from both applications. The resulting price is the highest possible transport price at which consumers are willing to use the second application. Call this price p_{2max}. This price enables the provider to earn transport revenue from both applications (figure 6.2, right). While the provider extracts all consumer surplus associated with the second application, it can only capture a fraction of the surplus that consumers derive from using the first application. As a result, consumers keep a surplus of $p_{1max} - p_{2max}$ with respect to the first application. The exact form of consumers' preferences will determine which strategy maximizes the network provider's profits.

In contrast, the network provider in a discriminatory network can choose different transport prices for the two applications: it sets the transport price for the first application at p_{1max} and the transport price for the second application at p_{2max}, gains transport revenue from both applications, and captures all consumer surplus. The resulting transport revenue is greater than the transport revenue under each of the options described above.

The difference in available pricing strategies has implications for application developers' incentives to innovate.[227] Consider the surplus a consumer would derive from a particular application if it paid for transport but got the application for free. If the application is offered in the end-to-end network at all,[228] this surplus is higher (or at least the same[229]) in an end-to-end network than in a discriminatory network. This surplus, however, denotes the maximum surplus an application developer can extract through its pricing of the application.

Thus, in an end-to-end network, more consumer surplus is available for extraction by application developers. Consequently, relative to a discriminatory network, an end-to-end network may earn application developers higher profits, thereby increasing their incentives to innovate.[230]

This analysis applies only if the network provider has some market power in the market for Internet services. If it does not have the ability to profitably raise the transport price above marginal cost, then the bandwidth-adjusted transport price—and, consequently, the consumer surplus available for extraction by application developers—will be the same in both networks.

Price Discrimination

Available Strategies The owner of a discriminatory network can also use its power to exclude applications from its network to price discriminate between customers. A provider in an end-to-end network lacks this option, since it cannot detect which applications run over its network and cannot control their execution.

Price discrimination can maximize profits by setting prices charged to different consumers on the basis of their individual willingness to pay.[231] Imagine two groups of potential customers. Group 1 has a low willingness to pay for the product; group 2 has a high willingness to pay. If the seller has to set a uniform price for all customers, it has two options: it can set a low price and sell to all customers, or it can set a high price and sell only to customers with a high willingness to pay. Which option is more profitable will depend on the sizes of the two groups and on their respective willingness to pay, but regardless of this the seller cannot capitalize on the differences between individual consumers' willingness to pay. In contrast, if it was able to charge members of group 1 a lower price than members of group 2 it could sell to each group of customers at their maximum willingness to pay, thus extracting more consumer surplus and earning more profit than if it had to charge a uniform price.

To practice price discrimination, a seller must have some market power (i.e., ability to profitably set price above marginal costs).[232] Otherwise, it would not be able to charge any consumer more than the competitive price. Thus, the network provider must be an oligopolist or a monopolist to use the following strategy.[233]

By excluding certain types of applications from its network and enabling their use for a higher price, a provider in a discriminatory network can practice "second-degree" price discrimination.[234] Under this type of discrimination, a seller knows that there are groups of consumers willing to pay different amounts, but the seller cannot identify which group an individual consumer belongs to. To deal with this, the seller offers products that differ in features and in price and that target different groups of consumers. The differences between products are designed to induce an individual consumer to choose the product intended for his or her group; the price for a product is based on the targeted group's willingness to pay.[235] As a result, the seller can capture more of each group's consumer surplus than if it sold only one good at a uniform price.

To practice second-degree price discrimination, a network provider may use consumers' eagerness to use specific types of applications as an indicator of consumers' willingness to pay for Internet services.[236] The provider offers two types of Internet service: a low-priced version that enables consumers to use the Internet but blocks a particular type of application, and a high-priced version that enables consumers to use all applications. If this strategy is to be used as a method of price discrimination, consumers' desire to use the blocked application must be positively correlated to their willingness to pay for Internet services (or, stated differently, the consumers eager to use the application must be those willing to pay high amounts for Internet services). Under these conditions, the provider can separate consumers into two groups willing to pay different amounts, thus allowing it to price different types of Internet service in a way that extracts as much surplus from each group as is possible.

To see how this might work, consider an example.[237] Telecommuters (employees who work from their homes) usually connect to the employer's computer system using an application called a *virtual private network*. In contrast, a typical home user, who uses the Internet in her free time to surf the Web and check e-mail, probably does not consider virtual private networks an essential element of Internet use. Additionally, telecommuters generally are willing to pay more than home users for Internet services. If a provider disables the use of virtual private networks in the "basic" version of Internet service and allows them in a "premium" version, telecommuters will choose the premium version, which can be priced to exploit their higher willingness to pay. Users who do not value the ability to use virtual private networks enough to pay for the premium version will choose the basic version. As a result, the network provider can capture more consumer surplus than if it was forced to offer only one version of Internet service at a uniform price.

This method does not require the provider to monopolize the complementary market. Customers of the "premium" service are free to use whatever application they prefer. The monopolist does not have to participate in the market for the "blocked" application; it simply blocks basic users from accessing applications that fall into this category.

Implications for Innovation   In a discriminatory network, but not in an end-to-end network, a network provider can use the strategy described above to price discriminate between consumers in the market for Internet services. The difference in available strategies affects application developers' incentives to innovate if their profits will be lower with discriminatory pricing than without it. This question hinges on detailed knowledge about consumers' preferences and market and cost structures, but some general observations are possible.[238]

We just saw that, relative to the profit-maximizing uniform price, the discriminatory pricing always increases the monopolist's profit from Internet services.[239]

Discriminatory pricing policies introduce distortion into the overall market for Internet applications by disadvantaging certain classes of applications.[240] Whereas developers of the blocked application can sell only to buyers of the premium version of Internet services, developers of other applications can sell to all Internet-service consumers. Thus, for producers of the blocked application, discriminatory pricing results in a smaller market—and potentially in lower profits. Their profits will be reduced if there are consumers of the basic version who would have bought the application if there was a uniform price for Internet services but who do not value it enough to pay the higher price for premium service in the non-uniform pricing scheme. These consumers are also worse off under the network provider's discriminatory pricing policy,[241] because they are not able to use an application that they value. Two conditions must be met for this situation to occur. First, there must be some consumers who choose the basic version of Internet services in the non-uniform pricing scheme and who are not priced out of the market for Internet services under the uniform price. These consumers buy Internet services under both pricing schemes, but are excluded from the market for the blocked application under the non-uniform pricing scheme. Second, under the uniform price for Internet services, it must be profitable for the blocked application's developers to sell their application to some of these consumers, using either a uniform or a non-uniform pricing scheme—for example, by offering a basic version to consumers with a low willingness to pay and a premium version targeted at consumers with a higher willingness to pay.[242]

In addition, the discriminatory pricing in the market for Internet services may decrease the profits of all applications' developers, because the non-uniform pricing scheme enables the network provider to capture more consumer surplus in the market for Internet services than if it was forced to charge a uniform price. As a result, the fraction of consumer surplus available for extraction in the complementary market will decrease.[243]

Charging Providers of Complementary Products
A network that deviates from the broad version of the end-to-end argument may also contain functionality that would let a network provider charge fees to providers of complementary products for the right to reach the provider's Internet-service customers. These fees could take many forms. For example, Comcast could charge Yahoo a one-time access fee for the right to be accessed by Comcast's Internet-service customers, Comcast could demand a share of the profits that Yahoo realizes from Comcast's Internet-service customers, or Comcast could charge a fee every time one of its Internet-service customers accesses Yahoo. The Internet does not currently offer the fine-grained accounting infrastructure that would be necessary to implement the last of these options, but a network provider may be able to implement some access charges using its ability to exclude: the network provider could threaten to exclude a specific application from its network unless the application's provider pays an access charge. Some network-neutrality proposals would ban these types of access charges.[244]

Network providers' ability to charge providers of complementary products for the right to be accessed by the network provider's Internet-service customers transforms the market for Internet access services into a two-sided market.[245] In such a market, one or more platforms (here, the Internet-service offerings) enable interactions between two types of users, which form the two sides of the market. In our case, Internet-service customers (one side of the market) would like to use applications or content, which are offered by providers of the complementary product (the other side of the market). Not every market that enables buyers and sellers to interact constitutes a two-sided market.[246] For a market to be two-sided, the volume of interactions between users on both sides must depend on the structure of fees charged each side, not only on the overall level of fees charged by the platform. This condition is met if users on one side of the market cannot directly pass on the fees charged by the platform provider (for example, because transaction costs prevent this). In the Internet context, application providers and content providers may not be able to pass network providers' access charges on to end users; the transaction costs associated with setting up and administering a payment infrastructure for micropayments on the content provider side, and entering payment-related information on the end-user side, may be prohibitively high.[247]

A complete analysis of the implications of network providers' ability to charge content or application providers is beyond the scope of this book; however, two observations can be offered. First, charging content or application providers enables network providers to directly extract some of the profits that application and content providers make, so this strategy directly reduces the profits of providers of applications and content. Second, research on two-sided markets indicates that the profits of these providers may be reduced disproportionately, because the network provider has an incentive to charge monopoly prices to them. The provision of Internet transport is a two-sided market in which end users are "single-homers" (that is, they are only connected to one network, their Internet access network), whereas application and content providers are "multi-homers" (they can reach customers on all access networks). The literature on two-sided markets predicts that in a market where one side is single-homing and the other is multi-homing, the platform owner (in our case, the network provider) will charge monopoly prices to the multi-homing side even if the platforms compete for the single-homers.[248] Thus, the literature predicts that network providers will charge monopoly prices to content and application providers even if there is competition on the end-user side of the market for Internet services.[249]

A platform owner has a terminating monopoly over access to its single-homing customers. This monopoly will exist whether or not single-homers have several platforms from which to choose. If a consumer gets his broadband access through AT&T, a content provider such as Yahoo can reach him only through the AT&T access network. This gives AT&T a monopoly over access to the consumer, which enables AT&T to charge monopoly prices to content and application providers even if AT&T is competing with other network providers for Internet-service customers.

Charging monopoly prices to content and application providers reduces their profits and may reduce their incentives to innovate below the social optimum.[250] If the resulting reduction in content innovation and application innovation reduces consumers' demand for Internet services, an individual network provider does not bear the full cost of this reduction; some of the reduced demand will affect competing network providers or network providers in other local markets. As a result, by increasing access charges for content providers, the network provider exerts a negative externality on other network providers that prevents it from fully internalizing the effect of higher access charges on content provision and leads it to set inefficiently high access charges.

If platforms compete for single-homers, this may affect how much of the monopoly profits that a platform makes on the multi-homing side will be passed on to the single-homing side, but it will not reduce the prices charged to multi-homers.[251] Thus, any problems that this pricing structure creates for the provision of content and applications will not be eliminated by increasing competition in the Internet-services market.

Conclusion on Pricing Strategies

A network provider in a discriminatory network can set different transport prices for different applications, and can also exclude applications from running over its network in order to price discriminate between customers. Additionally, a provider in a discriminatory network can charge content and application providers directly. These pricing strategies are not available in end-to-end networks.

Since these strategies may reduce the profits of independent developers of complementary products (relative to the profits they would earn in the absence of these strategies), the difference in available pricing strategies reduces independent developers' incentives to innovate. All strategies increase the profits of the network provider in the market for Internet services.

Conclusion

A discriminatory network offers network providers opportunities for strategic behavior against independent developers of complementary products, and increases the range of available pricing strategies in the market for Internet services.

Although a network provider does not generally have an incentive to discriminate against independent providers of content, applications, or portals, as this chapter has highlighted, in many circumstances a network provider has an incentive to use the power provided by the architecture to engage in noncooperative strategic behavior in order to increase its profits. In most cases, exclusion of all independent developers of complementary products is not necessary for a network provider to increase its profits. Instead, it will often be profitable to exclude complementary products that directly compete with one of its own complementary products. The network provider may also have an incentive to exclude complementary products that do not compete with one of its own products—for example, to manage bandwidth on its network or to exclude unwanted content. In any event, the exclusion will usually reduce or eliminate the profits of the producers of an excluded good.

Similarly, whereas the pricing strategies available in a discriminatory network are capable of increasing a network provider's profits, they usually reduce the profits of independent developers of complementary products, thus reducing their incentives to innovate.

A discriminatory network may enable a network provider to gain more profits in the market for Internet services or complementary products than an end-to-end architecture. The same strategies that increase the network provider's profits will usually reduce the profits of at least some independent developers of complementary products. Thus, independent developers of applications, portals, and content will tend to earn higher profits under an end-to-end architecture.

IV   The End-to-End Arguments and Application Innovation

7 Network Architectures and the Economic Environment for Application Innovation

Chapters 4–6 highlighted three mechanisms by which an architecture may influence economic actors' incentives and ability to innovate. By affecting the transaction and coordination costs associated with organizing initial component development and subsequent innovation in arm's-length relationships, an architecture affects the ability of independent economic actors other than system architects to innovate (chapter 5). An architecture's modifiability influences the cost of developing an innovation, which not only affects incentives to innovate but also may determine *who* can innovate (chapter 4). The range of strategies an architecture supports influences the potential benefits from innovating—and these potential benefits, in turn, affect the incentives to innovate (chapter 6). Chapters 4–6 also used these insights to examine the effect of the Internet's original architecture, highlighting the many ways in which an architecture can influence the economic environment for innovation. Together, these influences determine the overall effect of architecture on innovation.

Drawing on these insights, the present chapter explains how the gradual transition from a network architecture based on the broad version of the end-to-end arguments to a core-centered network architecture that sits at the other end of the spectrum from pure end-to-end to fully deviating from end-to-end changes the economic environment for application-level innovation. By assessing how deviations from the broad version of the end-to-end arguments affect independent innovators' and network providers' incentives to innovate, and how they affect other aspects of the economic environment for innovation such as the size and diversity of the innovator pool or the control over the development and deployment of applications, this chapter will help us understand how deviations from the broad version of the end-to-end arguments affect the nature and the amount of application-level innovation.

Potential Deviations from the End-to-End Arguments

An architecture can deviate from the broad version of the end-to-end arguments along two dimensions: it can become more "opaque" by implementing more application-specific functionality in the network's core, or it can become more "controllable" by increasing network providers' ability to control applications and content on their networks. As we will see, changes along these two dimensions affect the economic environment for innovation in different ways.

The broad version of the end-to-end arguments requires the lower layers of the network to be very general; they should not be optimized in favor of specific applications. Moving along the first dimension increasingly optimizes the network for existing applications by placing more and more application-specific functionality in the network's core. As we saw in chapter 2, the network engineers developing these changes and the network providers deploying them may move in this direction to optimize the performance of the network or save costs in the short term while disregarding the effects of their actions on the long-term evolvability of the network. In the Internet, the deployment of asymmetric DSL service and the introduction of firewalls and network-address translators are examples of changes along this dimension.[1]

As we saw in chapters 2 and 3, increasing the amount of application-specific functionality in the network makes it more difficult to deploy new applications. The more application-specific functionality the network's core contains, the more likely it is that new applications cannot be deployed without first making changes to the network. Whereas an architecture based on the broad version of the end-to-end arguments results in a network that is transparent for new applications, changes along this dimension make the network more opaque.

While changes along the first dimension aim to increase performance, changes along the second dimension aim at increasing control. A network based on the broad version of the end-to-end arguments is application-blind; as a result, network providers are not able to see which applications are using their networks and then control their execution. Network architects move along this dimension by adding application-specific functionality in the network's core that increases network providers' ability to monitor and control what is happening on the network. Small movements in this direction may involve adding devices that make the network more application-aware, thereby enabling the network provider to monitor (but not control) the network at an increasing level of granularity. Further movements would add tools for control that would become increasingly powerful and granular. In the Internet, the introduction of deep packet inspection—that is, the deployment in the network of devices that can look into data packets, determine the application or content whose data the packets are carrying, and process the packets on the basis of that information—is an example of movement in this direction. Network providers move in this direction mostly to increase their profits. However, as we saw in chapter 2, changes that let a network provider monitor what is happening on the network may also help the network provider to make the network more secure, to manage traffic on the network, or to assess the evolution of the network's use for the purpose of planning upgrades.[2]

Generally, moving in this direction does not reduce the network's ability to support new applications. Apart from the application-specific functionality needed for monitoring and control, the network is still general and still able to support a large variety of applications. But, contrary to a network based on the broad version of the end-to-end arguments, the network provider is able to block some or all applications. Thus, in general, the network does not have to be changed to allow the deployment of new applications. However, applications blocked by a network cannot run on that network unless the network provider removes the block.

The Four Network Architectures

To better understand how deviations from the broad version of the end-to-end arguments affect the economic environment for application-level innovation, let us focus on four generic network architectures that differ with respect to the nature and the amount of application-specific functionality within the network. All architectures are assumed to provide the general functionality of an Internet; that is, they enable computers attached to different physical networks to communicate with one another. Starting from an architecture based on the broad version, we will first move along the second dimension and gradually increase the controllability of the network; we will then move along the first dimension and increase the opaqueness of the network (figure 7.1). In line with the analysis so far, let us assume that the users control which applications are installed on their end hosts.

The first architecture is based on the broad version of the end-to-end arguments and is therefore application-blind and open for new applications. I will call this architecture *end-to-end architecture*.

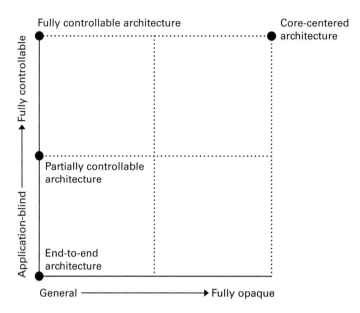

Figure 7.1
The four network architectures.

The second and third architectures deviate from the end-to-end arguments by increasing the network provider's ability to monitor and control applications on its network. I will call these architectures *controllable architectures*. Though technically open for new applications, they include application-specific functionality that can distinguish between different applications and control applications' execution. Architectures of these kinds, which can discriminate among specific applications or content, figured prominently in chapter 6.

The second architecture, which is "partially controllable," is generally open to new applications, but can be used to block them selectively; the third, which is "fully controllable," is generally closed to new applications, but can enable them selectively. To put this differently, the operator of a network having the second architecture must act to *block* new applications, while the operator of a network having the third architecture must act to *enable* them. In addition, the "fully controllable" architecture enables the network provider to charge application-specific prices to users or content providers, providing the opportunity to implement sophisticated pricing schemes.[3] Relative to the end-to-end architecture, we can think of the "fully controllable" architecture as being located on the other end of the spectrum from complete application-blindness to full awareness of and control of applications.

Finally, in addition to the functionality present in the fully controllable architecture, the fourth architecture contains a considerable amount of application-specific functionality in the core of the network. Owing to this functionality, the network is not generally open to new applications. Deploying a new application usually requires extensive changes to the core of the network. I will call this architecture *core-centered architecture*. Compared to the end-to-end architecture, it occupies the other end of the spectrum from full transparency to total opaqueness and from complete application blindness to complete awareness of and control of applications.

Analysis

Independent Application Developers' Incentives to Innovate
Independent application developers' incentives to innovate depend on the expected costs and benefits of innovation. Different network architectures may afford different costs and benefits. Innovators bear the costs of development, testing, production, and distribution. In addition, there may be costs associated with the deployment and with the ongoing operation of an application—e.g., negotiating network access and paying access fees. The expected benefits of an innovation depend on how an innovator expects to use her innovation. For example, if an innovator expects to benefit by selling the innovation to others, the benefits are the expected profits; if she expects to benefit primarily from using the innovation herself, the benefit is the expected increase in utility that the innovation offers.

In general, moving from the end-to-end architecture to the core-centered architecture increases the relative costs of innovation and decreases the relative benefits for independent innovators. As a result, independent developers' incentives to innovate decrease.

Developing and testing new applications in an end-to-end architecture requires no physical capital apart from investing in access to an end host, access to the application programming interfaces of the network protocols, and programming tools. Thus, the main costs of development under the first architecture are the costs of designing, programming, and testing the new application. For a non-commercial innovator, the only cost will be the opportunity costs of the time spent designing, programming, and testing the application. For a firm, the costs are those associated with paying employees to perform these tasks. Since applications in an end-to-end network consist of software that needs to be implemented only on end hosts, the applications can be produced and distributed over the network at almost no cost. Because the network is open to new applications, the network provider need not incur any costs to enable the deployment of the application.

Because the network cannot distinguish among applications or control their execution, an application developer does not have to consider the possibility that the network provider may discriminate against her application. Neither does she have to consider the possibility that her negotiations for access may break down, or that her profits may be reduced by access fees. Finally, as we saw in chapter 6, since in the end-to-end architecture the network provider is not able to set application-specific transport prices for users, more consumer surplus is available for extraction in the complementary market than in an architecture in which the network provider can set application-specific transport prices. Thus, under the end-to-end architecture an independent application developer can expect to reap more of the benefits of an innovation than she can expect to reap under one of the other architectures.

Since the partially controllable network is able to discriminate against applications, a developer must take into account the possibility that the network provider will discriminate against her application. (As was discussed in chapter 6, there are many situations in which a network provider may have an incentive to do so.) Relative to an end-to-end architecture, this reduces the expected benefits, reducing the developer's incentives to innovate.

Moving from the partially controllable to the fully controllable network increases the costs of developing and testing the new application and reduces the expected benefits. As the fully controllable network blocks new applications by default, the new application cannot simply be tested on the operational network. Instead, the developer must have access to a test network. In addition, the developer must negotiate access to the network (which may require costly legal support) and may have to pay an access fee. If the network provider chooses to charge application-specific transport prices to users, less consumer surplus will be available for extraction by the application developer. The developer must also consider the possibility that bargaining will break down and the possibility that the network provider will discriminate against his application. If this occurs, the application will never be able to access the network, and the developer will not benefit from the innovation at all. These possibilities all reduce the profits that a developer can expect to reap from an innovation.

Finally, as was explained in chapter 4, the costs of developing and testing a new application will be significantly higher in a core-centered network whose core has a lot of application-specific functionality than in an end-to-end network. Often the network's core will have to be changed to enable the new application to operate. As a result, the total costs of innovation are substantially higher than under any of the other architectures; they include not only the costs of developing and testing the application itself, but also the costs of developing and testing the changes to the network's core and the subsequent changes to applications that relied on the former version of the network's core. Because the application cannot run on the operational network, the innovator must have access to a test network. If the changes to the network's core include changes to hardware, the new hardware must be manufactured and physically distributed. Thus, the costs of production and distribution also may be higher under this architecture. Finally, the developer may incur considerable costs while trying to convince the network provider of the usefulness and commercial viability of the new application and negotiate any necessary changes to the network's core and to other existing applications. She also must consider the possibility that she will fail to convince the network provider of the usefulness and commercial viability of the application; accounting for this possibility reduces the expected benefits. Ultimately, these costs may be so overwhelming that independent innovators lose the ability to innovate.

Network Providers' Incentives to Innovate at the Application Level

Moving from an end-to-end network to a fully controllable network gradually increases the network provider's incentives to innovate. The transition to a core-centered network, however, sharply reduces his incentives to innovate—probably below the level of incentives in an end-to-end network.

For the network provider, the costs of innovation are the same in each of the first three networks. The network provider's own applications are not affected by the network's ability to block new applications. A network provider does not have to negotiate access or pay access fees to get access to his own network; he can simply remove the block. In addition, a network provider can test his new applications over the operational network.

At the same time, the benefits that network providers can expect to reap from innovation increase from the end-to-end architecture to the fully controllable architecture. In the two controllable networks, the network provider can discriminate against competing applications in order to improve the competitive positions of his own applications. As a result, his expected profits increase. The fully controllable network offers more benefits than the partially controllable network, because the fully controllable network enables a network provider to extract users' surplus by setting application-specific transport prices and to extract some of the profits that application and content providers make by setting sophisticated access charges.

Moving from the fully controllable network to the core-centered network sharply reduces the network provider's incentive to innovate, owing to the significant increase in the costs associated with developing a new application.[4]

Range of Potential Innovators

As was noted above, moving from an end-to-end network to a core-centered network increases the requirements that potential innovators must meet. Whereas developing applications for use in an end-to-end network requires only programming knowledge and access to an end host, developing applications for use in the other networks requires additional investments and capabilities. In the partially controllable network, in the fully controllable network and in the core-centered network, application developers may have to negotiate access or even sue the network provider for access, which can be difficult or impossible without legal support. In the fully controllable network and in the core-centered network, application developers must have access to a test network, as the operational network blocks new applications by default. They also must have funds (or higher ongoing profits) to pay any access fees. Finally, an application developer in a core-centered network may need detailed knowledge about the operation of the network's core in order to assess the feasibility of her application and develop the necessary changes. In addition, she must be able to convince the network provider that her application is valuable enough to merit changes to the network, and she must have sufficient manpower and processes to coordinate the development and deployment of the application and the necessary changes to the network with the network provider.

Thus, whereas in an end-to-end network the pool of potential innovators includes anyone with knowledge of a programming language and access to an end host, subsequent networks reduce the size and diversity of the innovator pool. The first developers to lose the ability to participate in innovation may be non-commercial innovators who lack the capability to negotiate access, to pay access fees, or to gain entry to a test network. Thus, the move to a more controllable network results in an increasing professionalization of innovation. Small firms with little capital may also lose the ability to innovate as the controllability or opaqueness of the network increase. Finally, in a core-centered network, the technical and coordinational obstacles to application development may become so large that network providers are the only remaining potential innovators.

Control over Application Innovation, Deployment, and Use

As we saw in chapters 5 and 6, the owner of an end-to-end network can neither prevent nor impede development, deployment, or use of a new application. Instead, each application developer independently decides on her approach to innovation. Since users can deploy an application simply by installing it on their end host, application deployment and (consequently) the success of the resulting applications are in the hands of users.

In the two controllable architectures, users deploy an application by installing it on their end hosts; in the fully controllable architecture, the network provider must also participate in deployment by unblocking the application before it can run on the network. Although the network provider does not have to participate in deployment in the partially controllable architecture (because the network is open to all applications that are not blocked), it can influence an application's chances of being deployed by discriminating against new applications or excluding them completely. Through the same mechanism, a network provider in the two controllable architectures can influence the development of applications, as the threat of discrimination reduces independent innovators' expected profits and consequently reduces their incentives to innovate. Since network providers can monitor and control the applications running over their network, they control the use of the network.

In the core-centered architecture, network providers control the development of new applications, since their power over the network makes them the only remaining potential innovators. They also directly control the deployment of new applications, since deployment requires changes to end hosts and to the network's core. Owing to the controlling functionality in the network, network providers are able to control the use of the network. In a purely opaque architecture, network providers have some control over the use of the network through their control over the deployment of new applications. Once changes to the network that enable a new application to run have been made, an opaque network does not give the network provider additional control over the extent to which users actually use the applications.

Thus, the transition from an end-to-end network to a more controllable or more opaque network shifts control over application development from developers to network providers, and shifts control over the deployment and the use of applications from users to network providers. As the controllability or the opaqueness of the network increases, control over application-level innovation and network use becomes more centralized.

Relative Costs of Application Deployment

In an end-to-end network, deploying a new application (that is, making all the changes to the operational network and to the end hosts that have to be made before the application can be used for the first time) requires no changes to the network's core.[4] New applications can be deployed incrementally by installing them at an end host. Starting in the third network, deploying a new application requires action by the network provider to unblock the application. The associated costs will be rather low. In addition, users must install the application at an end host. Finally, deploying a new application in a network that implements a large amount of functionality in the network's core probably will require costly changes to the network's core. Users cannot deploy an innovation incrementally; the network provider must change the network first. If the deployment context consists of numerous network providers (as in the commercial Internet), all networks must be changed before the application can run across the Internet.

Thus, the transition from an end-to-end network to a core-centered network also increases the relative costs that economic actors other than the innovator must incur before they can begin to use the new application. This has two implications. First, it increases the threshold for the overall benefit an innovation must provide to make adoption worthwhile. Second, it may affect what kinds of applications will be deployed under the various architectures. As we saw in chapter 4, the architecture and the economic system in which the network is used jointly influence what innovations will be deployed. A network's architecture affects what components will have to be changed to deploy an innovation (that is, what components have to be changed before the innovation can be used for the first time) and what the costs and benefits of deployment will be. The economic system in which the network is used influences who controls the components that must be altered and what incentives these actors may have to make these changes. For example, in the commercial Internet, end hosts are generally controlled by users, whereas the network's core is controlled by many different providers. Thus, in an end-to-end network with a deployment context similar to the commercial Internet, the small costs of deploying an application are borne by users who gain the immediate benefit of being able to use the application. Thus, only users must be convinced of the potential usefulness of the application; at the same time, the low costs of downloading and installing new applications make it easy to try new things. Because a new application can be deployed incrementally, users can decide whether to deploy it one by one. This is particularly important for innovations that take time to spread (for example, because they require users to develop new practices before the application is useful). In contrast, in an opaque network facing the same deployment context, network providers may have to make substantial investments to enable an application to run on their network—and must do so before it is clear whether users will even value the application enough for the provider to recoup her investments. These differences make it much more likely that new and unproven applications will be deployed in an end-to-end network than in a non-end-to-end network, owing to the uncertainty associated with their adoption. Similarly, applications catering to small, widely dispersed audiences may be deployed in an end-to-end network, but not in a non-end-to-end network. In the end-to-end network, only the users interested in these applications have to make changes. In contrast, the small number of potential users of the application among a specific network provider's Internet-service customers may not promise enough benefits to the network provider to justify the costs of changing the network, even if the overall number of potential users across all network providers would be large enough to justify the development of the application.

In sum, other things being equal, the different network architectures result in very different economic environments for innovation in applications. Before we can assess how these differences affect the overall amount, quality, and type of innovation, we need to understand how differences in the size and the diversity of the innovator pool and differences in control over application innovation and deployment influence how much innovation will occur. This is the topic of the next chapter.

8 Decentralized versus Centralized Environments for Application Innovation

As we saw in chapter 7, the transition from a network architecture based on the broad version of the end-to-end arguments to a core-centered network architecture gradually changes the economic environment for innovation at the application level. As the amount of application-specific functionality in the network increases, independent application developers' incentives to innovate can be expected to decrease. Network owners' incentives to innovate at the application level increase with the ability to control the network, but then decrease sharply as the rising amount of application-specific functionality in the core of the network increasingly prevents the deployment of new applications without extensive changes to the core of the network. The range of possible innovators decreases too—from anyone with access to an end host and the ability to learn a programming language (in an end-to-end network) to mostly commercial innovators able to negotiate and finance access to test networks and operational networks (in controllable networks) to the network owners (in the core-centered network). At the same time, control over the development and deployment of innovations in applications and the ability to innovate at this level gradually shifts to the owner of the network. Finally, the costs of adopting new or improved applications increase, both for users and for network owners.

Thus, moving from an end-to-end architecture to a core-centered architecture gradually reduces the number of potential innovators and changes the environment for application-level innovation from decentralized to centralized. Under the network architecture based on the broad version of the end-to-end arguments, independent application developers as well as network operators independently identify and realize opportunities for innovation. Users independently choose the applications they want to use. Thus, network operators are not able to control independent application developers' approaches to innovation or their ultimate success in the

Table 8.1
Decentralized versus centralized environments for application innovation.

	End-to-end network	Core-centered network
Control over application innovation	Application developers	Network providers
Control over application deployment	Users	Network providers
Innovator pool	Large and diverse	Small and homogeneous

marketplace. At the other extreme, under the core-centered architecture, only the network operators can engage in innovation at the application level. Because they have to change the network before an application can be deployed, they also determine which applications are made available to users. As a result, control over application-level innovation and deployment is centralized in the hands of the network operators.

This chapter focuses on how the differences in the number and type of innovators and in the different allocations of control over development and deployment of innovation affect the nature and the amount of innovation (table 8.1). Does decentralized innovation by many innovators offer specific advantages that cannot be achieved by a potential increase in centralized application-level innovation by a few network providers?

Effects of Differences in Innovator Diversity and in Control over Innovation

The Value of Many Innovators

To isolate the consequences of centralized innovation (with only network providers innovating) vs. decentralized innovation (with many more potential innovators), suppose the costs of innovation under the end-to-end architecture and the core-centered architecture were the same. How would the differences between centralized and decentralized innovation affect the amount and type of innovation?[1]

If we look at the question through the lens of neoclassical economic theory, the differences in the number and the type of potential innovators may not appear particularly relevant.[2] In line with the usual behavioral and cognitive assumptions used in neoclassical economic theory, neoclassical models usually assume that all actors know all potential opportunities for innovation, and only need to choose among them. To account for the inherent uncertainty of innovation, the models assume that actors know and agree on the probabilities of the various outcomes a particular project and a particular approach may produce.[3] Given this information, potential innovators are assumed to choose between different projects and approaches by conducting a cost-benefit analysis. The theory assumes that a potential innovator will choose the project (or the set of projects and approaches), that maximizes the expected net benefit.[4] These assumptions imply that it is possible to determine *ex ante* how many innovation projects, and which ones, should be pursued.

In the world of these models, there is not much value in having different economic actors perform this choice. After all, other things being equal, their decision will be the same.[5] Given these basic assumptions, it is not surprising that in many neoclassical models parallel innovation by different economic actors constitutes a wasteful duplication of efforts that would better be avoided.[6] As a result, central control over innovation appears beneficial, because it enables a coordinated approach to innovation that avoids duplication of efforts.[7]

Evolutionary and neo-institutional theories of economic change reach a different conclusion. According to them, decentralized innovation by diverse economic actors leads to a more diverse set of approaches to innovation, and this diversity is often socially beneficial.[8]

Drawing on numerous studies of specific innovations, these theories contend that the neoclassical models just described fail to capture crucial aspects of innovation, such as the effect of firm heterogeneity under uncertainty.[9] As countless studies of specific technologies and innovation show, often no one knows for sure what the best uses for a new technology may be, what consumers really want, or what the best technical approach to a certain problem may be. Under these circumstances, economic actors do not know the complete set of options available to them, nor can they foresee all potential outcomes of a specific project. While each actor may have a view on the likely probabilities of the outcomes of the options he sees, these views will differ across actors and will be shaped by actors' past experiences and theories about the world.[10] Theories of innovation that account for this fundamental uncertainty predict that different economic actors, when confronted with the same situation, will see different opportunities for innovation, will differ in their assessment of the value of the same opportunities, and consequently will select different projects, or different approaches to similar projects.[11] *Ex post*, some approaches will turn out to be successful and others will not, but it is not possible to determine the best or most efficient approaches to innovation in advance.[12]

As a result, if different economic actors can independently choose their innovation projects, the range of projects will reflect the various actors' idiosyncratic perceptions and judgments. In contrast, if only one economic actor chooses innovation projects, the project portfolio will reflect only that actor's view of the opportunities. In view of these differences, the projects pursued by multiple independent innovators probably will be more diverse than the projects pursued under the central control of a single economic actor.[13]

Thus, under fundamental uncertainty, it matters who makes the choice. At the same time, it is not possible to know in advance which choice will be the right one. In view of these two facts, proponents of evolutionary and neo-institutional theories of innovation suggest that trying a variety of approaches and waiting to see which turns out to be the best is better than trying only one. These theories do not deny that it would be more efficient if the best allocation of resources to innovation could simply be imposed. But since the best allocation cannot be known in advance, it seems desirable to explore a wide range of alternatives so as to increase the chance that a good solution will be found.[14]

In these theories, the differences between decentralized and centralized innovation become more profound as uncertainties about technology or market demand increase. The higher the uncertainty, the greater the effect of differences among potential innovators will be—and, consequently, the more likely it will be that different economic actors will make different choices, and the less possible it will be to objectively identify the best projects and approaches in advance. In contrast, in relatively mature industries it may be quite obvious to market participants which innovative efforts may be feasible and profitable, and different economic actors may be less likely to select different projects than they would be in a highly uncertain environment.[15] Similarly, as the complexity of the problem to be solved increases, it becomes less likely that economic actors will be able to foresee the various outcomes perfectly, and less likely that they will assess the underlying probability distributions correctly. Differences in assessment will then lead them to choose different approaches to the same problem.[16] Finally, the effect of differences between actors may increase with the heterogeneity of customers.[17]

As this chapter will show, the history of application-level innovation on the Internet strongly supports the second set of theories. Throughout the history of the Internet, innovation in applications has often been afflicted by the type of fundamental uncertainty described above. Even when they have had access to the same information, different innovators, investors, or observers have often disagreed on the prospects of specific projects. That even the innovators themselves were unable to predict the success of particular innovations in advance is a recurring theme in the history of many applications. In light of this fundamental uncertainty, differences between innovators were highly relevant. In line with the predictions of evolutionary and neoclassical theories of innovation, different actors often chose different applications or approaches, and these choices were often highly idiosyncratic.

All this suggests that the differences in the number and type of innovators between the two architectures will have important implications for the amount and type of application-level innovation. If, as in the end-to-end architecture, different economic actors can independently choose their innovation projects, the range of projects will reflect the different actors' idiosyncratic perception and judgment. In contrast, if, as in the core-centered architecture, only a few network providers choose innovation projects, the project portfolio will reflect only their view of the opportunities. In view of these differences, the projects pursued by multiple independent innovators probably will be more diverse than the projects pursued under the central control of a few network providers. Moreover, as we will see, even if we ignore the differences in innovation costs between the two architectures, letting everyone with access to an end host choose independently whether and how to innovate will result not only in a more diverse set of projects but also in a larger set of projects than if a few network providers and their employees are the only potential innovators. Not only will a large, diverse group of potential innovators discover a larger number of opportunities for innovation than a small group of homogeneous network providers; they will also realize a larger number of the opportunities that were discovered.

First, a large and diverse group of potential innovators will discover a larger number of opportunities for innovation than a small group of homogeneous network providers. Network providers may not see all innovative opportunities. This problem is neglected by neoclassical models of innovation which often assume that all actors know the potential opportunities for innovation.[18] In reality, discovering opportunities for innovation is the first step in the innovative process.[19] Often it is not immediately apparent how a new technology could be used, or that customers have unmet needs that a new or improved product could fill. This problem is particularly pronounced for relatively general technologies, such as the Internet, that can be put to a wide variety of uses. For these technologies, identifying ways in which the technology could be used is an important kind of innovation. As history has shown again and again, it is usually not possible to decide in advance which new uses will become successful.[20] Most Internet applications that later became highly successful either weren't envisaged by the designers of the network or were met by widespread skepticism when they first became available. For example, that e-mail would become one of the most popular applications for the ARPANET (the Internet's predecessor) was not envisaged by its planners or by its funders (box 8.1).[21] For years, Tim Berners-Lee and Robert Cailliau failed to convince the relevant committees at CERN that Berners-Lee's vision of the World Wide Web was something CERN should pursue. Though Berners-Lee managed to pursue the project informally with the consent of his immediate boss, Berners-Lee and Cailliau were not able to get the project accepted as a formal project, or to obtain the manpower they would have liked (box 8.2). In 1995, when Pierre Omidyar first developed eBay, friends and

Box 8.1
The Unexpected Success of E-Mail

The first working networked e-mail application was developed by Ray Tomlinson, a programmer at Bolt, Beranek and Newman, in 1971 (box 8.5). According to the ARPANET's Draft Completion Report, the success of e-mail was "unplanned, unanticipated, and mostly unsupported."[a] In 1967, Lawrence Roberts, who oversaw the development of the ARPANET as assistant director and later as director of the ARPA Information Processing Techniques Office,[b] had written, in an article describing the ARPANET, that the ability to "handle interpersonal message transmissions" was "not an important motivation for a network of scientific computers."[c] The ARPANET was intended to support resource sharing, i.e., to allow users to remotely access and share computing resources, software programs, or databases available on different computers attached to the network. In a 1990 interview, Frank Heart, who led Bolt, Beranek and Newman's ARPANET team, recalled: "When the mail was being developed, nobody thought at the beginning it was going to be the smash hit that it was. People liked it, they thought it was nice, but nobody imagined that it was going to be the explosion of excitement and interest that it became."[d] But by 1973, two years after the first e-mail had been sent over the ARPANET, 75 percent of ARPANET's traffic was email.[e]

a. Heart, McKenzie, McQuillan, and Walden 1977, Draft ARPANET Completion Report, p. III-67, as cited by Abbate (1999, p. 109).
b. Abbate 1999, p. 46.
c. Roberts 1967, p. 3/1.
d. Interview by Judy O'Neill, as cited by Abbate (1999, pp. 108–109).
e. Tuomi 2002, p. 139.

Box 8.2

The World Wide Web

Tim Berners-Lee, a physicist by training, developed his vision of the World Wide Web while working as a hardware and software engineer in the data control and acquisitions group at CERN, the European laboratory for particle physics.[a] He envisioned a decentralized global hypertext system that would enable researchers who came to CERN to run their experiments and then returned to their home institutions to add all sorts of documents to the system and link to related information. Berners-Lee repeatedly submitted his proposal to his boss and to other people at CERN in 1989 and 1990, but he did not get a reaction. Working with Robert Cailliau (a colleague in the Electronics and Computing for Physics division) and a student intern, he built the first versions of a browser and a server in an informal project that was justified internally as a way to test the operating system and software-development environment on a new NeXT computer. But when he and his co-workers were trying to encourage people in the Computing and Networking division to use the system to document their projects, Berners-Lee recalls, "they didn't seem to see how it would be useful."[b] In the spring of 1991, enthusiastic researchers and librarians at the Stanford Linear Accelerator set up the first Web server outside CERN after seeing the system during a visit at CERN. Berners-Lee's boss arranged for Berners-Lee to present the World Wide Web to the CERN Computer Centre Coordination Committee, which consisted of the managers of the main services of CERN's IT department, in order to explain the usefulness of the Web and get more funding. In his book, Berners-Lee recalls: "What we hoped for was that someone would say, 'Wow! This is going to be the cornerstone of high-energy physics communications! It will bind the entire community together in the next ten years. Here are four programmers to work on the project and here's your liaison with Management Information Systems. Anything else you need, you just tell us.' But it didn't happen."[c] Hoping to find programmers interested in improving the program, Berners-Lee made the documentation and code for the World Wide Web available on the Internet in August 1991, in particular on a newsgroup for hypertext enthusiasts. Berners-Lee later characterized this as a "water-shed event."[d] Those enthusiasts downloaded the code, found bugs, suggested features, and put up their own servers. As of the summer of 1991, content was being created, and CERN's server was getting 10 to 100 hits a day.

a. The account in the text is based on Berners-Lee and Fischetti 2000.

b. Ibid., p. 34.

c. Ibid., pp. 50–51.

d. Ibid., p. 51.

potential investors could not imagine that ordinary people would be willing to buy from or sell to complete strangers in an online auction.[22] At the time, even established companies had difficulties attracting customers willing to use their credit cards online, and it was not clear whether e-commerce would ever take off. Similarly, in the mid 1990s people in the Internet industry had severe doubts whether operating a search engine was a sustainable business at all. "Back in those days," Joe Kraus (a co-founder of Excite, one of the first search engines for the Web) recalled, "it was legitimate to [think] 'Why would I use a search engine more than a couple of times to find the sites that I like? Then I'll bookmark those sites and never go back to a search engine again.'"[23]

Even successful innovators are not necessarily able to predict in advance which uses will take off. For example, Max Levin and Peter Thiel started Confinity, the company that later became PayPal, to write cryptographic software for handheld computers. They went through several unsuccessful products until arriving—almost accidentally—at the product PayPal offers today, which allows people to make and receive online payments. At the time, their company was offering an application to transfer money from one handheld computer to another. To get people interested in buying the application, they built a "demo" for the company's website that let people do everything on the website that they could do on a handheld computer. After a while, they became aware that people were using the demo version to actually transfer money, and that the website was much more successful than their "real" product.[24]

When Ludicorp launched Flickr, it was an online photo-sharing application that enabled users to share photos and chat about them in real time. Users, however, wanted to share their pictures with others who were not online at the same time. The Flickr team had assumed that users would want to limit access to their pictures to family members and friends. Instead, most users left their photos public (box 8.3).

Uncertainty does not end once new uses are identified. Often it is not clear which technical approach will be the best for a particular use, which features users may want, or which business model might be the most appropriate. Under these circumstances, actors' past experiences, the context in which they are operating, their ties to other actors, or characteristics such as alertness to innovative opportunities influence what opportunities people see and what approaches they find valuable.[25]

For example, innovators often discover a potential opportunity for innovation when they realize that some difficulty they are experiencing might be problematic for others, too. For example, Sabeer Bhatia and Jack Smith

Box 8.3
Flickr

Flickr became a social network almost by accident.[a] It was launched in February 2004 as a place for people to chat about photos, but user feedback encouraged its evolution into a platform that lets people share their pictures with the world. From a business perspective, the idea that a photo-sharing website could be profitable standing alone stood in stark contrast to the business models of existing photo-sharing applications that were loss leaders for photo-printing websites.

In 2002, Caterina Fake and her husband, Stewart Butterfield, founded Ludicorp to build a Web-based multi-player online game called Game Neverending. Inspired by Neopets (a game in which children can interact with other children while tending to virtual pets), they wanted to build a game in which people could build a community and interact in whimsical ways. In late 2003, they found themselves at the point where "we're six months behind on back-end development[, we're] trying to raise venture capital[, and we're] trying to figure out what furniture we should sell to make payroll."[b]

While waiting for the "back-end" developers to catch up, the "front-end" developers had developed a feature that enabled players to drag and drop objects so as to "give" them—that is, show them—to other players. That feature inspired the original version of Flickr. The idea was to expand that feature so that photos could be dragged and dropped into a chat and onto chat participants' desktops in the same way as game objects to create real-time interaction around photo sharing. Since "we only had money for one last shot, and we knew we could deploy Flickr faster than the game," the team took a vote and decided to work on Flickr.[c] When Ludicorp launched Flickr (in February 2004), it enabled users to chat and share photos in real time; technically, the flash-based application was based on a stripped-down version of the Game Neverending user interface. Owing to the real-time nature of the application, people who wanted to share photos with each other had to be online at the same time, which limited Flickr's usefulness. Users preferred a website that would let them save photos that others could see at a later stage, so the Flickr team (which was closely following the discussions in user forums) added a website where people could upload and store pictures that others could view at a unique URL.[d] The Flickr team had assumed that users would use the site to store and organize photo collections and share them with their families and friends. When the team built a "social network" into Flickr, the idea was that it would allow people to limit access to their photos to family and friends. But they were surprised to find that about 80 percent of Flickr photos were left public. High-quality photographers began to see Flickr as a place to show their work. When Fake and Butterfield became aware that people

Box 8.3
(continued)

---

were using Flickr to share their photos with the public, their background in communal gaming and social software became their big advantage. It allowed them to capitalize on this trend as soon as they saw it by using open APIs, making it easy to integrate pictures into blogs, enabling the tagging program to allow people to pull together groups around certain types of photos, and unobtrusively finding ways to feature some of the best photos.

a. The account in this box is based on the following sources: Garrett 2005; Fitzgerald 2006; Gabbay 2006; Hawk 2005; Herron 2006; Naughton 2008; Fake 2007; Livingston 2007.

b. Fitzgerald 2006.

c. Ibid.

d. The website was far more popular than the real-time application, which was phased out.

---

got the idea for Hotmail, one of the first Web-based e-mail systems, when they were working on another project. While working at a start-up firm named FirePower, they were trying to come up with a "killer app" that would make their fortunes. Their original idea was to create a Web-accessible relational database tool, which they named JavaSoft. They worked on the coding for JavaSoft while they were employed full-time at Fire-Power.[26] They ran into trouble developing the database, though, because they had difficulty communicating when they weren't in the same locations. They didn't want their bosses to discover this project, so they were using their personal e-mail accounts, but FirePower's corporate firewall prevented them from "dialing out" to reach those accounts. The solution came to Smith one day in December 1995: Web-based email would let them access their e-mail from any computer, not just from home or at work. Since HTTP can easily traverse firewalls, firewalls would not be a problem, either. Bhatia thought the idea was perfect, and they began working on it immediately.[27] Others discover an opportunity for innovation when they watch others experience a need, and start thinking about potential solutions. For example, Shawn Fanning started thinking about Napster, the first digital file-sharing application, after his roommate repeatedly complained about the difficulty of finding MP3 files for download on the Internet.[28]

Often, innovators' ideas are inspired by the innovators' backgrounds. For example, the decision by Niklas Zennström and Janus Friis to develop

Skype, an Internet-telephony application based on a peer-to-peer architecture, was influenced by their desire to leverage their intimate knowledge of peer-to-peer applications. The pair had already created another highly successful peer-to-peer application: Kazaa, a peer-to-peer file-sharing application that enabled users to share files and was used mostly to share MP3 music files.[29] Friis recalls: "After Niklas Zennström and I did Kazaa, we looked at other areas where we could use our experience and where P2P technology could have a major disruptive impact. The telephony market is characterized both by what we think is rip-off pricing and a reliance on heavily centralized infrastructure. We just couldn't resist the opportunity to help shake this up a bit."[30]

Jim Clark's and Marc Andreessen's decision to develop the first commercial browser for the World Wide Web was deeply influenced by Andreessen's background, which gave him intimate knowledge of the inner workings (and the limitations) of the most successful browser to date, a recognition of the growing importance of the World Wide Web, and, potentially, a desire to get back at his former employer. Together with a colleague, Andreessen had developed the first user-friendly and widely successful browser, Mosaic, while working as a student at the University of Illinois' National Center for Supercomputing Applications (NCSA). After Mosaic had been released, the relationship between the NCSA and Andreessen had deteriorated, and Andreessen had moved to Palo Alto, where he met Clark (box 8.4).

Others discover opportunities for innovation when they perceive that a technology they are or were working with may be useful in another context. For example, the idea for the first working e-mail program for the ARPANET was born when Ray Tomlinson, a programmer at Bolt, Beranek and Newman, realized that the application he was working on (a program for sending e-mail messages between users of a single mainframe computer) could be improved using another application he had been working on earlier—a program for transferring files on the ARPANET (box 8.5). Similarly, the Google search engine was an unexpected application of an algorithm that Larry Page and Sergey Brin had developed for a different goal in their PhD work (box 8.6).

All this suggests that the discovery of opportunities for innovation is often highly idiosyncratic. As we just saw, some of today's most important applications (e.g., e-mail, search, the World Wide Web) have idiosyncratic roots. Under the end-to-end architecture, anyone with access to an end host can become an innovator. Though network providers—the only potential innovators under a core-centered architecture—can try to hire employees with diverse backgrounds and experiences, the wide range of backgrounds,

Box 8.4

Netscape

In April 1994, Jim Clark and Marc Andreessen founded Mosaic Communications Corporation (which later became Netscape) to develop the first commercial browser for the World Wide Web.[a]

Andreessen, 22 years old, had just graduated from the University of Illinois Urbana-Champaign. With a colleague, Eric Bina, he had created the first version of the Mosaic browser while working as a student at the University of Illinois' National Center for Supercomputing Applications (NCSA). Mosaic was not the first browser (the first one had been developed by Tim Berners-Lee, and other researchers had developed browsers too), but it became the first widely popular browser. Unlike most other browsers at the time, Mosaic was easy to install and use, and it had a clean interface. Whereas existing browsers displayed graphics in a separate window, Mosaic could display graphics as part of a webpage, making websites look more like magazine pages. Its point-and-click interface made it easy to surf the Web. Mosaic was first released in January 1993. Distributed freely, it quickly became popular. The NCSA, noting the success of the Unix version developed by Bina and Andreessen, decided to also develop versions for the PC and the Macintosh, making Mosaic the first cross-platform browser. Suddenly every PC or Mac user with an Internet connection could surf the Web, even if he did not understand HTML or TCP/IP. In the months following Mosaic's release, the Web quickly took off. In January 1993 there were 50 known Web servers; by October there were more than 500; by June 1994 there were 1,500.[b]

After Mosaic was released, relations between the NCSA and Andreessen quickly unraveled. The NCSA, wanting to make Mosaic more corporate, began to "marginalize" the engineers from the project. Eventually they asked Andreessen to stop working on Mosaic. Rather than stay at the NCSA in some other capacity, Andreessen moved to Palo Alto, took a job at Enterprise Integration Technologies, and eventually met Jim Clark.

Clark was a Silicon Valley entrepreneur who had founded Silicon Graphics. His new interest was in how to make money off the Internet—a relatively new idea in 1994. He was looking for a technical whiz with big ideas that he could help turn into reality. Someone mentioned Andreessen's name to him. He contacted Andreessen, and they agreed to start collaborating.

Initially, the two were not sure what they wanted to develop. Clark was interested in interactive TV and wanted to create something like an online Nintendo. Andreessen wasn't convinced. After a while, Andreessen's lingering bitterness toward the NCSA resurfaced. "We could always create a Mosaic killer—just build a better product and build a business around it," Clark

Box 8.4

(continued)

---

later remembered Andreessen saying.[c] Clark agreed to the idea. Both were convinced that cross-platform browsers would be important for the Internet, and that they might even replace operating systems.[d] They quickly hired most of the Mosaic team from the University of Illinois and formed Mosaic Communications. (They later changed the name to Netscape to avoid battles with the NCSA.)

a. The account in this box is based on Wolfe 1994, Berners-Lee and Fischetti 2000, Kaplan 1999, and Hamm 1998. Who had the idea to develop a browser that would be user-friendly and easy to use is contested. Kaplan (1999) and Hamm (1998) attribute the idea to Andreessen; Deutschman (1997) attributes it to Dave Thompson, a full time-employee of the NCSA. All accounts agree that Andreessen and Bina developed the Mosaic browser.

b. Wolfe 1994.

c. Hamm 1998.

d. Afuah and Tucci 2001, p. 203.

Box 8.5

The First E-Mail Program

Ray Tomlinson, a programmer at Bolt, Beranek and Newman, got the idea for the first working networked e-mail application in late 1971 while he was working on the TENEX operating system, an operating system for Digital Equipment Corporation's PDP-10 mainframe computer.[a] (A mainframe is a large computer that is shared by a number of users who access the system from different terminals.) At the time, most mainframes had mail programs that enabled users of the same mainframe to exchange messages. Tomlinson was improving TENEX's mail program when he realized that he could add functionality that would let users connected to different mainframes on the ARPANET send e-mail to one another by modifying code from an experimental file-transfer protocol for the ARPANET that he had worked on earlier. Instead of transferring files from one ARPANET computer to the other, the new mail program would transfer e-mail messages from one ARPANET computer to the other and add them to a user's mailbox.

a. The account in this box is based on the following sources: Tomlinson, undated b; Crocker, undated; Abbate 1999, p. 106; Partridge 2008b.

Box 8.6
Google

In 1995, Larry Page and Sergey Brin were studying the link structure of the World Wide Web in the course of their PhD work in computer science at Stanford University.[a] Because it was easy to see the links leaving a website but difficult to see the links pointing to the same site, they thought it might be interesting to find and analyze the links linking to a site. Their goal was to develop a system (to be named BackRub) that, if given the URL for a website, would list all the websites that linked to this site, —the "backlinks"—ranked by importance. To rank the backlinks, Page and Brin developed PageRank, an algorithm that would assign a rank to a website on the basis of the number of websites linking to this site, taking into account the relative importance of these sites. The idea was that if there were a large number of backlinks, BackRub would show the most important backlinks first. While Page and Brin were studying the results of their system, it occurred to them that the rank of a page might be useful for purposes other than ranking backlinks—in particular, for searching. To test this intuition, they wrote a rudimentary search tool based on PageRank. When it yielded results far superior to those yielded by existing search engines, they decided to focus their energy on building a real, full-text search engine that would use the PageRank algorithm to help determine how to order search results. They named it Google.

a. The account in this box is based on Battelle 2005 and on Page et al. 1999.

---

experiences, and contexts of potential innovators under an end-to-end architecture cannot be replicated within a few network providers' organizations. As we saw, experiencing or watching a need that may be met by using the Internet in a new or different way is an important way of identifying new uses for the Internet. A few network providers likely cannot re-create the use contexts of all the various areas of business and society within their organizations. Thus, by increasing the range of actors who can discover opportunities for innovation and act on them, the decentralized environment for innovation provided by an end-to-end architecture greatly increases the number of opportunities that will be discovered.

Second, a larger, diverse group of potential innovators will realize a greater number of the opportunities that were discovered. Even if a network provider sees an opportunity, it may not find that opportunity attractive. If there is fundamental uncertainty of the type described above, where different innovators cannot agree on the prospects of the various options, potential innovators' perceptions of the likely costs and benefits may differ; owing to these differences, the innovation may appear profitable to some of the innovators, but not to others (box 8.7).

Beyond differences in perception, different cost structures may make a project profitable for some innovators but not for others. Consider an individual programming at home in her free time, a start-up firm, and a larger firm (perhaps a network provider). To make their funds last longer, start-ups often cut costs in a number of ways—for example, the founders may work from their homes, or may rent only cheap office space, keep administrative overhead low, or forgo a part or all of their salary.[31] All this may enable them to produce their application at lower costs than an established larger firm. For example, for the first six months of its existence Amazon was run from a converted garage in the house Jeff Bezos lived in. Meetings with third parties were held in a nearby café.[32] Even after eBay had moved into rented offices, desks for new employees were picked up

Box 8.7
How Differences in Perception Affect the Number of Projects

To think more formally about how differences in perception affect the number of innovative ideas that will be realized, assume that there are a number of potential projects that have the same probability of success.[a] Suppose the various innovators differ in their beliefs about the likely success of projects, and that the probability that a particular innovator thinks a project will be successful (and therefore decides to pursue this project) is δ for all innovators, with $0 < \delta < 1$. Also assume that the probability that a particular approach is successful is ε, with $0 < \varepsilon < 1$. In this case, the probability that a particular project is pursued by at least one innovator is δ under centralized innovation, and it is $1 - (1 - \delta)^n$ under decentralized innovation with n innovators.

Because $\delta < 1 - (1 - \delta)^n < 1 - (1 - \delta)^{(n+1)}$ for all $n \geq 2$, the probability that a particular project is pursued by at least one innovator rises with the number of innovators. Intuitively, the larger the number of potential innovators, the more likely it is that at least one innovator will eventually choose a particular project. In this example, the expected ratio of successful approaches under decentralized innovation vs. centralized innovation is $[1 - (1 - \delta)^n]/\delta$, which is potentially very large. Thus, centralized innovation is likely to result in substantially less successful innovation than decentralized innovation.[b]

a. Similar models are used by Cohen and Klepper (1992, pp. 7–8) and by MacKie-Mason, Shenker, and Varian (1995, pp. 20–21).
b. It will also result in substantially more unsuccessful innovation. See below.

by an eBay employee using her uncle's truck and then assembled by the employees.[33] It is easy to imagine projects whose expected benefits are larger than the costs incurred by the programmer or the start-up firm, but lower than the costs incurred by a larger firm.

Even if the benefits are larger than the costs for all different potential innovators that see the opportunity, the size of the potential benefits may make the project unattractive for the network provider and other large firms.[34] Successful companies need to continue to grow in order to maintain their share prices and to provide the opportunity for employees to expand the scope of their responsibilities. As growth rates are expressed as a percentage of the current market valuation, the additional revenue required to maintain a particular growth rate increases with the size of the company. The larger a firm, the higher the additional revenue required to maintain a particular growth rate. For example, while a project with potential revenue of $10 million will let a $50 million company grow at a rate of 20 percent, it will let Comcast, whose market capitalization at the time of this writing (June 2008) is $63.66 billion,[35] grow at a rate of 0.00015 percent; for AT&T, whose market capitalization at this writing is $214.71 billion, the relative contribution to growth would be even smaller.[36] Because the overall number of projects a firm can pursue is usually limited (box 8.8), it will prefer projects that contribute a significant portion of the additional revenue needed to maintain its growth rate to projects that will lead to revenues that are too small to help the company achieve its growth rate. Thus, the project with potential revenue of $10 million probably will not be attractive to a larger company (such as Comcast or AT&T) but may be quite attractive to a start-up or a smaller firm. Similarly, the prospect of getting bought for $5 million, $10 million, or $20 million may be attractive for an entrepreneur who financed a project herself or through angel investors, but may not motivate a venture-capital firm to invest in the project.[37] Users who innovate to use the resulting application themselves may not care about the size of the market at all; they may care only about the potential benefit from using the program. Moreover, as we will see below, network providers and other established firms may have a bias against specific kinds of projects that may lead them to not select such a project even if they see the opportunity. Finally, strategic interests may make network providers and other established firms less interested in certain projects than other actors. For example, phone companies may be deterred from aggressively pursuing innovation in Internet telephony by the fear of cannibalizing their existing revenues from traditional telephony, and cable companies may be deterred from innovating in Internet video by the fear of cannibalizing their revenues from their traditional cable offerings.

Box 8.8

Limits of Firm Size

The number of projects that a firm can pursue internally is usually limited. Though it is difficult to pin down where exactly these limits are (they may also be changing with organizational form, or with technical advances that facilitate information sharing and coordination), most researchers agree that there are limits to how large a firm can become.[a] For example, it may be more difficult to monitor performance and maintain incentives in larger organizations. At some stage, increasing the scope of the firm will require adding hierarchies, which is costly and may make it more difficult for relevant information to travel to the top. Larger organizations may also incur higher influence costs, since the larger amount of resources available may motivate the larger number of stakeholders within the firm to compete more vigorously for their share of existing resources.[b]

In addition, the architecture may limit the number of projects that a firm can pursue. For example, developing a new application in the core-centered architecture will often require changes to the network. The complexity of making changes to the network and keeping track of the interactions between the changes required for different applications will limit the concurrent number of new application projects that a network provider can pursue.

a. See, e.g., Williamson 1975, chapters 7, 8; Williamson 1985, chapters 6, 11; Milgrom and Roberts 1992, pp. 571–575; Besanko, Dranove, and Shanley 2000, pp. 87–91.

b. See, e.g., Milgrom and Roberts 1992, pp. 571–575.

As we saw in chapter 5, the low costs of application innovation under an end-to-end architecture let innovators with all sorts of motivations innovate: the user who wants to get the application she needs, the volunteers who cooperate (often remotely) to develop an application, the potential entrepreneur who tests his idea as a side project while making money in his day job, the small company without outside funding whose owners want to be profitable, but value control over their company's destiny more than the opportunity of getting insanely rich, firms funded by venture capitalists, larger existing companies. Though the diversity of funding sources available to potential innovators may differ from country to country or even from region to region (for example, the availability of venture capital varies considerably across countries or regions), the broad range of cost structures, perceptions, and motivations able to support innovation under an end-to-end architecture makes it more likely that someone will find it attractive to realize an innovation even if the network provider does not find it attractive.

In sum, a large, diverse group of potential innovators, with diverse motivations and with access to diverse types of funding, not only will discover more opportunities for innovation than a small group of homogeneous network providers; it also is likely to realize a larger number of the opportunities that are discovered.

Having a larger and more diverse set of innovation projects, in turn, guarantees a more complete search of the problem space, reducing the chance that beneficial uses (or approaches to specific problems) will not be detected. If the various innovators pursue different technical approaches to the same problems or explore different business models, having a larger number of innovators increases the likelihood that at least one of them will be successful and increases the expected quality of the winner.[38] The benefits of diversity increase with uncertainty. Intuitively, if uncertainty is high, it is not likely that a single approach will yield a really good result. The more independent approaches are tried, the higher the probability that one of them will turn out to be really good. Certain innovators' idiosyncratic experiences or capabilities may further improve the expected quality of the outcome.

For example, Skype was not the first Internet-telephony application; it was not even the first one based on a peer-to-peer architecture. But the experience that the Skype team had gained developing Kazaa and a clear focus on voice quality and ease of use resulted in an application that surpassed the quality of existing Internet-telephony applications and was offered for free (box 8.9). Similarly, Flickr was not the first photo-sharing application; however, for reasons that were tightly linked to the circumstances surrounding its inception and the founders' backgrounds, it evolved into an offering with distinctive features—a platform for photo sharing with elements of social networking—that were central to its success (box 8.3).

Having several innovators approach a particular problem may also increase the overall quality of innovations through spillovers.[39] By watching others experiment, innovators can gain valuable insights about what works and what doesn't work without having to try the same approaches themselves, and can use these insights to improve their own approaches.[40] For example, providers of search engines initially struggled to find a good business model. The lack of a good business model was one of the main things that deterred potential investors from investing in search engines. The business model that Google pioneered, which dominates the industry today, evolved in a series of steps that involved substantial trial and error.

Box 8.9

Skype

When Niklas Zennström and Janus Friis began developing Skype, most of the existing Internet-telephony applications were based on a client-server architecture and used the Session Initiation Protocol, which didn't handle broadband users behind firewalls and network-address translators well. One company, PGPfone, was peer-to-peer, but couldn't work around firewalls.[a] Most of the services were difficult to use, and the voice quality of the services was relatively low.[b] Zennström and Friis decided to base Skype on a proprietary protocol, to use a peer-to-peer architecture, and to focus on call quality and ease of use. They hired the team of Estonian programmers that had developed Kazaa for them to adapt the technology underlying Kazaa for Internet tele-phony. Thanks to their experience with Kazaa, the programmers were able to overcome the problem of network-address translator and firewall traversal, something that Zennström perceives as critical to Skype's success.[c] The low ongoing costs associated with a peer-to-peer application (in 2004, it cost Skype only one-tenth of a cent to add a new user, as Skype needed only servers from which the application could be downloaded and an authentication server) and the viral nature of the software (since Skype uses a proprietary protocol, Skype users can talk only to other Skype users, which gives users an interest to convince their friends to use Skype, too) enabled Zennström and Friis to make the software available for free and to charge only for premium features. In contrast, Vonage and other companies that used the Session Initiation Protocol and a client-server architecture had to use a subscription model, because of the costs of operating the server infrastructure and the higher costs of marketing (in 2004, it cost Vonage $400 to add a new customer).[d] Because it enabled people to make high-quality phone calls for free with a program that was easy to install and easy to use, Skype was an instant success.

a. McCullagh 2003.
b. Charny 2003.
c. Mohney, undated; Maney 2006.
d. The costs of adding a customer to Vonage or Skype are taken from Roth 2004.

Over time, Google and other actors within the industry tried a variety of different approaches. At each step along the way, Google not only reacted to its own experience but also built on the experiences gained by others in the industry (box 8.10). In general, innovators can learn from other innovators' successes or failures, and such learning reduces the social costs of failure.

Box 8.10
The Evolution of Google's Business Model for Search

In 1999, when Larry Page and Sergey Brin secured their first venture-capital funding for Google, receiving $25 million from Sequioa Capital and Kleiner Perkins Caulfield and Byers, they had not yet found a business model.[a] At the time, existing search engines were either using banner advertising or diversifying into portals. Brin and Page argued that banner ads would cause the Google page to load slower, and that irrelevant ads would distract from the search results. Instead, Google first tried to make money by syndicating its search technology to large websites for a fee, in addition to offering it to consumers directly. But that approach was not very successful, so at the end of 1999 Page and Brin decided to try a variant of the dominant advertising model. As the providers of other search engines did, they would sell advertising space on their site, basing the price on the number of users seeing the ad (this method of pricing is called *cost per thousand impressions*). Unlike the others, however, they would show only text-based ads that were relevant to the topic of the search.[b] To prevent any confusion, paid ads were clearly separated from the normal search results. The system worked, but it did not provide enough revenue. In particular, it did not scale well, since the advertising deals were negotiated in person. In 2000, to remove the bottleneck and increase revenue, Google introduced AdWords, an automated system that let advertisers buy text ads online using a credit card. With AdWords, Google's revenue grew considerably, but GoTo, a competitor in the search market, was growing much faster.

GoTo, which later changed its name to Overture, had had been founded by Bill Gross as a commercial search engine. Whereas other search engines used algorithms or humans to rank search results, the order in which GoTo's search results were shown was determined by how much the owners of the corresponding websites were willing to pay. GoTo's business model contained two major innovations. One was that advertisers would pay only if a user actually clicked on their ad (a model now known as "pay per click"); the other was that advertising prices would be determined through an online auction in which advertisers could bid to be shown when searchers searched for particular keywords.

Although observers and industry participants had been highly skeptical when it was launched,[c] GoTo became very successful. Because users who search for something are really interested in it and, if their query is related to commercial activity, willing to act, advertisers found that users searching for relevant keywords were often clicking on their ads and then buying something. As a result, advertisers on GoTo were willing to pay much more than they paid for undifferentiated traffic from other websites. GoTo also syndicated the top paid results (as determined by the amount that advertisers were willing

Box 8.10
(continued)

to pay) to other search engines or portals, sharing the advertising revenue with them. Even though the market for display advertising crumbled after the NASDAQ crash in the spring of 2000, advertisers continued to advertise on GoTo, and GoTo became profitable while other search engines and portals were struggling from the slowdown in display advertising. The fact that GoTo was able to offer its syndication partners substantial revenue per search when the traditional model of display advertising had broken down fueled its syndication business and motivated others to imitate its approach.

Google executives, who had been following Overture's success, determined that Google's lack of auction-based pay-per-click pricing for its paid ads was an important reason for the difference in the growth of the two businesses.[d] In February 2002, Google introduced AdWords Select, which was based on Overture's model but which differed from it in important ways. As in Overture's system, the advertising price was determined by an auction, and advertisers paid only for actual clicks. But whereas Overture based the order in which ads were shown on the advertisers' bid, Google's system also considered the likelihood of users' clicking on the ad. Thus, an advertiser who bid $1 per click but had a large number of users clicking on its ad would be ranked higher than an advertiser who bid $2 per click but had few users clicking on its ad. Relative to Overture's system, these differences not only made ads more relevant for search users but also led to higher revenue for Google. (In April 2002, Overture filed a lawsuit claiming that Google had infringed Overture's patent covering its ad-placement method. The suit was settled out of court in 2004 after Yahoo acquired Overture. As part of the settlement, which also settled another claim by Yahoo, Google gave Yahoo 2.7 million shares of its stock in exchange for a fully paid, perpetual license to Overture's patents.[e]) Finally, whereas in Overture's system content providers' or advertisers' payments determined the placement in the search engine's main search results, Google only used the pricing mechanism to determine the order in which its paid links were shown on the site, and continued to clearly separate between the organic search results produced by Google's search algorithm and the paid results produced by AdWords Select. The new system not only made Google's own search website highly profitable, it also enabled Google to change its syndication model. Instead of syndicating its algorithmic search results to third parties for a fee, Google now syndicated both algorithmic and paid search results to other websites, offering them a share of the revenue. Today, this general approach is still at the core of Google's highly successful business model. Yahoo and Microsoft, Google's two biggest competitors in the search-engine market, adopted similar approaches.[f]

Box 8.10
(continued)

---

a. The account in this box is based on the following sources: Business Wire 1999; Google 2000; Bowman 2002; Festa 2002; Kane 2002a,b; Olsen 2002a,b,d; Sullivan 2002a,b; Wolverton 2002; Battelle 2005, pp. 88–146; Vise and Malseed 2005, pp. 62–69, 82–129.

b. Google's sales chief had used a similar approach in his previous job at Netscape, combining cost-per-million pricing with showing advertising results based on keywords (Battelle 2005, p. 124).

c. See, e.g., Pelline 1998; Sullivan 1998.

d. In 2001, Gross approached Brin and Page to discuss a potential merger, but Brin and Page did not approve the mixing of paid advertising with normal search results (Battelle 2005, pp. 115–116).

e. Olsen 2002c, 2004.

f. Yahoo did not use a relevancy factor such as click-through rates until it introduced its new search marketing system Panama in early 2007. The lack of such a factor is usually viewed as one important reason for the gap in search-engine monetization between Google and Yahoo. Another reason is the different number of users. See chapter 6 above, subsection "Complementary Product Source of Outside Revenue."

Finally, if consumers are heterogeneous, having a larger and more diverse group of potential innovators is likely to result in applications that better meet the needs of different consumer groups.[41] Because innovators often discover opportunities for innovation that are related to their backgrounds or to the context they are operating in, letting anyone with programming knowledge and access to an end host become an innovator makes it more likely that a specific user need is recognized. More innovators will not only discover more opportunities for innovation, they probably will also realize more of the opportunities that are discovered. For reasons discussed above, there will be many potential applications or services that users may want but which a network provider may not pursue. For example, catering to a niche market with relatively low profit margins may be interesting for a small software company with little overhead whose owners are happy to be just profitable, but not for larger companies with different cost structures that look for larger profit opportunities.[42] By enabling a wide range of actors with diverse backgrounds and diverse motivations to innovate, the end-to-end architecture makes it more likely that someone will find it attractive to cater to a particular group of consumers, even if this would not be attractive for the network provider. If no one else is interested in meeting their needs, users can always realize the application themselves.

To better understand when and why a larger and more diverse pool of innovators increases the amount of innovation, let us look at three specific types of innovators: new entrants, companies backed by venture capital, and users. These innovators are able to innovate under an end-to-end architecture, but may lose their ability to participate in innovation as an architecture moves away from the broad version of the end-to-end arguments. As we will see, these innovators often have an incentive to innovate in situations where the network provider does not have such an incentive. When these types of innovators lose the ability or incentive to innovate as a result of deviation from the broad version, this innovation will be lost. In addition, innovation by these types of innovators offers specific benefits that a network provider cannot replicate. Thus, the following subsections focus on these types of innovators, because they are able to innovate under an architecture based on the broad version, but they are not necessarily able to innovate under an architecture deviating from it. The resulting differences in the size and diversity of the innovator pool, in turn, may result in differences in the amount and the type of innovation under these alternative architectures. The focus on these types of innovators is not meant to imply, however, that they are the only potential innovators, or the only important types of innovators. For example, large and established firms may have specific advantages that a start-up firm cannot match. Large firms often benefit from economies of scale and scope, from economies of specialization, or from established business relationships with other firms. As we saw above, they are part of the pool of potential innovators under an end-to-end architecture. Their perspectives and specific advantages enable them to focus on projects that other types of innovators may neglect or may not be as good at, which contributes to the diverse set of innovations that will occur under such an architecture. Large, established firms will, however, often be less affected by deviations from the broad version of the end-to-end arguments, so their contribution to application innovation is not necessarily lost as a result of such deviations. Therefore, they are less important to the overall argument of this chapter. This is not meant to discount their importance to application innovation; it only reflects the specific focus of the analysis in this chapter and in this book.

The Value of Innovation by New Entrants

Different network architectures let new firms influence the rate and the direction of innovation in different ways. Under network architectures that centralize control over innovation, the rate and the direction of innovative activity are determined by a few network providers—established firms already operating in the industry. Either new entrants are blocked from innovating or their freedom to innovate is restricted by the need to get permission from the incumbent. In contrast, under the decentralized environment for innovation provided by an end-to-end architecture, incumbents and new entrants independently determine the rate and direction of innovation.

Throughout the history of the Internet, important new applications have often been developed by new entrants, not by established firms. For example, the online auction site eBay was started by Pierre Omidyar, not by a newspaper or a major Internet service provider. In the early years, the members of the eBay team constantly feared that an Internet service provider (e.g., AOL, CompuServe, or MSN) or one of the big portals would start competing with them. They felt that online auctions were a logical next step from the online classified sections that the big ISPs had developed. But none of the major ISPs entered the field.[43] Web-based e-mail was pioneered by startups (including Hotmail and Four11, which developed Rocketmail), not by the big portals. Instant messaging was invented by the Israeli startup ICQ, not by a portal or an ISP. Online music distribution was revolutionized by Shawn Fanning's Napster, not by the record companies.

In general, it took established firms who had been in the industry before the Internet became popular longer to realize the commercial potential of the Internet. For example, the most successful online bookshop, Amazon.com, was started by Jeff Bezos, a former senior vice president at a quantitative hedge fund who had a degree in computer science and electrical engineering, in the garage of his newly rented house in Seattle in June 1994. Amazon.com started selling books on the Internet in July 1995.[44] Barnes & Noble, the first major brick-and-mortar bookseller to sell books on the Internet, opened its first online store in the spring of 1997, after Amazon.com had become so successful that its success could not be ignored.[45] (In May 1996, a front-page article in the *Wall Street Journal* reported that Amazon was on its way to selling more than $5 million in books in 1996. Sales were growing by 20–30 percent every month, and Amazon's sales revenue that year surpassed $15 million.[46])

Another incumbent, Microsoft, initially failed to understand the growing importance of the Internet and the World Wide Web.[47] The commercial potential of providing software with which to access the World Wide Web was recognized by Netscape, a start-up firm, not by Microsoft. After the 1993 release of the Mosaic browser, the Web grew rapidly. Jim Clark and

Marc Andreessen founded Netscape in April 1994 to produce the first commercial Web browser. After October 1994, when Netscape released the first version of its browser, Netscape quickly garnered a dominant market share. In May 1995, Sun launched Java, a programming language that enabled programs to run within a browser, making the programs independent of the computer's operating system. Websites were using server programs such as the NCSA's HTTPD (released in mid 1993), Netscape's commercial server (launched in December 1993), and the open-source Apache server (released in April 1995), creating the prospect of an Internet free of Microsoft products. Meanwhile, Microsoft was focusing on finishing Windows95, WindowsNT, and Microsoft Network (an online service designed to compete with AOL). Although Bill Gates assigned the Internet "the highest level" of importance in an internal memo in 1995, changing Microsoft's strategy in response to the Internet and the competitive threat posed by Netscape and Java was delayed until after the launch of Windows95 and Microsoft Network. When Windows95 was shipped in August 1995, it included TCP/IP support, so that computers running the Windows95 operating system could connect to the Internet, but it did not include a browser. (Customers could buy Internet Explorer 1.0 as part of the Microsoft Plus add-on, though.) Microsoft Network went live using proprietary standards, not Web standards. In response to the threat posed by Netscape, Microsoft included Internet Explorer 2.0 with the operating system in November 1995 and released its first Web server in February 1996.

Other incumbents were offered the chance to commercialize important innovations, but declined. In line with CERN's "buy, don't build" policy, Tim Berners-Lee initially tried to get hypertext firms to work with him to build the World Wide Web. Existing commercial hypertext editors already let users open, display, and modify hypertext documents. Berners-Lee felt that these editors could easily be turned into the browsers he envisioned for the World Wide Web by adding functionality that could send hypertext documents across the Internet. However, none of the firms he approached wanted to pursue the idea, so Berners-Lee decided to write a browser and a server himself.[48]

Sergey Brin and Larry Page, the founders of Google, originally did not want to form their own company, but tried to sell or license their search technology to existing portals. Between 1996 and 1998 they offered their search-engine technology to the major portal and search-engine companies, but all declined. At the time, all the existing search-engine companies (including AltaVista and Excite) had become portals that made money from advertising. Search was just one of many services they wanted to provide, and not a particularly important one; after all, the portals' goal was to keep users on the portal, where they would create more advertising revenue or commissions for online sales. A search engine that by design led people away from the portal did not fit with this strategy. Thus, the existing search-engine companies had no interest in acquiring a better search-engine technology; search had to be only "good enough." For the same reasons, Yahoo, MSN, AOL, and other portals that did not have their own search engines were uninterested. For them, search was something to be outsourced to a third party, not a cornerstone of their competitive advantage.[49]

Research in management strategy suggests that this pattern was no accident. There seem to be systematic differences between firms that have been successful in an industry for some time and firms that are new to an industry, and these factors influence the relative abilities of the incumbent and the entrants to perceive the value of specific new technologies and to exploit them.[50] Moving from an end-to-end architecture that lets new entrants innovate to a network architecture that lets only established firms innovate would result in the loss of innovation by newcomers. (I do not mean to imply that established firms generally fail to take advantage of new technical opportunities. In fact, established firms may have an advantage with respect to innovations that require a large amount of resources. They may benefit from economies of scale or scope, or they may be able to build on existing business relationships. For example, when Google develops new applications, it can take advantage of its existing data centers or of its existing network infrastructure in a way that a new entrant who lacks these resources cannot. The argument is, rather, that there are certain opportunities for innovation that established firms may find unattractive, and that these innovations would not be realized under a non-end-to-end architecture under which only network providers or other established firms can innovate.)

The research reveals that a firm's competitive position is crucially influenced by its resources and capabilities, and that resources and capabilities may be difficult to both acquire and change.[51] Firms that have been successful in an industry for some time have optimized their resources and capabilities for the technological and competitive circumstances in the industry; in fact, this is the basis of their success. For example, the engineers of such a firm may be experts in the leading technology and its particular application in the company's products, and the firm's organizational structures and processes may be optimized to enable efficient product development and improvement based on the leading technology and on the needs of the customers in the firm's current market. But the assets that originally created the firm's competitive advantage may become disadvantageous in the face of particular types of technical change. If such a change occurs, incumbent firms may find it difficult to recognize the implications of the new technology or to change their resources and capabilities to take advantage of the new situation. New entrants whose perceptions and capabilities have not been shaped by the existing situation have an advantage in recognizing the value of the new technology and in mustering the resources and capabilities to exploit it.[52] Thus, this research predicts that incumbent firms will be good at pursuing innovations that fit their resources, their capabilities, and their economic position, but that they will be less able than new entrants to see the value of a new technology and adopt it if it is incompatible with incumbent firms' capabilities at the technological level, at the organizational level, or with respect to its economic position in the industry.

At the technological level, a new technology may require radically new technological competences that the incumbent is unable to acquire. Because that is more likely to occur with technological change involving radically new technology than with incremental changes, scholars of management strategy predict that new entrants may have an advantage with respect to radical technological change.[53]

At the organizational level, a firm's organizational structure may prevent it from seeing the significance of certain types of technological change and adapting to it. For example, the organizational structure of a firm often mirrors the architecture of its product, with different organizational units responsible for different components. Knowledge about the relationships and interdependencies between components shapes the organizational structures and processes that guide interactions among different organizational units. Even though a new technology might improve the overall quality of the product by improving the product architecture, the significance of this fact may get lost in the organizational structures and processes shaped by the existing architecture. Even if an established firm recognizes the value of the new technology, changing its organizational structures and processes may be difficult; owing to organizational inertia, it is usually more difficult to change established structures and processes than to build new ones from scratch. Thus, scholars of management strategy predict that technologies that require or enable changes at the architectural level of a product architecture will pose more of a challenge to leading firms than changes at the component level that leave the overall architecture of the product unchanged. New entrants whose organizational structures are not yet shaped by the existing architecture may have an advantage in perceiving the value of architecture-level innovations and in realizing them.[54]

Finally, and most importantly in the current context, a firm's economic position in the market may influence its perception of the value of different opportunities for technological innovation.[55] Firms often operate in differentiated product markets where the definition of quality differs considerably among groups of consumers; stated differently, consumer groups base their purchasing decision on very different criteria. For example, large corporations with dedicated project managers value project-management software with a rich set of features that let them produce Gantt charts or identify the critical path of the project; they do not mind the one-time effort to learn to navigate the complex software. In contrast, a small business that cannot afford to assign one person to project management full-time needs simple software that lets project members cooperate and track progress. Since no one can focus on this task full-time, the software has to be intuitive and easy to use.[56] As the example of project-management software shows, different quality attributes are often mutually exclusive, forcing firms to focus on a particular group of customers with common valuation of quality attributes. In this case, such characteristics of the competitive environment as typical cost structures and available profit margins are determined by the competition between the firms that compete for the same group of customers. In such a setting, a leading firm that has been successful for some time is successful because its resources, technological capabilities, organizational structures, and processes are well adapted to meet the distinctive needs of the group of customers it has decided to serve; it has found a way to outperform its competitors given the cost structures and available profit margins that are typical of its sub-industry. In other words, a successful firm's resources, technological capabilities, organizational structures, and processes are optimized to the specific characteristics of the competitive environment in which it operates.[57]

Although integral to the firm's success, this optimization constrains an established firm's perception of the value of different opportunities for technological innovation.[58] Contrary to an entrant, it is constrained by five factors: its existing group of customers, its existing cost structure and profit margins, its size, the incentive structure of its managers, and the firm's processes for managing innovation. As we will see, these constraints will bias an established firm in favor of products that let it better meet the needs of mainstream customers in its current market or that enable it to move into established markets with higher profit margins; they will bias it against products that do not meet the needs of customers in the firm's current market, that must be commercialized in new or emerging markets, or that are afflicted with significant business uncertainty.[59] New entrants that do not share these constraints will view such projects more favorably. Thus, understanding how these constraints affect the way in which successful firms assess potential opportunities for innovation will help us understand better which types of projects they may reject. Although potentially attractive for a new entrant, these projects would not be realized under an architecture in which only network providers or other established firms can innovate.

First, a successful established firm is constrained by its existing group of customers. A firm is successful in an industry if it can give its customers what they want.[60] Even though this orientation toward existing customers is the basis of the firm's success (the firm is successful precisely because it is puts a lot of effort into identifying the needs of its customers and evaluates potential projects based on how well they meet these needs), it biases the firm in favor of projects that let it better meet the needs of these customers.

Second, a firm's existing cost structure and profit margins influence the type of projects it finds attractive, biasing it to favor projects that increase its profit margins,[61] a natural way to increase profits. Projects with lower profit margins than existing products would require the firm to cut costs in order to maintain the current level of profitability. Successful companies probably already have cost structures that let them outperform their competitors in the current market. As a result, it may not be possible to cut costs and remain competitive in the current market. In any event, cost cutting is usually difficult and painful, making projects with lower profit margins unattractive. These considerations also influence the markets an established firm finds attractive: moving into markets with higher profit margins enables the firm to earn higher profit margins based on its current cost structure and potentially gives it a cost advantage over firms already operating in that market. In contrast, moving into markets with lower profit margins would require the firm to cut costs to maintain its current level of profitability. As a result, established firms have a tendency toward upmarket mobility and downmarket immobility.

Third, a firm's size influences the type of projects it considers valuable.[62] As we saw above, the size of a firm determines the additional amount of revenue a firm must earn in order to maintain its desired growth rate. As a result, a firm will prefer projects that contribute a significant portion of the additional revenue needed to maintain its growth rate to projects that will lead to revenues that are too small to help the company achieve its growth rate. On the basis of these considerations, an established firm will prefer projects targeting large markets to projects aimed at small markets.

Fourth, in established companies, proposals for innovation are evaluated at various levels of the organizational hierarchy. When evaluating proposals, managers also consider the potential effect of these decisions on their own careers. This biases managers against projects afflicted with considerable market uncertainty. A failure in the product market due to lack of consumer demand happens after investment in product development, manufacturing, marketing, and distribution has been made, and is therefore considerably more costly and publicly observable than failures in the early stages of an innovative project due to technological problems. As a result, such a failure is far more detrimental to a manager's career than a failure due to technological problems. At the same time, the reward from successful innovation (e.g., a bonus or a raise) is usually limited. As a result, a manager will tend to support projects directed toward well-known customer needs in established markets for which market uncertainty is low.[63]

Finally, the processes used to plan and manage innovation for well-known customer needs in established markets are not appropriate for managing innovation in emerging markets.[64] In established markets, consumers' needs and market sizes are usually well known; as a result, market uncertainty is low. In this situation, sophisticated marketing, investment, and management processes that require a wealth of data can be used to plan and control the innovation and product development process. Emerging markets, with their inherent uncertainty about consumer demand and market evolution, are not amenable to methods that require detailed data on consumers' needs and reliable forecasts on market development. Thus, the same processes that are crucial to managing innovation in established markets leave companies ill-equipped for dealing with emerging markets.

Given these constraints, an established firm will value technologies or innovations that let it better meet the needs of mainstream customers in its current market or that enable it to move upmarket into established markets with higher profit margins.[65] These technologies have the potential to increase profit margins on the basis of the firm's current cost structure. In established markets in which customers' needs are well known, market uncertainty is low. In addition, established markets are large enough to contribute the amount of revenue that a large company needs to sustain its growth, making them attractive targets for innovation.

In contrast, an established firm will be biased against innovations that do not meet the needs of customers in the firm's current market, that must be commercialized in new or emerging markets, or that are characterized by significant business uncertainty. Disruptive technologies are an important example of such innovations. Disruptive technologies typically do not meet the needs of customers in the firm's current market today, but they have the potential to evolve to a point where they better meet the needs of customers in this market in the future.[66] Products based on disruptive technologies are usually cheaper and simpler than existing products, resulting in lower profit margins. As they initially underperform established products in mainstream markets, they cannot be used in these markets, but must be commercialized in new or insignificant markets. Such markets do not solve the growth needs of a large successful company.[67] Finally, the uncertainty associated with creating new markets requires very different approaches to managing product development than facilitating innovation in established markets.[68] Consider Internet telephony, or video over the Internet. When the first Internet-telephony applications were developed, voice quality was lower than on the wireline network. Calls were less reliable and often required a running computer. Similarly, video-over-the-Internet transmissions often do not have the same high resolution that customers have come to expect from conventional television; it may take a moment until the video starts playing, and the video may stop unexpectedly to wait for more data. Sitting in front of a computer screen is not as relaxing as sitting on a couch in front of a large-screen television. As a result, these applications originally did not or still do not meet the needs of mainstream customers in the markets for telephony and video broadcast. As network and application technologies evolve, they may offer competitive performance. Owing to their initial quality, Internet telephony and video over Internet had to be commercialized in new markets. Given the uncertainty associated with emerging markets and the profit and growth needs of established companies, it is not surprising that Internet telephony and video-over-Internet applications were originally developed by new entrants, not by incumbent phone companies or cable providers.[69]

Contrary to an established firm, an entrant was not active in the industry before the advent of a new technology. As a result, an entrant's approach to innovation is not constrained by an existing group of customers, an existing cost structure, existing profit margins, and large size. Consequently, the entrant may be better able to identify the value of disruptive technologies and to exploit them.[70] More generally, a new entrant may find it easier to find new applications and markets for a new technology. A new entrant is not already dedicated to a particular group of customers.

As a result, it can evaluate the potential of the technology without reference to the needs of a particular group of customers. Instead, it can look for a group of customers that actually values the characteristics of the new technology.[71] Contrary to an established firm, a new entrant is not constrained by an existing cost structure, but can adapt the cost structure of the organization to the profit margins that the technology enables.[72] Finally, a new entrant is small and therefore needs less revenue than a large established firm to grow at a particular rate. Thus, for a new entrant, an emerging or insignificant market may constitute a viable growth engine.[73] As a result, an entrant may see attractive opportunities for innovation where an established firm sees none.

The Value of Venture-Capital-Backed Innovation

Under an end-to-end architecture, anyone, including a company financed by venture capitalists, can be an innovator. But at some stage along the path from an end-to-end architecture to a more centralized environment for innovation, firms backed by venture capital lose their ability to innovate. Under the core-centered architecture, network providers are the only remaining innovators.

Venture capital can be defined as "equity or equity-linked investments in young, privately held companies, where the investor is a financial intermediary who is typically active as a director, an adviser, or even a manager of the firm."[74] Venture capitalists raise funds from investors and use these funds to make equity or equity-linked investments in young, privately held companies. Thus, venture capitalists act as financial intermediaries between outside investors and young, privately held companies that need financing. Their function goes beyond providing funds. Once the decision to invest in a company has been made, venture capitalists closely monitor and control the company's progress, providing strategic advice, reputation, and contacts.[75]

Throughout the history of the Internet, companies backed by venture capitalists have commercialized important new applications. Netscape, Yahoo, eBay, Amazon.com, Excite, ICQ, Hotmail, Rocketmail, Google, Napster, PayPal, Skype, Vonage, Friendster, MySpace, Facebook, and deli. cio.us were all funded by venture capitalists at some stage in their history. Many of these firms pioneered completely new types of applications. This is not an accident. Venture capitalists specialize in high-risk, high-return projects that established companies often reject. In addition, innovation by venture-capital-backed firms offers specific benefits that other companies may not be able to replicate. When deviating from the broad version of the end-to-end arguments increases the costs of innovation so much that firms backed by venture capitalists lose the ability to innovate, these innovations and the associated benefits will be lost.

Compared to innovative employees and middle managers in established firms, entrepreneurs and venture capitalists face very different incentives, which lead them to pursue very different types of projects.

Though innovative employees and middle managers in established firms usually benefit from a successful innovation, the rewards are relatively limited. They may get a raise or a bonus, and their prospects for promotion may increase. At the same time, if a project fails for lack of market demand, the results are usually very expensive and public and thus probably will have a negative effect on the reputation and career of the middle manager who backed it. Thus, whereas the personal gain from backing a successful project is limited, the personal risk associated with backing a project that is afflicted with significant market uncertainty is high. Owing to this incentive structure, middle managers are believed to be averse to risk when choosing inventions for commercial development.[76] In particular, they will prefer a project with low market uncertainty and a moderate return over a project with high market uncertainty and high potential gains.

In contrast, entrepreneurs and venture capitalists retain a significant proportion of the gains associated with successful projects. Their compensation is directly linked to the firm's success. A considerable fraction of the compensation of managers and critical employees in venture-capital-backed firms consists of equity or stock options.[77] Similarly, venture capitalists usually receive a proportional share (traditionally around 20 percent) of the profits when the investment in a firm is liquidated.[78] Successful projects can create enormous profits. Thus, entrepreneurs and venture capitalists can make a lot of money if a firm is successful. But the personal loss from unsuccessful projects is limited. For an entrepreneur, failure of a firm is not necessarily regarded as a personal failure. If the firm fails as a result of circumstances the entrepreneur cannot influence, he may well be able to get funding for a new promising venture.[79] Similarly, owing to the high risk associated with investment in young, innovative companies, unsuccessful investments are regarded as inevitable in the venture-capital business. As a result, a venture capitalist's reputation is based on her overall track record, not on the failure of isolated investments.[80] Owing to this incentive structure, entrepreneurs and venture capitalists are usually believed to be "skewness lovers"—that is, to be motivated by the relatively low probability of an extremely high reward.[81]

Thus, venture capitalists have an incentive to invest in companies (and indirectly in projects) that they believe to have the potential to yield attractive returns. Contrary to middle managers in established companies, they will not be deterred by the uncertainty surrounding such projects or be biased by existing customers, cost structures, and business lines, because the management structures and processes of venture capitalists are designed to deal with high-risk, high-return projects (box 8.11).[82] Historically, venture capitalists concentrated most of their investments in early-stage companies in high-technology industries, where the perceived opportunities for innovation-based growth are huge and where the problems caused by uncertainty and information asymmetry are particularly profound.[83] For example, in the early 1980s venture capitalists made a large fraction of their investments in computer hardware and semiconductor electronics. Venture capitalists also invested heavily in the emerging computer software, biotechnology, Internet, and telecommunications industries.[84] For example, in 1999, 39 percent of all venture disbursements were directed at Internet investments, and 17 percent of all venture disbursements at telecommunications investments.[85] Between 1994 and 2007, venture capitalists made more than $218 billion in Internet-related investments in 19,664 US companies.[86] In 2007, 38 percent of all venture investments in US companies were directed at Internet-related investments.[87]

Thus, venture capitalists enable independent innovators to pursue high-risk, high-return projects that established firms, for whatever reason, reject. As a result, the ability of venture-capital-backed firms to participate in innovation widens the range of innovative projects and increases the probability that projects directed toward new or emerging markets will be adopted.

Apart from influencing the type of innovation, firms backed by venture capital may also create innovations of higher quality. Like all start-up founders, entrepreneurs in venture-capital-backed companies face strong incentives to innovate. Entrepreneurs, critical employees of the firm, and venture capitalists have high-powered compensation schemes that closely link their compensation to the performance of the firm and potentially enable them to reap enormous profits. Owing to the high incentive intensity, all parties are likely to expend greater effort than employees in an established firm, who do not similarly profit from successful projects.

Relative to start-up innovators using other forms of financing,[88] however, entrepreneurs whose companies are backed by venture capitalists may be better able to realize and commercialize their innovation thanks to the financial and other support provided by their venture capitalists. Venture

Box 8.11
Venture-Capital Mechanisms for Managing Uncertainty

Venture capitalists have developed management structures and processes that enable them to deal with the specific problems associated with high-risk, high-return ventures. To manage the risk associated with such investments, they carefully screen investment proposals to identify promising opportunities for investment, using their knowledge of the industry and a wide network of contacts.[a] Usually one venture-capital firm invests together with a similarly experienced venture-capital firm (syndication), so as to get a second opinion and so as to reduce the chance of funding unsuccessful projects.[b]

Venture capitalists also use mechanisms to minimize potential losses. Apart from providing a second opinion, syndication lets a venture-capital firm invest in more companies, reducing the exposure to any single investment.[c] Once the decision to invest in a company has been made, venture-capital firms disperse funds in stages. They evaluate the progress of the funded firm at each stage and decide whether to continue funding. They can thus monitor and control the progress of the funded firm and terminate funding if the firm's prospects turn negative, thereby capping potential losses.[d] Finally, venture capitalists actively support the operation of the firm to increase the probability of success.[e]

Finally, venture capitalists have developed mechanisms to address potential agency problems between the entrepreneur and the investors.[f] Through day-to-day involvement with his firm, the entrepreneur has more information than venture capitalists or investors about the progress of the company and its future viability. To reduce the possibility that the entrepreneur exploits this informational asymmetry to the detriment of investors, the venture capitalists closely monitor and control the progress of the firm[g] and structure the compensation of the entrepreneur and important employees to align the incentives of managers and investors.[h]

---

a. See, e.g., Kaplan and Strömberg 2001, pp. 427–428; Gompers and Lerner 2001a, pp. 44–46.
b. See, e.g., Gompers and Lerner 2004, pp. 166–167 and chapter 11.
c. Gompers and Lerner 2004, p. 167.
d. For a theoretical and empirical analysis of this practice, see Gompers and Lerner 2004, chapter 8.
e. See, e.g., Hellmann and Puri 2000; Kaplan and Strömberg 2001; Hellmann and Puri 2002.
f. For an overview of the theoretical literature on agency problems between the entrepreneur and the investors, see Gompers and Lerner 2004, pp. 157–163.
g. See, e.g., Kaplan and Strömberg 2001, pp. 428–429.
h. See, e.g., Gompers and Lerner 2001a, pp. 50–51, 53–58.

capitalists can give reliable and predictable financial support. This lets the firm focus on the efficient realization of their innovation without being impeded by a lack of funding or being distracted by the need to organize more financing.[89] Apart from providing the funds necessary to pursue the project, venture capitalists support the firms in their portfolio in a variety of ways; for example, they provide contacts and reputation that gives the firm access to other sources of financing or to important strategic business partners.[90] During the 1990s, Kleiner Perkins Caulfield and Byers, one of the leading venture-capital firms in Silicon Valley, became well known for fostering connections between the companies in Kleiner's portfolio and supporting strategic alliances among them.[91] Intuit, Sun Microsystems, Macromedia, and Netscape had all been funded by Kleiner Perkins at some point in their history. Shortly after the Netscape browser was launched, Intuit released a new version of its personal finance software Quicken that was tightly integrated with a special version of the Netscape browser. Sun Microsystems integrated Netscape's server software into its server offerings, while Netscape licensed Sun's Java programming language and integrated Java support into its browser. Netscape integrated Macromedia's director player, which enabled users to view multimedia files created using Macromedia's software, into the browser as well. Under a deal with Sun, Macromedia would license Java and integrate Java support into Macromedia's multimedia products.

Venture capitalists are used to the problems of young firms operating in uncertain environments and can help them adopt viable product-development, marketing, and finance strategies. They support the professionalization of the firm's internal organization in a number of ways: they help select the management team, help professionalize the recruitment and human resource processes, and foster the adoption of stock option plans.[92] For example, Kleiner Perkins Caulfield and Byers and Sequoia Capital had only agreed to fund Google on the condition that Brin and Page would hire an experienced chief executive officer. When Eric Schmidt, at the time CEO of Novell, was not interested in Brin's invitation to interview for the CEO position, John Doerr, one of the partners at Kleiner, convinced him to accept. Schmidt became chairman of Google's board in March 2001 and CEO in July 2001, forming a triumvirate with Brin and Page.[93] When their initial collaboration turned out to be a bit rocky, Doerr suggested the three get some informal mentoring from Jim Campbell, former CEO and current chairman of the board at Intuit and a board member at Apple. The three agreed, and observers credit Campbell with helping them find ways to work together and make decisions.[94]

Finally, venture capitalists help a firm decide when to go public, and prepare the initial public offering.[95] The importance of this non-financial support is highlighted by the stories of Netscape and eBay. Although the two firms did not depend on venture capitalists to fund their firms (Jim Clark, co-founder of Netscape, had the financial means to finance the firm himself; eBay was profitable from the beginning), both firms chose venture-capital financing for the non-financial support associated with it.[96]

The evidence shows that the support of venture capitalists pays off. Empirical studies demonstrate that companies backed by venture capitalists bring their products to market faster than similar entrepreneurial companies with other types of financing.[97] Firms that receive venture-capital financing grow more quickly and tend to be considerably younger at their IPO dates than non-venture companies.[98] Finally, venture-capital-backed firms continue to outperform non-venture-capital-backed companies even after the IPO.[99]

In a large number of market categories related to hardware or software for personal computers or the Internet, venture-capital-backed firms have become market leaders or acquired dominant positions. Intel, Microsoft, Cisco Systems, America Online, Yahoo, Adobe,[100] eBay,[101] Amazon, Google, and PayPal all received funding from venture capitalists in their early stages.[102] In 2000, in the computer software industry, firms that had been funded by venture capitalists in their early stages represented more than 75 percent of the software industry's market value; in the computer hardware industry, such firms represented 78 percent of the industry's value.[103]

Finally, there is some evidence that venture capital fosters innovation: for example, in the biotechnology industry, venture capitalists provided financing to 450 out of 1,500 firms between 1978 and 1995. These 450 firms, however, "accounted for over 85 percent of the patents awarded and drugs approved for marketing."[104] In another study, researchers used data covering twenty US manufacturing industries over three decades to assess the effect of venture capital on innovation.[105] According to their statistical calculations, "one dollar of venture capital appears to stimulate patenting three times more than a dollar of traditional corporate research and development does. This finding suggests that venture capital, even though it averaged less than 3% of corporate R&D from 1983 to 1992, drove a much greater share—about 8%—of US industry innovations over that decade."[106]

Network providers cannot replicate the advantages associated with venture-capital funded firms, for example by having their own corporate venture-capital funds. In recent years, a number of companies have created their own corporate venture-capital funds. While this may improve the situation compared to a world where only network providers can innovate, this will not necessarily solve all problems.

First, it is difficult to replicate the incentives and structural safeguards of independent venture capitalists within a firm.[107] For example, companies are often hesitant to pay their employees in a corporate venture-capital division the same share of the profits that an independent venture-capital firm would provide, since it may distort the company's pay structures. As a result, venture-fund managers within a firm may be less motivated than independent venture capitalists; it may also be harder for the firm to compete for the best fund managers. Empirical studies show that corporate venture funds often perform worse than independent funds and do not last as long—with one exception: corporate venture funds showed a comparable performance if there is a strategic overlap between the corporate investor and the funded firm. Thus, a few corporate venture firms associated with network providers would not match the breadth of expertise and investment activity that a large number of independent venture capitalist firms would provide.

Second, diversity among venture capitalists is as important as diversity among innovators. In the face of uncertainty, venture capitalists may have different views on a venture's potential. Having a large number of venture capitalists may be beneficial because it increases the chances that at least one venture capitalist may find the innovation worthwhile. Many companies that were eventually funded by venture capitalists (including eBay, Google, and Skype) were first rejected by other venture capitalists.[108]

The Value of User-Driven Innovation

Scholars of innovation have long classified potential innovators on the basis of their functional relationship to the innovation—that is, on the basis of how they benefit from the innovation.[109] A "manufacturer" benefits from an innovation by selling it to others; a "user" benefits by using it herself.[110] For example, 37signals (an independent software vendor that sells the project collaboration and management software it develops to customers) is a manufacturer; a bank that develops market-analysis software in-house to use the software in its day-to-day operations is a user.

Under architectures that centralize control over application development and deployment in the hands of the network provider, the network provider is a manufacturer with respect to most applications; it innovates to sell the resulting applications or services to consumers. In contrast, under an end-to-end architecture, manufacturers (including the network provider) as well as users have the ability to innovate.

Research suggests that there are situations in which users may have an incentive to innovate but a manufacturer may not. In addition, innovation by users may provide specific social benefits that innovation by a network provider cannot replicate. These innovations and benefits will be realized under an end-to-end architecture, but they will not be realized under a non-end-to-end architecture in which users cannot innovate.

Because users and manufacturers have different functional relationships to innovation, their relative costs and benefits and the criteria they use to determine whether to innovate differ.

Consider the example of Mark Fletcher, who developed Bloglines, a Web-based news-aggregation service that was later acquired by Ask Jeeves. Fletcher, who was running an anti-spam company at the time, had bookmarked more than 100 sites that he visited every day to see whether they had been updated. Clicking on 100 bookmarks only to see that the corresponding website or blog had not been updated took up a considerable amount of his time, so he began to look for an alternative way of doing this. At the time, there were some programs that would aggregate the information from the different sites in one place; however, these programs, which ran on the user's computer and were not synchronized between different computers, were not useful to Fletcher, who was using several computers during the day. A software engineer with a background in building server applications, he figured that a Web-based aggregator would solve his problem. He decided to program one for himself in his free time.[111]

David Heinemeier Hansson was developing a Web-based project-management application called Basecamp as a contractor for the small US firm 37signals while working toward a bachelor's degree in computer science and business at Copenhagen Business School. While programming the application, he realized that parts of the code constituted generic solutions to recurring problems and could be extracted for future use. The result was Ruby on Rails, a "toolbox" that can be used to build applications in the Ruby programming language more quickly and more effectively. Programmers at 37signals (where Heinemeier Hansson became a partner after graduation) have used Ruby on Rails to create other products, including a Web-based to-do list, a personal information manager, and an intranet for small businesses.[112]

In the late 1990s, legal scholars at Harvard Law School's Berkman Center for Internet and Society, unhappy with the choices offered by the commercial teaching software provided by the law school, developed software applications that helped them teach better. For example, the online discussion forum provided by the commercial software offered by the law school did not encourage students to respond to others' contributions. To remedy this, Jonathan Zittrain, a Lecturer at Harvard Law School and Executive Director of the Berkman Center at the time, conceived an online tool that linked random pairs of class participants for a point-counterpoint exchange and worked with two students to develop a Web-based application with that functionality.[113]

Like Fletcher, Heinemeier Hansson, or Zittrain, users often discover opportunities for innovation during their normal activities.[114] They experience a problem, and start thinking about a solution. They may have an incentive to realize their idea if the tools necessary to solve the problem are available to them, the benefits from solving and having solved the problem are greater than the associated costs, and existing solutions either aren't available or offer a lower net benefit.

A user may benefit from innovating in several ways. The user gets a solution that is tailored exactly to her needs.[115] This may let her perform her task better or more efficiently, and thus may let her be more productive. The user may also derive benefits from the process of innovating itself, such as learning or a sense of fulfillment.[116]

The costs of innovating consist of the costs of investing the resources necessary to develop and realize the innovation and the associated opportunity costs of not being able to use the resources for other purposes. As we saw earlier, in the original architecture of the Internet the resource costs of developing a software application consist mostly of the costs of programming and testing the application.[117] As a result, the only costs that the user who develops an application to solve her own problems incurs is the opportunity cost of the time spent designing, programming, and testing the application.[118] While working on the innovation, she is unable to do something else. If she is working on it in her free time, she forgoes other recreational activities; if she is working on it as part of her employment relationship, she is giving up the opportunity to work on other employment-related tasks. As we saw in chapter 4, the widespread availability of open-source programming tools and open-source software components has considerably reduced the costs of developing new applications (even if they are Web-based), making it more likely that the benefits of developing an application will be larger than the costs.

Some of the most important applications in the history of the Internet have been developed by users. For example, throughout the 1970s and the 1980s, most of the programs used to read and send e-mail were developed by researchers on the ARPANET who were unhappy with existing programs.[119]

Tim Berners-Lee developed the World Wide Web to better support the distributed community of CERN researchers and staff (box 8.2).[120]

The dominant Web server on the Internet at the time of this writing, the Apache Web Server, was originally developed by a small group of webmasters who needed server software for the websites they were administrating (box 8.12).[121] And like Ruby on Rails, many of the major programming languages used in Web development today, including Perl, PHP, and Ruby, were originally developed by programmers who were unhappy with existing programming languages. Later, they often released their software in open-source form.[122]

The likelihood that the expected benefits will be larger than the costs will be even higher for users who innovate on open-source software.[123] Like Brian Behlendorf and the webmasters who needed a server to run their sites, users contribute to open-source projects whose results they would like to use. For example, a lot of the programmers who contribute to the development of Ruby on Rails use the framework in their daily work.[124] More generally, when exploring the motivations of contributors to open-source projects, one study found that "facilitating my work due to better software" was ranked as the most important benefit.[125] In another study, 59 percent of contributors ranked use of the output they create as one of their three most important reasons to innovate.[126] Because the effort needed to produce the program is shared among the group of contributors, contributors to open-source software have to contribute only a portion of the effort needed to produce the full program, but get the benefits of being able to use a full program.

Other users innovate by modifying the source code according to their needs. The source code for open-source software can be downloaded from the Internet free of charge. Open-source licenses explicitly allow people to use and modify the program. By adapting open-source software to their specific needs, users can get a tailored solution without having to create a complete program from scratch.[127] Thus, a webmaster who needs a specific feature that the Apache server does not offer can download the Apache software and add the desired feature, even if she did not contribute to the Apache software in the first place. This lets her get a complete but tailored solution while incurring only the costs of the modification. Thus, relative to users who innovate on their own to produce an application they need from scratch, users of open-source software may incur lower costs for the same benefit.[128]

Box 8.12
The Apache Web Server

A Web server is a software application that can be used to provide content on the World Wide Web. The architecture of the Web consists of two types of application programs that are implemented on end hosts and which communicate with each other to provide the overall functionality. A browser such as Mozilla's Firefox or Microsoft's Internet Explorer retrieves particular documents or content from the Web. Web server software, located on computers that host the documents and content available on the Web, services requests from browsers for particular documents or content. In performing these tasks, today's Web servers also perform additional functions such as security and authentication of users or gateways to databases. Thus, whereas the Web browsers are used by those who view content, Web servers are used by those who provide content.

In 1995, the most popular Web server was NCSA httpd, developed in 1993 by Robert McCool, an undergraduate systems administrator working at the National Center for Supercomputing Applications at the University of Illinois. McCool wrote the code at the request of Marc Andreessen, who was developing the Mosaic browser at the NCSA. Andreessen thought that the availability of good Web servers would facilitate the adoption of the Web and, in turn, of his browser. The NCSA made early versions of the server source code available for free and released them with a non-restrictive license.

Soon webmasters all over the world were using the software to run their sites. When they found bugs, they either reported them back to McCool at the NCSA or fixed them themselves, sharing their patches with McCool and other website administrators through a mailing list administered by CERN. When McCool left the NCSA to work for Netscape, in mid 1994, the NCSA stopped maintaining the server code. As a result, the number of patches that had not been integrated into the latest NCSA version of the source code grew rapidly. Webmasters willing to use the software had to download the latest NCSA version, try to find all available patches, and manually integrate them into the source code. Not only did this result in a lot of duplication of efforts, the same bug being fixed again and again; it also created conflicts between different patches. To solve this problem, one of the webmasters proposed to a small group of webmasters that they produce their own updated version of the NCSA server code. Brian Behlendorf, who was chief engineer at HotWired at the time, set up a mailing list to collect the patches and to coordinate work on the source code and a shared workspace. The webmasters collected the available patches, integrated them into the code, tested them on their servers, and released them to the public in April 1995. During the summer of 1995, Robert Thau designed a new server architecture and a new code base that made the code more modular and solved problems that had plagued the

Box 8.12
(continued)

> existing version of the server. Version 1.0 of the Apache software, which was based on this code, was released to the public in December 1995. Although changes to the Apache versions of the source code are controlled by a core group of developers, anyone can download the source code and make modifications. Less than a year after the group's founding, the Apache Web server was the most popular server on the Internet. Not only was the software available for free; it also offered functionality that was not available in commercial servers offered by Netscape or Microsoft, such as the ability to host a large number of websites on a single server ("virtual hosting"). If a webmaster needed functionality that was missing, she was free to modify the source code and add the functionality.[a]
>
> a. The account in this box is based on the following sources: Moody 2001; Osterlie 2002; Apache Software Foundation 2008a,b.

In sum, there may be a variety of circumstances in which a user's benefits from innovating exceed the costs. This does not mean that users wouldn't prefer to buy the innovation from a manufacturer. In fact, a user would prefer to buy the innovation if the manufacturer's solution offered a higher net benefit.[129] The manufacturer, however, may not always have an incentive to innovate.

First, a manufacturer may fail to perceive the opportunity for innovation. Information about users' needs is costly to acquire. Whereas users discover their needs as a by-product of their normal activity at no incremental cost,[130] manufacturers need to spend considerable effort to acquire use-related information. Although there are many ways in which a manufacturer can acquire such information, including surveys, focus groups, and interacting with users,[131] these come at considerable cost. Information related to users' needs usually is "sticky"—that is, costly to transfer from its point of origin at the user's site to the manufacturer in usable form.[132] Thus, the relative costs of identifying users' needs are usually significantly higher for manufacturers than for users.[133]

Second, even if a manufacturer is aware of users' particular needs, it may not necessarily have an incentive to meet them.[134] In making the decision to innovate, users focus on how valuable it is to them to be able use an innovation themselves. In contrast, a manufacturer benefits from an innovation by selling it to others; the potential benefits often rise with the number of potential customers. As a result, given limited resources, a manufacturer will choose to work on those innovations that deliver the most expected profit. Working on projects that fulfill the needs of a large number of users will often be more profitable than working on projects that fulfill the needs of a small number of users.[135] Thus, even if the benefits of a project exceed its costs, a manufacturer may not necessarily pursue it.

In developing a product that appeals to as many customers as possible, manufacturers often focus on the needs of the *average* customer.[136] If customer heterogeneity is high, manufacturers may divide the market into segments of customers with broadly similar needs. Different products are then targeted to the average customer in each segment.[137] Still, this method may leave a considerable number of users' needs unserved.[138]

All this suggests that there will be circumstances under which users may pursue an opportunity to innovate to meet their own needs and a manufacturer may not. The more specific the needs of a particular user and the smaller the potential market consisting of users with similar needs, the more likely such a situation is to occur. The ability to innovate themselves may also be particularly important to so-called lead users, who experience certain needs well in advance of most other users.[139] Since they are so much further ahead, they need solutions when the nature, risks, and potential size of the overall market are difficult or impossible to forecast. As we saw earlier, this uncertainty often reduces the incentives of manufacturers to pursue the innovation in question.[140]

Enabling users to innovate offers three specific social benefits that innovation by manufacturers alone does not offer. First, innovation by users meets demand that would otherwise have remained unserved. Network architectures that do not let users innovate leave users at the mercy of products offered by innovating manufacturers. In an end-to-end architecture, users whose needs are not met by existing products can help themselves and innovate. If users have the ability to innovate and at least some of them have an incentive to do so, a higher fraction of consumers' needs will be met under an end-to-end architecture than under an architecture that rules out innovation by users. The size of such benefits is difficult to estimate. Surveys indicate, however, that today's standard commercial products may, on average, leave between 46 percent and 54 percent of customer needs unserved.[141] The size of this potential benefit increases with the heterogeneity of consumers. The greater that heterogeneity and the higher the uncertainty about consumers' needs, the more likely it is that some consumers' needs may not be served.[142]

Second, depending on the application in question, the adoption of the innovation by the user may have other beneficial effects. If the programmers at 37signals use Ruby on Rails to write new applications, their productivity increases.[143] If the legal scholars who developed teaching software use it in their teaching, the quality of their classes increases.

Finally, unlike manufacturers, users often choose to voluntarily reveal their innovations to others for free.[144] This may be done in a variety of ways. Some users let others use the application for free without giving away the program itself. For example, Mark Fletcher let others use Bloglines for free, but did not make the software or its source code available for download.[145] Others make the application software available for download, but not the source code. Others also make the source code available for free, enabling others to modify the software according to their needs.[146] For example, Tim Berners-Lee published the specifications for the protocols underlying the World Wide Web on the first Web server and made the source code for the first browsers and server publicly available. In 1993, CERN released the property rights to the protocols of the World Wide Web into the public domain, making it possible for anyone to use the protocols for free.[147] The Apache project was run as an open-source project from the beginning (box 8.12). David Heinemeier Hansson released his Ruby on Rails Web application framework in open-source form in July 2004; it is now maintained by a group of programmers including Heinemeier Hansson. Anyone can download the Ruby on Rails source code from the Ruby on Rails website for free.[148] Similarly, the programmers who originally developed the popular programming languages Perl, PHP, and Ruby to meet their own needs later made them available in open-source form for free. Free revealing is an inherent feature of open-source development projects; contributors to those projects invest their own private resources in developing source code and make their contributions publicly available by posting them on the projects' websites. Under the open-source software licenses, anyone can download, use, and modify open-source software for free. The size of these activities should not be underestimated. For example, in August 2008, Sourceforge.net, an infrastructure provider and repository for open-source software projects, listed more than 180,000 open-source software projects and more than 1.9 million registered users.[149] Although free revealing was at first surprising to economists, researchers have made progress in explaining why users may have an incentive to freely reveal their innovations (box 8.13).

If users voluntarily reveal their innovation for free, others can reap the benefits associated with use of the innovation without incurring the costs of innovating. In contrast, manufacturers often do not find it in their interest to freely reveal their innovation to others.[150] From the point of

Box 8.13

The Theory of Free Revealing

At first, the fact that users freely reveal their innovations puzzled economists. After all, conventional economic theory assumes that an innovator, in order to have sufficient incentives to innovate, must have the right to exclude others from using his innovation. Otherwise, he would not be able to reap the financial rewards necessary to cover the costs of innovation, which would remove his incentives to innovate.[a] If people will be able to use an innovation developed by others for free, why should anyone incur the costs of developing the innovation? On this reasoning, society rewards innovators with intellectual-property rights—limited sets of rights that give them a temporary monopoly over their innovation.[b] In this context, uncompensated spillovers of proprietary knowledge to third parties constitute a loss to the innovator, since they reduce his ability to profit from the innovation.[c]

Recent research has made some progress in understanding the incentives that drive users to freely reveal their innovations.[d] Explanations usually start with the insight that for the user innovator the main benefit from innovating is the ability to subsequently use the innovation. Thus, in order to make free revealing rational, the associated benefits do not have to cover the costs of innovating – these costs usually are covered by the benefits associated with using the innovation. Instead, the benefits associated with free revealing must exceed the costs of free revealing. If the costs of free revealing are low, the associated benefits need not be very large.[e] Thus, innovation and free revealing by users are easier to explain than innovation and free revealing by other types of non-commercial innovators.

The costs of free revealing consist of the costs of making the innovation available and the costs associated with giving up or not enforcing intellectual-property rights to the innovation.

Because software is a digital good, an innovator who is connected to the Internet can make it available for download by posting it on a website, or can distribute it using peer-to-peer file-sharing applications. Thus, the costs of reproducing and distributing the innovation are very low.

The opportunity costs of not enforcing intellectual-property rights to an innovation consist of (1) forgone profits that might have been available from selling the innovation and (2) any advantage that competitors of the innovator can gain through "free riding" on the invention. For users, both of these costs will often be low. Often the transaction costs and risks associated with licensing or selling the innovation are quite high. As a result, benefiting from the commercial exploitation of intellectual property will often not be a practical alternative for users.[f] Whether the innovator loses a competitive advantage if others are able to adopt the innovation for free depends on the degree of rivalry between the innovator and potential adopters and on the importance

Box 8.13
(continued)

of the innovation for any competitive advantage in the market in which the innovator and potential adopters compete. This suggests that free revealing by users may be more common if the perceived rivalry between the innovator and potential adopters is low.[8] Indeed, an empirical study indicates that the willingness of sports enthusiasts to freely reveal sports-related innovations decreases with an increase in competition between members of the sporting community.[h]

Thus, if the innovation can be made available on the Internet and the perceived rivalry between the user innovator and potential adopters is low, the costs of free revealing will be very low. As a result, a small benefit from free revealing may be sufficient to motivate that user innovator to make the innovation available.

Recent research has identified a variety of such benefits that may operate simultaneously. First, in many cases, at least some adopters of an innovation may provide valuable feedback or suggestions for improvement. This benefit has been highlighted in studies of open-source projects and online games.[i] Second, in the case of open-source software, free revealing is a prerequisite to having the functionality developed by the innovator included in the standard version of the open-source software that is maintained and distributed by the open-source project. Consider a webmaster who has developed a new feature for the Apache Web server. If the code for the feature is incorporated in the standard version, it will continue to be included in future updates of the program. Otherwise, the webmaster may not automatically be able to use the feature with future versions of the program, and may even have to rewrite it.[j] Third, the innovator may also expect that if he offers his innovation today and thereby benefits others, he may be able to benefit from another user's innovation in the future.[k] Finally, free revealing may also serve to increase the innovator's reputation among peers. This will be particularly relevant if there is a community of users, such as the community of those contributing to a particular open-source project or the community of online gamers of a particular computer game. In the case of open-source software, the innovator may also be interested in establishing a reputation among potential employers or venture capitalists.[l]

Researchers also suggest that user innovators will be less concerned about free riders than conventional economic theory assumes. First, as indicated above, while free riding on the innovative effort itself, at least some adopters may perform testing and other important functions.[m] Second, conventional economic theory assumes that innovators and free riders benefit equally from using the innovation. This assumption may not be correct in all cases. For example, innovators may derive a higher benefit from using the innovation,

Box 8.13
(continued)

---

since it exactly matches their needs.[n] They may also derive benefits from the process of innovating, such as learning, enjoyment, or a sense of ownership and control.[o] Studies suggest that learning is an important output of research and development projects. Knowledge acquired through a project may enable an individual to better benefit from innovations in the future.[p] The resulting combination of intrinsic rewards and more tangible direct and indirect benefits will often be sufficient to cover the low costs of free revealing.

a. See, e.g., Arrow 1962.

b. See, e.g., Arrow 1962. For a short introduction to this line of reasoning, see Carlton and Perloff 2005, chapter 16. For an in-depth analysis of the economic rationale underlying intellectual-property law, see Landes and Posner 2003.

c. See, e.g., Tirole 1988, p. 400.

d. On free revealing by users in general, see Harhoff, Henkel, and von Hippel 2003 and von Hippel 2007. As has become apparent, free revealing plays an important role in open-source projects. Research aimed at understanding the motivations to contribute to open-source projects is therefore applicable in the present context. For attempts to reconcile the empirical findings on open-source with economic theory, see Benkler 2002, Lerner and Tirole 2002, and von Hippel and von Krogh 2003.

e. See, e.g., von Hippel 2007, p. 304; von Hippel and von Krogh 2003, pp. 214–215.

f. For arguments along these lines, see von Hippel 2007, pp. 304–306; Harhoff, Henkel, and von Hippel 2003, pp. 1754–1756; von Hippel and von Krogh 2003, pp. 214–215. For an analysis of the circumstances under which user innovators may switch roles and become manufacturers, see Shah and Tripsas 2004.

g. See, e.g., Harhoff, Henkel, and von Hippel 2003, p. 1757; von Hippel 2007, p. 307.

h. Franke and Shah 2003, pp. 170–172.

i. See, e.g., von Hippel and von Krogh 2003, p. 218; Jeppesen and Molin 2003, pp. 374–376.

j. See, e.g., Harhoff, Henkel, and von Hippel 2003, p. 1759.

k. Franke and Shah (2003, pp. 172–173) call this motivation "generalized exchange behavior." See also Harhoff, Henkel, and von Hippel 2003, p. 1757.

l. See, e.g., Lerner and Tirole 2002, pp. 212–220.

m. See, e.g., von Hippel and von Krogh 2003, p. 218.

n. See, e.g., Harhoff, Henkel, and von Hippel 2003, p. 1760.

o. See, e.g., von Hippel and von Krogh 2003, pp. 216–217.

p. See, e.g., Cohen and Levinthal 1990.

view of potential adopters, however, buying an innovation is more costly than getting it for free. As a result, there may be less diffusion of the innovation if only the manufacturer innovates than if a user innovates and makes the innovation available for free.[151] Because widespread adoption of an innovation throughout the economy is a prerequisite for the innovation to positively affect economic growth,[152] increased adoption resulting from free revealing by users may provide significant social benefits. For example, releasing Ruby on Rails as open-source software enabled many developers to create Web-based applications with less time and effort. The framework has been widely adopted. Among the best-known applications are Twitter (which enables users to send short, text-based messages to others who have signed up to receive them), the Yellow Pages website, and the Web-based productivity applications developed by 37signals.[153] A number of open-source programs have been diffused widely; for example, according to the July 2008 Netcraft survey, 49.5 percent of the nearly 175 million Internet domains surveyed used Apache Web server software.[154] The Firefox browser, an open-source program, had a market share of 21 percent in November 2008, which made it the second most popular browser after Internet Explorer (which had 70 percent of the market).[155] Sendmail, an open-source software program for routing e-mail on the Internet, was estimated in 2008 to handle about 65 percent of all Internet e-mail traffic.[156] Linux, an open-source computer operating system for personal computers, is estimated to have between 7 million and 16 million users worldwide.[157] All these products compete with commercial off-the-shelf alternatives. Firefox, Sendmail, and Linux are not necessarily examples of user-driven innovation alone. And not all open-source software exemplifies user-driven innovation; companies have developed hybrid models that enable them to benefit from open-source software.[158]

In addition, free revealing often reduces the costs of second-generation innovators who are interested in improving an innovation. Instead of licensing the right to use the innovation for a fee or spending time and effort creating a comparable solution on which to build, innovators interested in improving an existing application can directly build on it and incur only the incremental costs associated with improving it.

The Possibility of Innovators' Contracting with Network Providers

So far we have assumed that, in the core-centered architecture, network providers and their employees are the only remaining innovators. One may ask whether the few network providers that control innovation can replicate the advantages of decentralized innovation by a diverse set of

Table 8.2
Different environments for application innovation and deployment.

	End-to-end network	Non-end-to-end network with network provider contracting	Core-centered network
Control over application innovation	Application developers	Network providers	Network providers
Control over application deployment	Users	Network providers	Network providers
Innovator pool	Large and diverse	Large and diverse	Small and homogeneous

innovators, for example by contracting with independent innovators (table 8.2).[159] (Thinking about this question will also help us understand whether and why it is important if application developers other than the network provider can innovate independently without needing permission or cooperation from the network provider.) Contracting with independent innovators may enable a network provider to benefit from opportunities discovered by such innovators, to take advantage of their differing capabilities, motivations, or cost structures, or, in some architectures, to overcome the fact that only a limited number of projects can be pursued within the firm.[160] Though such a strategy would increase the amount of innovation over what network providers alone would realize, it would not create as much innovation as a decentralized environment for innovation.[161]

First, if there is uncertainty, any increase in the number of decision makers that must approve an innovation reduces the chances that the innovation is realized.[162] A network provider will see no need to contract for applications that it perceives as infeasible, as not viable, or as counter to its strategic interests. These projects would be realized under an end-to-end architecture, but not under contracting.

Second, an innovator has to disclose its innovation as part of the contract negotiations. If the innovation is not protected by intellectual-property rights, there is a danger that the network provider may appropriate the innovation without paying for it, which may reduce the innovator's incentive to innovate in the first place.

Third, bargaining costs and strategic behavior may prevent a contractual solution.

Fourth, the incentives for independent innovators who can directly commercialize their innovation are higher owing to the possibility of exceptionally large gains. If the innovators depend on contracting with a network provider in order to commercialize their innovation and cannot gain access to the market on their own, they do not have any bargaining power. In fact, the network provider will be in a monopsony or oligopsony position, which leads to very low prices. In this case, the innovators will have to bear the risk of failure or bargaining breakdown, and will receive only modest compensation if they succeed. Such an incentive structure will probably not be sufficient to motivate innovators or their investors to put up with the risk.

Finally, if innovators have to contract with the network provider before they can innovate, they may be less able to react to new developments once they have started their project. Throughout the history of the Internet, successful innovators have often changed course repeatedly—for example, in response to feedback from consumers, or in response to an unexpected scarcity of funding. For example, in January 1999 Meg Hourihan and Evan Williams founded Pyra Labs to develop Web-based project-management software for geographically distributed project members to use in managing and coordinating their work. Users, however, were much more interested in Blogger, an application that enabled them to post entries to weblogs. Pyra Labs had made Blogger available for free to attract users to their project-management product.[163] Since they did not have enough resources to focus on both products, they finally decided to focus their efforts on Blogger (box 8.14).

Similarly, Caterina Fake and Stewart Butterfield, the founders behind Flickr, had not planned to develop a website for online photo sharing with social networking elements. They had founded their company, Ludicorp, to build a Web-based online game for a very large number of players. A shortage of funds motivated them to switch their focus to creating, instead, an application that would enable people to chat about photos. In response to consumer feedback, this application then evolved, through a series of changes, into a platform for sharing photos (box 8.3).

More generally, starting with one approach and then adapting it as events unfold may be the only way to successfully navigate fundamental uncertainty.[164] In a network that requires innovators to coordinate their activities with the network provider, this may not be possible. The transaction-cost and coordination-cost theories discussed in chapter 5 predict that deciding what to do in response to new developments is much more difficult and more time-consuming across firm boundaries than within a single firm. This is because firms have differing perspectives on how to react, and

Box 8.14

Blogger

Meg Hourihan and Evan Williams founded Pyra Labs in January 1999 to develop Web-based project-management software that would enable geographically distributed project members to manage and coordinate work.[a] In 1998, the first weblogs were started. But weblogs were the province of the technically sophisticated. The aspiring weblogger had to set up and find a host for a website and had to maintain the software using an FTP client or command-line prompts. A few weblogs, like Arts and Letters Daily, had captured some mass attention, but it was still relatively rare to keep or read a weblog.[b]

Williams had written some software for his personal weblog that automated the task of posting entries to a blog. The members of the Pyra Labs team used this software to post thoughts and information to an internal weblog that they used to coordinate their work, and later wrote software that let them cross-post some of these entries to the company's external weblog. Thinking that this tool might be attractive to website developers (the audience they were targeting with their main application), they decided to add it to their project-management software as an additional application and give it away for free, hoping that it would attract users to their main product.

People began using Blogger immediately. It became much more successful than the Pyra Labs team had expected, which created a problem for the company. People were using Blogger instead of Pyra Labs' "real" product. Though the team was convinced that users would be willing to pay for the project-management application, they could not figure out how to make money from Blogger. They tried to work on both products for a while, but this strained the resources of their small team. After Blogger's user base grew steadily for more than 9 months, they decided to focus their efforts on Blogger and drop their original project.

a. Livingston 2007, pp. 111–125; McKinnon 2001; Mead 2000.
b. Hourihan 2005; Mead 2000; Galant 2005.

---

the lack of efficient mechanisms for inter-firm decision making and dispute resolution may make the differences difficult to resolve.

Thus, relative to architectures in which innovators can innovate independently, architectures that force innovators to contract or otherwise coordinate with a network provider before they can innovate not only constrain independent innovators' ability and incentives to start a project. They also limit innovators' ability to react to new developments during the lifetime of the project—a limitation that is particularly detrimental under uncertainty.

The Costs of Diversity

Diversity is not without costs. Each approach incurs costs, and not every project will turn out to be successful. Because successful projects cannot be identified in advance, these costs seem to be unavoidable.[165] For the innovators' decision to innovate to be rational in expectation, the innovators must, on average, be sufficiently compensated from successful projects to compensate for the risk of losses associated with unsuccessful projects.[166] Empirical evidence on investment in high-technology ventures indicates that this is the case. For example, one study showed that, of the projects under analysis, the median project yielded less than the capitalized cost of capital funds invested, but that losses on the majority of projects were more than offset by gains from the most successful projects.[167] From society's point of view, the social costs of failed projects may be reduced by two factors. For people experimenting in their free time, the main cost is the opportunity cost of not doing other things that one normally does in one's free time. If the innovator had otherwise engaged in unproductive uses of her time, such as watching television, the social cost of the failed experiment may not be very high.[168] More generally, failed projects may still produce social benefits through spillovers. Other innovators may learn a valuable lesson from one innovator's failure—a lesson that may allow them to save the expense associated with trying the same approach themselves, or to use insights offered by the failed approach to improve their own product.[169]

In sum, if there is uncertainty, or if users' needs are heterogeneous, a larger and more diverse group of innovators that independently decide on their approaches to innovation will realize a larger and more diverse number of applications than a few network providers that control which innovative ideas can be realized. The larger and more diverse number of innovative projects, in turn, guarantees a more complete search of the problem space and increases the chance that beneficial applications or approaches will be detected. It increases the probability of success and increases the expected quality of the best results. Thus, diversity increases the amount and quality of innovation. If users' needs are heterogeneous, diversity will also result in a greater variety of products that better meet users' needs.

Effect of Differences in Control over Deployment

In the end-to-end architecture, innovators independently choose which applications to realize; in the core-centered architecture, only network providers make this selection. In the end-to-end architecture, users decide which applications are deployed and used by installing them on their computers and using them; in the core-centered architecture (and in the controllable architectures), network providers control which applications can be deployed and used. So far, we have focused on how differences in control over application development affect innovation. But what is the effect on innovation of differences in control over deployment?

Users' and network providers' decisions to deploy applications may differ for two reasons. First, network providers' interests may differ from users' interests, which can lead them to reject applications that users would find attractive. (As was shown in chapter 6, factors such as a concentrated market structure or market power due to switching costs or incomplete information may enable network providers to reject applications without being disciplined by the threat of customers' switching to another provider.) Whereas users choose the applications that best suit their needs, network providers may use different criteria. For example, as we saw in chapter 6, under certain conditions network providers may have an incentive to exclude an application that competes with one of their own applications.[170] Apple's behavior toward iPhone applications illustrates this possibility. Before any application can be sold in the iPhone App Store, Apple must approve it. Since the iPhone App Store is the exclusive distribution medium for iPhone applications, this enables Apple to control which applications can be deployed.[171] Apple has rejected several applications for the iPhone, claiming that they duplicated functionality provided by existing Apple applications. For example, MailWrangler, an application that enabled users to manage their GMail accounts from within the iPhone browser, was rejected for duplicating the iPhone's e-mail application. Another application, Podcaster, let users listen to podcasts and download podcasts over the air directly to the iPhone. In September 2008, Apple rejected that application, arguing that users could already download podcasts on their computer and load them on their iPhones. In December 2008, Apple itself introduced Podcaster's functionality. In both cases, users, developers, and observers argued that the functionality differed from and met their needs better than Apple's existing applications.[172] Thus, Apple blocked applications that competed with its own products, or with products it hoped to create, even though at least some users clearly preferred the blocked product. Similarly, when choosing to exclude an application in order to manage bandwidth, network providers may consider whether the application is easy to detect, whether their preferred vendor's products can detect the application, or whether blocking or throttling the application has a noticeable effect on traffic (ironically, the last criterion makes popular applications particularly attractive targets for this type of bandwidth management). As Comcast's blocking of the popular file-sharing application BitTorrent shows, the fact that an application is popular with users does not necessarily prevent the network provider from interfering with it. Instead, the network provider may simply try to interfere with the application in a way that is less noticeable by the user.

Second, decisions by users and by network providers to deploy applications may differ for another reason. Even in cases where network providers would like to deploy applications that users want, they are not necessarily able to do so. As we saw above, new applications are often afflicted with considerable uncertainty. No one knows which applications or features users will find attractive. Often users themselves do not know whether they like a specific application or find it useful until they have tried it or seen others using it. Thus, letting users choose applications replaces network providers' guesses about what users may like with a decision by users, who best know their current preferences and needs. It gives applications whose usefulness or attractiveness is not immediately apparent a chance, and it allows users' preferences and practices to evolve as a result of exposure to or experimentation with a new application. In addition, giving application developers direct access to users lets them experiment and change their product offerings in response to user feedback. The stories of PayPal and Flickr have shown how important this can be.[173] Being able to choose themselves is also important for users or user groups whose needs are idiosyncratic, since their needs may not be known to or may not be important to the network provider.

Overall Effect of Architectural Differences on Application Innovation

Thus, the mechanism that produces innovation in applications under an end-to-end architecture has two components: widespread experimentation by a large and diverse group of innovators who independently select whether to realize their innovative ideas and user choice among the resulting applications. Under uncertainty or consumer heterogeneity, this mechanism will produce more and better results than innovation in network architectures that concentrate control over innovation or deployment in the hands of a few network providers.

Together with the results of chapter 7, these insights help us predict how the differences between architectures based on the broad version of the end-to-end arguments and architectures deviating from it affect the overall amount and quality of innovation. The overall amount of innovation is determined jointly by the effects of changes in the costs and benefits of innovation (which may affect network providers and independent innovators differently), changes in the size and diversity of the innovator pool, and changes in the allocation of control over innovation and deployment.

With an architecture based on the broad version of the end-to-end arguments such as the Internet's original architecture taken as a baseline, making the network more opaque increases the costs of innovation for network providers and independent innovators alike (although ultimately network providers are better able to deal with the situation; in the extreme case, they are the only remaining potential innovators). The private benefits of application-level innovation will usually stay the same; they may increase or decrease slightly if the reduction in the number of innovators reduces competition in the market for an application.[174] Relative to the end-to-end architecture, this reduces the number of innovations that innovators will find worth realizing for both network providers and independent innovators. As we saw in chapter 4, the increase in costs may particularly affect innovators' ability to continue to serve niche markets or low-value markets, and may reduce their willingness to take risks. As the pool of innovators becomes smaller and less diverse, and as control over application innovation and deployment shifts to network providers, the amount and the quality of innovation are reduced further, and more user needs are left unserved.

Again taking the end-to-end architecture as a baseline, increasing the controllability of the network increases network providers' general profits and their expected benefits from their own application-level innovation, while independent innovators' expected benefits decrease. While network providers' costs stay the same, independents' costs of innovation increase. As a result, network providers' incentives to innovate increase, while independent innovators' incentives to innovate decrease. As costs and the requirements that potential innovators must meet increase, the size and the diversity of the innovator pool decrease. As this chapter has shown, the increase in innovation by a few network providers cannot offset the reduction or elimination of innovation by a large number of independent innovators.

Thus, under uncertainty or consumer heterogeneity, deviations along both dimensions reduce the overall amount and quality of innovation, and leave more user needs unserved. Relative to a fully opaque architecture, network providers' incentives to innovate will be higher under a fully controllable architecture. Also, although their incentives to innovate decrease, not all independent innovators will lose their ability to innovate. As a result, the overall amount of innovation will be higher under a fully controllable architecture than under a fully opaque one. Since the core-centered architecture combines the characteristics of a fully controllable and a fully opaque architecture, it will produce the least amount of innovation.

9 Public and Private Interests in Network Architectures

Different network architectures shape the economic environment for application innovation in different ways. In particular, a network architecture's compliance with or deviation from the broad version of the end-to-end arguments affects who can innovate and what incentives they have to do so. Ultimately (other things such as the set of actors exposed to the architecture and the set of constraints [i.e., laws or norms] under which they operate all being equal), these differences will result in different amounts, different qualities, and different kinds of innovation in applications.

But just because there are differences, legislators and regulators do not have to care about them. Therefore, this chapter evaluates how the differences among network architectures that comply with or deviate from the broad version of the end-to-end arguments relate to the public interest. If the values fostered by architectures based on the broad version are in the public interest, can we rely on the market to produce these architectures, or is there a wedge between the public's and network providers' private interests in network architectures?

Public Interests in Network Architectures

Social Benefits

As we saw in chapter 8, architectures based on the broad version of the end-to-end arguments provide an economic environment that is more conducive to application innovation than architectures that deviate from it. Apart from differences in the costs and benefits of innovation, the architectures allow different types of innovators to innovate. If there is technological uncertainty or market uncertainty, or if users' needs are heterogeneous, allowing innovators other than network providers to innovate increases the amount and the quality of innovation. If users' needs are heterogeneous, increasing the size and diversity of the innovator pool will also result in higher product variety that better meets users' needs. In the current Internet, technological uncertainty, market uncertainty, and user heterogeneity are still high. The technology of the network and the technologies for the development of applications are still evolving, creating considerable technological uncertainty. As more people and more businesses connect to the Internet, the population of Internet users will become more diverse. In an ideal situation, if a country manages to bridge the digital divide, the heterogeneity of Internet users will mirror the heterogeneity of society. As a result, the heterogeneity of users' needs is bound to increase. Thus, the conditions under which increases in the size and in the diversity of the innovator pool under an end-to-end architecture result in increases in the amount and the quality of innovation and in applications that better meet users' needs are still met. As a result, other things being equal, an architecture that is based on the broad version of the end-to-end arguments will foster more and better application innovation than an architecture that deviates from that version.

But is more innovation in applications socially beneficial? This question can be approached in several ways. First, one may ask whether the amount of innovation is generally lower than the social optimum. In this case, more innovation would be socially beneficial.[1] In dealing with such questions, economists often note that the link between innovation and social welfare is theoretically ambiguous.[2] On the one hand, some economic models highlight the possibility that firms, in their desire to capture the rents from innovation, may increase the level of investment in research and development above the socially efficient amount.[3] On the other hand, innovators may not be able to completely appropriate the social gains from innovation, which would lead them to invest less than the socially optimal amount in innovation.[4] For example, innovators may not be able to capture all the consumer value created by their innovation, or other firms may be able to exploit the innovation without compensating the original innovator, either of which will lead to uncompensated spillovers. While the theory is ambiguous, empirical studies indicate that there is too little innovation, because private firms are typically unable to appropriate all social gains from the innovation.[5]

Second, one may ask whether in the specific case of the Internet there is likely to be less innovation than the socially optimal amount. The Internet is a platform product that may be used with a large number of complementary products.[6] Innovation in platform products and in complementary products is subject to two types of externalities that are likely to reduce the amount of innovation below the social optimum.[7] The first externality operates vertically between the platform product and each complementary product; the second operates horizontally among different complementary products.

Owing to the complementarity between the platform product and complementary products, innovation in complementary products usually increases demand for the platform product, and vice versa. If the platform product and the complementary product are developed by different economic actors, the innovator in a complementary component does not appropriate his innovation's positive effects on the platform product, and vice versa.[8] On the Internet, new applications usually make Internet services more attractive, but an independent application developer does not capture this increase in value.

Innovation in one complementary product usually increases demand for the platform product, which may in turn positively affect demand for other complementary products. If different economic actors pursue innovation in the different components, each actor does not appropriate his innovation's positive effects on the other components. As a result, each actor's incentives to innovate will be lower than the social optimum. In the case of the Internet, application developers do not capture the beneficial effect of their innovation on other, unaffiliated applications.

A common solution to the problems caused by such externalities is integration among all affected parties. The resulting integrated entity internalizes the externalities and therefore has higher incentives to innovate.[9] In the context of the Internet, this is not a feasible solution, since a few network providers will not be able to identify and realize all beneficial uses of the platform.[10]

All this suggests that there will be too little application innovation, and that an increase in application innovation is socially beneficial. Moreover, application innovation is crucial for enabling the Internet to realize its economic, social, cultural, and political potential.

As a general-purpose technology, the Internet has the potential to contribute disproportionately to economic growth.[11] Fostering innovation in applications is critical to realizing this potential. Technological progress is the most important engine of growth for modern economies. Economists have estimated that as much as 70 percent of the growth in output per hour in the United States between 1950 and 1993 can be attributed to technological growth.[12] Exactly how and to what degree specific technological advancements contribute to economic growth, however, is less clear.

Research in economics indicates that technological inventions do not contribute equally to economic growth. Instead, over extended periods of time, technical progress and economic growth seem to be driven by a few general-purpose technologies; some examples are the steam engine, the electric motor, semiconductors, and information technology.[13] General-purpose technologies offer generic functionalities that can potentially be applied in a large number of sectors within the economy. As the use of a general-purpose technology spreads throughout the economy, use of the technology increases productivity in the sectors in which the technology is applied. At the same time, new applications of the technology or adoption of the technology in additional sectors of the economy increase the returns to innovation in the general purpose technology, triggering new advances in the general-purpose technology itself. These advances, in turn, may spawn the adoption of the general-purpose technology in additional sectors of the economy, or may lead to new or improved applications in sectors that already use the technology. Thus, the adoption of general-purpose technologies exhibits increasing returns to scale. The ongoing dynamic interactions among new or improved uses of the technology, adoption of the technology in additional sectors of the economy and advances in the general purpose technology can create enormous increases in economic growth.[14]

Owing to the general nature of a general-purpose technology, the mere existence of such a technology is not sufficient to have a positive effect on economic growth. A general-purpose technology's effects on growth stem from its adoption in more and more sectors of the economy and from the resulting increases in productivity. Owing to the general nature of the technology, however, its potential applications and uses are not immediately obvious. Instead, realizing a general-purpose technology's inherent promises in a specific sector of the economy requires a considerable amount of innovative activity in order to identify and realize potential uses. Thus, adoption of a general-purpose technology in a specific area is an important innovative activity in its own right; for this reason, such activity is often called *co-invention*.[15]

As a result, the rate at which a general-purpose technology can affect economic growth depends on the rate of co-invention, not primarily on the rate of technological innovation in the general-purpose technology itself. Thus, the cost of co-invention is an important determinant of the speed with which the social benefits of the general-purpose technology can be realized.[16] In fact, the empirically found delay with which firms' investments in information technology lead to increases in economic growth[17] is usually explained by the high costs of co-invention—that is, by the costs of finding the best ways to apply the new technology in a firm's daily operations, the costs of developing the appropriate software, and the costs of changing organizational structures and processes in response to the new opportunities.[18]

Thus, on the one hand, general-purpose technologies have the potential to contribute disproportionately to economic growth—that is their promise. On the other hand, the rate at which a general-purpose technology can contribute to this growth is limited by the rate at which *new* uses of the technology can be identified and realized.

These insights help us think about the importance of application innovation for economic growth.[19] As a general-purpose technology, the Internet has the potential to contribute disproportionately to economic growth. The ability to communicate cheaply and cost-effectively with computers all over the world may be usefully applied in a large number of contexts. The higher the number of uses, the higher the aggregated increases in productivity and the higher the effect of the Internet on economic growth.[20] The rate at which the Internet can contribute to economic growth, however, depends on the rate of co-invention—that is, the rate at which potential uses for the Internet are identified and applications that enable or support these uses are developed, deployed, and used.[21] Measures that increase the cost of co-invention or otherwise reduce the amount of co-invention can harm social welfare significantly. Specifically, increasing application-level innovation increases economic growth; in contrast, limiting application-level innovation may significantly limit the Internet's ability to contribute to economic growth.

The importance of innovation in applications goes beyond its role in fostering economic growth. As the literature on general-purpose technologies reminds us, the Internet, as a general-purpose technology, does not create value through its existence alone. It creates value by enabling users to do the things they want or need to do.[22] Applications are the tools that let users realize this value. For example, the Internet's political, social, or cultural potential—its potential to improve democratic discourse, to facilitate political organization and action, or to provide a decentralized environment for social and cultural interaction in which anyone can participate[23]—is tightly linked to applications that help individuals, groups, or organizations do more things or do them more efficiently, and not just in economic contexts but also in social, cultural, or political contexts.[24] For example, e-mail, instant messaging, Internet telephony, video chat, or social networking applications let us maintain or deepen our existing relationships with family members, friends, and colleagues, but also establish new relationships with people who share similar interests or goals, or with people who are interesting to us for other reasons.[25] Other applications enable us to organize and coordinate a multitude of tasks—for example, shopping, a class reunion, a fundraiser for a preschool, or a major political campaign—more efficiently.

The World Wide Web, weblogs, open-source programming languages, and audio and video processing software enable anyone who is willing and able to invest the time and effort necessary to master these applications to become a creator of information products at costs low enough to support a wide range of motivations and strategies. E-mail, mailing lists, content versioning systems, and wikis allow loosely joined and geographically distributed individuals to work together to create all sorts of information products, whether they are open-source programs or online encyclopedias. Such applications greatly increase our capacity to produce things alone or in groups, outside the realm of the market. As Yochai Benkler has shown, this capacity to be a speaker, not just a listener, and to actively shape our environment instead of just being at the receiving end, is central to the Internet's potential to enhance individual freedom, to provide a platform for better democratic participation, to foster a more critical and self-reflective culture, and potentially to improve human development everywhere.[26]

Across all these domains, new and better applications may open up new or better opportunities for users, increasing the Internet's potential to create value. Innovation in applications alone is not sufficient to create value; applications merely increase the potential for value creation. The value promised by applications is realized when users adopt and use these applications to realize their goals.

The kind of value that is realized may differ depending on the type of use. The value of consumptive uses (or uses preparing for consumptive uses) is realized when the user consumes the good. For example, I am entertained when I watch my favorite television show online. The use of a search engine to find the product I want to buy or an online shop to buy the product creates value by preparing my ultimate consumptive use of the good in a way that is more cost-efficient or time-efficient for me, or that helps me find a product that better meets my needs.[27]

The value of productive uses is more difficult to determine and to measure.[28] Consider someone who improves an article on Wikipedia or contributes an article to a website devoted to a certain subject. This person will realize certain benefits from doing so, including the pleasure of being creative and the potential to become recognized as an expert in the field. But the value created by such use of the Internet goes beyond that. People who read this person's article may learn something. People can benefit from his article even if they are not themselves Internet users. For example, a teacher could use the article to teach her class, or could print it out and distribute it to her students as supplemental reading. The article's beneficial effect may even affect those who never read the article, whether online or offline, if the higher level of education on this topic ultimately helps to improve societal conditions.

Similarly, political bloggers may realize some value resulting from their own blog entries. The political value created beyond that may be relatively tangible when the blogging directly influences the way political events unfold. For example, in 2002, Trent Lott, the US Senate's Republican Majority Leader, resigned from his position after he had commented at Senator J. Strom Thurmond's hundredth-birthday party that, in the words of a journalist, "the United States would have avoided 'all these problems' (Lott) if then-segregationist Strom Thurmond had been elected president in 1948."[29] The mainstream media originally ignored Lott's remark, although it had been broadcast on the cable channel C-SPAN. They began to focus on the remark only after it had triggered intense debate and criticism among bloggers. In other cases, bloggers have contributed "talking points" that were later used by members of the US Congress in speeches. Bloggers also made it more difficult for President George W. Bush to gain some support from Democrats for his proposed Social Security reforms by publicly identifying and criticizing Democrats who were thinking of supporting Bush's proposal.[30] Debates in the "blogosphere" also may help to highlight interesting or emerging issues for journalists working for traditional media, which in turn may frame the public discourse on those issues.[31] Most generally, blogs and other forms of online discourse may improve the political discourse on a subject, thereby benefiting even members of society who have not participated in the deliberations.[32]

Thus, productive Internet uses often create positive externalities that benefit not only other Internet users but also people who do not use the Internet.[33]

Whether users can realize the value promised by particular applications, or, more generally, whether the Internet can fulfill its economic, social, cultural, and political potential, depends not only on the availability of applications, but also on the way in which the architecture of a network shapes the environment for the use of the network.

As we have seen throughout this book, a network's architecture shapes the economic system for the design, development, and production of the network's components by imposing constraints on those who design, develop, and produce the components. Similarly, an architecture affects the social systems for the use of the network—the actors in these systems, the relationships among them, the governance structures through which they interact, and their behavior—by imposing constraints on those using the network. Of course, architecture is not the only constraint that shapes the options available to users of the system and affects the costs and benefits associated with these options. Architectural constraints interact with other constraints (including laws, norms, and more traditional economic constraints) to establish the set of constraints under which system users operate. The ultimate effect of an architecture on the environment for the use of the system at a specific place and time depends not only on the set of constraints, but also on the characteristics of the actors exposed to the architecture and on their existing and expected relationships with other actors. Depending on these other factors, the same architecture may result in very different actual environments for the use of the network.[34]

Whereas other scholars have highlighted the role of law, particularly intellectual-property law, in realizing the Internet's political and cultural potential,[35] I focus in this book on the specific effect of architecture. To isolate the effect of architecture, I neglect the effect of potential differences in actors or non-architectural constraints and focus on the technological possibilities afforded by or constrained by different architectures without implying that such possibilities can be or will be realized by everyone or everywhere. Although tracing how exactly design principles such as the broad version of the end-to-end arguments shape the environments for the economic, social, cultural, and political uses of the Internet is beyond the scope of this book, a few observations can be offered.

First, network architectures influence who controls which applications and what content can be used. In a network with an architecture based on the broad version and with a deployment context in which users control their end hosts, users can determine independently which applications or what content they want to use. Since the network is application-blind, network providers cannot interfere with users' choices. In contrast, network providers whose networks deviate from the broad version have at least some control over the use of their network. As we saw in chapter 7, this control is maximized in a fully controllable architecture. Most generally, the value of the Internet for users is maximized when they can do the things they need or want to do, using the applications or accessing the content that best suits their needs. Users know best what these are. In contrast, as we saw in chapters 6 and 8, if network providers can control the use of the network, decisions about which applications and what content to support or exclude may be driven by motivations that are not necessarily identical with users' preferences, preventing users from acting on their preferences and using the Internet in the way that creates the most value for them. For example, if I am working on an open-source project that uses BitTorrent to distribute its source code, and the network provider chooses to single out BitTorrent to manage bandwidth on its network, I am not able to use the application that best meets my needs or to use the Internet in the way that is most valuable to me. Thus, network architectures (such as architectures based on the broad version of the end-to-end arguments with a deployment context in which users control the end hosts) that allow users to decide how they want to use the network will let users realize more of the Internet's potential value for themselves than architectures in which network providers control the use of the network. I am not claiming that users' choices maximize the Internet's value for society. As we saw above, users do not appropriate many of the positive benefits that their productive uses create for other users or for those who do not use the Internet. At the same time, under flat-rate pricing users will not sufficiently consider the negative effects of their uses on other users (for example, negative effects due to congestion). Whether the positive or the negative externalities dominate on balance is difficult to determine. Identifying and implementing ways to encourage users to consider at least some of the negative externalities without overly stifling positive externalities would increase the likelihood that the balance is positive.[36] I argue, though, that having users choose applications or content provides more value to society as a whole than having network providers choose for them. This is because, taken together, network providers' limited ability to completely appropriate their users' benefits from the different uses or to appropriate the positive externalities these uses create for users of other Internet service providers or for those not using the Internet, as well as the various other biases and wedges between users' and network providers' interests and the public's and network providers' interests (discussed in chapters 6 and 8 and throughout this chapter), create a larger wedge between the public's interests and the network providers' private interest than is created by the fact that in countries with flat-rate pricing users do not internalize the congestion externalities during times of congestion.

Second, network architectures influence the environment for the use of the network by affecting the ease with which users (whether individuals, groups, firms, or other organizations) can adopt and use new applications that increase their productivity. The ease of adoption, in turn, influences the rate at which the Internet can contribute to economic growth.[37] As we saw in chapters 4 and 7, network architecture influences the costs and requirements for adopting new applications, for example by influencing whether new applications can be adopted incrementally. In this respect, a network architecture based on the broad version establishes the lowest hurdles for adopting applications by letting users adopt new applications incrementally (i.e., independently of other users) at very low costs—the costs of installing the application on their computer.

Third, network architectures influence the Internet's ability to realize its social, political, or cultural potential in subtler ways. As other scholars have shown, the individual's ability to speak and be heard, to be a producer and not just a consumer, and to have access to a wide variety of diverse sources that are not selected or controlled by a central gatekeeper who has its own motivations are central to the Internet's political and cultural potential.[38] All these aspects may be affected by the ways in which a network architecture shapes the environment for the use of the system.

Consider some of the ways in which network architectures shape the environment for political uses of the Internet. A network architecture based on the broad version of the end-to-end arguments is not optimized in favor of specific applications. In particular, it is not optimized in favor of end-user applications that receive a lot of data but do not send a lot of data. Such an environment equally supports an individual's ability to speak and listen. In contrast, an architecture that is optimized in favor of applications that download a lot of data but do not upload a lot of data (for example, by providing asymmetric bandwidth to and from the home) favors listening over speaking, consuming over producing, and consumptive uses over communicative uses (such as video chatting or video conferencing) that entail sending and receiving large amounts of data.[39]

More generally, given that network providers aim to maximize their profits, there is a danger that if network providers are allowed to optimize the network in favor of specific applications they will optimize the network in favor of uses that create observable value that they can appropriate over uses that create less observable and appropriable benefits. As we saw above, the value of consumptive uses is realized by the user itself and is relatively well defined, whereas productive uses often create external benefits for other users (and even for non-users) that neither the productive user nor the network provider can appropriate. This may lead network providers to optimize the network in favor of consumptive uses over productive uses.[40]

Architectures that enable network providers to control the applications and the content on their network give them the power to shape the information environment according to their private interests. If I am interested in content that my network provider happens to restrict, my ability to educate myself, my ability to contribute to a discussion on this subject, and my ability to make informed decisions are impeded. Instead, ISPs gain the power to shape public discourse based on their own interests and idiosyncratic content policies. This may affect users in their capacity as speakers and listeners.

Network architectures deviating from the broad version of the end-to-end arguments may also make it more difficult for non-commercial actors to participate in democratic or cultural discourse. For example, by using peer-to-peer file-sharing applications instead of a central server to distribute information goods, these actors can reduce their costs of distribution by shifting some of these costs to users of the file-sharing application who contribute their own bandwidth to assist in the distribution of the file. Network architectures in which network providers manage bandwidth by throttling or excluding these file-sharing applications may reduce the ability of these actors to participate in democratic or cultural discourse by making it more costly for them to make their information available to others.

In sum, network architecture affects the Internet's potential to create economic, social, cultural, and political value not only by fostering or impeding application innovation, but also by shaping the environment for the use of the network. In particular, applying the broad version of the end-to-end arguments ensures user choice, non-discrimination, and non-optimization all of which contribute directly to characteristics of the Internet (such as enabling users to listen, speak, consume, and produce, and to do so without intervention by the network provider) that are central to the Internet's social, cultural, and political potential.[41]

Social Costs
Using the broad version also has social costs.

First, as we saw in chapter 2, optimizing the network for particular applications or uses may create cost savings or performance gains for the applications for which the network is optimized. Keeping the network general, as the broad version requires, means forgoing these benefits.

Second, as we saw in chapters 6 and 7, deviating from the broad version by increasing the controllability of the network increases network providers' profits. Lower profits may reduce network providers' incentives to deploy more and better broadband networks. I am not convinced that the relatively lower profit in a network architecture based on the broad version reduces network providers' profits so significantly that they will no longer be able to deploy more and better broadband networks, or that network providers would really use the additional profits to deploy more networks instead of using the money for other things such as increasing dividends. But until we have data with which to better assess whether this is a real problem, it is safer to assume that network providers' incentives to deploy more and better broadband networks will be reduced to some degree.

Third, some scholars have argued that the end-to-end arguments constrain the needed evolution of the network's core by preventing Quality of Service, restricting the amount of state in the network, or requiring the network to be simple. As we saw in chapter 3, these assumptions are unfounded. The broad version provides much more room for network evolution than its critics recognize. It does, however, constrain the evolution of the network to some degree by requiring the network to be general, or by allowing only some forms of Quality of Service.

Finally, critics argue that the broad version makes it more difficult, or impossible, to make the network secure. Some seem to think that the broad version of the end-to-end arguments requires all functions related to security to be implemented at the end hosts. On this perception, some have argued that a network based on the broad version makes it impossible to defend against distributed denial-of-service attacks, in which distributed attackers flood the target (which may be a link or an end host) with unwanted traffic that exceeds the target's capacity to handle it, making it impossible for the target to properly handle its legitimate traffic. This argument is based on the view that distributed denial-of-service attacks can be identified only in the network, since only the network can recognize traffic patterns that may indicate an attack.[42]

Others have argued that the broad version of the end-to-end arguments, by assigning responsibility for security to the end hosts, creates challenges for users who have little knowledge of how to best secure their computers. Jonathan Zittrain has argued that the existence of a large number of unsecured end hosts may facilitate a catastrophic security attack that will have widespread and severe consequences for affected individual end users and businesses. In the aftermath of such an attack, Zittrain claims, users may be willing to completely lock down their computers so that they can run only applications approved by a trusted third party.[43] Given that general-purpose end hosts controlled by users rather than by third-party gatekeepers are an important component of the mechanism that fosters application innovation in the Internet,[44] Zittrain argues, following the broad version of the end-to-end arguments may threaten the Internet's ability to support new applications more than deviating from the end-to-end arguments and implementing some security functions in the network, because, according to Zittrain, following the broad version will ultimately result in a world in which end hosts are effectively controlled by third parties, through the sequence of events just described.[45] Again, this argument relies heavily on the assumption that the end-to-end arguments prevent the implementation of security-related functions in the network.[46]

The perception that the broad version of the end-to-end arguments requires "security" to be implemented at the end hosts is too strong.[47] The broad version provides guidelines for the placement of individual functions, not groups of functions belonging to a certain category. Thus, whether the broad version requires a function to be implemented at the end hosts or in the network must be determined function by function.[48]

For example, if it is true that distributed denial-of-service attacks can be identified and stopped only in the network,[49] the broad version clearly allows the implementation of the associated functions in the network. After all, the broad version does not prevent functions from being implemented in the network if they cannot be completely and correctly implemented at the end hosts only.[50]

In contrast, according to the broad version, a function (such as encryption) that can only be completely and correctly implemented end-to-end between the original source and ultimate destination of data should not be implemented in the network. This is because "a function or service should be carried out within a network layer only if it is needed by all clients of that layer, and it can be completely implemented in that layer."[51]

Thus, depending on the function, the broad version may not require that the function be implemented at the end hosts. But even if the broad version requires a function to be implemented at the end hosts, considerations such as those advanced by Zittrain may require a deviation from the broad version. More generally, if end users' inability to secure their end hosts makes it impossible to provide "effective" security by implementing functions solely at the end hosts, it may be necessary to implement them in the network even if the broad version would generally require these functions to be implemented on end hosts.[52] As we saw in chapter 2, the broad version is based on the assumption that long-term evolvability, reliability, and application autonomy are more important than the performance gains or cost savings resulting from the short-term optimization of the system. For reasons that were set out in detail in chapter 2, factors that were considered in this trade-off usually cannot justify a deviation from this rule. For example, the performance gain from implementing a certain application-specific function in the network cannot usually justify a deviation from the broad version, as the loss of these benefits has already been factored into the trade-off underlying the decision to use the design principle. In contrast, the effect of the broad version on the security of the system was not similarly considered as part of the original trade-offs (i.e., the trade-off underlying the design principle and the trade-off underlying the decision to use this design principle for a particular system). Insofar as maintaining the security of the Internet is a value that fundamentally affects the usefulness of the Internet for its users, and ultimately for society as a whole, deviating from the broad version of the end-to-end arguments for certain security-related functions may be justified.

This does not mean that any implementation of security-related functions in the network is automatically justified. Some solutions may affect the evolvability of the network and its ability to foster innovation more than others, and it is worth investing the time, money, and effort required to find solutions that maintain the Internet's openness to new applications as much as possible.[53] As a negative example, firewalls (which deviate from the broad version) have been particularly harmful for application development, and, together with network-address translators (which also deviate from the broad version), have made it difficult if not impossible to deploy new transport-layer protocols or certain types of new applications.[54] Thus, whether a specific security-related function should be implemented in the network although the broad version of the end-to-end arguments requires that this function be implemented at the end hosts can only be determined case by case after careful consideration of the consequences for the evolvability of the network. The discussion above shows, however, that the broad version is able to interact with and adapt to other requirements in a way that is flexible enough to maintain the design principle's usefulness in the face of changing requirements for the Internet.

In sum, the broad version of the end-to-end arguments constrains solutions to security problems much less than is often assumed. Still, protecting the evolvability of the system constrains the range of potential solutions more than architectures deviating from the broad version, in which concerns about evolvability do not play a role.

Trade-Offs

Thus, there are four potential social costs of using the broad version of the end-to-end arguments: the forgone benefits of short-term optimization (e.g. performance gains or cost savings), some limits on the evolvability of the network's core, some constraints on how security problems can be solved, and potentially lower incentives for network providers to deploy more and better broadband networks relative to network providers in more controllable network architectures.

These social costs must be traded off against the social benefits identified above: other things being equal, network architectures based on the broad version result in more and better application innovation and in applications that better meet the needs of Internet users. As we saw, fostering innovation in applications is not only critically important for economic growth. More applications also increase the Internet's potential to create value in the social, cultural, and political domains. In addition, network architectures based on the broad version let users realize more of the Internet's potential value, both for themselves and for society as a whole. Finally, the broad version directly influences characteristics of the environment for the social, cultural, and political uses of the Internet that are central to the Internet's potential to enhance individual freedom, provide a platform for better democratic participation, foster a more critical and self-reflective culture, and potentially improve human development everywhere.[55]

How should we compromise among these values? It may help to think about them in two steps. In a way, the first three costs constitute the price of having a system that can evolve. A system can either be optimized for the short-term or be evolvable, but not both. The trade-off closely resembles the technical trade-off underlying the broad version as a design principle that trades off the benefits of long-term evolvability against the advantages of short-term optimization. Is this fundamental trade-off still appropriate? If we believe that all important applications have been realized, there is no need to incur the costs of keeping the Internet open for new applications. If, however, we believe that there are many more potential applications waiting to be discovered and developed, it is a comparably low cost to forgo the benefits of optimization, or to live with some limits on the evolvability of the network's core.[56]

It would be premature to say that the only improvements left to make on applications are incremental. As the Internet permeates more and more areas of society and the economy, its potential uses come to mirror the diversity and variety of human life. Apart from being used to support existing activities, Internet applications may enable activities that were not possible before. In addition, new peripherals and advances in the services provided by the Internet infrastructure (e.g., the mobile Internet, the potential introduction of Quality of Service, or increases in available bandwidth and computer processing power) continuously create new opportunities for applications that take advantage of these features. Together, these ongoing technical developments at all layers of the Internet, in addition to increases in the number and the diversity of users and potential uses, make it likely that existing applications have only begun to tap the Internet's vast potential.

This leaves the more fundamental trade-off between broadband deployment and the benefits associated with the broad version of the end-to-end arguments.

Without access to broadband networks, users cannot realize the value of the broadband Internet and cannot benefit from the new applications that better broadband networks enable. Thus, widespread broadband deployment is clearly an important social goal. At the same time, for a variety of reasons (including spillovers), network providers do not capture all of the value created by broadband networks. All this suggests that network providers' private interests in deploying broadband networks may be lower than the social optimum.[57]

Thus, both social benefits *and* social costs of the broad version represent important social values, which makes it difficult to resolve the trade-off. Exploring whether the social benefits associated with one architecture could be realized even if this architecture is rejected may help. If we maintain the broad version of the end-to-end arguments so as to realize its social benefits, are there other ways to solve the problem of network deployment? Although it is non-trivial to finance and foster investment in infrastructure, the problem can be solved in a number of ways. If we truly believe that network providers need more profits to motivate them to deploy broadband networks, tax cuts on broadband investments or direct subsidies may be an option. An alternative solution may be to think about public provision of infrastructure.

If we let network providers increase the controllability of their networks in order to get more broadband networks with higher capacity, can we realize the benefits associated with the broad version in other ways? As we saw in chapter 8, under uncertainty or consumer heterogeneity, the two crucial ingredients for creating successful innovation in applications are (1) independent, low-cost application innovation by a large and diverse set of innovators and (2) user choice among the resulting applications. Letting network providers discriminate against applications or letting them increase the costs of innovation through access charges breaks this mechanism. Recreating a similar mechanism through other means (e.g., through subsidies targeted at potential application innovators) does not seem feasible. On the one hand, in an architecture based on the broad version, almost anyone is a potential innovator. On the other hand, no one can identify successful innovators and innovative ideas in advance.

Similarly, both the Internet's value for individual users and for society and the Internet's potential to realize important social, cultural, or political values depend fundamentally on user choice, non-discrimination, and non-optimization of the network, all of which are achieved by applying the broad version of the end-to-end arguments. Thus, letting network providers increase their profits by increasing the controllability of the network removes the very features of the network that make the Internet valuable.

Thus, whereas it is possible to have a network architecture based on the broad version, realize the associated social benefits, and then solve the deployment problem through other means, it is not possible to have a controllable architecture and realize the benefits associated with the broad version through other means.

Under these circumstances, sacrificing the very aspects that drive the Internet's value in order to get more broadband networks seems too high a price to pay; as Tim Wu put it, it is like selling the painting to get a better frame.[58] All this suggests that the trade-off among the social costs and benefits associated with the broad version is positive, so that the broad version of the end-to-end arguments is in the public interest.

Network Providers' Private Interests in Network Architectures

If using the broad version of the end-to-end arguments is in the public interest, do network providers share this interest, or do their private interests make them prefer architectures that deviate from the broad version?

As we saw in chapter 6, increasing network providers' ability to monitor and control applications and content on their networks increases their profits. They can increase the profitability of their own applications or content by excluding or discriminating against competing applications. In addition, the more sophisticated pricing strategies supported by more controllable architectures let them extract more of the value realized by users or by providers of applications and content. Network providers seem to be moving rapidly in this direction. They increasingly deploy devices for deep packet inspection in their networks that let them monitor and control the applications on their network. These devices can be used to slow down or exclude specific applications and content, to implement sophisticated pricing schemes, or to offer Internet-service packets that allow consumers to use some applications but not others.[59] Large network providers in the United States, in the United Kingdom, and in Germany have publicly stated their desire to charge applications or content providers for the right to have their applications or content travel over the network providers' "last-mile" networks to reach the network providers' Internet-service customers.[60] And incumbent network providers (including AT&T and Verizon in the United States and BT in the United Kingdom) have begun to deploy in their wireless and wireline networks a technology called *IP Multimedia Subsystem (IMS)* that adds to conventional IP networks functionality that gives network providers fine-grained information about and perfect control over the applications and the content on their networks. IMS also provides sophisticated charging capabilities that let the network provider charge both end users and providers of applications or content.[61] White papers by industry vendors laud IMS's ability to support flexible monetization models that convert the network from a "data highway to a data tollway."[62] Thus, in the terminology of chapter 7, IMS is an example of a "fully controllable architecture."

At the same time, the network has become more opaque. Recent years have seen a proliferation of technical solutions, driven by the short-term interests of particular actors, that do not take account of their effects on the long-term evolvability of the Internet. They solve the problem at hand, but at the same time they reduce the generality of the Internet, with significant costs for application-level innovation.[63] For example, residential broadband networks provide asymmetric bandwidth for uploads and downloads, creating problems for applications that send and receive equal amounts of data.[64] Network-address translators and firewalls deployed by network providers and users have made it increasingly difficult to deploy new transport-layer protocols or new applications whose behavior deviates from that of traditional client-server applications.[65] Network providers are using deep packet inspection to single out and slow down specific applications in order to manage bandwidth on their networks.[66] Though asymmetric bandwidth seems to have been motivated by the available cost savings, the other deviations from the end-to-end arguments seem to occur as a by-product of some actors' attempts to solve specific technological problems without considering the effect on the evolvability of the Internet as a whole. Often, as in the case of network-address translators and firewalls, the negative consequences take some time to become apparent.

Thus, the evidence suggests that network providers have an interest in deviating from the broad version. This may be surprising. After all, the broad version fosters application innovation. More applications make a network provider's Internet service more attractive, which should enable the network provider to sell more Internet service or increase its price. But if following the broad version increases network providers' profits, shouldn't this lead them to *prefer* the broad version over architectures that deviate from that version? This line of thought neglects that the potential increase in profits from more application innovation is not the only aspect network providers consider when choosing network architectures. Network providers compare the private costs and benefits of complying with the broad version with the private costs and benefits of deviating from it. Although more application innovation may increase their profits, increasing the controllability of the network may increase their profits even more. And whereas the economic and non-economic benefits of application innovation for society weigh heavily in the trade-off among the social benefits and the social costs, network providers consider their private costs and benefits, which may be different.

Although network providers receive some benefits from application innovation, two factors will lead them to undervalue the benefits of application innovation compared to the social optimum. First, they do not appropriate all the gains from application innovation. Second, the gains they are able to capture are uncertain and will be realized in the future, which may lead them to take even less account of those gains.

Network providers do not appropriate all of the gains from application innovation if they innovate themselves, much less if the application has been developed by someone other than the network provider. If consumers value the application differently, network providers cannot appropriate the entire consumer surplus associated with the use of the application. As we saw in chapter 6, this inability is particularly marked in an architecture that is based on the broad version of the end-to-end arguments, which forces the network provider to charge a uniform per-packet transport price that does not vary depending on the application being used. Because the network provider isn't able to collect access charges under an end-to-end architecture, it cannot extract all the value that application developers realize from the application, nor can it capture the positive externalities resulting from its users' productive uses that accrue to users of other Internet service providers and even to people who do not use the Internet at all. Finally, it does not capture the increase in the value of other network providers' Internet service resulting from additional application innovation. Thus, a network provider's private gain from an application innovation will often be much lower than the social benefits associated with that innovation. As a result, network providers value the increase in application innovation brought about by the broad version less than is socially optimal.

In addition, intertemporal biases (that is, biases affecting decisions involving trade-offs among outcomes that will have their effects at different times)[67] may bias network providers or their decision makers toward short-term outcomes. Whereas the private benefits of deviating from the broad version are realized immediately, most of the private benefits of complying with the broad version are uncertain and will be realized in the future. Given this intertemporal distribution of network providers' private benefits, a bias in favor of short-term gains would further exacerbate the wedge between network providers' interests and the interests of the public.

First, research in behavioral economics shows that individuals often discount future benefits more than rational discounting would suggest—a bias known as "hyperbolic discounting."[68] In the extreme case, this bias may cause individuals deciding whether to deviate from the broad version of the end-to-end arguments to prefer the smaller *current* private benefits associated with deviating (i.e., the performance gains, or the increase in profits from discrimination or pricing strategies that extract more of the value realized by users or independent application developers) over comparatively larger *future* private benefits associated with following the broad version (such as the increase in profits from Internet service due to increases in the number and variety of applications), even if rational discounting would lead them to prefer the future benefits. If under rational discounting the private current benefits of deviating from the broad version were larger than the private future benefits of using it, this bias would further reinforce network providers' preference for deviating from the broad version.

Second, since the future applications that may make network providers' Internet service more valuable are not known, it is difficult to know their worth. Uncertainty about the future further reduces the weight that future developments receive in current decision making.[69]

Third, researchers suggest that firms may generally be biased toward the short term.[70] For example, theoretical research and some empirical evidence suggest that the stock market favors short-term benefits over long-term gains.[71] If the stock market exhibits such a bias, we should expect network providers to follow the same valuation in order to please the stock market. Alternatively, managers' desire to enhance their reputation quickly may lead them to focus on actions that create high and observable short-term gains, without caring about the long-term effect, if they expect to have left the firm or their specific position when the long-term consequences of their actions occur.

Finally, network providers that currently dominate the market may not know whether they will be able to sustain their lead. For example, technical developments may reduce the costs of deploying broadband networks. Lower costs may motivate additional firms to enter the market, or may motivate regulators to artificially introduce competition. In both cases, network providers' expected share of benefits from innovation in applications will be lower in the future, when they have a less dominant position, which again would lead them to discount their share of future benefits from application innovation more.

All this suggests that network providers will often resolve the trade-off between the increased profits, performance gains, or cost savings from deviating from the broad version of the end-to-end arguments and the potential loss of application innovation in favor of deviating. Thus, the public's and the network providers' interests in network architecture diverge, creating a market failure regarding the evolution of the architecture.

Conclusion

Many people have a pragmatic attitude toward technology: they don't care how it works, they just want to use it. With regard to the Internet, this attitude is dangerous. As this book has shown, different ways of structuring the Internet result in very different environments for its development, production, and use. If left to themselves, network providers will continue to change the internal structure of the Internet in ways that are good for them, but not necessarily for the rest of us—individual, organizational or corporate Internet users, application developers and content providers, and even those who do not use the Internet. If we want to protect the Internet's usefulness, if we want to realize its full economic, social, cultural, and political potential, we need to understand the Internet's structure and what will happen if that structure is changed.

The End-to-End Arguments

The original architecture that governed the Internet from its inception to the early 1990s was based on a design principle called *the end-to-end arguments*. There are two versions of the end-to-end arguments, and both of them shaped the Internet's original architecture. The narrow version was first identified, named, and described by Saltzer, Reed, and Clark in 1981.[1] The broad version was the focus of later papers by these authors.[2] Although Saltzer, Reed, and Clark never explicitly drew attention to the change in definition, there are real differences between the two versions—differences in scope, in content, and in validity—that make it preferable to distinguish between the two.

The narrow version applies solely to functions (called *end-to-end functions*) that can only be completely and correctly implemented end-to-end—that is, between the original source and ultimate destination of data. This version can be summarized as follows: A function should not be implemented in a lower layer if it cannot be completely and correctly implemented at that layer. Sometimes an incomplete implementation of the function at the lower layer may be useful as a performance enhancement.[3] The narrow version prescribes that, for reasons of correctness, these functions must be implemented at a layer where a complete and correct implementation is possible—that is, at a higher layer that operates end-to-end between the original source and ultimate destination of data. Also implementing a necessarily incomplete version of these function at a lower layer is redundant and usually constitutes an inefficient use of system resources, but the narrow version recognizes that in some cases an additional, necessarily incomplete implementation at the lower layer may be justified as a performance enhancement.

Whereas the narrow version applies only to functions that cannot be completely and correctly implemented at lower layers, the broad version provides a general rule for distributing functionality in a multi-layer system and for dividing functionality between end systems and the network's core in multi-layer communication networks. According to the broad version, lower layers of the system—the network's core—should provide only general services that can be used by all applications. The network should not be optimized to better support specific higher-layer applications. Though this may increase the performance of particular applications, it is an unnecessary and therefore inefficient feature for applications that do not need this function; it may even rule out the implementation of applications not foreseen at the time of design. Finally, the broad version advises that application-specific functionality be concentrated in the higher layers of the system, at the end hosts. The broad version does not prevent functions from being implemented in the network if they cannot be completely and correctly implemented at the end hosts only.

In the context of the broad version, "end hosts" and "core of the network" denote a purely functional relationship between users and providers of communication services. Whereas end hosts run application programs that use the communication services provided by the network, computers in the core of the network provide these services. The terminology does not refer to topological relationships or to administrative ownership and control.

Whereas the narrow version, if it applies, must be followed for reasons of correctness, the broad version has other justifications. For all functions other than end-to-end functions that must be implemented end-to-end for reasons of correctness anyway, the broad version's design rules emerge from a trade-off. They prioritize long-term system evolvability, application autonomy, and reliability over short-term performance optimizations.

Thus, it is appropriate to use the broad version only if the system's requirements imply that this trade-off is justified. If the system's requirements imply a different resolution of this trade-off, the broad version should not be applied.

Although the broad version of the end-to-end arguments does not explicitly prohibit the core of the network from being aware of the applications running over it or being capable of controlling their execution, applying this design principle results in a network that does not have this functionality. Thus, though the broad version does not directly require the network to be non-discriminatory or "neutral," there is a causal relationship between the broad version and "network neutrality." A neutral network (that is, a network in which network providers cannot interfere with the applications and content on their network) is a direct consequence of applying the broad version. This characteristic represents a benefit for independent application developers, for users of the Internet, and for society as a whole. From the point of view of network owners, it constitutes a cost of architectures based on the broad version.

The End-to-End Arguments and the Original Architecture of the Internet

The original architecture of the Internet resulted from a combination of a variant of the layering principle called *relaxed layering with a portability layer* and the end-to-end arguments. Layering, in turn, is a special form of modularity.

The architecture of the Internet consists of four layers: the link layer (the lowest layer), the Internet layer, the transport layer, and the application layer.

The application of "relaxed layering with a portability layer" imposes constraints on the interactions among protocols belonging to different layers and on the number of protocols that may populate a layer. The Internet layer is designated as the portability layer. Layers above the Internet layer are allowed to invoke the services of protocols in the same layer or in any layer below them, down to the Internet layer, but they are not allowed to directly invoke the services of protocols in a layer below the Internet layer. Lower-layer protocols are not allowed to invoke the services of higher-layer protocols. Whereas the Internet layer is restricted to a single protocol (the Internet protocol), other layers may host a variety of different protocols.

Designating the Internet layer as the portability layer influenced the design of the Internet protocol, since a portability layer aims to provide a technology-independent interface to the services of the network.

During the initial design of the Internet's architecture, the end-to-end arguments shaped the division of functionality between the Internet layer and the transport layer. Whereas the narrow version required implementing functions such as reliable data transfer, duplicate suppression, and reordering end-to-end between the original source and ultimate destination of data (i.e., end-to-end between end hosts), the broad version influenced the division of functionality between the Internet layer and the transport layer.

The Internet's designers chose to implement such end-to-end functions as reliable data transfer, duplicate suppression, and reordering at the transport layer. This design fulfils the narrow version's requirement for an end-to-end implementation of these functions if the transport-layer protocols operate end-to-end between the original source and ultimate destination of data and no events falling into the responsibility of the function occur after the data leaves the transport layer.

The broad version of the end-to-end arguments shaped the Internet's original architecture by determining the following design choices. First, the functionality required to transfer data from host to host is separated from the end-to-end functionality required to control the end-to-end transmission of data. The two groups of functionality are placed in separate layers: the Internet layer and the transport layer. The Internet layer is the highest layer running on computers in the core of the network and provides a general service that is broadly useful across applications: unreliable connectionless datagram service. The transport layer is the lowest layer that only has to be implemented on end hosts and is the lowest layer implementing application-specific functionality.[4] Second, functionality provided end-to-end by the transport layer is not duplicated in the Internet layer. In particular, the Internet layer does not implement additional hop-by-hop error control.

Apart from guiding the division of functionality between the Internet layer and the transport layer, both versions of the end-to-end arguments influenced, and continue to influence, the design of individual applications.

If the transport-layer protocols do not operate end-to-end between the original source and the ultimate destination of data, or if events falling into the responsibility of the end-to-end function occur after data leaves the transport layer, the narrow version requires end-to-end functions to be implemented in layers above the transport layer, ultimately in the application itself.

The broad version constrains the design of individual applications by requiring that application-specific functionality be implemented in higher layers at the end hosts, not in the core of the network. Within these boundaries, designers are free to choose any application designs they like.

The use of the end-to-end arguments and of relaxed layering with a portability layer shields transport-layer protocols and application-layer protocols from changes below the Internet layer. At the same time, since the broad version of the end-to-end arguments concentrates application-specific functionality in higher layers, lower-layer protocols are not affected by changes in applications or other protocols above the Internet layer. Thus, the Internet layer divides the protocol stack into two quasi-independent subsystems that can evolve independently.

The Broad Version of the End-to-End Arguments and Innovation in the Original Architecture of the Internet

Network architectures (and the design principles that shape them) influence the economic system that develops and produces the Internet in a variety of ways. In particular, they affect which actors can innovate and what incentives they have to do so.

Applying the broad version of the end-to-end arguments creates an environment that is more conducive to application innovation than architectures that deviate from this design principle. The gradual transition from a network architecture based on the broad version of the end-to-end arguments to one that implements a considerable amount of application-specific functionality in the network's core significantly increases the costs of innovation for independent application developers. It reduces their incentives to innovate, limits the range of potential innovators, and gradually shifts control over the development and deployment of application-level innovation from application developers and users to network owners. In a network architecture based on the broad version of the end-to-end arguments, anyone with access to an end host and the ability to learn a programming language is a potential innovator. At the same time, innovators independently decide how they want to innovate. Users independently decide which applications they want to deploy. In contrast, in a network with a significant amount of application-specific functionality in the network's core, network owners may be the only remaining potential innovators. They also control which applications get deployed. At the same time, the costs of adopting new applications rise for both users and for network owners. As we saw in chapters 8 and 9, these changes significantly reduce the overall amount, the type, and (potentially) the quality of innovation, at significant costs to society. If there is market uncertainty, business uncertainty, or user heterogeneity, the effects of differences in the size and diversity of the innovator pool and of differences in control over application development and deployment are particularly profound.

Thus, the mechanism that produces innovation in applications under an end-to-end architecture has two components: widespread experimentation by a large and diverse group of innovators who independently select whether to realize their innovative ideas and user choice among the resulting applications. Under uncertainty or user heterogeneity, this mechanism will produce more and better applications than innovation in network architectures that concentrate control over innovation or deployment in the hands of a few network providers. If users' needs are heterogeneous, it will also produce more diverse applications that better meet users' needs.

The broad version's various influences on innovation in applications can be traced back to two features of end-to-end architectures. First, developing and deploying applications requires changing only end hosts that want to use the application. It does not require any changes to the network's core. As a result, innovators can decide independently whether to realize their ideas for an application, and can do so at low costs. Second, the network cannot discriminate against the applications running over it and cannot exclude applications. As a result, independent application developers need not fear that their application will be excluded or discriminated against, or that the network provider will try to extract their profits through access charges. Through mechanisms that were examined in chapters 4–6 and 8, these features influence the ability of economic actors other than network owners to participate in application-level innovation, their incentives to do so, and the types of applications they will develop.

Though the broad version of the end-to-end argument also affects innovation in the core of the network, it constrains the design and evolution of the core of the network less than is often assumed. The broad version requires the network to provide only general services that are useful for a large variety of existing and potential future applications. It prohibits optimizing the network in favor of specific applications and implementing application-specific functionality in the network's core. It does not require the core of the network to be "stupid" or simple. It does not constrain the amount of state in the network. Finally, it does not generally prevent Quality of Service, although it does constrain how Quality of Service can be realized. Thus, it leaves considerable room for innovation at the Internet layer and below.

There are, however, two other mechanisms that make it very difficult to change the core of the network. First, the large number of higher-layer protocols that use the Internet protocol constrain its potential evolution by creating large costs of system adaptation. Second, the deployment context provided by the commercial Internet constrains the Internet layer's evolution even more than an analysis based on the structural dependencies among the Internet's components would suggest.

Contrary to other potential network architectures, the original architecture of the Internet facilitates innovation below the Internet layer by designating the Internet layer as a portability layer. Since the Internet protocol provides a technology-independent interface to the services provided by the network, and because higher-layer protocols are not allowed to directly access protocols below the Internet layer, the underlying physical network technologies can evolve freely without requiring changes in protocols above the Internet layer as long as the service interface provided by the Internet layer stays the same.

End-to-End Arguments in the Current Internet

In recent years, the architecture of the Internet has evolved in ways that challenge both versions of the end-to-end arguments.[5] For one thing, many application services have evolved, or are evolving, toward a more distributed structure with application-level intermediaries that are topologically in the network and under the administrative control of a network provider or a third-party service provider. In addition, recent years have seen a proliferation of intermediary devices in the path between two end hosts that are not an intended part of the application executed between the two hosts, but perform functions other than the normal, standard functions of an IP router on the datagram path between a source host and a destination host.

Mature application services often evolve toward a more distributed structure, with application-level intermediaries that are topologically in the network and under the administrative control of a network provider or a third-party service provider (figure 3.7).[6] E-mail servers and Web caches are examples of such intermediaries. (For a description of the structure of e-mail, see box 3.6.) If such an intermediary is an integrated part of the application, correctly terminates the protocol stack, and implements its functionality above the Internet layer, this evolution does not pose any problems for the broad version of the end-to-end arguments.[7] After all, designers are free to design their applications in any way they want, as long as the application-specific functionality is completely contained in layers above the Internet layer. Since all the application-specific functionality is restricted to end hosts, an application with such intermediaries does not interfere with the deployment of new applications over the Internet.

From the perspective of the narrow version of the end-to-end arguments, these developments are highly relevant. Implicitly, the original architecture of the Internet was based on the assumption that application-layer and transport-layer protocols would operate directly between the two ultimate end systems of an application session (figure 3.3). Under these assumptions, the implementation of end-to-end functions (i.e., of functions that can only be completely and correctly implemented between the original source and ultimate destination of data) in the transport layer met the requirements of the narrow version of the end-to-end arguments for most applications, if no additional events relevant to the correct execution of the functions occurred after the data left the transport layer.

Today these assumptions are not automatically justified. The distributed application services described above consist of a concatenation of application-layer connections (and, consequently transport-layer connections); as a result, the transport-layer protocols no longer operate end-to-end between the ultimate end systems of the application. With respect to the path between the original source and ultimate destination of data, the transport-layer protocols operate hop-by-hop (figure 3.4). In this context, we cannot assume that end-to-end functions are executed correctly just because the application layer uses a transport-layer protocol that implements these functions. Instead, the narrow version of the end-to-end arguments requires that the end-to-end functions be implemented at a layer operating end-to-end between the original source and the ultimate destination of data, ultimately in the application itself.[8]

Though the increasing delegation of functions to parts of an application that are under the control of third parties such as network providers or service providers does not affect how easily the network can evolve, it raises important questions about the autonomy, the control, and the trust of end users.[9] Some have suggested that these new concerns make the old functional distinction between "end hosts" and "network" as users and providers of communication services underlying the broad version irrelevant.[10] I do not agree with this assessment. The broad version focuses on the evolvability of the network. In this context, a functional interpretation of "end hosts" and "the network" is still appropriate. As we have seen throughout this book, keeping the network general and open for new applications is still an acute and important problem. Just because new developments raise new issues that are orthogonal to the question of network evolvability does not mean that the old questions have become irrelevant.[11]

Furthermore, recent years have seen a proliferation of intermediary devices in the path between two end hosts that are not an intended part of the application, but which perform functions other than the normal, standard functions of an IP router on the datagram path between a source host and a destination host.[12] Most of these devices are topologically close to the edge of the network.

A large group of devices are explicitly aimed at controlling the execution of applications running over the network. Not surprisingly, these devices violate the broad version of the end-to-end arguments: they operate at the Internet layer, but they access parts of the datagram that contain the messages passed between higher-layer protocols. They then use the information gained through this layer violation to determine how to treat the datagram. To determine the appropriate treatment, they must implement application-specific functionality in the network.[13] Their reasons for existing differ. Some, such as firewalls, are intended to improve security. Others, such as devices for deep packet inspection, are explicitly intended to give network owners the ability to influence how applications run over their network.

Finally, the perceived shortage of IPv4 addresses has led to the emergence of so-called network-address translators (NATs) that let a number of end hosts simultaneously share the same Internet address.[14] NATs operate at the Internet layer and are intended to be transparent to the applications that traverse them. To perform their function, they access and modify parts of the datagram that contain the messages passed between higher-layer protocols—a clear layer violation.[15] In addition, they need to know how higher-layer protocol data messages are formatted in order to function correctly, which violates the broad version of the end-to-end arguments.[16]

Whereas devices that let network providers influence the applications and content on their networks affect application innovation by reducing independent application and content developers' incentives to innovate, devices such as NATs and firewalls directly impede the development and deployment of new applications and transport-layer protocols by increasing the costs of developing applications and forcing innovators to coordinate their innovations with others. The effect of these devices goes beyond their ability to block applications they are intended to block.[17] They can have unwanted side effects. Designers developed these devices with the needs of client-server applications such as the World Wide Web in mind. Applications with different characteristics often cannot pass through the device; in this case, users behind the firewall or NAT will not be able to use the application. For example, peer-to-peer applications, applications that use UDP, and applications that use one signaling connection to set up a second connection may have difficulties passing through NATs or firewalls.[18] To let these applications traverse the device, software specifically written for each particular application must be installed at the device. This not only complicates application design; it also may be very difficult to realize in practice. Often, commercial NATs and firewalls are closed boxes running proprietary software. As a result, application designers who want to let their applications traverse through such a device have to convince the device's vendor to write and distribute the necessary software. Obviously, device vendors may not be very motivated to do so for new applications with an unknown market base.[19] To deal with these problems, developers of affected applications develop complex workarounds or try to design their application in ways that make it as similar to HTTP as possible. This significantly impedes application development—for example, the developers of Skype spent a considerable amount of the overall development time developing mechanisms that would enable Skype to work through NATs and firewalls.

Moreover, NATs and firewalls have made it almost impossible for new transport-layer protocols to be deployed.[20] The designers of transport-layer protocols face a "chicken and egg" problem: an application using this protocol can run on a computer only if the protocol is deployed on that computer (usually transport-layer protocols are implemented as part of the operating system).[21] Since they would like their application to work for all potential users, application designers will not write applications using the new protocol unless it is widely deployed and can be expected to work end-to-end. Operating system vendors will implement a new transport-layer protocol only if they expect application developers to use it. And NAT and firewall vendors do not have an incentive to add support for a new transport protocol if it is not part of a commonly used operating system. Without support, the new transport-layer protocol will not be able to work for users behind firewalls and NATs, and this prevents application developers from using it. Even if firewall and NAT vendors decide to add support for the protocol to their devices, it will take a long time until devices with the new software have been ubiquitously deployed.

These examples show how seemingly minor deviations from the broad version to solve specific technical problems can add up to severely constrain the evolvability of the Internet's architecture.

Though the broad version does not establish any requirements for the end hosts, a sufficient number of end hosts must be general (that is, able to support a large variety of applications), and must be under the control of application developers and end users, if the mechanism that produces application innovation under an end-to-end architecture is to work. This suggests that widespread replacement of general-purpose end hosts controlled by users with specialized appliances controlled by the manufacturer or the network provider (e.g., mobile phones, video game controllers, TiVos), should it occur, might be problematic.[22]

Policy Implications

The architecture of the Internet changes in ways that deviate from the broad version of the end-to-end arguments. These changes have direct consequences for public interests because Internet architectures based on the broad version of the end-to-end arguments shape how the Internet is developed, produced, and used. As a general-purpose technology, the Internet does not create value through its existence alone. It creates value by helping users do what they want to do, or letting them do so more efficiently. Applications are the tools that let users realize this value. By fostering innovation in applications, the broad version of the end-to-end arguments increases the potential of the Internet to create even more value in the future. In addition, fostering application innovation is critically important for economic growth.

In a network based on the broad version, users, not network providers, decide how to use the network. Network providers cannot interfere with these uses, nor can they optimize the network for specific uses. By enabling users to use the Internet in the way that creates the most value for them, the broad version not only maximizes the value of the Internet for users, it also increases the Internet's overall value to society.

But the social value of architectures based on the broad version goes beyond that. The Internet has the potential to enhance individual freedom, provide a platform for better democratic participation, foster a more critical and self-reflective culture, and potentially improve human development everywhere.[23] The Internet's ability to realize this potential, however, is tightly linked to features—user choice, non-discrimination, non-optimization—that result from the application of the broad version of the end-to-end arguments. Though a network based on the broad version may reduce network providers' incentives to deploy more and better broadband networks to some degree, letting network providers deviate from the broad version by increasing the controllability of the network considerably reduces the Internet's value to society. Given that there are other ways to foster broadband deployment that are not similarly harmful, I resolve this trade-off in favor of the social benefits resulting from the broad version.

Network providers' interests point in a different direction. They capture only a small part of the social value resulting from the broad version, and the fact that this value is uncertain and will be realized in the future leads them to further discount their private benefits associated with respecting the broad version. They have an incentive to increase the controllability of the network to make more profits. They also have an incentive to optimize the network for specific applications or find easy solutions for technical problems, making the network more opaque. Insofar as network providers control the evolution of the network's core, it is not surprising that the network is moving away from its original end-to-end design.

Given this gap between network providers' private interests and the public's interests, we face an important choice. Leaving the evolution of the network to network providers will significantly reduce the Internet's value to society. If no one intervenes, network providers' interests will drive networks further away from the broad version. With this dynamic, doing nothing is not enough to preserve the status quo, let alone to restore the full potential of the Internet.

If the Internet's value for society is to be preserved, policy makers will have to intervene. How to best do so without over-restricting the evolution of the network or locking in design choices that may not remain appropriate in the future is a difficult question. Law and architecture may interact in different ways. Some issues can be solved through regulation after technology has been deployed. For example, even if a network contains devices that let network providers control the applications and content on their networks, non-discrimination rules can forbid them from using these devices. In contrast, some issues can be solved only at the level of technology. For example, an optimization in favor of specific applications, such as the asymmetric bandwidth to and from most residential homes, can be overcome only through new technology; it cannot be undone by a law. In these cases, regulators need to shape the technology *before* it is deployed.

All this suggests that potential policy interventions will have to be more sophisticated than simply requiring network providers to adhere to the broad version of the end-to-end arguments, or to maintain the Internet's original architecture.

But what does all this mean for the future of the broad version as an engineering design principle? After all, though we may object to regulators imposing specific design principles through regulation, network architects do have to choose design principles that help them realize their goals.

Design principles are tools to achieve certain ends: an architecture with a specific set and prioritization of characteristics. The broad version of the end-to-end arguments may not be the only design principle that can create an architecture that is evolvable or that realizes the social benefits that the broad version makes possible. We know, however, that the broad version has these effects. At the same time, the broad version provides much more flexibility for the evolution of the network's core than is often assumed. As the discussion of its potential interaction with security requirements in chapter 9 showed, the broad version is also able to react to other requirements that were not considered in the trade-offs underlying this design principle. Since the fundamental trade-off underlying the broad version is still appropriate (there are many more applications that have yet to be invented, which makes the long-term evolvability of the network more important than short-term performance optimizations), the broad version is at least a serious contender to be one of the design principles for the future Internet. Still, even if the broad version is chosen to shape the future Internet, its interaction with changed or new requirements will most likely result in an architecture that differs from the Internet's original architecture.

Though the focus of this book was on the effect of architecture on the economic system, the relationship between architecture and the economic system is not a one-way street. If architecture has economic implications, we can expect economic actors to begin exploiting the economic effect of architecture by engaging in strategic design—that is, attempting to shape architectures in their favor. The move by network providers toward next-generation networks and technologies such as the IP Multimedia Subsystem is an example of strategic design. From the perspective of network providers, the IP Multimedia Subsystem corrects perceived deficiencies of the Internet's original architecture (such as the lack of control and sophisticated charging capabilities) while maintaining the Internet's perceived benefits (e.g., the benefits of innovation by actors other than the network provider) (table C.1).[24]

Traditionally, actors have tried to influence laws, norms, or economic constraints to improve their positions. Architecture has become another tool that actors can use to further their interests.

For example, Google is currently trying to recreate the conditions that characterized the economic environment for the development, production, and use of the original Internet for the mobile Internet (tables C.2

Table C.1

Differences between network architectures.

	Intelligent telephone network	IP multimedia subsystem	Original Internet
Potential innovators	Few	Many	Many
Control over network use	Network providers	Network providers	Users
Sophisticated charging capabilities	Yes	Yes	No

Table C.2

Differences between the traditional mobile Internet and Google's vision of the mobile Internet.

	Traditional mobile Internet	Google's vision of mobile Internet	Original Internet
Specificity of end hosts	Application specific	General	General
Control over end hosts	Network providers, handset makers	Application developers and users	Application developers and users
Control over network	Network providers	Users	Users

Table C.3

Differences in end hosts for the mobile Internet.

	General	Application-specific
Controlled by users	Android	
Controlled by network providers and handset makers	Apple iPhone	Traditional cell phone

and C.3). In the past, the economic environment in which the mobile Internet was developed, produced, and used differed considerably from the economic environment in which the original Internet was developed, produced, and used, both at the handsets and in the network.[25] In the original Internet, users control which applications are running on their end hosts. Standardized application programming interfaces that give developers access to the full capabilities of the end hosts are available at low cost. In contrast, mobile phones have been traditionally controlled by handset providers and carriers. Users usually cannot freely install applications on their cell phones in the same way they can on their personal computers. Application programming interfaces for handsets were propri- etary, varied widely, and were costly to access, and often they provided only limited access to the phone's technical capabilities. Whereas users of the Internet can freely attach their computers to the Internet and can freely decide how they want to use the network, mobile carriers contractually or technically restrict which phones can be used on their networks and control the use of the network through contractual or technical means. As a result, in the mobile network, it has been difficult to develop new applications; network providers control the handsets and the use of the network. In contrast, networks based on the broad version of the end-to-end arguments make it easy to develop applications and enable users, who control their end hosts and the use of the network, to freely choose application and services.

Why is Google seeking these changes? If browsing on a cell phone becomes as convenient as browsing on a PC, Google will benefit from consumers' cell-phone searches just as it benefits from their PC searches.[26] To realize its goal, Google uses a mix of architectural, legal, and economic strategies.

At the core of Google's architectural strategy is Android, a new software platform and operating system for mobile phones that Google developed in a business coalition with handset makers, hardware vendors, and soft- ware vendors. Android is available to anyone for free and lets programmers create applications in the well-known Java programming language. Though carriers and handset makers can still cripple the functionality of a phone, Android is designed to give control of cell phones to users and application developers.

Some consequences of the broad version cannot be recreated by Android. Making it easier for developers to develop applications and letting users install them does not help users if carriers do not let the user's phone access the mobile network. Android also cannot protect against discrimination by the network. Google's legal strategy tries to solve these problems through regulation. Working with partners, Google has been lobbying heavily for regulations that would let people use any cell phone on a mobile network as long as it does not harm the network and would ban mobile network providers from interfering with the applications and content on the network. When the Federal Communications Commission decided to auction off spectrum in the 700-MHz band, Google asked for the rules just described as well as for rules that would require the winners of the spec- trum auction to license the spectrum to other providers on a wholesale basis in order to increase competition in the market for mobile carriers. (These latter regulations would have influenced the market structure in the market for mobile networks, which according to popular theory, would also reduce carriers' incentives to discriminate.) Google promised to bid for a portion of the 700-MHz spectrum in exchange for the imposition of its desired regulations.[27] When the FCC imposed two of the desired regulations on one block of spectrum in the 700 MHz auction, triggered by a certain reservation price, Google participated in the auction and bid the price up to the reservation price to make sure the regulations were triggered.[28]

These architectural and legal strategies were complemented by a more traditional economic strategy. Google got involved in the market for broadband wireless Internet service by investing in Clearwire, a company that provides wireless broadband Internet services, alongside with cable companies and Intel. Through its influence on the strategies of one wireless broadband provider, Google may be able to cause mobile carriers to change their behavior.

The IP Multimedia Subsystem was originally developed for mobile networks. Thus, in a way, wireline network providers try to make the traditional wireline Internet more similar to the closed and controlled wireless cellular Internet, while Google tries to make the cellular Internet more like the traditional Internet.

Influencing architecture can be a powerful way to pursue one's interests. Corporate actors such as network providers or Google have recognized this. Those protecting the public interest need to do so, too.

Notes

Introduction

1. Miniwatts Marketing Group 2009. This number reflects the estimated number of Internet users as of June 30, 2009. (N.B.: In the United States, a billion is a thousand million, i.e., 10^9.)

2. This argument was pioneered by the law professors Mark Lemley and Lawrence Lessig in an *ex parte* submission to the Federal Communications Commission in the AT&T-MediaOne merger proceeding (Lemley and Lessig 1999; see also Lemley and Lessig 2001). On the end-to-end arguments and network neutrality, see Lessig 2001; Lessig 2002; Wu and Lessig 2003; Wu 2003a; Lessig 2006; Lessig 2008b.

3. Network neutrality rules prevent network providers from interfering with the applications and content on their networks. Open access rules require the owners of broadband networks to allow independent Internet Service Providers to offer their services over these networks. Rules regarding network management in broadband network constrain network providers' ability to manage their networks. They may, for example, require network providers to use non-discriminatory mechanisms for managing their networks, if possible. For more on these debates, see chapter 6 below.

4. Since the 1990s, scholars of management strategy have explored the economic effect of modular and integrated architectures. See Langlois and Robertson 1992; Garud and Kumaraswamy 1993; Garud and Kumaraswamy 1995; Ulrich 1995; Sanchez 1995; Chesbrough and Teece 1996; Sanchez and Mahoney 1996; Baldwin and Clark 1997; Sanchez 1999; Baldwin and Clark 2000; Schilling 2000; Fixson and Sako 2001; Schilling and Steensma 2001; Christensen, Verlinden, and Westerman 2002; Langlois 2002; Sako 2002; Sturgeon 2002. The effect of the Internet's original architecture on innovation was first highlighted by Lemley and Lessig (1999). For a more detailed analysis, see Lessig 2001.

5. Researchers of business strategy have long recognized the strategic importance of architecture. See Ferguson and Morris 1993; Morris and Ferguson 1993; Gawer and Cusumano 2002; Baldwin and Clark 2006a; Woodard 2006; Woodard 2008.

6. More precisely, when talking about the original architecture of the Internet, I refer to the network architecture that was specified in the DARPA Internet Program protocol specifications for the Internet Protocol and the Transmission Control Protocol, RFC 791 (Postel 1981a) and RFC 793 (Postel 1981b). David Clark described this architecture in an important 1988 article on the design philosophy of the DARPA Internet protocols (D. D. Clark 1988).

7. See, e.g., Carpenter 1996, paragraph 2; Computer Science and Telecommunications Board and National Research Council 2001, pp. 36–38; Braden et al. 2000, p. 15; Moors 2002; Blumenthal and Clark 2001, p. 70; Clark et al. 2002, section 4.1.

8. Lemley and Lessig 2001, p. 928.

9. Solum and Chung 2004, p. 845.

10. Ibid., p. 844.

11. Sandvig 2002, p. 21.

12. Sandvig 2006, p. 235.

13. See, e.g., Yoo 2004, pp. 26, 41–46.

14. Saltzer, Reed, and Clark 1981. The 1981 paper was a conference paper. When referring to the original paper that first identified the end-to-end arguments, researchers usually cite the revised version (Saltzer, Reed, and Clark 1984) that appeared in the *ACM Transactions on Computer Systems* in 1984. I generally follow this convention too.

15. See, e.g., Reed, Saltzer, and Clark 1998.

16. A network that provides "Quality of Service" (QoS) offers different types of service to different data packets. For example, it may guarantee a minimum bandwidth or maximum delay, or it may give some traffic priority over others without giving absolute guarantees. See Peterson and Davie 2007, pp. 499–525.

17. In part III of the book, this thread focuses on how the broad version of the end-to-end arguments affects application-level innovation and neglects other aspects of the effect of the Internet's architecture on innovation explored in that part. Readers interested in this thread should skim chapter 1 for an introduction to the framework that underlies the more detailed analysis covered by this threat.

Chapter 1

1. This observation is often summarized as "code is law" (Lessig 1999a, p. 6). The argument is developed in detail in Lessig 1999a. For a shorter exposition of the argument, see Lessig 1999b. Lessig builds on the work of a number of scholars; see Mitchell 1995, p. 111; Katsh 1996, pp. 335, 338; Johnson and Post 1996, pp. 1378–1387; Boyle 1997, p. 177; Reidenberg 1998, p. 553; Shapiro 1998, pp. 715–723.

2. The slogan is usually attributed to Mitchell Kapor, co-founder of the Electronic Frontier Foundation. See Barlow 1992, p. 25; Lessig 1999a, p. 242, note 7 to chapter 1.

3. This use of the word follows Lessig's terminology. In general, Lessig (1999b, p. 507) uses 'architecture' to refer to "the physical world as we find it, even if 'as we find it' is simply how it has already been made." In the context of the Internet, Lessig (ibid., pp. 506, 509) uses 'architecture' and 'code' interchangeably to denote "the software and hardware that constitute cyberspace as it is."

4. This definition is equivalent to one often used in regard to software architecture: "The software architecture of a program or computing system is the structure or structures of the system, which comprise software components, the externally visible properties of those components, and the relationships among them. 'Externally visible' properties refers to those assumptions other components can make of a component, such as its provided services, performance characteristics, fault handling, shared resource usage, and so on." (Bass, Clements, and Kazman 1998, p. 23) This definition is widely quoted in the literature on software architecture—see van Vliet 2000, pp. 255–256; Bosch 2000, p. 11; Bengtsson et al. 2000, p. 3; Hofmeister, Nord, and Soni 2000, pp. 4, 6. For alternative definitions, see Bass, Clements, and Kazman 2003, pp. 23–24.The architecture of a complex software-intensive system usually consists of several structures that represent different aspects of the architecture. Each structure describes the system in terms of components, their externally visible properties, and the relationships among them, but each structure addresses different engineering concerns (e.g., the conceptual decomposition of the system, the design's concurrency and synchronization aspects or the mapping of the software onto the hardware elements). The representation of such a structure is usually called a *view* of the architecture. The terminology and the number of views differ across authors. This book's analysis focuses on the view of architecture that describes the decomposition of the system into subsystems and modules and the management of dependencies between them. Hofmeister, Nord, and Soni (2000, pp. 11–13, 97–124) call this view "the module view." Kruchten (1995, pp. 45–46) calls it "the development view." For more on the use of views in software architecture design, see Hofmeister, Nord, and Soni 2000, pp. 9–16; Bass, Clements, and Kazman 2003, pp. 35–42.

5. This definition does not prescribe a particular method of decomposition. Often, decomposition takes place on a functional basis, as in engineering design and traditional software design. In a functional decomposition, the overall functionality of the system is decomposed into a number of subfunctions, each of which solves part of the problem. These subfunctions, or subfunctions thereof, are then assigned to components. Thus, when functional decomposition is used, designing the architecture consists of allocating functionality to structure. The above definition also accommodates an object-oriented approach to design, which concentrates on the data on which the system will operate. As a result, the system is decomposed into collections of objects and relationships among them. (For a short overview of object-oriented analysis and design, see van Vliet 2000, 351 ff.)

6. In definitions of software architecture, this is often called the "physical view" (Kruchten 1995, pp. 46–47) or the "deployment view" (Bass, Clements, and Kazman 2003, pp. 38–39). In the terminology of Hofmeister, Nord, and Soni (2000, pp. 11–12), the mapping of functional components to the hardware is part of the "execution view".

7. Ulrich and Eppinger 2000, pp. 182–183.

8. The hierarchical structure described in the text is a common feature of complex systems. See Simon 1969, pp. 86–88.

9. Christensen and Rosenbloom (1995, p. 238) describe this structure as a nested hierarchy: "In other words, products which at one level can be viewed as complex architectured systems act as components in systems at a higher level. Viewed in these terms, a given system-of-use comprises a hierarchically nested set of constituent systems and components."

10. See Bass, Clements, and Kazman 2003, p. 72.

11. For a detailed explanation of these and other qualities in the context of software architecture, see Bass, Clements, and Kazman 1998, pp. 75–88. For an overview of existing taxonomies of quality attributes in software engineering, see van Vliet 2000, pp. 110–119. Definitions of quality characteristics for software are also contained in ISO/IEC Standard 9126: Software Quality Characteristics and Metrics (ISO 1997), which is reproduced in part on pp. 117–119 of van Vliet 2000.

12. The following two paragraphs draw heavily on p. 78 of Bass, Clements, and Kazman 1998.

13. This is due to the overhead incurred in inter-component communication.

14. Because it is possible to counter good architecture with bad subsequent design or implementation, "a good architecture is necessary, but not sufficient, to ensure quality" (Bass, Clements, and Kazman 1998, p. 32). See also Hofmeister, Nord, and Soni 2000, p. 3.

15. On conflicts between quality attributes and the resulting need for trade-offs, see Bass, Clements, and Kazman 1998, pp. 127–129; Bosch 2000, p. 31. For an abstract overview of different ways to resolve conflicts between requirements or qualities, see Hofmeister, Nord, and Soni 2000, p. 6.

16. For a detailed analysis of this trade-off in the context of a client-server architecture, see Kazman et al. 1998, sections 4–10 .

17. Conceptually, this decision is not a part of architectural design, but belongs to the specification of requirements. Because some conflicts between quality requirements become apparent only during architectural design, there probably will be some iteration between the requirements specification and architectural design.

18. The exact nature of a design principle's architectural guidelines may differ. Whereas some design principles contain abstract rules for allocating functionality to components, others are mainly concerned with structural choices. For example, much research in software architecture focuses on identifying, analyzing, and documenting "architectural styles" (or "architectural patterns"), i.e., design principles that influence the structure of an architecture. A specific architectural style consists of a collection of component types, a description of the potential patterns of interaction among them, and a set of constraints on how these elements can be combined. The constraints may limit the behavior of components, restrict the kind of interaction allowed among the different types of components, or impose restrictions on the topological layout of the system. Architectural styles usually do not describe how system-specific functionality is allocated to component types. Other design principles may provide guidelines on how to allocate the functionality of the system under design to instances of the component types given by the architectural style. The seminal work on architectural styles (or architectural patterns) is Shaw and Garlan 1996. For encyclopedic coverage, see Buschmann et al. 1996 and Schmidt et al. 2000. The research on architectural patterns has been strongly influenced by the work of the architect Christopher Alexander. (See Alexander et al. 1977; Alexander 1978.) For an introduction to Alexander's work for software engineers, see Lea 1994.

19. How using the design principle affects the properties of the resulting system may be described in more or less detail. In the literature on software architecture, descriptions of a design principle usually include an informal description of the advantages and disadvantages of using it, an account of how it has been used historically, and qualitative reasoning to explain why its use results in a system with the specified properties. (For some examples concerning architectural styles, see Shaw and Garlan 1996, chapter 2. For a description of different architectural styles and the corresponding rules of thumb for choosing an architectural style, see chapter 5 of Bass, Clements, and Kazman 1998 or pp. 270–281 of van Vliet 2000.) There are efforts, however, to associate design principles with frameworks for more detailed qualitative or quantitative reasoning. For example, research on "attribute-based architectural styles" seeks to link the description of an architectural style with an analysis of that style with respect to a particular quality attribute such as modifiability or performance (see Klein and Kazman 1999). Research on "quality attribute design primitives" or "architectural tactics" seeks to describe architectural building blocks that are smaller and more fundamental than architectural styles and to combine them with a quality-attribute-specific analysis. On quality attribute design primitives, see Bass, Klein, and Bachmann 2000. On architectural tactics, see Bachmann, Bass, and Klein 2002 and chapter 5 of Bass, Clements, and Kazman 2003.

20. For case studies demonstrating this point, see Shaw and Garlan 1996, pp. 33–38; Bass, Clements, and Kazman 1998, pp. 117–121; van Vliet 2000, pp. 258–270. For additional examples, see Shaw and Garlan 1996, chapter 3.

21. See Bass, Clements, and Kazman 1998, pp. 113–117.

22. In practice, compliance with design principles may be very difficult to enforce. In major software projects, system architects can force designers to abide by the design principles by rejecting designs that violate the chosen design principles. In larger systems without a hierarchical relationship between system architects and component designers, system architects may be unable to enforce the design principles and are dependent on designers following them on a voluntary basis. In case of a system that is standardized in a standard-setting organization, the organization can reject standards solutions that violate the design principles, but this does not necessarily prevent someone from developing such solutions outside the standard-setting process. For example, though the Internet Engineering Task Force may reject certain technical solutions, that does not prevent individual vendors from incorporating these solutions into their products or network providers or users from deploying them. The emergence and deployment of devices for deep packet inspection is an example of this phenomenon.

23. The constraints described in the text are examples of different types of constraints that affect human behavior. Laws include constitutional and judicial rules, rules that directly regulate behavior, and economic rules such as the legal rules governing property rights (North 1990; Posner 1998b). Laws are an example of "formal constraints" (North 1990, chapter 6); other formal constraints include regulations, bylaws, and individual contracts. Social norms are informal rules that govern behavior within a community (Ellickson 1991; Posner 2000). Contrary to law, a norm is "neither promulgated by an official source, such as a court or legislature, nor enforced by the threat of legal sanctions, yet is regularly complied with" (Posner 1997, p. 365). Together with codes of conduct and conventions, social norms are a type of "informal constraint" (North 1990, chapter 7). The technical and natural environment includes the climate or natural resources in a given area (Diamond 1997), the current technical, scientific, economic, political, and cultural knowledge about the world (Nelson and Winter 1982; Rosenberg 1982; Freeman and Louca 2001; Perez 2002; Nelson 2005), the architectural layout of cities (Lessig 1998; Katyal 2002), and the digital environment established by the hardware and software of the Internet (Lessig 1999a). See, generally, North 1990 and Lessig 1998.

24. See North 1990; Hall and Soskice 2001.

25. The framework described in the text is used by researchers in economics (North 1990; Aoki 2001; Furubotn and Richter 2005; Greif 2006), political science (Hall and Taylor 1996; Thelen 1999; Peters 2005); law (Sunstein 1996a; Lessig 1998; Benkler 2006), and sociology (Powell and DiMaggio 1991; DiMaggio 1998; Scott 2000).

26. For an overview of the literature, see Lessig 1998.

27. See Posner 1996b.

28. For general analyses of the issues that may arise if law regulates other structures of regulation to reach policy goals, see Lessig 1998, pp. 686–691; Lessig 1999b, pp. 536–541. For an analysis of the negative consequences of various efforts to regulate technical aspects of the Internet to reach specific goals, see Solum and Chung 2004.

29. For these and other ways of influencing market constraints, see Viscusi, Harrington, and Vernon 2005, pp. 357–368.

30. Weakening the effect of a norm and providing incentives to break it is the first step toward changing a norm. See Sunstein 1996b, p. 930; Posner 1996a, p. 1729; Lessig 1995, pp. 1010–1012. For general discussions of different techniques of norm regulation, see Lessig 1995; Posner 1996a; Sunstein 1996b; Cooter 1998; Posner 1998a.

31. For general overviews of methods by which governments can influence technical systems in cyberspace, see Reidenberg 1998; Lessig 1999b; Kesan and Shah 2005. For critical reviews of specific efforts to regulate behavior by directly or indirectly regulating technical aspects of the Internet, see Zittrain 2003; Solum and Chung 2004. Similarly, governments can influence the physical environment in order to affect behavior in real space. For some interesting historical examples, see Lessig 1999a, pp. 91–92. Different ways in which government can influence the architecture of cities, neighborhoods, and individual buildings to reduce criminal activity and some of the associated problems are analyzed in Katyal 2002.

32. The architecture of a system can also influence other economic and non-economic activities, for example the use of the system, or political speech. See the discussion in chapter 9 below.

33. This is the standard definition of 'innovation' used in the literature. See Hall 1994, p. 2; Beije 1998, pp. 1–2.

34. See, e.g., Hall 1994, pp. 17–19.

35. This is the central assumption underlying economic theory: People react to changes in the costs and benefits associated with certain behavior in a way that is observable and predictable, and economic theory can be used to predict how people react to such changes. While different economic theories differ in their predictions as to how exactly people react to changes in incentives, they agree that, on average, an activity that becomes less costly is likely to be pursued to a greater extent and that an activity that becomes more costly will be reduced or eliminated. See Jolls, Sunstein, and Thaler 2000, p. 17.

36. North 1990, p. 5; Arrow 1974, p. 224; Thelen 1999, pp. 377–378.

37. Economists usually treat resources and cost structures as constraints. Since they are specific to the individual actor, I mention them here. See also Ostrom 2005, p. 828; Furubotn and Richter 2005, pp. 308–309.

38. See, generally, Ostrom 2005, pp. 828–829; Furubotn and Richter 2005, pp. 3, 308–309.

39. On the need to consider the joint effect of all constraints to determine the effect on an individual, see Lessig 1998, pp. 663–664; Lessig 1999b, pp. 509–510.

40. For an in-depth analysis of this issue from an economic perspective and pointers to the literature, see Landes and Posner 2003.

41. For a detailed discussion of this possibility, see chapter 5. This part of the framework also allows the integration of insights from sociology about the effect of existing social or economic relationships on economic behavior. See, e.g., the research on embeddedness (e.g., Granovetter 1985; Uzzi 1996) or on the importance of organizational fields for firms' organizational choices (e.g., DiMaggio and Powell 1983). On the relevance of embeddedness within organizations, cultures, or network connections for innovation, see Saxenian 1994; Castilla et al. 2000; Saxenian 2002; Powell et al. 2002; Powell and Grodal 2005; Porter, Bunker Whittington, and Powell 2005.

42. For a similar argument, see Lipsey, Carlaw, and Bekar 2005, p. 16.

43. Venture capitalists specialize in providing funding to high-risk, early-stage ventures. See Gompers and Lerner 2006. Normal banks are less well equipped than venture capitalists to identify promising investment opportunities and are less likely to finance new ventures even if they are promising. If the existing framework of constraints (or, in the terminology of the new institutional economics, the institutional framework) is sufficiently flexible, though, new forms of financing may arise in response to changes in the architecture. See Baldwin and Clark 2000, pp. 416–417. On the importance of an economic system's ability to adapt to new circumstances for the performance of an economy, see North 1990, pp. 81–83, 135–137.

44. For a theory along these lines, see Baldwin and Clark 2000. Based on the theory of complex adaptive systems and the theory of real options, they develop a theory of how designers' search for value drives architectural evolution in modular architectures, which in turn drives industry evolution; they use this theory to explain the evolution of the computer industry. I will discuss the relationship between architectures and real options in chapter 4.

45. More precisely, when talking about the original architecture of the Internet, I refer to the network architecture that was specified in the DARPA Internet Program protocol specifications for the Internet Protocol and the Transmission Control Protocol, RFC 791 (Postel 1981a) and RFC 793 (Postel 1981b). As I have already mentioned, David Clark described this architecture in his 1988 article on the design philosophy of the DARPA Internet protocols (D. D. Clark 1988).

46. In reality, this may happen if an architecture that has been in use in a specific country is changed while the other constraints stay the same.

47. Rational-choice theory is the theory that economists have traditionally used to model human behavior (see Kreps 1990, chapters 2–4). Though the details may differ, rational-choice theory usually assumes that human actors have well-defined interests ("preferences") that can be described by individual utility functions, and that they seek to maximize their utility. Bounded rationality takes account of the fact that human actors may have limited knowledge and limited cognitive capabilities (Williamson 1975; Williamson 1985; Simon 1957). Behavioral economics takes account of the systematic deviations from rational-choice theory that have been found empirically (Kahneman and Tversky 2000; Camerer, Loewenstein, and Rabin 2004).

Chapter 2

1. System architects create the architecture of a system. Software development projects for larger systems often have dedicated "software architects." For systems developed through standardization, the architecture is often developed as part of the standardization process; in this case, the system architects are those who work on defining the architecture within the standard-setting process.

2. To some readers, characterizing design principles as "rules that system architects must follow" may seem too strong. After all, if the system architects choose the design principles, they can also choose to deviate from them. Although this is correct, deviating from a design principle often compromises the ability of the final system to realize the qualities that the design principle fosters. Thus, though system architects can decide for themselves how closely they want to comply with the constraints imposed by the principle, this should be a deliberate decision that seriously considers the consequences. Seemingly minor deviations may add up and may severely compromise the system's ability to meet its quality goals.

3. This analysis of modularity draws heavily on the ideas Carliss Baldwin and Kim Clark develop in their 2000 book *Design Rules*. For an application of Baldwin and Clark's approach to software design, see Sullivan et al. 2001.

4. At first sight, this description looks different from the one usually provided in the computer science literature, where modularity entails decomposing the system into smaller components with well-defined interfaces. (See van Vliet 2000, p. 299.) Smaller components with well-defined interfaces, however, result from the second step of a modular design (described in the text) that addresses and resolves all remaining dependencies among components. Though the traditional definition does not contain any rules concerning the decomposition of the system, descriptions of modularity usually proceed to argue that effective or good modularity is reached by decomposing the system in a way that minimizes dependencies between modules, which is equivalent to the first step of designing a modular architecture as described in the text. See Pressman 1997, pp. 357–361; Sommerville 1996, p. 218. Thus, the definition used in the text is equivalent to the traditional definition of a

"good modular architectural design." As described here, modularity as a design strategy is not restricted to particular approaches to design. For example, components with well-defined interfaces that realize the principle of information hiding also are characteristic of object-oriented systems (Sommerville 1996, p. 215). The definition of 'modularity' used in the text is often used to describe modularity in the context of physical products too (Sanchez and Mahoney 1996, pp. 65–66; Baldwin and Clark 2000, pp. 63–64). For a review of the literature on different definitions of the concept of modularity in the context of assembled hardware products, see Fixson 2001.

5. See Baldwin and Clark 2000, p. 63; Schilling 2000, p. 312; Ulrich and Eppinger 2000, p. 184.

6. See Baldwin and Clark 2000, pp. 63–64. Abstraction, information hiding, and the separation of concerns are fundamental principles of software design. On abstraction in software design, see Bass, Clements, and Kazman 1998, p. 125; van Vliet 2000, pp. 296–299. On separation of concerns, see Bass, Clements, and Kazman 1998, p. 124. The seminal paper on information hiding is Parnas 1972.

7. With respect to the following, see Baldwin and Clark 2000, pp. 72–76.

8. My interpretation of interfaces as the resolution of all remaining cross-component interdependencies follows Baldwin and Clark 2000, pp. 70–76. See also Sullivan et al. 2001, section 3.2. Sullivan et al. apply Baldwin and Clark's approach to software design.

9. For example, a module's interface describes the services provided by the module and how they can be invoked and specifies all functional and non-functional properties of the module that may be relevant for other modules using its services. This may include statements about the quality of service provided by the module or its performance, availability, or security. Access to the services of a module can occur only through its interfaces. As a result, each interaction between two modules is reflected in the interface of the module whose services are used. In present-day software architecture design, one also specifies the services the module needs from the system to perform its services as part of its interface definition. This part of the interface definition is usually called the *required interface*. In this case, each interaction is reflected in the corresponding interfaces of both modules: once in the "provided interface" of the module that provides the service, and once in the "required interface" of the module that uses the service (Hofmeister, Nord, and Soni 2000, p. 110; Bosch 2000, pp. 220–224). This fact is subsumed in the text for expositional clarity. Changes to the provided or required part of a module's interface have very different consequences: changing the interface provided by a module requires subsequent changes to all modules that use this interface. In contrast, if the internal implementation of a module uses existing interfaces in a new or different way, the "required interface" of this module has to change to reflect the change in dependencies, but this does not affect any module in the rest of the system.

10. See Ulrich 1995, p. 435; Baldwin and Clark 2000, pp. 52, 91; Sanchez 1995, pp. 145–147. For an analysis of the organizational implications of this fact, see chapter 5 below.

11. Changes to an architecture's visible information are usually very costly, as all modules that depended on the changed information have to be changed as well to enable the system to continue to operate. See chapter 4 below.

12. Baldwin and Clark 2000, p. 52.

13. See Baldwin and Clark 2000, pp. 68–89; Sullivan et al. 2001, sections 5 and 7.

14. Thus, a modular design introduces a hierarchical dependency into the system. Hidden design parameters depend on visible design parameters (Baldwin and Clark 2000, pp. 64–76).

15. For an example, see Sullivan et al. 2001, sections 5.1. and 5.3. For an empirical study of the relationship between the level of coupling and the evolvability of a system, see MacCormack, Rusnak, and Baldwin 2007.

16. Stevens, Myers, and Constantine 1999, p. 241. For factors balancing this effect, see ibid., pp. 241–243.

17. See e.g., Bass, Clements, and Kazman 1998, pp. 32, 78, 79.

18. Similarly, for physical products, modularity may improve local performance (e.g., because of the ability to replace modules with better versions or due to the reduction in complexity in the design of individual modules), but may hurt global performance by preventing the joint optimization of the design of different modules necessary to optimize global performance with respect to heat or space by hiding aspects of a module's implementation, see Ulrich 1995, pp. 432–434.

19. The terminology sometimes differs. See Sanchez and Mahoney 1996, p. 65 ("Methodology of Constrained Optimization"); Ulrich and Eppinger 2000, p. 184 ("Integral Architecture"); Baldwin and Clark 2000, pp. 49–52, 64–68 ("Interconnected Design"). For descriptions of this approach in the context of physical products, see Baldwin and Clark 2000, pp. 49–52, 64–68; Sanchez 1999, p. 95; Ulrich and Eppinger 2000, p. 184.

20. See Pressman 1997, pp. 359–361; Sullivan et al. 2001, section 3.1. For sources of interdependencies between components of a physical system, see Baldwin and Clark 2000, pp. 34–39; Sanchez 1999, p. 93, note 3.

21. On physical products see Baldwin and Clark 2000, pp. 39–40. On software see Sullivan et al. 2001, section 3.1.

22. This process will usually require a considerable amount of "cycling" and iteration. See Baldwin and Clark 2000, pp. 49–52; Sanchez 1999, p. 95.

23. See Sanchez 1999, p. 95.

24. This strategy is known as "geometric nesting." See Ulrich 1995, p. 433.

25. The use of layering is very common in modern software development. See Hofmeister, Nord, and Soni 2000, chapter 5. For discussions of layering in the context of architectural styles, see Shaw and Garlan 1996, p. 25; Bass, Clements, and Kazman 1998, pp. 100–101; Bosch 2000, pp. 119–120; van Vliet 2000, pp. 277–280; Sommerville 1996, pp. 232–233.

26. Hofmeister, Nord, and Soni 2000, p. 101.

27. In modern software architecture design, the description of a layer's interface to lower layers is also part of a layer's visible information. The interface to lower layers describes which lower-layer services or functionality the layer requires to correctly fulfill its responsibilities. While the interface to higher layers is called the *provided interface* (it specifies the services provided by the layer), the interface to lower layers is called the *required interface* (it specifies the services required by the layer). See Hofmeister, Nord, and Soni 2000, p. 113. The required interface is not important in the context of this book and is therefore neglected in the text for expositional clarity. (See note 9 above.)

28. See Bass, Clements, and Kazman 1998, p. 100; Hofmeister, Nord, and Soni 2000, p. 113; Bosch 2000, p. 119.

29. See Bass, Clements, and Kazman 1998, p. 100; Bosch 2000, p. 119.

30. See Bass, Clements, and Kazman 1998, p. 83. Following Clark (1997), a portability layer is also called a *spanning layer*. See, e.g., Messerschmitt 2000, pp. 185–186; Kavassalis and Lehr 2000, pp. 209–211.

31. See Tanenbaum 2008, pp. 4–6, 63–64.

32. In early operating systems, applications were sometimes able to access hardware functions directly. For example, in MS-DOS, application programs were able access hardware-specific device drivers to write directly to the hardware. See Silberschatz, Galvin, and Gagne 2005, p. 59.

33. See Shaw and Garlan 1996, p. 25; Hofmeister, Nord, and Soni 2000, p. 102. In the context of networking, see Comer 2000, p. 178; Peterson and Davie 2007, p. 20.

34. This problem is often mentioned in discussions of layering in the context of networking. See Comer 2000, p. 192; Kurose and Ross 2008, p. 48. It may be overcome by offering additional, potentially optional interfaces that selectively expose additional lower-layer information; see Eggert and Eddy 2006. See also Coulson et al. 1999; Herbert 1990.

35. See Bosch 2000, p. 121; Klein and Kazman 1999, p. 63. In the context of networking, see Peterson and Davie 2007, p. 37. See also Clark and Tennenhouse 1990.

36. For example, by associating processes (in some operating systems, a process is called a *thread*) with events instead of with layers, the amount of time-consuming context switches between processes may be reduced. A context switch occurs when the operating system "stops one process from executing on the CPU and starts up another one" (Peterson and Davie 2007, p. 37). This technique is often used in implementations of layered network protocols. Instead of implementing one process per protocol, protocol implementors associate processes with the messages that pass through the layers. (See ibid., pp. 37–39.) It is also possible to increase performance by reducing the amount of copying when passing messages between layers. (See ibid., pp. 39–40.) For an in-depth treatment of network architecture and design in the context of high-speed networking, see Sterbenz and Touch 2001.

37. Today, the use of layered network protocols is the generally accepted approach to network architecture. For discussions of layering and protocols in the context of network architecture, see Peterson and Davie 2007, pp. 20–25; Tanenbaum 2003, pp. 26–37; Comer 2000, chapter 11; Kurose and Ross 2008, pp. 45–51. For an alternative proposal that seeks to achieve modularity through a non-layered protocol paradigm called *role-based architecture*, see Braden, Faber, and Handley 2003. The proposal is intended to address the problems of layer violations and unintended feature interactions between layers that plague the current architecture of the Internet.

38. With respect to the following, compare Peterson and Davie 2007, p. 9; Tanenbaum 2003, p. 19; Kurose and Ross 2008, pp. 9–11; Blumenthal and Clark 2001, pp. 71–72, 80–81.

39. This description glosses over the fact that in some network architectures, the end hosts may not only use, but also offer network services. In the Internet, the computers on the network (or end hosts) also participate in the operation of the network through the protocols at the Internet layer and below. Thus, one may say that in the Internet, computers on the network form the network, too. A more precise description of the Internet would focus on layers: the layers up to the Internet layer are "in" the network, while the layers above the Internet layer are "on" the network. See, e.g., Comer 2000, p. 186; Sterbenz and Touch 2001, p. 350.

40. Throughout this book, "the core of the network" will be used to denote the set of computers "in the network," or, in the case of the Internet, the lower layers up to, and including, the Internet layer. (See preceding note.) For a similar use, see Blumenthal and Clark 2001, pp. 71–72. Sometimes (but not in this book), "core network" is used to denote the part of a hierarchical telecommunications network that provides the highest level of aggregation, such as the backbone network, as opposed to the intermediate part of the entire network, the backhaul, that connects the core network with the access networks or edge networks.

41. See Blumenthal and Clark 2001, pp. 80–81. The functional, topological, and administrative views of the meaning of "in the network" are explicitly distinguished

by Sterbenz and Touch (2001, p. 350). According to Sterbenz and Touch (ibid.), "the topological view has to do with whether or not functions and resources are collocated with network nodes or located with subscriber end systems."

42. The networking literature uses the word 'protocol' in different ways. Following the terminology used by Peterson and Davie (2007, pp. 20–25), this book uses 'protocol' to denote the collection of abstract entities at a certain layer that are distributed among different computers and cooperate with each other provide a particular service to the layer above. Others use 'protocol' more narrowly, to denote the rules governing the interaction among the communicating entities on different computers (see e.g., Tanenbaum 2003, pp. 36–37; Kurose and Ross 2008, pp. 8–9). Thus, in the terminology of this book, they use 'protocol' to denote a protocol's horizontal peer interface, as defined below.

43. Protocol peers are the instances of a protocol on different computers that communicate with each other. They are not the same as peer-to-peer applications. Peer-to-peer applications are applications in which the computers running the application act as both client and server. In contrast, in client-server applications, a computer running the application acts either as a client or as a server.

44. On the different uses of 'protocol', see note 42 above.

45. When protocols are defined in the Internet Engineering Task Force, only the peer interface, that is the form and meaning of the messages exchanged between the communicating protocol entities, and the services the protocol provides to higher layers are specified. The specification of the exact interface through which higher-layer protocols can invoke the services is left to those who implement the protocol. On IP, see Postel 1981a, section 3.3; Comer 2000, p. 413. On TCP, see Postel 1981b, section 1.4; Comer 2000, p. 216.

46. In the terminology of network engineering, these messages that protocol peers at a particular layer (layer n) send to each other are called *layer n-protocol data units*. See Sterbenz and Touch 2001, p. 43.

47. In the terminology of network engineering, the part of a message in layer $n - 1$ that consists of data to be delivered to layer n (that is, that consists of either the complete layer n-message or parts of it), is called the *layer n – 1 payload*. See Sterbenz and Touch 2001, p. 43.

48. In the terminology of network engineering, the part of a message in layer $n - 1$ that tells the receiving-layer $n - 1$ peer what to do is called a *header* or a *trailer*, depending on whether it is inserted before or after the payload. See Sterbenz and Touch 2001, p. 43. Thus, the layer $n - 1$ protocol data unit is created by adding a header or a trailer to the layer $n - 1$ payload—that is, to the layer n protocol data unit, or parts of it. Because the layer n protocol data unit is encapsulated in the layer $n - 1$ protocol data unit created by the layer n protocol, the process of protocol data unit creation is also called *encapsulation*. See Peterson and Davie 2007, pp. 24–25.

49. Comer 2000, pp. 187–189; Kruse 1999, abstract and section 2; Sterbenz and Touch 2001, pp. 42–43.

50. Some researchers seem to imply that the layering principle prohibits the modification of higher-layer messages by lower-layer protocols. (See Kruse 1999, section 2.) This statement, however, is not accurate. In order to perform their lower-layer services, lower layers may temporarily modify the messages passed to them by a higher layer. For example, lower layers may split or compress the messages passed to them by a higher layer in order to perform their services. (See Peterson and Davie 2007, pp. 24–25.) The layering principle requires that all these modifications are completely reversed before the message is delivered to the higher-layer protocol at the receiving computer. For example, the Internet Protocol may split a data packet passed to it by a transport-layer protocol and encapsulate it into several datagrams. The Internet Protocol implementation at the receiver, however, will completely reverse this split and deliver the complete data packet to the transport-layer protocol at the receiver. (See Peterson and Davie 2007, pp. 239–242.) Thus, it seems more accurate to say that the layering principle prohibits lower-layer protocols from permanently modifying higher-layer messages.

51. See Peterson and Davie 2007, p. 22; Tanenbaum 2003, pp. 26–30; Sterbenz and Touch 2001, p. 44; Kurose and Ross 2008, pp. 47–51.

52. See Comer 2000, p. 187; Tanenbaum 2003, p. 30.

53. Tanenbaum 2003, p. 448; Peterson and Davie 2007, pp. 24–25; Kruse 1999, abstract and section 2.

54. The applicability of the end-to-end arguments is not restricted to communication networks. In fact, according to Reed, Saltzer, and Clark (1998, p. 70) the end-to-end arguments originally arose from the authors' research on secure operating system kernels and on end-to-end transport protocols in local area networks and the Internet. For additional examples of end-to-end arguments in the design of other systems, see Saltzer, Reed, and Clark 1984; Reed, Saltzer, and Clark 1998.

55. The terms "end hosts" and "core of the network" and the differences between higher-layer and lower-layer protocols were explained in the section of this chapter titled "Modularity and Layering in Network Architectures."

56. With respect to the International Standards Organization's Open Systems Interconnection reference model (the transport layer and higher layers are typically implemented on end hosts, not on the intermediate switches or routers), see Peterson and Davie 2007, p. 28; Tanenbaum 2003, p. 40; Sterbenz and Touch 2001, pp. 41–42. With respect to the architecture of the Internet (end hosts implement all layers, while IP routers typically implement only lower layers, up to and including the Internet layer), see pp. 51–52 of Kurose and Ross 2008. In practice, routers may implement higher layers to terminate routing protocols such as BGP or management protocols.

57. Saltzer, Reed, and Clark 1981. The 1981 paper was a conference paper. When referring to the original paper that first identified and described the end-to-end arguments, researchers usually refer to the revised version (Saltzer, Reed, and Clark 1984) that appeared in *ACM Transactions on Computer Systems* in 1984. See, e.g., Moors 2002, p. 1214. I generally follow this convention too. For a discourse-oriented analysis of the end-to-end arguments and their subsequent role in political, social, and legal debates, see Gillespie 2006.

58. See Peterson and Davie 2007, pp. 52–53, 387.

59. See Carpenter 1996, section 2; Computer Science and Telecommunications Board and National Research Council 2001, pp. 36–38; Braden et al. 2000, p. 15; Moors 2002; Blumenthal and Clark 2001, p. 71; Clark et al. 2005, section VI.A.

60. Reed, Saltzer, and Clark 1998.

61. Blumenthal and Clark 2001; Clark and Blumenthal 2007.

62. Saltzer 1999; Reed 2000.

63. I first described the differences between the two versions in chapter 6 of van Schewick 2004.

64. Peterson and Davie (2007, p. 387) use a similar phrase, rephrasing the definition given in the original paper (Saltzer, Reed, and Clark 1984, p. 278): "The function in question can completely and correctly be implemented only with the knowledge and help of the application standing at the endpoints of the communication system. Therefore, providing that questioned function as a feature of the communication system itself is not possible. (Sometimes an incomplete version of the function provided by the communication system may be useful as a performance enhancement.)"

65. Reed, Saltzer, and Clark 1998, p. 69 (emphasis added).

66. Reed, Saltzer, and Clark (1998, p. 69), after referring to the 1984 paper, simply introduce the "new" second version quoted above as "the end-to-end principle."

67. For two recent exceptions, see Moors 2002 and Kempf and Austein 2004. Moors notes that the original paper emphasized an end-to-end argument "relating to correctness of function," referring to the version called *the narrow version* in the text. In addition to this version, Moors identifies a number of additional end-to-end arguments in the two end-to-end papers by treating each line of reasoning against the low-level implementation of functions as a separate "end-to-end argument." As a result of this increase in the number of end-to-end arguments, however, the notion of "end-to-end arguments" becomes arbitrary and loses any prescriptive value. This does not seem desirable, given that it is possible to identify two distinct design principles that provide clear guidelines for design in their respective areas of applicability and that are supported by the various arguments presented in the two end-

to-end papers. According to the interpretation advanced in the text, the different arguments against the implementation of application-specific functionality in lower layers of the system are relevant in two ways: first, in the context of the narrow version, they need to be considered in order to decide whether an additional, necessarily incomplete low-level implementation of end-to-end functions is justified. This decision is the trade-off mentioned in the original paper. See the discussion of the narrow version below. Second, in the context of the broad version, these arguments form the justification of the design rule established by the broad version. See the discussion of the broad version below. Kempf and Austein (2004, section 1) also note changes in the interpretation of the end-to-end principle: "The end-to-end principle was originally articulated as a question of where best not to put functions in a communication system. Yet, in the ensuing years, it has evolved to address concerns of maintaining openness, increasing reliability and robustness, and preserving the properties of user choice and ease of new service development as discussed by [Blumenthal and Clark (2001)]; concerns that were not part of the original articulation of the end-to-end principle." According to Kempf and Austein (2004, section 2.2), "the original articulation of the end-to-end principle—that knowledge and assistance of the end point is essential and that omitting such knowledge and implementing a function in the network without such knowledge and assistance is not possible—took a while to percolate through the engineering community, and had evolved by this point to a broad architectural statement about what belongs in the network and what doesn't." This observation is similar to the distinction between the narrow and the broad version made by this book. Contrary to this book, however, Kempf and Austein associate the end-to-end principle as a broad architectural statement with the question of "what kind of state is maintained where"— a point of view that is criticized in chapter 3 below. Finally, although Kempf and Austein emphasize the continuing importance of the end-to-end principle for the architecture of the Internet, it is difficult to see to which of the different interpretations of the end-to-end principle this statement is meant to apply. Thus, they fail to provide clear guidelines for the application of the end-to-end principle that can be used in network design.

68. See Peterson and Davie 2007, p. 387.

69. The perception of the end-to-end arguments in policy debates has been deeply influenced by Mark Lemley and Lawrence Lessig's description of "the end-to-end principle" in their 1999 *ex parte* letter to the FCC (Lemley and Lessig 1999, sections 16–17): "16. The end-to-end principle organizes the placement of functions within a network. It counsels that that [*sic*] 'intelligence' in a network be located at the top of a layered system—at its 'ends', where users put information and applications onto the network—and that the communications protocols themselves (the "pipes" through which information flows) be as simple and general as possible. 17. One consequence of this design is a principle of nondiscrimination among applications. Lower level network layers should provide a broad range of resources that are not

particular to or optimized for any single application—even if a more efficient design for at least some applications is thereby sacrificed." (See also Lemley and Lessig 2000, pp. 8–9.) As will become apparent below, this description refers to the broad version of the end-to-end arguments. For similar descriptions, see Lessig 2001, pp. 34–37 ("End-to-end says to keep intelligence in a network at the ends, or in the applications, leaving the network itself to be relatively simple"); Yoo 2002, p. 270; Solum and Chung 2004, p. 844. For descriptions of the broad version of the end-to-end arguments in the context of descriptions of the Internet's architecture, see Computer Science and Telecommunications Board and National Research Council 2001, p. 36 ("Aimed at simplicity and flexibility, this argument [i.e., the end-to-end argument] says that the network should provide a very basic level of service—data transport— and that the intelligence—the information processing needed to provide applications—should be located in or close to the devices attached to the edge of the network"), Carpenter 1996, section 2.1 ("However, in very general terms, the community believes that the goal is connectivity, the tool is the Internet Protocol, and the intelligence is end to end [sic] rather than hidden in the network"), and Carpenter 1996, section 2.3 ("The network's job is to transmit datagrams as efficiently and flexibly as possible. Everything else should be done at the fringes[,] in the context of the discussion of "the end-to-end argument").

70. See Carpenter 1996, section 2.3.

71. Kempf and Austein (2004) advance this interpretation. See note 67 above.

72. The terminology does not reflect the differences in the content of the rules.

73. A complete comparison of the two versions can be found in the subsection of this chapter titled "Comparison of the Two Versions."

74. In the paper, "communication system" is specified as follows (Saltzer, Reed, and Clark 1984, p. 278): "In a system that includes communications, one usually draws a modular boundary around the communication subsystem and defines a firm interface between it and the rest of the system. When doing so, it becomes apparent that there is a list of functions each of which might be implemented in any of several ways: by the communication subsystem, by its client, as a joint venture, or perhaps redundantly, each doing its own version."

75. Ibid., p.278.

76. Peterson and Davie (2007, p. 387) use similar phrasing.

77. The division of functionality between the layers has implications for the division of functionality between end hosts and the core of the network. The choice between layers, however, is not always equivalent to the choice between end systems and core of the network. See figure 2.6.

78. Although texts describing the narrow version agree that it only applies to certain functions (see Saltzer, Reed, and Clark 1984, p. 278; Moors 2002, p. 1214), the

literature does not contain a general description of the type of functions and of the circumstances under which the argument applies. Instead, texts list one or more specific functions to which the argument applies. For example, according to Saltzer, Reed, and Clark (1984), the (narrow) version applies to error control, "encryption, duplicate message detection, message sequencing, guaranteed message delivery, detecting host crashes and delivery receipts" (p. 278). Kempf and Austein (2004, section 2.1) and Peterson and Davie (2007, p. 387) also list specific functions to which the narrow version applies. A more general characterization of functions to which the argument applies seems desirable to enable designers to determine the applicability of the argument in their specific case. Building on the examples highlighted by the literature, the following treatment aims at providing such a general description.

79. Sterbenz and Touch (2001, pp. 39–41, 346–348) emphasize this case in their treatment of the end-to-end arguments.

80. Sterbenz and Touch 2001, pp. 39–41, 346–347; Moors 2002, p. 1214. For an empirical study confirming the introduction of errors by faulty hardware or software in routers or end hosts, see Stone and Partridge 2000.

81. Sterbenz and Touch 2001, pp. 39–41, 346–347. Even with end-to-end error control, data integrity cannot be absolutely guaranteed. This is due to the probabilistic nature of integrity checks. See Stone and Partridge 2000, section 2; Moors 2002, p. 1215.

82. Sterbenz and Touch 2001, pp. 39–41, 346; Moors 2002, p. 1215.

83. This case generalizes the example of reliable file transfer as well as other examples provided in the original end-to-end paper: as Saltzer, Reed, and Clark (1984, p. 280) note, even if the communication system can guarantee reliable data transmission within its boundaries, it cannot protect the application against threats to data integrity that occur outside the boundaries of the communication system. A similar reasoning about the possibility of threats to the function outside the boundaries of the communication system underlies the argument with respect to delivery guarantees (p. 282), secure transmission of data (pp. 282–283), or suppression of duplicate messages (p. 283).

84. Ibid., pp. 278–280.

85. Ibid., pp. 282–283.

86. This choice is also related to trust. See Moors 2002, pp. 1215, 1218–1219; Clark and Blumenthal 2007, pp. 2–6.

87. For example, according to the original paper, a file-transfer application must implement end-to-end error control itself in order to eliminate all threats to data integrity that may occur after the data leaves the communication system. For example, data may get corrupted when it is stored on the disk (Saltzer, Reed, and

Clark 1984, p. 280; Border et al. 2001, section 4.1.3). In spite of this insight, most applications today do not implement such functionality, but use the reliable-data-transfer functionality provided by transport-layer protocols such as TCP. On error control in higher layers, see box 3.2 below.

88. Saltzer, Reed, and Clark 1984, pp. 280–282.

89. Sometimes, the additional lower-layer implementation may reduce the performance of the system. For example, encrypting data at a lower layer that has already been encrypted at a higher layer may reduce the strength of the end-to-end encryption (Sterbenz and Touch 2001, pp. 423–424).

90. For a more detailed overview of the positive and negative effect of local implementations on performance, see Moors 2002, pp. 1216–1217.

91. Saltzer, Reed, and Clark 1984, p. 281. See also Sterbenz and Touch 2001, pp. 347–348.

92. See Saltzer, Reed, and Clark 1984, p. 281; Moors 2002, pp. 1216–1217. See also Wischik 2007, pp. 8–9.

93. For a discussion of these examples, see Sterbenz and Touch 2001, pp. 347–348.

94. Saltzer, Reed, and Clark 1984, pp. 281–282.

95. Ibid., p. 281.

96. See, e.g., the abstract of the original paper (Saltzer, Reed, and Clark 1984, p. 277): "This paper presents a design principle that helps guide placement of functions among the modules of a distributed computer system. The principle, called the end-to-end argument, suggests that functions placed at the lower levels of a system may be redundant or of little value when compared with the cost of providing them at that low level."

97. See, e.g., the quotations from Reed, Saltzer, and Clark 1998 and Blumenthal and Clark 2001 in the text. See also Saltzer 1999 ("The end-to-end argument says 'don't force any service, feature, or restriction on the customer; his application knows best what features it needs, and whether or not to provide those features itself.'"); Reed 2000 ("In that paper [meaning Saltzer, Reed, and Clark 1984] we argued that many functions can only be completely implemented at the end points of the network, so any attempt to build features in the network to support particular applications must be viewed as a trade-off. Those applications that don't need a particular feature will have unnecessary costs imposed on them to support the other applications that benefit. We argued that building in such functions is rarely necessary, and that systems designers should avoid building any more than the essential and common functions into the network."); Clark et al. (2005), p. 471 ("One of the most respected and cited of the Internet design principles is the end-to-end arguments which state that mechanism should not be placed in the network if it can be placed at the end

node, and that the core of the network should provide a general service, not one that is tailored to a specific application [Saltzer, Reed, and Clark 1984].")

98. Blumenthal and Clark 2001, p. 71.

99. Reed, Saltzer, and Clark 1998, p. 69.

100. Ibid., p. 70.

101. Blumenthal and Clark 2001, p. 80 (citing personal communication with Jerome Saltzer).

102. Reed 2002.

103. Reed, Saltzer, and Clark 1998, p. 70; Reed 2000.

104. Saltzer, Reed, and Clark 1984, pp. 281, 284–285; Reed, Saltzer, and Clark 1998, p. 70; Reed 2000; Moors 2002, p. 1217.

105. Reed, Saltzer, and Clark 1998, p. 70; Blumenthal and Clark 2001, p. 71; Reed 2000; Moors 2002, pp. 1217–1218; Clark et al. 2005, p. 472.

106. Though humans can hear a broader frequency range, this is the range which they need so that they can understand speech clearly.

107. See Moors 2002, p. 1217, citing Lucky 1997.

108. Apart from asymmetric bandwidth, dynamic IP addresses, network-address translators (NATs) and firewalls are examples of this trend. See Minar and Hedlund 2001, pp. 13–15. On NATs and firewalls, see my concluding chapter.

109. See Kurose and Ross 2008, p. 84.

110. See ibid., pp. 14–15.

111. The problems resulting from asymmetric bandwidth were clearly described in several reports by the Computer Science and Telecommunications Board and National Research Council (1994, p. 87; 1996, pp. 52, 71–77, 89–93).

112. The text assumes that the network only offers a single service to all applications, so that all applications have to use that service. It may be possible to offer different functions in the network among which applications can choose. Such a solution increases the complexity of the network and makes it more difficult to predict how the network will behave. This lower transparency constitutes a cost that is borne by all applications. Whether such a solution complies with the end-to-end arguments, has to be decided on a case-by-case basis. See Reed, Saltzer, and Clark 1998 (commenting on active networking and end-to-end arguments). A current example of a network service that is only provided to transport-layer connections that explicitly request it is Explicit Congestion Notification (ECN), where routers signal congestion to transport-layer connections by setting a code point in the IP packet, see Ramakrishnan, Floyd, and Black 2001.

113. Saltzer, Reed, and Clark 1984, pp. 281, 286–287; Reed, Saltzer, and Clark 1998, pp. 69–70; Moors 2002, p. 1217.

114. Saltzer, Reed, and Clark 1984, pp. 286–287.

115. Ibid., p. 281; Moors 2002, p. 1217.

116. See Peterson and Davie 2007, p. 558. The source of this example is Moors 2002, p. 1217.

117. Reed, Saltzer, and Clark 1998, p. 70.

118. Not every application of the broad version automatically results in decentralized control by users (instead of centralized control by a few network providers), though; it only results in decentralized control if end users control the end hosts. Thus, control over a network can be centralized even if the network is designed according to the broad version, if a central entity controls the end hosts. For example, an enterprise network based on the TCP/IP protocol suite where applications can only be installed by system administrators is based on the broad version, but centrally controlled.

119. Blumenthal and Clark 2001, p. 71; Clark et al. 2005, p. 472.

120. Blumenthal and Clark 2001, p. 71; Clark et al. 2005, p. 472. However, a network provider may prefer to provide functions in the network, where he controls their execution, instead of relying on users or third parties to execute them correctly. See Abbate 1999, pp. 156–161.

121. Blumenthal and Clark 2001, p. 71; Clark et al. 2005, p. 472; Computer Science and Telecommunications Board and National Research Council 2001, p. 37.

122. This is particularly common in contributions to the policy debate. See Wu 2003a, p. 146: "For these reasons, Internet Darwinians argue that their innovation theory is embodied in the 'end-to-end' design argument, which in essence suggests that networks should be neutral as among applications. [Saltzer, Reed, and Clark 1984]"

123. See Lemley and Lessig 1999: "16. The end-to-end principle organizes the placement of functions within a network. It counsels that that [sic] "intelligence" in a network be located at the top of a layered system—at its "ends," where users put information and applications onto the network—and that the communications protocols themselves (the "pipes" through which information flows) be as simple and general as possible. 17. One consequence of this design is a principle of non-discrimination among applications." (p. 8 in Lemley and Lessig 2000)

124. Blumenthal and Clark 2001, pp. 82–83.

125. In this context, "message" denotes the data that the higher-layer protocol wants to pass on to its peer.

126. For similar observations, see section 2 of Kruse 1999 and p. 846 of Solum and Chung 2004.

127. See the section of this chapter titled "Modularity and Layering in Network Architectures." Such mechanisms would introduce a dependence on higher layers. That lower layers must not depend on higher layers, however, is the central requirement for a layered architecture. If it is violated, changes at higher layers may require subsequent changes at lower layers, if the lower layer is to function correctly. This is exactly what the layering principle wants to prevent.

128. This consequence of an end-to-end design was first identified by Mark Lemley and Lawrence Lessig in their 1999 *ex parte* letter to the FCC (Lemley and Lessig 1999, reprinted as Lemley and Lessig 2000). But because the end-to-end arguments are just a design principle and network providers are not required to comply with them, nothing prevents the network providers from deploying devices in the network that enable them to control the traffic on their network, even if these devices violate the broad version.

129. For an overview of the debate and pointers to the literature, see chapter 6.

130. For a representative example of this view with respect to open access regulation, see Lemley and Lessig 1999, reprinted as Lemley and Lessig 2000. With respect to network neutrality rules, see Wu and Lessig 2003; Wu 2003a.

131. For two representative examples of this view, see Speta 2000a,b.

132. The two arguments are mutually exclusive. If network owners do not have an incentive to discriminate against independent applications anyway, the imposition of the network neutrality regime that prevents such discrimination will not reduce their profits. If it does not reduce their profits, however, it cannot reduce their incentives to invest in upgrades of their network infrastructure in the future.

133. For a representative example of this view, see Thierer 2004.

134. See Odlyzko 1998, pp. 40–41; Blumenthal and Clark 2001, pp. 74, 96; Clark et al. 2005, p. 467. As Jonathan Zittrain has pointed out, this makes it more difficult to adequately protect PCs from viruses, spyware, and other malware. The resulting security risk may be exploited in a global security attack which harms Internet users all over the world. In the aftermath of such an attack, users may call for countermeasures which may result in a lock-down of PCs, making them unable to run applications that have not been certified by a gatekeeper before. Such a development would considerably reduce the ability of users and application innovators to experiment with new applications. For a detailed description of this argument and possible solutions, see Zittrain 2008. For an analysis of the effect of the broad version on security, see the subsection of chapter 9 titled "Social Costs."

135. For a similar argument in a slightly different context, see p. 467 of Clark et al. 2005 and section 4.1.1 of Kempf and Austein 2004. A widespread move toward

"software as a service" and appliances, which enables software providers and appliance producers to control their product's functionality and even change it retroactively, may reduce the ability of users and application developers to experiment with new applications. For an analysis of the problem, see Zittrain 2008, chapter 5. For potential solutions, see Zittrain 2008, part III.

136. See Blumenthal and Clark 2001, pp. 77–78, 86; St. Johns and Huston 2003, section 3; Clark et al. 2005, p. 472. For an overview of principles of traffic engineering in the Internet today, see Awduche et al. 2002.

137. See Peterson and Davie 2007, p. 633; Blumenthal and Clark 2001, p. 80; St. Johns and Huston 2003, section 4.

138. For example, the IP protocol header contains a "protocol" field that indicates which higher-layer protocol at the destination host to deliver the data to. In other words, the "protocol" field indicates the higher-layer protocol that invoked the services of IP at the originating host. Thus, if an application does not use a transport protocol but invokes IP directly, the IP header will carry information about the application. This field is used solely for de-multiplexing at the destination host and does not influence the treatment of datagrams within the network. The numbering of protocols used in the protocol field is standardized across the entire Internet. The relevant numbers are contained in an online database located at www.iana.org. See Tanenbaum 2003, p. 435; Peterson and Davie 2007, p. 239. For an overview of the use of port numbers in TCP and UDP, see Comer 2000, pp. 197–206, 216–218.

139. See Blumenthal and Clark 2001, pp. 77–80, 86. The Internet Architecture Board has recently commented on this practice and highlighted some of the long-term problems associated with mechanisms that are not restricted to gathering information, but are intended to filter or prevent the transmission of traffic based on this information (St. Johns and Huston 2003).

140. Kruse 1999, section 2.

141. The proliferation of such devices creates huge problems in the current Internet. For example, such devices may affect the end-to-end integrity of data, may prevent the use of end-to-end IPSec or require the maintenance of state in the device, violating the principle of fate-sharing and introducing single points of failure. Most important in the context of this book, these devices may prevent or impede the deployment of new applications. The analysis of these problems is beyond the scope of this book. For a short overview of the problems for innovation, see the concluding chapter of this book. The Internet Engineering Task Force has analyzed these issues in a number of requests for comments. See Kaat 2000; Carpenter 2000; Carpenter and Brim 2002. Legal scholars have analyzed the policy implications of requiring the use of packet-filtering devices for regulatory purposes. See Solum and Chung 2004; Zittrain 2003.

142. For example, there may be instances when the cost reductions resulting from a low-level implementation are so large and the costs to applications with different

needs are so small, that an implementation of application-specific functionality in the network may be justified. In their second joint paper, Reed, Saltzer, and Clark mention the provision of network-level multicast as an example of such reasoning (1998, p. 69, note 1).

143. For a more detailed version of this argument in a slightly different context, see Solum and Chung 2004, pp. 854–865.

144. Braden et al. 2000, pp. 6–9.

145. See the discussion in my concluding chapter.

146. This trade-off is particularly apparent in Reed, Saltzer, and Clark 1998 (p. 70), in Blumenthal and Clark 2001 (pp. 71–72), and in Reed 2000.

147. Yoo 2004, pp. 40–43. The conflict results from the different ways in which the narrow version and the broad version approach partial implementations of application-specific functionality in the network. See the discussion in the subsection of this chapter titled "Comparison of the Two Versions."

Chapter 3

1. See Comer 2000, pp. 53–55.

2. See Comer 2000, p. 63.

3. Kurose and Ross 2008, pp. 526–544; Peterson and Davie 2007, pp. 137–143.

4. Kurose and Ross 2008, pp. 469–480; Peterson and Davie 2007, pp. 116–124.

5. See Peterson and Davie 2007, p. 234.

6. The global Internet is denoted by 'Internet' (capitalized); 'internet' (lower case) usually refers to an arbitrary collection of networks interconnected to provide a universal communication service. See Comer 2000, p. 1.

7. See Peterson and Davie 2007, p. 234.

8. The standards describing the protocols that are part of the Internet's architecture are developed and standardized by the Internet Engineering Task Force. A list of the current "Official Internet Protocol Standards" is available at http://www.rfc-editor .org; the list is updated daily. The Internet-standards process used by the Internet Engineering Task Force is described in Bradner 1996. For a short overview of that process, see Computer Science and Telecommunications Board and National Research Council 2001, pp. 134–135. For introductions to the architecture of the Internet, see Comer 2000; Peterson and Davie 2007; Tanenbaum 2003.

9. The description in the text follows the TCP/IP reference model used by the Internet Engineering Task Force (see Peterson and Davie 2007, pp. 28–30; Tanenbaum 2003, pp. 41–44; Comer 2000, pp.183–185). The terminology regarding the names

of the layers follows Comer 2000, pp. 183–185. As Comer notes, the link layer is sometimes called the *network interface layer*. An alternative reference model, the Open Systems Interconnection (OSI) Reference Model was developed by the International Organization for Standardization (ISO) (see Tanenbaum 2003, pp. 37–41; Peterson and Davie 2007, pp. 26–28). For a comparison of the two reference models, see Tanenbaum 2003, pp. 44–49; Comer 2000, pp. 185–186. For a discussion of the history of the OSI reference model, see Abbate 1999, pp. 167–179.

10. The link layer also includes protocols for transporting data packets across a point-to-point link. The use of the term "link layer" follows Comer 2000, p. 184. In the OSI reference architecture, this layer corresponds to two layers: the *physical layer* and the *data link layer*. The physical layer is responsible for transmitting raw bits over a communications link. The data link layer builds on the services of the physical layer to transmit data packets called *frames* from one end host to another end host on the same physical network. See Tanenbaum 2003, pp. 85–182 (discussing the physical layer) and 183–342 (discussing the data link layer).

11. On this division (end hosts implement all layers, while IP routers typically implement only lower layers, up to and including the Internet layer), see Kurose and Ross 2008, pp. 51–52. Although higher layers do not have to be implemented on routers, in practice routers implement higher layers to terminate management and routing protocols.

12. For a description of the service provided by IP, see Comer 2000, p. 97; Peterson and Davie 2007, pp. 236–237.

13. For empirical studies measuring the amount of packet re-ordering or packet loss in the Internet, see Paxson 1999; Jaiswal et al. 2007.

14. For overviews of IP interconnection and routing, see Comer 2000, pp. 56–60, 115–126; Peterson and Davie 2007, pp. 234–235, 250–254.

15. In reality, routers have an IP address for each physical network to which they attach. The same is true for "multi-homed hosts" that are connected to two or more physical networks. For details, see Comer 2000, p. 65. For overviews of IP addressing, see Comer 2000, pp. 63–75; Peterson and Davie 2007, pp. 248–250.

16. If the destination host is attached to the same physical network, the IP protocol at the source host does not send the datagram to the nearest router; it sends the datagram directly to the destination host, using the link-layer protocol of the physical network. This differs from networking technologies, such as GPRS or DOCSIS, in which two hosts can never send data directly to each other. By requiring hosts to send data via computers in the network, these technologies effectively make the existence of a network operator a technical requirement.

17. In many operating systems, a running application program is called a *process*, a *user process*, or a *task*. See Comer 2000, p. 197; Kurose and Ross 2008, pp. 85–86.

18. For a description of the mechanism (multiplexing and de-multiplexing) used to realize this goal, see Comer 2000, pp. 197–206, 243.

19. See Kurose and Ross 2008, pp. 195–199.

20. On this division (end hosts implement all layers, while IP routers typically implement only lower layers, up to and including the Internet layer), see pp. 51–52 of Kurose and Ross 2008. In practice, routers may implement higher layers to terminate routing protocols such as BGP or management protocols.

21. See the subsection of this chapter titled "The End-to-End Arguments and the Division of Functionality between the Internet Layer and the Transport Layer. The Broad Version."

22. For descriptions of the service provided by TCP, see Peterson and Davie 2007, pp. 384–385, 387, 410–411; Comer 2000, pp. 209–211.

23. For descriptions of the service provided by UDP, see Peterson and Davie 2007, pp. 382–384; Comer 2000, pp. 197–207.

24. Thus, there is a difference between the application (the program that implements the protocol specification) and the protocol specification (which describes the protocol's peer and service interface). See Kurose and Ross 2008, pp. 81–85.

25. More precisely, the format of the messages exchanged between different entities belonging to the protocol and the actions the receiver of a message is supposed to take are defined as part of the peer interface of the protocol.

26. The application layer in the reimbursement example in chapter 2 consists of only one application (reimbursement processing). Different protocol entities, such as the employee and the administrator in the reimbursement department, exchange messages according to rules, which constitute that protocol's peer interface.

27. See Comer 2000, p. 577.

28. Following Clark (1997), a portability layer is also called a *spanning layer*. (See Messerschmitt 2000, pp. 185–186; Kavassalis and Lehr 2000, pp. 209–211.) The role of the Internet layer as a spanning or portability layer populated by a single protocol is discussed by Clark (1997, pp. 134–135) and by Kavassalis and Lehr (2000, pp. 209–211). The proposal for an Open Data Network Architecture for the National Information Infrastructure by the Computer Science and Telecommunications Board and National Research Council (1994, pp. 47–55) also proposes a technology-independent portability layer below the transport layer called the *open bearer service*, noting that the Internet Protocol is the analogue of the bearer service in the TCP/IP protocol suite. See Computer Science and Telecommunications Board and National Research Council 1994, p. 54.

29. See Comer 2000, pp. 575–579; Peterson and Davie 2007, pp. 28–30.

30. See Comer 2000, pp. 577–578; Peterson and Davie 2007, pp. 29–30; Computer Science and Telecommunications Board and National Research Council 2001, pp. 126–130. The "hourglass" metaphor is often ascribed to the Computer Science and Telecommunications Board and National Research Council 1994, pp. 51, 53. (See Clark 1997, pp. 134–135.) According to Carpenter and Brim (2002, section 7 at [HOURG]), however, it was first used by John Aschenbrenner in 1979, with reference to the ISO Open Systems Interconnection model.

31. On the effect of the use of the Internet layer as a technology-independent portability layer, see Clark 1997, pp. 134–135; Kavassalis and Lehr 2000, pp. 209–211; Computer Science and Telecommunications Board and National Research Council 2001, pp. 126–130. For a detailed discussion of the benefits of such an approach, see Computer Science and Telecommunications Board and National Research Council 1994, pp. 50–55.

32. Saltzer, Reed, and Clark 1981 (narrow version); Reed, Saltzer, and Clark 1998 (broad version).

33. This point is taken up in more detail in the section on misconceptions below.

34. See the subsection of this chapter titled "The End-to-End Arguments and the Division of Functionality. . . : The Broad Version" below.

35. See Sterbenz and Touch 2001, pp. 351–352.

36. This aspect of the narrow version (i.e., that a function must sometimes be implemented at a higher layer at the end host, potentially in the application itself to guarantee a correct execution, if threats to the function may occur after the data leaves the communications subsystem) was already well established when the Internet's architecture was developed. In their paper describing the narrow version, Saltzer, Reed, and Clark (1984) describe a number of earlier systems that were designed during the 1960s and the 1970s in which the designers used this argument to justify the ultimate placement of the function under consideration in the application.

37. Comer 2000, p. 210.

38. Implementing functions such as reliable data transfer or duplicate suppression in TCP also complies with the broad version. These functions are application-specific functions, which, according to the broad version, should be implemented in a higher layer at an end host.

39. The approach is summarized in a critical statement by John Postel (1977a, p. 1): "Specifically we are trying to use TCP to do two things: serve as a host level end to end [sic] protocol, and to serve as an Internet packaging and routing protocol." For technical descriptions of the initial monolithic protocol, see Cerf and Kahn 1974 (the first published description), Cerf 1977, and Cerf and Postel 1978.

40. Originally, the designers assumed that the Internetwork Transmission Control Protocol could be designed to support any needed type of service, not just reliable

data transfer. The initial TCP attempted to provide two types of reliable data transfer with different combinations of throughput and delay. The designers came to the conclusion that accommodating all types of services in a single protocol would be too complex. See D. D. Clark 1988, pp. 107–108.

41. Even if the implementation of the function constituted only a partial implementation of the function (e.g., in cases where the Internet layer does not operate end-to-end between the original source and ultimate destination of data, or if events falling into the responsibility of the function may occur after data leaves the Internet layer), the narrow version would still have allowed the implementation of the function at the Internet layer as a performance enhancement.

42. See discussion in the next subsection.

43. See discussion in the next subsection.

44. See references cited in note 39 above.

45. See discussion in note 40 above.

46. See generally Reed 2000, box 3.3 below, and references cited in notes 51–53 below.

47. See Reed, Saltzer, and Clark 1998, p. 70. Also see the discussion of the broad version in chapter 2 above.

48. See Sproull and Cohen 1978, p. 1382; Boggs et al. 1980, pp. 615–616. For an overview of the needs of different applications, see Kurose and Ross 2008, pp. 88–94; Peterson and Davie 2007, pp. 499–505.

49. See Saltzer, Reed, and Clark 1984, p. 282, note 1; Kurose and Ross 2008, p. 589.

50. See D. D. Clark 1988, pp. 108–109.

51. See Sproull and Cohen 1978, pp. 1377, 1379, 1382; Boggs et al. 1980, p. 615; Saltzer, Reed, and Clark 1984, pp. 284–285. Similarly, computer-to-computer communications that exchange single packets in a simple request-response pattern do not need a separate acknowledgment from a lower-layer protocol that the request was received correctly. If the receiver sends the reply, this is acknowledgment enough. If the receiver does not reply, the sender can simply send another request. See Clark, Pogran, and Reed 1978, p. 1511; Boggs et al. 1980, p. 615.

52. See Sterbenz and Touch 2001, pp. 131–132, where connectionless and connection-oriented packet switching are compared. Also see Peterson and Davie 2007, pp. 410–411, where the signaling overhead associated with setting up and closing connections in TCP is discussed.

53. See Clark, Pogran, and Reed 1978, pp. 1511–1512; Reed 2000. See also box 3.3 below.

54. Boggs et al. 1980, p. 613; D. D. Clark 1988, pp. 108–109, 112; Reed 2000. See also box 3.3 above. Critics have argued that the service provided by the Internet's original architecture—unreliable, connectionless, best-effort datagram service—is not general enough, because the Internet Protocol does not offer Quality of Service. This argument is discussed in box 4.3 below.

55. For a description of the mechanisms used by the Transmission Control Protocol to provide reliable data transfer based on the unreliable data transfer provided by the Internet Protocol, see Kurose and Ross 2008, pp. 252–260.

56. Following the meeting where the decision to split was made, the proposals for the headers for the two protocols were made in Cerf 1978a and in Cerf 1978b. The first full specifications of TCP and IP after the split were the specification of the Internet Datagram Protocol Version 4 (Postel 1979a) and of the Transmission Control Protocol—TCP (Version 4) (Postel 1979b). See also Cerf 1980a, abstract and p. 4. The User Datagram Protocol (UDP) was also discussed at the meeting on January 30–31, 1978; the first specification of UDP was prepared by David Reed and Jon Postel (Reed and Postel 1978). See Postel 1978a, pp. 12–13; Reed 2006a,b.

57. See Cohen 1979, pp. 178–179; Boggs et al. 1980, pp. 613–614; D. D. Clark 1988, pp. 108–109; Reed 2000. See also box 3.3 below.

58. See Cerf and Kirstein 1978, pp. 1397–1398; Cerf 1980b, p. 11; Boggs et al. 1980, pp. 615–616; D. D. Clark 1988, pp. 108–109.

59. This implies a need for some suitable form of addressing. See D. D. Clark 1988, p. 109.

60. D. D. Clark 1988, pp. 109–110; Peterson and Davie 2007, p. 237; Computer Science and Telecommunications Board and National Research Council 2001, p. 37, note 14; Computer Science and Telecommunications Board and National Research Council 1994, pp. 54–55; Kurose and Ross 2008, pp. 323–324.

61. Cerf 1980b, p. 11; D. D. Clark 1988, pp. 107–108; Carpenter 1996, section 2.3.

62. The term "fate-sharing" was coined by David Clark (1988, p. 108).

63. For example, under Jon Postel's (1977a, pp. 5, 7) proposal for splitting the Internetwork Transmission Control Program into two protocols, end-to-end error control would have been removed from the Internet layer and provided by individual higher-layer protocols at the end hosts, but the Internet Protocol would still have performed error control hop-by-hop.

64. "The internet protocol does not provide a reliable communication facility. There are no acknowledgments either end-to-end or hop-by-hop. There is no error control for data, only a header checksum. There are no retransmissions. There is no flow control." (Postel 1979a, pp. 2–3) For the justification, see Postel 1981a, section 3.2: "There are some applications where a few data bit errors are acceptable while retrans-

mission delays are not. If the Internet Protocol enforced data correctness such applications could not be supported."

65. See the subsection of this chapter titled "The End-to-End Arguments and the Division of Functionality. . . . : The Narrow Version" above.

66. Solum and Chung 2004, pp. 844–845.

67. See also Felten 2003.

68. See the discussion of the layering principle in chapter 2 above.

69. See Saltzer, Reed, and Clark 1984, p. 287.

70. Reed, Saltzer, and Clark 1998, p. 69.

71. For a description of the X.25 protocol suite and its relationship to the ISO reference model of Open System Interconnection, see Comer 2000, pp. 182–183. For a comparison of the X.25 protocol suite and the TCP/IP protocol suite, see Comer 2000, pp. 185–186; Peterson and Davie 2007, p. 387.

72. See subsection "The End-to-End Arguments and the Division of Functionality . . . : The Broad Version" above.

73. This view is very common in the Internet community. Kempf and Austein (2004, section 2.2) mention it explicitly as one "formulation of the end-to-end principle": "The end-to-end principle in this formulation is specifically about what kind of state is maintained where." For another example of this view, see Gaynor 2003, p. 36.

74. Carpenter 1996, section 2.3.

75. See Chiappa 2002; Reed 2001.

76. David 2001, pp. 171–174; Frischmann 2005, pp. 1010–1011; Weiser 2008, pp. 277–278.

77. For a similar argument, see Reed 2001.

78. See Peterson and Davie 2007, pp. 499–525.

79. For a similar argument that also differentiates between the request for quality of service and the actual provision of the service, see Solum and Chung 2003, pp. 109–111.

80. See Kurose and Ross 2008, p. 199.

81. Blumenthal and Clark 2001, p. 80 (citing personal communication with Jerome Saltzer).

82. For a description of the corresponding technology, see Anderson 2007. For a specific example of such technology, see Cisco Systems 2005.

83. See the discussion of application-blindness in chapter 2 above. Also see Solum and Chung 2003, p. 114.

84. See Lessig 2001, pp. 37–38; Solum and Chung 2004, p. 829; Gaynor 2003, pp. 35–39.

85. Reed 2001.

86. Sandvig 2002, pp. 20–21. See also Gaynor et al. 2000, pp. 3, 4; Gaynor 2003, p. 45. Gaynor argues that applications with a decentralized management structure comply with the end-to-end arguments, while applications with a centralized management structure do not. According to Gaynor (2003, p. 26), "centralized management occurs when users cross organizational boundaries by accessing a server managed by someone unrelated to the users, or a centralized server manages the users [*sic*] data."

87. In the text, the term "edge of the network" is meant to describe the collection of end hosts, not the access networks.

88. According to Gaynor, applications where a part of the application is controlled centrally will be less innovated upon. See Gaynor 2001, pp. 32–36; Gaynor 2003, pp. 47–72, 245–249; Gaynor et al. 2000. I am not sure this is necessarily correct. An application with a server that is controlled and operated by the application provider may be able to evolve more quickly (at least in the server part) than an application whose parts are distributed among a number of different parties, since changes are easier to deploy. See chapter 4 below.

89. See chapter 2 above. Also see Reed 2002.

90. Saltzer, Reed, and Clark 1981; Reed, Saltzer, and Clark 1998.

91. Work on the Internet's architecture started in the early 1970s; the specifications of what I call the Internet's "original architecture" were published in 1981 (Postel 1981a,b). The argument described in the text has been made by Solum and Chung (2004, pp. 844–845).

92. See, e.g., the introductory paragraph of the 1984 paper (Saltzer, Reed, and Clark 1984, p. 277): "This paper discusses one class of function placement argument that has been used for many years with neither explicit recognition nor much conviction. However, the emergence of the data communication network as a computer system component has sharpened this line of function placement argument by making more apparent the situations in which and the reasons why it applies. This paper articulates the argument explicitly, so as to examine its nature and to see how general it really is."

93. Saltzer, Reed, and Clark 1984, pp. 285–287; Reed, Saltzer, and Clark 1998, p. 70.

94. See Reed 2000; Blumenthal and Clark 2001, pp. 71–72.

95. Saltzer, Reed, and Clark 1984, pp. 278–286.

96. Reed, Saltzer, and Clark 1998, p. 70.

Chapter 4

1. In a software-intensive system, the total amount of change corresponds to the total number of lines of code that need to be changed across all components. Thus, even if the overall number of lines of code that must be changed is the same, the costs of change are larger if these lines of codes are distributed over a number of components than if they are concentrated in one component.

2. Once a software system reaches a certain size, changing software components may become more expensive than changing hardware components, since testing becomes more and more expensive as a software system's size and complexity increase.

3. For example, some innovators may intend to sell their innovation; others may innovate to use it for themselves. Some actors may be motivated by pecuniary rewards; others may be motivated by intrinsic hedonic rewards or social-psychological rewards. For a discussion of how actors may differ in their preferences for these types of rewards and an analysis of the effect of these differences, see Benkler 2002, pp. 426–434.

4. For a similar assumption, see p. 68 of Lipsey, Carlaw, and Bekar 2005.

5. The costs of realizing an innovation differ from the costs of adopting an innovation. The costs of adopting an innovation are the costs that a user (and potentially other economic actors) must incur in order to be able to use the innovation.

6. See Sanchez 1999, p. 95; Ulrich 1995, pp. 426–428.

7. Adding a new interface to a component without changing existing interfaces or adding a new component to an existing system that uses the services of existing components in order to provide its own services constitutes an autonomous change, although it adds visible information to the architecture. Because a new interface is not yet used by other components, other components cannot have come to depend on it. Therefore, the addition of a new interface does not affect existing components in the rest of the system.

8. In practice, a system architect may still be involved for other reasons. If system architects want to encourage third-party innovators to produce new or improved components that are complementary to the platform component offered by the system architect, they often provide tools and advice that make it easier to innovate. For example, Intel, Microsoft, and Apple all provide information on new interface specifications of their products (and, sometimes, prototype implementations of the platform component) to third-party developers, hold forums and conferences for

third-party developers, and provide development tools that make it easier to build complementary components. See Gawer and Cusumano 2002, pp. 55–67 (describing Intel's efforts) and 150–151 (describing Microsoft's efforts), and Evans, Hagiu, and Schmalensee 2006, pp. 98–101 (describing Microsoft's and Apple's efforts).

9. Adding a new interface to an existing component does not change the architecture's existing visible information. Since it does not trigger adaptation costs, it constitutes an autonomous innovation. See note 7 above.

10. This does not mean that the new screen technology will never find its way into the iMac. Though the improvement in a single technology may not justify a complete redesign, at some stage the sum of the benefits associated with improvements in different technologies may exceed the costs of a complete redesign.

11. On options theory, see Hull 2002; Luenberger 1997; Merton 1992. For a short overview of the main concepts, see Sullivan et al. 1999, pp. 224–225.

12. See Dixit and Pindyck 1994; Trigeorgis 1996; Amram and Kulatilaka 1999.

13. See Sullivan et al. 1999, pp. 224–225.

14. See Amram and Kulatilaka 1999, chapter 2; Sullivan et al. 1999, p. 224.

15. See Amram and Kulatilaka 1999, pp. 14–20, 79–80; Sullivan et al. 1999, p. 225.

16. The seminal articles in this area are Black and Scholes 1973 and Merton 1973b.

17. Real options were first identified by Myers (1977). For an introduction to the theory of real options, see Dixit and Pindyck 1994; Trigeorgis 1996; Amram and Kulatilaka 1999. For a short overview of the history of the field, see Sanchez 1991, pp. 17–19; Sullivan et al. 1999, pp. 223, 226.

18. These conditions have been derived from the discussions in chapter 2 of Amram and Kulatilaka 1999 and in chapter 1 of Sanchez 1991.

19. This is based on the assumption that a firm that seeks to maximize its economic value will seek to maximize its net present value, and therefore choose the set of real options that maximizes the net present value of the firm. See Sanchez 1991, pp. 25–26, 71–72.

20. See Amram and Kulatilaka 1999, chapters 4 and 5.

21. See ibid., pp. 28, 81–82.

22. The following analysis is based on Baldwin and Clark 2000 and Sanchez 1991.

23. Baldwin and Clark 2000, pp. 234–235, 252–255.

24. Enkel, Perez-Freije, and Gassmann 2005, p. 426; Souder, Sherman, and Davies-Cooper 1998, pp. 521–522.

25. See Baldwin and Clark 2000, pp. 255–257.

26. This follows from the assumption that innovators will not pursue projects whose expected benefits are lower than their expected costs.

27. See Sanchez 1991, pp. 25–26; Baldwin and Clark 2000, pp. 250–251.

28. Baldwin and Clark 2000, pp. 259–260.

29. Ibid., pp. 255–257.

30. See Baldwin and Clark 2000, pp. 236–237; Garud and Kumaraswamy 1995, pp. 96–98; Ulrich 1995, pp. 426–432.

31. Depending on the system, it may also be possible to mix and match different components so that a variety of systems can be built from a set of components that adhere to the same architecture. In addition, a modular architecture can evolve at the architectural level through gradual changes to its visible information. Although these changes are more costly than isolated changes at the module level, they probably will still be less costly than the redesign of an integrated architecture, as all components unaffected by the changes can be reused. See Garud and Kumaraswamy 1995; Sanchez 1995; Ulrich 1995; Baldwin and Clark 2000.

32. Thus, an innovator must have an existing version of the module or must be able to fall back on an existing textbook solution to the problem before she can realize the option value associated with a modular architecture. This is because without access to such an existing solution the innovator cannot cut her losses by continuing to use the existing solution if the experiment fails. See Baldwin and Clark 2000, p. 252, note 5.

33. Baldwin and Clark 2000, pp. 257–260; Sullivan et al. 2001, p. 102.

34. Merton 1973a.

35. Baldwin and Clark 2000, pp. 259–260. Baldwin and Clark have developed a model that quantifies the difference between the option value of a modular architecture and the option value of an equivalent integrated architecture for modular architectures consisting of modules of equal size and of asymmetric size; see Baldwin and Clark 2000 (p. 259 for the symmetric case and p. 261 for the asymmetric case). Their model does not include the costs of creating the modular architecture. My analysis in the text considers only the option value of modular and integrated architectures. In comparing the value of an integrated and a modular architecture, an individual company will also consider what portion of the option value it expects to be able to capture for itself. This portion may be higher under an integrated architecture, since in an integrated architecture the system architect controls subsequent innovation and may therefore be better able to appropriate the gains from subsequent innovation than in a modular architecture, in which control over module-level innovation may move to the designers of individual modules. This is discussed further in chapter 5 below.

36. For example, the success or failure of a particular technical approach to improving screen technologies probably is not related to the success or failure of approaches that would increase the storage capacity of hard disks.

37. Baldwin and Clark 2000, pp. 285–286.

38. See ibid., chapters 10, 12, and 13; Sanchez 1991, part III.

39. Baldwin and Clark 2000, chapter 12.

40. See ibid., p. 312.

41. Ibid., p. 313.

42. It also depends on the diversity of the approaches. See note 55 below.

43. This is because the incremental benefit from an additional approach decreases with the number of approaches. See the discussion later in this subsection.

44. How many approaches will be pursued also depends on the market structures of the design and product markets, and on innovators' and investors' expectations with respect to competitors' actions (such as the level of entry), the nature of the subsequent competition, or the total rewards that may be expected. See the discussion later in this subsection.

45. The approach described in the text can also be used to assess the effect of differences in modules within a certain modular architecture on the distribution of innovation among the modules of that architecture. See Baldwin and Clark 2000, chapter 11.

46. The following analysis is based on Baldwin and Clark 2000, Sanchez 1991, and Krengel 1991.

47. In the model described in the text, the costs of comparing the result of the experiment with the existing version of the module are part of that module's core costs of innovation. See Baldwin and Clark 2000, p. 286. The model assumes that the relative quality of the innovation can be determined using module-level tests. See next note.

48. This statement embodies certain assumptions about the resolution of uncertainty. This modeling assumes that the uncertainty can be resolved by testing the module using module-level tests. In other words, the modeling assumes, first, that module-level tests are available that make it possible to evaluate the quality of a module based on the module without having to integrate the module into the larger system. This requirement may not be met for all systems. Often module-level tests are not available until designers have gained some experience with a system. On the importance of module-level tests, see Baldwin and Clark 2000, pp. 271–280. Second, the modeling assumes that the uncertainty can be resolved using module-level tests. This is a reasonable assumption for technical uncertainty

if the module-level tests can determine which outcome is the best. If the uncertainty results from uncertainty about consumers' preferences, it may not be possible to resolve the uncertainty using module-level tests in all cases. Though it may be possible to resolve market uncertainty through the use of focus groups, sometimes market uncertainty can be resolved only by putting the product on the market.

49. A random variable is a function that associates a unique numerical value with every outcome of an experiment. Random variables can be described by probability distributions that provide information about the probability with which different values of the random variable may occur (for discrete random variables) or about the probability that the value may fall within a certain interval (for continuous random variables).

50. Formally, the expected value is the sum of all potential values of the random variable, weighted by their associated probabilities.

51. This formulation reflects the loss-limiting characteristic of the option. Although the value of the best of k experiments can be better or worse than the existing module version, the calculation of the option value considers only the potential outcomes of the best of k experiments that are better than the existing module (technically, the option value equals the expected value of the positive value portion of the probability distribution of the random variable describing the best of the k experiments). For outcomes where the best of k experiments is worse than the existing module, the innovator continues to use the existing module, and its payoff is zero. See box 4.2.

52. Baldwin and Clark 2000, pp. 252–255.

53. In a normal distribution, about 68% of the outcomes fall within one standard deviation σ from the mean; in other words, 68% of the values lie between $\mu - \sigma$ and $\mu + \sigma$. About 5% are more than two standard deviations away from the mean; that is, 5% of the values are smaller than $\mu - (2 \times \sigma)$ or larger than $\mu + (2 \times \sigma)$.

54. The variance of a random variable is a non-negative number that gives an idea of how widely spread the values of the random variable are likely to be. The larger the variance, the further individual values of the random variable tend to be from the mean, on average. The smaller the variance, the closer individual values tend to be to the mean, on average. In other words, if the variance is large, it is more likely (relative to a probability distribution with the same mean and smaller variance) that the result of an experiment will be far away from the mean. In practice, measuring uncertainty may be quite a challenge. On how one type of uncertainty (market uncertainty) may be measured, see Gaynor 2003, pp. 86–91.

55. In reality, approaches may not be completely independent. Whereas approaches that are essentially similar, with only slight variation, might provide a more limited

set of results, a more varied set of approaches might provide a greater variety of results and therefore an increased likelihood of discovering a module that is better than the existing one. Owing to the reduction in the expected value of additional experiments, correlation across experiments would reduce the number of experiments that innovators would pursue. In the model, such correlation could be modeled by reducing σ_i, the parameter that models uncertainty. See Baldwin and Clark 2000, p. 357. In addition, over several generations of experiments on a module, innovators may gain experience with the module, which may also reduce uncertainty. For a formal model of this effect of learning, see Gaynor 2001, pp. 141–155.

56. For a formal definition of $Q(k)$, see box 4.2. See Baldwin and Clark 2000, p. 264, note 17.

57. $Q_i(k)$ is monotonically increasing and concave in k. See Baldwin and Clark 2002, p. 7, note 6.

58. This terminology is taken from pp. 75 and 225 of Baldwin and Clark 2000.

59. For a detailed analysis of the effect of different market structures and of differing expectations, see Baldwin and Clark 2000, chapter 14. For an analysis of decision rules under different market structures, see Baldwin and Clark 2000, pp. 410–411.

60. In reality, firms probably would not know exactly how many competitors had already started an experiment.

61. Baldwin and Clark (2000, pp. 287–288, 293–299) use a variant of the net option value formula described in the text to calculate differences in net option value for different modules in two hypothetical architectures. The results of the simulation support the conclusions reached in the text.

62. The visibility of a module increases with the number of other modules that directly or indirectly depend on this module.

63. See also Gaynor 2003, pp. 266–267.

64. At this point, an actor that is a monopolist in the design and product market would stop mounting additional approaches. Actors in markets with free entry into the design market and winner-take-all competition in the product market would start additional approaches as long as the net option value is greater than zero.

65. The loss-limiting characteristic of options applies only if the innovator already has an existing version of the component that it can continue to use if the result of the innovation is worse. Otherwise, the option value of innovating on the module will be realized only in the second generation of the module. See Baldwin and Clark 2000, p. 252, note 5; Baldwin and Clark 2002, p. 7.

66. For example, in simulation based on a variant of the model described in the text, Baldwin and Clark (2000, pp. 287–288, 293–299) found that modules that were visible to 50% of the system did not justify any innovation on their visible information.

67. See Baldwin and Clark 2000, pp. 289–293.

68. Throughout this book, the costs of innovation are the costs of developing and producing the first complete version of the system that contains the new or improved good or service. In networking, innovating may consist of a number of stages, so the costs of innovation may be borne by different actors. Innovating on networking protocols or technologies consists of, first, specifying the protocol's visible information such as its service and peer interfaces; conceptually, this step corresponds to the design of the architecture of the protocol. For protocols that undergo standardization, this step is usually performed within the standardization organization. Subsequent stages are detailed design, which is followed by implementation (if the protocol is implemented in software) or production (if the protocol is implemented in hardware) of the first version of the protocol. These steps are usually performed by actors other than the standardization organization.

69. Conceptually, the costs of deployment are not costs of innovation, but costs of adoption. They can be incurred only after the first version of the innovation has been produced. The costs of deployment are different from the costs of using the innovation. The costs of deployment are the one-time costs that must be incurred before the innovation can be used. See Thaler and Aboba 2008, p. 6 (noting the difference between deployment and use of a protocol).

70. The economic system in which the network is used consists of the actors who use and operate the network, the relationships among them and the governance structures through which they interact.

71. I use the term "commercial Internet" to denote the economic system for the operation and use of the Internet in the US and elsewhere as it has existed since the mid 1990s. In this system, the Internet backbones (i.e., the bigger networks used to interconnect smaller networks attached to the Internet) and the access networks that users use to connect to the Internet are owned, operated, and controlled primarily by private actors who operate networks for a profit. Throughout its early history, much of the US portion of the Internet was owned, operated, and controlled by government agencies, including the Advanced Research Projects Agency and, later, the National Science Foundation. In the late 1980s, the NSF backbone became the main backbone of the Internet. The NSF's Acceptable Use Policy explicitly prohibited the use of the backbone for commercial uses. From 1990 to 1995, the Internet gradually transitioned to the commercial mode of operation that we know today. For a description of this process, see Abbate 1999, pp. 195–200; Kesan and Shah 2001, pp. 99–167.

72. See Isenberg 1998, p. 29; Isenberg 1997; Moors 2002, pp. 1217–1218.

73. See the subsection of chapter 3 titled "The End-to-End Arguments and the Division of Functionality. . . : The Broad Version" above.

74. Although Skype uses UDP as a default transport-layer protocol, it falls back on TCP when a user's network-address translator or firewall effectively blocks UDP

(Handley 2006, pp. 124–125; Kurose and Ross 2008, p. 609). As I will discuss in more detail in my concluding chapter, network-address translators and firewalls deviate from the broad version of the end-to-end arguments. When these devices force Skype to fall back on a transport-layer protocol with reliability controls, they effectively re-create the situation that the split between TCP and IP—or, more generally, the broad version of the end-to-end arguments—was designed to prevent.

75. Innovations that require only changes to end hosts can be tested on the operational Internet (or at least on a subset). If changes to computers in the core of the network are needed, an innovator cannot test his innovation on the operational network and must test its innovation on a simulated network or on a private testbed instead. See Computer Science and Telecommunications Board and National Research Council 1994, pp. 103–104. See also Peterson and Davie 2007, pp. 496–497.

76. The problems for innovations in the core of the network that require a coordinated deployment are discussed in more detail in the present chapter's subsection on "Internet Architecture and Innovation at the Internet and Transport Layer."

77. See Blumenthal and Clark 2001, p. 72.

78. Today applications often have a more distributed structure, with more than two protocol implementations cooperating to provide the functionality of the protocol.

79. In the Internet, the application programming interfaces through which applications access the Internet are publicly available for free or at low cost. This is an example of a non-architectural factor that interacts with the broad version of the end-to-end arguments to create a beneficial environment for application innovation in the Internet. In order to test the application, the innovator will have to find someone who is willing and able to install the application on a second end host. But having access to one end host with access to the Internet will probably enable the innovator to find such a person.

80. See von Hippel 2002, pp. 21–22.

81. Computer Science and Telecommunications Board and National Research Council 1996, pp. 77–78.

82. These ongoing costs associated with making an application available to others do not belong to the costs of innovation. Like the costs of production and distribution, they are discussed here because they determine the investment required for exploiting the innovation. The costs described in the text are the minimum costs associated with the exploitation of an innovation that define the minimum requirements for an innovator who writes an application that other people may use. Beyond that, an innovator may want to market the application or offer customer support.

83. Roth 2004. For a high-level description of Skype's architecture, see Kurose and Ross 2008, pp. 157–159.

84. Kraus 2005a; Buckman 2005; Helft 2006. In addition, search-engine marketing enables small companies to reach potential audiences at low cost.

85. Amazon offers a number of storage and computing services that are based on Amazon's own infrastructure to other firms. Amazon passes on some of the benefits of its own economies of scale to these companies (Reiss 2008).

86. See Isenberg 1998, p. 29.

87. The effect of differences in the costs and mode of application deployment is discussed in this chapter's subsection on "Internet Architecture and Innovation at the Internet and Transport Layer" and in chapter 7's section on "Relative Costs of Application Deployment."

88. Innovations that do not trigger changes to the network would still be possible.

89. This is because applications are placed in the highest layer of the protocol stack, and lower-layer protocols are not allowed to depend on higher layers.

90. In contrast, the high costs of producing and distributing physical products make it much more difficult to bring the product to market in order to test consumers' reaction to it.

91. See Computer Science and Telecommunications Board and National Research Council 1994, pp. 102–103.

92. The desire not to change the Internet Protocol's service interface to higher layers (see next section) effectively constrains the type of innovations that will occur at the layers below the Internet layer to those that make sense given the Internet Protocol's existing service interface. Most likely, innovators at the lower layers will not put a lot of effort into changes that could not be exposed to higher layers given the Internet Protocol's existing service interface.

93. On the use of the Internet layer as a technology-independent portability layer, see Clark 1997, pp. 133–135; Kavassalis and Lehr 2000, pp. 209–211; Computer Science and Telecommunications Board and National Research Council 2001, pp. 126–130. Another detailed discussion of the benefits of such an approach can be found on pp. 47–55 of Computer Science and Telecommunications Board and National Research Council 1994.

94. While wireless networks do not require any changes to higher-layer protocols at the application layer and the transport layer (i.e., higher-layer protocols work over wireless links attached to the Internet), the technical characteristics of wireless links challenge some of the assumptions on which higher-layer protocols are based. For a short description of the problem and possible solutions, see Kurose and Ross 2008, pp. 575–578.

95. See Comer 2000, chapter 3; Peterson and Davie 2007, pp. 234–235.

96. The economic system in which the network is used consists of the actors who use and operate the network, the relationships among them and the governance structures through which they interact.

97. It is interesting to note the difference between this design and the design of the Internet Protocol. As IP's service interface requires the higher-layer protocol to provide the IP address of the receiving end host, a change in the format of the IP address automatically affects the service interface. As a result, a change in the IP address requires changes to all higher-layer protocols that make use of the IP address, which entail huge costs of system adaptation.

98. Changing the implementation of an architectural component in a modular architecture without changing its visible information does not require any changes in the rest of the system. Consequently, changing the implementation of a protocol without changing its interfaces affects neither higher-layer protocols that use its services nor implementations of the same protocol at different computers with which it interoperates. Thus, it is possible to change the implementation of a protocol at one computer only; innovations of this type can be deployed incrementally. See Peterson and Davie 2007, p. 23.

99. See the examples discussed by Peterson and Davie (2007, p. 441) and Handley (2006, p. 120). An example is a series of refinements of the mechanism that TCP uses to decide whether to retransmit a segment. These refinements, however, did not change the format of the TCP header and could therefore be incorporated into implementations individually. See Peterson and Davie 2007, p. 435.

100. Fielding and Taylor (2002, pp. 118, 119) discuss this requirement in the context of the design of the World Wide Web.

101. For a discussion of mechanisms used by the designers of HTTP to support the extensibility of the protocol, see Fielding and Taylor 2002, pp. 138–140. For a critical voice on the mechanisms for extensibility provided by HTTP, see Mogul 2004. Clark et al. (2003, p. 248, note 1) note the implementation and validation overhead and interoperability problems that may be associated with the extended use of options.

102. See Peterson and Davie 2007, p. 441.

103. Because it is not realistic to assume that all network providers connected to the global Internet would switch to a new Internet-layer protocol at the same time, networking researchers have developed various mechanisms that would support a more incremental transition to new Internet-layer protocols. See, e.g., the overview of mechanisms that support the transition to IPv6 in Kurose and Ross 2008 (pp. 363–366) or the discussion of overlays as transitioning mechanisms in Peterson and Davie 2007 (pp. 693–696).

104. On multicast, see Diot et al. 2000; Sharma, Perry, and Malpani 2003. On Quality of Service, see Armitage 2003; Bell 2003; Burgstahler et al. 2003.

105. Anderson et al. 2005a, p. 34. For example, the invention of network-address translators that allow a number of end hosts to connect to the Internet using the same globally unique IP address has reduced network providers' and users' incentives to deploy IPv6. Network-address translators deviate from the broad version of the end-to-end arguments by implementing a considerable amount of application-specific functionality in the network. As will be discussed in my concluding chapter, this impedes the development of new applications considerably. Still, individual economic actors find it easier to install a network-address translator to deal with the shortage of IPv4 addresses (and impose a negative externality on application-level innovation) than to migrate their networks to IPv6, although all actors would be collectively better off as a result of the transition.

106. Anderson et al. 2005a, p. 34; Ratnasamy, Shenker, and McCanne 2005, p. 313; Handley 2006, pp. 121–122.

107. See generally Floyd 2002, p. 17.

108. See Diot et al. 2000; Sharma, Perry, and Malpani 2003; Bell 2003; Burgstahler et al. 2003.

109. Burness et al. 2005, pp. 2975–2977; Thaler and Aboba 2008, pp. 7–8.

110. Floyd 1998, pp. 2, 4; Burness et al. 2005, pp. 2974–2976; Thaler and Aboba 2008, p. 8.

111. Anderson et al. 2005a; Ratnasamy, Shenker, and McCanne 2005.

112. Anderson et al. 2005a,b; Turner and Taylor 2005; Roscoe 2006; Feamster, Gao, and Jennifer 2007. Anderson et al. (2005a) describe both approaches but do not take a position on which one is better. An architecture such as the one described in the text that enables several network architectures to coexist at the same time will form the core of a large-scale experimental networking testbed facility called Global Environment for Network Innovations (GENI). The GENI testbed will enable networking researchers to experiment with and test new network architectures in a large-scale testbed with realistic traffic. GENI is funded by the National Science Foundation in the US. See Anderson et al. 2005a,b; Clark, Shenker, and Falk 2007.

113. See North 2005, pp. 3–10, 73–91.

Chapter 5

1. The chapter does not explore how the existing organizational structures in which an architecture and its components are designed may affect the structure or evolution of the architecture. Three interesting studies of this question are Henderson and Clark 1990, MacCormack, Rusnak, and Baldwin 2008, and Fixson and Park 2008.

2. In addition, there may be some additional teams who are responsible for the integration at the system level. For an empirical example (the development of an aircraft engine), see Sosa, Eppinger, and Rowles 2002, p. 11.

3. Thompson 1967.

4. On product design, see McCord and Eppinger 1993; Sosa, Eppinger, and Rowles 2000, p. 3; Henderson and Clark 1990, p. 15. On software design, see Bass, Clements, and Kazman 2003, pp. 29, 167–168; van Vliet 2000, p. 92; Kruchten 1995, p. 45.

5. For an empirical example (the development of an aircraft engine), see Sosa, Eppinger, and Rowles 2002, p. 11.

6. Thompson 1967, p. 57. For the same prescription in the context of product development, see von Hippel 1990.

7. Thompson 1967, p. 58

8. Ibid., pp. 54–56.

9. Ibid., pp. 59–61.

10. See von Hippel 1990, p. 409.

11. See van den Bulte and Moenaert 1998; Tushman 1977; Sosa et al. 2002; Sosa, Eppinger, and Rowles 2002. For pointers to additional empirical studies that report similar results, see Sosa et al. 2002; Sosa, Eppinger, and Rowles 2002.

12. See Eppinger 1991, p. 284; Steward 1981; Baldwin and Clark 2000, pp. 43–47; Sanchez 1995, p. 145.

13. See Besanko, Dranove, and Shanley 2000, p. 109.

14. See Argyres 1996; Poppo and Zenger 1998; Combs and Ketchen 1999; Williamson 1999; Tsang 2000. This approach is also used by management strategy textbooks. See, e.g., Besanko, Dranove, and Shanley 2000, chapters 3–5.

15. See Poppo and Zenger 1998, p. 854; Besanko, Dranove, and Shanley 2000, pp. 139, 170.

16. For an overview of potential benefits of using the market, see Besanko, Dranove, and Shanley 2000, pp. 115–127.

17. See Williamson 1999, pp. 1102–1103.

18. See Williamson 1985, chapter 6; Williamson 1991, pp. 275–276, 279.

19. "As pointed out in the resource-based view of the firm, heterogeneity in such resources leads to differentiated capabilities among firms, putting them at a competitive advantage in some activities and at a disadvantage in others. Such differential returns from activities encourage firms to specialize in those activities in which their

rate of return is highest." (Schilling and Steensma 2001, pp. 1153–1154, references omitted). See also Jacobides and Hitt 2005, p. 466.

20. See Besanko, Dranove, and Shanley 2000, pp. 115–122.

21. On maintaining capabilities, see Sobrero and Roberts 2002. On other strategic considerations, see Baldwin and Clark 2006a and chapter 1 of Boudreau 2006.

22. For empirical studies examining the organizational separation of detailed design and production, see Monteverde 1995 and Ulrich and Ellison 2005.

23. See Thompson 1967, pp. 56, 64.

24. For a similar observation, see Gulati and Singh 1998 and Jacobides 2002.

25. Gulati and Singh (1998) use a framework similar to the one described in the text to explain the choice of different levels of hierarchical control in alliances between firms. Though coordination costs have long been used to explain organizational structures within the firm, they have only recently been identified as a distinct cost category influencing firms' governance choices with respect to vertical boundaries. (See box 5.1.)

26. Chesbrough and Teece (1996, p. 67) write: "Tacit knowledge is knowledge that is implicitly grasped or used but has not been fully articulated, such as the know-how of a master craftsman or the ingrained perspectives of a specific company or work unit. Because such knowledge is deeply embedded in individuals or companies, it tends to diffuse slowly and only with effort and the transfer of people. Established companies can protect the tacit knowledge they hold, sharing only codified information. They can be quite strategic about what they disclose and when they disclose it." See also von Hippel 1994, pp. 430–431.

27. Sosa et al. (2002, p. 48) write: "Media richness theory . . . ranks communication media according to their capacity to process ambiguous information. [According to this theory], face-to-face is a richer medium than telephone, and telephone is a richer medium than e-mail."

28. See Sosa et al. 2002, p. 48.

29. See Chesbrough and Teece 1996, p. 67; von Hippel 1994, pp. 429–432.

30. For empirical studies confirming the beneficial effect of co-location, see van den Bulte and Moenaert 1998 and Morelli, Eppinger, and Gulati 1995.

31. The emergence of firm-specific language and routines and their positive effects on the generation of new knowledge and its efficient dissemination have been well developed theoretically by proponents of the knowledge-based theory of the firm (Demsetz 1988; Monteverde 1995; Kogut and Zander 1996). This advantage of internal organization can be reduced or eliminated by the formation of common communication codes across firms (as in Silicon Valley and other regional networks).

Mechanisms that establish "common ground" (knowledge that is shared, and known to be shared, among partners in an outsourcing relationship) may also make it easier for firms to coordinate interdependent tasks across firm boundaries (Srikanth and Puranam 2007, 2008).

32. See Jacobides 2002, pp. 1–12.

33. See ibid., pp. 30–33.

34. See Gulati and Singh 1998, pp. 785–786.

35. See Williamson 1991, pp. 274–276; Besanko, Dranove, and Shanley 2000, pp. 161–162.

36. See Jacobides 2002, pp. 21–22.

37. See Novak and Stern 2003, p. 9; Besanko, Dranove, and Shanley 2000, pp. 132–134.

38. Thompson 1967, pp. 54–56.

39. Thompson's analysis does not cover complete independence. Instead, Thompson (1967, p. 54) analyzes a similar type of interdependency called *pooled interdependency*.

40. Thompson 1967, p. 54.

41. Ibid., pp. 54–55.

42. This type of coordination has been characterized as coordination by "standardization of work outputs." See van Vliet 2000, p. 89 (referring to a classification by Mintzberg).

43. See Thompson 1967, p. 56; van Vliet 2000, p. 89.

44. See Monteverde 1995, pp. 1628–1629.

45. See Sanchez 1995, pp. 145–146.

46. For a similar observation in the context of product development, see Sanchez 1995, pp. 145–146.

47. See Sobrero and Roberts 2001; Sobrero and Roberts 2002; Takeishi 2001; Sako 2004; Srikanth and Puranam 2007, 2008. Brusoni (2005, p. 1901) notes the emergence of projects as "a temporary administrative framework within which some form of hierarchical coordination replaces the market."

48. On the trade-off between efficiency and learning in R&D cooperation, see Sobrero and Roberts 2001.

49. See Dyer 1996, 1997; Takeishi 2001.

50. See Monteverde 1995.

51. Jacobides 2001; Jacobides 2002; Jacobides 2005.

52. Gulati and Singh 1998.

53. See the section "Integrated Design" in chapter 2 above.

54. See Sanchez 1995, pp. 145–146; Christensen, Verlinden, and Westerman 2002, pp. 958–960. For some examples, see Dyer 1996, 1997; Takeishi 2001; Sako 2004; Srikanth and Puranam 2007, 2008.

55. See Sanchez 1999, p. 95.

56. Baldwin and Clark 2000, pp. 64–72.

57. See Baldwin and Clark 2000, pp. 70–72, 372–375. Baldwin and Clark's (2000, pp. 61–62) definition of "block-hierarchical" corresponds to my definition of sequential interdependence. See the subsection of this chapter titled "Linking Task Interdependency to Governance Choices."

58. Ulrich 1995, pp. 435; Sanchez 1995, pp. 146–147; Baldwin and Clark 2000, p. 352; Christensen, Verlinden, and Westerman 2002, pp. 958–959.

59. Baldwin and Clark 2006a; Boudreau 2006, chapter 1.

60. Baldwin and Clark 2000, pp. 373–375.

61. Baldwin and Clark 2000, pp. 76–77. But see Brusoni and Prencipe 2001 (describing a more central role of system integrators).

62. See Sosa, Eppinger, and Rowles 2004; Sosa, Gargiulo, and Rowles 2007; Staudenmayer, Tripsas, and Tucci 2005.

63. Baldwin and Clark 2000, pp. 76–77, 86.

64. See Chesbrough and Teece 1996, p. 67.

65. As a module's internal design is hidden from the system's architects as well as from the designers of other modules, neither visible design parameters at the architectural level nor hidden design parameters in other modules depend on that information. As a result, changes to a module's hidden information cannot require changes in the rest of the system as long as the module's visible information is unaffected. To be able to interoperate with the rest of the system, the new design must comply with the relevant interface specifications. In this case, the innovation can occur completely independent of the rest of the system. As a result, internal organization and arm's-length relationships are equally feasible organizational choices.

66. See Baldwin and Clark 2000, pp. 267–269.

67. Ibid., pp. 267–269.

68. See Garud and Kumaraswamy 1995, pp. 100–101.

69. Williamson 1985, pp. 20–22. The origins of transaction-cost theory can be traced back to Ronald Coase (1937, 1960). The transaction-cost approach was operationalized by Oliver Williamson (1975, 1985). For a short overview of the history and content of Williamson's contributions to transaction-cost theory, see Masten 1999. For overviews of empirical studies testing the predictions of transaction-cost theory, see Rindfleisch and Heide 1997 and Shelanski and Klein 1999.

70. According to the traditional transaction-cost analysis, this factor shifts firms' preferences toward market-based organization if uncertainty, asset specificity, and measurement problems are below a certain threshold. See Williamson 1985, pp. 90–95.

71. For a comparison of the behavioral assumptions of transaction-cost economics with those of neoclassical economics, see Williamson 1985, pp. 44–52.

72. Simon (1961, pp. xxiv), cited by Williamson (1985, p. 45).

73. Williamson 1985, pp. 45–46.

74. Ibid., pp. 47–49.

75. With respect to the following, see Milgrom and Roberts 1992, pp. 126–131; Besanko, Dranove, and Shanley 2000, pp. 144–147.

76. For an econometric study of the relative importance of transaction costs and heterogeneous capabilities, see Jacobides and Hitt 2005.

77. On the effect of uncertainty, see Williamson 1985, pp. 56–63.

78. On the effect of asset specificity, see, e.g., Williamson 1985, pp. 52–63; Besanko, Dranove, and Shanley 2000, pp. 148–160; Milgrom and Roberts 1992, pp. 134–139.

79. See Williamson 1985, p. 78; Williamson 1991, p. 280.

80. Williamson 1975, p. 29.

81. Ibid., pp. 25, 37–39.

82. Ibid., p. 29.

83. Ibid., pp. 29–30, 35.

84. See Jacobides 2002, pp. 21–22.

85. See Alchian and Demsetz 1972, Jensen and Meckling 1976, and Barzel 1982. On moral hazard, principal-agent theory, and performance incentives in general, see chapter 6 of Milgrom and Roberts 1992.

86. See Alchian and Demsetz 1972, p. 780.

87. Holmstrom and Milgrom 1994.

88. Williamson 1975, p. 29.

89. For an overview of alternative governance structures in general, see Milgrom and Roberts 1992, pp. 561–569; Besanko, Dranove, and Shanley 2000, pp. 182–194.

90. Dyer 1997, p. 537.

91. See ibid., pp. 547–549.

92. Dyer (ibid., pp. 547–549) calls these mechanisms, which reduce transaction costs over a long period of time, "self-enforcing safeguards."

93. For an alternative explanation focusing on the difficulties associated with defining, counting, and compensating for each transaction at different points in the architecture, see Baldwin 2008.

94. See Dyer 1996, p. 275; Besanko, Dranove, and Shanley 2000, p. 163.

95. Besanko, Dranove, and Shanley (2000, p. 151) write: "Human asset specificity refers to cases in which a worker, or group of workers, has acquired skills, know-how, and information that are more valuable inside a particular relationship than outside it."

96. See Novak and Stern 2003, pp. 5–6, 9.

97. See also Baldwin 2008.

98. As we saw above, completely new or relatively young architectures may suffer from undetected cross-component dependencies, which increase uncertainty.

99. On module-level tests, see Baldwin and Clark 2000, pp. 77, 134–135, 272, 273, 277.

100. Garud and Kumaraswamy 1995, p. 103.

101. For a similar analysis, see Gawer 2000, pp. 64–65.

102. For in-depth analyses of the conditions under which an innovator may prefer selling its innovation in the "market for ideas" to entering the product market, see Gans and Stern 2000; Gans, Hsu, and Stern 2002; Gans and Stern 2003.

103. See Schilling and Steensma 2001; Jacobides and Hitt 2005; Sobrero and Roberts 2002; Baldwin and Clark 2006a; Boudreau 2006.

104. See also Sako 2002, pp. 14–15.

105. See Langlois and Robertson 1992; Baldwin and Clark 2000, chapter 14; Christensen, Verlinden, and Westerman 2002, p. 964.

106. Baldwin and Clark 2000, p. 351.

107. The word 'complementor', coined by Brandenburger and Nalebuff (1998, p. 16), denotes an economic actor that provides complements.

108. See Garud and Kumaraswamy 1995, p. 102.

109. See Baldwin and Clark 2000, p. 77.

110. See Christensen, Verlinden, and Westerman 2002, pp. 963–965.

111. Samuelson and Scotchmer 2002.

112. For some examples, see Gawer and Cusumano 2002 and Woodard 2008.

113. Langlois and Robertson 1992, pp. 302–306.

114. Christensen, Verlinden, and Westerman 2002, pp. 966–969.

115. Baldwin and Clark 2000.

116. Jacobides 2001, 2002, 2005.

117. Christensen, Verlinden, and Westerman 2002, pp. 971–972.

118. Fine 1998; Christensen, Verlinden, and Westerman 2002; Fixson and Park 2008.

119. For an overview and a discussion of existing explanations, see Fixson and Park 2008.

120. Baldwin and Clark 2000, pp. 105–106, 406, 414–417. For a formal theory of the "Silicon Valley model" and of the relationship between modularity and venture-capital financing, see Aoki 1999 and chapter 14 of Aoki 2001. For more on venture capital, see chapter 8 below.

121. See Gawer and Cusumano 2002, pp. 44–45.

122. See Baldwin and Clark 2000, pp. 267–269.

123. See ibid., chapter 7.

124. For an in-depth analysis of this problem and a detailed study of the mechanisms Intel uses to encourage the adoption of new specifications by independent developers of complementary products, see Gawer 2000. See also Gawer and Cusumano 2002 and Gawer and Henderson 2007.

125. For an analysis of externalities in platform systems, see chapter 9 below.

126. Gawer and Henderson 2007. For a model illustrating these problems, see Farrell and Katz 2000.

127. See Shapiro and Varian 1999, pp. 237–259.

128. Gawer and Cusumano 2002, pp. 18–28. For an analysis of the strategies used by Intel, Microsoft, Cisco, and other platform leaders to overcome these problems, see Gawer and Cusumano 2002. For an analysis of the problems associated with standard setting and standard evolution when firms compete under conditions of compatibility, see Shapiro and Varian 1999, chapter 8.

129. See Garud and Kumaraswamy 1995, pp. 100–101. If a standards body or a consortium coordinates architectural changes, that organization's rules determine who can participate in any efforts to change the architecture. For an overview of the dimensions along which standard setting organizations may differ, see West 2007.

130. The factors discussed in the text are not the only factors to be considered as part of the decision. For a detailed analysis of the strategic choices that a system architect in a modular architecture faces, see Gawer and Cusumano 2002. See also Boudreau 2006.

131. See Novak and Stern 2003, pp. 8–9.

132. See Fixson and Park 2008.

133. See Baldwin and Clark 2001, p. 8.

134. For an overview of standards and the Internet, see Weiser 2001.

135. The IETF's standard-setting process is described in Bradner 1996.

136. See Comer 2000, pp. 216, 413.

137. See Computer Science and Telecommunications Board and National Research Council 2001, pp. 124–125.

138. See Baldwin and Clark 2001, p. 8.

139. See Kavassalis and Lehr 2000; Computer Science and Telecommunications Board and National Research Council 1996, pp. 83–85; Rao 1999.

140. Also see chapter 4 above.

141. On the strategy pursued by Microsoft, see Gawer and Cusumano 2002, pp. 131–162.

142. On the strategy pursued by Cisco, see ibid., pp. 162–187.

143. Thus, the architecture of the Internet also enables modularity in use. On modularity in use, see box 2.1 above and p. 78 of Baldwin and Clark 2000.

144. See the section "Costs of Change in the Original Architecture of the Internet" in chapter 4 above.

145. See the subsection "The Broad Version of the End-to-End Arguments and Innovation at the Application Layer" in chapter 4 above.

146. See Isenberg 1998, p. 29; von Hippel 2007; Benkler 2002; Gaynor 2003, p. 40. In the Internet, the application programming interfaces through which applications access the Internet are publicly available for free or at low cost. This is an example of a non-architectural factor that interacts with the broad version of the end-to-end arguments to create a beneficial environment for application innovation in the Internet.

147. Lakhani and Wolf 2005, pp. 12–16. See also Benkler 2002. For analyses of the processes and mechanisms open-source projects use to coordinate their work, see Feller and Fitzgerald 2000; Yamauchi et al. 2000; Mockus, Fielding, and Herbsleb 2002; Scacchi 2002; Ulhøi 2004. For a short overview of literature on governance, organization, and innovation processes in open-source projects, see von Krogh and von Hippel 2006, pp. 979–980.

148. This type of innovation, in which users innovate to meet their own needs, is discussed in more detail in chapter 8 below.

149. Livingston 2007, pp. 127–130; Rapp 2006; Yahoo 2005. Since the traffic was slowing Stanford's network, Yan and Phyllo moved their servers to Netscape in early 1995 (Livingston 2007, p. 134).

150. Partridge 2008a.

151. Cohen 2002, pp. 3–4, 20–23, 29–30.

152. Cassidy 2006. Several people have claimed that Zuckerberg stole their idea. A dispute with three other Harvard students who had asked Zuckerberg to help them program a similar site in November 2003 was settled in court in June 2008. See Cassidy 2006; Markoff 2007; O'Brien 2007; Levenson 2008.

153. See also Kraus 2005a; Heinemeier Hansson 2005; Helft 2006; Buckman 2005.

154. Angel investors are individuals who invest capital in start-ups. The amount of money invested by angel investors is usually considerably smaller than that invested by venture capitalists; they are usually considered to be more flexible and less constraining than venture capitalists (Shah 2006; van Osnabrugge and Robinson 2000).

155. Spector 2000, pp. 62, 68, 70, 84–93.

156. Livingston 2007, pp. 260–261.

157. Ibid., pp. 112–113.

158. Joel Spolsky follows the same approach with his company FogCreek Software (Spolsky 2003; Livingston 2007, pp. 112–113).

159. On eBay, see Cohen 2002, pp. 60–65. On Google, see chapter 8 below. On ICQ, see Brooker 1999; Weisman 2005. On Blogger, see Kahney 2001; Livingston 2007, pp. 117–120.

160. Christensen and Raynor 2003, p. 256; Gompers and Lerner 2001a, p. 136.

161. Spolsky 2003; Helft 2006. See also Lerner 2002; Scherer 2001.

162. Gompers and Lerner 2006, pp. 14–17 (on 2000); Miller, 2008a,b (on 2008).

163. Kraus 2005a.

164. On ICQ, see Brooker 1999; Weisman 2005. On Google, see Battelle 2005, pp. 85–87; Vise and Malseed 2005, pp. 45–49.

165. Jason Fried and David Heinemeier Hansson of 37signals and Joel Spolsky of Fog Creek Software are particularly vocal advocates of the latter approach (Spolsky 2003; 37signals 2006, chapter 2; Heinemeier Hansson 2008; Fried 2008b). (N.B.: In the references, 37signals is alphabetized as if spelled out: Thirty-Seven Signals.) Other founders who (at times) have decided against using venture capital include Evan Williams (Blogger/Twitter), Stewart Butterfield, and Caterina Fake (both Flickr). See Chafkin 2008, Helft 2006, and p. 261 of Livingston 2007. The benefits associated with venture-capital funding are discussed in chapter 8 below.

166. For example, in the fall of 2003, when the venture-capital firms Benchmark Capital and Kleiner Perkins Caufield and Byers invested $13 million in Friendster, the first online social networking site, the site (which had been launched in March 2003) already had 3 million users and was widely viewed as "the next big thing." But the company was not successful. See Rivlin 2006 and Hutheesing 2004.

167. On eBay, see Cohen 2002, pp. 55–59.

168. Spector 2000, pp. 96–103.

169. Battelle 2005, pp. 85–87, 89–91; Vise and Malseed 2005, pp. 45–49, 60–69; Google 1999.

170. Apart from Bloglines and Del.icio.us, which had been completely self-funded before these events, all these companies had taken some angel investments earlier in their history.

171. See the subsection of chapter 4 above titled "The Broad Version of the End-to-End Arguments and Innovation at the Application Layer."

172. On the relevance of embeddedness within organizations, cultures, or network connections for innovation, see Saxenian 1994; Castilla et al. 2000; Saxenian 2002; Powell et al. 2002; Powell and Grodal 2005; Porter, Bunker Whittington, and Powell 2005.

173. The problems associated with this type of systemic innovation are discussed in the subsection of this chapter titled "Implications of the Link between Architecture and Feasible Governance Choices: Effect on Ability to Innovate."

Chapter 6

1. Whether a reduction in independent developers' incentives to innovate will be offset by the increase in network providers' incentives to innovate will be discussed in chapter 8.

2. Though some technology was available that enabled network providers to detect and control some applications, this technology could not detect Internet-telephony

applications yet. It took a while to develop technology that was able to detect and block Internet-telephony applications. See Cherry 2005. Today, detecting Skype is still difficult. See Bonfiglio et al. 2007.

3. See chapter 2 above.

4. The IP protocol header contains a "protocol" field that indicates to which higher-layer protocol at the destination host the data should be delivered. In other words, the "protocol" field indicates the higher-layer protocol that invoked the services of IP at the originating host. Thus, if an application does not use a transport protocol but invokes IP directly, the IP header will carry information about the application. This field, however, is used solely for de-multiplexing at the destination host, and does not influence the treatment of datagrams within the network. The numbering of protocols used in the protocol field is standardized across the entire Internet. The relevant numbers are contained in an online database located at www.iana.org. See Tanenbaum 2003, p. 435.

5. The original specification of IPv4 provided an application with the possibility of specifying the desired type of service in a "service type" field. For example, the application could ask for low delay, high throughput, or high reliability. Routers could then use this information when choosing among various paths to a destination. Even if the routers made use of this information, the Internet protocol did not guarantee to provide any particular type of service owing to its best-effort service model. Thus, in an Internet running IPv4, routers may treat datagrams differently. The treatment depends on the content of the service type field, not on the type or particular instance of application. In practice, routers often ignore the type of service field. In the 1990s, the meaning of the field was redefined to accommodate differentiated services. See Comer 2000, pp. 99–101; Tanenbaum 2003, p. 434.

6. On deep packet inspection in general, see Anderson 2007. For a specific example, see Cisco Systems 2005. For an extended description of the techniques used to perform discrimination, see Peha 2007, pp. 646–650.

7. Technologies now being developed, including the IP Multimedia Subsystem and Next Generation Networks, are intended to change this. On these technologies, see the section in chapter 9 titled "Network Provider's Private Interests in Network Architectures."

8. The definition follows Carlton and Perloff 2005, p. 351.

9. As was noted in chapter 5, 'complementor' denotes an economic actor that provides complements. See Brandenburger and Nalebuff 1998, p. 16.

10. In the context of the framework developed in chapter 1, this is an example how an actor's existing or expected economic relationships with other actors (here, the market structure in the market for Internet services) and other constraints (here, regulations) may influence an actor's reaction to an architectural constraint.

11. See, e.g., Internet Non-Discrimination Act of 2006 (2006), §4(a); Internet Freedom and Nondiscrimination Act of 2006 (2006), §28(a); Internet Freedom Preservation Act (2007), §12(a)(1). Academic proponents of network neutrality include Lessig (2001), Wu (2003a), Wu and Lessig (2003), Weiser (2003), van Schewick (2007), Frischmann and van Schewick (2007), and Herman (2006). Academic opponents of network neutrality include Yoo (2005), Sidak (2006), Hahn and Wallsten (2006), and Faulhaber (2007). For a short introduction to the debate, see van Schewick 2009.

12. This is a common argument used by opponents of regulation. See, e.g., Speta 2000a, pp. 76–88; Speta 2000b, pp. 995–1007. In this case, regulation may still serve an educational function and protect customers and providers of independent content, portals, and applications from discriminatory or exclusionary conduct by "incompetent incumbents" (Farrell and Weiser 2003, p. 114) that fail to recognize that discrimination is not in their best economic interest. (See, e.g., Farrell and Weiser 2003, pp. 114–117; Wu 2003a, pp. 154–156.) But in comparison with a threat of discrimination due to a real incentive to discriminate, this constitutes a weaker basis for regulatory intervention.

13. See, e.g., Yoo 2004, p. 67; Hahn and Wallsten 2006, p. 6; Baumol et al. 2007, p. 3; Wu 2006a, p. 7.

14. For an example of this view, see Yoo 2004, p. 67: "On the other hand, regulators can adopt a more humble posture about their ability to distinguish anticompetitive from pro-competitive behavior and attempt to resolve the problem by promoting entry by alternative broadband platforms. Once a sufficient number of alternative last-mile providers exists, the danger of anticompetitive effects disappears, as any attempt to use an exclusivity arrangement to harm competition will simply induce consumers to obtain their services from another last-mile provider." Also see Baumol et al. 2007, p. 3; Hahn and Wallsten 2006, p. 6.

15. An example of this line of reasoning can be found in the FCC memorandum and opinion in the AOL TimeWarner merger proceeding: "We believe that if unaffiliated ISPs receive non-discriminatory access to TimeWarner cable systems . . . the merged firm's incentives and ability to withhold unaffiliated content from its subscribers will be substantially mitigated." (Federal Communications Commission 2001, pp. 6594–6595, paragraph 107). See also Federal Communications Commission 2001, p. 6596, paragraph 112; Lemley and Lessig 1999 (reprinted as Lemley and Lessig 2000).

16. See Federal Communications Commission 2001, p. 6578, paragraph 74: "The relevant geographic markets for residential high-speed Internet access services are local. That is, a consumer's choices are limited to those companies that offer high-speed Internet access services in his or her area, and the only way to obtain different choices is to move. While high-speed ISPs other than cable operators may offer service over different local areas (e.g., DSL or wireless) or may offer service over

much wider areas, even nationally (e.g., satellite), a consumer's choices are dictated by what is offered in his or her locality." See also Hausman, Sidak, and Singer 2001, p. 135: "From a consumer's perspective, the relevant geographic market is local because one can purchase broadband Internet access only from a local residence. Stated another way, a hypothetical monopoly supplier of broadband Internet access in a given geographic market could exercise market power without controlling the provision of broadband access in neighboring geographic markets."

17. Thus, the analysis assumes that the network provider may be vertically integrated into the provision of at least some applications. Vertical integration, however, is not the only case to which the analysis applies. A similar analysis applies to other forms of close vertical relationships between the network provider and a provider of complementary products such as partial integration, partial equity investments, long-term contracts, or other forms of close affiliation.

18. This clearly is an unrealistic assumption, as antitrust law usually includes some rules that restrict monopolization. Still, participants in the network-neutrality debate do not agree on whether the existing laws in antitrust and communications law cover all relevant threats of discrimination or not. For a flavor of the debate, see, e.g., Shelanski 2007; Yoo 2007; Hemphill 2008; Weiser 2008; van Schewick 2009. On the European situation, see Cave and Crocioni 2007 and Chirico, van der Haar, and Larouche 2007.

19. See the description of the architecture of the Internet in chapter 3.

20. The "open access" debate focuses on the question whether the owners of broadband networks should be required to allow independent ISPs to provide Internet access services over their networks. For a flavor of the debate, see Lemley and Lessig 1999, reprinted as Lemley and Lessig 2000; Bar et al. 2000; Speta 2000a,b; Yoo 2002.

21. See, e.g., Bork 1993, pp. 372–375; Posner 2001, pp. 198–199. In general, two goods are complements, if a decrease in the price of one increases the demand for the other (Varian 1999, p. 112). If the two goods are used in variable proportions, the monopolist may have an incentive to monopolize the complementary market, as this creates greater flexibility in its relative pricing of both components. Through appropriate pricing, the monopolist may be able to extract more surplus from consumers. If it needs a monopoly over both products to price discriminate in this fashion, monopolizing the second market will increase its profits. See, e.g., Ordover, Sykes, and Willig 1985.

22. Farrell and Weiser 2003, p. 89.

23. See, e.g., Whinston 1990, pp. 840, 850–852; Farrell and Katz 2000; Farrell and Weiser 2003, p. 103.

24. See, e.g., Whinston 1990, pp. 850–852, 855.

25. This case is widely recognized as an exception to the "one monopoly rent" argument. See Bork 1993, p. 376; Ordover, Sykes, and Willig 1985, pp. 121–127. In the context of the "open access" debate, this case has been highlighted by Farrell and Weiser (2003, pp. 105–107) and by Speta (2000b, pp. 997–1000). This theory has been used to explain why AT&T had an incentive to monopolize the market for telecommunications equipment in the past (Farrell and Weiser 2003, pp. 105–107; Speta 2000b, pp. 997–1000) and why the Bell operating companies may have incentives to engage in non-price discrimination against their long-distance rivals today, if they are allowed to participate in the long-distance market. For discussions of this question in the context of the American telecommunications market, see Sibley and Weisman 1998; Weisman 1998; Schwartz 2000; Mandy 2000; Weisman and Williams 2001.

26. On the factors that may lead a price-regulated upstream monopolist with a downstream subsidiary to engage in non-price discrimination against its downstream rivals, see Mandy 2000.

27. The theory laid out below, developed by Whinston (1990, pp. 854–855), is widely accepted as an exception to the "one monopoly rent" argument. See, e.g., Carlton 2001, pp. 667–668; Choi and Stefanadis 2001, p. 55; Whinston 2001, p. 71; Carlton and Waldman 2002, p. 195. For a detailed application of this theory in the context of the "open access" debate, see Rubinfeld and Singer 2001. See also Farrell and Weiser 2003, p. 119.

28. Whinston's (1990) model does not consider the possibility that the primary-good monopolist may extract the complementary-good revenue for the "stand-alone market" through access charges. Assume, for a moment, that the primary-good monopolist can set access charges. If the producer of a complementary good has fixed costs, the monopolist could exclude it from the market by increasing the access charge. In this case, the complementary producer will be willing to pay an access fee less than or equal to its profits across both markets (i.e., the "systems market" and the "stand-alone market") to stay in the market. However, exclusion may still be more profitable than extracting profits through access charges. First, even if the primary-good monopolist could completely extract its rivals' profits across both parts of the market, the net gains from monopolizing the complementary market may be higher than the net gains resulting from an access charge, because of the presence of economies of scale or network effects in the complementary market, and the reduction in fixed costs under exclusion. In addition, if rivals know that their profits will be fully extracted, they may have fewer incentives to increase profits. Under such a scheme, the rivals' incentives to maximize profits may also be lower. Second, it is likely that the primary-good monopolist will be unable to perfectly implement access charges. Since the monopolist does not know its rivals' profit levels, it is difficult to set access charges. If the access charge is based on past profits, the firm may have an incentive to suppress profits or burn money in order to keep future access charges low (the "ratchet effect"—see, e.g., Weitzman 1980;

Freixas, Guesnerie, and Tirole 1985). This may make foreclosure preferable, as there is no information asymmetry.

29. Economies of scale exist if an increase in output causes long-run average total costs to decrease. In other words, the more output is produced, the lower the cost per unit. For example, economies of scale exist if fixed costs are large relative to marginal costs. In this case, an increase in output allows the firm to spread the fixed costs of production over greater amounts of output, lowering the costs per unit of output. See Hall and Lieberman 2001, pp. 177–178.

30. In markets subject to indirect network effects, this relates to product differentiation with respect to the primary good. Consumers' desire for variety in complementary markets leads them to prefer a larger network. If the benefits of product differentiation with respect to the network or primary good are strong enough, multiple incompatible networks may be able to coexist in equilibrium. Katz and Shapiro (1994, p. 106) write: "Consumer heterogeneity and product differentiation tend to limit tipping and sustain multiple networks. If the rival systems have distinct features sought by certain consumers, two or more systems may be able to survive by catering to consumers who care more about product attributes than network size. Here, market equilibrium with multiple incompatible products reflects the social value of variety."

31. Two technologies are incompatible if they cannot be used together. Thus, the users of the two technologies form two different networks. In a market with direct network effects, two technologies are incompatible, if consumers using one technology cannot interact with consumers using the other technology in the way that gives rise to the network effects in the first place. That is, users of one communication service will be unable to communicate with users of the other communication service. Similarly, users of one word-processing software will be unable to exchange documents with users of the other word-processing software. In a market with indirect network effects, two technologies are said to be incompatible, if the complementary products developed for one technology do not work with the primary product of the other technology, and vice versa. For example, users of the Microsoft Windows operating system will be unable to run application programs written for the Linux operating system, and vice versa. Users of Microsoft's media player will be unable to listen to music coded for RealNetworks RealPlayer, and vice versa. Compare Katz and Shapiro 1985, pp. 424–425.

32. Whether a firm wishes to make its products compatible with a competitor's technology is a strategic decision that results in very different forms of competition. If products are incompatible, firms compete for the standard. If products are compatible, firms compete within the standard. In general, owing to the huge gains from winning the competition between incompatible technologies (market dominance), a firm will tend to oppose compatibility, if it is confident to be the winner. In contrast, a firm that fears to lose in a competition for the standard will prefer compatibil-

ity and competition within the standard in order to avoid the huge costs of losing the competition for the standard. For an analysis of the factors influencing these choices and an overview of suitable strategies in the different forms of competition, see Besen and Farrell 1994; Katz and Shapiro 1985; Katz and Shapiro 1994; Shapiro and Varian 1999.

33. Often competitors will not be driven completely from the market. In particular, some customers with high switching costs or a unique preference for a competitor's product will prefer to stay with that competitor in spite of the strong network effects associated with the winning technology. See, e.g., Faulhaber 2002, p. 329, note 37.

34. "'Tipping' occurs," according to Faulhaber (2002, p. 316), "when a single provider reaches a critical mass of customers that are so attractive to others that competitors must inevitably shrink, in the absence of interoperation."

35. In network markets, consumer expectations about the future size of the network play a crucial role in determining the outcome of the competition. This is due to the costs of belonging to the losing network: A consumer who has chosen the losing network can either switch to the winner, which may be costly, or suffer from the lower value of a small network. To avoid this situation, the consumer will choose the network that it expects to be the winner. See, e.g., Besen and Farrell 1994, p. 118.

36. A substantial lead in installed base is not the only factor that influences the outcome of the competition. Owing to the huge benefits of belonging to the winning network, users have a strong desire to choose the technology that will ultimately prevail. Therefore, consumers expectations of who the winner will be are at least as important. Other factors that may influence customers' expectations and that may therefore result in a competitive advantage are an established reputation, a well-known brand name, or ready visible access to capital. Thus, an unknown firm with an early lead may be overtaken by a market leader that enters second, but has a well-known brand name and good reputation. See, e.g., Katz and Shapiro 1994, p. 107.

37. For example, if the rival produces a differentiated product, the rival's presence creates additional surplus, some of which the monopolist can extract through its sales of the primary good. Thus, the monopolist's profits in the "systems market" are increased if its rival is in the market.

38. See Whinston 1990, pp. 850–852, 855.

39. Owing to the cost structure of information products, the primary-good monopolist can profit from additional sales of the complementary information good, even if it does not have a monopoly in the complementary market. Thus, the network provider may have an incentive to exclude rivals in the complementary market, even if it cannot monopolize that market. See the subsection of this chapter titled "Profitability of Discrimination without Monopolization."

40. Carlton and Waldman 2002, pp. 206–207.

41. The market for broadband Internet access is considered a distinct market from the narrowband-access market, see, e.g.,, Hausman, Sidak, and Singer 2001, pp. 135–157; Federal Communications Commission 2001, pp. 6574–6577, paragraphs 68–73.

42. For residential high-speed Internet access service, the relevant market is local. See note 16 above. According to FCC data, 34% of ZIP codes have one or less cable or ADSL provider who serves at least one subscriber living within the ZIP code as of June 2007 (Federal Communications Commission 2008b, table 16, line "ADSL and/or Cable Modem"). As the United States Government Accountability Office (2006) has pointed out, this measure (i.e., the number of providers reporting at least one subscriber in a certain ZIP code) overstates the level of competition to individual households.

43. Breznick 2003; AOL 2008a,b.

44. Microsoft Online Services 2009.

45. Beardsley, Doman, and Edin (2003) report statistics showing that "so far, . . . faster and better access to the Internet is the sole killer application of broadband." Thus, the scenario described in the text may be quite common. This possibility is also highlighted by Farrell and Weiser (2003, p. 119).

46. The marginal cost of production is the incremental cost of producing an additional unit of the good. Thus, the marginal cost of production does not include the costs of product development (see, e.g., Hall and Lieberman 2001, pp. 168–169). In the case of software applications, Internet content and portals, the marginal cost of production is the cost of making an additional digital copy of the product, which is typically very low.

47. The average cost of production indicates a firm's total cost per unit of output. In other words, it denotes the total cost associated with a particular product divided by the quantity of output produced. Thus, contrary to the marginal cost of production which does not include the cost of developing the first unit of the product, the average cost of production includes the cost of development divided by the total number of copies. See, e.g., Hall and Lieberman 2001, p. 168.

48. This cost structure (low marginal costs relative to average costs), which results in significant economies of scale, is generally viewed as a key economic characteristic of the markets for these products. On information goods in general, see Shapiro and Varian 1999, pp. 3–4; on software, see Katz and Shapiro 1999, pp. 34–36; on Internet content, portals and software, see Posner 2001, pp. 245–246; on broadband portals, see MacKie-Mason 2000, p.14; on broadband content, see Rubinfeld and Singer 2001, p. 307.

49. The existence of direct or indirect network effects is a fundamental economic characteristic of many software markets. See, e.g., Evans and Schmalensee 2002, pp. 9–10; Katz and Shapiro 1999, pp. 32–34.

50. E.g., Faulhaber 2002.

51. E.g., MacKie-Mason 2000, p. 16.

52. See, e.g., Rubinfeld and Singer 2001, pp. 310–313.

53. For a numerical example, see Rubinfeld and Singer 2001, pp. 310–313. That paper assesses the likelihood of content discrimination (i.e., blocking or degrading the quality of outside content) by a broadband network provider that is vertically integrated into the market for broadband content and portals in the context of the merger between AOL and TimeWarner.

54. This theory is new and has not been covered by the existing literature.

55. If firms in the complementary market sell access to the users of their product to advertisers or other third parties they have two potential sources of revenue from two different sides of the market: the consumer side of the market, and the third-party side of the market. Such markets are known as two-sided markets; the good in the middle, here the complementary good, is known as a platform product. In a two-sided market, one or more platforms enable interactions between two different types of users, which form the two sides of the market, and the volume of interactions between users on both sides of the market depends on the structure of fees and not only on the overall level of fees charged by the platform (Rochet and Tirole 2006, p. 645). In our case, the complementary product enables interactions between consumers of the complementary product on the one side and advertisers on the other side; an interaction occurs when a consumer of the complementary product views an ad. Platform products that enable interactions between consumers of the platform good and advertisers are a special case of two-sided markets: In most two-sided markets, the two sides of the market want to interact with each other, resulting in positive network effects between the two sides. For example, the users of a video game console (the platform product) would like to play video games written for the console, and prefer a console that is compatible with more video games. Video game developers, the other side of the market, want to sell their video games to users of the console and prefer to write video games for a console that has more users. In contrast, the benefits that end users receive from the platform product may or may not increase with the amount of advertisers associated with the platform product. For example, consumers of yellow pages have been shown to prefer yellow pages with more advertising (Rysman 2004, p. 508). Researchers often assume that television viewers prefer to watch stations with less advertising (Anderson and Coate 2005, p. 951). However, this depends on the situation—more than a quarter of viewers of the Super Bowl tune in for the ads (Markillie 2005, p. 3). The more easily consumers can avoid advertising in a particular medium, the more likely that the ads provided in that medium are utility-enhancing, because otherwise consumers would simply choose to ignore the ads (Becker and Murphy 1993, p. 962). On the Internet, advertisers clearly benefit from additional consumers using the platform, but end users may or may not benefit from an increased number of advertisers.

56. The conditions under which this pricing structure will arise are explored by the literature on two-sided markets (Armstrong 2006; Rochet and Tirole 2003; Rochet and Tirole 2006).

57. A common set of tactics forces rival producers of the complementary good to lower the quality-adjusted price of their product (e.g., Farrell and Katz 2000, pp. 414–415). This increases the consumer surplus available for extraction in the primary market. In another tactic, the monopolist imposes an access charge on rivals who wish to participate in the complementary market (ibid., p. 422). Of course, the monopolist must actually have the power to do so because of intellectual-property rights or because rivals' access to the primary good requires the monopolist's cooperation.

58. This may be an unrealistic assumption. See note 28 above.

59. More formally, assume that the monopolist's (M's) complementary product has x customers and a rival's (R's) complementary product (before the exclusion) has y customers. Let $f_M(u)$ and $f_R(u)$ represent the advertising revenues that the monopolist and the rival can realize if they sell access to u customers of their respected version of the complementary good. Finally, assume that after exclusion z customers demand the monopolist's complementary product. If $f_M(z) > f_M(x) + f_R(y)$, the monopolist will generate more advertising revenue by excluding its rival from the complementary market and selling access to all users of the complementary good directly than by having its rivals stay in the market and extracting the advertising revenue from them, even if it is able to extract all such revenues.

60. Monopolizing the market for the complementary good directly monopolizes sales to the end-user side of the market. As access to end users is monopolized, the primary-good monopolist becomes the only supplier of access to these customers through the complementary good and the advertiser side of the market is also monopolized. Of course, advertisers may find other ways to market their offerings to users of the primary good, for example through other media, so the exclusion of rivals from the complementary market will not necessarily confer market power over advertisers on the primary-good monopolist and the primary-good monopolist may not be able to raise advertising prices. Whether market power is conferred or not will depend on the specific circumstances of the advertising market and the characteristics of the consumers of the complementary good.

61. With multiple auctions the third parties may have been able to bid in different auctions, thereby reducing competition in any given auction.

62. Ultimately, higher prices on the third-party side of the market will harm consumers, as firms will pass on at least some of the increased costs to their customers. For example, higher advertising fees will ultimately lead to higher prices for the goods that are advertised. See Rubinfeld and Singer 2001, p. 316; MacKie-Mason 2000, p. 23.

63. See, e.g., Shapiro and Varian 1999, pp. 34–35.

64. Theoretically, the monopolist could always increase the value of complementary market by sharing this information with all the firms in the complementary market (so that they could share it with their advertisers and increase their advertising fees) and then extract these additional rents. However, data protection may prevent this information being shared on a disaggregated basis or the primary-good monopolist may consider such information a valuable business secret that it does not wish to disclose.

65. Under the analysis above, foreclosure may be welfare enhancing or destroying. Generally, the reduction of fixed costs and of costs associated with access charge administration and negotiation under foreclosure will increase welfare. The increased value of advertising space from network effects and additional information provided by the monopolist will also generally increase welfare. However, the increased rents that can be extracted through increased monopoly power are likely to reduce welfare. As prices on the third-party side of the market increase, third parties are likely to demand less access to the complementary market's customers and this may reduce welfare in the standard way that a monopoly reduces welfare. As a side effect of foreclosure, welfare is likely to be reduced if the complementary goods market was differentiated. In this case, the reduction in choice is likely to reduce consumer surplus which directly reduces welfare. In addition, this may feed through to lower demand in the complementary market, also reducing producer surplus (in the notation of note 59 above, $z < x + y$). Overall, the static welfare effects of foreclosure are likely to be ambiguous. This book's argument, however, is based on the dynamic welfare effects of foreclosure, in particular the reduction in innovation in complementary markets. See the discussion in chapter 9.

66. Theoretically, the primary-good monopolist may be able to set an access charge that extracts its rivals' advertising profits across the "stand-alone market" and the "systems market." Whether access charges are an option at all, depends on the markets under analysis. Even if they are possible, exclusion may enable the monopolist to realize higher profits than access charges. First, we just saw that the total profits available in the complementary market may be higher under foreclosure than under access charges. Second, access charges may distort incentives for rivals in the complementary market. Third, the monopolist may be unable to extract the full revenue because of information asymmetry about profit levels. See note 28 above.

67. Afuah and Tucci 2001, p. 56; Shapiro and Varian 1999, pp. 162–163.

68. Google 2008, p. 39.

69. Time Warner 2008, p.1; Yahoo 2008b, p. 35.

70. See Schiesel 2002 with respect to a contract between AOL and AT&T Comcast.

71. See, e.g., Rubinfeld and Singer 2001, p. 316; MacKie-Mason 2000, p. 23.

72. Rashtchy et al. 2007, p. 117.

73. Holahan 2006.

74. By excluding competing providers of the complementary product from access to its Internet-service customers, the network provider monopolizes the customer side of the market and becomes the exclusive provider of access to its Internet-service customers through the complementary good. However, this will only translate into an ability to raise prices on the advertiser side of the market when advertisers cannot get access to equivalent end users at the current price through another medium. See note 60 above.

75. For example, comScore, a market research company, estimated Google's market share of the US search-engine market in February 2007 at 59%, Yahoo's at 22%, and Microsoft's at 10% (comScore 2008).

76. For example, SearchIgnite, a firm that offers technology that helps advertisers and advertising agencies manage paid search campaigns, reported that revenue per search for ads by all marketers in June 2007 was $21 for Google, $15 for Microsoft, and $9 for Yahoo. Revenue per search for ads by large brand marketers in June 2007 was $25 for Google, $21 for Microsoft, and $16 for Yahoo. (SearchIgnite and RBC Capital Markets 2007, pp. 3–4.) According to SearchIgnite (ibid., p. 3), "revenue per search (RPS) takes into account how well [search] engines generate revenue from search ad impressions—specifically, factoring in search ads' cost-per-click (CPC) and click-through-rate (CTR) to measure the revenue per every 1,000 ad impressions servered."

77. Varian 2006, p. 178.

78. Ibid., pp. 186–188; Lohr 2008; Holahan 2007; Rashtchy et al. 2007, pp. 169, 174.

79. Of course, for the higher number of advertisers to create larger value to users, the search engine needs to be able to identify and display those ads that are most relevant to the users.

80. In early 2007, Yahoo introduced a similar system called Panama in order to increase the revenue from search. While this system has increased the click-through rate of ads on Yahoo's search engine, Yahoo said in a presentation to investors in March 2008 that Panama had improved Yahoo's revenue per search for searches in the United states by 30% in the first nine months of 2007, but that it still earned 60–70 percent less for searches than Google (Yahoo 2008a, Exhibit 99.2, p. 14). See also Rashtchy et al. 2007, pp. 169, 174, 195–196; Holahan 2007.

81. This assumes that the users' demographic characteristics are similar across search engines. If users' demographic characteristics differed across search-engine providers and advertisers were willing to pay more for access to Google's users because they value the particular demographic characteristics of Google's users, having the users

of other search engines use Google may make Google's demographics worse and may reduce Google's revenue per search. It also assumes that a sufficient number of users that had used Microsoft's or Yahoo's search engine before the exclusion would use Google's search engine after the exclusion (instead of stopping to use search engines altogether).

82. Hansell 2008b.

83. Unless otherwise noted, the analysis in this paragraph is based on Hansell 2008a, Gapper 2008, and Evans and Noel 2007.

84. Rashtchy et al. 2007, pp. 276, 241–242. The gap between advertising revenue may decrease in the future with the introduction of behavioral targeting methods by advertising networks. These methods would enable advertising networks to track users' behavior across websites, enabling them to sell highly targeted ads. Still, the website on which the ad is ultimately placed will most likely get only a share of the advertising revenue that the advertiser pays to the ad network. For example, Tacoda, an advertising-network company using behavioral marketing that was acquired by AOL in 2007, keeps 40% of the revenue from a targeted ad; 40% go to the site on which the ad is ultimately placed, and 20% go to the site that enabled Tacoda to identify specific interests of a user (Holahan 2006). Thus, this still makes it likely that the advertising revenue that a network provider could extract from an independent website will be lower than the advertising revenue that the network provider can realize if the users visit its own website instead of the independent website (assuming the network provider's website is part of a larger conglomerate).

85. Yahoo has an ad network, partnering in a revenue-sharing model with AT&T in the United States, BT in the United Kingdom, and Rogers Cable in Canada; in addition, it sells co-branded Internet services with a number of other providers (Yahoo 2008b, p. 12). For details of such a deal, see Kaye 2008.

86. Holahan 2006.

87. Even if those rivals require consumers to register before using their product or service, they have no way to verify the information, unless they require payment; in this case, they can verify the information as part of the billing process. See Shapiro and Varian 1999, pp. 34–35; MacKie-Mason 2000, p. 11. Theoretically, the network provider could share this information with providers of complementary goods. This would enable them to charge higher advertising fees which the network provider could extract through access charges. However, data protection may prevent this information being shared on a disaggregated basis or the network provider may consider such information a valuable business secret that it does not wish to disclose.

88. For example, in the notation of note 59, if there is one complementary good rival to a vertically integrated monopolist before exclusion, the net gains in the complementary market are positive if $f_M(z) - c_M(z) > f_M(x) - c_M(x) + f_R(y) - c_R(y)$, with $c_M(u)$ representing the monopolist's fixed and variable costs of serving u

complementary good customers and $c_R(u)$ representing the rival's fixed and variable costs of serving u complementary good customers. To make exclusion profitable overall, the net gains in the complementary market must be larger than the reduction in profit in the Internet-services market.

89. If the costs were sunk (i.e., non-recoverable) instead of fixed, existing providers would stay in the market as long as the network provider would let them keep enough revenue to cover their variable costs. However, future applications and content providers would not make the start-up investment, because they would anticipate it being appropriated by the network provider. Thus, the network provider would have to let existing providers keep their sunk costs in order to motivate future applications providers to enter the market.

90. See the references cited in note 48 above. On economies of scale in search engines, see Varian 2006.

91. While the reduction in fixed costs and transaction costs under foreclosure may be welfare enhancing, exclusion may not be welfare enhancing overall. See note 65 above.

92. Thanks to Robert Pepper for highlighting this example.

93. See Nuechterlein and Weiser 2005, pp. 49–50, 53–54, 195, 204, 294.

94. The access charge is lost if the call is placed using VoIP, regardless of whether VoIP is provided by the network provider or by an independent provider. Thus, the network provider has an incentive not to have VoIP used on its network at all.

95. In theory, network providers may be able to realize the same or higher profits as under blocking by setting an access charge that all providers of Internet-telephony applications must pay. However, the costs of setting up a system for these access charges and the potential political fallout may make it preferable to simply block (or secretly slow) the Internet-telephony applications and continue to realize regulated access charges through the existing system. In addition, for reasons discussed in note 28 above, a network provider may prefer to realize profits himself over extracting them from others via access charges.

96. See Federal Communications Commission 2005b,c; Charny 2005b; McCullagh 2005; Madison River Communications 2006.

97. On international settlement charges and the US regulatory regime governing these charges, see, e.g., Federal Communications Commission 2007; Einhorn 2003; Stanley 2000.

98. Sources: Cherry 2005 (Saudi Telecom); Charny 2005a (Mexico); PriMetrica 2008 (United Arab Emirates).

99. See, e.g., Salop and Romaine 1999, pp. 625–626; Carlton and Waldman 2002, p. 195.

100. On this type of monopoly maintenance in general, see, e.g., Carlton 2001, pp. 668–671; Farrell and Weiser 2003, pp. 109–112; Salop and Romaine 1999, pp. 625–626. For specific models, see, e.g., Carlton and Waldman 2002; Choi and Stefanadis 2001.

101. See, e.g., Carlton 2001, pp. 669–670.

102. E.g., U.S. Department of Justice and Federal Trade Commission 1984, §4.212 (promulgated in 1984 and reaffirmed in 1992 and 1997) ("The relevant question is whether the need for simultaneous entry to the secondary market gives rise to a substantial incremental difficulty as compared to entry into the primary market alone. If the entry at the secondary level is easy in absolute terms, the requirement of simultaneous entry to that market is unlikely adversely to affect entry to the primary market.").

103. For an argument along these lines, see Williamson 1979, pp. 962–964; U.S. Department of Justice and Federal Trade Commission 1984, §4.212.

104. U.S. Department of Justice and Federal Trade Commission 1984, §4.212.

105. Carlton and Gertner 2003; Choi and Stefanadis 2001.

106. For a definition of indirect network effects, see box 6.4.

107. Gilbert and Katz 2001, p. 30 (referring to operating systems and application programs). Under the label "applications barrier to entry," this line of reasoning has featured prominently in the Microsoft case. See, e.g., *United States v. Microsoft*, 253 F.3d 34, 54–56 (D. C. Cir. 2001); Gilbert and Katz 2001, pp. 28–30.

108. In addition to offering its own content and applications to the customers of its Internet service, the monopolist may also "allow" independent producers of these products to offer their products to the customers of its Internet service, as long as they agree to offer their products exclusively to these customers. Stated differently, instead of depriving a potential entrant into the market for Internet services of a source of complementary products by driving rival content and application producers from the market, the monopolist could deprive the potential entrant of a source of complementary products by signing exclusive contracts with independent content and application producers. Whether a monopolist could profitably impose such an exclusivity provision, has been the subject of considerable debate. The Chicago school denied such a possibility, arguing that the other party to the exclusive contract would not agree to contracts that made it worse off. (See, e.g., Bork 1993, p. 309.) More recent research has shown that this argument is incomplete: it does not consider the possibility that the exclusive contract imposes harm on third parties that are not parties to the contract, while not making the contracting parties worse off. In other words, the exclusive contract gives rise to a negative externality on third parties, and because of this externality signing an exclusive contract is jointly optimal for the contracting parties. For discussions of this question with pointers to the literature, see Gilbert and Katz 2001, pp. 31–33; Whinston 2001, pp. 66–70.

109. Usually, this theory is applied to cases in which the entrant's primary good is technically unable to take advantage of the set of applications developed for the monopolist's primary good. For example, software applications make use of a specific operating system's application programming interfaces and therefore run only on this operating system. As a result, customers of the entrant's operating system are technically unable to use applications developed for the incumbent's operating system. In contrast, as long as an application complies with the specifications of the Internet protocol, it can run over any physical network that supports the Internet protocol. As a result, applications adhering to that standard can be used by anyone connected to the Internet. Thus, from a technical point of view, the applications offered by the monopolist could be used by customers of a rival network provider as well. Therefore, the entrant's inability to use the monopolist's applications and content is not due to technical differences or incompatibility between the Internet services offered by the monopolist and a potential entrant, but results from the monopolist's business decision to offer its content and applications exclusively to customers of its own Internet service.

110. The strategy described here requires that the monopolist does not offer the content, application or portal to consumers outside its network; in contrast, in the "primary good not essential" strategy, the inability to earn monopoly profits on its sales to consumers outside its network is the reason that leads the monopolist to monopolize the complementary market as well. See the subsection titled "Primary Good Not Essential."

111. The potential anti-competitive implications of such a strategy are explored by, e.g., MacKie-Mason 2000, pp. 23–25; Rubinfeld and Singer 2001, pp. 313–316.

112. Alternatively, the monopolist could reach the same result by allowing independent producers of applications, content, and portals to offer their products to the customers of its Internet service, if they agree to provide the products exclusively to its customers. See note 108 above.

113. For example, compared to PCs, mobile handsets have small screens, limited keypads, and not a lot of storage. See, e.g., Deprez, Rosengren, and Soman 2002, p. 97, note 4.

114. Finally, one may imagine a situation in which the nationwide market for Internet services consists of a collection of local monopolies who all bundle their content, portal, and applications exclusively with their Internet service. In this case, a new entrant into the market for Internet services would have to enter the market for content, portals, or applications as well.

115. See, e.g., Niewijk, Songhurst, and Todd 2003, section "Moving towards partnerships."

116. That the costs of capital may increase with the amount of entry costs that are sunk is discussed by Viscusi, Harrington, and Vernon (2005, pp. 169–170, 173).

117. Deprez, Rosengren, and Soman 2002, pp. 96–97.

118. For example, as of March 2008, the Top 19 cable and phone broadband providers account for 94% of the US market; the seven smallest of these providers had between 227,900 (Cincinnati Bell) and 911,000 (Windstream) subscribers (Leichtman Research Group 2008).

119. E.g., Speta 2000a, pp. 83–84.

120. See the subsection of this chapter titled "Primary Good Not Essential."

121. See box 6.4.

122. An ISP could reach the same effect (i.e., reintroduce indirect network effects with respect to its own network) by using proprietary protocols inside its network, see, e.g., Computer Science and Telecommunications Board and National Research Council 2001, pp. 147–149. An alternative strategy may be the provision of quality of service only within an Internet provider's network, see, e.g., Shapiro and Varian 1999, p. 187.

123. On a similar situation in the context of provider-specific indirect network effects due to the use of proprietary protocols inside the network, see Computer Science and Telecommunications Board and National Research Council 2001, pp. 147–149.

124. As was highlighted in note 108 above, an alternative way of deterring entry would be to sign exclusive contracts with independent producers of applications, content, and portals. Such a strategy would have the advantage that the monopolist does not have to bear losses with respect to its Internet-service fees, as its customers would have access to all existing applications, content, and portals.

125. This theory has not been used as an exception to the "one monopoly rent" argument before. It generalizes from an argument that was used by the Federal Communications Commission in the AOL/TimeWarner merger proceeding with regard to instant messaging (Federal Communications Commission 2001, pp. 6603–6629, paragraphs 128–200) and subsequently analyzed by Faulhaber (2002).

126. See the subsection of this chapter titled "Primary Good Not Essential."

127. On dynamic or "Schumpeterian" competition, see, e.g., Evans and Schmalensee 2002; Shelanski and Sidak 2001, pp. 10–15; Carlton and Gertner 2003, pp. 45–48.

128. See e.g., Evans and Schmalensee 2002, pp. 3–13.

129. Federal Communications Commission 2001, pp. 6603–6629, paragraphs 128–200. For an in-depth analysis of the economic rationale underlying this condition, see Faulhaber 2002.

130. The fifth exception, "monopoly preservation in the primary market," requires that rival producers of excluded complementary products are driven from the market.

131. For a similar argument in the context of a general analysis of the profitability of exclusionary conduct, see Elhauge and Geradin 2007, pp. 498–499, 548–549.

132. For an economic model demonstrating this effect (i.e., if marginal profits in the complementary market are positive, a primary-good monopolist or duopolist may have an incentive to engage in exclusionary conduct in the complementary market if this increases its number of sales in this market, even if the conduct does not monopolize the complementary market) in the context of tying, see DeGraba 1996. In DeGraba's model, oligopolists sell a differentiated good (the primary good) and a homogenous good (the complementary good) that are used in fixed proportions to produce the final good. The homogenous good can be produced at constant marginal cost by any firm incurring a certain fixed cost. The homogenous market is characterized by free-entry Cournot competition. In such a market, the zero-profit price of the good is greater than the marginal cost, since each firm has to make a positive profit on each sale to cover the fixed costs of production. As a result, the oligopolist in DeGraba's model will tie in order to increase the sales of the complementary good, which increases profits (although the tying does not monopolize the complementary market). Note that this model does not require the complementary good to be a differentiated good. In deGraba's model, tying increases welfare by reducing competition in the complementary market, which reduces the wasteful replication of fixed cost expenditures. As products in the downstream market are homogeneous, there is no scope in this model for the reduction in choice harming consumers. Were products modeled as heterogeneous in the downstream market then it is likely that the static welfare effects would be ambiguous. Moreover, deGraba does not consider the dynamic effects on innovation, which are the focus of this book. See the discussion in chapter 9 below.

133. If the price were equal to marginal costs, firms would not be able to cover their fixed costs and would earn negative profits. In the long run, firms would not operate in such a market. Thus, even if all firms earn zero profit per unit in long-run equilibrium, equilibrium prices are above marginal costs.

134. Shapiro and Varian 1999, p. 161. The importance of market share and number of units sold in knowledge-based products is also described by Afuah and Tucci (2001, pp. 52–54). For an economic model demonstrating this effect in the context of tying, see DeGraba 1996. For a discussion of DeGraba's model, see note 132 above.

135. Katz and Shapiro 1999, p. 41.

136. See the subsection of this chapter titled "Primary Good Not Essential."

137. As outlined in the subsection "Primary Good Not Essential," the conditions are as follows: The network provider has a monopoly in the primary market (i.e., the market for Internet services). The primary good is not essential (i.e., there are uses of the complementary product that do not require the primary good). This condition is met when the ISP offers its complementary product not only to its

Internet-service customers, but to customers nationwide. The complementary market is subject to economies of scale or network effects, a condition that is met in most markets for applications, content, or portals. The monopolist has a mechanism at its disposal that enables it to exclude its rivals from access to its primary-good customers. In the Internet context, technology that enables the network provider to distinguish between applications running over its network and to control their execution provides the network provider with this capability.

138. See the subsection of this chapter titled "Complementary Product Source of Outside Revenue."

139. Even if those rivals require consumers to register before using their product or service, they have no way to verify the information, unless they require payment; in this case, they can verify the information as part of the billing process (Shapiro and Varian 1999, pp. 34–35; MacKie-Mason 2000, p. 11).

140. Access charges may not be similarly effective. (See notes 28 and 66 above.) This is particularly likely if, as discussed in the text, the amount of advertising revenue in the complementary market is larger if the monopolist realizes the advertising revenue itself rather than through access charges.

141. See the subsection of this chapter titled "Complementary Product Source of Outside Revenue."

142. See the subsection of this chapter titled "Monopolist's Complementary Product Source of Outside Revenue."

143. See the subsection of this chapter titled "Monopoly Preservation in the Complementary Market."

144. For a similar argument with respect to the profitability of monopoly preservation through exclusionary conduct in new economy markets, if the monopoly is of intellectual property, see Posner 2001, p. 254.

145. Under tying, a sale of a product is conditioned on the purchase of another (Carlton and Perloff 2005, pp. 675–677; Posner 2001, pp. 197–207). Under exclusive dealing, a firm forbids the firm it supplies to sell products of competing firms (Carlton and Perloff 2005, pp. 672–673; Posner 2001, pp. 229–232, 251–256). In a vertical merger, a firm merges with a firm belonging to another stage in the production or distribution chain (Carlton and Perloff 2005, pp. 669; Posner 2001, pp. 223–229).

146. E.g., Posner 2001, p. 195; Yoo 2002, p. 188. Similarly, some sort of market power or political power is considered to be a prerequisite for strategies that raise rivals costs; see, e.g., Carlton and Perloff 2005, p. 371.

147. For an important exception to this point, see the literature on the exercise of aftermarket power by a firm that faces competition in the foremarket. This literature focuses on the question whether primary market competition precludes

anti-competitive aftermarket actions. For an analysis of these issues with pointers to the literature, see MacKie-Mason and Metzler 1999.

148. See, e.g., Yoo 2002, pp. 249–250, 253, in the context of the "open access" debate ("I conclude that the structure of the broadband industry renders it unlikely that such combinations will pose any significant anti-competitive threat"), and Yoo 2005, p. 61, in the context of the network-neutrality debate ("This suggests that for most of the country, competition should remain sufficiently robust to ameliorate concerns of anticompetitive effects").

149. E.g., Speta 2000b, p. 986, in the context of the "open access" debate.

150. See the references cited in note 13 above.

151. The analysis assumes that the network provider competes with at least one other network provider; thus, it is not restricted to the duopoly situation. Farrell (2006) calls this market structure "duopoly +/–."

152. See also Farrell (2006). Farrell argues that limited competition may not necessarily remove network providers' incentives to discriminate. For a similar argument in the context of the debate over censorship by private proxies, see Kreimer 2006, pp. 33–36. Kreimer argues that competition between ISPs may not be sufficient to discipline ISPs that disable content needlessly on the basis of arguments very similar to the ones advanced above.

153. There may be other reasons that justify these proposals, though. For example, according to Lemley and Lessig (1999, pp. 21–25) the reduction in application-level innovation by independent providers resulting from the threat of discrimination constitutes only one of three arguments in favor of open access.

154. This assumption reflects the reality in the broadband market for residential customers in the US. According to a recent study by the United States Government Accountability Office (2006, p. 18), the median number of broadband providers available to residential users is two.

155. See subsection "Primary Good Not Essential."

156. But even if the network provider does not manage to drive complementary goods producers from the market completely, it may still have an incentive to discriminate. See subsection "Profitability of Discrimination without Monopolization."

157. See subsection "Profitability of Discrimination without Monopolization."

158. See subsection "Profitability of Discrimination without Monopolization."

159. See subsection "Profitability of Discrimination without Monopolization: More Sales at Market Prices."

160. DeGraba's (1996) model, which demonstrates this effect in the context of tying, supports this analysis. In the model, the producer of the primary good has

an incentive to tie in order to increase the number of sales of the secondary good, although it competes with another producer in the primary market. Thus, in the model the incentive to exclude independent competitors from the secondary market is not dependent on a monopoly position in the primary market. The model is discussed in note 132 above.

161. See subsections "Complementary Product Source of Outside Revenue" and "More Outside Revenue."

162. Federal Communications Commission 2001, p. 6594, paragraph 106; pp. 6593–6594, paragraphs 104–106.

163. See subsections "Monopolist's Complementary Product Source of Outside Revenue" and "More Outside Revenue."

164. See subsection "Monopoly Preservation in the Complementary Market."

165. See the references in note 13 above.

166. Wu (2003a, p. 153) makes a similar point in his discussion of the costs of a discriminatory pricing scheme that prohibits customers of a network provider's basic Internet service from using specific applications.

167. See, e.g., Rubinfeld and Singer 2001, p. 310.

168. See ibid., p. 310.

169. See the references in note 13 above.

170. See, e.g., Rubinfeld and Singer 2001, pp. 312–313.

171. See, e.g., Rubinfeld and Singer 2001, pp. 310, 313.

172. See, e.g., Craswell 1982; Bar-Gill 2006.

173. At the end of March 2008, Comcast provided about 40% of cable broadband Internet and 20% of all broadband Internet in the US (Leichtman Research Group 2008).

174. Eckersley, von Lohmann, and Schoen 2007; Topolski 2008. Comcast stopped using this method of interfering with peer-to-peer file-sharing applications in 2008.

175. Reardon 2007; Schoen 2007a.

176. Sandvine 2004, p. 14.

177. Mennecke 2005; Hellweg 2003; Sandvine 2004, pp. 5–6. See also National Cable and Telecommunications Association 2007, p. 31 ("cable operators will not go down the path of blocking access to video or P2P services. Blocking such services would be a recipe for . . . massive dissatisfaction among consumers, which would lead to loss of customers to our competitors.")

178. See Hausman, Sidak, and Singer 2001, p. 164; Kreimer 2006, pp. 34–35; Nuechterlein and Weiser 2005, p. 156.

179. For an in-depth overview of the economic literature on switching costs, see Farrell and Klemperer 2007. For a short overview, see Varian 1999, pp. 603–605. For a treatment of switching costs in the context of information goods, see Shapiro and Varian 1999, chapters 5 and 6.

180. E.g., Varian 1999, pp. 604–605; Hausman, Sidak, and Singer 2001, p. 164.

181. Switching costs do not protect the network provider from losing business from new customers.

182. For example, HearUsNow.org, a project of the Consumers Union, found that a number of the top broadband providers in the United States charge early-termination fees. For example, at the time of the survey in March 2007, Qwest charged a $200 early-termination fee on a two-year contract for high-speed Internet service, Earthlink charged a $149 early-termination fee on a one-year contract for DSL service, and AT&T (including SBC and BellSouth) charged a $99 early-termination fee (Consumers Union 2007; Dunbar 2007).

183. The customer may switch his whole bundle to the new provider, but that creates other problems, for example by making the decision to switch more complex, or by resulting in the loss of the preferred service offering for example in television or telephony.

184. Providers have considerable influence over this cost. For example, in 2005, AOL paid $1.25 million in fines as part of a settlement with the state of New York, because AOL's customer service representatives were incentivized to dissuade customers from switching away from America Online, "by either making the cancellation process so painful for the customers that they could not bear to continue, or by simply ignoring their requests" (Stross 2005).

185. On the use of provider-specific e-mail addresses as a way to increase switching costs in Internet services, see Shapiro and Varian 1999, pp. 109–110. In other telecommunications markets such as wireline telephony and mobile telephony, regulation often requires providers to provide number portability, i.e., to enable a customer to keep its phone number when he switches providers. The Federal Communications Commission currently has to consider a petition to require e-mail providers to forward e-mail to a new e-mail address for a limited time (Mortenson 2007).

186. Stross 2005.

187. For example, an empirical study of competition between cable television and direct broadcast satellite (DBS) multi-channel services showed that while customers generally tend to switch from cable to DBS when the quality-adjusted price of cable increases substantially, the availability of regional sports channels reduced DBS penetration, either because it raised consumers' switching costs or because it

increased product differentiation between the two types of services (Wise and Duwadi 2005, pp. 695, 699–700).

188. DW Staff 2006.

189. This is a hypothetical example. At the time of this writing, Deutsche Telekom offers customers of other ISPs the opportunity to subscribe to the soccer content for a monthly fee (Deutsche Telekom 2008).

190. That product differentiation may provide sellers with some degree of market power is well established in the literature (Carlton and Perloff 2005, pp. 203–205).

191. Ranaweera and Prabhu 2003.

192. Burnham, Frels, and Mahajan 2003.

193. Status quo bias seems to result from a number of factors. For example, contrary to rational-choice theory, consumers often take past sunk costs into account when making consumption decisions (Samuelson and Zeckhauser 1988, pp. 37–38). Choosing one option and rejecting the other also creates cognitive dissonance, which is reduced by subsequent rationalization that the chosen option is more desirable than it was *ex ante* (Brehm 1956, p. 389). Finally, people tend to regret bad outcomes that are a result of their own action more than bad outcomes that are the result of their inaction, which again leads to a bias for doing nothing (Kahneman and Tversky 1984, pp. 343–344).

194. Trial subscriptions with a low introductory price that automatically convert to a higher price, or other contracts with automatic renewal also exploit the cognitive bias that people tend to overestimate their future willingness to incur the then immediate costs of switching (or terminating the contract) in order to reap the future benefits (i.e., the savings) resulting from switching (or terminating the contract) (DellaVigna and Malmendier 2004, pp. 381–393).

195. In addition, open-access regulations (regulations that require the owners of broadband networks to allow independent ISPs to offer their services over these networks) usually do not protect against cases in which the provider of the underlying physical network infrastructure discriminates against a specific application in all traffic that is running over its network, independent of which ISP the traffic belongs to. This is because open-access regulations usually only require the network provider to treat ISPs in a non-discriminatory way, not to treat applications and content in a non-discriminatory way. A recent case in Canada exemplifies this concern. Bell Canada slowed down all peer-to-peer file-sharing traffic on its network, regardless of which ISP the traffic belonged to. In November 2008, the Canadian regulator subsequently denied an application by the Canadian Association of Internet Providers to order Bell Canada to cease and desist this practice (Anderson 2008a,b).

196. Yoo (2006) argued that singling out specific applications or classes of applications and blocking them is a socially efficient way to manage congestion. Brett

Frischmann and I have taken up this argument (Frischmann and van Schewick 2007). As we show, not only is Yoo's theory based on the false assumption that it is currently impossible to meter subscribers' Internet use; Yoo also neglects the significant social costs associated with the blocking of specific applications to manage congestion.

197. In DSL networks, end users do not share the link between the DSL modem and the Digital Subscriber Line Access Multiplexer (DSLAM), but they share the link from the DSLAM which aggregates data traffic from a number of subscribers onto a single high-speed data link to the ISP. See, e.g., Mervana and Le 2001, pp. 189–197.

198. This is obvious if the network provider has a transit agreement with the other network; in a transit agreement, the smaller network pays a price for data transport that is based on use. Under a peering agreement, the networks usually do not compensate each other for the exchange of traffic. Peering agreements are based on the assumption that both networks will send and receive an equal amount of data. If this assumption does not hold any more, for example because new applications lead to an imbalance between the amount of traffic sent and received, network providers may be required to pay under a peering agreement as well. See Weiss and Shin 2004, pp. 43–46; van der Berg 2008; MIT Communications Futures Program and Cambridge University Communications Research Network Broadband Working Group 2005, pp. 5, 7.

199. The Broadband Working Group of the MIT Communications Futures Program has characterized this as the "Broadband Incentive Problem." See MIT Communications Futures Program and Cambridge University Communications Research Network Broadband Working Group 2005.

200. Eckersley, von Lohmann, and Schoen 2007; Svensson 2007; Schoen 2007b. Comcast stopped using this method of interfering with peer-to-peer file-sharing applications in 2008.

201. See, e.g., Aggarwal et al. 2004, pp. 219–220; Karagiannis, Rodriguez, and Papagiannaki 2005, pp. 63–64, 67–68; Aggarwal, Feldmann, and Scheideler 2007, pp. 31–32.

202. Mennecke 2005; Hellweg 2003.

203. See notes 173–177 above and accompanying text.

204. In particular, the Internet Policy Statement states that "consumers are entitled to access the lawful Internet content of their choice" and "to run applications and use services of their choice, subject to the needs of law enforcement" (Federal Communications Commission 2005a, p. 14988).

205. See, e.g., van Schewick 2008; Frischmann and van Schewick 2007.

206. See, e.g., Yoo 2006. The social costs associated with such a rule are discussed in Frischmann and van Schewick 2007.

207. Free Press and Public Knowledge 2007; Free Press et al. 2007; Federal Communications Commission 2008a.

208. The account in the text is based on the following sources: CBC News 2005; Barrett 2005; OpenNet Initiative 2005; Geist 2005, pp. 5–6; Miller 2005.

209. Barrett 2005.

210. The account in the text is based on the following: Hansell 2006; Olsen 2006; Karr 2006.

211. The account in the text is based on the following: Liptak 2007a,b; Public Knowledge et al. 2007.

212. All quotations are from Jones 2007.

213. For a comprehensive overview of the state of Internet Filtering, a description of the tools and techniques used in Filtering, and detailed regional and country reports based on empirical tests, see Deibert et al. 2008.

214. Discrimination to manage bandwidth or exclude unwanted content does not depend on the network provider offering a competing application.

215. For a similar argument with respect to the profitability of monopoly preservation through exclusionary conduct in new economy markets, if the monopoly is of intellectual property, see Posner 2001, p. 254.

216. The exclusionary conduct hurts independent producers of excluded complementary products in several ways: first, they are excluded from the part of the complementary market that consists of the network provider's Internet-service customers. As a result, they are not able to make any sales in that market. In addition, owing to economies of scale and, potentially, network effects in the production of their products, the exclusion from a part of the market may put them at a competitive disadvantage in the rest of the market as well. In the worst case, they may be forced to exit the complementary market completely. If they had made at least some sales to the network provider's Internet-service customers in the absence of the exclusionary conduct, the exclusion will reduce their profits.

217. Similarly, the network provider may fail to assess the situation correctly and discriminate against or exclude an independent provider of complementary products, even if none of the conditions under which this conduct would be profitable apply. Farrell and Weiser (2003, pp. 114–117) call this problem "incompetent incumbents" and include it in their list of exceptions to their version of the "one monopoly rent" argument.

218. Miller 2007.

219. Ibid.

220. E.g., Christensen 2000. For a full discussion of these reasons, see the discussion in chapter 8 below.

221. On the ability of antitrust law to capture all instances of discrimination that proponents of network neutrality are concerned about, see also van Schewick 2009, pp. 36–37; Frischmann and van Schewick 2007, p. 414, note 119.

222. More precisely, the bandwidth-adjusted transport prices may differ between applications. The following analysis expands on an argument by MacKie-Mason, Shenker, and Varian (1995), who examine the effect of application-blind and application-aware architectures on content provision and content creation, focusing on the ability to select different transport prices for different applications. See also MacKie-Mason, Shenker, and Varian 1996.

223. More precisely, the bandwidth-adjusted transport price is the same for all applications.

224. MacKie-Mason, Shenker, and Varian 1995, p. 7.

225. The difference is similar to the difference between a uniform price and a non-uniform pricing structure. A seller with some degree of market power who can charge different prices to different consumers can capture more consumer surplus than if it had to charge the same price to all customers. See the subsection of this chapter titled "Price Discrimination."

226. The analysis also assumes that all consumers assign the same value to a particular application.

227. See also MacKie-Mason, Shenker, and Varian 1995, pp. 19, 22.

228. Applications for which users' willingness to pay is lower than the general transport price will not be produced in an end-to-end network. See also MacKie-Mason, Shenker, and Varian 1995, p. 7.

229. If the profit-maximizing transport price for an individual application in the discriminatory network is equal to the uniform transport price in the end-to-end network, the remaining surplus is the same in both architectures.

230. Applications for which users' willingness to pay is lower than the general transport price, however, will not be produced in such a network. See MacKie-Mason, Shenker, and Varian 1995, p. 7.

231. It is difficult to find a precise definition that encompasses all types of price discrimination; see, e.g., Tirole 1988, pp. 133–134; Varian 1989, pp. 598–599. For general treatments of price discrimination, see Varian 1989; Tirole 1988, chapter 3; Carlton and Perloff 2005, chapters 9–10. For an introduction to price discrimination in the context of information goods, see Shapiro and Varian 1999, chapters 2 and 3.

232. See, e.g., Carlton and Perloff 2005, p. 294.

233. Price discrimination is also feasible in monopolistically competitive industries, i.e., in industries characterized by the presence of significant product differentiation, relatively free entry and zero long-run profits. See Varian 1989, pp. 641–643.

234. For treatments of second-degree price discrimination, see, e.g., Varian 1989, pp. 611–617; Tirole 1988, pp. 135, 142–152; Carlton and Perloff 2005, chapter 10. For a treatment of second-degree price discrimination in the context of information goods, see Shapiro and Varian 1999, chapter 3.

235. In choosing products and prices, the firm is subject to a self-selection constraint: the firm must design products and prices such that consumers in any group do not prefer a product intended for another group. See, e.g., Tirole 1988, pp. 134–135, 142–162.

236. This strategy is also described by Wu and Lessig (2003, pp. 4, 15) and by Wu (2003a, pp. 151–154). Those authors present evidence for the use of this strategy by broadband operators. (See next note.)

237. Wu (2003a) presents evidence from the year 2001 showing that Comcast, an operator of broadband cable networks, had implemented the discriminatory pricing policy described in the text: customers of Comcast's "basic high-speed Internet service" were not allowed to use virtual private networks. Customers who wanted to use virtual private networks were offered the higher-priced "Comcast @Home Professional product" to which this contractual restriction did not apply. See Wu 2003a, pp. 151–152, 165. After this policy was made public and used as an example of "discriminatory behavior" by broadband cable operators in the debate over network-neutrality regulation, Comcast eliminated the ban on virtual private networks from its subscriber agreements and terms of service in 2003. See Wu 2003a, p. 156; Wu and Lessig 2003, p. 4. For a survey of contractual and technical restrictions on certain classes of applications employed by the ten largest cable operators and the six largest DSL providers in the United States, see Wu 2003a.

238. In general, the welfare effects of second price discrimination are theoretically ambiguous and can only be determined empirically on the basis of detailed knowledge about consumers' preferences and market and cost structures. See, e.g., Tirole 1988, pp. 149, 158; Varian 1989, p. 617. The general analysis of the welfare effects, however, focuses on stand-alone products and considers only allocative or static efficiency. As the text shows, in the case of platform products consisting of a primary product that can be used with various complementary products, price discrimination in the primary product based on the use of specific complementary products may have negative consequences for dynamic efficiency that are not captured by the conventional analysis. For a similar observation, see Wu 2003a, pp. 152–153.

239. Increasing profits is the objective of price discrimination. See, e.g., Carlton and Perloff 2005, pp. 293–94, 338. For a similar argument in the context of restrictions

on home networking that require that home networking equipment be purchased and installed by the cable operator, see Wu and Lessig 2003, p. 8.

240. For a similar argument, see Wu and Lessig 2003, p. 15; Wu 2003a, pp. 168–169.

241. For a similar observation in the context of restrictions on home networking that require that home networking equipment be purchased and installed by the cable operator, see Wu and Lessig 2003, p. 8.

242. Stated differently, at least some of the consumers who are excluded from the market for the blocked application under the discriminatory pricing policy would buy the blocked application under the uniform price for Internet services.

243. MacKie-Mason, Shenker, and Varian (1995, pp. 19, 22) make a similar argument when analyzing the effect of the ability to set different Internet transport prices for different applications on content creators' incentives to innovate.

244. See the references cited in notes c–f to box 6.1. The debate mostly focuses on whether network providers should be allowed to charge application or content providers for better service (e.g., for Quality of Service or higher bandwidth), but some proposals would ban any type of access charges.

245. Economides and Tåg 2007; Ralph 2006; Lee and Wu 2009. Note that applications and content providers pay user fees to their ISP who connects them to the Internet. Similarly, end users pay their ISP for access to the Internet. The providers of the access networks, in turn, compensate the backbone providers connecting the two access networks according to the interconnection agreements between them. In the scenario discussed in the text, the network providers of the end users who use the application or content would charge the providers of application or content for transport over the end users' access networks. For an introduction to the inter-provider compensation mechanisms used in the Internet, see van der Berg 2008.

246. With respect to the following, compare Rochet and Tirole 2003, pp. 1017–1020; Rochet and Tirole 2006, pp. 648–650.

247. Rochet and Tirole 2006, p. 650.

248. See generally Armstrong 2006, pp. 669–670, 677–689. Wright (2002) develops the same result in the context of cellular networks.

249. Ralph 2006. For a similar observation, see Weiser 2008.

250. See generally Wright 2002. For an application of this line of reasoning to the network-neutrality context, see pp. 2–3 of Ralph 2006.

251. See generally Armstrong 2006, pp. 669–670, 677–689; Wright 2002; Wright 2004, pp. 48–49.

Chapter 7

1. On asymmetric bandwidth, see my discussion of the broad version in chapter 2. On network-address translators and firewalls, see my concluding chapter, section "End-to-End Arguments in the Current Internet."

2. See chapter 2, subsection "Costs of the Broad Version of the End-to-End Arguments."

3. In theory, the functionality in the second network would enable the network provider to extract fees from providers of applications or of content by threatening to exclude them unless they pay an access charge. The architecture does not, however, provide the fine-grained accounting and billing infrastructure necessary to implement sophisticated pricing schemes.

4. Moving from the fully controllable to the core-centered architecture may increase the network providers' benefits from application-level innovation: as fewer innovators are able to participate in application-level innovation (in the extreme case, network providers are the only remaining innovators), it is more likely that network providers will have market power over a specific application, which would enable it to increase prices. As a theoretical matter, the effect of market structure on incentives to innovate is ambiguous. Even if the increase in profits from market power increases network providers' incentives to innovate, this effect probably will not offset the significant increase in the cost of developing new applications.

Chapter 8

1. A similar problem is at the heart of the debate about the scope of patents in intellectual-property law. The debate focuses on whether an innovator whose invention has a potential for significant subsequent improvement and variegation should be granted a patent of broad scope that would enable her to control subsequent innovations in the field opened by her invention. The article that started the debate was Kitch 1977. Subsequent contributions include Klemperer 1990; Merges and Nelson 1990; Scotchmer 1991; Merges 1994; Merges and Nelson 1994; Green and Scotchmer 1995; Matutes, Regibeau, and Rockett 1996; Scotchmer 1996; Lemley 1997; and Cohen and Lemley 2001. For an overview of the debate, see Jaffe 2000, pp. 549–552.

2. For an overview of the behavioral and cognitive assumptions underlying neoclassical approaches to innovation and an overview of different models, see Merges and Nelson 1994, pp. 3–5. See also Nelson 2005, pp. 9–38 (discussing neoclassical growth models). For a detailed comparison of neoclassical and evolutionary accounts of innovation, see Lipsey, Carlaw, and Bekar 2005, chapter 2. For some newer neoclassical growth models, see Grossman and Helpman 1990; Romer 1990; Aghion and Howitt 1992. For overviews of neoclassical models of innovation, see Reinganum 1989 and Scotchmer 2004.

3. If actors in these models disagree about the probability of success, this is attributed to asymmetric information. In other words, these models assume that once the different actors share their information, their views regarding the probability of success will be the same. This assumption, called the *common prior assumption* or the *Harsanyi doctrine*, is a fundamental assumption in many neoclassical models dealing with subjective probabilities (Kreps 1990, pp. 110–111).

4. For a prototypical example of the neoclassical approach to innovation described in the text, see the economic models in Dasgupta and Maskin 1987 or those in Farrell, Gilbert, and Katz 2003.

5. Lipsey, Carlaw, and Bekar 2005, p. 30. Newer neoclassical models of patent races acknowledge that different market positions (e.g., incumbent monopolist vs. new entrant) or different cost structures may lead to different incentives to innovate. For an overview of these models, see Gilbert 1989 or Reinganum 1989.

6. See Dasgupta and Maskin 1987.

7. See Kitch 1977, pp. 276, 278–279.

8. See Nelson and Winter 1977, p. 47; Nelson and Winter 1982, pp. 389–390; North 1990, pp. 80–82; Merges and Nelson 1994, p. 6; Rosenberg 1994, pp. 87–108; Rosenberg 1996; Cohen and Malerba 2001. On the link between the end-to-end architecture of the Internet and evolutionary theories of innovation, see Wu and Lessig 2003, pp. 5–7; Wu 2003a, pp. 145–146; Wu 2004, section II.A. Researchers working on the "open innovation" paradigm have used arguments similar to the ones described in the text to highlight the value to individual firms of using not only internal, but also external sources of innovation. See, e.g., Chesbrough 2003, 2006 and Chesbrough, Vanhaverbeke, and West 2006.

9. See Rosenberg 1996, pp. 334–336; Nelson 1991, pp. 64–70; Nelson 2005, pp. 11–12. (These sources all criticize new neoclassical growth models.)

10. See Rosenberg 1996; Holbrook et al. 2000; Shane 2000; Murmann 2003; Nelson 2005; Greenstein 2007b. The type of uncertainty described in the text is also called *Knightian uncertainty*. See Knight 1971; Rosenberg 1996, p. 340; Lipsey, Carlaw, and Bekar 2005, pp. 29–32; Nelson 2005, pp. 11, 21.

11. See Lipsey, Carlaw, and Bekar 2005, pp. 29–32, 44, 72–73. Scholars of innovation often model decision making under the type of uncertainty described in the text as a heuristic search (e.g., Nelson and Winter 1982) or with models of bounded rationality (e.g., North 1990, pp. 80–82; Nelson 2005, p. 37). However, models based on rational-choice theory can reach the same result by allowing the actors that have access to the same information to have different prior probability distributions over the success of different innovations, i.e., different subjective beliefs about the probability of success (e.g., Scotchmer 2004, pp. 56, 59–61).

12. See Nelson and Winter 1982, pp. 28, 61, 186–187; Merges and Nelson 1994, pp. 5–6.

13. See Nelson and Winter 1982, pp. 186–187, 389; Merges and Nelson 1994, p. 6; MacKie-Mason, Shenker, and Varian 1996, p. 215; Cohen and Klepper 1992; Cohen and Malerba 2001.

14. See Nelson and Winter 1977, p. 47; Nelson and Winter 1982, pp. 389–390; North 1990, pp. 80–92; Merges and Nelson 1994, p. 6; Rosenberg 1996, pp. 352–353.

15. See Dosi and Nelson 1994, p. 158: "But when put this way, rational choice theory would seem applicable to contexts to which the actors can be presumed familiar, and evolutionary theoretic arguments can be understood as an attempt to deal with situations where this presumption does not seem applicable. In particular, evolutionary theory can be argued to be needed for analyses of behavior in contexts that involve significant elements of novelty, so that it cannot be presumed that good responses already have been learned, but rather that they are still to be learned. . . . This line of argument would appear to preserve for neoclassical theory the analysis of decisionmaking in situations that are relatively stable and actions repetitive." See also Rosenberg 1996, pp. 352–353; Lipsey, Carlaw, and Bekar 2005, pp. 72–73.

16. See Boudreau, Lacetera, and Lakhani 2008.

17. See the discussion later in this subsection.

18. E.g., Kihlstrom and Laffont 1979.

19. E.g., Kirzner 1997; Shane 2000; Shane and Venkataraman 2000; Sarasvathy et al. 2003.

20. E.g., Rosenberg 1996.

21. The following account is based on pp. 83–111 of Abbate 1999.

22. Cohen 2002, pp. 3–4, 26, 31, 64, 74.

23. Livingston 2007, p. 68.

24. PayPal's origins can be traced to two different companies: Confinity (founded in December 1998 by Max Levchin, Peter Thiel, and Luke Nosek) and X.com (founded in March 1999 by Elon Musk). The two companies merged in March 2000, focusing on e-mail payments under the name paypal. The company later changed its name to PayPal. See Livingston 2007 and Denton 2007.

25. For qualitative studies of specific innovations or industries, see Holbrook et al. 2000; Shane 2000; Murmann 2003. For theoretical analyses, see Merges and Nelson 1994; Ardichvili, Cardozo, and Ray 2003; Lipsey, Carlaw, and Bekar 2005.

26. Afuah and Tucci 2001, p. 259.

27. Bronson 1999, pp. 78–79; Livingston 2007, pp. 18–19.

28. King 2002; Honan 2008.

29. Roth 2004; Maney 2006.

30. Charny 2003.

31. Livingston (2007) provides ample evidence of such behavior.

32. Spector 2000, pp. 37, 47–48, 64.

33. Cohen 2002, p. 49.

34. See Christensen 2000, pp. 128–130.

35. Yahoo Finance 2008b. (Again, in the United States a billion is a thousand million, i.e., 10^9.)

36. Yahoo Finance 2008a.

37. Helft 2006; Spolsky 2003; Stephenson 2005.

38. More formally, if success is not guaranteed, increasing the number of attempts may increase the likelihood of success. This fact is well known from probability theory. For example, assume that the probability that an approach will be successful is δ for all approaches. Let n be the number of independent approaches to the same problem. Then the probability that at least one approach will be successful is $1 - (1 - \delta)^n$, which increases with n, the number of approaches (MacKie-Mason, Shenker, and Varian 1995, p. 20). Similarly, the more independent approaches, the higher the expected quality of the winner. This expectation too is familiar from probability theory. (See chapter 4 above.) This effect has been confirmed by empirical studies (Cohen and Malerba 2001; Leiponen and Helfat 2005). Although earlier research in economics predicts that an increase in the number of agents may reduce the level of effort incurred by the individual agent, the increase in the quality of the best result resulting from the parallel search effect seems to outweigh the effect of individual reductions in effort at least for complex problems. For a theoretical model, see Terwiesch and Xu 2008. For empirical confirmation of this result, see Boudreau, Lacetera, and Lakhani 2008.

39. Spillovers are uncompensated benefits that one person's activity provides to another (Frischmann and Lemley 2006, p. 102). That innovators need to engage in economic experiments to reduce the business uncertainty regarding what consumers want and what business models may be appropriate has been emphasized by Rosenberg (1994), by Stern (2005), and by Greenstein (2007a,b). Greenstein, in particular, highlights how actors learn not only from their own economic experiments, but also from competitors' successes and failures.

40. The ability to monitor experiments by others may differ depending on the type of experiment. For example, innovators may be able to keep technical experiments performed "in house" secret, but consumers' reaction to a product's feature or price or the success of a firm's business model usually is visible to other market participants, at least to some degree.

41. See the qualitative studies by Holbrook et al. (2000) and Shane (2000).

42. Spolsky 2000; Stephenson 2005; Kraus 2005b.

43. Cohen 2002, pp. 44, 59, 72.

44. Spector 2000, pp. 1–70. Amazon.com was not the first online bookstore. Computer Literacy Bookstores, Inc., a small independent bookstore in Silicon Valley that specialized in books for computer engineers and scientists, had set up a website and started selling books via e-mail in 1991 (Spector 2000, pp. 21–22). Book Stacks Unlimited, an online bookstore that had been founded by Charles Stack, a lawyer who had become a software engineer, had started selling books online through a bulletin board service in 1992 and launched an online bookstore in October 1994 (Spector 2000, pp. 29; Klein 1999; Rayport and Louie 2001, p. 5).

45. Barnes & Noble became the exclusive bookseller on AOL's marketplace in March 1997 and opened an online store open for the general public in May 1997 (Quistagaard 1997a,b; Knecht 1996). In an interview, Stephen Riggio, CEO of Barnes & Noble, claimed that his company had followed the evolution of Internet bookstores from the beginning (Schrage 1997).

46. Knecht 1996; Rayport and Louie 1998.

47. The account of Microsoft's reaction to the Internet is based on Rebello, Cortese, and Hof 1996a,b.

48. Berners-Lee and Fischetti 2000, pp. 28–30, 49.

49. Battelle 2005, pp. 82–84; 102; Vise and Malseed 2005, pp. 40–43, 85–86; Livingston 2007, pp. 132–133.

50. In addition, a rich literature in economics analyzes how incentives to innovate may differ between an incumbent monopolist and a new entrant. For an overview, see Reinganum 1989.

51. These assumptions are at the core of the resource-based theory of the firm and the dynamic capabilities framework. On the resource-based theory of the firm, see Wernerfelt 1984; Barney 1991; Peteraf 1993. On the dynamic capabilities framework, see Teece, Pisano, and Shuen 1997.

52. See Christensen and Rosenbloom 1995.

53. This argument has been advanced by K. B. Clark (1985) and is supported by empirical evidence (Tushman and Anderson 1986, 1990; K. B. Clark 1988).

54. For a detailed exposition of this argument and an application to the semiconductor photolithographic alignment equipment industry, see Henderson and Clark 1990. For other industry studies supporting this view, see the pointers to the literature on pp. 236–237 of Christensen and Rosenbloom 1995.

55. This theory has been developed by Christensen. For a detailed exposition of the theory, see Christensen 2000. For a short overview, see Christensen and Rosenbloom 1995. The theory is based on substantial evidence. In particular, evidence from a wide variety of industries supports the theory that new entrants have an advantage over established firms in perceiving and exploiting the value of disruptive technologies. This theory has been successfully applied to explain why new entrants overtook market leadership from established firms in the hard disk drive industry, the mechanical excavator industry, the steel industry, the retail industry, the printer industry, the personal digital assistant industry, the electric motor control industry, the motorcycle industry, the logic circuitry industry, the computer industry, the accounting software industry, and the insulin industry. See Christensen 2000. For alternative theories explaining when and why established firms may find it difficult to react to new developments, see Kaplan and Henderson 2005; Barnett and Pontikes 2008.

56. Hedlund 2005.

57. See Christensen and Rosenbloom 1995, pp. 238–242; Christensen 2000, p. 98.

58. See Christensen 2000, pp. xxii–xxiii.

59. See ibid., pp. 44–45.

60. See ibid., pp. 101–104.

61. See ibid., pp. 79–84.

62. See ibid., pp. 128–130.

63. Ibid., pp. 82, 104, 155–156.

64. See ibid., pp. xxi–xxii, 143–159.

65. See ibid., pp. 44–45. Christensen (ibid., p. xv) writes: "Most new technologies foster improve product performance. I call these sustaining technologies. Some sustaining technologies can be discontinuous or radical in character, while others are of an incremental nature. What all sustaining technologies have in common is that they improve the performance of established products, along the dimensions of performance that mainstream customers in major markets have historically valued."

66. On disruptive technologies, see ibid., p. xv.

67. See ibid., pp. 121, 128–130.

68. See ibid., pp. 143–159.

69. In addition, incumbent providers may have been more interested in protecting their existing dominant positions and highly profitable margins against competition by lower margin competitors. See the discussion in chapter 6.

70. Christensen 2000, p. 55.

71. Ibid., pp. 70–71, 101–117.

72. Ibid., p. 132.

73. Ibid., pp. 128–130.

74. This definition is taken from p. 676 of Kortum and Lerner 2000.

75. For an in-depth treatment of theoretical and empirical research on venture capital, see Gompers and Lerner 2004. For a more practical treatment, see Gompers and Lerner 2001a. For a short overview with pointers to the literature, see Gompers and Lerner 2001b.

76. See Christensen 2000, pp. 82–84, 104; Scherer 2001, p. 20.

77. See Gompers and Lerner 2004, p. 161; Gompers and Lerner 2001a, pp. 53–58.

78. In recent years, successful funds have demanded higher proportions. For an overview of the compensation structure used in limited partnership venture funds, the most prominent organizational structure of venture-capital funds, see Gompers and Lerner 2004, chapter 5; Gompers and Lerner 2001a, pp. 100–102.

79. See Aoki 2001, pp. 368–369.

80. For venture capitalists, this incentive structure may even lead to excessive risk-taking. For some of the mechanisms used to mitigate this threat, see Gompers and Lerner 2001a, p. 106.

81. Scherer 2001, pp. 15–19, 20. Aoki (2001, chapter 14) arrives at a similar conclusion on the basis of a game-theoretic model.

82. For a theoretical deduction of this insight from agency theory and an empirical study supporting it, see Gompers and Lerner 2004, chapter 8.

83. Ibid., pp. 164, 177–183.

84. For a historical breakdown of venture capital of investment by industry and stage of development, see Gompers and Lerner 2001a, pp. 72–73, table 4-5. See also Gompers and Lerner's analysis of a random sample of 794 firms that received venture-capital financing between January 1961 and July 1992 (2004, pp. 177–183).

85. See Gompers and Lerner 2002, p. 26.

86. National Venture Capital Association 2008, p. 27, figure 3.16.

87. Ibid., p. 30, figure 3.22.

88. For an overview of other sources of financing, see Gompers and Lerner 2001a, pp. 9–11.

89. See ibid., p. 62.

90. See ibid., pp. 21–23.

91. Moukheiber 1996; Netscape 1995a–d.

92. In an empirical study of 170 young high-technology firms in Silicon Valley, Hellmann and Puri (2002) find that companies that obtain venture capital are more likely or faster to professionalize along these dimensions.

93. Battelle 2005, pp. 134–137; Vise and Malseed 2005, pp. 103–109.

94. Heilemann 2005; Vise and Malseed 2005; Reingold 2008.

95. See Gompers and Lerner 2004, p. 355.

96. On Netscape, see Gompers and Lerner 2001a, p. 22. On eBay, see Afuah and Tucci 2001, pp. 286–287; Cohen 2002, pp. 73–77.

97. Hellmann and Puri (2000) make this finding using a hand-selected data set of 173 start-up companies in Silicon Valley.

98. Gompers and Lerner 2001a, pp. 62–64.

99. Gompers and Lerner 2004, chapter 20; Gompers and Lerner 2001a, pp. 64–66.

100. On Adobe, see Scherer 2001, p. 11.

101. On eBay, see Afuah and Tucci 2001, pp. 286–287.

102. According to Gompers and Lerner (2001a, pp. 5, 70), these companies were funded by venture capitalists. Gompers and Lerner do not discuss Adobe and eBay.

103. Gompers and Lerner 2001a, p. 70.

104. Lerner 2000, p. 204.

105. See Kortum and Lerner 2000. The article focuses on manufacturing industries, since survey evidence suggests that the reliance on patenting as a means of appropriating new technological discoveries as opposed to, e.g., trade secrecy or first-mover advantages is much higher in these industries. Patenting is thus likely to be a better indicator of the rate of technological innovation in the manufacturing sector (Kortum and Lerner 2000, p. 678). For an accessible discussion of the findings of this study, see Gompers and Lerner 2001a, pp. 74–77.

106. Gompers and Lerner (2001a, p. 77) summarize the results of Kortum and Lerner (2000) this way: "Given the continued rise in venture funding since 1992, and assuming that the potency of venture funding remained consistent with the measured impact of venture capital and patenting rates, the calibrations imply that, by 1999, venture capital investment accounted for about 18% of US innovative activity."

107. The following account is based on Gompers and Lerner 2001a and Gompers and Lerner 2000.

108. On eBay, see Cohen 2002, p. 74. On Skype, see Rangar 2005. On Google, see the subsection of the present chapter titled "The Value of Innovation by New Entrants."

109. The seminal work in this area is von Hippel 1988.

110. See von Hippel 1988, pp. 3–4; von Hippel 2005, p. 3. Depending on its functional relationship to the innovation, an innovator can be a manufacturer with respect to some innovations and a user with respect to others. For example, if Google improves its search-engine algorithm, we would categorize it as a manufacturer, as it profits from the search engine by making it available to users. In contrast, if Google develops software to better manage its server farms, we would consider it a user.

111. Livingston 2007, pp. 233–234.

112. Grimmer 2006; Livingston 2007; Park 2008.

113. Spicer 1998.

114. See Luethje, Herstatt, and von Hippel 2005, pp. 962–964.

115. See von Hippel and von Krogh 2003, p. 214; von Hippel 1998, p. 630; Luethje, Herstatt, and von Hippel 2005, p. 953. In a Web-based survey that was administered to 684 software developers in 287 free or open-source software projects, 58.7% reported use of the output they produce for work or non work-related needs as one of their three most important motivations to innovate. See Lakhani and Wolf 2005. For an empirical study showing higher satisfaction of users of the open-source Apache Web server software who customized their software compared to users who did not customize, see Franke and von Hippel 2003, pp. 1209–1210.

116. For a short overview of the theoretical literature on intrinsic and extrinsic motivation, see Lakhani and Wolf 2005, pp. 4–5. In a Web-based survey that was administered to 684 software developers in 287 free or open-source software projects, 44.9% ranked "project code is intellectually stimulating to write" as one of the top three motivations. 41.8% were motivated by the improvement in programming skills resulting from their involvement in the project. See Lakhani and Wolf 2005.

117. See chapter 4 above.

118. For a more detailed analysis of the opportunity costs incurred by programmers working on an open-source software development project, see Lerner and Tirole 2002, p. 213.

119. Being able to use the resulting software often seems to have been the initial motivation. In addition, improving the application often involved research, which

was fun. During the time of the ARPANET, people who developed successful applications were highly regarded, so the desire to improve their reputation may have motivated these researchers as well. See Partridge 2008a.

120. Berners-Lee and Fischetti 2000, pp. 16–19. His idea for the World Wide Web emerged from Enquire, a simpler program that Berners-Lee had written during an earlier employment as a contractor at CERN to help him keep track of relationships among people, equipment, and programs. Foreshadowing the websites and links of the World Wide Web, Enquire made it possible to store pieces of information and to establish links between them. See Berners-Lee and Fischetti 2000, pp. 10–12.

121. In July 2008, Apache's market share was 49%, Microsoft's was 36%, and Google's was 10% (Netcraft 2008).

122. Moody 2001, pp. 130–139; chromatic and Sheppard 2008. According to the PHP Group (2008), "PHP/FI was created by Rasmus Lerdorf in 1995, initially as a simple set of Perl scripts for tracking accesses to his online resume," and Lerdorf "named this set of scripts 'Personal Home Page Tools.'" Yukihiro Matsumoto, developer of Ruby, recalled: "I wanted a scripting language that was more powerful than Perl, and more object-oriented than Python. That's why I decided to design my own language." (Stewart 2001)

123. For a short introduction to the history and characteristics of open-source software, see von Hippel and von Krogh 2003, pp. 209–212; Lerner and Tirole 2002, pp. 200–207. For views on the open-source movement from some important participants, see DiBona, Ockman, and Stone 1999; Raymond 1999.

124. For biographies of the members of the core developer group of Ruby on Rails, see Ruby on Rails 2008.

125. The average level of respondents' agreement with that statement was 4.7 on a scale of 5. See von Hippel 2007, p. 297.

126. Lakhani and Wolf 2005.

127. Owing to these characteristics of open-source software, a particular open-source software program and open-source tools for software design and testing constitute a complete tool kit for user innovation for users of this program in the sense described by von Hippel (2001). This observation is made by Franke and von Hippel (2003, p. 1204) with respect to the Apache Web server software.

128. For unfamiliar users, the costs of understanding and modifying an existing code base may be significant. For such users, it may be more cost-effective to use sub-optimal software or to hire someone else to learn and modify the code for them.

129. In making this make-or-buy decision, the user faces a trade-off that is well known from the literature on make-or-buy decisions with respect to software (e.g.,

Messerschmitt 2000, pp. 286–278). Buying the product from the manufacturer is usually less costly, since the development costs are spread over a number of sales; however, the manufacturer's product is standardized to meet the needs of the average user and may leave some of the user's needs unserved. For example, SAP R/3 (a standardized software for business applications with extensive options for customization) is said to meet about 80% of most users' needs (Bancroft, Seip, and Sprengel 1998, p. 141). In contrast, when making the software itself, the user bears the complete development costs and the development risk, but gets software that exactly meets its needs. In this situation, the user will often prefer to buy from the manufacturer. This is not an option, however, if there is no standardized product available in the market or the existing products are not satisfactory. As will be set out below, such a situation may well occur for applications supporting specific needs of an individual user or a small group of users. In this situation, the ability of the user to develop the innovation herself becomes highly relevant. For an analysis of a user's decision whether to innovate herself or to buy the product from a manufacturer of custom products, see von Hippel 2005, chapter 4.

130. See Luethje, Herstatt, and von Hippel 2005, pp. 963–964.

131. For a short overview of common approaches to this problem and pointers to the literature, see e.g., Jeppesen 2005, pp. 349–351.

132. The term "sticky information" was coined by von Hippel (1994). For an overview of the reasons for information stickiness, see von Hippel 1994, pp. 430–432; von Hippel 1998, pp. 630–631.

133. See von Hippel 1998, pp. 630–631; von Hippel 2001, pp. 248–249.

134. See von Hippel 1998, p. 630; Franke and von Hippel 2003, pp. 1199–1202.

135. Of course, there may be small markets whose consumers have a very high willingness to pay.

136. See Franke and von Hippel 2003, pp. 1199–1202. Benkler (2000, p. 576) describes the same phenomenon in the context of professional content provision.

137. Franke and von Hippel 2003, pp. 1199, 1201.

138. Based on surveys of literature on market segmentation studies, Franke and von Hippel (2003, pp. 1199, 1201–1202) find that current practice in market segmentation studies may leave about half of customers' needs within a segment unaddressed. Intuitively, one might expect the problem to be less profound in software, where the costs of coding additional functionality may not be very high, which may make it easier to respond to individual customers' needs. Adding additional functionality increases the complexity of the product, which considerably increases the amount of testing and support. Because most of the cost of software comes from testing, debugging, and customer maintenance (according to a study by Cusumano (1991, p. 65), testing, debugging, and maintenance account for 82% of the cost of

software), software vendors have the same incentive to limit the number of additional features and focus on the need of the average consumer as the manufacturer innovators of physical products.

139. According to von Hippel (1988, p. 107), lead users are defined by two characteristics: "1. Lead users face needs that will be general in a marketplace, but they face them months or years before the bulk of that marketplace encounters them, and 2. Lead users are positioned to benefit significantly by obtaining a solution to those needs." On lead users in general, see ibid., chapter 8.

140. See the subsection of this chapter titled "The Value of Innovation by New Entrants." See also von Hippel 2007, p. 302.

141. See Franke and von Hippel 2003, pp. 1200–1201. In two surveys of market segmentation studies described in the literature, the authors found that the current market segmentation techniques leave unaddressed, on average, 54% (survey 1) and 46% (survey 2) of the total variation of customer needs within a segment.

142. For a detailed analysis of the welfare effects of user innovation in the context of the economic literature on product diversity, innovation, and welfare, see Henkel and von Hippel 2005, pp. 76–81. For a complementary view on the importance of user involvement in innovation, see Bar and Munk Riis 2000.

143. Grimmer 2006; Livingston 2007; Park 2008.

144. The literature on free revealing by users usually defines free revealing as follows: "When we say that an innovator 'freely reveals' proprietary information, we mean that all existing and potential intellectual property rights to that information are voluntarily given up by that innovator and all interested parties are given access to it—the information becomes a public good. Thus, we define the free revealing of information by a possessor as the granting of access to all interested agents without imposition of any direct payment." (Harhoff, Henkel, and von Hippel 2003, pp. 1753–1754) In the case of the Internet, this definition is not fully accurate—software is usually released under a license that describes the restrictions associated with the software.

145. After Bloglines continued to grow, Fletcher decided to focus on it full-time. In February 2005, Bloglines was acquired by Ask Jeeves (Livingston 2007, pp. 233–236). That user innovators end up commercializing their innovation once it becomes successful is not uncommon on the Internet. Other examples of this phenomenon are the blogging software Movable Type (ibid., pp. 405–417) or the online bookmarking service del.icio.us (ibid., pp. 223–232).

146. The source code is usually not made available without any restrictions, but released under a license which specifies what exactly programmers are allowed to do with the code. For an overview of different licenses and an empirical study regarding their use, see Lerner and Tirole 2005b.

147. Berners-Lee and Fischetti 2000, pp. 32, 50–53, 80.

148. Grimmer 2006.

149. SourceForge.net 2008.

150. See von Hippel and von Krogh 2003, pp. 212–213.

151. See von Hippel 2007, p. 306.

152. For a more detailed analysis of the positive welfare effects of free revealing by users, see Henkel and von Hippel 2005, pp. 81–82.

153. Park 2008; Slater 2008.

154. Netcraft 2008. The Netcraft survey includes parked domains (i.e., Internet domains that point to a server, but that are not actively used as websites) and may therefore overestimate the number of websites (Varghese 2003).

155. Net Applications 2008.

156. This includes commercial versions of Sendmail that are distributed by the company Sendmail, Inc. (Sendmail 2008).

157. Lerner and Tirole 2002, p. 210.

158. Lerner and Tirole 2005a, pp. 102–107.

159. In the context of the patent scope debate, this argument is made by Kitch (1977, pp. 277–278).

160. In the core-centered architecture, the number of concurrent application projects is limited for reasons independent of the usual reasons for the limits of internal organization. See box 8.8.

161. For an overview of the factors that may impede or prevent a contractual solution, see, for example, Lemley 1997, pp. 1048–1067, in the context of the patent scope debate. For an analysis of the conditions under which innovators may prefer selling their innovation to an incumbent in the "market for ideas" to competing with the incumbent in the product market, see Gans and Stern 2000; Gans, Hsu, and Stern 2002; Gans and Stern 2003.

162. To see this, assume that the probability that one decision maker will not approve the innovation is ß, with $0 < ß < 1$, and that the number of decision makers is n. In order for the project to be realized, all decision makers must approve the project. In this case, the probability that at least one decision maker will not approve the project, and, consequently, the project will not be realized, is $1 - (1 - ß)^n$, which increases with n, the number of innovators.

163. Livingston 2007, pp. 111–125.

164. See Christensen and Raynor 2003, chapters 7 and 8; Amram and Kulatilaka 1999; Chesbrough 2003, pp. 12–13.

165. See Nelson and Winter 1982, pp. 389–390; Merges and Nelson 1994, p. 6; Rosenberg 1996, p. 353.

166. MacKie-Mason, Shenker, and Varian 1995, p. 21.

167. See, e.g., the empirical studies on the distribution of gains for new drug chemical entities and investments in high-technology start-ups reported by Scherer (2001) or the empirical study on the returns to investments in the software industry by Lerner (2002). The empirical study on the return to invention by independent inventors by Åstebro (2003) arrives at similar findings.

168. For a similar argument in the context of peer production, see Benkler 2002, p. 423.

169. Rosenberg 1994; Greenstein 2007a,b.

170. Network providers will exclude such an application, if the reduction in profit in the Internet-service market due to the reduction in application variety (which is also dependent on factors such as switching costs and the network providers' ability to use discrimination instead of exclusion) is offset by the increase in profit in the application market.

171. Thus, although Apple is not acting as a network provider here, it is acting as a central gatekeeper that controls which applications users can deploy.

172. Arthur 2008; Hadar 2008; Manjoo 2008; Wilson 2008.

173. On PayPal, see the discussion early in this chapter. On Flickr, see box 8.3.

174. See note 4 to chapter 7.

Chapter 9

1. The analysis in this paragraph and in the next 11 paragraphs draws on pp. 383–386 of van Schewick 2007.

2. See Reinganum 1989; Tirole 1988, pp. 399–400; Katz 2002, pp. 329–331.

3. For an overview of this literature, see Reinganum 1989. For a particular example of such a model, see Dasgupta and Maskin 1987.

4. See Tirole 1988, pp. 399–400.

5. See Mansfield et al. 1977; Jones and Williams 1998.

6. Lichtman 2000, p. 615.

7. This observation is made, in different contexts, by Bresnahan and Trajtenberg (1995) and Lichtman (2000).

8. See Farrell and Katz 2000, p. 414 and appendix; Bresnahan and Trajtenberg 1995, p. 94.

9. For some important refinements to this statement, see Farrell and Katz 2000. As Farrell and Katz demonstrate, integration between two firms that each are the sole supplier of a component that is complementary with the other does not necessarily increase the incentives to invest in socially valuable research and development. (See ibid., appendix.) In addition, they show that integration between a monopoly supplier of one component with one of several suppliers of a complementary component may inefficiently lower independent suppliers' incentives to innovate.

10. On platform products, see Bresnahan and Greenstein 2001 and Lichtman 2000.

11. See the explanation in this paragraph and the next five. For an alternative explanation of how the Internet contributes to economic growth, see Crawford 2007, part II.

12. Jones (2002, p. 229) attributes this percentage of growth to "a rise in the stock of ideas produced by researchers throughout the G-5 countries." See also Helpman's (2004, pp. 47–48) description of Jones's results.

13. On general-purpose technologies, see Bresnahan and Trajtenberg 1995, Bresnahan and Greenstein 2001, and Helpman 1998.

14. See Bresnahan and Trajtenberg 1995 and Helpman and Trajtenberg 1998b.

15. See Bresnahan and Trajtenberg 1995, pp. 86–88; Bresnahan and Greenstein 2001, p. 96.

16. Bresnahan and Greenstein 2001, p. 97.

17. For empirical evidence suggesting that the US productivity acceleration observed in the mid to late 1990s is linked to information technology, see Brynjolfsson 1996, Oliner and Sichel 2000, Jorgenson 2001, and Jorgenson, Ho, and Stiroh 2008. For a more critical statement, see Gordon 2000. For an overview of the debate, see Litan and Rivlin 2001, pp. 12–17.

18. See David 1990. For similar explanations, see Brynjolfsson and Hitt 2000, Bresnahan and Greenstein 2001, Brynjolfsson and Hitt 2003, and Basu and Fernald 2007. Owing to the time and cost needed for co-invention to take place, delay between the time of investment in a general-purpose technology and the time when its effect on economic growth can be measured may be a general feature of general-purpose-technology-based growth. See Helpman and Trajtenberg 1998a,b.

19. See Harris 1998.

20. Current ways of measuring economic growth may underestimate the economic value created by the Internet. As Brynjolfsson and Saunders (2009) point out, traditional measures of output (which in turn are used for gross domestic product and productivity accounting) do not adequately capture the value created by information technology and the Internet for two reasons: First, the gross domestic product

generally does not include economic activity that takes place outside the market, or market transactions in used goods and services. As a result, applications or content that are made available online for free (e.g., Wikipedia or search engines) do not count as output for the gross domestic product. The same applies for applications or services that facilitate transactions in used goods (e.g., eBay or Amazon's market for used books). (See ibid., pp. 21–25, 91–93, 120–121.) Second, traditional measures of input and output do not adequately capture the value created by "new products, quality improvements, increased product variety, [and] improved timeliness" (ibid., p. 122). Research that attempts to quantify the value of consumer surplus from specific products or online markets indicates that this value is huge. However, it does not appear in the gross domestic product. For example, studies have shown that the value to consumers of greater variety and choice in the online book market is about a billion dollars; that the estimated total value of consumer surplus from transactions on eBay was about $7 billion in 2003; or that the overall increase in consumer surplus from Amazon's used book markets was about $67 million per year. (See ibid., pp. 25–38, 109–115, 120–122.)

21. For a similar observation, see Litan and Rivlin 2001, pp. 104–107.

22. See also Frischmann 2005. Frischmann's work on infrastructure has fundamentally shaped my thinking on this issue. According to Frischmann, infrastructure resources are general-purpose resources that generate value primarily as inputs "into a wide range of goods and services, including private goods, public goods and nonmarket goods." For the full definition, see ibid., p. 956.

23. My analysis focuses on the possibilities afforded by these applications. It makes a claim about the Internet's potential which may or may not be realized. It is not meant as a description of current reality. In reality, differences in class, socioeconomic status, race, literacy or geographic location may result in a much more hierarchical and less open environment than the one described in the text (see Barney 2000; Hindman 2008).

24. In Internet policy debates, some scholars criticize other researchers' focus on application innovation as too narrowly focused on economic issues. The criticism seems to neglect that applications are necessary to enable users to create value from the Internet in all areas of society. Thus, a focus on application innovation does not automatically imply a focus on economic effects only.

25. Benkler 2006, chapter 10; Boase et al. 2006; Griffith and Fox 2007; Lenhart 2009.

26. Benkler 2006, pp. 129–355. The list in the text cites from a similar list by Benkler (ibid., p. 2).

27. This story is more complicated than it appears in the text. As the "long tail" literature has shown, lower costs of producing and distributing information goods, the ability to offer a much larger number of products online than is possible in

conventional stores, and lower search costs have made it possible to create and offer consumers access to much greater product variety online than was possible before the Internet. Thus, applications such as search engines or product marketplaces may create value not just by enabling people to find what they want, but also by enabling more product variety (Anderson 2006; Brynjolfsson, Hu, and Smith 2006; Brynjolfsson, Hu, and Simester 2006). Empirical research suggests that the value of increased product variety online may be even larger than the value resulting from lower prices online, see Brynjolfsson, Hu, and Smith 2003.

28. For an attempt to describe the externalities associated with speech more generally, see Frischmann 2008, pp. 310–321.

29. Mercurio 2002.

30. For descriptions of these cases and others, see Drezner and Farrell 2008, pp. 2–6.

31. Farrell and Drezner 2008, pp. 23–27.

32. Mutz 2006.

33. According to Frischmann (2005), Internet users create these externalities when they engage in the creation of public and non-market goods.

34. For a similar description of the role of technology, see Benkler 2006, pp. 16–18; Lipsey, Carlaw, and Bekar 2005, pp. 16–19.

35. See Balkin 2004; Balkin 2008; Benkler 2006; Fisher 1988; Fisher 2001; Lessig 2001; Lessig 2004; Lessig 2008a.

36. On how to best get users to internalize at least some of the negative externalities created by their uses, and on the effect such measures may have on the positive externalities created by users, see Frischmann and van Schewick 2007, part II.

37. The cost of adopting new uses of the general-purpose technology contributes to the costs of co-invention.

38. Benkler 2006; Balkin 2004, 2008; Fisher 1988, 2001.

39. It may be possible to work around this limitation if the user can upload his information product to a server that makes the work available to others. However, even uploading long text, photos or video once is more difficult and time-consuming with small upstream bandwidth than with symmetric bandwidth.

40. For a detailed exposition of this argument, see Frischmann 2005. For a shorter summary, see Frischmann and van Schewick 2007.

41. Strictly speaking, applying the broad version only ensures user choice in a deployment context in which users control the end hosts. See note 118 to chapter 2 and accompanying text.

42. Others point out that if the denial of service attack is intended to overwhelm a specific end host by sending more traffic than this host can process, or by overloading the link to the end host, stopping the attack requires stopping the traffic before it reaches the end host, which may require stopping it in the network.

43. Zittrain 2008.

44. See the section titled "Effect of Differences in Control over Deployment" in chapter 8 above. See also Gillett et al. 2001 and Zittrain 2008, chapter 5 and pp. 162–168.

45. Zittrain 2008, pp. 163–167. See also Zittrain 2009.

46. Zittrain (2008, pp. 164–165) ascribes this requirement to "end-to-end theory," criticizing those who "cling to a categorical end-to-end approach." Although Zittrain uses a slightly different terminology ("end-to-end theory"), he seems to be referring to the (broad version of the) end-to-end arguments (ibid., pp. 164–165 and note 24). In this case, his description of the broad version is overly broad. For an interpretation similar to mine, see Reed 2009b. Ultimately, the results of Zittrain's approach (he suggests replacing "strict loyalty to end-to-end neutrality" with "a new generativity principle, a rule that asks that any modifications to the Internet's design or to the behavior of ISPs be made where they will do the least harm to generative possibilities" —2008, p. 165) may be similar to the results of the trade-off I suggest below.

47. See also Reed 2009b.

48. See also Reed 2009b.

49. Whether distributed denial of service can be identified and stopped only in the network is subject to debate. For example, Stavrou et al. (2005) propose an approach that, according to them, would work completely on end hosts. Gligor (2005) describes denial of service attacks that can only be mitigated at the end hosts. For an overview of solutions that require support from the network, see Xiaowei, Whetherall, and Anderson 2005, p. 242.

50. Blumenthal and Clark 2001, p. 80 (citing personal communication with Jerome Saltzer).

51. Reed, Saltzer, and Clark 1998, p. 69. See also Saltzer, Reed, and Clark 1984, pp. 282–283; Bradner 2006, p. 77. The latter two sources discuss what I call the narrow version of the end-to-end arguments.

52. One may wonder whether implementing such a function in the network may be justified by the broad version itself. If implementing the function solely at the end points does not provide "effective" security in practice, one could argue that the function cannot be completely and correctly implemented at the end hosts alone. Under such an interpretation, "completely and correctly implemented" would refer not only to technical correctness (the traditional interpretation), but would also refer to the effectiveness of the solution in practice. Broadening the

interpretation of "completely and correctly implemented" in this way, however, replaces a relatively clear criterion (the technical correctness of the solution) with a criterion that is open to debate. Such an interpretation may have unwanted side effects by broadening the range of functions that could be implemented in the network even in cases that are unrelated to security, and may create unnecessary debates about "effectiveness in practice." In contrast, the solution advanced in the text (allowing deviations from the broad version case by case on the basis of a trade-off) clearly shows that this decision requires a trade-off, and invites debate about the relevant question how this trade-off should be resolved.

53. Generally, and for one such attempt to reconcile the change from a network connecting a small number of users that trust each other to a global network connecting millions of users whose trustworthiness is often unclear with the end-to-end arguments, see Clark et al. 2003, pp. 6, 39–61, 71–74.

54. See my concluding chapter. See also Handley 2006 and Rosenberg 2008.

55. See Benkler 2006, pp. 129–355. The list in the text cites from a similar list by Benkler (ibid., p. 2).

56. This argument assumes that the lack of optimization does not make it impossible for some applications to use the network. This is exactly what the broad version tries to prevent by keeping the network general. Some scholars criticize the Internet Protocol for offering only "best effort" service and not guaranteeing bandwidth, jitter, or delay. As was discussed in box 4.3., this may create problems for applications that strictly require guaranteed bandwidth, jitter, or delay. To the extent that there is a problem (in the current Internet, real-time applications have been able to function without these guarantees), it does not result from a lack of optimization, though. Instead, it results from the fact that the service provided by the Internet layer may not be general enough, because there is a class of applications it cannot support. As we saw in chapter 3, the broad version of the end-to-end arguments does not generally prevent the provision of Quality of Service. Thus, insofar as there is a problem, it results from the way the broad version was applied; it is not a problem of the broad version of the end-to-end arguments as such. Finally, technologies that would enable the Internet to offer Quality of Service have been standardized by the Internet Engineering Task Force. As we saw in chapter 4, these technologies have been implemented by the vendors of routers and of operating systems for end hosts, but they have not been widely deployed in the operational Internet. Thus, the fact that the current operational Internet mostly does not offer Quality of Service is attributable to a lack of deployment, not to a lack of available Internet technology.

57. For a detailed analysis of the positive externalities of broadband infrastructure, see Atkinson 2007.

58. Wu 2006b.

59. Anderson 2007.

60. O'Connell 2005; Maier 2008; Oates 2006.

61. On IMS, see Camarillo and Garcia-Martin 2008. On session control and charging in IMS, see Cuevas et al. 2006 and Camarillo and Garcia-Martin 2008. On IMS deployments, see Taylor and Hettick 2008 (on Verizon), Buckley 2007 (on AT&T), and Crane 2007 (on BT).

62. Cisco Systems 2006, p. 8.

63. Braden et al. 2000, pp. 6–9.

64. On asymmetric bandwidth, see the discussion of the broad version in chapter 2 above.

65. On network-address translators and firewalls, see my concluding chapter.

66. On discriminatory bandwidth management, see chapter 6 above.

67. The definition of intertemporal bias in the text mirrors Read's (2004, p. 425) definition of "intertemporal choice."

68. See Loewenstein and Prelec 1992; Frederick, Loewenstein, and O'Donoghue 2002; Read 2004.

69. E.g., Read 2004, p. 431.

70. For an overview of the potential explanations, see Laverty 1996 and Marginson and McAulay 2007.

71. See Cuthbertson, Hayes, and Nitzsche 1997 and Bushee 2001.

Conclusion

1. Saltzer, Reed, and Clark 1981. The 1981 paper was a conference paper. A revised version of the paper was published in the *ACM Transactions on Computer Systems* as Saltzer, Reed, and Clark 1984. The later version is commonly cited as the paper that first identified and described the end-to-end arguments.

2. See Reed, Saltzer, and Clark 1998.

3. For a similar summary of the narrow version, see p. 387 of Peterson and Davie 2007.

4. On this division (end hosts implement all layers, while IP routers typically implement only lower layers, up to and including the Internet layer), see Kurose and Ross 2008, pp. 51–52. In practice, routers may implement higher layers to terminate routing protocols such as BGP or management protocols.

5. The forces behind the increasing pressure on the end-to-end design of the architecture of the Internet have been described by Blumenthal and Clark (2001). Most

subsequent literature summarizes Blumenthal's and Clark's analysis (see, for example, Kempf and Austein 2004, section 3; Yoo 2004, pp. 34–37). The problems resulting from the increasing number of architectural solutions that deviate from the original design principles of the Internet have also been covered by the IETF in a series of Requests for Comments. See, e.g., Kaat 2000; Carpenter 2000; Carpenter and Brim 2002; Floyd 2002; Kempf and Austein 2004. See also Saltzer 1999; Reed 2000; Moors 2002; Clark et al. 2002.

6. See Clark et al. 2002, p. 354.

7. As has been indicated above, the fact that parts of the application run on end hosts that are topologically in the core of the network and under the administrative ownership of third parties is irrelevant: the broad version only focuses on the functional relationship between users and providers of communication services. See chapter 3 above.

8. See Sterbenz and Touch 2001, pp. 351–352.

9. The moves toward Web-based applications and cloud computing are examples of this trend. For an application of "end-to-end" reasoning to these issues, see Clark and Blumenthal 2007. See also Clark et al. 2003, pp. 47–61; Zittrain 2008, p. 167.

10. Zittrain 2008, pp. 167–168.

11. Clark and Blumenthal (2007) take a similar position.

12. Such devices are called *middleboxes*. See Carpenter and Brim 2002.

13. See Kruse 1999, pp. 1–2; Blumenthal and Clark 2001, pp. 83–84.

14. On NATs, see Srisuresh and Holdrege 1999 and Srisuresh and Egevang 2001.

15. See Kruse 1999, section 2; Tanenbaum 2003, p. 448.

16. See Blumenthal and Clark 2001, p. 83.

17. Apart from the negative effect on innovation, the proliferation of middleboxes creates a number of other problems: for example, such devices may affect end-to-end data integrity, may prevent the use of end-to-end IPSec, or may require the maintenance of state in the device, violating the principle of fate sharing and introducing single points of failure. See Kaat 2000; Carpenter 2000; Hain 2000; Carpenter and Brim 2002. IPSec (Internet Protocol Security) is a suite of protocols, standardized by the IETF, that provides various security services (such as encryption or authentication) at the Internet layer. In end-to-end IPSec, IPSec is used between the endpoints of an IP connection.

18. On the problems for applications caused by NATs, see Hain 2000, Senie 2002, Holdrege and Srisuresh 2001, and Dutcher 2001. On the problems for applications caused by firewalls, see Freed 2000 and Cheswick, Bellovin, and Rubin 2003.

19. In a way, NATs and firewalls that create the necessity to coordinate an innovation with a large number of economic actors that produce or operate devices in the core of the network convert the Internet to an anticommons. In an anticommons, "multiple owners are each endowed with the right to exclude others from a scarce resource, and no one has an effective privilege of use. When too many owners hold such rights of exclusion, the resource is prone to underuse—a tragedy of the anticommons." (Heller 1998, abstract) The concept of an anticommons has been developed by Heller (ibid.) and mirrors the concept of common property. On the tragedy of the commons, see Hardin 1968. On commons and anticommons, see Buchanan and Yoon 2000.

20. See Handley 2006 and Rosenberg 2008.

21. To work around the problem, an application that wants to use a new transport-layer protocol can include an implementation of the transport-layer protocol as part of the application. As transport-layer protocols work best when they are implemented as part of the operating system, this strategy often comes with a performance penalty.

22. For more detailed discussions, see Gillett et al. 2001 and Zittrain 2008. See also note 118 to chapter 2 and accompanying text.

23. Benkler 2006, pp. 129–355. The list in my text cites from a similar list from p. 2 of the same work.

24. See Camarillo and Garcia-Martin 2008, pp. 6–8.

25. For an overview of the obstacles of developing applications in the traditional mobile Internet, see Wu 2007.

26. For a detailed analysis of Google's motivations and for a history of Android, see Roth 2008.

27. Google 2007.

28. See Whitt and Faber 2008. Google had also asked for a fourth condition, which would have required a licensee of 700-MHz spectrum to allow third parties (such as Internet service providers) to interconnect at any technically feasible point in the wireless network of that licensee.

References

Abbate, J. 1999. *Inventing the Internet*. MIT Press.

Afuah, A., and Tucci, C. L. 2001. *Internet Business Models and Strategies: Text and Cases*. McGraw-Hill/Irwin.

Aggarwal, V., Bender, S., Feldmann, A., and Wichmann, A. 2004. Methodology for Estimating Network Distances of Gnutella Neighbors. Paper presented at Workshop GI-16, INFORMATIK 2004.

Aggarwal, V., Feldmann, A., and Scheideler, C. 2007. Can ISPs and P2P Users Cooperate for Improved Performance? *Computer Communication Review* 37(3): 31–40.

Aghion, P., and Howitt, P. 1992. A Model of Growth through Creative Destruction. *Econometrica* 60(2): 323–351.

Alchian, A. A., and Demsetz, H. 1972. Production, Information Costs, and Economic Organization. *American Economic Review* 62(5): 777–795.

Alexander, C. 1978. *The Timeless Way of Building*. Oxford University Press.

Alexander, C., Ishikawa, S., Silverstein, M., Jacobson, M., Fiksdahl-King, I., and Angel, S. 1977. *A Pattern Language: Towns, Buildings, Construction*. Oxford University Press.

Allen, F., and Gale, D. 2001. *Comparing Financial Systems*. MIT Press.

Almeroth, K. C. 2000. The Evolution of Multicast: From the MBone to Interdomain Multicast to Internet2 Deployment. *IEEE Network* 14(1): 10–20.

American Registry for Internet Numbers. 2007. ARIN Board Advises Internet Community on Migration to IPv6. https://www.arin.net/announcements/2007/20070521 .html.

Amram, M., and Kulatilaka, N. 1999. *Real Options: Managing Strategic Investment in an Uncertain World*. Harvard Business School Press.

Anderson, C. 2006. *The Long Tail: Why the Future of Business Is Selling Less of More*. Hyperion.

Anderson, N. 2007. Deep Packet Inspection Meets 'Net Neutrality, CALEA. *Ars Technica*, July 25. http://arstechnica.com/articles/culture/Deep-packet-inspection-meets-net-neutrality.ars.

Anderson, N. 2008a. Canadian ISPs Furious about Bell Canada's Traffic Throttling. *Ars Technica*, March 25. http://arstechnica.com/news.ars/post/20080325-canadian-isps-furious-about-bell-canadas-traffic-throttling.html.

Anderson, N. 2008b. Canadian Regulators Allow P2P Throttling. *Ars Technica*, November 20. http://arstechnica.com/news.ars/post/20081120-canadian-regulators-allow-p2p-throttling.html.

Anderson, S. P., and Coate, S. 2005. Market Provision of Broadcasting: A Welfare Analysis. *Review of Economic Studies* 72(4): 947–972.

Anderson, T., Peterson, L., Shenker, S., and Turner, J. 2005a. Overcoming the Internet Impasse through Virtualization. *IEEE Computer* 38(4): 34–41.

Anderson, T., Peterson, L., Shenker, S., and Turner, J. 2005b. *Report of NSF Workshop on Overcoming Barriers to Disruptive Innovation in Networking.*

Aoki, M. 1999. Information and Governance in the Silicon Valley Model. Working paper, Stanford University.

Aoki, M. 2001. *Towards a Comparative Institutional Analysis.* MIT Press.

AOL. 2008a. AOL, Select the Plan That's Right for You!—AOL Dial-up Advantage. http://free.aol.com/thenewaol/plan_choice.adp.

AOL. 2008b. AOL, Select the Plan That's Right for You!—AOL High-Speed Essentials. http://free.aol.com/thenewaol/plan_choice.adp.

Apache Software Foundation. 2008a. About the Apache HTTP Server Project. http://httpd.apache.org/ABOUT_APACHE.html.

Apache Software Foundation. 2008b. Apache History—Timeline. http://www.apache.org/history/timeline.html.

Ardichvili, A., Cardozo, R., and Ray, S. 2003. A Theory of Entrepreneurial Opportunity Identification and Development. *Journal of Business Venturing* 18(1): 105–123.

Argyres, N. S. 1996. Evidence on the Role of Firm Capabilities in Vertical Integration Decisions. *Strategic Management Journal* 17(2): 129–150.

Armitage, G. J. 2003. Revisiting IP QoS: Why Do We Care, What Have We Learned? ACM SIGCOMM 2003 RIPQOS Workshop Report. *Computer Communication Review* 33(5): 81–88.

Armstrong, M. 2006. Competition in Two-Sided Markets. *Rand Journal of Economics* 37(3): 668–691.

Arrow, K. J. 1962. Economic Welfare and the Allocation of Resources for Invention. *The Rate and Direction of Inventive Activity: Economic and Social Factors. A Conference of the Universities–National Bureau Committee for Economic Research and the Committee on Economic Growth of the Social Science Research Council.*

Arrow, K. J. 1974. *The Limits of Organization.* Norton.

Arthur, C. 2008. Things Are Rosy in Apple's Walled Garden—For Some. *The Guardian,* September 25.

Asia Pacific Network Information Centre. 2007. JPNIC Releases Statement on IPv4 Consumption. June 26. http://www.europe-ipv6.net/index.php?page=news/newsroom&id=3043

Åstebro, T. 2003. The Return to Independent Invention: Evidence of Unrealistic Optimism, Risk Seeking or Skewness Loving? *Economic Journal* 113 (January): 226–239.

Atkinson, R. D. 2007. Framing a National Broadband Policy. *Commlaw Conspectus* 16(1): 145–177.

Awduche, D., Chiu, A., Elwalid, A., Widjaja, I., and Xiao, X. 2002. Overview and Principles of Internet Traffic Engineering. Request for Comments 3272. IETF.

Bachmann, F., Bass, L., and Klein, M. 2002. Illuminating the Fundamental Contributors to Software Architecture Quality. Technical Report CMU/SEI-2002-TR-025, ESC-TR-2002-025, Carnegie Mellon Software Engineering Institute.

Baldwin, C. Y. 2008. Where Do Transactions Come From? Modularity, Transactions, and the Boundaries of Firms. *Industrial and Corporate Change* 17(1): 155–195.

Baldwin, C. Y., and Clark, K. B. 1997. Managing in an Age of Modularity. *Harvard Business Review* 75(5): 84–93.

Baldwin, C. Y., and Clark, K. B. 2000. *Design Rules: The Power of Modularity,* volume 1. MIT Press.

Baldwin, C. Y., and Clark, K. B. 2001. Modularity after the Crash. Working Paper 01-075, Harvard Business School.

Baldwin, C. Y., and Clark, K. B. 2002. The Technology of Design and Its Problems. Working Paper 02-076, Harvard Business School.

Baldwin, C. Y., and Clark, K. B. 2006a. Architectural Innovation and Dynamic Competition: The Smaller "Footprint" Strategy. Working Paper 07-014, Harvard Business School .

Baldwin, C. Y., and Clark, K. B. 2006b. Between "Knowledge" and "The Economy": Notes on the Scientific Study of Designs. In B. Kahin and D. Foray, eds., *Advancing Knowledge and the Knowledge Economy.* MIT Press.

Balkin, J. M. 2004. Digital Speech and Democratic Culture: A Theory of Freedom of Expression for the Information Society. *New York University Law Review* 79(1): 1–58.

Balkin, J. M. 2008. Media Access: A Question of Design. *George Washington Law Review*, 76(4): 101–118.

Bancroft, N. H., Seip, H., and Sprengel, A. 1998. *Implementing SAP R/3: How to Introduce a Large System into a Large Organization*, second edition. Manning.

Bar, F., Cohen, S., Cowhey, P., DeLong, B., Kleeman, M., and Zysman, J. 2000. Access and Innovation Policy for the Third-Generation Internet. *Telecommunications Policy* 24(6–7): 489–518.

Bar, F., and Riis, A. M. 2000. Tapping User-Driven Innovation: A New Rationale for Universal Service. *Information Society* 16(2): 99–108.

Bar-Gill, O. 2006. Bundling and Consumer Misperception. *University of Chicago Law Review* 73 (winter): 33–61.

Barlow, J. P. 1992. The Great Work. *Communications of the ACM* 35(1): 25–28.

Barnett, W. P., and Pontikes, E. G. 2008. The Red Queen, Success Bias, and Organizational Inertia. *Management Science* 54(7): 1237–1251.

Barney, D. 2000. *Prometheus Wired: The Hope for Democracy in the Age of Network Technology*. University of Chicago Press.

Barney, J. 1991. Firm Resources and Sustained Competitive Advantage. *Journal of Management* 17(1): 99–120.

Barrett, T. 2005. To Censor Pro-Union Web Site, Telus Blocked 766 Others. *The Tyee*, August 4. http://thetyee.ca/News/2005/08/04/TelusCensor/.

Barzel, Y. 1982. Measurement Cost and the Organization of Markets. *Journal of Law and Economics* 25(1): 27–48.

Bass, L., Clements, P., and Kazman, R. 1998. *Software Architecture in Practice*. Addison-Wesley Longman.

Bass, L., Clements, P., and Kazman, R. 2003. *Software Architecture in Practice*, second edition. Addison-Wesley.

Bass, L., Klein, M., and Bachmann, F. 2000. Quality Attribute Design Primitives. Technical Note CMU/SEI-2000-TN-017, Carnegie Mellon Software Engineering Institute.

Basu, S., and Fernald, J. 2007. Information and Communications Technology as a General-Purpose Technology: Evidence from US Industry Data. *German Economic Review* 8(2): 146–173.

Battelle, J. 2005. *The Search*. Penguin.

Baumol, W. J., Cave, M., Cramton, P., Hahn, R., Hazlett, T. W., Joskow, P. L., et al. 2007. Economists' Statement on Network Neutrality Policy. Working Paper RP07-08, AEI-Brookings Joint Center .

Beardsley, S., Doman, A., and Edin, P. 2003. Making Sense of Broadband. *McKinsey Quarterly* 2003(2): 78–87.

Becker, G. S., and Murphy, K. M. 1993. A Simple Theory of Advertising as a Good or Bad. *Quarterly Journal of Economics* 108(4): 941–964.

Beije, P. 1998. *Technological Change in the Modern Economy: Basic Topics and New Developments.* Elgar.

Bell, G. 2003. Failure to Thrive: QoS and the Culture of Operational Networking. *ACM SIGCOMM Workshop on Revisiting IP QoS: What Have We Learned, Why Do We Care?*

Bengtsson, O., Lassing, N., Bosch, J., and van Vliet, H. 2000. *Analyzing Software Architectures for Modifiability.* Research Report 1/00, Department of Software Engineering and Computer Science, University of Karlskrona.

Benkler, Y. 2000. From Consumers to Users: Shifting the Deeper Structures of Regulation Towards Sustainable Commons and User Access. *Federal Communications Law Journal* 52(3): 561–579.

Benkler, Y. 2002. Coase's Penguin, or, Linux and the Nature of the Firm. *Yale Law Journal* 112(3): 369–446.

Benkler, Y. 2006. *The Wealth of Networks: How Social Production Transforms Markets and Freedom.* Yale University Press.

Berners-Lee, T., and Fischetti, M. 2000. *Weaving the Web: The Past, Present and Future of the World Wide Web by Its Inventor.* Orion Business.

Besanko, D., Dranove, D., and Shanley, M. 2000. *Economics of Strategy,* second edition. Wiley.

Besen, S. M., and Farrell, J. 1994. Choosing How to Compete: Strategies and Tactics in Standardization. *Journal of Economic Perspectives* 8(2): 117–131.

Black, F., and Scholes, M. 1973. The Pricing of Options and Corporate Liabilities. *Journal of Political Economy* 81(3): 637–654.

Blackshaw, R. E., and Cunningham, I. M. 1980. Evolution of Open Systems Interconnection. *Fifth International Conference on Computer Communication.*

Blumenthal, M. S., and Clark, D. D. 2001. Rethinking the Design of the Internet: The End-to-End Arguments vs. the Brave New World. *ACM Transactions on Internet Technology* 1(1): 70–109.

Boase, J., Horrigan, J. B., Wellman, B., and Rainie, L. 2006. The Strength of Internet Ties. Report, Pew Internet and American Life Project.

Bochmann, G. V., and Goyer, P. 1977. *Datagrams as a Public Packet-Switched Data Transmission Service.* Report for the Department of Communications of Canada, University of Montreal. Internet Engineering Note 17.

Boehm, B. W., and Sullivan, K. J. 2000. Software Economics: A Roadmap. *Conference on the Future of Software Engineering. International Conference on Software Engineering.*

Boggs, D. R., Shoch, J. F., Taft, E. A., and Metcalfe, R. M. 1980. Pup: An Internetwork Architecture. *IEEE Transactions on Communications* 28(4): 612–624.

Bolt Beranek and Newman Inc. 1974. *Network Design Issues.* Report 2918.

Bonfiglio, D., Mellia, M., Meo, M., Rossi, D., and Tofanelli, P. 2007. Revealing Skype Traffic: When Randomness Plays with You. *Computer Communication Review* 37(4): 37–48.

Border, J., Kojo, M., Griner, J., Montenegro, G., and Shelby, Z. 2001. Performance Enhancing Proxies Intended to Mitigate Link-Related Degradations. Request for Comments 3135. IETF.

Bork, R. H. 1993. *The Antitrust Paradox: A Policy at War with Itself.* Free Press.

Bosch, J. 2000. *Design and Use of Software Architectures: Adopting and Evolving a Product-Line Approach.* Addison-Wesley.

Bosch, J., and Bengtsson, P. 2001. Assessing Optimal Software Architecture Maintainability. *Fifth European Conference on Software Maintenance and Reengineering.*

Boudreau, K. J. 2006. How Open Should an Open System Be? PhD dissertation, Massachusetts Institute of Technology.

Boudreau, K. J., Lacetera, N., and Lakhani, K. R. 2008. Parallel Search, Incentives and Problem Type: Revisiting the Competition and Innovation Link. Working Paper 09-41, Harvard Business School .

Bowman, L. M. 2002. Google Unveils New Pay-for-Play Plan. *CNET News,* March 28. http://news.cnet.com/Google-unveils-new-pay-for-play-plan/2100-1023 _3-841348.html.

Boyle, J. 1997. Foucault in Cyberspace: Surveillance, Sovereignty, and Hardwired Censors. *University of Cincinnati Law Review* 66(1): 177–203.

Braden, B., Faber, T., and Handley, M. 2003. From Protocol Stack to Protocol Heap—Role-Based Architecture. *Computer Communication Review* 33(1): 17–22.

Braden, R., Clark, D., Shenker, S., and Wroclawski, J. 2000. Developing a Next-Generation Internet Architecture. Introductory Paper, NewArch Project.

Bradner, S. 1996. The Internet Standards Process—Revision 3. Request for Comments 2026. IETF.

Bradner, S. 2006. The End of End-to-End Security? *IEEE Security and Privacy* 4(2): 76–79.

Brandenburger, A. M., and Nalebuff, B. J. 1998. *Co-Opetition*. Doubleday.

Brehm, J. 1956. Postdecision Changes in Desirability of Alternatives. *Journal of Abnormal and Social Psychology* 52(3): 384–389.

Bresnahan, T. F., and Greenstein, S. 2001. The Economic Contribution of Information Technology: Towards Comparative and User Studies. *Journal of Evolutionary Economics* 11(1): 95–118.

Bresnahan, T. F., and Trajtenberg, M. 1995. General-Purpose Technologies: Engines of Growth. *Journal of Econometrics* 65(1): 83–108.

Breznick, A. 2003. AOL Shifts Broadband Strategy. *Cable Datacom News*, January 1. http://www.cabledatacomnews.com/jan03/jan03-3.html.

Briand, L. C., Lounis, H., and Wüst, J. 1999. Using Coupling Measurement for Impact Analysis in Object-Oriented Systems. *IEEE International Conference on Software Maintenance*.

Briand, L. C., Wüst, J., Daly, J. W., and Victor Porter, D. 2000. Exploring the Relationships between Design Measures and Software Quality in Object-Oriented Systems. *Journal of Systems and Software* 51(3): 245–273.

Briand, L., Devanbu, P., and Melo, W. 1997. An Investigation into Coupling Measures for C++. *19th International Conference on Software Engineering*.

Bronson, P. 1999. *The Nudist on the Late Shift*. Random House.

Brooker, K. 1999. No Sales? No Profits? No Problem. *Fortune* 139(3): 163–169.

Brusoni, S. 2005. The Limits to Specialization: Problem Solving and Coordination in 'Modular Networks'. *Organization Studies* 26(12): 1885–1907.

Brusoni, S., and Prencipe, A. 2001. Unpacking the Black Box of Modularity: Technologies, Products and Organizations. *Industrial and Corporate Change* 10(1): 179–205.

Brynjolfsson, E. 1996. The Contribution of Information Technology to Consumer Welfare. *Information Systems Research* 7(3): 281–300.

Brynjolfsson, E., and Hitt, L. M. 2000. Beyond Computation: Information Technology, Organizational Transformation and Business Performance. *Journal of Economic Perspectives* 14(4): 23–48.

Brynjolfsson, E., and Hitt, L. M. 2003. Computer Productivity: Firm-Level Evidence. *Review of Economics and Statistics* 85(4): 793–808.

Brynjolfsson, E., Hu, Y. J., and Smith, M. D. 2003. Consumer Surplus in the Digital Economy: Estimating the Value of Increased Product Variety at Online Booksellers. *Management Science* 49(11): 1580–1596.

Brynjolfsson, E., Hu, Y. J., and Smith, M. D. 2006. From Niches to Riches: Anatomy of the Long Tail. *MIT Sloan Management Review* 47(4): 67–71.

Brynjolfsson, E., Hu, Y. J., and Simester, D. 2006. Goodbye Pareto Principle, Hello Long Tail: The Effect of Search Costs on the Concentration of Product Sales. Working paper, MIT Center for Digital Business.

Brynjolfsson, E., and Saunders, A. 2009. *Wired for Innovation: How Information Technology Is Reshaping the Economy*. MIT Press.

Buchanan, J. M., and Yoon, Y. J. 2000. Symmetric Tragedies: Commons and Anti-commons. *Journal of Law and Economics* 43(1): 1–13.

Buckley, S. 2007. AT&T's Converged IMS Vision. *Telecommunications Online*. October 5. http://www.telecommagazine.com/article.asp?HH_ID=AR_3566.

Buckman, R. 2005. Many Internet Start-ups Are Telling Venture Capitalists: "We Don't Need You." *Wall Street Journal*, October 31.

Burgstahler, L., Dolzer, K., Hauser, C., Jähnert, J., Junghans, S., Macián, C., et al. 2003. Beyond Technology: the Missing Pieces for QoS Success. *ACM SIGCOMM Workshop on Revisiting IP QoS: What Have We Learned, Why Do We Care?*

Burk, D. L., and Cohen, J. E. 2001. Fair Use Infrastructure for Rights Management Systems. *Harvard Journal of Law and Technology* 15(1): 41–92.

Burness, A.-L., Eardley, P., Akhtar, N., Callejo, M. A., and Colas, J. A. 2005. Making Migration Easy: A Key Requirement for Systems Beyond 3G. *IEEE 61st Vehicular Technology Conference*.

Burnham, T., Frels, J., and Mahajan, V. 2003. Consumer Switching Costs: A Typology, Antecedents, and Consequences. *Journal of the Academy of Marketing Science* 31(2): 109–126.

Buschmann, F., Meunier, R., Rohnert, H., Sommerlad, P., and Stal, M. 1996. *Pattern-Oriented Software Architecture. A System of Patterns*, volume 1. Wiley.

Bushee, B. J. 2001. Do Institutional Investors Prefer Near-Term Earnings over Long-Run Value? *Contemporary Accounting Research* 18(2): 207–246.

Business Wire, 1999. EarthLink Signs GoTo.com as Its Default Search Provider: Two-Year, $10 Million Premiere Partnership Puts GoTo.com on EarthLink's Top Web Properties. *Business Wire*, October 14. http://findarticles.com/p/articles/mi_m0EIN/is_1999_Oct_14/ai_56280327.

Calomiris, C. W. 2000. *U.S. Bank Deregulation in Historical Perspective*. Cambridge University Press.

Camarillo, G., and Garcia-Martin, M. A. 2008. *The 3G IP Multimedia Subsystem (IMS): Merging the Internet and the Cellular Worlds*, third edition. Wiley.

Camerer, C. F., Loewenstein, G., and Rabin, M., eds. 2004. *Advances in Behavioral Economics*. Princeton University Press.

Carlton, D. W. 2001. A General Analysis of Exclusionary Conduct and Refusal to Deal: Why Aspen and Kodak Are Misguided. *Antitrust Law Journal* 68(3): 659–683.

Carlton, D. W., and Gertner, R. H. 2003. Intellectual Property, Antitrust and Strategic Behavior. In A. Jaffe, J. Lerner, and S. Stern, eds., *Innovation Policy and the Economy*, volume 3. MIT Press.

Carlton, D. W., and Perloff, J. M. 2005. *Modern Industrial Organization*, fourth edition. Pearson.

Carlton, D. W., and Waldman, M. 2000. The Strategic Use of Tying to Preserve and Create Market Power in Evolving Industries. Working paper, University of Chicago.

Carlton, D. W., and Waldman, M. 2002. The Strategic Use of Tying to Preserve and Create Market Power in Evolving Industries. *Rand Journal of Economics* 33(2): 194–220.

Carney, W. J. 1997. Large Bank Stockholders in Germany: Saviors or Substitutes? *Journal of Applied Corporate Finance* 9(4): 74–80.

Carpenter, B. 1996. Architectural Principles of the Internet. Request for Comments 1958. IETF.

Carpenter, B. 2000. Internet Transparency. Request for Comments 2775. IETF.

Carpenter, B., and Brim, S. 2002. Middleboxes: Taxonomy and Issues. Request for Comments 3234. IETF.

Cassidy, J. 2006. Me Media. *The New Yorker*, May 15. http://www.newyorker.com/archive/2006/05/15/060515fa_fact_cassidy.

Castilla, E. J., Hwang, H., Granovetter, E., and Granovetter, M. 2000. Social Networks in Silicon Valley. In C.-M. Lee, W. Miller, M. Hancock, and H. Rowen, eds., *The Silicon Valley Edge: A Habitat for Innovation and Entrepreneurship*. Stanford University Press.

Cave, M., and Crocioni, P. 2007. Does Europe Need Network Neutrality Rules? *International Journal of Communication* 1, 669–679.

CBC News. 2005. Telus Cuts Subscriber Access to Pro-Union Website. *CBC News*, June 9. http://www.cbc.ca/story/canada/national/2005/07/24/telus-sites050724.html.

Cerf, V. G. 1977. TCP (Version 2) Specification. Internet Engineering Note 5.

Cerf, V. G. 1978a. A Proposal for TCP Version 3.1 Header Format. Internet Engineering Note 27.

Cerf, V. G. 1978b. A Proposed New Internet Header Format. Internet Engineering Note 26.

Cerf, V. G. 1980a. Final Report of the Stanford University TCP Project. Internet Engineering Note 151.

Cerf, V. G. 1980b. Protocols for Interconnected Packet Networks. *Computer Communication Review* 10(4): 10–11.

Cerf, V. G., and Kahn, R. E. 1974. A Protocol for Packet Network Intercommunication. *Transactions on Communications* 22(5): 637–648.

Cerf, V. G., and Kirstein, P. T. 1978. Issues in Packet-Network Interconnection. *Proceedings of the IEEE* 66(11): 1386–1408.

Cerf, V. G., and Postel, J. B. 1978. Specification of Internetwork Transmission Control Program. TCP. Version 3. Internet Engineering Note 21.

Chafkin, M. 2008. Anything Could Happen. *Inc.*, March 1. http://www.inc.com/magazine/20080301/anything-could-happen.html.

Charny, B. 2003. Why VoIP Is Music to Kazaa's Ear. *CNET News*, September 11. http://www.news.com/Why-VoIP-is-music-to-Kazaas-ear/2008-1082_3-5074558.html.

Charny, B. 2005a. Mexico Telephone Operator under VoIP Fire. *ZDNet News*, April 25. http://news.zdnet.com/2100-1035_22-5681542.html.

Charny, B. 2005b. Vonage Says Broadband Provider Blocks Its Calls. *CNET News*, February 14. http://news.cnet.com/Vonage-says-broadband-provider-blocks-its-calls/2100-7352_3-5576234.html.

Cherry, S. 2005. The VOIP Backlash. *IEEE Spectrum*, 42(10): 61–63.

Chesbrough, H. W. 2003. *Open Innovation: The New Imperative for Creating and Profiting from Technology*. Harvard Business School Press.

Chesbrough, H. W. 2006. *Open Business Models: How to Thrive in the New Innovation Landscape*. Harvard Business School Press.

Chesbrough, H. W., and Teece, D. J. 1996. When Is Virtual Virtuous? Organizing for Innovation. *Harvard Business Review* 74(1): 65–73.

Chesbrough, H., Vanhaverbeke, W., and West, J., eds. 2006. *Open Innovation: Researching a New Paradigm*. Oxford University Press.

Cheswick, W. R., Bellovin, S. M., and Rubin, A. D. 2003. *Firewalls and Internet Security: Repelling the Wily Hacker*, second edition. Addison-Wesley.

Chiappa, J. N. 2002. Will the Real "End-End Principle" Please Stand Up? http://mercury.lcs.mit.edu/~jnc/tech/end_end.html

Chirico, F., van der Haar, I., and Larouche, P. 2007. Network Neutrality in the EU. TILEC Discussion Paper DP 2007-030, Tilburg University.

Choi, J. P., and Stefanadis, C. 2001. Tying, Investment, and the Dynamic Leverage Theory. *Rand Journal of Economics* 32(1): 52–71.

Christensen, C. M. 2000. *The Innovator's Dilemma: When New Technologies Cause Great Firms to Fail.* Harper Business.

Christensen, C. M., and Raynor, M. E. 2003. *The Innovator's Solution: Creating and Sustaining Successful Growth.* Harvard Business School Press.

Christensen, C. M., and Rosenbloom, R. S. 1995. Explaining the Attacker's Advantage: Technological Paradigms, Organizational Dynamics, and the Value Network. *Research Policy* 24(2): 233–257.

Christensen, C. M., Verlinden, M., and Westerman, G. 2002. Disruption, Disintegration and the Dissipation of Differentiability. *Industrial and Corporate Change* 11(5): 955–993.

chromatic and Sheppard, D. 2008. A Beginner's Introduction to Perl 5.10. April 23. http://www.perl.com/pub/a/2008/04/23/a-beginners-introduction-to-perl-510 .html.

Cisco Systems. 2005. Network-Based Application Recognition and Distributed Network-Based Application Recognition. Documentation. http://www.cisco.com/ univercd/cc/td/doc/product/software/ios122/122newft/122t/122t8/dtnbarad.pdf.

Cisco Systems. 2006. *Supporting the IP Multimedia Subsystem for Mobile, Wireline, and Cable Providers.* White paper.

Clark, D. D. 1985. The Structuring of Systems Using Upcalls. *Tenth ACM Symposium on Operating Systems Principles.*

Clark, D. D. 1988. The Design Philosophy of the DARPA Internet Protocols. *Computer Communication Review*, 18(4): 106–114.

Clark, D. D. 1997. Interoperation, Open Interfaces, and Protocol Architecture. In *White Papers: The Unpredictable Certainty: Information Infrastructure through 2000.* National Academy Press.

Clark, D. D., and Blumenthal, M. S. 2007. The End-to-End Argument and Application Design: The Role of Trust. Paper presented at 35th Research Conference on Communication, Information and Internet Policy.

Clark, D. D., Pogran, K. T., and Reed, D. P. 1978. An Introduction to Local Area Networks. *Proceedings of the IEEE* 66(11): 1497–1517.

Clark, D. D., Shenker, S., and Falk, A. 2007. GENI Research Plan (Version 4.5). GENI Research Coordination Working Group and GENI Planning Group. GDD 06-28

Clark, D. D., Sollins, K., Wroclawski, J., and Faber, T. 2003. Addressing Reality: An Architectural Response to Real-World Demands on the Evolving Internet. *ACM SIGCOMM Workshop on Revisiting IP QoS: Why Do We Care, What Have We Learned?*

Clark, D. D., Sollins, K., Wroclawski, J., Katabi, D., Kulik, J., Yang, X., et al. 2003. *NewArch: Future Generation Internet Architecture*. Final Technical Report, NewArch Project.

Clark, D. D., and Tennenhouse, D. L. 1990. Architectural Considerations for a New Generation of Protocols. *ACM Symposium on Communications Architectures and Protocols.*

Clark, D. D., Wroclawski, J., Sollins, K. R., and Braden, R. 2002. Tussle in Cyberspace: Defining Tomorrow's Internet. *Computer Communication Review* 32(4): 347–356.

Clark, D. D., Wroclawski, J., Sollins, K. R., and Braden, R. 2005. Tussle in Cyberspace: Defining Tomorrow's Internet. *IEEE/ACM Transactions on Networking* 13(3): 462–475.

Clark, K. B. 1985. The Interaction of Design Hierarchies and Market Concepts in Technological Evolution. *Research Policy* 14(5): 235–251.

Clark, K. B. 1988. Managing Technology in International Competition: The Case of Product Development in Response to Foreign Entry. In A. Spence and H. Hazard, eds., *International Competitiveness*. Ballinger.

Coase, R. 1937. The Nature of the Firm. *Economica* 4(16): 386–405.

Coase, R. H. 1960. The Problem of Social Cost. *Journal of Law and Economics* 3(1): 1–44.

Cohen, A. 2002. *The Perfect Store: Inside eBay*. Little, Brown.

Cohen, D. 1979. On Interconnection of Computer Networks. In K. Beauchamp, ed., *Interlinking of Computer Networks: Proceedings of the NATO Advanced Study Institute held at Bonas, France, August 28–September 8, 1978*. Reidel.

Cohen, J. E., and Lemley, M. A. 2001. Patent Scope and Innovation in the Software Industry. *California Law Review* 89(1): 1–57.

Cohen, W. M., and Klepper, S. 1992. The Tradeoff between Firm Size and Diversity in the Pursuit of Technological Progress. *Small Business Economics* 4(1): 1–14.

Cohen, W. M., and Levinthal, D. A. 1990. Absorptive Capacity: A New Perspective on Learning and Innovation. *Administrative Science Quarterly* 35(1): 128–152.

Cohen, W. M., and Malerba, F. 2001. Is the Tendency to Variation a Chief Cause of Progress? *Industrial and Corporate Change* 10(3): 587–608.

Combs, J. G., and Ketchen, D. J. 1999. Explaining Interfirm Cooperation and Performance: Toward a Reconciliation of Predictions from the Resource-Based View and Organizational Economics. *Strategic Management Journal* 20(9): 867–888.

Comer, D. E. 2000. *Internetworking with TCP/IP: Principles, Protocols, and Architectures*, fourth edition. Prentice-Hall.

Computer Science and Telecommunications Board and National Research Council. 1994. *Realizing the Information Future: The Internet and Beyond.* National Academy Press.

Computer Science and Telecommunications Board and National Research Council. 1996. *The Unpredictable Certainty: Information Infrastructure through 2000.* National Academy Press.

Computer Science and Telecommunications Board and National Research Council. 2001. *The Internet's Coming of Age.* National Academy Press.

comScore. 2008. comScore Releases February 2008 U.S. Search Engine Rankings. Press release, March 19. http://www.comscore.com/press/release.asp?press=2119.

Consumers Union. 2007. The Next Big Thing in Broadband: Early Termination Penalties. HearUsNow.org Blog. April 9. http://www.consumersunion.org/blogs/hun/2007/04/the_next_big_thing_in_broadban.html.

Cooter, R. D. 1998. Expressive Law and Economics. *Journal of Legal Studies* 27(S2): 585–608.

Coulson, G., Blair, G. S., Davies, N., Robin, P., and Fitzpatrick, T. 1999. Supporting Mobile Multimedia Applications through Adaptive Middleware. *IEEE Journal on Selected Areas in Communications* 17(9): 1651–1659.

Crane, P. 2007. A New Service Infrastructure Architecture. *BT Technology Journal* 23(1): 15–27.

Craswell, R. 1982. Tying Requirements in Competitive Markets: The Consumer Protection Issues. *Boston University Law Review* 62(3): 661–700.

Crawford, S. C. 2007. The Internet and the Project of Communications Law. *UCLA Law Review* 55(2): 359–407.

Crocker, D. undated. Email History: How Email Was Invented. http://livinginternet.com/e/ei.htm.

Cuevas, A., Moreno, J., Vidales, P., and Einsiedler, H. 2006. The IMS Service Platform: A Solution for Next Generation Network Operators to Be More Than Bit Pipes. *IEEE Communications Magazine*, 44(8): 75–81.

Cusumano, M. A. 1991. *Japan's Software Factories: A Challenge to U.S. Management.* Oxford University Press.

Cuthbertson, K., Hayes, S., and Nitzsche, D. 1997. The Behaviour of UK Stock Prices and Returns: Is the Market Efficient? *Economic Journal* 107(443): 986–1008.

Dasgupta, P., and Maskin, E. 1987. The Simple Economics of Research Portfolios. *Economic Journal* 97(387): 581–595.

David, P. A. 1990. The Dynamo and the Computer: An Historical Perspective on the Modern Productivity Paradox. *American Economic Review* 80(2): 355–361.

David, P. A. 2001. The Evolving Accidental Information Super-highway. *Oxford Review of Economic Policy* 17(2): 159–187.

DeGraba, P. 1996. Why Lever into a Zero-Profit Industry: Tying, Foreclosure, and Exclusion. *Journal of Economics and Management Strategy* 5(3): 433–447.

Deibert, R., Palfrey, J., Rohozinski, R., and Zittrain, J. L., eds. 2008. *Access Denied: The Practice and Policy of Global Internet Filtering*. MIT Press.

DellaVigna, S., and Malmendier, U. 2004. Contract Design and Self-Control Theory and Evidence. *Quarterly Journal of Economics* 119(2): 353–402.

Demsetz, H. 1988. The Theory of the Firm Revisited. *Journal of Law Economics and Organization* 4(1): 141–162.

Denton, N. 2007. An Alternate History According to Elon Musk. *Valleywag*, January 19. http://valleywag.com/tech/paypal/an-alternate-history-according-to-elon-musk-230076.php.

Deprez, F., Rosengren, J., and Soman, V. 2002. Portals for All Platforms. *McKinsey Quarterly* 2002(1): 93–101.

Deutsche Telekom. 2008. Allgemeine Geschaftsbedingungen und Preise: Bundesliga Insider.

Deutschman, A. 1997. Imposter Boy. *Gentlemen's Quarterly*. January. http://web.archive.org/web/20030212202753/http://www.chrispy.net/marca/gqarticle.html.

Diamond, J. M. 1997. *Guns, Germs, and Steel: The Fates of Human Societies*. Norton.

DiBona, C., Ockman, S., and Stone, M., eds. 1999. *OpenSources: Voices from the Open Source Revolution*. O'Reilly.

DiMaggio. 1998. The New Institutionalism: Avenues of Collaboration. *Journal of Institutional and Theoretical Economics* 154(4): 696–715.

DiMaggio, P. J., and Powell, W. W. 1983. The Iron Cage Revisited: Institutional Isomorphism and Collective Rationality in Organizational Fields. *American Sociological Review* 48(2): 147–160.

Diot, C., Levine, B. N., Lyles, B., Kassem, H., and Balensiefen, D. 2000. Deployment Issues for the IP Multicast Service and Architecture. *IEEE Network* 14(1): 78–88.

Dixit, A. K., and Pindyck, R. S. 1994. *Investment under Uncertainty*. Princeton University Press.

Dosi, G., and Nelson, R. R. 1994. An Introduction to Evolutionary Theories in Economics. *Journal of Evolutionary Economics* 4(3): 153–172.

Drezner, D. W., and Farrell, H. 2008. Blogs, Politics and Power: A Special Issue of Public Choice. *Public Choice* 134(1–2): 1–13.

Dunbar, J. 2007. Pulling Plug on Net Service Not Easy. *USA Today*, April 9. http://www.usatoday.com/tech/techinvestor/industry/2007-04-09-net-fees_N.htm?POE=TECISVA.

Dutcher, B. 2001. *The NAT Handbook: Implementing and Managing Network Address Translation.* Wiley.

DW Staff. 2006. Bundesliga Agrees on Massive Sponsorship Deal with T-Com. *Deutsche Welle*, June 8. http://www.dw-world.de/dw/article/0,2144,2046790,00.html.

Dyer, J. H. 1996. Specialized Supplier Networks as a Source of Competitive Advantage: Evidence from the Auto Industry. *Strategic Management Journal* 17(4): 271–291.

Dyer, J. H. 1997. Effective Interfirm Collaboration: How Firms Minimize Transaction Costs and Maximize Transaction Value. *Strategic Management Journal* 18(7): 535–556.

Easterbrook, F. H. 1997. International Corporate Differences: Markets or Law? *Journal of Applied Corporate Finance* 9(4): 23–29.

Eckersley, P., von Lohmann, F., and Schoen, S. 2007. *Packet Forgery by ISPs: A Report on the Comcast Affair.* Electronic Frontier Foundation. November 28. http://www.eff.org/files/eff_comcast_report2.pdf

Economides, N., and Tåg., J. 2007. Net Neutrality on the Internet: A Two-sided Market Analysis. Working Paper 07-45, NET Institute.

Edwards, J. S. S., and Fischer, K. 1994. *Banks, Finance and Investments in Germany.* Cambridge University Press.

Eggert, L., and Eddy, W. M. 2006. Towards More Expressive Transport-Layer Interfaces. *First ACM/IEEE International Workshop on Mobility in the Evolving Internet Architecture.*

Einhorn, M. A. 2003. US Settlement Reform: An Historical Review. In G. Madden, ed., *Traditional Telecommunications Networks*, volume 1. Elgar.

Elhauge, E., and Geradin, D. 2007. *Global Antitrust Law and Economics.* Foundation Press.

Ellickson, R. C. 1991. *Order Without Law: How Neighbours Settle Disputes.* Harvard University Press.

Enkel, E., Perez-Freije, J., and Gassmann, O. 2005. Minimizing Market Risks through Customer Integration in New Product Development: Learning from Bad Practice. *Creativity and Innovation Management* 14(4): 425–437.

Eppinger, S. D. 1991. Model-Based Approaches to Managing Concurrent Engineering. *Journal of Engineering Design* 2(4): 283–290.

Erdogmus, H., Boehm, B. W., Harrison, W., Reifer, D. J., and Sullivan, K. J. 2002. Software Engineering Economics: Background, Current Practices, and Future Directions. *24rd International Conference on Software Engineering.*

Eubanks, M. 2006. Multicast Business Models (PowerPoint Presentation). Multicast Workshop, SANOG 7.

Evans, D. S., Hagiu, A., and Schmalensee, R. 2006. *Invisible Engines: How Software Platforms Drive Innovation and Transform Industries.* MIT Press.

Evans, D. S., and Noel, M. D. 2007. Defining Markets That Involve Multi-Sided Platform Businesses: An Empirical Framework with an Application to Google's Purchase of DoubleClick. Working Paper 07-18, Reg-Markets Center.

Evans, D. S., and Schmalensee, R. L. 2002. Some Economic Aspects of Antitrust Analysis in Dynamically Competitive Industries. In A. Jaffe, J. Lerner, and S. Stern, eds., *Innovation Policy and the Economy,* volume 2. MIT Press.

Fake, C. 2007. The History of Flickr. *IT Conversations,* February 12. http://itc .conversationsnetwork.org/shows/detail1755.html.

Farrell, H., and Drezner, D. W. 2008. The Power and Politics of Blogs. *Public Choice* 134(1–2): 15–30.

Farrell, J. 2006. Open Access Arguments: Why Confidence Is Misplaced. In T. Lenard and R. May, eds., *Net Neutrality or Net Neutering: Should Broadband Internet Services Be Regulated?* Springer.

Farrell, J., Gilbert, R. J., and Katz, M. L. 2002. Market Structure, Organizational Structure, and R&D Diversity. In R. Arnott, B. Greenwald, R. Kanbur, and B. Nalebuff, eds., *Economics for an Imperfect World: Essays in Honor of Joseph E. Stiglitz.* MIT Press.

Farrell, J., and Katz, M. L. 2000. Innovation, Rent Extraction, and Integration in Systems Markets. *Journal of Industrial Economics* 48(4): 413–432.

Farrell, J., and Klemperer, P. 2007. Coordination and Lock-in: Competition and Switching Costs and Network Effects. In M. Armstrong and R. Porter, eds., *Handbook of Industrial Organization,* volume 3. Elsevier.

Farrell, J., and Weiser, P. J. 2003. Modularity, Vertical Integration, and Open Access Policies: Towards a Convergence of Antitrust and Regulation in the Internet Age. *Harvard Journal of Law and Technology* 17(1): 85–134.

Faulhaber, G. 2002. Network Effects and Merger Analysis: Instant Messaging and the AOL-Time Warner Case. *Telecommunications Policy* 26(5–6): 311–333.

Faulhaber, G. R. 2007. Network Neutrality: The Debate Evolves. *International Journal of Communication* 1: 680–700.

Feamster, N., Gao, L., and Rexford, J. 2007. How to Lease the Internet in Your Spare Time. *Computer Communication Review* 37(1): 61–64.

Federal Communications Commission. 2001. Applications for Consent to the Transfer of Control of Licenses and Section 214 Authorizations by Time Warner Inc. and America Online, Inc., Transferors, to AOL Time Warner Inc., Transferee. Memorandum Opinion and Order. FCC 01-12. *Federal Communications Commission Record* 16: 6547–6612.

Federal Communications Commission. 2005a. Appropriate Framework for Broadband Access to the Internet over Wireline Facilities. Policy Statement. *Federal Communications Commission Record* 20: 14986–14988.

Federal Communications Commission. 2005b. Madison River Communications, LLC and Affiliated Companies. Consent Decree. *Federal Communications Commission Record* 20: 4296–4299.

Federal Communications Commission. 2005c. Madison River Communications, LLC and Affiliated Companies. Order. *Federal Communications Commission Record* 20: 4295–4295.

Federal Communications Commission. 2007. International Settlements Policy and U.S.-International Accounting Rates. *International Bureau*, February 20. http://www .fcc.gov/ib/pd/pf/account.html.

Federal Communications Commission. 2008a. Formal Complaint of Free Press and Public Knowledge Against Comcast for Secretly Degrading Peer-to-Peer Applications. Memorandum Opinion and Order. FCC 08–183.

Federal Communications Commission. 2008b. *High-Speed Services for Internet Access: Status as of June 30, 2007*. Report.

Federal Trade Commission. 2008. Commission Announces Revised Jurisdictional Thresholds for Section 8 and Section 7A of the Clayton Act. January 18. http://www .ftc.gov/opa/2008/01/clayton.shtm.

Feller, J., and Fitzgerald, B. 2000. A Framework Analysis of the Open Source Software Development Paradigm. *Twenty First International Conference on Information Systems*.

Felten, E. W. 2003. Layers. *Freedom to Tinker*, June 18 (updated September 11, 2003). http://www.freedom-to-tinker.com/blog/felten/layers.

Ferguson, C. H., and Morris, C. R. 1993. *Computer Wars: How the West Can Win in a Post-IBM World*. Times Books.

Festa, P. 2002. GoTo Gains Amid Web Pains. *CNET News*, January 2. http://news.cnet.com/GoTo-gains-amid-Web-pains/2100-1023_3-257328.html.

Fielding, R. T., and Taylor, R. N. 2002. Principled Design of the Modern Web Architecture. *ACM Transactions on Internet Technology* 2(2): 115–150.

Fine, C. H. 1998. *Clockspeed: Winning Industry Control in the Age of Temporary Advantage*. Perseus Books.

Fisher, W. W., III. 1988. Reconstructing the Fair Use Doctrine. *Harvard Law Review* 101(8): 1659–1795.

Fisher, W. W., III. 2001. Theories of Intellectual Property. In S. Munzer, ed., *New Essays in the Legal and Political Theory of Property*. Cambridge University Press.

Fitzgerald, M. 2006. How We Did It: Stewart Butterfield and Caterina Fake, Cofounders, Flickr. *Inc.*, December. http://www.inc.com/magazine/20061201/hidi-butterfield-fake.html.

Fixson, S. K. 2001. Three Perspectives on Modularity—A Literature Review of a Product Concept for Assembled Hardware Products. Working Paper EDS-WP-2001-06, Engineering Systems Division, MIT.

Fixson, S. K., and Park, J.-K. 2008. The Power of Integrality: Linkages between Product Architecture, Innovation, and Industry Structure. *Research Policy* 37(8): 1296–1316.

Fixson, S., and Sako, M. 2001. Modularity in Product Architecture: Will the Auto Industry Follow the Computer Industry? Paper presented at Annual Meeting of International Motor Vehicle Program.

Fligstein, N., and Freeland, R. 1995. Theoretical and Comparative Perspectives on Corporate Organization. *Annual Review of Sociology* 21: 21–43.

Floyd, S. 1998. Internet Research: Comments on Formulating the Problem. Unpublished.

Floyd, S. 2002. General Architectural and Policy Considerations. Request for Comments 3426. IETF.

Franke, N., and Shah, S. 2003. How Communities Support Innovative Activities: An Exploration of Assistance and Sharing among End-Users. *Research Policy* 32(1): 157–178.

Franke, N., and von Hippel, E. 2003. Satisfying Heterogeneous User Needs Via Innovation Toolkits: The Case of Apache Security Software. *Research Policy* 32(7): 1199–1215.

Franks, J., and Mayer, C. 1997. Corporate Ownership and Control in the U.K., Germany, and France. *Journal of Applied Corporate Finance* 9(4): 30–45.

Frederick, S., Loewenstein, G., and O'Donoghue, T. 2002. Time Discounting and Time Preference: A Critical Review. *Journal of Economic Literature* 40(2): 351–401.

Free Press, Public Knowledge, Media Access Project, Consumer Federation of America, Consumers Union, Information Society Project at Yale Law School, et al. 2007. Petition for Declaratory Ruling to Federal Communications Commission. WC Dkt. No. 07–52. November 1.

Free Press and Public Knowledge. 2007. Formal Complaint to Federal Communications Commission. November 1.

Freed, N. 2000. Behavior of and Requirements for Internet Firewalls. Request for Comments 2979. IETF.

Freeman, C., and Louca, F. 2001. *As Time Goes By: From the Industrial Revolutions to the Information Revolution.* Oxford University Press.

Freixas, X., Guesnerie, R., and Tirole, J. 1985. Planning under Incomplete Information and the Ratchet Effect. *Review of Economic Studies* 52(2): 173–191.

Fried, J. 2006. Bezos Expeditions Invests in 37signals. *Signal vs. Noise*, July 20. http://www.37signals.com/svn/archives2/bezos_expeditions_invests_in_37signals.php.

Fried, J. 2008a. Ask 37signals: Does "Getting Real" Work in This Economy? *Signal vs. Noise*, November 14. http://www.37signals.com/svn/posts/1398-ask-37signals-does-getting-real-work-in-this-economy.

Fried, J. 2008b. Start a Business, Not a Startup. *Signal vs. Noise*, April 25. http://www.37signals.com/svn/posts/997-start-a-business-not-a-startup.

Frischmann, B. M. 2005. An Economic Theory of Infrastructure and Commons Management. *Minnesota Law Review* 89 (April): 917–1030.

Frischmann, B. M. 2008. Speech, Spillovers, and the First Amendment. *University of Chicago Legal Forum*, 2008: 301–333.

Frischmann, B. M., and Lemley, M. A. 2006. Spillovers. *Columbia Law Review* 100(2): 101–143.

Frischmann, B. M., and van Schewick, B. 2007. Network Neutrality and the Economics of an Information Superhighway: A Reply to Professor Yoo. *Jurimetrics Journal* 47 (summer): 383–428.

Furubotn, E. G., and Richter, R. 2005. *Institutions and Economic Theory: The Contribution of the New Institutional Economics*, second edition. University of Michigan Press.

Gabbay, N. 2006. Flickr Case Study: Still about Tech for Exit? August 27. http://www.startup-review.com/blog/flickr-case-study-still-about-tech-for-exit.php.

Galant, G. 2005. Venture Voice Show #7—Evan Williams of Odeo. *Venture Voice*, July 26. http://www.venturevoice.com/2005/07/vv_show_7_-_eva.html.

Ganjam, A., and Zhang, H. 2005. Internet Multicast Video Delivery. *Proceedings of the IEEE* 93(1): 159–170.

Gans, J. S., Hsu, D. H., and Stern, S. 2002. When Does Start-Up Innovation Spur the Gale of Creative Destruction? *Rand Journal of Economics* 33(4): 571–586.

Gans, J. S., and Stern, S. 2000. Incumbency and R&D Incentives: Licensing the Gale of Creative Destruction. *Journal of Economics and Management Strategy* 9(4): 485–511.

Gans, J. S., and Stern, S. 2003. The Product Market and the Market for "Ideas": Commercialization Strategies for Technology Entrepreneurs. *Research Policy* 32(2): 333–350.

Gapper, J. 2008. Haze May Obscure Microsoft's Path. *FT.com*, February 6. http://www.ft.com/cms/s/0/27a2794e-d4d9-11dc-9af1-0000779fd2ac.html?nclick_check=1.

Garber, L. 1999. Steve Deering: Multicast Waits for Its Killer App. *IT Professional* 1(2): 78–80.

Garlick, L. L., Rom, R., and Postel, J. B. 1977. Issues in Reliable Host-to-Host Protocols. Internet Engineering Note 12.

Garrett, J. J. 2005. An Interview with Flickr's Eric Costello. *adaptive path*, August 4. http://adaptivepath.com/ideas/essays/archives/000519.php.

Garud, R., and Kumaraswamy, A. 1993. Changing Competitive Dynamics in Network Industries: An Exploration of Sun Microsystems Open Systems Strategy. *Strategic Management Journal* 14(5): 351–369.

Garud, R., and Kumaraswamy, A. 1995. Technological and Organizational Designs for Realizing Economies of Substitution. *Strategic Management Journal* 16 (special issue, summer): 93–109.

Gawer, A. 2000. The Organization of Platform Leadership: An Empirical Investigation of Intel's Management Processes Aimed at Fostering Complementary Innovation by Third Parties. PhD dissertation, Massachusetts Institute of Technology.

Gawer, A., and Cusumano, M. A. 2002. *Platform Leadership: How Intel, Microsoft, and Cisco Drive Industry Innovation*. Harvard Business School Press.

Gawer, A., and Henderson, R. 2007. Platform Owner Entry and Innovation in Complementary Markets: Evidence from Intel. *Journal of Economics and Management Strategy* 16(1): 1–34.

Gaynor, M. 2001. The Effect of Market Uncertainty on the Management Structure for Network-Based Services. PhD dissertation, Harvard University.

Gaynor, M. 2003. *Network Services Investment Guide: Maximizing ROI in Uncertain Times*. Wiley.

Gaynor, M., Bradner, S., Iansiti, M., and Kung, H. T. 2000. The Real Options Approach to Network-Based Service Architecture. http://people.bu.edu/mgaynor/papers/IEEE-special.pdf.

Geist, M. 2005. *Telecommunications Policy Review Submission*. University of Ottawa Faculty of Law.

Gilbert, R. J. 1989. Mobility Barriers and the Value of Incumbency. In R. Schmalensee and R. Willig, eds., *Handbook of Industrial Organization*, volume 1. Elsevier.

Gilbert, R., and Katz, M. L. 2001. An Economist's Guide to US v. Microsoft. *Journal of Economic Perspectives* 15(2): 25–44.

Gillespie, T. 2006. Engineering a Principle: 'End-to-End' in the Design of the Internet. *Social Studies of Science* 36(3): 427–457.

Gillett, S. E., Lehr, W. H., Wroclawski, J. T., and Clark, D. D. 2001. Do Appliances Threaten Internet Innovation? *IEEE Communications Magazine* 39(10): 46–51.

Gligor, V. D. 2005. Guaranteeing Access in Spite of Distributed Service-Flooding Attacks. In B. Christianson et al., eds., *Security Protocols*. Springer.

Gompers, P. A., and Lerner, J. 2000. The Determinants of Corporate Venture Capital Success: Organizational Structure, Incentives, and Complementarities. In R. Morck, ed., *Concentrated Corporate Ownership*. University of Chicago Press.

Gompers, P. A., and Lerner, J. 2001a. *The Money of Invention: How Venture Capital Creates New Wealth*. Harvard Business School Press.

Gompers, P. A., and Lerner, J. 2001b. The Venture Capital Revolution. *Journal of Economic Perspectives* 15(2): 145–168.

Gompers, P. A., and Lerner, J. 2002. Short-Term America Revisited? Boom and Bust in the Venture Capital Industry and the Impact on Innovation. In A. Jaffe, J. Lerner, and S. Stern, eds., *Innovation Policy and the Economy*, volume 3. MIT Press.

Gompers, P., and Lerner, J. 2004. *The Venture Capital Cycle*. MIT Press.

Gompers, P., and Lerner, J. 2006. *The Venture Capital Cycle*, second edition. MIT Press.

Google. 1999. Google Receives $25 Million in Equity Funding. Press release, June 7. http://www.google.com/press/pressrel/pressrelease1.html

Google. 2000. Google's Targeted Keyword Ad Program Shows Strong Momentum with Advertisers. Press release, August 16. http://www.google.com/press/pressrel/pressrelease31.html.

Google. 2007. Google Intends to Bid in Spectrum Auction If FCC Adopts Consumer Choice and Competition Requirements. Press release, July 20, 2007. http://www.google.com/intl/en/press/pressrel/20070720_wireless.html.

Google. 2008. *Form 10-K for the Fiscal Year Ended December 31, 2007.*

Gordon, R. J. 2000. Does the "New Economy" Measure up to the Great Inventions of the Past? *Journal of Economic Perspectives* 14(4): 49–74.

Granovetter, M. 1985. Economic Action and Social Structure: The Problem of Embeddedness. *American Journal of Sociology* 91(3): 481–510.

Green, J. R., and Scotchmer, Suzanne. 1995. On the Division of Profit in Sequential Innovation. *Rand Journal of Economics* 26(1): 20–33.

Greenstein, S. 2007a. *Economic Experiments and Neutrality in Internet Access.* Working Paper 13158, National Bureau of Economic Research.

Greenstein, S. 2007b. Economic Experiments in Internet Access Markets. *First Monday*, 12(6). http://firstmonday.org/htbin/cgiwrap/bin/ojs/index.php/fm/article/view/1902/1784.

Greif, A. 2006. *Institutions and the Path to the Modern Economy: Lessons from Medieval Trade.* Cambridge University Press.

Griffith, M., and Fox, S. 2007. Hobbyists Online. Data Memo, Pew Internet and American Life Project.

Grimmer, L. 2006. Interview with David Heinemeier Hansson from Ruby on Rails. *My SQL Developer Zone,* February. http://dev.mysql.com/tech-resources/interviews/david-heinemeier-hansson-rails.html.

Grossman, G. M., and Helpman, E. 1990. Comparative Advantage and Long-Run Growth. *American Economic Review* 80(4): 796–815.

Gulati, R. 1998. Alliances and Networks. *Strategic Management Journal,* 19(4), 293–317.

Gulati, R., Lawrence, P. R., and Puranam, P. 2005. Adaptation in Vertical Relationships: Beyond Incentive Conflict. *Strategic Management Journal* 26(5): 415–440.

Gulati, R., and Singh, H. 1998. The Architecture of Cooperation: Managing Coordination Costs and Appropriation Concerns in Strategic Alliances. *Administrative Science Quarterly,* 43(4), 781–814.

Hadar, A. 2008. Apple Probably Stealing the Idea, Rejects MailWrangler from the App Store. *MacBlogz,* September 21. http://www.macblogz.com/2008/09/21/apple-rejects-mailwrangler-from-the-app-store-probably-stealing-the-idea/.

Hahn, R. W., and Wallsten, S. J. 2006. The Economics of Net Neutrality. *The Economist's Voice* 3(6): Article 8.

Hain, T. 2000. Architectural Implications of NAT. Request for Comments 2993. IETF.

Hall, P. 1994. *Innovation, Economics and Evolution: Theoretical Perspectives on Changing Technology in Economic Systems.* Harvester Wheatsheaf.

Hall, P. A., and Soskice, D. 2001. An Introduction to Varieties of Capitalism. In P. Hall and D. Soskice, eds., *Varieties of Capitalism: The Institutional Foundations of Comparative Advantage*. Oxford University Press.

Hall, P. A., and Taylor, R. C. R. 1996. Political Science and the Three New Institutionalisms. *Political Studies* 44(5): 936–957.

Hall, R. E., and Lieberman, M. 2001. *Economics. Principles and Applications*, second edition. South-Western College Publishing.

Hamm, S. 1998. The Education of Marc Andreessen. *Business Week*, April 13. http://www.businessweek.com/1998/15/topstory.htm.

Hammock, R. 2006. The Next Small Thing. *mybusinessmag.com*, August/September. http://www.mybusinessmag.com/fullstory.php3?sid=1413.

Handley, M. 2006. Why the Internet Only Just Works. *BT Technology Journal* 24(3): 119–129.

Hansell, S. 2006. Plan for Fees on Some E-Mail Spurs Protest. *New York Times*, February 28.

Hansell, S. 2007. Google Keeps Tweaking Its Search Engine. *New York Times*, June 3. http://www.nytimes.com/2007/06/03/business/yourmoney/03google.html.

Hansell, S. 2008a. How Google Could Keep Yahoo From Microsoft. *New York Times*, February 4. http://bits.blogs.nytimes.com/2008/02/04/how-google-could-keep-yahoo -from-microsoft/.

Hansell, S. 2008b. The Open Way Yahoo Could Do a Search Deal with Google. *New York Times*, April 15. http://bits.blogs.nytimes.com/2008/04/09/the-open-way-yahoo -could-do-a-search-deal-with-google/.

Hardin, G. 1968. The Tragedy of the Commons. *Science* 162(3859): 1243–1248.

Harhoff, D., Henkel, J., and von Hippel, E. 2003. Profiting from Voluntary Information Spillovers: How Users Benefit by Freely Revealing Their Innovations. *Research Policy*, 32(10), 1753–1769.

Harris, R. G. 1998. The Internet as a GPT: Factor Market Implications. In E. Helpman, ed., *General Purpose Technologies and Economic Growth*. MIT Press.

Hausman, J. A., Sidak, G. J., and Singer, H. J. 2001. Residential Demand for Broadband Telecommunications and Consumer Access to Unaffiliated Internet Content Providers. *Yale Journal on Regulation* 18(1): 129–173.

Hawk, T. 2005. Flickr and WebShots: A Classic Web2.0 Case. *Thomas Hawk's Digital Connection*, November 25. http://thomashawk.com/2005/11/flickr-and-webshots -classic-web20-case.html.

Hedlund, M. 2005. The Builders of Basecamp. *O'Reilly Network*, March 3. http://www .oreillynet.com/pub/a/network/2005/03/10/basecamp.html.

Heilemann, J. 2005. Journey to the (Revolutionary, Evil-Hating, Cash-Crazy, and Possibly Self-Destructive) Center of Google. *GQ*, March. http://www.gq.com/news -politics/newsmakers/200502/google-larry-sergey

Heinemeier Hansson, David. 2005. Entrepreneurs, Angels, and the Cost of Launch. *Signal vs. Noise*, June 30. http://www.37signals.com/svn/archives2/entrepreneurs _angels_and_the_cost_of_launch.php.

Heinemeier Hansson, David. 2008. It Doesn't Have to Be All or Nothing with a Startup. *Signal vs. Noise*, June 11. http://www.37signals.com/svn/posts/1078-it -doesnt-have-to-be-all-or-nothing-with-a-startup.

Helft, M. 2006. Yearning for Freedom ... From Venture Capital Overlords. *New York Times*, November 24.

Helft, M. 2008. The Humans behind the Google Money Machine. *New York Times*, June 2. http://www.nytimes.com/2008/06/02/technology/02google.html?partner=rssnyt.

Heller, M. A. 1998. The Tragedy of the Anticommons: Property in the Transition from Marx to Markets. *Harvard Law Review* 111(3): 621–688.

Hellmann, T., and Puri, M. 2000. The Interaction between Product Market and Financing Strategy: The Role of Venture Capital. *Review of Financial Studies* 13(4), 959–984.

Hellmann, T., and Puri, M. 2002. Venture Capital and the Professionalization of Start-Up Firms: Empirical Evidence. *Journal of Finance* 57(1): 169–197.

Hellweg, E. 2003. The Kazaa Conundrum: The RIAA's Lawsuits Have Split the Broadband ISP Industry and Will Likely Split Investors as Well. *CNN Money.com*, September 10. http://money.cnn.com/2003/09/10/technology/techinvestor/hellweg/ index.htm.

Helpman, E. 2004. *The Mystery of Economic Growth*. Belknap.

Helpman, E., ed. 1998. *General Purpose Technologies and Economic Growth*. MIT Press.

Helpman, E., and Trajtenberg, M. 1998a. Diffusion of General Purpose Technologies. In E. Helpman, ed., *General Purpose Technologies and Economic Growth*. MIT Press.

Helpman, E., and Trajtenberg, M. 1998b. A Time to Sow and a Time to Reap. Growth Based on General Purpose Technologies. In E. Helpman, ed., *General Purpose Technologies and Economic Growth*. MIT Press.

Hemphill, C. S. 2008. Network Neutrality and the False Promise of Zero-Price Regulation. *Yale Journal on Regulation* 25(2): 135–180.

Henderson, R. M., and Clark, K. B. 1990. Architectural Innovation: The Reconfiguration of Existing Product Technologies and the Failure of Established Firms. *Administrative Science Quarterly* 35(1): 9–30.

Henkel, J., and von Hippel, E. 2005. Welfare Implications of User Innovation. *Journal of Technology Transfer* 30(1–2): 73–87.

Herbert, A.J. 1990. ANSA Approach to the Design of Distributed Systems. *IEE Colloquium on Building Distributed Systems*.

Herman, B. D. 2006. Opening Bottlenecks: On Behalf of Mandated Network Neutrality. *Federal Communications Law Journal* 59(1): 103–156.

Herron, C. 2006. Caterina Fake and Meg Hourihan Share Flickr, Blogger Lore. *Christine(.net)*, August 16. http://www.christine.net/2006/08/caterina_fake_a.html.

Hindman, M. 2008. *The Myth of Digital Democracy*. Princeton University Press.

Hofmeister, C., Nord, R., and Soni, D. 2000. *Applied Software Architecture*. Addison-Wesley.

Holahan, C. 2006. Why Yahoo's Panama Won't Be Enough. *BusinessWeek.com*, December 26. http://www.businessweek.com/print/technology/content/dec2006/tc20061226_633699.htm.

Holahan, C. 2007. Panama's Promising Early Results. *BusinessWeek.com*, March 8. http://www.businessweek.com/print/technology/content/mar2007/tc20070307_187360.htm.

Holbrook, D., Cohen, W. M., Hounshell, D. A., and Klepper, S. 2000. The Nature, Sources, and Consequences of Firm Differences in the Early History of the Semiconductor Industry. *Strategic Management Journal* 21(10–11): 1017–1041.

Holdrege, M., and Srisuresh, P. 2001. Protocol Complications with the IP Network Address Translator. Request for Comments 3027. IETF.

Holmstrom, B., and Milgrom, P. 1994. The Firm as an Incentive System. *American Economic Review* 84(4): 972–991.

Honan, M. 2008. Photo Essay: Unlikely Places Where Wired Pioneers Had Their Eureka! Moments. *Wired*, March 24. http://www.wired.com/culture/lifestyle/multimedia/2008/03/ff_eureka.

Hosseini, M., Ahmed, D. T., Shirmohammadi, S., and Georganas, N. D. 2007. A Survey of Application-Layer Multicast Protocols. *IEEE Communications Surveys and Tutorials* 9(3): 58–74.

Hourihan, M. 2005. Meg Hourihan Interview. *Memory Lane*, May 17. http://itc.conversationsnetwork.org/shows/detail541.html.

Huston, G. 2008. IPv4 Address Report, generated May 11. http://ipv4.potaroo.net.

Hull, J. C. 2002. *Options, Futures, and Other Derivative Securities*, fifth edition. Prentice-Hall.

Hutheesing, N. 2004. Corporate Inter-Face-Time. *Forbes*, March 22. http://www
.forbes.com/best/2004/0322/002.html.

IETF. 2008. Hypertext Transfer Protocol Bis (httpbis) Working Group Overview.
August 28. http://www.ietf.org/html.charters/httpbis-charter.html.

IETF. 2009. Official Internet Protocol Standards. September 17. http://www.rfc-
editor.org/rfcxx00.html.

Internet Freedom and Nondiscrimination Act of 2006. H.R. 5417. 109th Congress,
2nd Session. 2006.

Internet Freedom Preservation Act. S. 215. 110th Congress, 1st Session. 2007.

Internet Non-Discrimination Act of 2006. S. 2360. 109th Congress, 2nd Session.
2006.

Isenberg, David. 1997. Rise of the Stupid Network: Why the Intelligent Network Was
Once a Good Idea, but Isn't Anymore. One Telephone Company Nerd's Odd Perspective on the Changing Value Proposition. *Computer Telephony*, August: 16,18, 20,
24, 26.

Isenberg, David S. 1998. The Dawn of the "Stupid Network." *netWorker* 2(1): 24–31.

ISO. 1997. *International Standard ISO/IEC 9126: Software Quality Characteristics and
Metrics. Part 1: Quality Characteristics and Sub-Characteristics. Part 2: External Metrics.*
International Organization for Standardization. International Electrotechnical
Commission.

Jacobides, M. G. 2001. Revisiting Vertical Scope: Capabilities, Integration and Profitability in the Mortgage Banking Industry. Working Paper 01-16, Wharton Financial
Institutions Center, University of Pennsylvania.

Jacobides, M. G. 2002. Where Do Markets Come From? Working Paper CNE
WP06/2002, Centre for the Network Economy.

Jacobides, M. G. 2005. Industry Change through Vertical Disintegration: How and
Why Markets Emerged in Mortgage Banking. *Academy of Management Journal* 48(3):
465–498.

Jacobides, M. G., and Hitt, L. M. 2005. Losing Sight of the Forest for the Trees? Productive Capabilities and Gains from Trade as Drivers of Vertical Scope. *Strategic
Management Journal* 26(13): 1209–1227.

Jaffe, A. B. 2000. The U.S. Patent System in Transition: Policy Innovation and the
Innovation Process. *Research Policy* 29(4–5): 531–557.

Jaiswal, S., Iannaccone, G., Diot, C., Kurose, K., and Towsley, D. 2007. Measurement
and Classification of Out-of-Sequence Packets in a Tier-1 IP Backbone. *IEEE/ACM
Transactions on Networking* 15(1): 54–66.

Jaspers, F., and van den Ende, J. 2006. The Organizational Form of Vertical Relationships: Dimensions of Integration. *Industrial Marketing Management* 35(7): 819–828.

Jensen, M. C., and Meckling, W. H. 1976. Theory of the Firm. Managerial Behavior, Agency Costs and Ownership Structure. *Journal of Financial Economics* 3(4): 305–360.

Jeppesen, L. B. 2005. User Toolkits for Innovation: Consumers Support Each Other. *Journal of Product Innovation Management* 22(4): 347–362.

Jeppesen, L. B., and Molin, M. J. 2003. Consumers as Co-developers: Learning and Innovation Outside the Firm. *Technology Analysis and Strategic Management* 15(3): 363–383.

Johnson, D. R., and Post, D. 1996. Law and Borders—The Rise of Law in Cyberspace. *Stanford Law Review* 48(5): 1367–1402.

Jolls, C., Sunstein, C. R., and Thaler, R. H. 2000. A Behavioral Approach to Law and Economics. In C. Sunstein, ed., *Behavioral Law and Economics*. Cambridge University Press.

Jones, C. I. 2002. Sources of U.S. Economic Growth in a World of Ideas. *American Economic Review* 92(1): 220–239.

Jones, C. I., and Williams, J. C. 1998. Measuring the Social Return to R&D. *Quarterly Journal of Economics* 113(4): 1119–1135.

Jones, K. C. 2007. Pearl Jam Blasts AT&T for Cut Lyrics in Lollapalooza Webcast. *InformationWeek*, Aug. 9. http://www.informationweek.com/shared/printableArticle.jhtml?articleID=201310731.

Jorgenson, D. W. 2001. Information Technology and the US Economy. *American Economic Review* 91(1): 1–32.

Jorgenson, D. W., Ho, M. S., and Stiroh, K. J. 2008. A Retrospective Look at the U.S. Productivity Growth Resurgence. *Journal of Economic Perspectives* 22(1): 3–24.

Kaat, M. 2000. Overview of 1999 IAB Network Layer Workshop. Request for Comments 2956. IETF.

Kahneman, D., and Tversky, A. 1984. Choices, Values and Frames. *American Psychologist* 39(4): 341–350.

Kahneman, D., and Tversky, A., eds. 2000. *Choices, Values, and Frames*. Cambridge University Press.

Kahney, L. 2001. Dot-Com Begs for Bucks. *Wired*, January 4. http://www.wired.com/techbiz/media/news/2001/01/40979.

Kane, M. 2002a. Overture Bows to Google in AOL Deal. *CNET News*, May 27. http://news.cnet.com/2100-1023-896152.html.

Kane, M. 2002b. Overture Bullish Despite Earthlink Loss. *CNET News*, May 27. http://news.cnet.com/Overture-bullish-despite-EarthLink-loss/2100-1023_3-831496.html.

Kaplan, D. A. 1999. *The Silicon Boys and Their Valley of Dreams*. William Morrow.

Kaplan, S., and Henderson, R. 2005. Inertia and Incentives: Bridging Organizational Economics and Organizational Theory. *Organization Science* 16(5): 509–521.

Kaplan, S. B., and Strömberg, P. 2001. Venture Capitalists as Principals: Contracting, Screening, and Monitoring. *American Economic Review* 91(2): 426–430.

Karagiannis, T., Rodriguez, P., and Papagiannaki, K. 2005. Should Internet Service Providers Fear Peer-Assisted Content Distribution? *Internet Measurement Conference 2005*.

Karr, T. 2006. AOL Censors Opposition Site. *MediaCitizen*, April 14. http://www.freepress.net/news/14960.

Katsh, M. E. 1996. Software Worlds and the First Amendment: Virtual Doorkeepers in Cyberspace. *University of Chicago Legal Forum*, 1996: 335–360.

Katyal, N. K. 2002. Architecture as Crime Control. *Yale Law Journal* 111(5): 1039–1140.

Katz, M. L. 2002. Intellectual Property Rights and Antitrust Policy: Four Principles for a Complex World. *Journal on Telecommunication and High Technology Law* 1: 325–353.

Katz, M. L., and Shapiro, C. 1985. Network Externalities, Competition, and Compatibility. *American Economic Review* 75(3): 424–440.

Katz, M. L., and Shapiro, C. 1994. Systems Competition and Network Effects. *Journal of Economic Perspectives* 8(2): 93–115.

Katz, M. L., and Shapiro, C. 1999. Antitrust in Software Markets. In J. Eisenach and T. Lenard, eds., *Competition, Innovation, and the Microsoft Monopoly: Antitrust in the Digital Marketplace*. Kluwer.

Kavassalis, P., and Lehr, W. 2000. The Flexible Specialization Path of the Internet. In E. Bohlin, K. Brodin, A. Lundgren, and B. Thorngren, eds., *Convergence in Communications and Beyond*. Elsevier.

Kaye, K. 2008. Yahoo's Revamped AT&T Deal Aligns with Display Ad Network Goal. *The ClickZ News*, February 1. http://www.clickz.com/showPage.html?page=3628297.

Kazman, R., Klein, M., Barbacci, M., Longstaff, T., Lipson, H., and Carriere, J. 1998. The Architecture Tradeoff Analysis Method. *Fourth International Conference on Engineering Complex Computer Systems*.

Kempf, J., and Austein, R. 2004. The Rise of the Middle and the Future of End-to-End: Reflections on the Evolution of the Internet Architecture. Request for Comments 3724. IETF.

Kesan, J. P., and Shah, R. C. 2001. Fool Us Once Shame on You—Fool Us Twice Shame on Us: What We Can Learn from the Privatizations of the Internet Backbone Network and the Domain Name. *Washington University Law Quarterly* 79(1): 89–220.

Kesan, J. P., and Shah, R. C. 2005. Shaping Code. *Harvard Journal of Law and Technology*, 18 (spring), 319–404.

Kihlstrom, R. E., and Laffont, J.-J. 1979. A General Equilibrium Entrepreneurial Theory of Firm Formation Based on Risk Aversion. *Journal of Political Economy* 87(4): 719–748.

King, B. 2002. The Day the Napster Died. *Wired*, May 15. http://www.wired.com/gadgets/portablemusic/news/2002/05/52540?currentPage=all.

Kirzner, I. M. 1997. Entrepreneurial Discovery and the Competitive Market Process: An Austrian Approach. *Journal of Economic Literature* 35(1): 60–85.

Kitch, E. W. 1977. The Nature and Function of the Patent System. *Journal of Law and Economics* 20(2): 265–290.

Klein, D. S. 1999. Visionary in Obscurity. *SmartBusiness*, April. http://www.sbnonline.com/Local/Article/3592/82/0/Visionary_in_obscurity.aspx.

Klein, M., and Kazman, R. 1999. *Attribute-Based Architectural Styles*. Technical Report CMU/SEI-99-TR-022, ESC-TR-49-022, Carnegie Mellon Software Engineering Institute.

Klemperer, P. 1990. How Broad Should the Scope of Patent Protection Be? *Rand Journal of Economics* 21(1): 113–130.

Knecht, G. Bruce. 1996. Reading the Market: How Wall Street Whiz Found a Niche Selling Books on the Internet. *Wall Street Journal*, May 16.

Knight, F. H. 1971. *Risk, Uncertainty and Profit*. Reprint: University of Chicago Press.

Kogut, B., and Zander, U. 1996. What Firms Do? Coordination, Identity, and Learning. *Organization Science* 7(5): 502–518.

Kolasky, W. J. 1999. Network Effects: A Contrarian View. *George Mason Law Review* 7(3): 577–615.

Kortum, S., and Lerner, J. 2000. Assessing the Contribution of Venture Capital to Innovation. *Rand Journal of Economics* 31(4): 674–692.

Krantz, M. 2002. Web of Board Members Ties Together Corporate America. *USA Today*, November 25.

Kraus, J. 2005a. It's a Great Time to be an Entrepreneur. *Bnoopy*, June 29. http://bnoopy.typepad.com/bnoopy/2005/06/its_a_great_tim.html.

Kraus, J. 2005b. The Long Tail of Software. Millions of Markets of Dozens. *Bnoopy*, March 9. http://bnoopy.typepad.com/bnoopy/2005/03/the_long_tail_o.html.

Kreimer, S. F. 2006. Censorship by Proxy: The First Amendment, Internet Intermediaries, and the Problem of the Weakest Link. *University of Pennsylvania Law Review* 155(1): 11–95.

Krengel, U. 1991. *Einführung in die Wahrscheinlichkeitstheorie und Statistik*. 3rd ed. Vieweg.

Kreps, D. M. 1990. *A Course in Microeconomic Theory*. Princeton University Press.

Kruchten, P. B. 1995. The 4+1 View Model of Architecture. *IEEE Software* 12(6): 42–50.

Kruse, H. 1999. Protocol Interactions and Their Effects on Internet-Based E-Commerce. Paper presented at Second International Conference on Telecommunications and Electronic Commerce.

Kurose, J. F., and Ross, K. W. 2008. *Computer Networking: A Top-Down Approach*, fourth edition. Pearson/Addison-Wesley.

Lakhani, K. R., and Wolf, R. G. 2005. Why Hackers Do What They Do: Understanding Motivation and Effort in Free/Open Source Software Projects. In J. Feller, B. Fitzgerald, S. Hissam, and K. Lakhani, eds., *Perspectives on Free and Open Source Software*. MIT Press.

Landes, W. M., and Posner, R. A. 2003. *The Economic Structure of Intellectual Property Law*. Belknap.

Langlois, R. N. 2002. Modularity in Technology and Organization. *Journal of Economic Behavior and Organization* 49(1): 19–37.

Langlois, R. N., and Robertson, P. L. 1992. Networks and Innovation in a Modular System: Lessons from the Microcomputer and Stereo Component Industries. *Research Policy* 21(4): 297–313.

Latin American and Caribbean Internet Addresses Registry. 2007. LACNIC Announces the Imminent Depletion of the IPv4 Addresses. June 20 http://lacnic.net/en/anuncios/2007_agotamiento_ipv4.html.

Laverty, K. J. 1996. Economic "Short-Termism": The Debate, the Unresolved Issues, and the Implications for Management Practice and Research. *Academy of Management Review* 21(3): 825–860.

Lea, D. 1994. Christopher Alexander: An Introduction for Object-Oriented Designers. *ACM SIGSOFT Software Engineering Notes* 19(1): 39–46.

Lee, R. S., and Wu, T. 2009. Subsidizing Creativity through Network Design: Zero-Pricing and Net Neutrality. *Journal of Economic Perspectives* 23(3): 61–76.

Leichtman Research Group. 2008. Over 8.5 Million Added Broadband from Top Cable and Telephone Companies in 2007. March 3. http://www.leichtmanresearch.com/press/030308release.html.

Leiponen, A., and Helfat, C. E. 2005. Innovation Objectives, Knowledge Sources, and the Benefits of Breadth. Working paper.

Lemley, M. A. 1997. The Economics of Improvement in Intellectual Property Law. *Texas Law Review* 75 (April): 989–1084.

Lemley, Mark A., and Lawrence Lessig. 1999. Ex Parte to Federal Communications Commission. CS Dkt. No. 99–251.

Lemley, M. A., and Lessig, L. 2000. Open Access to Cable Modems. *Whittier Law Review* 22(1): 3–34.

Lemley, M. A., and Lessig, L. 2001. The End of End-to-End: Preserving the Architecture of the Internet in the Broadband Era. *UCLA Law Review* 48(4): 925–972.

Lemley, M. A., and McGowan, D. 1998. Legal Implications of Network Economic Effects. *California Law Review* 86(3): 479–611.

Lenhart, A. 2009. Adults and Social Network Websites. Data Memo, Pew Internet and American Life Project.

Lerner, J. 2000. Small Business, Innovation, and Public Policy in the Information Technology Industry. In E. Brynjolfsson and B. Kahin, eds., *Understanding the Digital Economy: Data, Tools, and Research*. MIT Press.

Lerner, J. 2002. The Returns to Investments in Innovative Activities: An Overview and an Analysis of the Software Industry. In D. Evans, ed., *Microsoft, Antitrust and the New Economy: Selected Essays*, volume 2. Kluwer.

Lerner, J., and Tirole, J. 2002. Some Simple Economics of Open Source. *Journal of Industrial Economics* 50(2): 197–234.

Lerner, J., and Tirole, J. 2005a. The Economics of Technology Sharing: Open Source and Beyond. *Journal of Economic Perspectives* 19(2): 99–120.

Lerner, J., and Tirole, J. 2005b. The Scope of Open Source Licensing. *Journal of Law Economics and Organization* 21(1): 20–56.

Lessig, L. 1995. The Regulation of Social Meaning. *University of Chicago Law Review* 62(3): 943–1045.

Lessig, L. 1998. The New Chicago School. *Journal of Legal Studies* 27(2): 661–691.

Lessig, L. 1999a. *Code and Other Laws of Cyberspace*. Basic Books.

Lessig, L. 1999b. The Law of the Horse: What Cyberlaw Might Teach. *Harvard Law Review* 113(2): 501–549.

Lessig, L. 2001. *The Future of Ideas: The Fate of the Commons in a Connected World.* Vintage Books.

Lessig, L. 2002. Testimony before the United States Senate, Committee on Commerce, Science, and Transportation, at Its Hearing on: The Government's Role in Promoting the Future of Telecommunications Industry and Broadband Deployment, October 1. 107th Cong., 2nd Session.

Lessig, L. 2004. *Free Culture: How Big Media Uses Technology and the Law to Lock Down Culture and Control Creativity.* Penguin.

Lessig, L. 2006. Testimony before the United States Senate, Committee on Commerce, Science, and Transportation, at Its Hearing on: Network Neutrality, February 2. 109th Cong., 2nd Session.

Lessig, L. 2008a. *Remix: Making Art and Commerce Thrive in the Hybrid Economy.* Penguin.

Lessig, L. 2008b. Testimony before the United States Senate, Committee on Commerce, Science, and Transportation, at its Hearing on: The Future of the Internet, April 22. 110th Cong., 2nd Session.

Levenson, M. 2008. Facebook, ConnectU Settle Dispute. *Boston Globe*, June 27. http://www.boston.com/business/technology/articles/2008/06/27/facebook _connectu_settle_dispute/.

Lichtman, D. G. 2000. Property Rights in Emerging Platform Technologies. *Journal of Legal Studies* 29(2): 615–648.

Liebowitz, S. J., and Margolis, S. E. 2001. *Winners, Losers and Microsoft: Competition and Antitrust in High Technology*, revised edition. Independent Institute.

Lindgren, B. W. 1962. *Statistical Theory.* Macmillan.

Lipsey, R. G., Carlaw, K. I., and Bekar, C. T. 2005. *Economic Transformations: General Purpose Technologies and Long-Term Economic Growth.* Oxford University Press.

Liptak, A. 2007a. Verizon Rejects Text Messages of Abortion Rights Group. *New York Times*, September 27.

Liptak, A. 2007b. Verizon Reverses Itself on Abortion Messages. *New York Times*, September 28. http://www.nytimes.com/2007/09/28/business/28verizon.html?th &emc=th.

Litan, R. E., and Rivlin, A. M. 2001. *Beyond the Dot.coms: The Economic Promise of the Internet.* Brookings Institution.

Livingston, J. 2007. *Founders at Work: Stories of Startups' Early Days*. University of California Press.

Loewenstein, G., and Prelec, D. 1992. Anomalies in Intertemporal Choice: Evidence and an Interpretation. *Quarterly Journal of Economics* 107(2): 573–597.

Lohr, S. 2008. Yahoo Offer Is Strategy Shift for Microsoft. *New York Times*, February 2. http://www.nytimes.com/2008/02/02/technology/02soft.html.

Lucky, R. W. 1997. When Is Dumb Smart? *IEEE Spectrum* 34(11): 21.

Luenberger, D. G. 1997. *Investment Science*. Oxford University Press.

Luethje, C., Herstatt, C., and von Hippel, E. 2005. User-Innovators and "Local" Information: The Case of Mountain Biking. *Research Policy* 34(6): 951–965.

MacCormack, A., Rusnak, J., and Baldwin, C. 2007. The Impact of Component Modularity on Design Evolution: Evidence from the Software Industry. Working Paper 08-038, Harvard Business School.

MacCormack, A., Rusnak, J., and Baldwin, C. Y. 2008. Exploring the Duality between Product and Organizational Architectures: A Test of the Mirroring Hypothesis. Working Paper 08-039, Harvard Business School.

MacKie-Mason, J. 2000. *An AOL/Time Warner Merger Will Harm Competition in Internet Online Services*. Report submitted to the U.S. Federal Trade Commission.

MacKie-Mason, J., and Metzler, J. 1999. Links between Vertically Related Markets: Kodak. In J. Kwoka Jr. and L. White, eds., *The Antitrust Revolution: Economics, Competition, and Policy*, third edition. Oxford University Press.

MacKie-Mason, J., Shenker, S., and Varian, H. 1995. Network Architecture and Content Provision: An Economic Analysis (June 29, 1996). 23rd Telecommunications Policy Research Conference.

MacKie-Mason, J. K., Shenker, S., and Varian, H. R. 1996. Service Architecture and Content Provision. The Network Provider as Editor. *Telecommunications Policy* 20(3): 203–217.

Madison River Communications. 2006. Who We Are. Madison River Communications. http://www.madisonriver.net/about_us/who_we_are.php

Maier, A. 2008. Exklusiv: Gebührenpflicht auf der Datenautobahn. Briten bieten Google die Stirn. *Financial Times Deutschland*, July 16. http://www.ftd.de/technik/it_telekommunikation/:Geb%FChrenpflicht%20Datenautobahn%20Briten%20Google%20Stirn/386651.html.

Mandy, D. M. 2000. Killing the Goose That May Have Laid the Golden Egg: Only the Data Know Whether Sabotage Pays. *Journal of Regulatory Economics* 17(2): 157–172.

Maney, K. 2006. Disrupter Man Goes after TV This Time. *USA Today*, December 6.

Manjoo, F. 2008. The Cell Phone Wars. *Slate*, September 25. http://www.slate.com/id/2200914/.

Mansfield, E., Rapoport, J., Romeo, A., Wagner, S., and Beardsley, G. 1977. Social and Private Rates of Return from Industrial Innovations. *Quarterly Journal of Economics* 91(2): 221–240.

Marginson, D., and McAulay, L. 2007. Exploring the Debate on Short-Termism: A Theoretical and Empirical Analysis. *Strategic Management Journal* 29(3): 273–292.

Markillie, P. 2005. Crowned At Last. *The Economist*, April 2, 3–6.

Markoff, J. 2007. Who Founded Facebook? A New Claim Emerges. *New York Times*, September 1. http://www.nytimes.com/2007/09/01/technology/01facebook.html.

Masten, S. E. 1999. About Oliver E. Williamson. In G. R. Carroll and D. J. Teece, eds., *Firms, Markets, and Hierarchies: The Transaction Cost Economics Perspective*. Oxford University Press.

Matutes, C., Regibeau, P., and Rockett, K. 1996. Optimal Patent Design and the Diffusion of Innovations. *Rand Journal of Economics* 27(1): 60–83.

McCord, K. R., and Eppinger, S. D. 1993. Managing the Integration Problem in Concurrent Engineering. Working Paper 3594-93-MSA, MIT Sloan School of Management.

McCullagh, D. 2003. Skype's VoIP Ambitions. *CNET News*, December 2. http://www.news.com/2008-7352-5112783.html.

McCullagh, D. 2005. Telco Agrees to Stop Blocking VoIP Calls. *CNET News*, March 3. http://news.cnet.com/Telco-agrees-to-stop-blocking-VoIP-calls/2100-7352_3-5598633.html.

McKinnon, M. 2001. King of the Blogs. *Shift*, summer. http://www.matthewmckinnon.com/kingoftheblogs.html.

Mead, R. 2000. You've Got Blog. *The New Yorker*, November 13: 102.

Mennecke, T. 2005. DSL Broadband Providers Perform Balancing Act. *Slyck News*, November 1. http://www.slyck.com/news.php?story=973.

Mercurio, J. 2002. Lott Apologizes for Thrumond Comment. *CNN*, December 10. http://archives.cnn.com/2002/ALLPOLITICS/12/09/lott.comment/.

Mercuro, N., and Medema, S. G. 2006. *Economics and the Law: From Posner to Postmodernism and Beyond*, second edition. Princeton University Press.

Merges, R. 1994. Intellectual Property Rights and Bargaining Breakdown: The Case of Blocking Patents. *Tennessee Law Review* 62(1): 75–106.

Merges, R. P., and Nelson, R. R. 1990. On the Complex Economics of Patent Scope. *Columbia Law Review* 90(3): 839–916.

Merges, R. P., and Nelson, R. R. 1994. On Limiting or Encouraging Rivalry in Technical Progress: The Effect of Patent Scope Decisions. *Journal of Economic Behavior and Organization* 25(1): 1–24.

Merton, R. C. 1973a. An Intertemporal Capital Asset Pricing Model. *Econometrica* 41(5): 867–887.

Merton, R. C. 1973b. Theory of Rational Option Pricing. *Bell Journal of Economics* 4(1): 141–183.

Merton, R. C. 1992. *Continuous-Time Finance*. Blackwell.

Mervana, S., and Le, C. 2001. *Design and Implementation of DSL-Based Access Solutions*. Cisco Press.

Messerschmitt, D. G. 2000. *Understanding Networked Applications: A First Course*. Morgan Kaufmann.

Microsoft Online Services. 2009. MSN Dial Up: Overview. http://get.msn.com/?prod =dialup.

Milgrom, P., and Roberts, J. 1992. *Economics, Organization and Management*. Prentice-Hall.

Miller, C. C. 2008a. I.P.O. Crisis Could Have Lingering Effect on Start-Ups. *New York Times*, October 3. http://bits.blogs.nytimes.com/2008/10/03/ipo-crisis-could-have -lingering-effect-on-start-ups/.

Miller, C. C. 2008b. Venture Capital Exit Drought Continues. *New York Times*, October 1. http://bits.blogs.nytimes.com/2008/10/01/venture-capital-exit-drought -continues/.

Miller, D. A. 2007. Invention under Uncertainty and the Threat of Ex Post Entry. *European Economic Review* 52 (April): 387–412.

Miller, D. K. 2005. The Continuing Telus Website Blocking Saga. *penmachine.com*, July 27. http://www.penmachine.com/2005/07/continuing-telus-website-blocking -saga.html.

Minar, N., and Hedlund, M. 2001. A Network of Peers: Peer-to-Peer Models through the History of the Internet. In *Peer-to-Peer: Harnessing the Benefits of Disruptive Technologies*, ed. A. Oram. O'Reilly.

Miniwatts Marketing Group. 2009. Internet Usage Statistics. The Internet Big Picture. World Internet Users and Population Stats as of June 30, 2009. http://www .internetworldstats.com/stats.htm.

MIT Communications Futures Program and Cambridge University Communications Research Network Broadband Working Group. 2005. *The Broadband Incentive Problem.* White Paper.

Mitchell, W. J. 1995. *City of Bits: Space, Place, and the Infobahn.* MIT Press.

Mockus, A., Fielding, R. T., and Herbsleb, J. D. 2002. Two Case Studies of Open Source Software Development: Apache and Mozilla. *ACM Transactions on Software Engineering and Methodology* 11(3): 309–346.

Mogul, J. C. 2004. Clarifying the Fundamentals of HTTP. *Software, Practice and Experience* 34(2): 103–134.

Mohney, D. undated. Niklas Zennstrom, Founder of Kazaa, Skype and Joost Interview. *vonmag.com.* http://vonmag.com/editorial/pioneer/niklas-zennstrom-founder-of-kazaa-skype-and-joost-interview.

Monteverde, K. 1995. Technical Dialog as an Incentive for Vertical Integration in the Semiconductor Industry. *Management Science* 41(10): 1624–1638.

Moody, G. 2001. *Rebel Code: Linux and the Open Source Revolution.* Penguin.

Moors, T. 2002. A Critical Review of 'End-to-End Arguments in System Design.' *IEEE International Conference on Communications.*

Morelli, M. D., Eppinger, S. D., and Gulati, R. K. 1995. Predicting Technical Communication in Product Development Organizations. *IEEE Transactions on Engineering Management* 42(3): 215–222.

Morris, C. R., and Ferguson, C. R. 1993. How Architecture Wins Technology Wars. *Harvard Business Review* 71(2): 86–96.

Mortenson, G. M. 2007. Petition for Rulemaking to Federal Communications Commission, July 20.

Moukheiber, Z. 1996. Kleiner's Web. *Forbes* 157(6): 40–42.

Murmann, J. P. 2003. *Knowledge and Competitive Advantage: The Coevolution of Firms, Technology, and National Institutions.* Cambridge University Press.

Mutz, D. C. 2006. *Hearing the Other Side: Deliberative Versus Participatory Democracy.* Cambridge University Press.

Myers, S. 1977. Determinants of Corporate Borrowing. *Journal of Financial Economics* 5(2): 147–175.

National Cable and Telecommunications Association. 2007. Comments to Federal Communications Commission. WC Dkt. No. 07–52. June 15.

National Venture Capital Association. 2008. *Yearbook 2008.*

Naughton, J. 2008. How Flickr Developed into a Classic Web 2.0 Success. *The Observer,* March 9: 16.

Nelson, R. R. 1991. Why Do Firms Differ, and How Does It Matter? *Strategic Management Journal*, 12 (special issue: Fundamental Research Issues in Strategy and Economics): 61–74.

Nelson, R. R. 2005. *Technology, Institutions and Economic Growth.* Harvard University Press.

Nelson, R. R., and Winter, S. G. 1977. In Search of Useful Theory of Innovation. *Research Policy* 6(1): 37–76.

Nelson, R. R., and Winter, S. G. 1982. *An Evolutionary Theory of Economic Change.* Belknap.

Net Applications. 2008. Browser Market Share. November. http://marketshare .hitslink.com/firefox-market-share.aspx?qprid=0&sample=28.

Netcraft. 2008. *July 2008 Web Server Survey*, July 7. http://news.netcraft.com/ archives/2008/07/07/july_2008_web_server_survey.html

Netscape. 1995a. Intuit to Provide Internet Access Directly From Quicken. Press release, October 19. http://cgi.netscape.com/newsref/pr/newsrelease55.html.

Netscape. 1995b. Macromedia and Netscape Combine Technologies to Bring True Multimedia to the Internet. Press release, June 5. http://cgi.netscape.com/newsref/ pr/newsrelease28.html.

Netscape. 1995c. Netscape and Sun. Press release, April 11. http://cgi.netscape.com/ newsref/pr/newsrelease23.html.

Netscape. 1995d. Netscape to License Sun's Java Programming Language. Press release, May 23. http://cgi.netscape.com/newsref/pr/newsrelease25.html.

Network Neutrality Act of 2006. H.R. 5273. 109th Congress 2nd Session. 2006.

Niewijk, R., Songhurst, C., and Todd, P. 2003. Why European ISPs Need Partners. *McKinsey Quarterly*, February. http://www.mckinseyquarterly.com/Why_European _ISPs_need_partners_1280

North, D. C. 1990. *Institutions, Institutional Change and Economic Performance.* Cambridge University Press.

North, D. C. 2005. Institutions and the Performance of Economies over Time. In C. Menard and M. M. Shirley, eds., *Handbook of New Institutional Economics.* Springer.

Novak, S., and Stern, S. 2003. The Impact of Technological Interdependency on Contracting Complementarities: Evidence from Automobile Product Development. Working paper, Northwestern University.

Nuechterlein, J. E., and Weiser, P. J. 2005. *Digital Crossroads: American Telecommunications Policy in the Internet Age.* MIT Press.

O'Brien, L. 2007. Poking Facebook. *02138*, November/December. http://www
.02138mag.com/magazine/article/1724.html.

O'Connell, P. 2005. Online Extra: At SBC, It's All about Scale and Scope. *Business Week*, November 7. http://www.businessweek.com/@@n34h*IUQu7KtOwgA/magazine/content/05_45/b3958092.htm.

Oates, J. 2006. Germans Want to Charge Google. *The Register*, February 27. http://www.theregister.co.uk/2006/02/27/deutche_telekom_google/.

Odlyzko, Andrew. 1998. Smart and Stupid Networks: Why the Internet Is Like Microsoft. *netWorker* 2(5): 38–46.

Oliner, S. D., and Sichel, D. E. 2000. The Resurgence of Growth in the Late 1990s: Is Information Technology the Story? *Journal of Economic Perspectives* 14(4): 3–22.

Olsen, S. 2002a. Google Challenges Pay-For-Play Search. *CNET News*, May 27. http://news.cnet.com/2100-1023-830123.html.

Olsen, S. 2002b. MSN, Overture Test Paid Listings. *CNET News*, January 7. http://news.cnet.com/MSN,-Overture-test-paid-listings/2110-1023_3-801374.html.

Olsen, S. 2002c. Overture Sues Google over Search Patent. *CNET News*, May 27. http://news.cnet.com/2100-1023-876861.html.

Olsen, S. 2002d. Yahoo Plays Overture's Paid Search Listings. *CNET News*, May 27. http://news.cnet.com/2100-1023-275821.html.

Olsen, S. 2004. Google, Yahoo Bury the Legal Hatchet. *CNET News*, August 9. http://news.cnet.com/Google,-Yahoo-bury-the-legal-hatchet/2100-1024_3-5302421.html.

Olsen, S. 2006. AOL Charged with Blocking Opponents' E-mail. *ZDNet News*, April 13. http://news.zdnet.com/2100-9595_22-6061089.html.

OpenNet Initiative. 2005. OpenNet Initiative: Bulletin 010. Telus Blocks Consumer Access to Labour Union Web Site and Filters an Additional 766 Unrelated Sites. August 2. http://opennet.net/bulletins/010/.

Ordover, J. A. Sykes, A. O., and Willig, R. D. 1985. Nonprice Anticompetitive Behavior by Dominant Firms toward the Producers of Complementary Products. In *Antitrust and Regulation: Essays in Memory of John J. McGowan,* ed. F. M. Fisher. MIT Press.

Osterlie, T. 2002. The User-Developer Convergence: Innovation and Software Systems Development in the Apache Project. Master's thesis, Norwegian University of Science and Technology.

Ostrom, E. 2005. Doing Institutional Analysis: Digging Deeper than Markets and Hierarchies. In C. Menard and M. M. Shirley, eds., *Handbook of New Institutional Economics*. Springer.

Page, L., Brin, S., Motwani, R., and Winograd, T.. 1999. *The PageRank Citation Ranking: Bringing Order to the Web*. Technical report, Stanford InfoLab.

Park, A. 2008. The Brash Boys at 37signals Will Tell You: Keep It Simple, Stupid. *Wired*, February 25. http://www.wired.com/techbiz/media/magazine/16-03/mf_signals.

Parnas, D. L. 1972. On the Criteria To Be Used in Decomposing Systems into Modules. *Communications of the ACM* 15(12): 1053–1058.

Partridge, C. 2008a. E-Mail to Barbara van Schewick. August 2.

Partridge, C. 2008b. The Technical Development of Internet Email. *IEEE Annals of the History of Computing* 30(2): 3–29.

Paxson, V. 1999. End-to-End Internet Packet Dynamics. *IEEE/ACM Transactions on Networking*, 7(3), 277–292.

Peha, J. M. 2007. The Benefits and Risks of Mandating Network Neutrality, and the Quest for a Balanced Policy. *International Journal of Communication* 1: 644–668.

Pelline, J. 1998. Pay-for-Placement Gets Another Shot. *CNET News*, January 2. http://news.cnet.com/Pay-for-placement-gets-another-shot/2100-1023_3-208309.html.

Penmachine. 2005a. The Continuing Telus Website Blocking Saga. July 27. http://www.penmachine.com/2005/07/continuing-telus-website-blocking-saga.html.

Penmachine. 2005b. Telus-Voices for Change Website Settlement Agreement. July 29. http://www.flickr.com/photos/penmachine/29590389/.

Perez, C. 2002. *Technological Revolutions and Financial Capital: The Dynamics of Bubbles and Golden Ages*. Elgar.

Peter, I. no date. On the Design of TCP/IP. *NetHistory: Internet History Project*. http://www.nethistory.info/Archives/tcpiptalk.htmls.

Peteraf, M. A. 1993. The Cornerstones of Competitive Advantage: A Resource-Based View. *Strategic Management Journal* 14(3), 179–191.

Peters, B. G. 2005. *Institutional Theory in Political Science: The New Institutionalism*, second edition. Continuum.

Peterson, L. L., and Davie, B. S. 2003. *Computer Networks: A Systems Approach*, third edition. Morgan Kaufmann.

Peterson, L. L., and Davie, B. S. 2007. *Computer Networks: A Systems Approach*, fourth edition. Morgan Kaufmann.

PHP Group. 2008. History of PHP and Related Projects. September 11. http://us2.php.net/history.

Poppo, L., and Zenger, T. 1998. Testing Alternative Theories of the Firm: Transaction Cost, Knowledge-Based, and Measurement Explanations for Make-or-Buy Decisions in Information Services. *Strategic Management Journal* 19(9): 853–877.

Porter, K., Bunker Whittington, K., and Powell, W. W. 2005. The Institutional Embeddedness of High-Tech Regions: Relational Foundations of the Boston Biotechnology Community. In S. Breschi and F. Malerba, eds., *Clusters, Networks, and Innovation*. Oxford University Press.

Posner, E. A. 1996a. Law, Economics and Inefficient Norms. *University of Pennsylvania Law Review* 144(5): 1697–1744.

Posner, E. A. 1996b. The Regulation of Groups: The Influence of Legal and Nonlegal Sanctions on Collective Action. *University of Chicago Law Review* 63(1): 133–197.

Posner, E. A. 1998a. Symbols, Signals, and Social Norms in Politics and the Law. *Journal of Legal Studies* 27(2, Part 1): 765–798.

Posner, E. A. 2000. *Law and Social Norms*. Harvard University Press.

Posner, R. A. 1997. Social Norms and the Law: An Economic Approach. *American Economic Review* 87(2): 365–369.

Posner, R. A. 1998b. *Economic Analysis of Law*, fifth edition. Aspen Law and Business.

Posner, R. A. 2001. *Antitrust Law*, second edition. University of Chicago Press.

Postel, J. 1977a. Comments on Internet Protocol and TCP. Internet Engineering Note 2.

Postel, J. 1977b. TCP Meeting Notes, 13 and 14 October 1977. Internet Engineering Note 66.

Postel, J. 1978a. Internet Meeting Notes, 30 and 31 October 1978. Internet Engineering Note 63.

Postel, J. 1978b. Meeting Notes, 1 February 1978. Internet Engineering Note 22.

Postel, J. 1979a. Internet Datagram Protocol Version 4. Internet Engineering Note 80.

Postel, J. 1979b. Transmission Control Protocol—TCP Version 4. Internet Engineering Note 81.

Postel, J. 1981a. Internet Protocol: DARPA Internet Program Protocol Specification. Request for Comments 791. IETF.

Postel, J. 1981b. Transmission Control Protocol: DARPA Internet Program Protocol Specification. Request for Comments 793. IETF.

Pouzin, L., and Zimmerman, H. 1978. A Tutorial on Protocols. *Proceedings of the IEEE* 66(11): 1346–1370.

Powell, W.W., Koput, K. W., Bowie, J. I., and Smith-Doerr, L. 2002. The Spatial Clustering of Science and Capital: Accounting for Biotech Firm-Venture Capital Relationships. *Regional Studies* 36(3): 299–313.

Powell, W. W., and DiMaggio, P. J., eds. 1991. *The New Institutionalism in Organizational Analysis*. University of Chicago Press.

Powell, W. W., and Grodal, S. 2005. Networks of Innovators. In J. Faberberg, D. C. Mowery, and R. R. Nelson, eds., *The Oxford Handbook of Innovation*. Oxford University Press.

Pressman, R. S. 1997. *Software Engineering: A Practitioner's Approach*, fourth edition. McGraw-Hill.

PriMetrica. 2008. VoIP Ban Remains for Now. March 11. http://www.telegeography. com/cu/article.php?article_id=22126&email=html.

Public Knowledge, Free Press, Consumer Federation of America, Consumers Union, Educause, Media Access Project, et al. 2007. Petition for Declaratory Ruling. WT Dkt. No. 08–7. December 11.

Quistagaard, K. 1997a. Amazon.com Upstages Barnes & Noble. *Wired*, March 17. http://www.wired.com/techbiz/media/news/1997/03/2609.

Quistagaard, K. 1997b. Online Book Wars Escalate Further. *Wired*, May 16. http:// www.wired.com/techbiz/media/news/1997/05/3925.

Ralph, E. K. 2006. Letter: Comment on the Economics of Network Neutrality. *The Economists' Voice*. http://www.bepress.com/ev/vol3/iss1/art6.

Ramakrishnan, K., Floyd, S., and Black, D. 2001. The Addition of Explicit Congestion Notification (ECN) to IP. Request for Comments 3168. IETF.

Ranaweera, C., and Prabhu, J. 2003. The Influence of Satisfaction, Trust and Switching Barriers on Customer Retention in a Continuous Purchasing Setting. *International Journal of Service Industry Management* 14(4): 374–395.

Rangar, B. S. 2005. Skype: Reflections for European Venture Capital. *Ariadne Capital Journal—Through the Maze*. http://www.ariadnecapital.com/journal/v5e3/outlook _alwayson.htm.

Rao, P. M. 1999. Convergence and Unbundling of Corporate R&D in Telecommunications: Is Software Taking the Helm? *Telecommunications Policy* 23(1): 83–93.

Rapp, D. 2006. Inventing Yahoo! *AmericanHeritage.com*, April 12. w2.eff.org/patent/ wanted/neomedia/reexam/ExhibitH_InventingYahoo!.pdf.

Rashtchy, S., Kessler, A. M., Bieber, P. J., Schindler, N. H., and Tzeng, J. C. 2007. *The User Revolution: The New Advertising Ecosystem and the Rise of the Internet as a Mass Medium*. PiperJaffray Investment Research.

Ratnasamy, S., Shenker, S., and McCanne, S. 2005. Towards an Evolvable Internet Architecture. *2005 Conference on Applications, Technologies, Architectures, and Protocols for Computer Communications.*

Raymond, E. S. 1999. *The Cathedral and the Bazaar: Musings on Linux and Open Source by an Accidental Revolutionary.* O'Reilly.

Rayport, J. F., and Louie, D. L. 1998. Amazon.com (A). Case 9-897-128, Harvard Business School.

Rayport, J. F., and Louie, D. L. 2001. barnesandnoble.com (A). Case 9-898-082, Harvard Business School.

Read, D. 2004. Intertemporal Choice. In N. Harvey and D. J. Koehler, eds., *Blackwell Handbook of Judgment and Decision Making.* Blackwell.

Reardon, M. 2007. Comcast Denies Monkeying with BitTorrent Traffic. *CNET News,* August 21. http://www.news.com/8301-10784_3-9763901-7.html.

Rebello, K., Cortese, A., and Hof, R. D. 1996a. Inside Microsoft (Part 1). *BusinessWeek,* July 15. http://www.businessweek.com/1996/29/b34841.htm.

Rebello, K., Cortese, A., and Hof, R. D. 1996b. Inside Microsoft (Part 2). *BusinessWeek,* July 15. http://www.businessweek.com/1996/29/b34842.htm

Reed, D. P. 2000. The End of the End-to-End Argument. http://www.reed.com/Papers/endofendtoend.html

Reed, D. P. 2001. [e2e] Where End-to-End Ends. E-Mail to end2end-interest@postel.org Mailing List. May 23, 12:35:41 PDT. http://www.postel.org/pipermail/end2end-interest/2001-May/000908.html.

Reed, D. P. 2002. [e2e] Clarifying the End-to-End Principle. E-Mail to end2end-interest@postel.org Mailing List. March 5, 06:10:17 PST. http://www.postel.org/pipermail/end2end-interest/2002-March/001853.html.

Reed, D. P. 2006a. "[ih] Date of RFC 791 for Celebration. E-Mail to internet-history@postel.org Mailing List. March 30, 05:55:09 PST. http://mailman.postel.org/pipermail/internet-history/2006-March/000555.html.

Reed, D. P. 2006b. [ih] UDP Creation (Was: Date of RFC 791 for Celebration). E-Mail to internet-history@postel.org Mailing List. March 31, 08:46:59 PST. http://mailman.postel.org/pipermail/internet-history/2006-March/000569.html.

Reed, D. P. 2009a. E-Mail to Barbara van Schewick. October 16.

Reed, D. P. 2009b. Re: [IP] ISPs helping with botnets. E-Mail to ip@v2.listbox.com Mailing List. October 13. http://seclists.org/interesting-people/2009/Oct/102.

Reed, D. P., and Postel, J. 1978. User Datagram Protocol. Internet Engineering Note 71.

Reed, D. P., Saltzer, J. H., and Clark, D. D. 1998. Commentaries on 'Active Networking and End-to-End Arguments'. *IEEE Network* 12(3): 69–71.

Reidenberg, J. R. 1998. Lex Informatica: The Formulation of Information Policy Rules through Technology. *Texas Law Review* 76(3): 533–594.

Reinganum, J. F. 1989. The Timing of Innovation: Research, Development, and Diffusion. In R. L. Schmalensee and R. D. Willig, eds., *Handbook of Industrial Organization*, volume 1. Elsevier.

Reingold, J. 2008. The Secret Coach. *Fortune* 158(2): 124–134.

Reiss, S. 2008. Cloud Computing. Available at Amazon.com Today. *Wired*, April 21. http://www.wired.com/techbiz/it/magazine/16-05/mf_amazon.

Rindfleisch, A., and Heide, J. B. 1997. Transaction Cost Analysis: Past, Present, and Future Applications. *Journal of Marketing* 61(4): 30–54.

Rivlin, G. 2006. Wallflower at the Web Party. *New York Times*, October 15.

Roberts, L. G. 1967. Multiple Computer Networks and Intercomputer Communication. *First ACM Symposium on Operating System Principles*.

Rochet, J.-C., and Tirole, J. 2003. Platform Competition in Two-Sided Markets. *Journal of the European Economic Association* 1(4): 990–1029.

Rochet, J.-C., and Tirole, J. 2006. Two-sided Markets: A Progress Report. *Rand Journal of Economics* 37(3): 645–667.

Roe, M. J. 1994. *Strong Managers, Weak Owners: The Political Roots of American Corporate Finance*. Princeton University Press.

Romer, Paul M. 1990. Endogenous Technological Change. *Journal of Political Economy* 98(5): S71–S102.

Roscoe, T. 2006. The End of Internet Architecture. *Fifth Workshop on Hot Topics in Networks*.

Rosenberg, J. 2008. UDP and TCP as the New Waist of the Internet Hourglass. Internet-Draft, February 11.

Rosenberg, N. 1982. *Inside the Black Box: Technology and Economics*. Cambridge University Press.

Rosenberg, N. 1994. *Exploring the Black Box: Technology, Economics and History*. Cambridge University Press.

Rosenberg, N. 1996. Uncertainty and Technological Change. In R. Landau, T. Taylor, and G. Wright, eds., *The Mosaic of Economic Growth*. Stanford University Press.

Roth, D. 2004. Catch Us If You Can. *Fortune* 49(3): 64–74.

Roth, D. 2008. Google's Open Source Android OS Will Free the Wireless Web. *Wired*, June 23. http://www.wired.com/techbiz/media/magazine/16-07/ff_android.

Rubinfeld, D. L., and Singer, H. J. 2001. Vertical Foreclosure in Broadband Access? *Journal of Industrial Economics* 49(3): 299–318.

Ruby on Rails. 2008. The Core Team. http://rubyonrails.org/core.

Rysman, M. 2004. Competition between Networks: A Study of the Market for Yellow Pages. *Review of Economic Studies* 71(247): 483–512.

Sako, M. 2002. Modularity and Outsourcing: The Nature of Co-Evolution of Product Architecture and Organisation Architecture in the Global Automotive Industry. Working paper, Said Business School, University of Oxford.

Sako, M. 2004. Supplier Development at Honda, Nissan and Toyota: Comparative Case Studies of Organizational Capability Enhancement. *Industrial and Corporate Change* 13(2): 281–308.

Salop, S. C., and Craig Romaine, R. 1999. Preserving Monopoly: Economic Analysis, Legal Standards, and Microsoft. *George Mason Law Review* 7(3): 617–671.

Saltzer, J. H. 1999. "Open Access" Is Just the Tip of the Iceberg. October 22. http://web.mit.edu/Saltzer/www/publications/openaccess.html.

Saltzer, J. H., Reed, D. P., and Clark, D. D. 1981. End-to-End Arguments in System Design. *2nd International Conference on Distributed Computing Systems*.

Saltzer, J. H., Reed, D. P., and Clark, D. D. 1984. End-to-End Arguments in System Design. *ACM Transactions on Computer Systems* 2(4): 277–288.

Samuelson, P., and Scotchmer, S. 2002. The Law and Economics of Reverse Engineering. *Yale Law Journal* 111(7): 1575–1664.

Samuelson, W., and Zeckhauser, R. 1988. Status Quo Bias in Decision Making. *Journal of Risk and Uncertainty* 1(1): 7–59.

Sanchez, R. 1995. Strategic Flexibility in Product Competition. *Strategic Management Journal* 16 (special issue, summer): 135–159.

Sanchez, R. 1999. Modular Architectures in the Marketing Process. *Journal of Marketing* 63: 92–111.

Sanchez, Ron and Joseph T. Mahoney. 1996. Modularity, Flexibility, and Knowledge Management in Product and Organization Design. *Strategic Management Journal* 17 (special issue, winter): 63–76.

Sanchez, R. A. 1991. Strategic Flexibility, Real Options and Product-Based Strategy. PhD dissertation, Massachusetts Institute of Technology.

Sandvig, C. 2002. Communication Infrastructure and Innovation: The Internet as End-to-End Network That Isn't. Paper presented at Symposium with the Next Generation of Leaders in Science and Technology Policy.

Sandvig, C. 2006. Shaping Infrastructure and Innovation on the Internet: The End-to-End Network That Isn't. In D. H. Guston and D. Sarewitz, eds., *Shaping Science and Technology Policy: The Next Generation of Research*. University of Wisconsin Press.

Sandvine. 2004. *Meeting the Challenge of Today's Evasive P2P Traffic: Service Provider Strategies for Managing P2P Filesharing*. Sandvine Inc.

Sarac, K., and Almeroth, K. C. 2005. Monitoring IP Multicast in the Internet: Recent Advances and Ongoing Challenges. *IEEE Communications Magazine* 43(10): 85–91.

Sarasvathy, S. D., and Dew, N. S., Velamuri, R., and Venkataraman, S. 2003. Three Views of Entrepreneurial Opportunity. In Z. J. Acs and D. B. Audretsch, eds., *Handbook of Entrepreneurship Research*. Kluwer.

Saxenian, AnnaLee. 1994. *Regional Advantage: Culture and Competition in Silicon Valley and Route 128*. Harvard University Press.

Saxenian, AnnaLee. 2002. *Local and Global Networks of Immigrant Professionals in Silicon Valley*. Public Policy Institute of California.

Scacchi, W. 2002. Understanding the Requirements for Developing Open Source Software Systems. *IEE Software Proceedings* 149(1): 24–39.

Scherer, F. M. 2001. The Innovation Lottery. In R. C. Dreyfuss, D. L. Zimmerman, and H. First, eds., *Expanding the Boundaries of Intellectual Property: Innovation Policy for the Knowledge Society*. Oxford University Press.

Schiesel, S. 2002. A New Model for AOL May Influence Cable's Future. *New York Times*, August 26.

Schilling, M. A. 2000. Toward a General Modular Systems Theory and its Application to Interfirm Product Modularity. *Academy of Management Review* 25(2): 312–334.

Schilling, M. A., and Kevin Steensma, H. 2001. The Use of Modular Organizational Forms: An Industry-Level Analysis. *Academy of Management Journal* 44(6): 1149–1168.

Schmidt, D. C., Stal, M., Rohnert, H., and Buschmann, F. 2000. *Pattern-Oriented Software Architecture: Patterns for Concurrent and Networked Objects*, volume 2. Wiley.

Schoen, S. 2007a. Comcast and BitTorrent. *EFF Deeplinks Blog*, September 13. http://www.eff.org/deeplinks/2007/09/comcast-and-bittorrent.

Schoen, S. 2007b. EFF Tests Agree with AP: Comcast Is Forging Packets to Interfere with User Traffic. *EFF Deeplinks Blog*, October 19. http://www.eff.org/deeplinks/2007/10/eff-tests-agree-ap-comcast-forging-packets-tointerfere.

Schrage, M. 1997. The IQ Q&A: Steve Riggio. *Adweek.com*, August 18. http://www
.adweek.com/aw/esearch/article_display.jsp?vnu_content_id=518353.

Schwartz, M. 2000. The Economic Logic for Conditioning Bell Entry into Long Distance on the Prior Opening of Local Markets. *Journal of Regulatory Economics* 18(3):
247–288.

Scotchmer, S. 1991. Standing on the Shoulders of Giants: Cumulative Research and
the Patent Law. *Journal of Economic Perspectives* 5(1): 29–41.

Scotchmer, S. 1996. Protecting Early Innovators: Should Second-Generation Products Be Patentable? *Rand Journal of Economics* 27(2): 322–331.

Scotchmer, S. 2004. *Innovation and Incentives*. MIT Press.

Scott, W. R. 2000. *Institutions and Organizations*, second edition. Sage.

SearchIgnite and RBC Capital Markets. 2007. *Market Share Trends Within the
Engines, and Their Impact on Brand Marketers*, July 17. http://www.searchignite.com/
whitepapers/rbc-searchignite-july07.pdf

Selby, R. W., and Basili, V. R. 1991. Analyzing Error-Prone System Structure. *IEEE
Transactions on Software Engineering* 17(2): 141–152.

Sendmail, Inc. 2008. Sendmail Corporate Fact Sheet. July.

Senie, D. 2002. Network Address Translator (NAT)-Friendly Application Design
Guidelines. Request for Comments 3235. IETF.

Shah, D. 2006. On Startups: Patterns and Practices of Contemporary Software Entrepreneurs. Master's thesis. Massachusetts Institute of Technology.

Shah, S., and Tripsas, M. 2004. When Do User-Innovators Start Firms? Towards a
Theory of User Entrepreneurship. Working paper, University of Illinois.

Shane, S. 2000. Prior Knowledge and the Discovery of Entrepreneurial Opportunities. *Organization Science* 11(4): 448–469.

Shane, S., and Venkataraman, S. 2000. The Promise of Entrepreneurship as a Field
of Research. *Academy of Management Review* 25(1): 217–226.

Shapiro, A. L. 1998. The Disappearance of Cyberspace and the Rise of Code. *Seton
Hall Constitutional Law Journal* 8(3): 703–724.

Shapiro, C., and Varian, H. R. 1999. *Information Rules: A Strategic Guide to the Network
Economy*. Harvard Business School Press.

Sharma, P., Perry, E., and Malpani, R. 2003. IP Multicast Operational Network
Management: Design, Challenges, and Experiences. *IEEE Network* 17(2): 49–55.

Shaw, M., and Garlan, D. 1996. *Software Architecture: Perspectives on an Emerging
Discipline*. Prentice-Hall.

Shelanski, H. A. 2007. Adjusting Regulation to Competition: Toward a New Model for U.S. Telecommunications Policy. *Yale Journal on Regulation* 24(1): 55–105.

Shelanski, H. A., and Klein, P. G. 1999. Empirical Research in Transaction Cost Economics: A Review and Assessment. In G. R. Carroll and D. J. Teece, eds., *Firms, Markets, and Hierarchies: The Transaction Cost Economics Perspective*. Oxford University Press.

Shelanski, H. A., and Sidak, G. J. 2001. Antitrust Divestiture in Network Industries. *University of Chicago Law Review* 68(1): 1–100.

Sibley, D. S., and Weisman, D. L. 1998. Raising Rivals' Costs: The Entry of an Upstream Monopolist into Downstream Markets. *Information Economics and Policy* 10(4): 451–470.

Sidak, J. G. 2006. A Consumer-Welfare Approach to Network Neutrality Regulation of the Internet. *Journal of Competition Law and Economics* 2(3): 349–474.

Silberschatz, A., Galvin, P. B., and Gagne, G. 2005. *Operating Systems Concepts*, seventh edition. Wiley.

Simon, H. A. 1961. *Administrative Behavior*, second edition. Macmillan. Original Publication: 1947.

Simon, H. A. 1969. *The Sciences of the Artificial*. MIT Press.

Simon, H. A. 1957. *Models of Man: Social and Rational*. Wiley.

Slater, M. 2008. Can Rails Scale? Absolutely! April 6. http://www.buildingwebapps .com/articles/6419-can-rails-scale-absolutely.

Sobrero, M., and Roberts, E. B. 2001. The Trade-Off between Efficiency and Learning in Interorganizational Relationships for Product Development. *Management Science* 47(4): 493–511.

Sobrero, M., and Roberts, E. B. 2002. Strategic Management of Supplier-Manufacturer Relations in New Product Development. *Research Policy* 31(1): 159–182.

Sobrero, M., and Schrader, S. 1998. Structuring Inter-firm Relationships: A Meta-analytic Approach. *Organization Studies* 19(4): 585–615.

Solum, L. B., and Chung, M. 2003. The Layers Principle: Internet Architecture and the Law. Public Law and Legal Theory Research Paper 55, University of San Diego School of Law.

Solum, L. B., and Chung, M. 2004. The Layers Principle: Internet Architecture and the Law. *Notre Dame Law Review* 79(3): 815–948.

Sommerville, I. 1996. *Software Engineering*, fifth edition. Addison-Wesley.

Sosa, M. E., Eppinger, S. D., Pich, M., McKendrick, D. G., and Stout, S. K. 2002. Factors That Influence Technical Communication in Distributed Product Development: An Empirical Study in the Telecommunications Industry. *IEEE Transactions on Engineering Management* 49(1): 45–58.

Sosa, M. E., Eppinger, S. D., and Rowles, C. M. 2000. Understanding the Effects of Product Architecture on Technical Communication in Product Development Organizations. Working Paper 4130, MIT Sloan School of Management.

Sosa, M. E., Eppinger, S. D., and Rowles, C. M. 2002. The Coupling of Product Architecture and Organizational Structure in Complex Product Development. Working Paper 2002/76/TM, INSEAD.

Sosa, M., Eppinger, S. D., and Rowles, C. M. 2004. The Misalignment of Product Architecture and Organizational Structure in Complex Product Development. *Management Science* 50(12): 1674–1689.

Sosa, M., Gargiulo, M., and Rowles, C. 2007. Component Connectivity, Team Network Structure and the Attention to Technical Interfaces in Complex Product Development. Research Paper 2007/68/TOM/OB, INSEAD.

Souder, W. E., Sherman, J. D., and Davies-Cooper, R. 1998. Environmental Uncertainty, Organizational Integration, and New Product Development Effectiveness: A Test of Contingency Theory. *Journal of Product Innovation Management* 15(6): 520–533.

SourceForge.net. 2008. What Is SourceForge.net? *SourceForge.net*, December 18. http://alexandria.wiki.sourceforge.net/What+is+SourceForge.net%3F.

Spector, R. 2000. *Amazon.com: Get Big Fast.* HarperCollins.

Speta, J. B. 2000a. Handicapping the Race for the Last Mile?: A Critique of Open Access Rules for Broadband Platforms. *Yale Journal on Regulation* 17(1): 39–92.

Speta, J. B. 2000b. The Vertical Dimension of Cable Open Access. *University of Colorado Law Review* 71(4): 975–1010.

Spicer, D. E. 1998. Online in Class: Melding Cyber and Realspace in a Law School Seminar.

Spolsky, J. 2000. Strategy Letter I: Ben and Jerry's vs. Amazon. May 12. http://www .joelonsoftware.com/articles/fog0000000056.html.

Spolsky, J. 2003. Fixing Venture Capital. June 3. http://www.joelonsoftware.com/articles/VC.html.

Sproull, R. F., and Cohen, D. 1978. High-Level Protocols. *Proceedings of the IEEE* 66(11): 1371–1386.

Srikanth, K., and Puranam, P. 2007. Coordination in Distributed Organizations. Working paper, London Business School.

Srikanth, K., and Puranam, P. 2008. Coordination in Business Process Offshoring. Druid Working Paper 08-16.

Srisuresh, P., and Egevang, K. 2001. Traditional IP Network Address Translator (Traditional NAT). Request for Comments 3022. IETF.

Srisuresh, P., and Holdrege, M. 1999. IP Network Address Translator (NAT) Terminology and Considerations. Request for Comments 2663. IETF.

Stanley, K. B. 2000. Toward International Settlement Reform: FCC Benchmarks Versus ITU Rates. *Telecommunications Policy* 24(10–11): 843–863.

Staudenmayer, N., Tripsas, M., and Tucci, C. L. 2005. Interfirm Modularity and Its Implications for Product Development. *Journal of Product Innovation Management*, 22(4), 303–321.

Stavrou, A., Keromytis, A. D., Nieh, J., Misra, V., and Rubenstein, D. 2005. MOVE: An End-to-End Solution To Network Denial of Service. *12th Annual Network and Distributed System Security Symposium*.

Stephenson, S. 2005. Side-Business Software: The Neglected Software Market. *Signal vs. Noise*, July 24. http://www.37signals.com/svn/archives2/sidebusiness_software _the_neglected_software_market.php.

Sterbenz, J. P. G., and Touch, J. D. 2001. *High-Speed Networking: A Systematic Approach to High-Bandwidth Low-Latency Communication*. Wiley.

Stern, S. 2005. Economic Experiments: The Role of Entrepreneurship in Economic Prosperity. In *Understanding Entrepreneurship: A Research and Policy Report*. Ewing Marion Kauffman Foundation.

Stevens, W.P., Myers, G. J., and Constantine, L. L. 1999. Structured Design (Reprint). *IBM Systems Journal* 38(2–3): 231–256.

Steward, D. V. 1981. The Design Structure System: A Method for Managing the Design of Complex Systems. *IEEE Transactions on Engineering Management* 28(3): 71–74.

Stewart, B. 2001. An Interview with the Creator of Ruby. *O'Reilly Linux Devcenter*, November 29. http://www.linuxdevcenter.com/pub/a/linux/2001/11/29/ruby .html.

St. Johns, M., and Huston, G. 2003. Considerations on the Use of a Service Identifier in Packet Headers. Request for Comments 3639. IETF.

Stone, J., and Partridge, C. 2000. When the CRC and TCP Checksum Disagree. *Computer Communication Review* 30(4): 309–319.

Stross, R. 2005. Why Time Warner Has Fallen in Love with AOL, Again. *New York Times*, September 25.

Sturgeon, T. J. 2002. Modular Production Networks: A New American Model of Industrial Organization. *Industrial and Corporate Change* 11(3): 451–496.

Sullivan, D. 1998. GoTo Going Strong. *Search Engine Watch*, July 1. http://searchenginewatch.com/showPage.html?page=2166331.

Sullivan, D. 2002a. Overture and Inktomi Out, Google In at AOL. *Search Engine Watch*, May 1. http://searchenginewatch.com/2164731.

Sullivan, D. 2002b. Overture Wins Yahoo, What Will Happen with Google? *Search Engine Watch*, May 6. http://searchenginewatch.com/2164811.

Sullivan, K. J., Chalasani, P., Jha, S., and Sazawal, V. 1999. Software Design as an Investment Activity: A Real Options Perspective. In L. Trigeorgis, ed., *Real Options and Business Strategy: Applications to Decision Making*. Risk Books.

Sullivan, K. J., Griswold, W. G., Cai, Y., and Hallen, B. 2001. The Structure and Value of Modularity in Software Design. *8th European Software Engineering Conference Held Jointly with 9th ACM SIGSOFT International Symposium on Foundations of Software Engineering*.

Sunstein, C. R. 1996a. On the Expressive Function of Law. *University of Pennsylvania Law Review* 144(5): 2021–2053.

Sunstein, C. R. 1996b. Social Norms and Social Roles. *Columbia Law Review* 96(4): 903–968.

Svensson, P. 2007. Comcast Blocks Some Internet Traffic. Associated Press, October 19. http://www.sfgate.com/cgi-bin/article.cgi?f=/n/a/2007/10/19/financial/f061526D54.DTL.

Takeishi, A. 2001. Bridging Inter- and Intra-Firm Boundaries: Management of Supplier Involvement in Automobile Product Development. *Strategic Management Journal* 22(5): 403–433.

Tanenbaum, A. S. 2003. *Computer Networks*, fourth edition. Prentice-Hall.

Tanenbaum, A. S. 2008. *Modern Operating Systems*, third edition. Prentice-Hall.

Taylor, S., and Hettick, L. 2008. Verizon: IP Multimedia Subsystem on the Cusp of Being Viable in 2008. *Network World*, January 2. http://www.networkworld.com/newsletters/converg/2008/1231converge2.html.

Teece, D. J., Pisano, G., and Shuen, A. 1997. Dynamic Capabilities and Strategic Management. *Strategic Management Journal* 18(7): 509–533.

Terwiesch, C., and Xu, Y. 2008. Innovation Contests, Open Innovation, and Multiagent Problem Solving. *Management Science* 54(9): 1529–1543.

Thaler, D., and Aboba, B. 2008. What Makes for a Successful Protocol? Request for Comment 5218. IETF.

Thelen, K. 1999. Historical Institutionalism in Comparative Politics. *Annual Review of Political Science* 2: 369–404.

Thierer, A. D. 2004. "Net Neutrality": Digital Discrimination or Regulatory Gamesmanship in Cyberspace? Policy Analysis 507, Cato Institute.

37signals. 2006. *Getting Real: The Smarter, Faster, Easier Way to Build a Successful Web Application.* 37signals, L.L.C.

Thompson, J. D. 1967. *Organizations in Action.* McGraw-Hill.

Time Warner. 2008. *Form 10-K for the Fiscal Year Ended December 31, 2007.*

Tirole, J. 1988. *The Theory of Industrial Organization.* MIT Press.

Tomlinson, R. undated-b. The First Email. http://openmap.bbn.com/~tomlinso/ray/firstemailframe.html.

Topolski, Robert M. 2008. Your Letter Addressed to FCC Chairman Martin, dated March 28, 2008. Letter to David Cohen. April 3.

Trigeorgis, L. 1996. *Real Options: Managerial Flexibility and Strategy in Resource Allocation.* MIT Press.

Troy, D. A., and Zweben, S. H. 1981. Measuring the Quality of Structured Designs. *Journal of Systems and Software* 2(2): 113–120.

Tsang, E. W. K. 2000. Transaction Cost and Resource-based Explanations of Joint Ventures: A Comparison and Synthesis. *Organization Studies* 21(1): 215–242.

Tuomi, I. 2002. *Networks of Innovation: Change and Meaning in the Age of the Internet.* Oxford University Press.

Turner, J. S., and Taylor, D. E. 2005. Diversifying the Internet. *IEEE GLOBECOM 2005.*

Tushman, M. L. 1977. Special Boundary Roles in the Innovation Process. *Administrative Science Quarterly* 22(4): 587–605.

Tushman, M. L., and Anderson, P. 1986. Technological Discontinuities and Organizational Environments. *Administrative Science Quarterly* 31(3): 439–465.

Tushman, M. L., and Anderson, P. 1990. Technological Discontinuities and Dominant Designs: A Cyclical Model of Technological Change. *Administrative Science Quarterly* 35(4): 604–633.

U.S. Department of Justice and Federal Trade Commission. 1984. Non-Horizontal Merger Guidelines. Originally issued as part of U.S. Department of Justice Merger Guidelines, June 14, 1984. http://www.usdoj.gov/atr/public/guidelines/2614.htm.

U.S. Senate Committee on Banking. 1999. *Financial Services Modernization Act. Gramm-Leach-Bliley. Summary of Provisions.*

Ulhøi, J. P. 2004. Open Source Development: A Hybrid in Innovation and Management Theory. *Management Decision* 42(9): 1095–1114.

Ulrich, K. 1995. The Role of Product Architecture in the Manufacturing Firm. *Research Policy* 24(3): 419–440.

Ulrich, K. T., and Ellison, D. J. 2005. Beyond Make-Buy: Internalization and Integration of Design and Production. *Production and Operations Management* 14(3): 315–330.

Ulrich, K. T., and Eppinger, S. D. 2000. *Product Design and Development*, second edition. Irwin McGraw-Hill.

United States Government Accountability Office. 2006. *Report to Congressional Committees; Telecommunications; Broadband Deployment Is Extensive throughout the United States, but It Is Difficult to Assess the Extent of Deployment Gaps in Rural Areas.* GAO-06-426.

Uzzi, B. 1996. The Sources and Consequences of Embeddedness for the Economic Performance of Organizations: The Network Effect. *American Sociological Review* 61(4): 674–698.

van den Bulte, C., and Moenaert, R. K. 1998. The Effects of R&D Team Co-Location on Communication Patterns among R&D, Marketing, and Manufacturing. *Management Science* 44(11, Part 2): S1–S18.

van der Berg, R. 2008. How the 'Net Works: An Introduction to Peering and Transit. *Ars Technica*, September 2. http://arstechnica.com/guides/other/peering-and-transit.ars/1.

van Osnabrugge, M., and Robinson, R. 2000. *Angel Investing: Matching Start-up Funds with Start-up Companies—The Guide for Entrepreneurs and Individual Investors.* Jossey-Bass.

van Schewick, B. 2004. Architecture and Innovation: The Role of the End-to-End Arguments in the Original Internet. PhD dissertation, Technical University Berlin.

van Schewick, B. 2007. Towards an Economic Framework for Network Neutrality Regulation. *Journal on Telecommunications and High Technology Law* 5(2): 329–391.

van Schewick, B. 2008. Written Testimony before the Federal Communications Commission at its Second En Banc Hearing on Broadband Management Practices, April 17.

van Schewick, B. 2009. Point/Counterpoint. Network Neutrality Nuances. *Communications of the ACM* 52(2): 31–37.

van Vliet, H. 2000. *Software Engineering: Principles and Practice*, second edition. Wiley.

Varghese, S. 2003. Survey Questions Business Relevance of Netcraft Web Server Data. November 26. http://www.theage.com.au/articles/2003/11/26/1069522639857 .html.

Varian, H. R. 1989. Price Discrimination. In R. L. Schmalensee and R. D. Willig, eds., *Handbook of Industrial Organization*, volume 1. Elsevier.

Varian, H. R. 1999. *Intermediate Microeconomics: A Modern Approach*, fifth edition. Norton.

Varian, H. R. 2006. The Economics of Internet Search. *Rivista di Politica Economica* 96(6): 177–191.

Varian, H. R. 2007. Kaizen, That Continuous Improvement Strategy, Finds its Ideal Environment. *New York Times*, February 8.

Viscusi, W. K., Harrington, J. E., Jr., and Vernon, J. M. 2005. *Economics of Regulation and Antitrust*, fourth edition. MIT Press.

Vise, D. A., and Malseed, M. 2005. *The Google Story*. Delacorte.

von Hippel, E. 1988. *The Sources of Innovation*. Oxford University Press.

von Hippel, E. 1990. Task Partitioning: An Innovation Process Variable. *Research Policy* 19(5): 407–418.

von Hippel, E. 1994. "Sticky Information" and the Locus of Problem Solving: Implications for Innovation. *Management Science* 40(4): 429–439.

von Hippel, E. 1998. Economics of Product Development by Users: The Impact of "Sticky" Local Information. *Management Science* 44(5): 629–644.

von Hippel, E. 2001. PERSPECTIVE: User Toolkits for Innovation. *Journal of Product Innovation Management* 18(4): 247–257.

von Hippel, E. 2002. Horizontal Innovation Networks—by and for Users. Working Paper 4366-02, MIT Sloan School of Management.

von Hippel, E. 2005. *Democratizing Innovation*. MIT Press.

von Hippel, E. 2007. Horizontal Innovation Networks—by and for Users. *Industrial and Corporate Change* 16(2): 293–315.

von Hippel, E., and von Krogh, G. 2003. Open Source Software and the "Private-Collective" Innovation Model: Issues for Organization Science. *Organization Science* 14(2): 209–223.

von Krogh, G., and von Hippel, E. 2006. The Promise of Research on Open Source Software. *Management Science* 52(7): 975–983.

Weiser, P. 2008. The Next Frontier for Network Neutrality. *Administrative Law Review* 60(2): 273–322.

Weiser, P. J. 2001. Internet Governance, Standard Setting, and Self-Regulation. *Northern Kentucky Law Review* 28(4): 822–845.

Weiser, P. J. 2003. Toward a Next Generation Regulatory Strategy. *Loyola University of Chicago Law Journal* 35(1): 41–85.

Weisman, D. L. 1998. The Incentive to Discriminate by a Vertically-Integrated Regulated Firm: A Reply. *Journal of Regulatory Economics* 14(1): 87–91.

Weisman, D. L., and Williams, M. A. 2001. The Costs and Benefits of Long-Distance Entry: Regulation and Non-Price Discrimination. *Review of Industrial Organization* 18(3): 275–282.

Weisman, R. 2005. ICQ Founder Has a New Message. *Boston Globe*, April 4.

Weiss, M. B., and Shin, S. J. 2004. Internet Interconnection Economic Model and Its Analysis: Peering and Settlement. *NETNOMICS: Economic Research and Electronic Networking* 6(1): 43–57.

Weitzman, M. L. 1980. The "Ratchet Principle" and Performance Incentives. *Bell Journal of Economics* 11(1): 302–308.

Wernerfelt, B. 1984. A Resource-Based View of the Firm. *Strategic Management Journal* 5(2): 171–180.

West, J. 2007. The Economic Realities of Open Standards: Black, White, and Many Shades of Gray. In S. Greenstein and V. Stango, eds., *Standards and Public Policy.* Cambridge University Press.

Whinston, M. D. 1990. Tying, Foreclosure, and Exclusion. *American Economic Review* 80(4): 837–859.

Whinston, M. D. 2001. Exclusivity and Tying in U.S. v. Microsoft: What We Know; and Don't Know. *Journal of Economic Perspectives* 15(2): 63–80.

Whitt, R., and Faber, J. 2008. Cone of Silence (Finally) Lifts on the Spectrum Auction. *Google Public Policy Blog*, April 3. http://googlepublicpolicy.blogspot.com/2008/04/cone-of-silence-finally-lifts-on.html.

Williamson, O. E. 1975. *Markets and Hierarchies: Analysis and Antitrust Implications.* Free Press.

Williamson, O. E. 1979. Assessing Vertical Market Restrictions: Antitrust Ramifications of the Transaction Cost Approach. *University of Pennsylvania Law Review* 127(4): 953–993.

Williamson, O. E. 1985. *The Economic Institutions of Capitalism: Firms, Markets, Relational Contracting.* Free Press.

Williamson, O. E. 1991. Comparative Economic Organization: The Analysis of Discrete Structural Alternatives. *Administrative Science Quarterly* 36 (June): 269–296.

Williamson, O. E. 1999. Strategy Research: Governance and Competence Perspectives. *Strategic Management Journal* 20(12): 1087–1108.

Wilson, M. 2008. Apple Rejects MailWrangler App for "Leading to User Confusion." *GIZMODO*, September 22. http://gizmodo.com/5053232/apple-rejects-mailwrangler -app-for-leading-to-user-confusion.

Wischik, D. 2007. Short Messages. Royal Society Workshop on Networks: Modelling and Control.

Wise, A. S., and Duwadi, K. 2005. Competition between Cable Television and Direct Broadcast Satellite: The Importance of Switching Costs and Regional Sports Networks. *Journal of Competition Law and Economics* 1(4): 679–705.

Wolfe, G. 1994. The (Second Phase of the) Revolution Has Begun. *Wired*, October. http://www.wired.com/wired/archive/2.10/mosaic.html.

Wolverton, T. 2002. GoTo.com to See Profit Sooner Than Expected. *CNET News*, January 2. http://news.cnet.com/GoTo.com-to-see-profit-sooner-than-expected/ 2100-1023_3-270585.html.

Woodard, C. J. 2006. Architectural Strategy and Design Evolution in Complex Engineered Systems. PhD dissertation, Harvard University.

Woodard, C. J. 2008. Architectural Control Points (Long Version, January 23). Working paper.

Wright, J. 2002. Access Pricing under Competition: An Application to Cellular Networks. *Journal of Industrial Economics* 50(3): 289–315.

Wright, J. 2004. One-sided Logic in Two-sided Markets. *Review of Network Economics* 3(1): 42–63.

Wu, T. 2003a. Network Neutrality and Broadband Discrimination. *Journal on Telecommunications and High Technology Law* 2: 141–175.

Wu, T. 2003b. When Code Isn't Law. *Virginia Law Review* 89(4): 101–169.

Wu, T. 2004. The Broadband Debate: A User's Guide. *Journal on Telecommunications and High Technology Law* 3(1): 69–95.

Wu, T. 2006a. Testimony before the House Committee on the Judiciary: Telecom and Antitrust Task Force at its hearing on: Network Neutrality: Competition, Innovation, and Nondiscriminatory Access. April 25. 109th Congress, 2nd Session.

Wu, T. 2006b. Why You Should Care about Network Neutrality. *Slate*, May 1. http:// www.slate.com/id/2140850.

Wu, T. 2007. Wireless Carterfone. *International Journal of Communication* 1: 389–426.

Wu, T., and Lessig, L.. 2003. Ex Parte Submission to Federal Communications Commission. CS Dkt. No. 02-52, August 22.

Xiaowei, Y., Whetherall, D., and Anderson, T. 2005. A DoS-Limiting Network Architecture. *Computer Communication Review* 35(4): 241–252.

Yahoo. 2005. The History of Yahoo!—How It All Started. http://docs.yahoo.com/ info/misc/history.html.

Yahoo. 2008a. *Form 8-K. March 18.*

Yahoo. 2008b. *Form 10-K for the Fiscal Year Ended December 31, 2007.*

Yahoo! Finance. 2008a. AT&T Inc. (T). *Yahoo! Finance,* June 21. http://finance.yahoo .com/q?s=T.

Yahoo! Finance. 2008b. Comcast Corp. (CMSA). *Yahoo! Finance.,* June 21. http:// finance.yahoo.com/q/ks?s=CMCSA.

Yamauchi, Y., Yokozawa, M., Shinohara, T., and Ishida, T. 2000. Collaboration with Lean Media: How Open-Source Software Succeeds. *2000 ACM Conference on Computer Supported Cooperative Work.*

Yoo, C. S. 2002. Vertical Integration and Media Regulation in the New Economy. *Yale Journal on Regulation* 19(1): 171–300.

Yoo, C. S. 2004. Would Mandating Broadband Network Neutrality Help or Hurt Competition? A Comment on the End-to-End Debate. *Journal on Telecommunications and High Technology Law* 3(1): 23–68.

Yoo, C. S. 2005. Beyond Network Neutrality. *Harvard Journal of Law and Technology* 19(1): 1–77.

Yoo, C. S. 2006. Network Neutrality and the Economics of Congestion. *Georgetown Law Journal* 94 (June): 1847–1908.

Yoo, C. S. 2007. What Can Antitrust Contribute to the Network Neutrality Debate? *International Journal of Communication* 1: 493–530.

Yourdon, E., and Constantine, L. L. 1975. *Structured Design: Fundamentals of a Discipline of Computer Program and Systems Design.* Prentice-Hall.

Zittrain, J. 2003. Internet Points of Control. *Boston College Law Review* 44(2): 653–688.

Zittrain, J. 2008. *The Future of the Internet and How to Stop It.* Yale University Press.

Zittrain, J. 2009. ISPs helping with botnets. E-Mail to ip@v2.listbox.com Mailing List. October 12. http://seclists.org/interesting-people/2009/Oct/95.

Index

HARD JUSTICE

CHAPTER ONE

When the doorbell rang, Fallon Wade's heart jumped into a beat so furious, it stole her breath. *He was here.* She wasn't ready, would never be ready, but she hadn't been given a choice.

Opening her bedroom door very quietly, she tiptoed to the staircase landing and peeked over.

Her father and mother stood before the man, in her line of vision. But it didn't matter. He towered over them and it'd take a giant to block him. Holy smokes. He had to be at least six-five.

Muscles bulged everywhere. Like...seriously. *Everywhere.* Shoulders, biceps, chest, neck; he stood in a casual pose, if a brick wall could ever be casual.

Dark hair stuck up in a messy faux hawk. An untrimmed goatee mixed with beard shadow covered a hard, square jaw. And his nose...well, his nose looked as if it had been broken. At least once.

Or maybe multiple times.

Oddly none of that detracted from his extremely rugged good looks, but rather added a dangerous, sexy edge. He certainly looked more than capable of providing protection.

While her father, no doubt a little shell-shocked, prattled on about what was and wasn't acceptable for his "precious daughter," the man shifted his weight, crossed his arms and, with polite impatience, listened.

Until he glanced up at her.

It was a passing glance at first, as if he'd felt her scrutiny and was only mildly curious. But then those dark sinner's eyes shot back and locked onto her.

Fallon couldn't have been more flustered if he'd reached out and touched her.

Her father, realizing he'd lost his audience, jerked around to see her, too, and then her mother, as well.

Busted.

With all eyes on her, Fallon cleared her very dry throat and squeaked, "I'll be down in a minute." Escaping back into her room with alacrity, she closed the door and collapsed against it.

Hand to her thundering heart, she thought, *potent*.

Definitely macho.

And big. Oh, so big.

Not at all what she'd been expecting.

Okay, maybe having a protection detail wouldn't be so bad after all. She had prepared to meet the usual Men in Black clone with the requisite suit, dark glasses and grim expression.

Instead, he wore sneakers, faded jeans and a graphic T-shirt with an open flannel for added warmth. If she hadn't heard her father lecturing, she would have assumed him to be someone else.

Maybe a landscaper.

Or, given his cross demeanor, something more nefarious— like a burglar.

It took Fallon a few seconds more to get her feet moving, then she darted to the closet with new excitement. Shoot, even having a bodyguard would be an adventure when the bodyguard looked like him.

She stepped into her flat-heeled shoes, found a cardigan to pull on over her top and chose a scarf to drape around her neck. She didn't particularly like the outfit, but no way would she make *him* wait while she went through her wardrobe.

After one last fluff of her brown hair and a quick swipe of gloss over her lips, Fallon squared her shoulders, filled her lungs with a fortifying breath for courage and ventured forth.

The second she stepped out, she heard his deep voice and paused to listen.

"No need to worry. I'll cover her."

Her father choked, turned it into a cough, and said with authority, "She is not to be alone. Not for a single second."

"Promise I'll stick real close."

Alarmed, her father corrected, "But not too close."

"Just close enough, then."

"No one is to get too cozy with her either."

"No cozy shenanigans," he said. "Got it."

"She's naive and doesn't understand that thugs—" here her father paused for effect, his narrowed gaze on the man "—might try to use her to get to her wealth."

"Yeah? That's happened before?"

"Well…no." Her father harrumphed in that familiar way that showed his annoyance. "But it's a very real concern."

"Anyone know her itinerary?" the man asked.

"Even *we* don't know it," her mother explained.

"That's good then. Not like anyone can plan to use her if they don't know where she'll be." The bodyguard sounded accepting of all the rules. "Don't sweat it."

Fallon strangled on a breath. Dear God, he'd just told her mother not to "sweat it." In her memory, no one had ever spoken to the refined Mrs. Rothschild Wade in such a way.

It was, Fallon decided, somewhat hilarious.

"I realize it all seems extreme," her father said. "But Fallon is delicate."

No, I'm not, Fallon wanted to shout. She'd never been *delicate,* or naive. It was her parents who couldn't deal, who couldn't move on. Their worry had all but crippled her—and she'd helped. In trying not to add to their burden, she'd made things worse. For their sake as well as her own, she had to make some changes.

With a note of humor, the big guy replied, "Promise I won't break her."

Fallon snickered, but her mother just stared, so her father rushed to reassure her. And Fallon just wanted to get out the door with her hunky new bodyguard before her parents had a complete meltdown.

Tonight was a meet and greet, and hopefully the path to fun and cutting loose and finally being free. *Safely.* If all went well, if the bodyguard suited her, she'd get to be on her own, living her life without the shackles of the past. Limited freedom, yes. There were some things that, for her, would never change.

She'd had a very sharp reminder of that lately.

However, she could change the scenery. She could change the outlook and her attitude. And she would.

When she reached the landing at the top of the curving staircase, she saw that he stood there at the bottom.

Waiting.

Again his gaze trapped her. He had a way of staring that consumed a person. Beside him her father looked small, even though Clayton Wade stood nearly six feet tall and looked very distinguished with his silver-tipped hair and impeccable manner.

Holding the handrail and attempting a smile, Fallon started down.

"You will remember your place," her father said to the man.

Oh, dear God. Mortified, Fallon wailed, *"Dad."*

"My place?" the man asked.

"As an *avuncular* escort who will, at all costs, ensure her safety."

Fallon wanted to disappear. Did her father honestly think that massive hunk of macho man would be attracted to her?

He looked merely confused, not insulted, so she rushed to move beyond her father's awkward reprimand.

"You're my protection detail?"

"Afraid so."

What did that mean? Did he regret the assignment already—or was he expecting her to regret *him*? She waited, but he said nothing else, just tracked her every step as she descended.

Her father broke the silence. "Justice Wallington, meet my daughter, Fallon Wade. Fallon, Mr. Wallington is the security I've hired from the very respected Body Armor Agency."

As she got closer, she said, "Mr. Wallington," in formal acknowledgment.

"Justice will do, Ms. Wade." His gaze skipped quickly down her body, then forcefully back to her face. He looked to be concentrating.

Did he just check me out? Fallon wasn't at all sure, but it felt like it and her voice went squeaky again. "All right. Then you must call me Fallon."

He tugged at a thickened ear. "Works for me. I'm not much for ceremony."

That prompted her father to start lecturing again. "She is not to be out of your sight."

"I'll keep an eye on her."

"If anything happens to her, we will hold you and the agency responsible."

"Nothing will."

Her father scowled. "Ms. Silver swears you're capable."

"That I am." Though Justice spoke to her father, he didn't look away from Fallon, and she shivered at the deepness of the voice that stroked over her skin like a warm caress.

"She also said you were a professional fighter," her father continued.

"Was once," Justice agreed. "I fought with the SBC, but I don't compete anymore."

"SBC?" her father asked.

"Supreme Battle Challenge. Best known fight organization there is."

Ah, a fighter. Fallon gave him another quick glance. She supposed that explained the damaged ear, crook in his nose and the outrageous hairstyle. "Not a boxer," she guessed.

"Mixed martial arts, so kicking, grappling, submissions, but yeah, I'm a pretty good boxer, too." He jokingly threw a few shadow punches, then, with a glance at her dad, quickly sobered. "Not to brag or anything."

With a critical eye, her father said, "Admittedly, you're not what I expected."

"You were looking for Rocky Balboa? The one in the later movies, not the first? He did get slick in the last few, huh? That's not me, though. Never will be."

Such an outpouring left her father stymied for a moment. "Well, my wife and Ms. Silver did suggest that you'd be able to blend in."

Fallon remained on the last step—and still Justice towered over her. She smiled up at him. "That was my stipulation. That you be able to blend, I mean. I didn't want a bodyguard to be super conspicuous. But seeing you now, I can't imagine you blending in too easily."

He crooked a brow. "Why not?"

"You're rather large to blend."

"Depends on where we go, right?" He took her elbow and very unnecessarily helped her down the last step. "Bar, club, steakhouse—no one will pay much attention to me. In this house?" He looked around as if a little put off by the grandeur. "Or a fancy party?" He rasped a big hand over his beard stubble. "I can shave, spiff up a little and force myself into a suit, but that still might not do the trick."

Fallon couldn't help but laugh; she found this bodyguard

completely delightful. "Well, we're lucky that there aren't any parties scheduled."

"Fallon," her mother said, her expression curious and expectant. "Are you absolutely certain—"

"Yes and yes," Fallon replied with enthusiasm, hoping to stem their concerns. Spinning around, she embraced her mother in a tight hug. "I'm *very* certain, Mother." Next, she embraced her father. "Please don't worry, Dad. It's absolutely fine. I promise you."

"What time will you be home?"

She smiled as she rolled her eyes. "I don't know, Dad. I'm twenty-four, so I might just stay out all night."

Appalled, her father again looked at the man. Her mother lifted her brows.

Wincing inwardly, Fallon glanced back and said, "That is, unless you have a—"

"I'm yours for the night. Keep me as late as you want."

Everything he said sounded somehow more personal, even intimate. Or maybe that was just her male-deprived brain doing some wishful thinking.

Her smile quavered, but this was too important to turn chicken now. "Perfect. Then if you're ready?"

The corner of his mouth quirked up. "Was born ready." He swept a hand toward the door in a ridiculously gallant gesture. "Ladies first."

Charmed, Fallon hitched her purse strap over her shoulder and started out. Normally she'd wear a coat, too, but late May in Ohio was unseasonably mild this year, even with the frequent rain.

And tonight she wanted to be different. Free.

Eventually, she wanted to be a woman, whole.

After a quick glance at Mr. Wade, who remained stiff and horrified by the sight of him, and Mrs. Wade, who looked like she was waiting for him to perform tricks, Justice went out and pulled the door closed behind him. Whew. Glad to have some fresh air, he inhaled deeply and rolled his neck to relieve the vibrating tension.

The freaking mansion had intimidated him. Who the hell needed a house that big? A few times there, he'd thought for sure his voice would echo back at him.

The obvious wealth had intimidated him, too. The ornate staircase alone probably cost more than what he got paid in a year. The rock on Mrs. Wade's finger had all but blinded him. He'd been half-afraid to move for fear he'd bump into some pricey shit and break it.

As if all that weren't enough, Fallon Wade's father had tried—unsuccessfully—to cow him. The man had a cold stare that probably made lackeys buckle. But behind that act, Justice had seen the real concern.

The man loved his daughter, spoiled as she might be.

Thinking of her...little Fallon was quite the surprise. He'd expected a princess, a snooty brat used to snapping her fingers and having her every wish granted. Instead, he'd looked up that sprawling staircase and found a curious mouse peeking through the rails... Then he'd caught her wicked grin and bursting enthusiasm and knew that looks were deceiving.

He watched now as Fallon Wade practically danced down the wide tiled steps to the circular drive where he'd parked. The printed scarf draping her neck blew out to the sides from an increasing wind.

Brown hair, parted on the side with wispy bangs over her forehead, skimmed just below her shoulders, bouncing with her every step. That hair looked silky enough to be liquid.

When he'd first seen her, he'd noticed the smooth, flushed cheeks, a small straight nose and rounded chin... Really nice mouth, too.

But it was her eyes that got him.

For an otherwise unremarkable face, her eyes were amazing, dark like a doe's, framed by long, thick lashes and gently arched brows.

The innocence and curiosity in her face was enough for a second look, but the body...

She wore a plain pink crewneck top tucked into a long black skirt, a darker pink cardigan sweater and that fancy scarf.

For a petite girl with slim legs and arms and a narrow waist, she still had curves. Hard to tell much about those curves in that particular outfit, but he had a feeling she'd be pretty sweet all over.

Following her down the steps to the SUV, Justice noticed she had some nice padding around back. There'd be no hiding that heart-shaped ass.

As she headed for his ride with a happy, brisk walk, her black skirt hugged her hips but swished around her knees.

Her face looked young, her body looked ripe and she behaved like a puppy just let off the leash.

Her parents treated her like she was ten instead of twenty-four. *Overprotective much?* Hell, it had smothered *him* to see the way they tried to harness her.

Somehow, Justice thought, he had to get a handle on the situation. He'd expected this to be an easy assignment, but so far, nothing added up.

In an effort to understand, Justice drew out his phone and pulled up the internet.

He was aware of Fallon Wade watching him before she asked, "Do you need privacy for your call?"

So even now she wouldn't complain about his lack of deference? He should be focusing solely on her, but first... "I'm just looking up a word."

She tipped her head. "What word?"

"Avuncular."

The wind carried her laugh until it surrounded him.

Smiling, Justice asked, "You think that's funny?"

Mirth danced in her dark eyes. "And a little embarrassing."

"Because I don't know the word?" It finally popped up on the screen.

"No, of course not." She looked wrecked by his conclusion. "I was in no way judging you."

That only made his smile widen. He didn't come off as the most professional person and he knew it. "Then why?"

She faced him from a good distance away. "Because my father felt the silly warning was necessary."

Avuncular: of or pertaining to an uncle, especially in kindness and manner. "Ah." Now he got it. "So your dad was warning me against making any moves?"

"It wasn't personal. Dad feels compelled to make similar warnings to everyone, even though it's never been an issue." She wrinkled her nose. "I'd hardly need to hire you if I had a string of big, strong guys taking me out, right?"

"Oh, I dunno." By the minute, she somehow got sexier. Justice didn't understand it, but maybe it was that quirky smile or those subtle curves she tried to downplay. She definitely didn't seem spoiled, and in fact was downright modest. "I think if you wanted it, you'd have plenty of guys hoping for a shot."

Her brows went up. "A shot?"

Justice gave her a long, heated look. "You know my meaning."

Her dark eyes widened. "Oh." Surprise, then embarrassment, had her ducking her face.

Damn it, why the hell was he flirting with her? "Sorry. I shouldn't have…" He shook his head. "Ignore me."

Appearing both amused and confused by his attitude, she started to speak, and instead lifted her arms out to her sides and turned her face up to the sky. "It's a beautiful night, isn't it?"

Dark clouds rolled over one another and humidity hung thick in the air. He liked storms.

They made him horny.

Though this time, he wasn't sure if it was the storm or the girl. "Sure." Lengthening his stride, more than ready to get the show on the road, Justice opened the door to the backseat of the SUV. "You want to tell me where we're going?"

"You mentioned a bar." She bit her lip. A nice full lip, he couldn't help but notice. "Is there one you'd recommend?"

Justice couldn't figure her out. Was she a practiced flirt? Too naive to know how she affected him? For sure, she made him forget himself. He kept focusing on her mouth—plump lips and that shiny gloss... She waited for an answer, but he'd forgotten the topic. "One what?"

"A bar?" She grinned, putting dimples into those pink cheeks. "I've never been before."

Justice took a step back. Naive then, and damn it, since when was that a turn-on? "You've never been to a bar?"

"No." She leaned closer in a conspiratorial way, her face turned up to his, her tone teasing. "Is it fun?"

Could be, depending on her idea of fun. But if she'd never been before, why pick now, tonight, with *him* of all people?

Suspicion got the better of him. "What are you hoping to do at this bar?"

"Drink a little." Her nose wrinkled again. "That'd be a first, too."

Justice folded his arms over his chest. "You've never had a drink?"

"Wine a few times at galas, but that was long ago." Though she still smiled, shadows suddenly saddened her expression.

Justice had the awful urge to comfort her. He resisted with stoic effort. "How can it have been long ago when you're so young?"

"Twenty-four isn't that young, and if you want me to be specific, I'll say that I haven't had wine since the night I turned nineteen. Besides, it isn't wine I want to try." The impish grin returned. "I want a beer."

"Beer?" She made beer sound scandalous. Every girl he knew occasionally had a beer, even if she didn't particularly like it.

"Yes."

Justice rubbed the back of his neck. "Okay, well, you can do that at every bar everywhere."

She laughed. "Let's see. I'd also like to dance. Maybe chat with new people. And I want to have fun."

How the hell did she figure to do any of that when her daddy didn't want anyone within spitting distance of her? A raindrop fell, then a few more...and Justice knew the skies would open up soon. He took her arm and tried to urge her into the backseat of the SUV.

She resisted. "I'll ride up front."

Taken by surprise, he did his parrot act and repeated, "Up front?" Clients never rode up front. Definitely not young female clients.

She stared at him with those big soul-sucking eyes. "Unless that's a problem for you."

The only problem, so far, was his reaction to her. But hell, as the client, she got to call the shots, so... "Suit yourself." He switched direction, closing the back door and opening the front.

The raindrops began pelting the ground in earnest, so she hurriedly seated herself.

Jogging around the hood, Justice narrowly avoided the sudden deluge. He checked that Fallon had on her seat belt, then, instead of driving, he returned to her earlier question. "There are a bunch of bars in the area. I don't know much about them, though."

"Really? I thought most guys...that is..." Her cheeks pinked. "You don't drink?"

"Sure. But usually I head back to Warfield to Rowdy's when I want to drink and relax with friends."

"Rowdy's?"

"A bar that's gotten popular with fighters."

"Fighters who are your friends?" she asked with interest.

He eyed her warily. "Yeah."

"I'd love to go there sometime."

A hint? Was she another groupie hoping to hook up with a fighter? God knew they came from all age ranges, backgrounds and interests. "It's a no-go for tonight." Hopefully Ms. Fancy-pants wouldn't insist. "I'd need to ensure first that things aren't too chaotic before I take you there. The bar has some rambunctious parties."

She sighed. "Yes, I suppose tonight we should stick closer to home."

"As to that, I should have been told your plans in advance so I could scope out any place you wanted to go."

Brows coming together, she said, "I've never heard that rule."

She sounded a bit stiff, and Justice bit back his smile. "Yeah, well, now you know."

The frown intensified. "Going forward, I'll plan accordingly."

"Good." Rain made the windows opaque and insulated them from everything outside the car. He could practically hear his own heartbeat, could definitely hear her soft breathing. The sense of intimacy made him uneasy. "So what are we doing now?"

"I'll settle for a more local bar. Anyway, it's probably a good idea that we don't travel too far, just in case."

"In case *what?*"

"In case we don't suit." She gave him a quick, firm glance. "If all goes well tonight, well then, there's a lot more I'd like to schedule."

He'd already been told that when he took the assignment, but still he repeated, "More?"

She ducked her face and pressed her hands over her skirt, smoothing an imaginary crease. "More...like every night? Did no one tell you this could be a month-long detail?"

"Yeah, I knew it." Why was she being so shy now? "I was told we'd be getting acquainted, but I thought most of that would be at your house with your mom and dad."

She laughed. "Nooo."

Yeah, it'd probably be impossible with those two hawks over-head. "So here's how it usually works. You tell me where you want to go, I find the best route to get there, then scope out the place in advance to ensure I know the different exits, if it's secure, stuff like that."

She flapped a hand. "That's not necessary. Honest. I mean, I suppose that makes sense for most people who need protection. But overall, my parents just wanted to ensure I could explore safely. There will be plenty of other people at the bar, right? Lots of people who visit daily?"

"Sure." Long as he didn't take her to a dive, it shouldn't be a problem.

"Why don't you pick one, and we'll give it a shot?" She grinned. "What could go wrong?"

Justice didn't bother answering. If the alarm bells going off in his head were any indication, he figured they'd both find out soon enough.

Fallon rejected Justice's first two choices. One was too swanky for the way she'd dressed, and the other looked more like a club. She wanted a regular, everyday bar with everyday people and, finally, on his third try, she agreed with his choice.

A multitude of fluorescent signs filled the big front window of The Broken Pony. People loitered outside, some openly mak-ing out, others smoking, groups talking. The parking lot across the street nearly overflowed.

Because it was still pouring, Fallon said, "Drop me off at the door, please." The thought of walking in there alone made her breathless with nerves, but otherwise she'd be soaked, so—

"No can do," Justice said. "I promised to stick like glue, re-member?" He swung the SUV into the lot, drove up one row then down another until he found an empty space a good distance from the bar.

"I'll get wet."

He paused in the process of turning off the car, blew out a long breath, then said evenly, "I've got an umbrella."

He reached around to the backseat, coming very close to her as he did so.

And oh, God, he smelled good. Not like aftershave, just like… man. Fallon tried to take a deep breath without being too obvious.

He gave her a look as he settled back, now with a black umbrella. "You okay?"

She nodded fast. "Yes."

Without looking convinced, he said, "Stay put. I'll come around."

After pocketing the keys, he opened the door, popped up the umbrella and circled the hood to her side of the car.

By necessity, she had to step out very near him to stay shielded under the umbrella. He didn't bother trying to protect himself from the storm.

"Come under with me," she insisted.

He hesitated.

"Please, Justice? I'll feel terrible otherwise."

Reluctantly, he moved up against her back, his arm around her as he tilted the umbrella to block the worst of the rain blowing toward them. "C'mon."

With every step, their bodies touched. She could smell him again, a rich masculine musk, and better than that, she felt his incredible heat.

Why, even if the bar turned out to be a bust, this alone was a wonderful new experience.

He kept her sheltered from the storm until they'd stepped into the bar, then he turned her so her back was against a wall and he stood in front. While closing the umbrella, he visually scoured the room.

Teasing, Fallon asked, "Safe to proceed?"

"Don't be a smart-ass." His grin took the sting from the comment. "How about those seats at the bar?"

The men to the left of the empty stools looked like a rough motorcycle club, and the men to the right could have been a college fraternity group. She *loved* the differences. "Yes, please."

"It's crowded, so stay close." He pulled her around in front of him and left one big, warm hand on her shoulder, guiding her as they maneuvered through the crowds. Soon as they reached the bar, he mean mugged the men on either side of them until they turned away.

"So what's it to be?" He helped her onto the high round stool. "Still want a beer?"

She could smell the alcohol in the air. In the background, loud music played. Belatedly, Fallon realized that she probably should have eaten something before now, but earlier she'd been too nervous. "Yes, please."

"You sure? 'Cuz you don't look sure."

Trying for more confidence, she said, "Beer."

"All right, then." He ordered one.

"You aren't going to drink with me?"

"I'm on duty."

"Working for me, yes? So I insist." She leaned close to ensure he'd hear her, then whispered, "I'll feel less awkward."

His gaze went from her eyes to her mouth, then away. "Hey, if you insist, who am I to argue?" He asked for another beer.

The man to her right glanced at her again, then turned for a closer look. Fallon didn't smile. She must have been too surprised by the attention.

The young man glanced at Justice next—then quailed. When she looked at Justice, she saw only an innocent expression, one brow raised. But she wasn't buying it, especially since the man turned back to his friends, spoke low, and together they vacated their seats.

"Hey," Fallon complained. "I was going to talk to him."

Justice snorted. "It wasn't talk he wanted."

"How do you know?"

"The way he looked you over? Besides, he was already crocked. You don't want to deal with that."

From the other side of her, a guy said, "I ain't crocked."

Justice narrowed his eyes. Fallon quickly turned to see the biker grinning at her. She had the fast impression of frazzled brown hair in a long ponytail, a ridiculous handlebar mustache, broad shoulders under a black T-shirt and leather vest.

Fallon said, "Hello."

"'Lo yourself, honey." He ignored Justice and asked, "What's up?"

Lifting her glass, Fallon said, "I'm having a beer."

His grin widened. "I'm guessing this ain't your usual place, is it?"

"Am I that transparent?"

"Little bit." Swinging around to face her, he said, "So besides riling the big guy, what's the plan?"

"Oh, I'm not trying to rile him." But one glimpse at Justice showed he was more than a little fired up. "Justice," she said. "Anything wrong?"

"Not yet." His eyes narrowed on the man. "And it's going to stay that way, isn't it?"

"What's happenin' here?" the biker asked. "You two a thing?"

"No," Fallon denied. "We're—"

"I'm watching out for her." Justice, too, smiled, but it wasn't a nice sight. More like a warning.

She sighed. "Justice is—"

"Look," Justice said, standing and taking her arm. "A booth opened up."

She barely had time to snatch up her beer before he led her

away. Two other men got to the seats at the same time, but Justice stared them down until they detoured away without a fuss.

"Really," Fallon said, a little irate. "Was that necessary? I'm here because I want to visit with people."

"Not those people," he said, and he downed his beer in one long impressive swallow.

Digging in, Fallon insisted, "Any people I choose," and she, too, tipped up her beer.

Then almost gagged.

She swallowed the big gulp rather than spit it back into the glass, then stuck her tongue out. "Gak. That's *awful*."

Justice looked at her, then grinned. "Did that quench your thirst?"

Her face still scrunched, Fallon hunted through her purse for a mint. Unfortunately she didn't have any.

Justice pushed the glass toward her. "Take another sip. It'll help."

"I'll vomit."

He chuckled. "Nah, you won't. Trust me."

She did want to learn, so she held her nose and sipped. It wasn't quite as bad since she'd taken such a small taste.

Wearing a lopsided smile, Justice asked, "Better?"

She shook her head, continued to hold her nose, and drank again. This time, Justice put a finger at the bottom of the glass and held it there, encouraging her to keep drinking.

When she'd finished it, she burped, covered her mouth and blushed.

He laughed. "There you go." He held up two fingers, and a minute later a very pretty waitress carried over two more beers.

Fallon eyed them with disgust, until it dawned on her that Justice had just given the woman money. "I need to pay for the drinks."

"Don't sweat it."

She snickered. "You said the same thing to my mom."

"Did I?" He settled back and watched her.

"No one, ever, has said anything like that to her. It cracked me up."

His expression warmed. "You already feelin' that beer?"

"No." She did feel sleepy though. Holding her nose once more, she again drank, but this time she sat back so Justice couldn't reach her drink. "At least it's cold, huh?"

For such a big guy, he looked awfully gentle as he smiled at her. "So what's the plan? Can you enjoy yourself without hitting on a thug?"

"Thug?" she asked. "Who?"

"Either one of those yahoos at the bar. That first kid was looking for trouble, and the other guy lives trouble."

"So neither one was safe?"

Idly turning the beer, he surveyed her, then shook his head. "Looking like you do, not sure anyone in here is safe. At least, not to daddy's standards."

Making air quotes with her fingers, Fallon mimicked his voice and said, "Daddy's standards." She started laughing and couldn't stop. "That's so funny."

"You think so?"

When she nodded, her vision swam, so she held her head. "Yes. Dad really is outrageous."

"How come? I mean, what's he so worried about?"

She clammed up, unwilling to give too much away. "We've only lived here a short while—" *like a year* "—and he's unfamiliar with the area."

Justice pushed her drink toward her again.

She dutifully sipped before looking around. "People are dancing. I want to dance."

Wary, Justice straightened and surveyed the gyrating bodies on the floor. "I don't know…"

But she'd already stood. She took one last drink of her nasty beer, then started for the floor.

Justice caught her hand.

Wow, another revelation. For such a big man he had a very gentle hold.

He released her. "Stay where I can see you."

With a sharp salute, she said, "Yes, sir."

She loved to dance but rarely had the opportunity, and never in a place like this. Here, in the boisterous crowd, no one would pay any attention to her.

That is, no one except Justice, because he never took his gaze off her.

CHAPTER TWO

She'd drunk only two and a half beers, but Justice had a feeling that was two beers too many for little Fallon Wade.

"Dance with me," she'd asked early on.

"I don't dance," he'd lied the first time.

Half an hour later, she'd asked again. "Dance with me."

"Not in my job description." He'd felt like a prick after saying it, but hoped it'd keep her from asking.

It didn't.

"No one else is dancing with me," she complained.

A few guys had tried to sidle up to her.

Justice had stared hard enough to send them all packing. In MMA, he'd learned the value of a really confident, mean, nearly tactile stare. There were times he'd won a fight before it ever started, just with his stare-down.

"Don't worry about it," he said. "Just enjoy yourself."

"I feel foolish."

"You shouldn't." A woman like Fallon stood out from the others, but in a good way. "Trust me, lots of guys are looking."

"Really?" She glanced around. "You're just saying that to make me feel better."

"Gospel truth." He crossed his heart.

Laughing, she rejoined the dancers.

Admittedly, Fallon looked a little lonely. All around her, people brushed against once another but never came within two feet of her.

Several times, the urge to join her burned in his blood.

He couldn't help thinking of her moving against him, the scent of her skin and how soft she'd feel. Twice he'd even gotten to his feet. But he held back.

The things he imagined with her were already taboo enough; he wouldn't cross the line in deed, as well.

So instead he kept his vigil—and tortured himself with carnal fantasies inspired by the rhythmic roll of her hips and the sway of her torso.

Repeatedly, Fallon returned to the booth to sip on her beer. Halfway through the third, she pronounced her words too precisely, a deep flush stained her cheeks, and her dark eyes had that glassy look. Hoping to discourage her, Justice scooted the remainder of the drink to the other side of the table.

It was nearing midnight when some random dude, no doubt guided by liquid courage, caught her in his sights.

Justice read the intent in his gaze, but Fallon, still dancing, remained oblivious.

When the guy elbowed one of his buddies, then pointed her out, his friends started egging him on.

Justice couldn't really blame the guy for trying.

The prim clothes and overprotective upbringing hadn't stifled Fallon's sensuality. Nope, that came out loud and clear in the way she moved.

The guy had almost reached her when Justice stepped into his path. "Don't," he growled into the idiot's startled face, and the guy literally fled the bar.

Fallon wanted to dance, so by God, she'd get to dance—without getting hassled.

At one o'clock, the crowd finally thinned. Justice took her purse from the seat, grabbed the umbrella and walked out to the dance floor to tell her it was time to go.

She tried to tempt him into dancing.

It wasn't easy, but he held firm. "We need to get going."

She fashioned a very sexy pout. "Why?"

"It's late, the storm let up and you're drunk."

She gave it some thought, then nodded. "I think you might be right."

"So you know you're plastered?"

"No, I meant that the rain has stopped." She grinned at him. "I think I've learned to like beer."

She still held her nose every time she drank, so no, she definitely didn't like it. "If you say so."

"Thank you for your patience."

"It's what I'm paid for." He handed her purse to her, waited while she got the strap up and over her shoulder, which took her three tries, then led her out into the dark night.

Not a single star showed. So much humidity hung in the air that halos formed around each streetlamp. There were a lot less people outside now, and they were more subdued than the earlier crowd, talking low in small groups.

The drone of rain dripping from every surface lent a light music to the night.

Though they no longer shared an umbrella, Fallon stayed very close to him, so he felt it when she shivered.

He was so warm, particularly because of her nearness, that he hadn't even thought about her getting chilled. He glanced down at her and realized she'd gotten dewy with all her dancing in the heated bar. In comparison, the temps outside were cool.

He paused to slip off his flannel shirt then carefully draped it around her shoulders. "Better?"

Surprise had her blinking before she gave him a beautiful

smile. "Yes, thank you." Then with concern, she asked, "You're not cold?"

Not even close. Hell, seeing the pleasure on her face sent his temp up a few more notches. "I'm fine."

She looked up at him, maybe gauging his sincerity, then put her palm against his left biceps. "You're actually warm," she whispered with awe.

Yeah, much more of that and he'd combust.

To get her moving and distract his misplaced lust, Justice put his arm around her and steered her forward.

They'd almost reached the car when three bodies slipped out of the shadows. Big, muscular—definitely not slouches. Well, hell.

"Got a cigarette?" the one in front asked.

"Don't smoke." Justice took a step in front of Fallon, planning to protect her as they proceeded, but the other two blocked him. With his patience strained, he loosened his stance. "You don't want to do this."

Ignoring that warning, the lead man said, "I'll take her purse."

"No," Justice replied evenly, "you won't. And if you try, you're gonna get hurt…bad."

The man to his right drew a knife. Justice heard Fallon's gasp, and it infuriated him. She stayed behind him, not even peeking around. Odds were stuff like this never happened in her world—because she didn't go to bars, didn't drink…didn't dance, visit friends or apparently have fun.

Pissed that her night out might end in violence, he growled, "Put that away before I stick it in your fucking ear."

Cowering behind him, Fallon's trembling increased.

The most brazen one laughed. "You're scaring her, dude. Just hand it over and we can all get on our way."

Fuck it. "You're right." He pivoted to the side, as if to face Fallon, but as she started to give him her purse, he kicked out fast, catching the bastard in the face with his heel. The crunch of cartilage satisfied Justice. Even in his sneakers, his kick had likely done more than break the guy's nose, given the way he dropped.

The knife wielder slashed out. With far faster reflexes, Justice ducked back and at the same time grabbed his wrist. With little effort, he broke it, then took the knife from his limp hand.

Remembering Justice's threat, the second attacker turned and, with his damaged arm held close, ran away as fast as he could.

The third man, now more than a little incredulous, eyed his buddy on the ground, then his fleeing friend.

"What do you think?" Justice said. "Make up your mind before I take the decision away from you."

Lifting his hands in submission, the man slowly stepped away until he disappeared back into the shadows.

"Oh, my God," Fallon whispered.

What he'd like to do, Justice realized, was walk away from the mess. But he was on official business with Body Armor, so he had to call it in.

Rule of the agency: don't dick with the law unless given prior permission. For sure Sahara would want him to follow the rules tonight, with a client like Fallon.

When he turned to her, he saw Fallon's eyes were enormous and her lips parted.

"You okay?" he asked.

She closed her mouth and gulped. "You pulverized them."

She sounded so surprised, a smile tried to steal away Justice's black mood. "Not even close, but it's hard to do when the pricks run off."

"You *terrified* them." She looked at where the first guy still sprawled on the ground, out for the count. "I've never seen anyone move that fast."

"Because you haven't watched professional MMA." In comparison to the best fighters, he was fucking slow.

"So impressive. Like…pow!" A little on the tipsy side, she tried to mimic his kick, and almost fell to her nicely rounded butt.

"Easy," Justice said, catching her under the arms and hauling her upright. Knowing he needed to get her in the car before anything else happened, he said, "Come on," and led the way.

As they passed the downed man, she gawked and asked, "Is he dead?"

"Don't be so bloodthirsty. He's just knocked out." At least, Justice hoped that was true. He got Fallon seated, tucked the flannel around her, then hit the automatic lock. "Don't open this for anyone but me."

As he started to close the door, she said, "Wait! What are you doing?"

"Calling the cops. I'll be right here, but I have to let them know."

"Are you sure?" She fretted with the strap of her purse. "I mean, Dad will have a conniption. If you thought he was over-protective before, this will seal my fate."

"You're twenty-four," Justice pointed out. "You're a grown woman and can do as you please." Or was she worried about losing daddy's money? She hadn't seemed that mercenary, but truth be told, he still didn't know shit about her, except that she looked hot as hell dancing and couldn't hold her beer.

"It's not that easy." She looked away. "But they…well, they've been through a lot and I'm all they have left."

The sincerity in her tone did him in. Justice glanced back at the guy he'd kicked. The fool was finally coming to. He staggered to his feet, likely with a broken jaw, but given how quickly he sneaked off, he'd live. The area was quiet; no one else was paying any attention.

Shit, he hated making decisions like this. Sometimes the "right thing to do" wasn't so clear-cut.

"Please, Justice?"

Now, how was he supposed to refuse her when she looked up at him like that?

Decision made, Justice nodded. "All right, fine. Get your seat belt on." Once they were on the road, they'd have a nice long talk about expectations. He'd explain his responsibilities and how he had to fulfill them not only for her father, as the client, but for the agency that employed him.

He drove for five minutes, getting his thoughts in order, deciding what he'd say and tamping down the adrenaline rush from kicking a little ass. He missed competing. Not that the stupid punks had offered any real challenge. Street thugs never did. Whenever possible, Justice avoided them.

But competition…even when he'd lost, he'd loved the sport. 'Course, winning was so much sweeter.

Rather than dwell on opportunities lost, he cleared his throat and glanced at Fallon, his lecture mentally prepared.

She was fast asleep. Deep, even breaths lifted her breasts. Her lips were slightly parted, her hands limp at her sides, her head lolling back against the seat.

Justice should have been disgruntled with her.

Instead, he spent the rest of the drive to her house with a stupid smile on his face.

"Wake up, sleepyhead."

From far away, Fallon heard the words. Too tired to care, she snuggled into her seat and sighed.

"Fallon, c'mon, girl. Up and at 'em."

That gruff voice teased her senses. She pulled the blanket up higher and frowned, trying to refuse.

Rough fingers stroked her cheek, and she heard, "Damn, you are so soft."

Well, that was nice. In fact, this might be the nicest dream she'd ever had.

A second later, a hard hand shook her shoulder. "Knock off

the sappy smile and *wake up*. Lights are coming on inside and I expect your dad to charge out here any minute."

Her dad? Fallon lifted her lashes—and found Justice staring into her face. She blinked to bring him into focus.

"Hello," he said with a lopsided grin. "You with me, Fallon?"

"Oh." She sat up, felt her head swim and closed her eyes again. "Yes. Sorry."

She heard his car door open and close again, then hers opened. "Let's go." He unhooked her seat belt for her and practically lifted her out.

More drunk than she'd realized, Fallon fell against him, and the security lights flashed on around them.

Justice groaned. "Now we're in for it."

"What in the world do you think you're doing?"

Shielding her eyes from the lights, Fallon straightened away from Justice, but kept a hand on his arm for necessary support. "Dad?"

Wrapped in his housecoat and wearing slippers, her father did indeed charge. The clothes, or lack thereof, and disheveled hair didn't diminish his stately presence. With haughty disgruntlement, he looked her over, then turned to glare at Justice with concentrated disapproval.

"You should know," Justice said fast, "I was all kinds of avuncular. But she drank a little too much and—"

Fallon gasped. "You big tattletale! I wasn't going to tell him I drank!"

With a roll of his eyes, Justice said, "It's not something you could have hidden from him when you can't even stand up straight."

"I can stand." She attempted to and teetered to the left. Both Justice and her father reached out. She caught her balance, lifted her chin in triumph...and slowly tipped over.

Justice got to her first, holding her steady. "Just hush now and let me explain."

Feeling very accusatory, Fallon demanded, "Are you going to tell him about the fight, too?"

This time Justice groaned. "Wasn't planning on it."

"Fight?" her father rasped, his face going ashen. He grabbed her shoulders, turned her this way and that to check her over. "Dear God, are you all right?"

"No one was hurt," Justice rushed to explain. "Fallon's fine."

Her father took that in, let out a shaky breath, then drilled them both with his patented stare. "There was a fight?"

"Skirmish," Justice soothed. "Nothing serious."

Well, since her father knew anyway... "He was *amazing*," Fallon gushed. Justice had impressed her and she was dying to share. "He kicked one guy in the face and put him down."

"One guy?" More apoplectic by the second, her father barked, "There was more than one?"

Justice squeezed her when she started to explain, then he took over. "Three knuckleheads wanted to take her purse, that's all. It wasn't a big deal."

A flush of anger replaced the pale disbelief. Through clenched teeth, her dad said, "I don't know where you took her, but you quite obviously used poor judgment."

When Justice started to speak, Fallon fell into him. "I need to sit down."

"Let's take you in, then your father and I can talk." He put an arm around her and led her forward.

She took one step and tripped over her own feet. The concrete drive rushed up at her face.

Before she made impact, Justice scooped her up into his arms. "Make a note, Fallon. You are *not* a beer drinker." He walked past her silently outraged dad.

Her mother, often more reasonable, stood at the door. "Fallon, what in the world have you done?"

"Two beers," Fallon explained. "I swear."

"Close to the truth," Justice said, stepping inside when her mother held the door open. "Add another half a beer to be exact."

Fallon looked at the long stairs, then at Justice. "I don't suppose you could carry me on up?" Her legs felt ridiculously wobbly, and besides, she liked being in his arms. He didn't look the least bit strained.

"No," her dad snapped. "He most definitely cannot. In fact, you will unhand her this instant."

"Clayton," her mother chastised. Then to Justice, "Put her right here."

He strode across the foyer to the small settee her mother had indicated and carefully lowered her to the seat.

Behind them, her father seethed. "You're fired. Leave and do not return."

Going stiff in the neck, Justice said, "She had a terrific time tonight. You know she's not done, and she's already familiar with me and—"

"*Fired!* Now get out."

"Dad!" No, no, no, Fallon thought. It couldn't end like this. "You can't blame him for—"

"If he doesn't leave this instant, I'll call the police and have him removed."

Justice stiffened. "Fine."

As he turned to go, Fallon panicked. "Justice?"

He paused only a second, sent her a look of frustrated regret, then kept on going...right out of her life.

"Shh," her mother told her before she could make a single sound of protest. "Pick your battles, honey, and time them well. Now is definitely not the time."

"But—"

"Come along. I'll help you upstairs."

The night had been so nice. How could she go from happy to devastated in a matter of minutes?

"You need to sleep it off," her mother whispered, "then we'll talk in the morning, I promise."

Behind them, her father glared. Never before had she seen him enraged like this. Certainly she'd never seen him enraged at her.

"Clayton will be fine," her mom assured her. "He's struggling with his own demons, and like you, he needs a little time. Morning will be soon enough to sort it all out."

God, she hoped so. Halfway up the stairs, Fallon said, "I had a nice time."

"I'm glad."

"Even though no one would dance with me."

Smiling, her mother said, "Perhaps Mr. Wallington wouldn't allow it?"

"Maybe," Fallon said. "He has this crazy death stare, way worse than dad's, and it terrified everyone. I don't think Justice knew that I noticed, but I did."

"Of course you did."

Thinking about the way Justice had watched her, Fallon admitted, "He was wonderful, Mom."

"Was he, now?" Supporting her, her mother kept her walking, up and up that never-ending staircase.

Tonight the stairs seemed a particular challenge. Fallon knew she'd never before overimbibed because this out-of-control feeling was entirely new. She couldn't get her limbs to coordinate, and worse, she felt like bawling.

Once in her room, her mother got out her nightgown and folded down her covers.

Feeling far too clumsy, Fallon finally got her clothes changed and didn't protest when her mother put them away. More than anything, she wanted to drop into bed. However, old habits died hard, so she first went into her bathroom to halfheartedly brush her teeth and wash her face.

When she stepped out, she found her mother sitting on the

side of the bed. Knowing that probably meant a talk, Fallon groaned, but dutifully got into bed.

"How do you feel?"

"Exhausted." And melancholy and excited and…too many emotions for her to differentiate. The night had been fun, but at times scary. Peaceful and exhilarating. And until she'd blundered, she'd felt so incredibly free.

She should never have given up on life, limited as it might be. Now that she'd had a small taste, she wanted more. God, she *craved* more. With new conviction, she decided that if she couldn't have it all, she'd at least take what she could get.

Her mother smiled, then said carefully, "Mr. Wallington is an interesting character."

He fascinated her. "Yes." Interesting, funny, strong, an unbelievable fighter, unique and so protective and gentle without smothering her as her parents often did.

After tucking the covers up around her, her mother smiled. "You know, I met with Ms. Silver and went over all the profiles before selecting Mr. Wallington as your guard."

That was news to Fallon. "You did?" She knew her mother and Ms. Silver had met via their social circles, but she'd assumed her father had made all the arrangements for the protection.

"Yes. Your father was put off by his appearance, but I specifically choose him because, well, I assumed you'd find him unattractive?"

With her mother watching her so closely, Fallon tried not to show any reaction, but inside, she scoffed.

The truth was that she found Justice almost too attractive to bear. But her mother waited for a reply, so Fallon said, "He's okay."

"Yes." Her mother smiled. "Anyway, whether you'd find him handsome or not, I decided his casual manner and dress would make him less obvious as a bodyguard."

Working up what she hoped would be a convincing smile,

Fallon said, "I'm glad you did." In the end, it didn't matter how sinfully gorgeous Justice might be: she understood her own limitations.

"I want you to be happy, Fallon."

Fallon sighed. Her mother had her hair loose, no makeup on her face, and still Fallon thought she looked very pretty. She also looked to be fishing.

"I am happy."

"Oh, honey." Her smile went sad. "You know you don't ever need to lie to me."

"I wouldn't." Yes, she could be happier, but she understood her lot. She had parents who loved her, financial security, a custom-made job that she enjoyed and all the comforts she wanted. "Just because I'm…"

"Expanding your horizons?"

Fallon nodded. That was a good way to put it. "It doesn't mean I'm unhappy." She hoped she could clear out the cobwebs sufficiently to reassure her mom.

Teasing, her mother mused aloud, "Now that I've met him in person, I'll admit that Mr. Wallington has a certain rugged appeal."

Rather than admit anything else inflammatory, Fallon pressed her lips together and shrugged.

"And, my Lord, the man is enormous, all of it brute strength. I imagine any young lady would find him striking on a very basic level."

Pretty much on any level, but Fallon said only, "Yes, so?"

"So he's your guard. It's not only your father he has to answer to, but also his employer. You're a beautiful woman, Fallon, but understand that Mr. Wallington could be completely discredited if he crossed the line while on the job."

"Mom." Heat rushed into her face. "It wasn't like that."

"I'm all for you dating again," her mother continued. "If Marcus doesn't suit—"

"Marcus most definitely does not." She'd see Marcus again, of course. They moved in the same social circle. But she'd never again be alone with him—and she'd never again trust him.

"If you want to talk about it—"

"No." Her mother didn't know the soul-crushing rejection Marcus had delivered, and Fallon hoped to keep it that way. Her way of dealing? Get out there and live without expectations. "I'm fine. Please don't worry."

"I'm a mother. I'm allowed to worry and I imagine I'll be doing so the rest of my life." She softened that with a hug. "Now, about Mr. Wallington."

Fallon would never again delude herself. A strong, confident man like Justice Wallington wouldn't give a woman like her a second look, except as an assignment.

And as a mere assignment, he'd never know her secrets.

"I have no illusions there."

"That's not at all what I'm saying," her mother corrected. "Mr. Wallington would be lucky to have you, and since he seems like a smart man, he probably realizes it. But Fallon, getting drunk and allowing the man to carry you in will only make it more difficult for him to resist you."

Fallon almost laughed. Her mother would be forever biased, no matter what. Justice had resisted her easily enough. "I know. It won't happen again. I promise."

Expression curious, her mother asked, "You think he'll suit as your protection?"

"Yes. He was really terrific, sticking close like Dad asked, but not once getting too familiar." Okay, that was stretching the truth just a tiny bit. She'd had guards before; none of them had been as familiar as Justice.

In fact, none of them had been anything at all like him.

Because of the circumstances, she assumed, as well as his manner, Justice was totally unique. He was far more rough-hewn than any other man she knew, and it showed in his speech, his expressions, his big gorgeous body and his naturally protective nature.

Her mother gave her a knowing look. "I would say carrying you in like an old-fashioned knight went a wee bit beyond familiar."

"That," Fallon assured her, "was entirely my fault." She twisted her mouth to the side. "Apparently two beers are far more potent than a single glass of wine." If she hadn't been so tipsy, she'd never have let him do that, most especially not in front of her father.

"It's late," her mother said with a laugh. "Get some sleep and in the morning you can tell me everything."

"Okay." She turned to her side and burrowed into her pillow. Tomorrow she'd work it out with her dad. She had to. She wasn't ready to let go of her new personal guard so soon. "Mom?"

"Hmm?"

Fallon closed her eyes. "I love you. You know that, right?"

"Yes," her mother said, "we know."

CHAPTER THREE

Justice called Leese Phelps on his drive home. He knew he shouldn't; it was the middle of the night and his buddy would be sleeping, but damn it, he needed to unload. Since Leese was the one who'd gotten him involved with Body Armor, was in fact the one who'd mostly trained him, he seemed the likely person to pester now.

Proving he'd checked the caller ID, Leese answered with, "Everything okay, Justice?"

"Yeah. Sorry for waking you."

"Cat and I went to bed late after a movie. We've only been asleep for a few hours."

Cat, short for Catalina, was Leese's new fiancée and a real peach. "Give her my apologies."

"It's fine. What's up?"

"I got fired."

There was a pause, then Leese asked, "She didn't like you?"

He honestly didn't know what Fallon thought or, once she got sober, if she'd mind that he was canned. "Was her dad who cut me loose." Justice's thoughts churned, interrupted only by the hiss of the tires over wet pavement. There were few people out this late on such a stormy night. "And maybe," Justice admitted, "he had good reason."

As he drove, Justice shared everything that had happened, including the skirmish in the parking lot that he hadn't reported.

When he finished, he waited for Leese to tell him the various ways he'd fucked up the assignment.

Instead, Leese said, "Sounds like it was out of your control."

It took Justice a second to soak that in. "You think?"

"Reporting an attempting mugging is routine, but if the client insists otherwise... I'd have done the same as you. Every so often, things go sideways and you just have to roll with it."

Justice grinned. He knew his friend had gone off script more than a few times where Catalina was concerned. She'd been a pretty damned challenging assignment.

"I have to be at the office tomorrow," Leese said. "Why don't you come on in and we'll talk with Sahara."

"You think Mr. Wade will ask Sahara to assign someone new?" Justice hated the idea of any other guy being Fallon's bodyguard, but still he asked Leese, "Maybe you?"

"Nah," Leese said. "I'm already on detail at the convention center for the outdoor show. Besides, if her dad was that pissed, odds are he'll not only switch guards, but agencies."

Justice winced. Sahara wouldn't be too happy about that. She prided herself on keeping clients happy. "I guess you're right." Having the whole agency lose out was even worse. Body Armor offered the best protection around. If Fallon's dad switched, Fallon would have to settle for second best.

"You should get a new assignment right away," Leese said. "Meet me tomorrow at nine and we'll work it out with Sahara. Another job will help you put this one behind you."

"Yeah, all right." Justice said his farewells and disconnected the call. Hopefully the new assignment would be something easier, maybe a dignitary dodging death threats. That, Justice thought, he could handle.

Hell, *anything* would easier than a nearly impossible to resist, far too innocent, curious and sexy girl...who looked at him with awe. So why did he already miss her?

Fallon woke early with a sinking sensation in her stomach. Not from the alcohol.

Awareness of how badly she'd blundered had her pulling the covers over her head. Good God, she'd gotten smashed and played the fool. When she thought of how carefree she'd been on the dance floor, her face heated.

When she remembered how many times she'd tried to coerce Justice into joining her, each time without success, humiliation made her groan.

He, at least, had behaved with decorum. What must he think of her now? Likely nothing good.

She'd compromised him. Rather than cower, she had to set things right.

The second Fallon left the bed, she realized she'd put her nightgown on backward. Grumbling to herself, she showered and dressed in record time, then entered the breakfast room, anxious to make amends.

Her father was already at the table, his tablet open in front of him as he read the morning news, a cup of hot tea at his elbow. Her mother, dressed in a pretty spring dress and her hair now up, nibbled on toast while typing in email replies for her insanely busy social calendar.

When Fallon cleared her throat, her mother looked up.

Her father did not.

"Fallon? Good morning, sweetheart. How are you feeling?"

Awkward. And anxious. Hopeful to the point of desperation. Fallon said only, "I'm fine, Mom. Thanks." She helped herself to tea, cautiously watching her father.

"No residual effects?"

"No. Except that I'm hungry."

Her mom laughed, but her father continued to ignore her.

Fallon let out a sigh. "Dad."

"Good morning," he said, his gaze still on the tablet.

"Dad," she complained as she took a seat beside him.

Frustration visible, he finally looked up. And waited.

Put on the spot, Fallon cleared her throat again. "I'm sorry about last night."

He nodded, and went back to reading.

"Really?" Fallon narrowed her eyes. "That's all you have to say?" She waited for his reciprocal apology.

After a deep breath, he pressed a button on the tablet to shut it down and gave her his undivided attention. "There's no reason to apologize, Fallon, and no reason to discuss it. Your mother and I talked and we both understand that you haven't had much opportunity to spread your wings. Last night was an aberration, better forgotten." He smiled. "We'll put it behind us as a lesson learned."

Incredulous and insulted, Fallon sucked in a breath. "I don't believe you."

"It's true." He reached out and patted her hand. "I officially dismissed Mr. Wallington first thing this morning. You don't need to worry."

Fury gathered as Fallon stared at her father. "Now I know you're joking."

Her mother interjected, "Unfortunately, Fallon, you know your father rarely jokes."

She flattened her hands on the tabletop. "You already called the agency?"

"And spoke with Ms. Silver herself. She, too, sends her apologies and offered a full refund."

Fallon shoved back her seat. "Call her back!"

"I'll do no such thing." Throwing down his napkin, her father pushed back his chair and he, too, stood.

Her mother quickly circled the table and positioned herself

between them. "I know Sahara Silver quite well. Lovely lady. Very shrewd. I'm sure she'll give the situation time to cool down before actually acting—"

"I told her my decision was final." Her father's expression pinched. "I also told her that her man had gotten you drunk to the point that he had to carry you in, and that he'd engaged in violence in your presence."

Fallon saw red. "The bar was *my* idea. I picked the place. I chose to drink. And Justice did exactly as you asked—he kept every other person a mile away." Hoping for a smidge of understanding, Fallon snapped, "I even had to dance alone! Isn't that what you wanted?"

Her father ignored most of what she'd said to focus on one thing. "Justice?" he repeated with a scowl. "Now you're on a first-name basis with the man?"

"Clayton," her mother reprimanded. "Of course they're on a first-name basis. This is a more casual assignment—"

"An assignment the two of you insisted on!" Fallon said, more than ready to fight her own battles. "I didn't need a bodyguard to be a normal person."

"Fallon..." Her father reached for her, but she stepped back.

"The fight wasn't his fault either. He was the perfect protection. I didn't even see what happened, it was over with so quickly. I only know that no one got near me because *he* didn't let them."

Not budging an inch, her father said, "What's done is done."

Giving up, Fallon realized that she wouldn't be able to reason with him. Whenever challenged, the inimitable Mr. Wade dug in. "Fine," Fallon said. "You don't want to hire him, then don't. I'll take care of it myself."

"Oh, dear," her mother whispered. "Fallon, honey, he's quite expensive."

"I have more than enough of my own money." Breathing

harder, Fallon said, "I'm twenty-four and it's time I lived my own life."

"I forbid it!"

Her eyes flared at her father's vehemence. "Why? Because then you won't have control?"

Silence fell around them. After several tense seconds, her father removed his reading glasses and rubbed at his forehead. "I've never yelled at you before. Not in anger."

Fallon saw his remorse. "I've never yelled at you either."

Using that as an opening, her mother said, "This is important to her, Clayton. Surely you see that."

Once again, the silence stretched out...until Fallon couldn't take it anymore.

"Dad, I understand how you feel. I really do." But she'd let that understanding isolate her to the point that her parents thought she needed a bodyguard just to go out. "The thing is, I'm doing this with or without your blessing." She clasped his hand. "I'd prefer it with."

Defeated, he nodded, and even managed a dim smile. "And I'd prefer to be the one who hires him."

Fallon almost groaned. Somehow, some way, she needed to gain her independence. "Dad—"

"I'll go call the agency now."

Disgruntled after a sleepless night filled with regret, Justice slouched in a seat in his boss's office at the posh Body Armor Agency. He'd only been on the job for four months. First he'd worked part of a case with Leese—a case that ended with Leese getting engaged. Then he'd had a longer stint with a movie star cast in an MMA movie roll. The duties of that job had been twofold: protect the client from rabid fans during the local shoots and teach him how to portray a fighter during the action scenes.

The first part was a piece of cake compared to the second. The dude, talented at acting but not so much at throwing punches,

had a hell of a time catching on. He'd been too arrogant to really learn, determined to think he could overcome the physical
aspect of the role—the right stance, the proper moves—with
added drama. Justice dreaded seeing the movie, since he knew
the actor was going to end up looking like a fool.

Or maybe, he hoped, selective editing and a more athletic
stand-in could make it all work. The upside of that job had been
the groupies who, when shot down by the star, were more than
happy to spend time with a bodyguard. He grinned, remembering how in awe they'd been of his résumé. Not many fighters
turned to protection, but for him, so far, it fit.

That is, until Fallon Wade.

His boss's number-one man, Enoch, delivered a tray of much
needed coffee and Sahara's favorite pastries.

Less tired and therefore more upright, Leese sat across from
Justice. Apparently the late-night call hadn't kept him up. Since
getting engaged, Leese looked satisfied more often than not.

Leese accepted coffee but, forever the fitness buff, passed on
the sweets. Leese might have left the fight world, but he'd yet
to abandon the training.

Sahara Silver, best boss ever, propped her very shapely rear
on the edge of her massive desk and, looking orgasmic, bit into
a jelly-filled doughnut. She'd dressed as classy as ever in a silky
blouse, skinny skirt and crazy-high heels.

He liked Sahara a lot and respected her even more. She was
a shark in business, a high-maintenance woman and a loyal
friend. After licking her lips and washing down the sugar with
a big drink of her coffee, Sahara turned to him, grinned and
said, "Buck up, buttercup."

"I got fired," Justice grouched back. "Don't expect me to be
happy about it."

"True, you did." She swung one foot. "But I'm guessing *someone* had a fit, because just as I was headed in to this little meet-

ing, Mr. Wade called to say he'd had a change of heart. You are
to report to their home at six this evening."

Very slowly, Justice straightened. "You're shi—" he quickly
censored himself and corrected "—kidding me?"

Sahara feigned an absurd look of innocence. "Would I do
that?"

"You think the daughter forced it?" Leese asked.

"Why else? When Mr. Wade called—at the crack of dawn,
by the way—he was most adamant that Justice was through. I
do believe he wanted me to hang him by his toenails...or some
other more vulnerable body part." She bobbed her eyebrows
while giving a pointed look at his crotch. "The man was entirely enraged and I only soothed him by telling him I'd give
Justice a strict reprimand."

Justice scowled.

"Consider yourself severely reprimanded, by the way." Sahara made him wait while she took another bite of her doughnut. "Funny thing, though, when Mr. Wade called back, he
was subdued to the point of being sullen. He snarled that he'd
reconsidered and the contract should stand."

Justice didn't know what to think. Had Fallon had a hissy?
That'd fit the princess role, but she hadn't seemed like the hissy
type to him.

Still, it wasn't like he knew her well. Shortly after meeting,
she'd gotten drunk and people could be very different then.

"None of this makes sense," Justice said. "I'm not even sure
why she needs protection."

While sipping coffee, Sahara shrugged. "Her father is wealthy.
Threats come out of nowhere."

"But it's more than that," Justice insisted. "They treat her like
she's a kid." He glanced at Leese. "She wanted to go to a bar
and drink beer. Said she'd never done either one before. What
twenty-four-year-old lady's never done that?" And now that he
thought of it, it made him wonder what else she hadn't done.

Not a good direction for his thoughts to take.

"That's where you took her?" Leese asked.

"Yeah." He couldn't help but half grin. "She got hammered right off the bat. It would have been funny if her dad wasn't breathing fire down my neck."

Leese gave him a long look. "Had she eaten?"

"I dunno."

The long look became disbelieving. "You didn't find out?" Leese sat forward, his elbows on his knees. "You took a twenty-four-year-old sheltered client on a drinking spree without asking questions first?"

Going on the defensive, Justice said, "'Course I asked questions. She just didn't give a lot of answers."

"Tell me you at least did your research beforehand."

"I told you last night, she didn't give me a chance. She laid out the agenda after I got there, not before."

Leese shook his head. "But you researched her, right?"

Starting to feel uncomfortable, Justice shifted. He knew Leese was big on digging up every bit of info he could, in every way he could. "What was there to research? It was a straightforward job. Just watch over her for a while."

Leese and Sahara shared a look of disappointment.

"What?" he demanded. "There wasn't any specific threat ever mentioned."

"You do your research, regardless." Leese stood. "You know that."

"Sure. But this time, it didn't seem necessary. I mean, I'm like a glorified babysitter or something." Except that now...yeah, now he wished he knew more about her.

"Let's go." Leese returned his coffee cup to the tray. "We'll do it now."

"We will?" Justice quickly gulped down his coffee and went to follow his friend. After all, Leese had fallen much more comfortably into this new gig. For him, it had been an easy transition.

For Justice, he still felt like he had a lot to learn...obviously.

"Yes," Sahara said. "Go, shoo. Do your jobs. Leave the rest of the pastries for me. And Justice? Let me know how it goes."

By the time Justice pulled through the gate to the Wade home, he felt like he had a better handle on things.

He now knew that Fallon had graduated at the top of her class, so she was obviously smart.

She didn't keep a Facebook page or Twitter account, so she wasn't much for social media—or she was super private. He'd bet on the latter.

The lack of an online persona made it tougher to get a handle on her personal preferences. Leese had thought they'd find out about her friends, past dates, the places she enjoyed hanging...but when they found nothing, they both decided it was her father's wealth that made it difficult to do the usual. Anyone could be tracked online, but as protective as her folks were, they wouldn't like making it easy.

Fallon was young for her job as a decorator for her father's hotel chain. She handled only the local hotels, though. Justice didn't know if that was out of an aversion to traveling or just convenience.

Since most rich people spent a bunch of their time jetting around, Leese had dug a little more, but even he couldn't find a single instance of Fallon leaving the city in years.

Curious, but what Justice found most interesting was an incident from five years ago when Fallon's sister, older by two years, had tragically died in a fire. That alone might be enough to prompt the parents to hover over her.

Losing a kid...he couldn't imagine anything worse than that. But yeah, it could make anyone more protective.

There weren't many details to go by. The parents were super private and had refused all interviews. All Leese could find was a report of the fire, started by accident, saying that the sister had died. Apparently the Wades had enough money and influence to keep their personal business out of the news.

To prepare for the assignment, Justice had left Leese to finish up his cursory research while he checked out all the local establishments that Fallon might want to visit. That had taken most of the afternoon. After figuring he had a handle on things, Justice had eaten his dinner and headed out.

Now that the storms had blown over, the spring day felt too warm and muggy. He'd dressed in a T-shirt and jeans with his usual gym shoes. This time of early evening, the sun settled like a blaze on the horizon, making sunglasses necessary as he drove along the landscaped private drive to the house.

First thing Justice noticed was a black Mercedes parked out front. Slick ride. Curious, he parked behind it, got out and started for the front door. Right before he reached the steps, the door opened and a suited GQ-looking guy got ushered out.

Tall, trim, blond—and obviously of the same moneyed ilk as Fallon's family.

Effectively backing him out the door, Fallon said, "Really, Marcus, I've been clear. I'm sorry, but it's over."

Huh. A boyfriend? Maybe *past* boyfriend, given Fallon's frown. Justice held back, watching and waiting.

Marcus took her hands. "Don't say that, Fallon. You can't mean it."

"I do." She tugged, but good ole Marcus didn't let her go.

That irked Justice big-time. He was about to intercede when Mr. Wade stepped out, and for once he looked pissed at someone other than Justice. "Go, Marcus. Don't make this more uncomfortable for her than it has to be."

"Please, sir, I need just a minute to speak with her."

"She doesn't want to talk to you," Mr. Wade insisted.

"Dad," Fallon complained. "I can handle this."

"I screwed up," Marcus rushed to say to her father, ignoring

Fallon's objection. "I know that and I'm sorry. It just...took me by surprise."

"Marcus!" Face going red, Fallon glanced at her father, who didn't budge. "You don't have to explain. Seriously." She tugged again, but blondie didn't let go. "I understand. But surely you see—"

"It won't happen again. I swear."

"What," her father asked with growling menace, "won't happen again?"

"*Dad,*" Fallon pleaded more urgently. Then to Marcus, "Don't do this. *Please.*"

Justice decided he'd had enough. Interrupting whatever Marcus would have said, he announced himself. "Hey, Fallon. You about ready?"

Finally noticing him, her face lit up, then pinched in irritation as she forcefully yanked her hands from Marcus. "Yes, of course. I'll need only a minute."

"Sure." As he strode up the steps, Justice pushed the glasses to the top of his head, letting them catch in the messy fauxhawk that he knew needed a good trim.

She looked nervously to her pushy swain. "Marcus..."

"I'm not leaving," Marcus insisted.

Yeah, Justice decided, he was. "Did I get here just in time to be useful?" His muscles clenched. He felt like cracking his knuckles—or the boyfriend's head.

"No! That is, everything's fine." Fallon floundered, then pulled back her shoulders and glared at Marcus.

"Fallon," the guy pleaded.

"Goodbye." After giving her dad a warning frown, Fallon sent a fast smile to Justice, then hurried inside.

Pinning his gaze to Marcus, Justice approached with as much menace as he could muster.

Marcus quickly stepped aside, caught himself and, instead of leaving, he struck an arrogant stance. "Who are you?"

"None of your business." Satisfied with Marcus's flustered reaction, Justice turned to her father with a cordial nod. "Mr. Wade."

"Mr. Wallington." He blocked the door. "I'd like a word please."

"All right." Justice had figured on getting an earful.

Mr. Wade turned to Marcus again. "Don't come back here uninvited or you'll find yourself out of a job."

Justice whistled low. Far as dismissals went, that was a brutal one.

Face going red, Marcus nodded. "As you wish." Trying to muster some dignity, he needlessly straightened his suit coat. "But I *will* speak with her again." He cast a cautious look at Justice, turned and left.

Both men watched, arms crossed, until Marcus had driven out of view.

Seeing a neutral opening, Justice asked, "Is he a threat?"

"Marcus? No, of course not." Mr. Wade closed the door behind him, giving them privacy outside. "You know that I fired you."

"Not something I would've missed." The man had shouted it at him in a rage.

"I hired you back only because Fallon insisted."

What was he supposed to say about that? No way would he thank him, so instead he settled on a simple, "Okay." He didn't want things to be more awkward than necessary, but hell if he'd grovel.

"I wouldn't have," Mr. Wade stated, "but she threatened to hire you herself. With her own money."

Fallon had enough of her own? Justice wasn't sure. Nothing in the research revealed her finances, and it didn't feel like an appropriate question to ask. Feeling his way, he said, "I gather you don't want her to do that?"

"No, I don't." Showing his frustration, Mr. Wade ran a hand

through his hair, disrupting the meticulous style. "But Fallon is independent."

Justice almost choked on that. He banked the skepticism when Mr. Wade glared at him.

"You don't understand," Mr. Wade continued. "I would love to indulge her, but other than agreeing to live at home, she rarely lets me. Even for holidays—her birthday, Christmas—she complains if we give her too many gifts. She buys casual department store clothes, drives an economy car—"

"So far," Justice said, "I don't see a problem." He kind of liked the idea that Fallon was so low-key. Made it easier for him to relate to her.

"I was remiss in explaining things to you." Locking his hands behind his back, Mr. Wade paced. "Fallon received a sizable trust fund from my parents. If she chose to, she could live a very comfortable, independent life off that. However, she almost never touches the money. For the most part, she makes do with her limited salary."

"So it's because of this big inheritance that you wanted her protected?"

"Not entirely, no." Mr. Wade looked off down the drive, visibly gathering his thoughts.

Justice waited for him to explain the threat.

Instead, he said, "I didn't want Fallon to finally spend the money...only to spite me."

Damn, how big of a spat had they had? Justice found himself in the awkward position of feeling bad for Mr. Wade. "Yeah, okay, I get that." He cleared his throat, searching for words to smooth things over. "Look, I don't want to be a bone of contention between father and daughter. If there are strict rules here, just let me know and I'll do my best. But if I can speak up?"

A touch of desperation held her father stiff. "By all means."

"Well..." Justice rubbed the back of his neck, completely out of his comfort zone. Hell, as a fighter, he'd hooked up with plenty of girls and never, not once, had he been forced through a heart-to-heart with a father. "Fallon's not a kid, right? The things she gets excited over, like drinking a beer? That's stuff she should've done years ago. Seems to me she's just spreading her wings a little, playing catch-up with other people her age. Why not let her? So she got a little drunk. You were mid-twenties once, right?"

After a moment, the slightest of smiles tweaked Mr. Wade's mouth. "Yes."

Somehow Justice couldn't see the staid man before him ever cutting loose, but whatever. "No harm was done. And that fight she mentioned wasn't much of a fight at all."

"She said the two of you were accosted by three men."

Bearing his own frustration, Justice propped his hands on his hips. "Yeah, but they were just bozos. I handled it, and I'll handle anything else that comes up." He threw caution to the wind and clapped a hand to the man's shoulder. "Let her cut loose in the way she wants—with me keeping her safe. You'll worry, sure. I get that dads do that."

Brows lifted, Mr. Wade looked first at the hand on his shoulder, then at Justice directly. "Your own father. Does he worry?"

"He passed when I was young. But my mom? That woman could worry paint off the wall." He grinned, gave the smaller man two strong shoulder slaps that left him staggering, then dropped his hand. "Thing is, Mom trusts me. I'm thinking you need to trust Fallon some, too."

"I do."

"Then how about trusting me? I come with good credentials." Not wanting to miss the opportunity, Justice moved on to more important matters. "So about this Marcus character…"

That soured the man's mood even more. "They used to date."

Yeah, he'd figured that much on his own. "Didn't work out?"

After only a second or two of hesitation, Mr. Wade confided

in him. "Marcus hurt her. I'm not sure how but they ended their relationship and she hasn't dated since."

Justice went rigid. "What do you mean, he hurt her?"

"Her feelings. He said or did something." In a low voice, Mr. Wade murmured, "Bastard."

Well, what do you know? He and Mr. Wade were finding common ground after all. "Did she date much before that?"

"Not since high school."

Which meant she hadn't dated in college? Why the hell not? "So when did she and Marcus meet?" To keep from sounding too personally interested, Justice said, "It helps if I know what's what, in case he shows up again."

"If he does, it won't go well for him. I meant it when I said I'd fire him."

"What did he do for you?"

Mr. Wade waved a hand. "Management position, created for him—which means he'd be easy to replace."

Hmm. "You think Fallon would be okay with that? I mean, I got the impression she wanted to handle it herself, not with your influence."

His shoulders dropped. "True." After a huff, he added, "And Rebecca is fond of him."

Fallon's mom? "So maybe you need to be just a little more subtle in how you scare him off."

Mr. Wade scrutinized him. "You?"

Why not? After all, his job was to protect her. "I can easily handle it, and since you're paying me..." Justice left that open-ended, and then waited.

"Keep him away from her," Mr. Wade instructed, "and I just might consider you valuable after all."

"I'll see to it." With pleasure. *What had the prick done to turn her against him?* Hands in his pockets, Justice asked, "You wanna give me any details?"

Mr. Wade grumbled to himself a moment, something about

a wasted promotion, then explained, "They were together for about four months and she seemed so happy. Fallon is private, so I don't know what Marcus did to screw it up, but it ended about six weeks ago."

Stalling the million and one questions Justice had, Fallon opened the door—and drew up short when she saw the two men in close conversation.

Suspicion lifted her brows, then animosity lowered them. In a chilling tone of warning, Fallon asked, "Dad?"

CHAPTER FOUR

Justice said, "Um…"

Hell, he felt like he'd just gotten caught with his hand in the cookie jar. In truth, Fallon had probably saved him because he'd been close to asking questions that had nothing to do with the job, and had everything to do with the odd protectiveness he felt toward Fallon as a woman.

It went beyond work ethic and nudged into…territorial.

Assignment, assignment, assignment. He'd remind himself as many times as necessary.

Being much smoother, Mr. Wade pasted on a tempered smile. "We were just passing the time until you finished getting ready, honey."

Fallon wasn't buying it. Her doubt showed in the way she looked at Justice out of the corner of her eye.

He grinned at her.

That seemed to confuse her. "I would have been ready if Marcus hadn't dropped in. I'm sorry for making you wait."

"Does he do that often?" *Shut up, Justice.*

"Um, no." She looked between him and her father. "But it did put me just a little behind."

"Not a problem," Justice promised. "I'm on your schedule, remember."

"And it gave us a chance to chat and get better acquainted." Mr. Wade pulled his daughter into an embrace, hugging her close. He looked at Justice over her head while he said, "Have fun, and be safe."

Next he offered his hand to Justice.

Huh. Maybe they really had smoothed over the rough waters. "Right. Better acquainted." Justice accepted the olive branch.

"I'm trusting you to take care of her." After that quiet acceptance, Mr. Wade went in.

Fallon scowled up at Justice. "What was that all about?"

Today she wore slim ankle-length jeans with flat shoes and a loose, blue striped sweater. She looked incredibly cute. "Just talking man to man." Rather than go into detail, Justice gestured for her to precede him to the car. "Where to tonight?"

"I checked out local attractions and found that there's a street fair nearby. It's open for a few more hours."

Justice tripped over his own feet. Damn it, he'd checked everything he could think of, but he hadn't even known about the fair. "Where?"

"It's downtown. Lots of crowds expected."

He grabbed for the door handle right before she could.

Once again, she sat up front.

Like déjà vu, he got behind the wheel but didn't pull away. "Will you need me tomorrow, too?"

She tipped her head. "Is that a problem?"

"Nope. But I'm thinking we save the fair till then."

"Why?"

"I don't know anything about it."

"It's a fair," she said. "There will be vendors, things to buy, food to try."

Justice figured it was past time they made some ground rules. "You need to understand, it's my job to make you secure. I gotta know what's happening a little beforehand, otherwise it's impossible. And when it's impossible, your dad gets pissed and I could end up canned again."

Not giving in, Fallon asked, "What could happen at a fair?"

No idea, but he knew better than to take chances. "Anything, I guess." He tugged at his ear. "See, what I do is figure out how to proceed in case anything does go wrong. Like, I need to know the quickest way out, the best route to take, the neighborhoods we'll go through—"

"You're taking this all too seriously."

"Yeah, says the girl who got shit-faced, had to be carried in, got me fired—"

"Stop!" Barely suppressing a laugh, she pressed her palms to her reddened cheeks. "That's not who I usually am."

Justice noticed how cute she looked with a blush. "Too bad, because that girl was fun."

She blinked at him. "Really?"

Too late to call back the words, Justice said, "I mean—"

"You don't think I was...pathetic?" So much heat now colored her cheeks, she looked scalded.

Bracing a forearm on the steering wheel, Justice turned to face her. The vulnerability in her dark eyes nearly broke his heart. Softly, he asked, "Why would you think that?"

She looked away, hesitated, then changed the subject. "Maybe we could do the art museum then. There's a special exhibit—"

He cut her off. "Same problem. I'd need to check it out first."

Disappointed, she clutched her hands in her lap. "So then what are we going to do? I'm not anxious to visit another bar."

That surprised him. "I thought you had fun." But maybe her daddy had put the kibosh on drinking.

"I did," she admitted. "But then I woke up this morning and remembered that no one had danced with me. Not that I expected guys to rush over or anything, but...not a single one?"

The smile tugged at his mouth. "You know why, right?"

Her shoulders sagged. "I assume—"

Justice took her hand. It was small in his, delicate. Hell, her dad was right—she was fragile.

Taboo, dude. Knock that shit off.

He retreated, but explained, "Guys tried, honey. More than a few. My job was to keep them away, so that's what I did."

Comprehension came slowly. "You're serious?"

Justice nodded. "Any guy who looked too long, or tried to cozy up, got my best 'back the ef off' stare. You were busy dancing—" *and turning me on in the process* "—so I guess you didn't notice."

She dropped back in her seat. "You actually warned men away?"

"With a mean stare, yeah." In his defense, Justice said, "They weren't your usual refined aristocrats, you know."

A slow simmering anger straightened her shoulders, tightened that soft mouth and narrowed her amazing eyes. "I didn't want to dance with an aristocrat. That's why I went to a local *bar.*"

She said it like she spoke to an idiot. Amused by the show of temper, Justice grinned. "Tell you what, if you have enough free time tonight, how about I take you to Rowdy's? I'm already familiar with it and I'm betting the guys I know will be around. If you want to dance with them, no sweat."

She looked tempted, and still riled. "I don't want you coercing anyone to do you a favor. I'm not a charity case."

"Far from it." Hell, he'd probably still have to read the riot act to any man—friend or not—who got too close. "So what do you say?" To help convince her, he added, "You can try another beer, but this time just one."

She stewed a minute more before finally nodding. "Well… all right. But, Justice, you have to trust me to do my own fending off, okay?"

Now that he had a destination, he started the car and pulled away. "That's a no-go. It's my job to—"

"You are only to protect me if things get out of hand!"

Yeah, she had a point. But with a woman like Fallon, that could happen in the blink of an eye.

They weren't on the road long when Justice cleared his throat. Over the next twenty minutes he did it several more times, repeatedly glancing her way, and Fallon assumed he was uneasy about her scolding.

Because he wore his mirrored sunglasses, she couldn't see his eyes. Not that she needed to. The tension in his big body, in his broad shoulders and the set of his jaw, told her he was on edge.

She remained a little irked at his high-handed attitude, but clearly that mood wasn't conducive to a nice evening so she decided to break the ice. With a slight huff, she faced him. "Something on your mind, Justice?"

A long exhale left his posture more relaxed. "Whew." He flashed her a relieved grin. "That silent treatment was getting to me."

Fallon hid her smile. For such a big, bulky guy, he'd really let one little disagreement bother him. "Then why don't we chat?"

As if he'd been waiting for that invitation, Justice said, "Good idea. Who's Marcus?"

Well, shoot. She'd walked right into that one. "Nobody important." Not anymore.

"Nah, don't give me that. He's somebody, or at least he was. You cut ties on him?"

"Yes." Or more like Marcus had cut ties—with his reaction.

He frowned. "Hung up on him still?"

Emphatic, she said, *"Noooo."*

"No?" he clarified.

"Not even a little." Marcus had bruised her pride, wounded her spirit and dashed her hopes, but she knew she'd never really loved him. "He was...convenient." She wrinkled her nose. "That sounds terrible, doesn't it? Very mercenary. The thing is, he works for my dad and my parents liked him. He was familiar with the family." And all her secrets. "It seemed easy to fall into a pattern with him." Easy, and oh, so stupid.

"Well, for what it's worth," Justice said, "I don't like him."

He sounded so sincere, she couldn't help but point out the obvious. "You don't even know him."

"Sure I do. See, fighters learn how to size people up real quick. You get in the cage with a guy and you have to know if he's quiet because he's afraid, or because he's that confident. Does he talk smack to counter insecurities, or because he knows he can back it up? I can read body language and Marcus is a putz."

Fallon laughed. "Sorry to disappoint you, but he really isn't. He's successful and engaging and people love him."

"Not me." Justice squeezed the steering wheel. "Not you."

Good point. "We're the exceptions, then."

"Nope. Your dad wasn't too keen on him either, let me tell you." Justice glanced in the rearview mirror, frowned, and then took an exit. "So what happened? What'd he do?"

She couldn't believe his audacity. "That's private, Justice."

He chewed his upper lip, rolled one shoulder, and said with complete seriousness, "I have to know these things. I mean, what if he shows up and tries to start trouble?"

Fallon laughed. "He won't. In all ways, Marcus is proper."

"Asshole wasn't all that proper today. Proper is letting a lady go when she asks."

"Justice!" It took all her control not to laugh. He did have a way of saying things.

Jaw working, Justice grumbled, "I wanted to cream him."

It was ridiculous, but his vehemence warmed Fallon's heart. She touched his rigid shoulder and said, "I'd prefer that you didn't."

"Okay, so help me out here—what's his crime? If I know, then maybe, *maybe*, I won't feel the need to stomp on him."

For the first time since the breakup, Fallon felt like talking about it. Oh, she wouldn't give him every detail. She'd learned her lesson on sharing too much. But given Justice's defense, and the fact he didn't know all her secrets, he might be the perfect person to listen.

"I'm on the edge of my seat here," he said. "Imagining all kinds of crazy stuff."

Belatedly, she withdrew her hand, but her palm continued to tingle. She curled her fingers into a fist, holding on to the sensation.

Justice's shoulder was boulder hard and so warm that she couldn't help but think about touching him again, wrong as she knew it would be.

"Honestly, it wasn't all that much." The hazy setting sun glared through the windshield, giving her a good excuse to hide behind her own sunglasses. *Now where to begin?* "Marcus and I started out as just friends. I...haven't done much dating."

What an understatement.

Not wanting him to ask about that, she quickly continued. "There are some occasions where you'd really like a date. Weddings, company parties, things like that," she explained. "I knew Marcus through the company, he was nice, others admired him..."

"And you bought into that shit?"

She bit back a smile. "My dad was really pleased when Marcus asked me to a company gathering."

"So what? Your dad didn't have to date him."

That time the laugh broke free. "For some reason you're biased."

"I told you, I'm a good judge of character."

Curiosity got the best of her. "So what do you think of me?"

Becoming uneasy again, Justice said, "Finish your story first."

Fallon thought about it, then decided he was right. Better to get it over with. "We did the whole friend thing for a while until finally, maybe a month later, Marcus wanted more than that, but my parents have been really overprotective."

"Noticed."

Of course he had. Not like he could have missed that. "I didn't have much experience with guys, and Marcus was...patient."

Interest sharpening, Justice growled, "You're talking about sex?"

She wished she could be as plainspoken as him. But his question alone made her face hot. Lifting a hand in a lame gesture, she said, "Stuff that comes before that."

"What stuff?"

Fallon shifted. "You know what I'm saying."

He chewed his lip again. "Okay, so we're talking foreplay, right? Making out, groping a little, testing the water so to speak."

"Yes, exactly." And all that had gone well enough as long as she left on her clothes. "We seemed to suit...until it came time for the deed."

He snorted a laugh. "The *deed*?" he mimicked. With a teasing glance, he asked, "We're still talking sex, right?"

"Yes," she growled, her eyes narrowed as Justice made her feel foolish.

"Let me tell you, if Marcus screwed that up, then good riddance."

Yes, he'd definitely screwed it up. The same strangling humiliation swamped her. "We found we didn't suit and that there could be no future between us. Not in any intimate way."

"Holy shit," Justice breathed. "He *did* screw it up. Jesus, what a putz."

"It wasn't like that."

He snorted another laugh. "If you say so. But now I just feel sorry for him." This time Justice reached out and patted her knee. "The idiot will be regretting that the rest of his life."

It blew her away that Justice seemed to consider her such a prize. "Why would he regret it? Because he works for my father? I don't think Dad would—"

"Yeah, your dad definitely would. But what I meant was that

he'd lost out with you." Justice got back on the expressway before saying, "You know you're a catch, right?"

He didn't know her well enough to make that judgment, but she enjoyed hearing it anyway. "You think so?"

"Know so. I mean, what's not to like, right?"

She half turned to face him. "So tell me, what do you consider my sterling qualities?"

He glanced in the rearview mirror again. "Would that be crossing a line? I mean, I don't look forward to your dad unloading on me again."

"I won't tell if you don't."

He grinned wide enough to put dimples in his whiskery cheeks. "Alrighty, then. For one thing, you're cute as hell. Big bedroom eyes, soft sexy mouth, and you have such a sweet little body."

Fallon ducked her head as guilt swamped her. "I don't."

"See, this is why I should pound on Marcus. Did that prick say or do something to make you—"

"No." Caught between wanting to laugh and dying of embarrassment, Fallon said, "And your language is deteriorating by the second."

"Let's blame Marcus," Justice grumbled. "He brings out the worst in me."

Shaking her head, Fallon said, "You're incorrigible."

"Just speaking the truth." He grew more serious. "You're also really nice. And smart. You have a good sense of humor. You're daring. And... I dunno. You're *genuine*." With a fast shrug, he added, "I didn't expect that. I thought with you being rich and all, you'd maybe be snooty or bitchy, but you're not. You're real down-to-earth."

Never in her life had she been so flattered. "Thank you, Justice." For obvious reasons, compliments to her character were far nicer than commenting on her physical appearance.

He gave a nod, then said, "You also look really great dancing. Too good, maybe."

Having no idea what he meant by that, Fallon said again, "Thank you. I haven't had much practice dancing either, but I enjoy it."

"I could tell that you did," he murmured. "Hell, every guy there could tell." Then he asked, "Marcus never took you dancing?"

"A few times. Not often." She didn't want to detail everything she hadn't done, so she switched gears. "While we're discussing Marcus, I should probably explain that none of this was his fault."

Justice snorted. "I saw him, remember? He was all butt-hurt and bossy, probably because he knew he'd screwed up."

Fallon choked. "Butt-hurt?"

He grinned again. "Yeah, you know. All pouty and belligerent."

"I've, ah, never heard the term."

He dismissed that with a shrug. "Take my word for it—men don't act that way unless they're butt-hurt. Not real men, anyway."

With Justice having been a fighter, his ideas of how real men should behave might differ from many others. "Could I ask you something now?"

"Shoot."

"Why did you give up fighting when you're so obviously good?"

"Ouch." He gave a theatrical wince. "Tough question. See, I'm not that good. Not good enough to win a title and that's what it's all about."

"But you're fast, and strong and—"

He grinned at her. "Keep going."

"Admittedly, I don't know that much about fighting, but I was certainly impressed."

"Because," he repeated, "you don't know that much about fighting. The dudes you'll meet tonight at Rowdy's? Some of them are top-notch. Championship quality. Without sounding too cocky, I am good, but only against untrained idiots. You could throw street thugs at me all day long and I wouldn't break a sweat. But in the cage…" He gave a small shake of his head. "Whole different ballgame."

Fascinated, Fallon thought about the men she'd meet, even while wanting to know more about Justice. "How so?"

He lifted one hand from the wheel and curled it into a tight fist. Muscles bulged all along his forearm, his biceps, shoulder and into his neck. "I have bricks for fists. Real knock-out power. Problem is, trained fighters aren't still long enough to let me hit them. MMA is a mixed fighting style, so it's not just boxing. It's grappling, too."

"Grappling?"

"Sort of a mix between wrestling, submission and strikes. My takedowns are too slow and once I'm on the ground the best fighters have an advantage over me with speed. If I get hold of a guy, or if I can land a punch or kick, I can put him down. That's my strength."

She agreed—he looked very strong.

"But any scenario other than that and I'd get in trouble. The losses I had were all submissions."

"How many losses did you have?"

"Twenty wins, six losses."

"Pfft. And for that you gave up?"

He scowled at her. "There wasn't a path to the belt. The heavyweight title holder is a beast. He beat me twice. If I lost weight and dropped down to light heavyweight, my buddy Cannon was in the way."

"You didn't want to fight a buddy?"

"Hell, I don't mind that. Guys compete with their friends all the time. It's a sport, not a grudge match."

He sounded disgruntled, making her smile. "Sorry, I didn't realize."

"I trained at Cannon's camp. I'd seen him fight plenty of

times, but even in training he was slicker than most. I knew I'd
only beat him with a lucky punch, and so far, no one's gotten a
lucky punch in on him. You'll like him."

"You don't sound resentful."

"Of Cannon?" He snorted. "No, 'course not. He's a great guy.
Not just at fighting either. That camp? It's his gym, a way for
fighters to learn new techniques from each other, but he also
runs classes for the neighborhood kids. Everyone in Warfield
idolizes him because that's the type of man he is."

She held silent for a bit, noticing that he again checked the
rearview mirror, then the side mirror. Just cautious, or was there
a problem? She checked her side mirror but saw nothing amiss,
just other cars on the road.

As the light faded from the horizon, streetlamps flickered on.
They each removed their sunglasses. The headlights automatically flicked on as Justice took another exit and turned down
a busy street.

"Do you miss fighting?"

"Yeah. A lot."

She heard the longing in his tone and it bothered her. "Why
switch to being a bodyguard then? I'd think if you enjoyed it
and you were good—even if not the best—it'd be worth it to
continue."

His hands tightened on the steering wheel. "I'm no good at
being second best. Too competitive. My last fight was a good
win. I was the underdog. Everyone expected me to get my
ass handed to me. Instead, I nailed a quick, clean knockout in
under thirty seconds. So I figured I'd go out on a high note,
you know?"

"Wow." But because she didn't know, she asked, "That's fast,
right?"

He laughed. "Yeah. Usually we go three five-minute rounds.
Championship fights are five five-minute rounds." He shifted,
popped his neck, then admitted, "Nine times out of ten, he'd

have beaten me. But he shot in, I threw a punch and *pow*, he went down for the count."

"I'd say there's luck, and then there's being ready. Clearly you took advantage of an opportunity. You were prepared and you did what you needed to do, when you needed to do it."

Grinning, he patted her knee again. "Yeah, that's how I tell it, too."

"Do you still train?"

"Sure. Once a gym rat, always a gym rat. But now I can eat burgers when I want." He patted his flat abdomen. "And drink an occasional beer."

Absurd for him to pretend he had any fat on his body. From what Fallon could tell, he was muscle layered on muscle. But given it was probably a somewhat new occurrence, she was ridiculously pleased that he'd drunk a beer with *her*.

"On top of being competitive, I like a challenge. Let me tell you, this gig is *real* challenging. Hell, every day I learn something new. Another fighter friend, Leese Phelps, was the first to cut out for personal security. He sort of paved the way." With another cocky grin, Justice added, "I still get to be a badass and have some interesting assignments. As a bonus, I get to carry a gun."

Startled, she asked, "You're carrying a gun?"

He gave her a "duh" look. "You thought I wouldn't?"

"I never thought about it either way." She looked him over, but didn't see—

"Want to see for yourself, huh?" He leaned forward a little, lifted his T-shirt and showed her a black automatic in a holster connected to his belt, situated at the small of his back.

It took her a second to find her voice. Justice had just flashed a swath of firm skin and muscle, and the waistband of black boxers riding low on his hips. Temperature rising, Fallon asked in a whisper, "Have you ever shot anyone?"

"Not so far, no." As he pulled up to a stoplight, he turned to look at her. "But I would if necessary."

She believed him.

Then he flashed another grin, flexed his arms to make massive muscles pop in his biceps. "But with guns like these, it's usually not necessary."

Fallon felt like fanning her face. Good Lord, he looked fine. Needing another switch, she said, "I'm sorry I'm not a more interesting assignment."

"You fit that 'challenge' part, and that keeps it interesting."

Before she could ask him what he meant, the light changed and he moved his foot off the brake.

"Before you," he said, "I worked with Mark Stricker."

Her jaw loosened. "The movie star?"

"Yeah. Let me tell you—that was interesting. Did you know he's, like, five-two?"

"Really? I thought he was taller."

"Me, too."

"In movies, he looks to be at least six feet tall."

"Yeah, but it's a trick. They put him on a platform when he's next to the taller female actors. Crazy, huh?"

"Fascinating." Curious why he'd been assigned to Stricker, she asked, "Was he in danger?"

"Nah. Mostly I helped him train for a new role as a fighter. But there were also times I had to keep the rabid fans away. I can't talk about it much. The deets on the film are still hush-hush."

"Okay, sorry." When he again checked his mirrors, Fallon huffed a breath. "Is there a problem, Justice?"

"What do you mean?"

"You keep checking behind us like you're expecting trouble."

"It's my job to expect trouble."

She started to relax...

Until he added, "Especially when we're being followed."

CHAPTER FIVE

Fallon looked so startled, Justice decided to distract her. "Tell me about your job now."

She twisted to stare out the rear window. "Justice—"

"Fair's fair. I answered your questions."

Glaring at him, she asked, "Who's following us?"

"Don't know. I'm willing to bet it's Marcus, though."

For a few seconds, she just stared at him—then laughed. "Don't be ridiculous." But she looked again. "Can you see his car?"

"No."

She relaxed back in her seat. "How do you know we're being followed?"

"I know." He took another look in the mirror before leaving the road and pulling into a restaurant lot.

"This is it?" she asked, sounding disappointed by the updated, casual, mom-and-pop diner.

"No." Justice did a U-turn in the lot to face the road, turned off the headlights and waited.

Fallon appeared to be holding her breath, so without taking his gaze off the road, Justice said, "Relax. You're fine."

In reply, she wrapped her arms around herself.

Justice wanted to comfort her but he'd already crossed too many lines. If he kept it up, he'd deserve to be canned.

A car drove past. A few trucks. And then he saw the fancy sports car.

Fallon seemed unaware as she stared through the windshield.

Was she afraid of Marcus? If so, that was reason enough for Justice to confront him. For some reason—crazy as it might be—he was itching to pulverize the guy.

After the slick black car sped past, Justice asked, "Does Marcus have a Corvette?"

"What?" Drawn from her thoughts, she shook her head. "No—or at least I don't think so. He's more a BMW or Mercedes type of man."

"I saw the Mercedes. Can he afford two cars? Maybe one for business and one for sport?"

"He could, yes. But, Justice, I'm sure that wasn't him. It's not his style to chase after anyone."

"Maybe." Justice stewed a minute more before deciding it would be best to get to their destination so Fallon could enjoy herself. He drove out of the lot, saying, "We'll be there in about five minutes."

"Rowdy's?"

"Yeah." So that he wouldn't make the same mistake twice, he asked, "You hungry? They have some killer burgers there."

She gave it quick thought and nodded. "Very hungry, in fact. Thanks."

Luckily Rowdy had opened up a separate lot adjacent to the bar because the place stayed packed, especially on a Saturday night. Justice kept Fallon close as he stepped inside the busy bar.

Avery, Rowdy's wife who usually worked as the bartender, bustled from table to table. When she spotted him, she got closer and said, "They're in back at the pool tables."

"Thanks. I'll join them in a bit, but we want to grab some food first."

"There's a booth that just emptied. Follow me."

Justice waited until they'd nabbed the seats before doing introductions. "Avery, this is Fallon. Fallon, Avery is married to the owner."

He let the ladies say their hellos before asking, "How come you're on the floor tonight?"

"One of our waitresses called in sick. Rowdy's working the bar and I'm doing my best to keep up here. Some days," she grumbled, "being popular is a bother."

Fallon smiled at her. "Is there some way we can help?"

Justice froze. If Avery said yes, how the hell would he keep track of her?

Luckily, Avery laughed, told Justice he had a "winner," then asked them if they needed to look at the menu.

Sorry that he couldn't lend her a hand, but relieved that Fallon would remain close, he said, "Loaded burgers, plate of fries and I'll take a chocolate milk shake. Fallon?"

"Works for me. Make it two shakes."

Avery's smile was slow and knowing. "Definitely a keeper. I'll get that out to you shortly."

"No rush," Fallon said.

After Avery left, Justice smiled at Fallon. "That was nice of you. To offer to help, I mean."

"I wouldn't mind." She glanced around the bar with a sort of wistful yearning. "In fact, it might be fun."

Yeah, right. "You ever work as a waitress?"

She twitched her mouth to the side. "Dad would have had a heart attack." With the tip of her finger, she traced the wood grain in the tabletop. "Going through school, I worked for him part-time as an apprentice. Now my job is decorating the local hotels he owns. Decor gets old quick in the industry. We like to keep things as fresh and updated as possible."

"The hotels are fancy, aren't they?"

"Not really. I mean, they're nice, but not super upscale or anything. I stay busy with it, but I got ahead on everything so right now I have a whole month off."

Time she'd built in to play. Curious about her, Justice asked, "You like the job?"

"I do. The different locations each have their own character and I get to reflect that in how I decorate them. I do only those in Ohio, Indiana and Northern Kentucky, though Dad has locations all across the country."

He'd wondered about that. "You don't like to travel?"

She shook her head and then deliberately tried to divert him. "What about you?"

Justice shrugged. "It's okay. I haven't traveled much for pleasure, but fighters go all over, either to compete or to support friends. Brazil, Japan, Canada, South Korea—"

"Wow. I had no idea." She folded her arms on the tabletop. "That's so exciting."

"Not if you're fighting. Let me tell you, the packing and travel and promo is a hassle. Then you have to adjust to the time zone and sometimes the altitude. It's not like you get much opportunity to be a tourist."

"I can't imagine all that running and prep and then having to perform. But I'm impressed."

Sheepish, Justice shook his head. "Don't be. I won in Japan, but not in South Korea or Brazil. Not that I got creamed or anything," he rushed to assure her. "Got bonus bucks for 'fight of the night' in Brazil. It was a real brawl, but I lost two of the three rounds."

"I would love to see a live fight sometime."

He was about to tell her it'd be too risky when Cannon spoke beside them. "You're in luck. Stack Hannigan is fighting next weekend and it's local. Have Justice bring you."

While Fallon stared up in awe at Cannon, Justice tried to signal him by slashing a finger across his neck.

Cannon ignored him. "Introduce me, Justice."

Armie strolled up next to him. "Yeah, introduce us."

"Jesus, Joseph and Mary," Justice mumbled. Did they think she was a date? "I was going to bring her to the pool room for introductions after we ate."

Showing up with the food, Avery bumped Cannon and Armie out of her way with her hip. She set the plates and drinks off her tray, then asked, "Anything else?"

"It smells perfect," Fallon gushed. "Thank you."

Armie said to Avery, "You sure you don't want me to lend a hand?"

"You're sweet," Avery said, "but Crissy just showed up. We're covered."

As soon as Avery got out of the way, Cannon and Armie muscled their way in. Cannon made Fallon scoot over and Armie would have sat on Justice's lap if he hadn't moved quick enough.

Deadpan, Justice asked, "Why don't you guys join us?"

They ignored his dry tone.

"Think I will," Armie said, stealing one of his fries. To Fallon he said, "I'm Armie. That's Cannon."

She looked…mesmerized, her eyes wide, watchful. "You're both fighters?"

Armie grinned. "Good guess."

"Oh, no. You both look as muscular as Justice."

Cannon grinned now, too. "And you are?"

She poked out a hand. "Fallon Wade."

While Cannon's hand completely swallowed hers, Armie said, "Nice, Eugene. She's a step up."

With surprise, Fallon turned to Justice. "Eugene?"

Cannon leaned near, saying in a loud stage whisper behind his hand, "That's his real name."

Giving Armie a shove that almost put him out of the booth, Justice growled, "You're both assholes, you know that, right?"

Chuckling, Armie righted himself. "Avery just said I was sweet."

"She has to be nice to you because you're a customer."

"Ah, c'mon, Eugene," Armie replied. "Don't be pissy."

"No one," Justice stressed to Fallon, "calls me that."

Armie raised his hand. "Just us A-holes." He slanted a look at Justice. "I, at least, know how to speak in front of a lady."

That was almost too hilarious, given Armie's rep, which wasn't all that distant yet. "Where are your wives? Rissy and Yvette would keep you in line."

"Rissy, Vanity and Cherry are visiting Yvette at our place," Cannon said. "The wives insisted we show up here for Stack's last weekend before the fight."

Justice explained to Fallon, "These two are new dads. Cannon has twins, a boy and a girl, and Armie has a daughter. Usually you can't pry them away from the babies."

"Look who's talking!" Cannon pointed at Justice. "This one does the whole baby-talk thing. It's hilarious."

"And nauseating," Armie chimed in. Then he shrugged. "But the babies adore him."

Justice grinned. "True enough. I'm one of their favorite people."

"There's only four months between our kids' ages." Cannon smiled with pride. "They'll grow up close."

For the next twenty minutes, Justice and Fallon ate while the men told stories.

Like a spectator at a tennis match, Fallon's head bobbed back and forth as she alternately listened to each man gush affectionately. It still amused Justice that the two of them were so affected by their kids. If one of the babies gurgled, they were on it. Drool didn't faze them and they changed diapers like a couple of champions, which they were.

Other than during training, or occasionally at Rowdy's, if you saw one of the men, you saw a baby.

Justice finally interrupted to say, "You get the feeling they're proud papas?"

Smiling, Fallon nodded. "Very. And I think it's lovely."

"So I'm sweet and lovely," Armie said. "I can't wait to tell Stretch."

"My sister will strangle you for calling her that," Cannon reminded Armie. Then to Fallon, he said, "She's almost as tall as me."

"But a lot prettier," Armie added, his eyebrows bobbing.

Justice noticed that Fallon had eaten at least half of the enormous burger and a good share of fries before she pushed back her plate and patted her mouth with the paper napkin.

"Dessert?" he asked her.

She lifted the shake. "This counts." Leaning in, she asked, "So, do you think we could see your friend's fight next weekend?"

Not a good idea. "I don't know," he hedged. "It's going to be crowded."

One brow lifted, Cannon sat back and watched him.

Armie slanted him a look of curiosity.

"I'll cover my own ticket," she promised. "That is, if tickets are still available."

"Not for any good seats."

Cannon and Armie waited to pounce; Justice knew that and tried to think of a way to deter them from interfering, but he came up blank. Wasn't like he could explain that Fallon was only an assignment—and he was already too close.

Finally, Cannon said, "I have tickets. Brand and Miles, friends you can meet in a minute, would be happy to—"

Justice growled, "If she goes, she goes with me."

Fallon's face went pink and she cleared her throat. "It's all ridiculous, but Justice is my bodyguard."

Groaning, Justice stared up at the ceiling. He could feel the guys eyeballing him, the bastards.

"Why's it ridiculous?" Armie asked.

"Because there's no threat against me. It's just that my parents anticipate a boogeyman around every corner."

"We were followed," Justice reminded her.

Cannon said, "You were?"

"Yeah." And now that he remembered, he realized that might be a good excuse to skip the fight at the arena. But before he could mention it, another voice intruded.

"There you are, you chickenshit bastard."

Fallon turned with a start, Armie grumbled and Cannon briefly closed his eyes as if aggrieved.

But Justice laughed as he extended his hand over the booth. "Look who crawled aboveground." He and Tom exchanged a quick, knuckle-breaking hand grip, then Justice did the introductions. "Fallon, this is Tom Nelson, aka Tomahawk."

Tom gave her a quick once-over. "Tell your boyfriend to quit ducking me."

Armie said, "He beat you, Hawk," shortening the man's nickname. "Soundly, in fact. Bellyaching now is pointless. Move on."

"It was a lucky punch and you know it," Tom countered.

"You got caught," Cannon said in that calm way of his. "That wasn't luck, but good training."

"Says the man who trained him." Without losing his good mood, Tom stared down at Armie. "As to moving on...ain't happening. Not until I get a rematch."

Justice ate another fry. "Told you, man, I retired. I'm out of the fight biz."

"Get back in," Tom insisted. Then just to provoke him, he added, "If you can work up the nerve."

As Fallon watched, the man pointed at Justice, grinned and sauntered away.

"Fucking doofus," Armie growled low.

"So much for knowing how to speak in front of a lady," Justice complained, sparing Fallon a glance.

"It's okay." Fallon noticed that Justice didn't seem nearly as bothered by the intruder as his friends were. "He's the one you beat early in the fight?"

Lifting his milk shake, Justice nodded. "None other."

"Tom doesn't want to accept it," Cannon explained to Fallon. "He tries to hide it with jokes, but he's still smarting over getting tuned."

"He's convinced he'd beat me if we fought again," Justice said by way of justification.

Armie gave a shove to Justice's shoulder, almost making him spit out his shake. "If it ever happened, my money would be on you."

Scowling, Justice drew off the straw, finishing his drink.

"People match up differently," Cannon said to Fallon. "A guy who beats everyone else can meet that one guy who gets him every time. Tomahawk's good, no doubt about it. But against Justice? I agree with Armie. Tom's not slick enough to duck those massive fists of his."

Justice gave a self-deprecating laugh. "Guys, really, she's not a date. You don't have to try to soften her up for me."

"He's so freaking humble, too," Armie said with a roll of his eyes.

"I can't beat Cannon."

"And that's your measuring stick?" Armie looked ready to shove Justice again. "Hell, man, there's a reason Cannon's a champion."

Wow. Fallon looked at the man next to her again. "Champion?"

"Light heavyweight."

"That's amazing." She noticed that Cannon leaned toward quiet confidence. He struck her as serious and kind—odd for a guy as big and honed as him.

Armie, on the other hand, was cocky to the extreme. She smiled at him. "What about you?"

"He's also a champion," Justice answered before Armie could. "You're in the presence of real talent."

"I don't understand." Finding this all very fascinating, Fallon twisted in her seat and propped her back against the wall. "Don't you become champion by beating everyone else? How can there be two?"

"Different weight classes." Cannon was happy to explain. "Armie's a middleweight."

"What are you?" she asked Justice.

"I *was* a heavyweight."

That made sense. All the men were big, but Justice towered over them.

"C'mon," Justice said, rudely shouldering Armie out of the booth. "If you want to learn about fighting, we'll join the others for a few games of pool and you can ask all the questions you want."

That sounded like an amazing idea to her.

An hour later, Fallon decided this was the best night of her entire life.

Fighters, she discovered, were hilarious and very friendly.

After Cannon explained the rules of the game, Justice taught her how to hold the cue stick and how to shoot. That in itself made the night memorable; he'd aligned his big body behind hers, surrounded her as he reached around to help her place her hands, then spoken softly into her ear.

She'd taken the shot awkwardly, almost scraping the felt on the tabletop. But no one teased her. The patient instruction continued until she got the hang of it—and once she did, she started sinking balls.

Who knew she had the knack for judging how one ball would rebound off another?

Armie declared her a natural, then immediately wagered five dollars.

She won.

Smiling with pride, Justice stood back, his shoulders braced on the wall, and encouraged her.

Before this very night, Fallon hadn't known she had a knack for shooting pool. Playful accusations of "pool shark" were called out after she'd won her third game.

Twice Avery came in to collect empties and refill drink orders. Though Fallon did indulge in another beer, she only sipped at it, making it last.

One, she decided, was her limit.

When she took the money she'd won and gave it to Avery for an additional tip, everyone cheered her.

Though she blushed, she loved it.

As soon as she declared she was done shooting pool, Justice's friend Miles whisked her away to dance.

Justice protested, but the rest of the guys heckled him so badly, he finally subsided. While he allowed the dance, he clearly didn't like it. Just as he'd done before, he kept her in his sights every second. The only difference now was that his friends paid no attention to his ruthless stares.

In fact, they seemed to enjoy them.

Grinning at her, Miles asked, "You sure you two don't have anything personal going on? Justice is acting mighty territorial."

Fallon didn't know Justice well enough to judge if that was true. She glanced at him, saw his concentrated expression, and wondered if he resented having to keep tabs on her.

Well, if he did, too bad. This was her time out and she intended to enjoy it.

"It's his job to be alert, that's all."

Miles smiled. "If you say so."

As they danced, more than a few ladies watched them. And why not? With his gentle green eyes, dark brown hair and crooked smiles, Miles was a real charmer, who'd instantly put her at ease. As a light heavyweight fighter, he was also as buff as the rest of them.

"Why do they call you the Legend?"

"My legendary sense of humor," he replied with a wink.

Fallon laughed. "I'm not buying that."

"Well, honey, the truth would make you blush."

Shoot, she blushed just from wondering what it could be!

That made his grin widen. "Come on. Spill. You and Justice have a secret fling going on, right?"

That he would think so flattered her. "I promise, we don't. Justice takes his responsibilities very seriously, that's all."

"Being a bodyguard, you mean?"

"Yes." Feeling Justice's alert intensity, she glanced at him again. "He doesn't yet understand that my parents are extreme about everything that concerns me. That doesn't mean a bodyguard is actually necessary."

Miles was about to question her more when Brand cut in.

Brand was another heavyweight. Not quite as tall as Justice, but just as broad in the shoulders. Though he smiled often, his dark eyes always looked a little distant, as if he held himself back.

"Having fun?" he asked as they moved to a fast song.

"Definitely."

"Did I hear that you'll be joining us at the fight next weekend?"

Because she doubted it, given Justice's hesitation on the idea, she asked, "Us?"

"We'll all be there. Front section, good seats." The music ended and everyone paused to wait for the next song. "The wives should be there, too. Have you met any of them yet?"

They all seemed to assume...something, but Fallon wasn't sure what. "This is my first time here, and it's about an hour and a half from where I live. I'm not sure I'll be around often enough to meet anyone else."

"That's a bit of a drive just to have drinks."

"Justice preferred this bar to those more local."

"Yeah, I just bet he did." Brand laughed. "He figures he has a better handle on the competition here."

Fallon tried to deny that. She understood, even if they didn't, that Justice wasn't worried about competition.

"Armie, Cannon, Stack, Denver and Gage are all married. When one of our own fights, we provide the cheering section."

It sounded amazing to Fallon. "I think Justice had other plans, so—"

Stepping in, Tom said, "If he doesn't agree, let me know and I'll bring you along." Then, as another song started, he said to Brand, "I'm cutting in."

This music was slower and Tom quickly caught her waist.

It startled Fallon. "Oh, um…" She watched as Brand got pulled into a dance with another lady. Drat.

"Something wrong?" Tom asked.

Yes, as a matter of fact, his earlier insults to Justice still annoyed her. Justice might not have minded, but she did. Good manners, however, kept her polite. "No, of course not."

He cuddled her closer.

She strained away.

Pretending not to notice, Tom asked, "So I heard you say you don't live nearby."

"I don't, but I'm glad we made the trip. This is a terrific place."

"Agreed. Rowdy and Avery run a good business." He turned a slow circle, and in the process brought her nearer. "I wasn't here before, but they say it was a real foul dive before Rowdy bought it. He did a big reno, kicked out the drug dealers and put in the pool room."

Drug dealers? Fascinated, Fallon asked, "Seriously?"

"Yeah. It's cool now, though. All the fighters hang out here, along with most of the neighborhood."

"You live in the area?" she asked.

"I'm staying here for a while to train. Fighters go to different camps to learn new techniques." He gave a boyish grin and added, "If I can ever sweet-talk Justice into competing again, I want to be ready so I last more than a heartbeat."

Perhaps she'd been wrong about Tom. "You think he will?"

"Fight again? I hope so." He gave her a brief hug and bent to whisper in her ear, "I'm still stung over that knockout."

She laughed with him. "I take it that was unusual for you?"

"To lose, no. Every fighter takes his knocks. But like that? Yeah, first time I was ever KO'd, and for it to happen so fast, well, let me tell ya, it sucked." He circled again and Fallon found herself plastered to his rock-hard body. "Justice has sledgehammers for fists, and that lucky punch caught me just right."

From directly behind her, Justice said, "Know what? I'm feeling pretty damned lucky again."

Fallon jumped; Tom did not, so apparently he'd seen Justice approach.

Keeping her trapped to his body, Tom smiled. Now that he again had Justice's attention, he reverted back to the insults. "One-trick ponies only go so far."

"Maybe you only saw the one trick because you haven't been paying attention. Besides, with you, one trick was all I needed."

"Ouch," Tom said with a grin. They'd stopped dancing, but he didn't let her go. "So that's what it takes to motivate you, huh? A little cuddle with your lady friend?"

"She's a client."

"You still sticking with that?"

"Hey!" Fallon finally caught on. Shoving her way free with a little more force than necessary, she glared up at Tom. "If you want to goad him into a fight, use someone other than me!"

She turned to march away, but Justice caught her hand and anchored her to his side, ruining her dramatic exit.

"Not just yet, Fallon," Justice said when she tugged against his restraint. "Tom has something he wants to tell you."

Oh, good grief. She didn't want to hear anything else he had to say.

Voice jovial, Tom said, "He's right. I promise I only wanted to dance, not incite violence. I'm sorry if my teasing made you think otherwise."

So...had she overreacted?

It didn't matter because Justice said, "She's off-limits."

Tom lifted a brow. "Yeah? For what?"

Sounding as if he chewed gravel, Justice growled, "Everything."

"Ah, I didn't realize." Still fighting a smile, Tom looked down at her. "Really, no insult intended, so will you forgive me?"

She felt like a spectacle. "Yes, of course."

Tom clapped Justice on the shoulder. "Call a truce, Justice. You're making her nervous."

Justice said nothing, but he nodded.

"Good. I want a rematch, you know that. But I don't want or need a barroom brawl. You gotta know I'm not after that."

Justice loosened his stance. "Yeah, I do."

"Thanks." Tom saluted them both and departed.

When she and Justice turned and headed toward a table, Cannon and Armie applauded.

After that, the guys razzed Justice endlessly about being a bodyguard. They heralded him for being oh-so-meticulous in his duties, calling him keenly thorough in exploring every possible threat, both real and imagined.

Fallon would have been offended for him again, except that the guys infused enough obvious respect in their tones for her to know it was only good-natured ribbing.

Justice grinned, in fact, when he gave them each a one-finger salute. Minutes later when the questions started, he patiently answered each one. Miles, especially, seemed interested in the different duties required of a bodyguard.

Fallon didn't mind any of it, until the talk turned to Marcus.

"Ex-boyfriend?" Cannon asked. "I've had some experience with those."

Armie raised his hand. "Me, too."

"No," Fallon denied. "He was never really—"

"He was," Justice interrupted. "But not anymore. Now he's just a pita."

"Pita?" Fallon asked.

"Pain in the ass," Justice explained.

Because she couldn't deny that, Fallon turned the topic to kids, and for the next forty minutes or so, the men talked about their babies. It seemed they had enough stories to last the night.

When Cannon got a text, he read it and stood. "The party finally broke up at my house. I'm heading home."

Armie was right behind him. "That means I can go now, too."

Stack, who she'd met earlier, shook his head at both of them, then finished his bottle of water. "Pathetic." He yawned elaborately and claimed his wife, Vanity, would be waiting for him.

Justice brought her to her feet. "You ready to call it a night?"

"I—" Her words got cut off as each of the men drew her around for a hug. She got passed from one big, hard body to the next, with praise on her pool shooting skills, her dancing, how she'd put Tom in his place, how well she handled Justice...on and on with invented qualities. Well, except for the games of pool. She really had done well there.

Lastly, Stack asked, "You'll be there next weekend for the fights? Vanity would enjoy meeting you."

She glanced at Justice in time to see him rolling his eyes.

Guessing that it was a special weekend for him to spend with his close friends, she knew she couldn't interrupt. "It's probably better if I don't—"

"You can all stop twisting my arm," Justice announced right before hauling her back over to his side. "She'll be there."

Fallon would have objected, but Justice hurried her out the door. She glanced back in time to see the others all grinning.

CHAPTER SIX

The following week passed in a near blur of happiness. As requested, Fallon presented Justice with an itinerary of the places she wanted to go. Because she'd listed a lot, she didn't expect to get to everything. She'd assumed Justice would pick and choose and let her know what was easiest.

Instead, he covered everything on her wish list, which meant they spent all day, every day, together.

Usually, he'd show up late morning to early afternoon after spending a few hours scoping out their immediate destination. Given the time of day, they'd head to lunch first thing. Justice arranged it so she got to visit nearly every area restaurant, from the mom-and-pop diners to the fast-food chains to the trendy spots. Fallon got him to try a few new things, and she learned the places he liked best.

They spent an entire day at the street fair and even got a caricature drawing of them together. Because the artist drew Justice so comically big, and her eyes so enormous, Fallon couldn't stop laughing over it.

Other days were spent at the art museum, a flower show, a butterfly show at the conservatory, a Star Trek exhibit and an outdoor sculpture display at a park. Justice enjoyed the Star Trek exhibit best, and she most enjoyed the flower show. But all of it was terrific.

Tomorrow would be his friend's fight and she was excited, so when Justice showed up late morning, she had a dozen questions ready for him.

When she opened the door and saw him, though, she forgot much of what she'd planned to ask. "You look tired."

Around a wide yawn, he said, "I'm fine."

"Fine my foot." Had she been running him too much? True, they'd been on the go almost nonstop for days. But he hadn't once complained.

It was only ten, a little earlier than usual, and bright sunshine poured over the steps and surrounding landscape, reflecting off the black SUV Justice drove. A perfect day for the river walk she'd planned, but Fallon was ready to call it quits. Justice, she decided, looked like he needed a nice long nap.

She was about to tell him the change in plans when her mother stepped up behind her and invited him in.

"Join us for a cup of tea."

He quickly removed the dark sunglasses, saying, "No thank you, ma'am. Not a tea drinker."

"Coffee then."

"I brought my own. It's in the car."

Her mother, unfortunately, wasn't taking no for an answer. "Fallon needs to get her sunscreen. Please, come in." Her mother held the door open and waited.

Hooking his glasses on the front of his T-shirt, Justice reluctantly stepped in, and immediately looked ill at ease.

"My husband is gone for the weekend or I'm certain he'd enjoy saying hello, as well."

Justice didn't look convinced. "Off on business?"

"Yes." She indicated a chair, leaving Justice no choice but to sit. "Fallon, honey, would you make some coffee?"

She didn't want to, but the kitchen was close enough to the sitting room that she'd be able to listen in. "All right." She rushed off to do the prep so she could rejoin them while it perked.

From a distance, she heard her mother say, "May I ask you something, Justice?"

"Shoot."

"Is that hairstyle popular among fighters?"

Fallon almost choked.

Justice just laughed. "Not sure I'd say it's popular anywhere, especially right now. I haven't trimmed it in a while. When I was fighting, though, I'd dye it orange."

"Orange? Somewhat like a…rooster?"

"Somewhat," he agreed, his tone teasing. "But there are a lot of words for rooster, ya know?"

Oh, dear Lord. Fallon dumped water into the coffeemaker and rushed back to the room. She got there in time to see her mother laughing.

Justice smiled at her, then ran a hand over his head. "Now that I'm not fighting, I've kinda lost interest. Guess I should either shape it up or shave it off."

"Well," her mother said, "I find it interesting. So please don't bother on my account."

His mouth quirked. "No, ma'am."

Horrified over the subject for several reasons, Fallon bit her lip. Luckily, he mother didn't seem scandalized, and Justice didn't look offended.

"The coffee will be ready in a minute." She studied Justice's face and saw the tiredness there. "We can reschedule for another day if you'd like to rest."

He clutched his heart and groaned. "Don't unman me in front of your ma. What would she think of me if you're all bushytailed and I'm pooped out when we've been doing the same thing?"

"Her ma," Mrs. Wade quipped, "would think you're hilarious."

For some reason, Fallon's face went hot. Probably from the
way he spoke so casually in front of her very formal mother—
and how her mother teased back. "We haven't been. You leave
earlier each day to inspect the route and venue and…whatever
else it is bodyguards do."

Justice gave her a level, very intense look. "I ensure your
safety. That's everything I do."

She had no reply for that, but it didn't matter because Justice
wasn't done yet anyway.

"And I go where you go. This is your time, so don't worry
about me." He stretched. "Besides, I'm tired because of my
grandma."

"Your grandma?" she asked.

"That coffee ready yet?"

"Oh, yes." With haste so she wouldn't miss the story, Fallon
filled a cup and brought it to him. Creamer and sugar were already on the table. "So," she said as she handed him the cup,
"what was that about your grandma?"

"She had to go into the hospital last night." He dropped a
spoonful of sugar into the coffee and sipped appreciatively. "I
spent the night there with her. My mother came up this morning, so I was able to leave."

Fallon and her mother both stared at him. He'd spent the
night with his grandmother at the hospital?

"I hope she's okay," Fallon finally thought to say.

"Yeah, she's a tough old bird. Insists on living alone and for
the most part, she gets around okay. But even though her eye-
sight is bad, she refuses to wear glasses, so it's no surprise that
she tripped over the stoop. We thought she might have broken
a hip in the fall. Since she gives the docs a really hard time, it's
always better if my mom or I are with her to sort of smooth
things over." He grinned. "Otherwise she might've gotten herself shoved out the door just for being so ornery."

"You say that with a great deal of affection," her mother noted.

"Yeah. Granny's a keeper." Justice drank more of his coffee, then sat back. Muscles rolled in his shoulders as he relaxed, and yet his abdomen stayed firm and flat beneath the T-shirt. "The doc came in to see her this morning right before my mom got there. She's bruised up real good, but no breaks, thank goodness. She and my mom were arguing when I left." He grinned.

"Arguing?" Fallon asked.

"Yeah, see, Mom says Granny has to come home with her until she's fit again, but Granny said she wasn't a baby and didn't need a sitter. Still, I'd put my money on Mom. She can be stubborn as a goat when the mood strikes her. Not stubborn enough to get Granny to wear her glasses, but otherwise, she usually wins."

"Why won't she wear her glasses?" her mom asked.

Justice shrugged. "Says it makes her look old."

Fascinated by this glimpse into his life, Fallon pulled out a chair. "How old is your grandmother?"

Justice rubbed his jaw. "Let's see. Mom's sixty now, so Granny must be eighty-five or thereabouts. It's hard to believe, with me being such a lug, but they're both itty-bitty things. Mom's maybe five-one, and now that she doesn't stand so straight, Granny's barely five feet."

"Amazing." Fallon's mother sat forward. "So your father is a large man?"

"Was. He died when I was real young. An accident at the factory where he worked. I was only three so I don't remember much about him, but Mom has the house full of photos and between her and Granny, I've heard every story there is about Dad, twice."

Sympathy left a knot in Fallon's chest. "I'm sorry. I didn't realize."

He shrugged. "It's okay."

"So…" Her mother faltered, cleared her throat, and continued with "*Granny* is your father's mother?"

"Nope. But she loved my dad, too, said he really made my mom shine." Justice smiled with some memory. "Dad and Granny liked to play poker. To hear my mom tell it, they had some serious competition going. Knowing my grandma, I can imagine it got loud and rowdy on occasion."

"Your mother never remarried?"

He laughed. "No. She said she started with the best and wasn't taking second pick for anyone. I think she's been content." After finishing off his coffee, he pushed back his chair and looked toward Fallon. "You ready to go?"

Lost to thoughts of Justice as a little boy, she jumped. "Oh, yes. Of course." She quickly gathered up their cups and carried them to the dishwasher.

Her mother protested. "You don't have to fool with that, honey. Lindsey will be in later today."

"I don't mind."

Minutes later, she and Justice got into the SUV. She noticed the shirts in the backseat and was going to ask him about it, but Justice diverted her.

"Who's Lindsey?"

Because she liked the woman a lot, Fallon smiled. "She helps out around the house."

"Helps out how?"

"During the first part of the week she only does light housekeeping, but on Friday she does the bigger stuff, like laundry and changing the sheets on the beds and grocery shopping. That's why I don't like to leave little messes for her to contend with. She's got enough to do today."

"I'm guessing in a house that size, you have other staff?"

"Yes." Fallon tipped her head, watching him drive. "We have a landscaper who takes care of the property. Lindsey's there every day except the weekends, and once a month a cleaning crew comes in to do the heavier work, like washing down all the walls, polishing the floors, things like that." Now that she said it, it sounded extravagant when she'd never really thought of it like that before. "Why do you ask?"

"Seems like there are a lot of people coming and going. I don't like it." His brows pulled together. "Mind giving me some names and their contact info?"

Unbelievable. The man looked exhausted, but he wanted to take on more work? Crazy.

Folding her arms across her chest, Fallon said, "Actually, yes. I mind." She didn't want things to get out of hand. "I promise you, my father is extremely diligent in ensuring all personal employees are vetted. You don't need to worry about it."

"But he's out of town for the weekend."

"That happens a lot, Justice. Dad travels often for business, plus he takes a lot of golfing trips."

She could see that Justice didn't want to let it go.

Sighing, Fallon added, "We have a top-of-the-line security system. You should realize that. I mean, look at how overboard Dad is about me going out anywhere."

They were almost out of the long drive when Marcus turned in.

Justice looked first stunned, then irate. He steered into the middle of the drive, blocking Marcus, and put the car in Park.

Uh-oh. "Do not start anything," Fallon warned.

"Wouldn't." The corners of his mouth lifted in a mean smile. "But he's not coming in. I heard your dad forbid him."

"Dad did *what?*" How come she didn't know about that?

"Told him not to come around uninvited."

She jumped on that. "So maybe my mother invited him."

Doubtful, he glanced at her. "You really think she might've?"

No, she didn't. Huffing, Fallon said, "How should I know?"

"You big faker." He reached out and tweaked her chin. "I'm

betting your mom doesn't like him enough to go against your dad's wishes."

Marcus got out of his idling car and slammed the door.

Fallon grabbed Justice's arm. "I mean it, Justice. Don't you dare do anything…physical."

"Afraid I'll smash the little worm?"

"No. You don't strike me as a bully."

"I'm not, so quit worrying about him."

Mostly she was afraid Marcus would humiliate her. But how could she end this peacefully? Both men looked ready to implode.

When Marcus started around to her side of the car, Justice muttered, "Like hell," and threw open his door.

Fallon hurriedly got out of the car, too. "Marcus," she said, her voice too high. "What are you doing here? Do you have an appointment with Mom?"

"What? No." Marcus kept flicking his gaze to Justice. "I came to see you."

"Well, as you can see, I'm on my way out." She tried to sound cheerful instead of panicked.

When Justice stopped beside her, massive arms crossed, posture relaxed as he leaned on the car, Marcus must have decided he wasn't a problem and finally gave her his full attention.

"We need to talk."

She didn't want to talk. "Another time, maybe."

"You keep dodging me."

"'Cuz she doesn't want to talk to you, you dipshit." Justice smiled at him. "Let it sink in, then go away."

Marcus turned on him. "Bodyguards are supposed to be respectful!"

"Not to dipshits," Justice muttered. "I'm plenty respectful to Fallon, which is more than I can say for you."

Marcus all but vibrated in frustration as he tried to focus on her again. "I'm sorry I hurt you. It was thoughtless and if I'd been better prepared—"

No, no, no. "It's fine," she squeaked. "I've already forgotten about it."

"Then—"

"We're done, Marcus. Over. Please, *please* get that through your head."

"I won't accept that." He reached for her—

And Justice moved. "Nope. Touch her and I'll break something. Or to be more specific, something on you. Like...an arm? Maybe just a hand. I dunno, yet."

"You cannot just go around threatening people!"

Unconcerned, Justice said, "Wasn't a threat."

Fallon pointed at Justice. "Get in the car!"

"Will when you do."

She glared at Marcus, saw he wouldn't budge, and turned to Justice again. "I'm going to speak to Marcus over there." She pointed to the side of the road. "You are not to intrude, do you understand me?"

"Long as he doesn't touch you, I can restrain myself." After cracking his knuckles, he lounged back against the side of the car again. "I won't like it, but I'll do as told."

"Like a trained ape," Marcus sneered.

Fallon gave him a shove. "Shut up or I won't talk to you at all. Ever again!"

Petulant, Marcus turned and stomped away to where she'd indicated, near a flowering hedge.

With one last warning look at Justice, who managed to appear amused, Fallon joined her ex.

The second she reached him, Marcus started to speak.

Fallon cut him off with a slash of her hand. "I don't want to hear it," she hissed low. "If you can't understand how I feel, at least respect what I say."

"Not when you keep saying it's over." He swallowed hard and whispered, "I love you, Fallon."

Her temples started to throb. "You don't," she replied gently. Of that much she was quite certain. "If you'd stop pretending to be wounded, you'd realize it." Again he tried to speak and again, she didn't allow it. "Men who love women are not repulsed by them."

"Oh, God, honey, I wasn't," he denied fervently. "It's just… I assumed your family had paid for…"

"There are some things money can't buy."

Frantically, he shook his head. "There are specialists who could—"

"No." Fallon had to make him understand. "Don't you see, Marcus? This is a problem for you, and it's not going away."

Determined, he squared his shoulders. "There are ways around it."

She didn't want to know what he might mean by that. Did he expect her to hide her entire life? No, she wouldn't.

Trying to reason with him, she put a hand on his arm. "I didn't know my father had banned you. If you promise to stop pursuing me, I'll get him to let up on that."

"You ask the impossible."

With her goodwill gone, she snapped, "Fine. Suit yourself. But I'm not discussing this anymore." Heart punching in slow, painful beats, Fallon pivoted on her heel and strode back toward Justice.

Marcus yelled, "Any man would have a problem with those scars!"

Oh, God.

Shoulders lifting, she froze, horrified and panicked. An invisible fist squeezed her heart, making her gasp.

Her gaze shot to Justice's.

Eyes narrowed, arms crossed, he leaned a hip against the car and watched her.

In that moment he reminded her of a coiled panther who only pretended to be at ease.

As Marcus rushed toward her, Justice moved—and reached her in two long steps. Before she could even draw breath, Justice stood behind her and he stopped Marcus's approach with one long, outstretched arm. His hand flattened on Marcus's shoulder.

"Word of advice." Justice sounded cold and furious. "Leave."

Hearing that tone, Marcus finally showed some sense.

She could feel Justice at her back, his big body emanating waves of anger. She prayed Marcus would go—and finally he did, stalking away with a muttered curse.

Fallon was still standing there, too mortified to move, when Marcus made a U-turn through the meticulously trimmed grass and sped out of the driveway. The sound of his revving engine gradually faded until all she could hear were the birds in the trees, the rustling of leaves and her own heartbeat pounding in her ears.

What would Justice say now? What would he do? She was oh so aware of him behind her, backing her up, protecting her from hurts he didn't know and probably wouldn't understand. She felt sick with worry, apprehensive of what would happen next.

Then Justice's big hands settled on her shoulders, softly massaging. He said nothing. Didn't question her, didn't force the issue.

He'd heard Marcus, she knew it.

She didn't know what to think.

Time ticked by and he only caressed her. By small degrees the panic quieted and her heartbeat returned to normal. She knew she couldn't remain a mute, trembling mess, so she cleared her throat, reached up to pat his hand and asked as casually as she could muster, "Are you ready to go?"

"Sure." Yet he didn't move.

Fearing her reprieve might be slipping away, she said hesitantly, "Justice..."

Suddenly his massive arms came around her, stunning her stupid. He drew her back against his chest and held her, enfolded in that delicious embrace.

Why was he always so warm? And oh my, how could she think when his scent of musk and sexy man surrounded her? Savoring it, she sucked in a long, slow breath.

Justice lowered his chin to the top of her head, gently hugging her. Voice pitched low and rough, he muttered, "Your dad would shoot me if he saw me doing this."

She strangled out, "This?"

"Comforting you."

Pride made her protest. "I don't need—"

He squeezed her quiet. "Holding you makes *me* feel better, okay? So just go with it."

She nodded, even managed to settle more comfortably against him. Never had a man so large held her so gently. Actually, she'd never known a man as large as him. His forearms, folded over her breasts, flexed with roped muscle when his thumbs brushed her skin. Fascinated, she lightly touched the soft hair there, then with one fingertip, she traced a line up to his bulging biceps.

He was so big, so hard.

And speaking of hard, against her back she felt—

His mouth touched her temple, and he muttered, "That's about enough of that or I'm gonna get carried away." Hands on her shoulders, he turned her toward him, studied her face and asked with concern, "You okay?"

The abrupt change was like a dash of ice water. *Now* he would ask about Marcus. "I'm fine."

He smiled at her crisp tone. "I don't know what that dumbass was blathering on about. Shh. I promise I won't ask." He tipped up her chin. "But know that you can talk to me, okay?"

He did that amazing "look into her soul" thing and it left her flustered. His eyes were so dark, so serious and too intense.

She nodded fast. "Yes, thank you. Now we should get going." Pulling away, she hurried to the car.

As usual, Justice reached the door before she could and opened it for her. "If he comes back, I want to know."

She wouldn't report to him, but it didn't seem worth arguing over, so she made a noncommittal sound of acknowledgment.

They were on the road a few minutes before she remembered the T-shirts in the backseat. "Taking your laundry somewhere?"

Distracted, he glanced at her, caught her meaning and grinned. "Those are for you. You'll be with the team tomorrow, so you need an official shirt. I brought a few different ones for you to choose from." Pretending to be stern, he added, "Most of the chicks wear them really tight and low. But I don't want to have to beat the guys away with a baseball bat, so the shirts I brought for you are crew necked. Hope that's okay."

Better than okay, it was preferable. "Thank you." She gestured at the shirts. "May I?"

"Sure."

She reached back and pulled four shirts into her lap. Two were black, one gray and one white. Each had a wolf head on the front. She read aloud, "'Howl for the Wolf.'"

"That's Stack. We'll all be rooting for him." He winked at her. "Now you're official."

"Why do they call him the Wolf?"

Justice laughed.

"There's a joke?"

"Nah, see, there're two meanings behind the name and I'm not sure you want to hear them both."

"But I do," she insisted.

He glanced at her two more times before shrugging. "All right then. He got the fight name because of the way he stalks his prey in the cage."

"Ah, like a wolf. I get it."

Justice's grin widened. "It was a good, legit, badass name. But then a bunch of ladies started rumors, and now most say he's called Wolf because of how he makes women howl in the bedroom."

Fallon blinked in surprise—and felt her mouth twitch. "You're serious?"

"Yup. Old Stack used to be a real player. That was before Vanity, though." He tried to put on a straight face as he said, "Now he only makes her howl."

When Fallon snickered, Justice laughed with her.

It felt…nice. Casual and easy. So very different from her relationship with Marcus, which despite their longer association had always felt somehow superficial, too polite and proper. "Now that I know, I'm going to feel silly wearing the shirt."

"Even guys will wear some version of it, so don't give it a thought. I'll be wearing the gray one."

"Okay, then I'll choose the black one." It had short sleeves, but that suited her. "With jeans?"

"Perfect."

For the rest of their drive, Justice detailed what she should expect at the venue. It would be a late night with a lot of raucous men in close quarters and, according to Justice, women hoping to "hook up" who would probably attend the after party at Rowdy's bar.

It all sounded very exciting, and yes, very fun.

She could hardly wait.

He hung back, keeping his distance until they finally parked near the river. So they'd be doing the river walk? That could take all day. Perfect.

Turning the car around, he went back the way they'd come. With them occupied, he'd have time to visit both residences.

He tightened his hands on the wheel and thought about things—then decided exactly what to do.

★ ★ ★

It was late when Justice brought Fallon home.

Today more than any other day, she'd been so damned hard to resist. Maybe because she was so natural, so sweet, and her smiles, man those smiles, they nearly did him in. He loved seeing her happy, relaxed. For much of the day, he'd barely been able to take his eyes off her.

They'd walked for miles and miles, and neither of them had complained. He enjoyed the way Fallon had appreciated each spring flower, cloud formations and various animals they encountered on the trails. She seemed to see everything, in ways he hadn't before.

Not until she showed him.

In one of the more wooded sections of the hike, he'd overturned a fallen log and found her a salamander. She'd admired it from five feet away, making him laugh. When she insisted he carefully replace the creature and the log, his heart had squeezed with a weird sensation of…respect. Yeah, he respected her. A lot. She was rich, but compassionate. Pampered, but vulnerable. Sweet, but also amazingly sexy.

They'd eaten picnic-style along the riverbank; hot dogs and bagged chips and cold colas had never tasted so good. He should have chosen a shadier spot, given her now-pink nose and cheekbones, but she hadn't protested. Some geese swam by, frogs occasionally sang and tiny fish glittered in the shallower water along the shore. Butterflies had been everywhere and the air smelled good, like wildflowers, water and… Fallon.

He taught her how to skip rocks and how to overhand throw. She wasn't very good at either, but they'd done a lot of laughing. Before they left, she'd chosen a smooth rock as a souvenir.

A rock. It still astounded him, and made her even more endearing.

Though the air had cooled now, they were both a little sweaty.

Justice couldn't remember the last time he'd taken so much pleasure in a day—hell, a week.

Something about Fallon made it impossible for him to be detached. The way she saw the world and her happy outlook, the simple joy she took in the smallest things, affected him.

And yeah, he liked the way she looked at him. She might not realize it, but she wore her heart on her sleeve. If she'd been anyone else, anyone other than a client, maybe someone just a tad more experienced, he'd have already made a move on her.

Instead, he'd repeated the facts in his head like a litany.

Client, innocent, inexperienced. Those three things made her as taboo as a woman could get.

Didn't stop him from thinking things, but for the most part it did help him to keep those thoughts to himself...and his hands off her.

The glow of the headlights from the SUV bounded around the area as he turned into her private drive—and that's when he saw it. At first glance he thought it was blood.

Everywhere.

Then he realized it was too bright, and the arcing splatter looked as if someone had literally thrown it from a paint can. He stopped the car.

Fallon, who'd looked to be dozing, her eyes closed, her mouth curled in a serene smile, turned to him. "What's the matter?"

Justice hated to ruin her day, but there was no way around it. He couldn't pull into the drive without getting the paint on the tires and further spreading it. He drew a slow breath and nodded at the destruction. "Someone is playing vandal, and I'm betting I know who it is."

CHAPTER SEVEN

Wide-eyed, Fallon started to open her car door.

Justice stopped her. "No. It could be a trap."

"A trap?" She looked shocked, unable to understand the concept.

Already backing out, Justice said, "We can't drive through, so it stands to reason we'd get out of the car. That could be the whole point."

She scoffed, but didn't argue. Justice drove farther down the road to the start of an upscale community, then pulled over to the side. Leaving the car running, he locked the doors and used hands-free dialing on the SUV's Bluetooth to dial 911.

"Is that necessary?" Fallon quickly asked. "It seems like such a fuss."

"It's necessary." As soon as he finished talking to the police, who promised to meet him shortly back at the house, he dialed the agency. Everyone was gone for the day, but he left a message that Sahara would get first thing in the morning.

Next he insisted on calling her mother.

"She'll be in bed."

"Probably. But won't you feel better once you know she's okay?"

Clearly she hadn't considered any other possibility, but as soon as he mentioned it, she agreed.

Mrs. Wade answered on the third ring, and she did indeed sound half-asleep.

"Mom?" Fallon said in a rush. "Are you okay?"

More alert, her mother said, "Fallon? What's wrong?"

Justice sighed and took over. "Everyone is okay, Mrs. Wade. Did we wake you?"

Bemused to realize she was on speaker, Mrs. Wade cleared her throat. "Yes. I'm sorry. What time is it?"

"It's late. I was just bringing Fallon home, but someone vandalized your entryway. There's red paint everywhere. I'm going to speak to the police, and then I'll walk her up to the door and arrange for someone to come clean it so it doesn't get tracked anywhere else."

There was a startled silence before Mrs. Wade said, "I'll be right there!"

"No," Justice insisted. "Let the cops do their thing first. They need to make sure no one is hanging around, and they might want to take a few pictures or something. I'll let you know when they're done."

"Oh, yes, I guess that makes sense." She paused. "Red paint, you said?"

"That's what it looks like to me." Justice assumed it was supposed to look like blood. But whatever idiot did it had no real clue how spilled blood should look.

Lights flashed behind them as a police car pulled up.

Justice said, "The cops are here. Gotta go. But I'll let you know what's happening as soon as I know."

It was another hour before Justice finally walked Fallon up to her front door. He'd left the car on the street and together they'd edged around the mess. A twenty-four-hour cleanup company would arrive shortly.

He would stay until the job was done, but he wanted to get Fallon inside, and let her mother get back to bed.

Mrs. Wade greeted them the second they got close, then she insisted that Justice come in.

The poor woman looked frazzled, so Justice tried his best to put her mind at ease. "The mess will be gone in no time. The cops agreed it's only paint. Likely just vandals." Not that he believed it. "Fallon says you have a terrific security system, but only on the house and nearby grounds."

"Yes. Clayton had it set up, but I doubt he ever considered a situation like this."

"No reason he should have." Now though, Justice thought, things had changed. "Any chance you can put a security camera at the street entrance in case anything like this ever happens again? In fact, I can take care of it if you want, since I know Mr. Wade is away for the weekend."

She reached out and touched his wrist. "Please, let's move on to first names. We're Rebecca and Clayton."

Reacting to her smile, Justice nodded. "All right, Rebecca. Thanks. Now about that security?"

"You don't think it can wait until Monday when Clayton returns?"

Aware of Fallon quietly watching him, he rubbed the back of his neck. "I'd rather not." Gesturing, he said, "With the paint being red, I think someone might've wanted us to think it was...blood."

"Oh, my God." Eyes wider, Rebecca put a hand to her throat. "But why?"

Justice was taking it as an implied threat, but he saw no reason to spook the two of them further. "No idea." Moving on from that, he asked, "Mind if I have a look at the security?"

"Oh, yes, of course." Dressed in a pretty robe and delicate

slippers, Rebecca led him around the first floor to all the security cameras.

He also checked the different locks on the doors and windows. "How about downstairs?"

"It's a finished rec area. Why?"

"Assuming there are doors and windows, I'd like to check it out, too."

She agreed, leading the way to what literally appeared to be a rec center. There was a theater room, bar and kitchen, game room, sauna, workout area and even an indoor pool. Trying not to feel intimidated again, Justice concentrated on the double doors that opened to an opulent outdoor entertaining area, and when he found them to be adequately secure, he checked all the windows.

"What do you think?" Rebecca asked him.

He smiled at her. "I'm reassured. Now about upstairs?"

"You already checked the main floor."

"I meant up from that. Those are bedrooms up there, right? Is there any way for someone to get in?"

She gave it some thought. "There are balconies off the bedrooms..."

"Let's have a look, okay?"

"All right."

It surprised Justice that Fallon's mom was so agreeable to letting him prowl the house. As he followed her up the stairs, he asked, "How many people have been through your house?"

"Up here? No one that I can think of. When we entertain at home, guests generally remain on the main floor."

The first room she led Justice to was her and Clayton's bedroom. It was so formal, he didn't know how the hell they managed to sleep—or get frisky. He sort of hated to even step in the room for fear he'd damage something.

Windows made up one entire wall with a remote to open and close the curtains and to darken the panes. He looked out and saw an amazing view of the grounds, leaving him almost speechless.

The windows were, of course, secure.

A decadent bathroom, sitting room and a closet big enough to live in completed the suite.

Irritated, with no idea why, Justice next viewed two guest bedrooms, an upstairs library and then, with a teasing smile, Rebecca led him into Fallon's room.

"She's still a little messy," Rebecca said. "And she certainly didn't expect anyone to be in here, so pay no mind to that."

Messy? Other than a pair of shoes not quite in the open closet, a cardigan draped over the arm of an oversize, padded rocking chair and a selection of jewelry atop a dresser, the room looked perfect.

Like Fallon.

"When we hired a designer, Fallon insisted on doing her own room." Pride glowed from her eyes. "She has a fresh style."

"Fallon is a decorator, but you hired an outsider?" That seemed curious to him—and insulting to Fallon.

Rebecca quickly turned away, but not before Justice saw a flash of regret, and something more, in her eyes.

"Fallon wasn't feeling well at the time." Proving she didn't want to be questioned on that, Rebecca rushed on. "She made the quilt herself. Isn't it beautiful?"

"Yeah." But Justice only gave a quick glance to the pretty quilt made in shades of blue that seemed to blend from light to dark. He was too busy watching Fallon's mom.

"As you can see, her windows also lock tight. She didn't want a whole wall of windows like her father and I have. But the architectural windows are nice, aren't they? To keep a balance in the outside view of the house, there's a wall of windows in the adjacent study."

Jabbering? Justice figured she really didn't want to focus on Fallon, so instead he dutifully looked over the locks on the two arched windows. Sheer curtains, also in layered shades of blue, would keep out the worst of the sunshine during the day, but wouldn't really provide any privacy at night.

The immense backyard, however, ensured there were no close neighbors to peek inside.

She, too, had a connecting bath, decorated all in cream with a plush rug in front of the claw-foot tub and another in front of the glass-walled shower. When Justice took a deep breath, he caught the scent of her shampoo and lotion.

Dangerous.

When he finished checking everything, he and Rebecca went back to the front door where a panel held the security code. In the basement he'd seen the panel that contained all the settings.

"The cameras are also accessible from our cell phones and tablets," Rebecca told him. "Our privacy is very important to us."

Speaking of privacy…it suddenly occurred to Justice that Fallon had disappeared. Where was she? He knew she hadn't gone to bed because he'd just been in her room. Was she peeved at him for something? Maybe thinking he was too high-handed in trying to keep her safe?

"Well?" Rebecca asked. "What do you think?"

"Mr. Wade did a great job. Everything is as safe as you can make it without around-the-clock guards. I know the system. It's top-of-the-line and easily customizable. Adding a few more cameras wouldn't be a big deal, or too costly." Not that they'd probably mind the expense. "I'll come by a few hours early tomorrow and take care of it. Tonight, though, make sure you lock up behind me, okay?"

"I will, and thank you for your concern."

He glanced around but still didn't see Fallon, so he asked, "Who else knows about your system? What it covers and doesn't cover?"

"I don't really know." She thought about it. "Fallon, of course."

"None of your employees? The people who work around the house?"

"No. Clayton would never tell them." She pursed her mouth and gave Justice close scrutiny while saying, "I believe Marcus is aware, since he and Fallon were practically engaged."

Whoa. That was news to him! Trying to sound neutral, he asked, "Engaged?"

"Yes. He'd often bring her home from events."

Marcus. Just thinking his name made Justice frown. "When's the last time you saw him?"

Brows lifted, Rebecca said, "Oh, he came by earlier today—not long after you and Fallon had left."

Tension crawled into Justice's shoulders. "Why?"

"He wants to work with me on the reading program for underprivileged kids. Marcus is very generous and gives freely of his time as well as his money."

It took some effort, but Justice managed not to snarl when he said, "I thought your husband disliked him."

She flapped a hand. "Clayton gets touchy when it comes to Fallon. Doesn't matter how old she gets, he still wants to treat her like his little girl." The way she said it told Justice that Rebecca didn't really see that as a flaw. "However, I trust her to make good choices. She and Marcus are no longer together, but Fallon has said there's no reason for us to break ties with him."

Justice wished he had a vote—he'd side with Clayton for sure. "You don't think it's a little coincidental that I ran him off, then he returned and now someone has vandalized your property?"

Her brows went up. "What do you mean, you ran him off?"

Carrying a tray with sandwiches and tea, Fallon chose that exact moment to return. She set the tray on the foyer table with a clatter that deliberately drew their attention.

After a cross glare at Justice, she said to her mother, "Marcus was being pushy. But *I'm* the one who sent him away."

Justice shrugged. She could tell that fairy tale if she wanted, but they both knew Marcus would have continued to press her if he hadn't intervened. "The point is, he was here, hassling you, then snuck in to see your ma after we left—"

"He didn't exactly sneak," Rebecca said.

"And now your driveway is splattered in bloodred paint."

Fallon shoved a plate at him.

He eyed the sandwich made from some small, round, fancy-type bread. Placed artfully beside it were a pickle spear and kettle chips. Until that moment, he hadn't thought about being hungry. "Thanks."

While handing a plate to her mother, Fallon said, "I'm sure Marcus had nothing to do with the paint."

Relieved, Rebecca nodded. "I can't imagine that he would."

"Bodyguards," Fallon added in an incriminating tone, "are apparently prone to melodrama."

Rebecca murmured, "I see," while attempting to hide her smile.

Justice snorted. "It's called doing my job." Then he ate the tiny sandwich in one big bite.

Bemused, Fallon watched him chew and swallow, looked at her own sandwich, and offered him half.

He grinned. "Nah, thanks. Even we melodramatic types know not to take other people's share."

"Fallon usually only eats half anyway," Rebecca offered, while ushering them to the dining room.

Each lady ended up putting half a sandwich on his plate. And true enough, he'd finished every bite while they were still nibbling on theirs. "So what do you say? I can grab what I need and get here in the afternoon. We won't need to leave for the fights until five."

Fallon hesitated with a chip almost to her mouth. "I thought the first fight started at eight."

"Prelims start at eight. Stack will be with the main event starting at ten. But I always get there early when someone from the same camp is fighting. Moral support and all that." It'd be interesting to see how Fallon fared in the loud, testosterone-laden atmosphere. Half hoping she'd decline, but also anxious to introduce her to his world, he asked, "That work for you?"

"Oh, sure. Whatever you want."

So accommodating, he mused, knowing she had no idea of everything he wanted. Not that he should be thinking about that, especially not with her mother watching him as if she, at least, knew exactly where his mind had gone.

The beeping of his cell saved him. He answered the call from the cleaning company, replied that he'd be right out and pushed back his chair.

"I'll stick around until they're done with the mess, but you two can go on to bed." *Yeah, shouldn't be thinking about Fallon curling up in that cozy-looking bed either.* "I'll bring you the invoice for the work tomorrow when I come by to add to the security."

"It's too much," Rebecca protested. "I can see to the—"

"No, ma'am. I'd rather you didn't." Melodramatic or not, at this point Justice chose to trust very few people. "Let me handle it, okay?"

She subsided. "If you wish. But, Justice?"

He lifted a brow.

"Thank you."

"Thank me by locking up behind me. And try not to let Marcus in until I've cleared him."

Rolling her eyes, Fallon abandoned her plate and stood to join him.

"He's persistent," her mother said, smiling at Justice as if she didn't mind.

"Seems so."

Folding his arms, Justice held his ground. "Promise me."

"Fine by me," Fallon grumbled. "I don't particularly want to see him anyway."

He'd noticed. *What scar could she possibly have?*

From what Justice could tell, she was physically perfect. Curved in all the right places, sleek in others. For sure her boobs were real; they didn't appear large, but the way they bounced when she walked nearly made him nuts.

Marcus was an idiot. *Did she have an appendectomy scar?*

He snorted again, gaining added attention from both women. Going for some cover, he said, "Your mom is working with the man." A fact Justice hated. "You're bound to see him."

"Going forward," Rebecca promised, "Marcus and I will hold our meetings elsewhere."

Better than nothing. Justice nodded. "Just be careful around him."

She treated him to an indulgent smile. "Yes, Justice."

Fallon grabbed his arm and practically dragged him from the room. Of course, he allowed the dragging. She looked extra cute when she got all riled up.

As soon as they were out of earshot, he asked, "Was your ma patronizing me?"

Releasing him at the door, she faced him with hands on her hips. "Yes, with good reason."

Justice frowned. He'd kind of liked having her hands on him. "How's that?"

"Oh, no, you don't. You're not going to divert me. I have something important I want to explain to you."

Her grave tone put his chin in the air with wary defiance. "What?"

She glanced back toward where they'd left her mother, then lowered her voice. "I'm trying to break away from insanely overprotective people."

"Your parents?" he asked, wanting to make sure.

She threw up her hands. "Yes, my parents. They love me—"

"But they smother you. Yeah, I get that."

"Then *get* that you're doing the same thing!"

"Shhh," he cautioned. "Your ma will hear and you'll hurt her feelings." Justice knew instinctively that Fallon wouldn't want to do that.

She drew a breath, then managed a thin smile. "This is important to me, Justice. For once I want to be free, not treated like an infant."

One of these days he'd understand her...maybe after he figured out why her folks were so watchful—and why she'd allowed it. "Trust me, honey, I know you're not a child."

The way her eyes flared, Justice knew he definitely shouldn't have said that.

Annoyed with himself, he started to explain. "I mean—"

"Thank you." Her expression softened. "I appreciate the sentiment and I'm glad that *someone* realizes I can take care of myself."

He hadn't said that, but he was glad she'd let him off the hook, so he muttered, "No problem."

"How about instead of worrying about me, you head home to get some much-needed rest?"

Rest? At least this time she hadn't insulted him in front of her mother. "Do I look frail to you?"

"No."

"Weak?"

"Of course not."

"Then why would you think I need to *rest?*"

She barely muffled a laugh. "You say it like a slur. Everyone needs to rest sometimes. You've had several busy days and—"

Thinking she needed to understand just how energetic he felt, he took a step closer—but caught himself before he did anything stupid. Like touch her. Or kiss her.

God, he wanted to kiss her.

Instead, he waffled. He'd never been this uncertain with a woman, but damn it, Fallon wasn't just a woman.

She was a client.

He needed to remember that.

Eyes big and dark, Fallon stared up at him, unsure of herself, her gaze searching his. "Justice?" she whispered, sounding a little breathless and completely on board for whatever he might want to do in that moment.

"Shit."

She blinked, the fog of interest clearing. "What?"

"Just…shit." He laughed at himself and ran both hands over his face. "I gotta roll. Lock this door behind me, and don't let anyone else in. I'll see you tomorrow."

He didn't wait to learn if she had anything else to say. Instead, he strode down the drive, which now felt a mile long, though he knew it wasn't. And with every step he felt her gaze on his back. He'd confused her.

But hell, she couldn't be more confused than him.

It took nearly two hours to clean up the paint. Luckily, it was a cheap, water-based paint and they were able to get it completely removed from the concrete drive. The lawn, however, looked like hell. The crew promised the paint wouldn't actually kill anything and that after mowing two more times, it wouldn't even be noticeable.

With the spring rains, even the grass should look good as new very soon.

By the time Justice got to the small house he'd recently purchased, he really was dragging. Thanks to Fallon feeding him, he needed only a quick shower and then he could fall into bed.

Soon as his headlights hit the front of the house, he realized he'd had a visitor.

Some asshole had stomped on all the new flowers he'd planted in the beds around the front porch.

Son of a bitch. The Wades weren't the only ones to be vandalized. Could that mean someone didn't like his connection to them? Probably, and as far as Justice was concerned, Marcus was his number-one suspect.

★ ★ ★

Sitting in the Body Armor Agency, ensconced in his boss's office with the requisite coffee and treats, Justice updated Leese and Sahara. Knowing they'd be curious, he'd even taken photos with his cell phone to better show the damage done to the houses.

They both frowned over the red paint and sympathized with him over his squished flowers.

"Sucks," Leese said. "But it still surprises me that you'd plant all those flowers."

"My granny and mom bought them for me. I didn't have much choice. They're both going to be pissed when they see the mess."

Sahara looked at him over her coffee cup, and when she finished her drink, she suggested, "Replant. Don't tell them."

"Maybe." The idea had merit, though he knew how disappointed his mom always got whenever he'd told her even the smallest lie. Still, she'd start in worrying if he didn't.

Absolutely *no one* could worry like his mom. She'd cornered the market. If Fallon wanted to see melodrama, he should introduce the two of them— No. *What the hell was he thinking?*

All kinds of crazy connotations went along with a girl meeting a guy's mom. He definitely couldn't go there.

"What?" Leese asked. "Did you think of something else?"

"No." Nothing that he could share with anyone.

Leese said, "I think more research is in order. There's probably a connection somewhere that we're missing."

"Fallon and her family swear there isn't any real threat. They just want her protected against anything that might come up."

"So maybe they don't know. Maybe they're overlooking something."

Sahara saluted Leese with her coffee. "You know, you're proving to be the best at research, often even better than my PI. You have an innate knack for knowing what trails to follow. If you have any free time, maybe you could lend Justice a hand. Just log in your hours for me."

Leese glanced at Justice. "I don't want to step on your toes. If you'd rather do some digging yourself—"

"Not offended," Justice promised. "I'm not nearly as good at it as you are, and I know it, so I welcome the help."

Leese smiled in anticipation. "Then consider it done."

"I'm glad that's settled." Sahara moved to sit behind her desk, dismissing them with a shooing motion of her hand. "Keep me updated," she said absently, already logging into her PC.

In silence, Justice and Leese walked out together and boarded the elevator. As soon as the doors closed, Leese asked, "You okay?"

Surprised by the question, Justice growled, "Yeah, 'course." But he stewed.

Leese snorted. "Give it up. You've got something on your mind. I can tell."

Should he tell? He'd found Leese to be a good confidant, but still, some shit should be kept private.

Folding his arms and resting back in the elevator, Leese waited.

Well, hell. Justice scowled. "Thing is, it's going to sound ridiculous." As melodramatic as Fallon had accused.

"Probably not as much as you're thinking."

Scrubbing a hand over his face, Justice tried to think of where to start, and finally just said it. "I don't feel like me anymore. Hell, I don't even know what I'm doing. It's like, for so long I was a fighter. End of story, ya know? I woke up and knew what I'd be doing that day. What I wanted to happen and how I'd work on it."

Leese nodded. "There's more of a routine to fighting. Training, travel, competition. Whether it goes good or bad, you know what to expect. With this job, not so much."

"Right," Justice agreed, jumping on his understanding of the situation. "I'm doing this shit and I like it. A lot. But the guy I used to know isn't there anymore. The things that come naturally to me, I can't do. The stuff I *can* do…well, it feels way too fucking natural. Like I was born to do it." Frustration crawled over him; he knew most of it centered around Fallon.

They stepped out of the elevator but didn't head for the front doors.

"I get it," Leese assured him.

"Do you?" Because Justice wasn't entirely sure he did, so how could Leese?

"I've gone through a few transformations myself." With a self-deprecating smile, Leese said, "I used to be a dick."

Justice tried to deny that. "You were just—"

"We both know it's true. Then I got involved in Cannon's camp and I finally felt focused. I gave my all to following what I thought I wanted—fighting."

"That *is* what you wanted," Justice countered. Hell, Leese had more heart than a lot of champions.

"No. Once I accepted reality, that I'd never be the best, I starting thinking about other options, and the stuff I enjoyed more."

"That's how you ended up at Body Armor?"

"Yeah." Leese looked as uncomfortable with the conversation as Justice. "And good thing, because now I know this is what I was always meant to do. It feels like the right fit, you know? Far more so than fighting ever did. It's more natural for me."

"See," Justice said, "that's sort of how I feel. Except there are conflicts, too."

Leese slowly smiled. "The girl? That's the conflict we're talking about, right?"

Would it be disloyal to Fallon to say so?

"I've been there, too," Leese reminded him. "I'm definitely not one to judge."

True. Leese was going to marry the girl he'd been conflicted over, so he'd been farther down the road than Justice planned to travel. After remembering that, he didn't need much prodding. He spilled his guts, telling Leese about Marcus, his mention of a scar and Fallon's reaction. "What do you make of that?"

Brows together, Leese gave it quick thought, then shared his advice. "I think I need to dig a little deeper into her background."

"I thought you already did that."

"I did a surface search looking for the obvious stuff, but now I might have more direction." He clapped Justice on the shoulder. "In the meantime, stay sharp—and make damned sure she's on board before you push for anything beyond a business relationship."

Justice put his hands on his hips. "S'that what you did with Catalina?"

Grinning, Leese said, "Catalina didn't give me much choice in the matter. I tried to resist, but she was pretty damned insistent."

After a shared laugh, they parted ways, with Leese heading to the shooting range in the basement and Justice heading for his car. He had a lot to accomplish before he went to the Wade house.

Unlike Catalina, he knew Fallon would never push for a relationship. She was too shy, too sheltered. That meant he had to concentrate on keeping it professional, no matter how difficult that might be.

CHAPTER EIGHT

Fallon was so excited, she couldn't contain her smiles. The parking lot would be jam-packed, Justice explained, so he parked in a pay lot a block from the venue. On their way in, they passed crowds of people ready for the fights, many of them wearing the same type of shirt as the one Justice had given to her, but with different fighters featured on the front.

Groups of young men hung together, already tipsy. Women, dressed to impress, flirted as they went by.

A couple of guys recognized Justice and asked for a photo with him. Even after he explained that he didn't compete anymore, they were still impressed and adoring, so he gave in, all while keeping Fallon close at hand.

He got them into the venue through a side door, away from the long line of people awaiting entry. They went down a hallway filled with men in shorts and T-shirts, some pacing, some hurrying along, others carrying supplies.

When passage got difficult, Justice took her hand, presumably so he wouldn't lose track of her. Whatever the reason, she felt a ridiculous thrill from his touch. His hand was easily twice the size of hers, strong and warm. Her heart started thumping hard, and when he glanced back at her with a cocky smile, she realized she was squeezing him.

They ducked through a closed door. She was surprised to find Cannon, Armie and Denver inside.

"You made it," Cannon said to her, coming forward for a greeting.

"It's so exciting," she whispered, then stalled when Cannon drew her in for a hug. Armie got her next, then passed her along to Denver.

If she lived to be a hundred, she'd never get used to how these big, ripped specimens were so demonstrative—and so gentle. It was enough to leave a woman with permanent heart palpitations.

Knowing she blushed, Fallon didn't object when Justice pulled her back to his side.

She stayed quiet as he asked the group, "How's Stack doing?"

"He's ready," Cannon said with confidence. "I'll be rejoining him in a few minutes." Then to Fallon he said, "There's food if you're hungry." He indicated a table filled with a variety of things to eat and drinks in a cooler. "Or if you're interested, Justice can show you around, introduce you to some people."

"Whatever Justice wants to do is fine by me."

All the men grinned at her while Justice rubbed the back of his neck. She realized what she'd said, twisted her mouth and added, "Within reason."

That made them laugh.

Armie nodded at her chest. "Nice shirt."

She looked down at it with a smile. "Justice gave it to me." She'd worn the oversize black fighter tee over a long-sleeved white shirt. Justice wore his gray shirt alone.

And my, how he filled it out. She had to admit, it looked much better on him than it looked on her.

Armie said, "When the ladies wear it, they tie it on the side." He smiled. "Mind if I show you?"

"Oh…um…" She glanced at Justice.

He rolled his eyes. "Do it," he said to Armie, "but make damned sure you're behaving."

"Stretch would have my hide if I didn't."

Stretch, she recalled, was Cannon's little sister and Armie's wife.

Armie stepped up to her, turned her to the side, then took the hem of the shirt and knotted it at her hip. It didn't affect the wolf design on front, but did make it fit her better and look more stylish.

He turned her toward a mirror and asked, "What do you think?"

Apparently Armie had many talents. "I like it. Thank you."

"You're going to get warm with that undershirt," Denver predicted. "It gets downright steamy about halfway through the night."

"Oh, well..." She couldn't lose the layer, so she merely shrugged and tried to act like it didn't matter. "It'll be fine, I'm sure."

Justice watched her until the door opened and more people stepped in. Clearly these were other fighters in the group and since she was the only woman, she started to feel like an intruder.

It got more awkward when one of the men asked if she was "with" Justice and he explained they weren't dating.

The man immediately tried to cozy up to her.

Justice immediately protested—and that had his friends all laughing.

Armie pulled him aside for a private conversation, and while Justice was otherwise occupied, two more men smoothly stepped in with questions about her availability. Fallon was both flattered and flustered. She'd never before garnered so much attention.

Even as she made excuses about why she shouldn't give out her phone number, she smiled until her cheeks hurt.

Minutes later, Justice rejoined her and that got rid of the interested men real quick.

It might have had something to do with Justice's sudden cross mood. He glared at everyone, including Armie, who kept snickering.

With the growled excuse that he'd show her around, Justice flipped off Armie, gave a halfhearted wave to the others and urged her from the room.

"What's going on?" Fallon asked.

"Nothing."

It was far too crowded to debate while walking in the hallway, so Fallon simply stopped. When Justice turned to her, she said, "*Something*, and I want to know what."

He stepped close, backing her to the wall and using his body to block her from passersby. He braced one thick arm on the wall above her head and leaned in. "Fine. You want to know what's got me irked?"

She'd never seen him in a mood like this. And, good Lord, he surrounded her! With every breath, she inhaled his hot scent, leaving her stomach filled with butterflies. No longer quite so certain, she whispered, "Yes?"

He angled closer still until his face was near hers and she could see her own reflection in his dark eyes. Then he said nothing.

His gaze dipped to her mouth.

Her heart went into her throat and her toes curled inside her shoes. "Justice?"

He drew a slow breath and his eyes met hers again. The impact was enough to weaken her knees.

Suddenly his mouth tilted. "Don't faint on me."

She shook her head, unwilling to make any promises.

"Guys are hittin' on you."

"They are?" Is that what bothered him?

"Yeah, and don't give me that innocent act." He tweaked her chin. "You liked it. But, honey, this isn't the place for it. Half the dudes here will be toasted by the end of the night, and half the ladies will be willing regardless. So Armie made a suggestion."

Was it the suggestion, then, that had him riled? Feeling very daring, she prodded him. "Let's hear it."

Justice took his time, tucking back her hair, then stroking her cheek with his thumb. "Tonight, if anyone asks, you're with me."

Going breathless, she repeated, "With you?"

"Yeah. That's the safest way for us to play it." He drifted the backs of his knuckles down her throat, then lightly cupped her shoulder. "So we'll be doing some of this tonight."

"This...what?"

"Touching. Teasing. Me making it clear to every yahoo out there that you're mine."

She had absolutely nothing to say to that. Little jittery explosions were going off in her body, making it hard to breathe, hard to think, but not to feel. Nope, she could feel just fine and the way he'd touched her...

"Okay?"

Well, shoot. He expected conversation. She managed a nod.

When Justice grinned, crinkles showed in the corners of his dark sinner's eyes. "You are so sweet." He looked her over, then playfully asked, "You sure you won't faint?"

No. "Pretty sure."

His grin widened. "You sound all raspy." He dipped his head, then said softly into her ear, "Don't get nervous. I won't be pushing the boundaries. We just need to convince everyone else."

Right. In order to protect her heart—and her pride—she seriously needed to remember that, for Justice, this was no more than a job. All the sudden flirting and intimacy was a game played to make the job easier. It would be beyond foolish for her to keep reacting to him so emotionally.

What she needed to do, she decided, was take advantage of the awesome opportunity now afforded her. How many big, buff, badass and sexy men would want to be this close to her? She could enjoy every second of it while keeping it in perspective by reminding herself that it wasn't real.

Play it cool, she told herself, but definitely go ahead and play. "Fallon?"

Justice's low, gruff voice and the way his warm breath teased her ear wasn't helping her to get control.

He stayed very near to her, and his scruffy jaw brushed hers. "Hmm?"

"You ready?"

For what? She didn't actually ask, because she knew whatever it was, yes, she was more than ready. Anxious even. She'd wanted some new experiences; now it appeared she'd get her money's worth.

In a lust-induced stupor, she nodded. Satisfied, he pressed his warm mouth to her temple in a brief kiss that made her breath catch.

"For anyone watching," he explained, then he levered back and slung his arm around her shoulders, keeping her close as he headed back down the wide hall.

Luckily they had a few minutes before she was expected to speak to anyone. The crowds got thicker, giving her time to get her wits together as they wended in and out of human congestion. Eventually they ended up near the "cage." Justice showed her where their seats would be, right behind the announcers. An entire section was roped off for the group.

Many people—fighters and their wives, past and present champions, a few celebrities who'd shown up to watch, referees and announcers—all greeted Justice like a friend. The scope of his social circle amazed her.

He introduced her each time and allowed people to make the assumption they were a couple. One man grinned and gave him a fist bump with the murmured praise, "Nice."

After the man walked away, Justice whispered, "He means you," and gave her an affectionate squeeze.

Fallon bit her lip, but the implied flattery still made her grin.

Once the fight started, many of the women sat together but

Justice didn't like that arrangement. He kept her at his side and she ended up sandwiched between him and Denver.

Since they were both gigantic men, she felt extra tiny and completely insulated from some of the jostling as people surged to their feet again and again to cheer or shout instructions. Fallon didn't think the men fighting heard all the yelling. If they did, they didn't acknowledge it. She figured the spectators just liked to give suggestions regardless.

Armie sat back with the ladies, including his wife. Fallon learned that Cannon's wife had stayed home with the babies. Apparently she and Armie's wife took turns on that.

Because Justice was so engrossed in the fight, Fallon asked Denver about Cannon. He explained that as an assistant coach, Cannon was in back with Stack, and when it came time for the fight, he'd be cage-side.

Trying to understand, she asked, "So Cannon not only runs a gym and fights, but he coaches, too?"

Denver started to lean close to reply and she suddenly found herself hauled up to Justice's side. He took over the explanations. "Cannon started the gym but everyone pitches in to help out there. And depending on who's fighting, different fighters step up as assistant coaches. They leave the real training to a dedicated, full-time coach, though." When the prelims ended, Justice went into more depth about the process, and the other guys chimed in, giving her a lot of insight.

The women, too, had much to say, and their perspectives, she found, were vastly different from the men.

Overall, she gathered that the fighters were something of a family. They stuck together, supported each other and accepted imperfections.

Even though he no longer competed, Justice was clearly still part of the family, and Fallon loved that for him. Her own family had always been small and after losing her sister—

"Son of a bitch."

Justice's muttered complaint drew her from her wayward thoughts. She glanced up—and found Marcus staring at her from across the aisle, several rows away. He, too, had good seats, but in a different section.

"That's Marcus," she said in surprise.

"Yeah, and I'll bet my ass the little weasel isn't an MMA fan." Justice sounded accusatory and more than furious.

"Maybe not," she rushed to say. "But it appears he's here with clients. Notice the other men around him? They're probably fans and Marcus is wooing them for business."

When he started their way, Justice said, "Let me handle this," with evil relish. He started out of the row.

"No." Fallon caught the back of his waistband, which was the only thing she could reach, and inadvertently got pulled from her seat. She almost tripped over a seat, but three pair of male hands caught her.

Mortified, she thanked everyone, then in a very low voice hissed to Justice, "Don't you dare embarrass me by causing a scene. I mean it."

Expression fierce, Denver said, "I wouldn't."

Already the others were staring at them, wondering what had happened. Fallon pasted on a smile before ushering Justice along. When they reached the aisle, she requested, "Give a minute."

He laughed like she was nuts. "Hell, no."

"Justice," she growled.

He cupped his hand around the nape of her neck, stalling her complaints. "With or without your boyfriend, I wouldn't let you out of my sight here. But I'll let you take the lead. How's that?"

Not good enough; however, debating it in front of everyone would only cause more conflict. So instead she said, "He's *not* my boyfriend," then looked at Marcus and pointed to the hall behind them.

He nodded and headed in that direction.

Giving Justice a stern frown, she said, "I'm trusting you to behave."

"Yes, ma'am." Keeping his hand on her nape, he walked with her to the very congested main hall.

Watching them together, he realized their relationship was more than client and bodyguard. Were they a couple? It sure appeared so.

Being classy, rich and pampered, Fallon Wade couldn't be Justice's usual type. Maybe the differences made her more appealing, perhaps even special to him.

If so, that'd make things easier. Justice was a real hard-ass who didn't feel the need to prove anything to anyone.

Women, however, had a knack for weakening even the strongest of men.

He'd definitely work this to his advantage.

Every locked door could be opened, as long as you had a key. He smiled, thinking he'd just acquired the key he needed.

"Good heavens, it's packed."

Justice pulled her closer, moving her in front of him and using his arms to shield her from being jostled. "Everyone is heading to get a drink before the main fights start."

"Is it always this busy?"

"Yeah." He steered her into a slight alcove near the fire exit. As they waited for Marcus, he figured he might as well set her straight. "This is your show—"

"Thank you."

"As long as he doesn't insult you."

She rounded on him with a lot of attitude. "If he insults me—"

"He'll get flattened."

"I'll handle it." Her eyes narrowed. "We've discussed this, Justice."

"Yeah." Justice had a hard time thinking straight. Out of necessity, he'd followed Armie's suggestion and kept her as close as he would a bed partner. But that just naturally led to him thinking more about her actually being one.

"And?" she asked, sounding a little breathless.

"I dunno." The longer he stared down at her, the less angry she seemed. He touched her cheek and found it every bit as soft and warm as he remembered.

She shifted, cleared her throat, licked her lips. "Justice?"

God he loved her eyes, so big and deep with emotion. And her mouth—all pink and wet... Without meaning to, he leaned a little closer, more than ready for a taste.

"What are you doing here?"

At Marcus's brusque question, Fallon jumped as if someone had goosed her. She whipped around, snapping, "Damn it!"

Marcus scowled.

"Fallon, Fallon," Justice playfully chided. "I had no idea you had such a potty mouth."

Her elbow connected with his gut.

Taken by surprise, he grunted, "Oof," then caught her arm. "Violent, too."

She forced a smile for Marcus. "I'm here to watch the fights of course."

Very deliberately, Marcus kept his gaze on Fallon. Even with Justice giving him a death stare, the bastard avoided his gaze.

Shoving his hands in his pockets, Marcus nodded. "I didn't know you were a fan."

"And you are?"

"Not really. But I have some potential donors for the literacy fund-raiser with me. When a friend had tickets he couldn't use, I bought them from him."

Justice propped a shoulder against the wall and suffered through the cordial conversation. He detested hearing Fallon talk so sweetly to her ex, and he especially hated that the ex was being reasonable for once.

He liked Marcus better as an asshole he could revile.

"So they enjoy the sport?" Fallon asked.

"I really don't know," Marcus said. "But they're competitive brothers and enjoy any kind of wager there is."

Fallon frowned. "They're betting on the fights?"

"They bet on everything, and they especially favor friendly wagers over sports of any kind." He made a face. "They've left it to me to keep a tally of the bets, since I'm not joining in the competition."

"I take it they have deep pockets?" Fallon teased.

"Yes, very deep. But they don't just gamble with money. I've seen them put up cars, houses and, a few times, women. Whoever loses always pays up."

Fallon stiffened. "Exactly how do you pay up with a woman?"

Marcus smiled slightly. "No one is being forced, I'm sure. When you're as well off as those two are, women are always available and willing to oblige."

She narrowed her eyes. "It's still wrong."

He shrugged. "I'm not disagreeing."

To switch the topic a bit, Justice spoke up. "You said they're businessmen?"

Face tightening, Marcus looked away. "They have a willingness to contribute."

Something in his tone and manner sharpened Justice's interest even more. "So *not* businessmen?"

"Of course they have businesses."

"And those are?"

Instead of answering, Marcus ignored him and asked Fallon, "Are you enjoying yourself?"

"Yes. It's so exciting. I'd never realized."

His expression warmed. "You wouldn't even watch boxing with me."

"In comparison, boxing seems boring."

"Boring?" he teased. "Maybe you need to give it another try."

Justice sawed his teeth together.

"From what I remember of boxing," Fallon said, "it's just punching. This is punching and kicking, elbows and knees, grappling and—"

Indulgent, Marcus smiled. "You've become an expert?"

"Far from it. But I am learning a lot from Justice's friends. In fact, one of his friends is the main fight of the night."

"Main event? Really?" There was no real surprise in Marcus's eyes when he looked at Justice again. "So you know Stack Hannigan?"

"Know him and gave Fallon the shirt."

Using both thumbs, Fallon pointed to her chest to show off the wolf logo.

Justice took her hand and lowered it. The last thing he wanted her to do was draw Marcus's attention to her boobs.

Unfortunately, he was too late.

With his gaze where it shouldn't be, Marcus swallowed. "Nice."

Resisting the urge to clock him, Justice said, "Damn, man, you must be one of Stack's more rabid fans the way you're drooling."

As if only then realizing where he'd been looking, Marcus snapped to. He coughed and tried to hurry along with a question. "I take it you'll be rooting for him?"

Pretending to miss the male conflict, Fallon nodded. "Yes. And Justice promises me that he'll win."

"Fact," Justice said.

"I'll pass along that inside info, then," Marcus promised. "The brothers will appreciate it." He glanced at Justice, glanced over his shoulder, then said to Fallon, "Do you think we could—"

Gleefully, Justice said, "Nope."

Since he held her arm, Fallon couldn't elbow him again. Instead, she tried to yank free of his hold. But Justice didn't let go, even when she tried to shake him off.

Naturally Marcus couldn't help but notice.

Eyes going flinty, the ex took a step forward. "Now wait just—"

To keep Marcus from interceding, Fallon did an immediate about-face. "Mother told me you'll be working with her on the literacy charity. That's very generous of you."

Divided, Marcus waffled between showing his anger and grabbing her olive branch.

Knowing which one he'd prefer, Justice waited.

Marcus finally settled on the branch. "Yes. It's a great cause." Voice softer, he said, "And I was hoping I'd get to see you."

Ha! Justice had guessed all along that Marcus had ulterior motives.

Staying firm, Fallon shook her head. "That's not going to happen."

"But—"

"Mother has agreed that she'll only meet with you away from our home."

Marcus turned his hate-filled glare on Justice. "I suppose that's what *he* wants?"

Justice gave an evil smile.

"It's what *I* want," Fallon hurried to say.

Done with the dramatics, Justice drew her into his side and draped his arm over her shoulders to keep her anchored there. "The fights will be starting soon. We should get back to our seats."

Luckily Fallon agreed, and for once, Marcus didn't kick up a fuss. He glanced over his shoulder again, nodded to Fallon and said, "I'll see you soon."

Something made Justice uneasy.

Maybe it was the wary way Marcus kept looking around, how he went the opposite direction from which he'd come. Skin prickling, Justice, too, did a quick survey of the area—and found one of Marcus's betting buddies standing a few yards away, arms crossed, watching them with too much interest.

In an instinctive move to meet a threat head-on, Justice stepped forward. Almost at the same time, Fallon turned into his path, probably to blast him—which, okay, he maybe deserved.

They collided.

Justice caught her upper arms to keep her from stumbling. She automatically braced her hands against his chest. They both went still.

Maybe it was Marcus hitting on her, or maybe it was all the other dudes trying to get her attention. Whatever the reason, he felt all territorial and determined to stake a claim.

Resisting a woman wasn't easy. Hell, it wasn't even natural. Resisting Fallon…now that was almost impossible, but he hung on by a thread.

Torturous, especially when she turned her face up to his.

The awareness in her eyes damn near knocked him over the edge.

Everything around him faded away as sexual tension sank in. Fallon's gaze dipped to his mouth, she licked her lips and, choosing to see that as an invitation, Justice gave in.

He cupped a hand to the back of her neck, drew her up and covered her mouth with his own. He couldn't say exactly what got into him, and he sure as hell couldn't justify it, but in that moment, he felt explosive with need.

Should'a made it a light kiss.

Should'a kept it quick.

But damn, her mouth was soft and damp, and with a shuddering breath she parted her lips.

He lost his head a little, especially when she melted against him and her small hands clutched at his chest.

Again on instinct, he turned them so that her back was against the wall, her front shielded by his body, ensuring no one could see her.

It was insane. Definitely wrong. But he had to taste her.

His tongue slipped over her lips, dipped inside to touch her teeth, then her tongue. She teased back with her own.

On a groan, he nudged her mouth open, deepening the kiss with a bold stroke of his tongue. Her mouth was warm and sweet, and he couldn't get enough.

Her soft sound of surprise gave him a second of sanity. *What the hell was he doing?*

He decided he had to stop, and tried to by lifting his head. He expected Fallon to say something, maybe even push him away. Instead, her breathing labored, she kept her eyes closed—her swollen mouth looked so pink, so wet...

This time he kissed her without any reserve at all. He couldn't get enough of her as he held her nape in one hand, and with the other, coasted down her narrow back to her hip.

In a sign of acceptance, her arms slid up and around his neck.

He pressed against her—

"Jesus, Justice, what are you doing?"

Harsh reality crashed into him. Oh, fuck.

Justice glanced over his shoulder and saw Leese scowling, Armie grinning. *Busted.* After clearing his throat, he asked, "When'd you get here?"

"Just now," Leese said, disapproval in his tone and expression.

Armie cocked a brow. "Really getting into the act, huh? It's convincing. No one will doubt that you're into each other."

"Yeah, um..." What to do? Fallon had tucked her face against his chest, clearly hiding, and damn, he could feel her hot breath even through his T-shirt. He also felt her trembling.

It took him a second to wrap his brain around the fact that he'd now be stopped cold, when seconds before he'd been smoldering.

The idea of watching Stack compete no longer seemed so important, but no way could he do what he really wanted, which involved finding someplace private and scoring big with sweet little Fallon Wade.

"Would you like a minute?" Armie asked with absurd formality. "Not to finish, you know. I mean, you're right here in the open. But maybe to make your apologies to the lady? To set up plans for later?"

"Fuck off, Armie."

That got his friend laughing. Clutching his hands together, Armie said, "Young love. So beautiful. So...lusty."

Leese shoved Armie, then scowled again at Justice. "Wrap it up," he suggested, his tone terse. With yet another shove, he prodded Armie along to give them privacy.

Feeling damned ridiculous, Justice turned back to Fallon.

She continued to hide against him, and now her shoulders shook.

Oh, shit. If he'd made her cry, he'd kick his own ass. "Fallon?" He tried to lift her chin.

She resisted by tucking tighter to him.

He didn't know what to do. He stroked her silky hair, then her back. He pressed a kiss to her temple—and got himself all hot and bothered again.

Frowning at his own lack of control, Justice whispered, "You okay, honey?"

Her hands fisted in his shirt, and she made this strangled sound that alarmed him.

"Fallon?"

He heard it again, not quite a sob, but maybe—

She looked up at him and Justice saw that her big doe eyes were bright with laughter, her cheeks hot, and she couldn't quit snickering.

Hilarity?

He quirked a smile of relief. "Tickled your funny bone, huh?"

Choking on her humor, she hugged him again.

God, she looked incredibly beautiful to him. "Get it together, woman. We're in public."

Around a chuckle, she admitted, "Right—*now* I remember!"

Meaning she'd forgotten, too? "You're not the one who had to face Leese and Armie."

She did more snickering before she could face him again. "Oh, God, that was *so* embarrassing."

But rather than blast him, she laughed? Nice. Justice liked that reaction. He tangled a hand in her hair, saying, "Trust me, Armie's done worse."

That only put her into a fit of giggles—until Justice murmured, "You taste good, Fallon."

With a sharp inhale, she stared at him and bit her lip.

Renewed need clenched his guts. As much to himself as her, he said, "We have to get back to our seats."

"Right." She looked away, smoothing her hair and shirt. "I guess that kiss was to help convince people we're together?"

Sure, and I got hard for the same reason.

No, he couldn't say that; it'd only make things worse.

But because he didn't have a good answer, and he didn't want to outright lie to her, he kissed her again instead.

This time he managed to keep it light and quick.

"Sorry I embarrassed you." With an arm around her, he steered her out of the alcove and along the wide hall to their aisle entrance. "Don't ask me to apologize, though."

"Okay."

Justice frowned. She shouldn't have been so damned agreeable. "Not for the kiss, I mean."

"I knew what you meant."

Damn it. "It was wrong to maul you like that, especially here and now, but—"

"Justice, I'm not complaining."

No, she wasn't.

He didn't know what to think about that.

Talking became impossible as they squeezed through the crowds returning to their seats. He noticed Marcus and his cronies were again seated, now with drinks in their hands.

Feeling more surly than ever, Justice looked at each of them. The same man who'd been eyeballing him earlier looked up to meet his gaze. The guy smiled, then lifted his drink in a mock toast.

Justice continued to stare at him—until Fallon tugged on his hand to get him seated. There was a lot of ribbing from the guys as they waited for the next fight. Justice ignored them until he saw Fallon blushing.

Then he tried to mean-mug them all—without much success.

"Aw, he's sensitive," Denver said in a loud stage whisper.

Armie grinned. "And damned indiscreet."

"Rude as hell, too," Leese added, "because he hasn't introduced me yet."

Fallon turned with a smile and took care of the introduction herself. For a few minutes she and Leese talked about the bodyguard business. Justice thought about Marcus and wondered how he could get the names of the men with him.

When Tom came up to him, he almost groaned with frustration, especially when Tom took the seat beside him.

"Good night of fights, so far."

"Yeah," Justice agreed, not exactly in a chatty mood.

Tom elbowed him. "Makes you want to get back in it, doesn't it?"

"No."

"Bullshit. It's in your blood, Justice."

Used to be. But now? He had so many other things on his mind that he—

Tom thwacked him hard on the shoulder. "Give me the word and I'll talk to the powers that be. They already promised they'd set us up quick. And you know fans would love it."

Justice tried ignoring him.

"Your little lady would love to see you compete."

Sitting back in his seat, Justice said, "Ain't happening. Let it go."

"Can't, man. You're part of the plan and you know it."

"Get a new plan."

Tom grinned widely, but the annoyance was there in his eyes. "Fallon, honey, wouldn't you like to see Justice in the cage?"

Being drawn into the discussion caused her to falter, but not for long. "Justice can make his own decisions."

"But you'd like to see it, right? Or maybe you don't, considering how badly he'll lose."

She took the bait, saying, "Maybe I'll just watch the fight where he already knocked you out."

"I have it recorded," Armie said. "You're welcome to it."

"That was a fluke," Tom scoffed. "If Justice was really so damned cocksure, he'd have already given me a rematch."

Armie laughed. "If you want to stick with that fluke story, a rematch is a bad idea."

"You chicken?" Tom leaned around Justice to see Fallon. "Normally I wouldn't believe that of him, but since he's dodging me…"

Justice took Fallon's hand to stifle her denial. "Believe what you want, but I'm still done."

Finally Tom's smile slipped. "Damn it, man. I can't accept that."

Justice looked him in the eyes. "That's your problem then."

Fallon glanced anxiously from one man to the other. Justice gave her hand a squeeze to let her know he wasn't bothered. But, yeah, that was a lie. Tom got to him—not enough to make him backtrack, though.

Just enough to make him want to throw a punch.

Then he saw the guys with Marcus watching with interest. No way could they hear anything being said, not from that distance, but body language alone probably showed a conflict, and it had caught their interest.

Tom said, "I'll give you half my pay." Then with quiet force, "Take the fucking fight."

Fed up, Justice half turned to face him. "Your ego wants to fight, but here's a news flash for you—I don't give a shit about your ego, so leave me the hell alone."

Tom looked surprised for just a moment, then his face split with a grin. "I'm wearin' you down, buddy, I can tell. No, don't start gnashing your teeth. I'll let it go—for now."

Luckily the music started as fighters made their entrance with deafening fanfare. This was the start of the main card with a lot of fan favorites competing.

Fallon held his hand and listened intently to the introductions. Leese, he noticed, kept a sharp watch everywhere else.

Did he feel the same thing Justice did? It must have been catching, because by the end of the fight, Armie and Denver were also more alert.

Something was happening, Justice only wished he knew *what*.

CHAPTER NINE

The excitement was contagious, and although Fallon didn't know any of the athletes, out of loyalty she cheered for whomever Justice preferred.

The competitions proved more thrilling than she'd ever imagined possible. Bloody, yes. Brutal, no question. But she noted a mesmerizing fluidity to the defense and offense of each fighter. It didn't take her long to understand the styles and to recognize when a fighter wanted to stay on his feet versus preferring a ground game.

She was glad they had the "good seats," given how many people milled around going for more beer. She found it very distracting even though they weren't passing in front of her.

Denver leaned toward her ear to ensure she'd hear him. "Too many people are here without any real interest in the fights. But you seem to be enjoying them."

"Oh, yes, definitely." Secretly, she kept imagining Justice competing and, each time, a secret thrill unfurled inside her. Then again, the brush of his arm against hers, the way he smiled, also affected her.

She watched as he shouted suggestions and enacted them from

his seat. He'd twist, tighten and duck as if he, himself, were in the fight.

Studying his profile, she asked, "Do you miss it?"

He glanced down at her. "What?"

"Competing. I know you said you didn't, but—"

"Sometimes," he admitted with a crooked grin. "But I have no intention of going back, so don't tell Tom or he'll be even more relentless."

Fallon didn't know Tom well, but she assumed, from what she'd seen so far, he'd be relentless anyway. If he ever did get Justice back in the cage, she'd put her faith in Justice every time. His modesty didn't matter. There was an amazing quiet confidence about him that she found incredibly appealing.

And good heavens, he knew how to kiss.

Just thinking about it now made her lips tingle and left her a little breathless.

She was so lost in daydreams, she almost missed a submission. When everyone surged to their feet, she shook off the sensual haze and jumped up, too.

Oh, it was awful!

She might have screamed...but then the referee called the fight and she watched as the poor guy who'd just gotten his arm cranked bounded to his feet with a low curse—before slapping his opponent on the shoulder.

Justice slipped his arm around her waist. Amused, he said, "You're on the squeamish side."

She made a face. "I thought his arm would break."

Tom leaned around Justice to say, "It happens on occasion."

Dear God. She blanched. "You're joking."

"Nope."

"I'm glad that didn't happen tonight."

"One more fight to go," Justice said. "But Stack's pretty good at avoiding submissions."

Tom stood. "I'm running out for a drink. Either of you want anything?"

Justice shook his head and Fallon said, "Thank you, but I'm fine."

With a nod, he left.

A few minutes later Armie returned and leaned forward, his arms braced on the back of her and Justice's seats. "So Tom knows your...friend?"

Fallon half turned. "My friend? Who?"

Armie tipped his head toward where Marcus had been sitting, but now the seats were empty.

Justice scowled. "What are you talking about?"

"Tom's out there with the three of them, chatting like they're old pals."

"The hell you say!" Justice surged to his feet before Fallon could stop him.

He'd only taken two steps when the intro music started for Stack's fight, making him hesitate. And then Marcus and his friends reentered—but not with Tom.

"Justice," she said, hooking her fingers over the back pocket of his jeans, which was the only part of him she could reach. "Why do you care?"

As he slowly turned to face her, the chilling anger left his eyes, replaced by something else. Something far from chilly.

His gaze shifted to her hand on his butt pocket, then to her face with a raised brow.

Armie started snickering. "Dude, you are in a bad way."

He'd had to shout to be heard over the music, and that got the attention of the other guys, who all started in with outrageous comments about their buddy being molested.

When she started to retreat, Justice laced his fingers with hers and stared toward Marcus and the others. He ignored his friends' provoking comments.

Finally Tom rejoined them, empty-handed, she noticed.

Justice didn't remark on it, but he was still scowling when he claimed his seat again.

Leese leaned past her to ask him, "What are you thinking?"

"That something's going on."

Fallon looked back and forth between the men. "What are you talking about?"

New music blared, and then Stack and his entourage, led by Cannon, entered the arena through a side door and all conversation died as the men raucously shouted for their fighter.

Clearly, Stack was a fan favorite. Most people were on their feet, some holding signs, many snapping pictures. Fallon forgot all about Tom and Marcus and whatever clandestine message had passed between Leese and Justice.

For this fight, anxiety riddled her. Everyone was so certain Stack would win, she kept wondering what would happen if he didn't. And of course, the other fighter had plenty of fans, too. How disappointed would they be?

She thought of Tom; clearly, he hadn't yet gotten over his loss.

With every punch or kick thrown, each takedown and submission attempt, she got more tense until she thought she might break. For once Justice was too caught up in the fight to notice how she fretted.

The torture lasted until the middle of the third round. Both fighters were battered. Stack had a severe black eye and the other guy had a cut on his forehead. Sweat covered their muscles, which had seemed to pump up with each punch thrown. Though Stack continued to breathe evenly, the other guy was getting gassed and it showed.

Earning his fight name, Stack prowled relentlessly forward, and when his opponent stepped back, Stack shot in. They ended in a tangle on the floor.

Beside her, Justice went nuts. The shouting from all the men nearly deafened her. She continually shifted her position to see around all the now-standing people and when she finally had a clear view again, she saw that Stack had a full mount. He landed four punches in a row, and the body beneath him went slack.

The ref called the knockout.

Pandemonium ensued while several of the fighters seated near her surged forward to the cage. Fallon could tell that Justice wanted to join them, but instead he swung her up in his arms and hugged her while laughing.

He held her as if she weighed nothing, and being in his arms made her nerve endings all go on alert.

As he set her back on her feet, she noticed that Armie had also stayed behind with the wives, who hugged each other, alternately laughing and crying.

They were such protective, considerate men, and she sighed in distraction.

Until Justice cupped the side of her face and pressed his mouth to hers.

It was no more than a celebratory smooch, there and gone too quickly for her to kiss him back, but her blasted knees almost buckled.

While congratulations and back slaps got passed around their triumphant group, Fallon subtly fanned her face. Justice talked with others, and her mind wandered—to kisses and handholding, protectiveness and affection.

The truth settled into her heart and she knew...she cared far too much for him.

For so long she'd tried to keep her private life just that—private. In doing so, she felt like Justice only knew bits and pieces of her. Nothing of depth.

Nothing *real*.

Now with new awareness, she decided he had a right to know why she'd never dated. He needed to understand her issues, awful as they would be to share. Whether he considered the touching and kissing tonight as part of an act, for her it was real.

How would he react once he knew all of her?

Denver returned to their row of seats to collect his wife, who threw herself into his arms. While cuddling her close, he said to Justice, "After party at the club."

Justice was already shaking his head. "Not this time."

Denver glanced at her, then nodded. "Got it. Well, if you're interested, we're all going to Cannon's place tomorrow to hang out."

"Celebrating Stack's win?"

Denver shrugged. "The plans were already made, but sure."

Laughing, Justice told her, "Anyone can get caught, so if he'd lost we'd get together to grumble."

"That's about it," Denver agreed.

Justice put his arm around her. "What do you think? Did you have any plans for Sunday?"

Thrilled that he would include her, she quickly shook her head. "I'm free."

After giving her a one-arm hug, he told Denver, "Then count us in."

With plans made, everyone began exiting in a crush far worse than when they'd entered. Because some of the guys and their wives went a different direction to join up with Stack, she and Justice were among strangers. He kept her in front of him, occasionally raising a forearm to keep anyone from bumping into her.

They'd finally made it to the main hall that led to an escalator when something happened. People began cursing and the sounds of a scuffle were heard. She tried to go on tiptoe to better see, but Justice immediately tucked her behind him, saying, "Hold on to me."

She flattened a hand to the middle of his back.

Muscles flexed under her palm; the man was so hard all over.

Then a guy behind her shoved past in excitement, saying, "Fight!" as if he relished the idea.

A woman pushed in front of her, separating her from Justice while pressing close to his back.

Someone else wedged past her, then more people—and more. In a matter of seconds, she couldn't even see Justice. Uncertainty gripped her as she got jostled left and right.

Thinking it might be a good idea to get out of the main flow of bodies, she edged to the side, hoping to stand against the wall until Justice came back for her.

She almost made it, too, until someone shouldered her hard and she lost her footing. Her purse got jerked off her shoulder. She stumbled.

Without even realizing she was near the stairs, she went down them, nearly taking a few other startled people with her. Her hip hit the rail, her shin cracked against a step.

At a short landing where the stairs took a turn before continuing down, she finally crashed into a corner wall, her body in a disheveled heap. Somewhere along the way, she must have clunked her head because stars danced in her vision. In a daze, she struggled to get her bearings.

"Hey now." Tom crouched down in front of her. "You okay, honey?"

His big body blocked others from crowding her. "Justice..."

"I'm sure he's coming." He put a hand to her shoulder when she started to stand. "How about you hold on just a sec? Catch your breath and let me see if anything's hurt?"

Honestly, everything hurt, especially her pride. People who'd given up on the escalator continued to gawk at her as they passed down the stairs.

She brushed her hair back and winced. Looking at her wrist, she saw the bruise starting.

Tom took her hand and gently turned it. "Did you brace yourself as you fell?"

"I don't know. It happened so fast."

She heard an enraged shout and a second later Justice shoved Tom aside. "Fallon? Ah, shit." He touched her face. "Baby, what happened?"

Feeling like an utter fool, Fallon reached for him.

He drew her up and against him.

"I fell," she said with a hot blush. She wished there weren't so many people around to witness her embarrassment.

Scowling darkly, Justice asked, "Down the steps?" He looked back at them.

"Yes. Don't ask me how. It just...happened."

He slowly tipped up her face. "Banged yourself up, too."

He didn't know the half of it. Her hip ached, her shin throbbed, but at least the twirling stars were gone.

Tom stepped close again. "Got her purse."

Fallon gave up her stranglehold on Justice, limped as she put her weight on her leg, and attempted a smile. "Thank you, Tom." She took her purse from him. "Stuff went everywhere—"

"So did you." Like Justice, Tom appeared furious. "I think I got most of it."

Justice kissed her temple, then said to Tom, "Sorry if I—"

"No worries." Tom bent to look at her. "You seemed a little loopy when I first got to you. You sure you're okay?"

"Yes. Just humiliated."

Tom said, "Want me to lead the way?"

Nodding, Justice kept her close as they continued slowly down the stairs, following the flow of people out a side door into a near empty lot.

"We're parked around front," Justice said with a frown. "Can you walk okay?"

"Of course." The brisk air helped to revive her and after a few more steps, the pain in her hip eased. To get the attention off her, she asked, "Was there a fight?"

His expression carved in stone, Justice said, "No. Just two idiots arguing." He continued to watch her closely, proving her ploy hadn't worked.

"Does that happen often?"

Tom answered her. "I've seen a few crowd disputes but they're usually over before they really get any steam."

"You've got a bruise on your cheek."

"I do?" Surprised by Justice's growl, Fallon touched her face.

He caught her hand and moved it down. "Don't prod it. We need to get some ice."

"Want me to go back in and grab an ice pack?" Tom offered.

Fallon answered before Justice could. "That's not necessary. I really am fine."

Neither man agreed.

Even after they reached the parking lot, they both looked far too grim.

Why was Tom still hanging around? "Are you parked close to us?" Fallon asked.

He shook his head. "Got a second?" he asked Justice. "I mean, maybe after you get her seated?"

Justice's expression tightened even more, and he nodded. He treated Fallon like breakable glass as she got into the car, then he closed the door and walked a small distance away to where Tom waited.

Knowing they deliberately excluded her irked Fallon. She wanted to protest, but even more than that, she wanted to take inventory of her injuries.

She found a large purpling bruise on her shin and a peek in the visor mirror showed a nasty swelling on her cheekbone. Checking her hip would have to wait until she had privacy. She wasn't about to pull down her pants with people so close to the car.

She glanced up and found Justice watching her intently as he listened to whatever Tom said. By the second his expression darkened until he looked quietly enraged.

The two men finished their conversation, briefly shook hands, and Justice started her way.

Ho, boy. Fallon didn't know what had made him so angry, but she assumed she was about to find out.

★ ★ ★

Someone had pushed her.

Justice still couldn't wrap his mind around it. Why would anyone want to hurt Fallon? And how the hell did Tom know what Fallon didn't?

He'd already demanded she tell him what had happened, but she repeatedly insisted that she'd lost her balance in the crush. No one, she promised him, had pushed her.

He wanted to believe that—only Tom had been adamant. He claimed he saw it, Fallon struggling to reach the wall but two men had deliberately corralled her nearer and nearer to the steps, then shouldered her hard.

Picturing it put Justice in a murderous rage.

He'd fucked up, letting her out of his sight, and that pissed him off, too. They were almost to her house when he growled in accusation, "You were supposed to be holding on to me."

She stiffened with indignation. "I was until people got in front of me. How could you have not noticed that I was gone?"

"I felt a hand on my back and I thought it was yours."

She snapped back, "Great to know I'm indistinguishable from the crowd."

Justice drew a slow breath, reaching for calm. "You're distinguishable, believe me."

"Oh, really?"

With that sarcastic tone, she sounded as pissed as him. "Yeah."

"So when exactly did you realize I wasn't with you?"

He cleared his throat. "When the chick cupped me from behind."

Fallon went rigid and in a deadly whisper, asked, "She did what?"

Shrugging, Justice explained, "Reached down between my legs and grabbed a handful. I about jumped a foot." He glanced at her. "Knew right then it wasn't you."

Agitation narrowed her eyes. "Of all the—"

"She only copped a quick feel. Then I saw you were gone..."
His own anger edged back in. "You could have been killed,"
he muttered.

"That's ridiculous. Bruised, yes. Dead? Doubtful."

Justice pulled to the side of the road less than a mile from
her home.

"What are you doing?"

"I want to talk to you." *And touch you.* "I want this resolved
before I let you go tonight."

"Justice." She softened her tone. "I promise, I'm fine."

Taking her hand in his, he kissed her sore wrist. "I should
have protected you better."

A little breathless, she whispered, "It wasn't your fault."

He didn't remind her that she'd just been blaming him for not
noticing sooner how they'd gotten separated. "Whether Tom is
right or not, I want you to be careful."

"I'm always careful."

No, she wasn't. Her exuberance kept her wide-eyed with
absorption, but not caution. At times it seemed to Justice as if
she rushed to soak up as many new experiences as she could,
as quickly as possible, as if she thought the opportunity would
only last so long.

In doing so, she also gave him a new perspective. He began
to notice things he'd long taken for granted.

Thanks to Fallon, he had a new outlook on life. Accepting
the necessary changes he'd made came easier than expected.
Hell, he was starting to feel as if he'd only just discovered what
he'd always meant to be.

Featherlight, he brushed his fingertips over her bruised cheek.
"I'm sorry." It pained him to see her hurt. He wanted to hold
her close, and he wanted to rage.

If it had been deliberate, he'd damn well find out.

She leaned into his palm.

That simple show of trust did crazy things to him. "Fallon..."

"Hmm?"

Using care, he tunneled his fingers into her silky hair, then nudged her closer. Trying again, he said, "Fallon."

She stared at him with those big, dark eyes, making him hard with need. "Yes?"

"God, you tempt me." There, let her deal with that.

Her eyes widened in surprise, then grew heavy lidded in understanding. She looked at his mouth—and did the unthinkable.

She leaned toward him in silent consent.

"Damn," he whispered, already dragging her closer and pressing his mouth to hers. He started slow and easy, but when she made a small, hungry sound, his good intentions snapped. He tilted his head, nudged her lips open, and tasted her with his tongue.

So sweet.

Justice told himself to pull back, but Fallon settled her hand on his shoulder, lightly dug her fingers into his muscles, and it set him off.

Crazy how such a simple touch from her affected him.

The kiss was a little wild in ways he hadn't known were possible. He knew good old chemistry, but this was something else.

From a *kiss.*

Because of Fallon.

He was supposed to be protecting her, not pawing her in the front seat of a car.

But before he could think better of it, his hand was on her breast, lightly cuddling. God almighty, she felt good. Even through the layers she wore, her stiffened nipple grazed his palm and that, too, fired his blood.

Her gasp of surprise turned into a throaty moan, proving she enjoyed the touch as much as he did.

While teasing his thumb over one thrusting nipple, Justice pulled back and put his forehead to hers. Their heavy breaths mingled.

"We need to stop," he murmured low, trying to convince himself as much as her. Despite that, he continued to play with her, loving how she trembled, how she clutched at him. Her breasts were sensitive and he knew if he ever got the chance to have her, he'd enjoy spending an extra amount of time there.

He was just about to get it together and retreat when she touched her lips to his again.

Approval had never felt so hot.

The damned center console was in his way, but still he managed to kiss her firmly enough to press her head back against her seat. Needing to feel her skin, he reached for the hem of her shirt.

Getting under the oversize SBC fighter T-shirt was easy, but she wore another shirt under that, tucked in. Continually kissing her and feeling like a bumbling high school boy again, Justice inched it away.

Fallon never once protested, but then, she seemed so involved in dueling with his tongue, so lost to sensation, Justice wasn't sure she even noticed.

When he finally stroked his palm over the soft, naked flesh of her waist—yup, she noticed that.

She jerked back with a yelp, frantically righting her shirts and retreating as far away from him as she could.

Justice was left holding air.

Breathing hard, he watched her, concerned, wary. "Guess I stepped over the line?" He wanted to kick his own ass. *Of course that was over the line.* Hell, he wasn't supposed to be kissing her, much less fondling her.

"I didn't realize... I can't..." She folded her arms around her middle and stared at him. "I can't."

Trying to figure out how to proceed, he nodded. "Okay." He had a raging boner and adjusted his jeans.

She watched his every move as if expecting him to pounce on her.

"I understand." He sat back, giving her as much space as he could. "Sorry. I didn't mean to rush you."

She said nothing.

Damn it, he couldn't take it and reached out to gently brush her cheek. "Honey, it really is okay. My bad. I shouldn't have let things get so far."

As if pained, she closed her eyes. "No, I'm the one who should apologize. I've overreacted. It's just…"

She looked so pained, he asked softly, "Just what?"

"I… I meant to talk to you. To explain."

He waited, but again she went silent. "You want to tell me something?"

"No. Not tonight." She dropped back in her seat, her posture far too defeated. Then just as quickly she sat forward and faced him. "Tomorrow. Could we talk tomorrow?"

Whatever it was, Justice didn't know if he wanted to hear it. "Sure. We're going to Cannon's, right?"

Immediately she shook her head. "No, it needs to be before that. Maybe over breakfast?"

Did she plan to fire him then? He probably deserved no less. Not that it'd matter. Whether working for her or not, he'd continue to protect her—and pursue her. At this point, he couldn't seem to help himself. "I had planned to do some gardening."

She blinked. "Gardening?"

"Yeah. The same time someone tossed paint on your driveway, my flowers got trampled."

"Flowers?"

Did she have to sound so disbelieving? "You know those colorful things you plant around the bushes?" He lifted his chin. "My mom and granny got them for me as a housewarming gift, so I used them in the landscaping. If Mom finds out they got destroyed, it'll upset her. So I'm going to replace them before she has a chance to visit." Defensively, he added, "I don't want her upset."

Very slowly the shock left Fallon's face and her brows pinched down. "What do you mean they got trampled?" And in a higher pitch, she added, "On *purpose*?"

"Looked like."

Getting riled, she demanded, "Why didn't you tell me?"

Confused by that reaction, Justice shrugged. "You had enough on your mind."

"Enough on…"

Sighing, he draped an arm over the steering wheel and looked her over. "You keep repeating my words. Did a little groping cause that, or was it the kissing?"

She drew back. "Neither!"

"Settle down," he soothed, relieved that she was no longer so withdrawn. He'd take her irritation over shock any day. "I just wondered."

"You had no right not to tell me! If your flowers were sabotaged, there's a good chance the two incidents are related."

Was there any doubt? "I assume so." Which meant there was definitely a threat, whether she wanted to see it or not.

As if she'd read his thoughts, Fallon huffed. "You keep thinking someone is harassing me, but did it occur to you that *you* could be the one being harassed?"

Justice snorted. "No." But now that she said it… He considered it only a second or two before saying, "I'm not worried about me. I can handle myself."

"Apparently you can't handle your flowers."

Boy, she really was in a snit. To smooth things over, he said, "Sorry I didn't tell you. You're right. The more you know, the more cautious you'll be." Hopefully, anyway.

The annoyance faded under grudging acceptance. "Thank you."

To seal the deal, he added, "If I get done in time, I can come by early and we can talk then."

He watched as she chewed her bottom lip.

"Or," she offered, "I could help you plant tomorrow?"

She looked very uncertain, as if she expected him to refuse. Shoot, he'd love the company. Problem was, a woman like Fallon shouldn't be digging in the dirt, especially not with her bodyguard. "I have about three dozen flowers to get in the ground and it's going to be warm tomorrow."

"I won't wilt."

He thought about it for only a second. He could best protect her by keeping her close—and yeah, that excuse worked as well as any, and was definitely more acceptable than just wanting her company. "If you're sure you don't mind, then I can pick you up in the morning."

Amazingly, her face lit up. "What time should I expect you?"

Damn it, he badly wanted to kiss her again. He had enough sense to resist, but it wasn't easy.

After they made their plans, he drove the rest of the way to her house and walked her up to the door. With his hands in pockets to keep from touching her, he said, "Put some ice on those bruises, okay?"

"All right." And still she stared up at him.

"Good night, Fallon."

Her gaze went to his mouth. "Good night." In a flash, she went on tiptoe to kiss him. Just a warm touch of her mouth to his before she darted into the house and shut the door.

His hands were still in his pockets, but a smile split his face.

Amazing how something so wrong could feel so right.

Goddamn it, he needed this win.

Rising frustration burned in his guts. Things weren't working out as quickly as he needed them to and his patience wore dangerously thin.

He was a man of action, a man who made things happen, but all he could do now was stay vigilant until he found the leverage he needed.

Why wouldn't Justice get on board?

Why did he have to be so goddamned stubborn?

By pure luck, he'd gotten ahead of them today. He'd waited in a driveway, headlights off, and he'd planned a clever accident for when Justice's car got close.

When they'd pulled over to the side of the road, he'd gotten diverted. From the bright moonlight, he'd watched them making out.

Interesting.

Apparently, the girl's spill down the stairs had sparked Justice's possessive instincts after all.

When they'd finally driven on, he'd made the split-second decision not to interfere. He'd hold on to his plans for the accident and use it another, more propitious night. The stakes grew higher with time, and that was in his favor.

Now that he knew he could use the girl as motivation, he didn't want to rush and risk a misstep.

He needed to plan carefully.

Finally, everything was falling into place.

CHAPTER TEN

Fallon knelt in the soft grass, gardening gloves on her hands, surrounded by pots of daffodils and pansies.

She loved Justice's home.

It was a moderately sized ranch with three bedrooms, two bathrooms, a one-car garage and a front porch that ran the length of the house.

"I painted everything after I moved in," he explained while opening a bag of fertilizer. "Used to be this dull army green."

"I love the yellow with white trim. And the black roof and shutters are classic. The front door is really beautiful, too. Is that also new?"

"Yeah. Used to be just a plain door, but I put in the sidelights and transom."

"It looks amazing."

Crouched next to her, Justice sat back on his heels. "The whole house is about the size of your garage."

"Size doesn't matter."

He snorted. "Depends on who you ask."

Catching on to his thoughts, she ducked her face. "You know what I mean."

"I do." He studied her. "The amazing part is that I think you really believe it."

"Of course I do." Carrying on a normal conversation wasn't easy. Today Justice wore athletic shorts and sneakers. When he'd picked her up, she'd admired his white T-shirt, but as soon as they reached his house he'd peeled it off and she admired his bare chest so much more.

The sight of him was enough to make her breathless. Add in the stirring aroma of his skin, amplified by the bright morning sunshine, and it was a wonder she could string together two words.

When she saw his mouth curl into a smile, she realized she'd been staring and quickly cleared her throat. "Besides, if you recall, that's my parents' house, not mine." She placed a cluster of daffodils into the prepared hole and gently pressed the rich soil around it.

Justice, too, got back to work and without looking at her, he said, "It's the type of house you're used to."

Is that what he thought? That she expected a mansion throughout her life? Softly, she shared a confession. "I've stayed there because it meant so much to Mom and Dad. But when I imagine moving out—and I will, eventually—it isn't into a mansion."

"What do you imagine?" he asked.

She glanced up at his home. She really did love it and the neighborhood seemed nice. The houses weren't too close together, but children would have friends to play with and that was a bonus.

But to be honest... "I've always thought about living someplace remote. Where I could step outside and there wouldn't be anyone around to see me. I could come and go without being... noticed."

He thought about that, nodded, and asked, "Why?"

With one plant done, she scooted down to work on another. The silence stretched out, but Justice didn't press her.

He'd always been patient. Too patient.

Fallon really wished he'd prod her. Now, in the light of day, she dreaded the talk and needed the encouragement.

"I'm just private." *Liar.* Being private was very different from hiding.

"Did your mom see your bruises?"

Glad for the temporary reprieve, Fallon shook her head. "She was asleep when I got home, and I was asleep when she left this morning. She peeked into my room long enough to tell me she wouldn't be home until supper. My father will be home by then, too." Using the back of her hand, she brushed perspiration from her brow. "Just as well that I tell them both together. They tend to flip out whenever I get injured."

"You've been injured before?"

A perfect opening, but her courage fled. Putting all her concentration on carefully removing another flower from a plastic pot without damaging the roots, she said, "If I skin my toe, they carry on."

He nodded. "Want me to stay with you when you explain?"

That was the nicest offer she'd ever gotten. Justice was her bodyguard, but he was also the most down-to-earth person she'd ever known. He'd kissed her. Repeatedly. And now he offered to face her disgruntled parents with her.

Her reticence melted away and she whispered, "Remember that talk I wanted to have?"

His head jerked up and he stared at her. "Yes."

She hadn't been prepared for that reaction. He'd seemed so relaxed about it, almost disinterested. But at the first mention he bit.

Because she couldn't maintain eye contact, Fallon went back to planting. It'd be easier if she wasn't looking at him when she bared her soul. "I had a sister who died in a fire."

Very gently, he said, "I knew that."

"You did?"

He nodded. "There weren't many details to be found. I'm guessing your folks kept as much of it out of the news as they could."

Fallon let a humorless laugh escape before she could stop it. *Dig*, she told herself. *Plant. Focus on something other than his sympathy.*

She moved on to a pansy. "It was five years ago. We were—"

"We?"

He'd jumped on that clarification pretty quickly. But then, she'd already noticed how he stayed so attuned to her.

A lump formed in her throat. "I was there." Because she concentrated so closely on the plant, she didn't realize Justice had stood and was now behind her, not until he caught her upper arms and pulled her to her feet.

He didn't force her to face him, but he did caress her, his big hands warm on her shoulders. "Go on."

Resisting the urge to lean back against him, she drew a breath and whispered her explanation. "It was five years ago. I was nineteen and Cindy was twenty-one. She was always a little... freer than me. Where I was shy, she was the life of the party."

"Were you close?"

"Very." Her smile hurt her heart and her voice cracked. "She wasn't only my older sister. She was also my best friend and my hero." It took several gulping breaths before she could admit the truth. "It's my fault she's dead."

Justice stilled, his hot hands firm on her shoulders, before pulling her closer. In a low, soothing voice, he asked, "Will you tell me what happened?"

Giving herself time to regain her control, Fallon nodded. It felt odd to stand out in the open, in Justice's small yard with other houses nearby and neighbors passing by, while talking about such a life-changing moment.

But she did it anyway—because he deserved to know.

"My parents had bought some new lakefront property. It came with a small fishing cabin. They planned to build a nice vacation home and figured the contractors could use the cabin until that was done, then they'd have it torn down. But since it was there, Cindy decided she and I should have a girls' weekend away."

"Just the two of you?"

"Yes." A bee buzzed near Fallon's face and she waved it away. The sun was so bright, almost blinding, giving her a good excuse to close her eyes. "We'd packed a bunch of junk food and our bathing suits and planned to just catch up. She'd been abroad and I'd missed her, so it sounded like a wonderful plan. Dad didn't like the idea much but we convinced him. And Mom always thought we were safe together."

Justice wrapped his arms around her, hugging her back to his chest, his chin on top of her head. "What happened?"

"Cindy brought a few joints and I was...shocked."

He hesitated. "It's not uncommon for someone her age—"

"I know. But Rebecca Rothschild Wade's daughters did not smoke pot." Another smile took Fallon by surprise. "That's what Mom said whenever we did something she disapproved of. I once got a D on a paper because I hadn't studied, and she gave me this look, then said, 'The daughter of Rebecca Rothschild Wade always does her best—and, Fallon, this is not your best.'"

Justice nuzzled her temple. "I like your mom."

"Me, too."

"So you girls were cutting loose a little, having fun, and something went wrong?"

"I didn't cut loose," she protested, twisting to see him. "I've never in my life smoked pot."

He smoothed back her bangs. "Such a good girl."

"No," she whispered. "I wasn't." A deep breath helped her to continue. "Cindy was teasing me, trying to egg me into trying it, calling me chicken and Goody Two-shoes. I decided to get even, so I went to the front window and pretended our parents had showed up. I acted all panicked, like we were caught."

Justice kept her close. "But they weren't there?"

"No. We were still very much alone on a deserted country road in an isolated area on a lake."

Worry darkened his expression. "Shit."

"Yeah." An understatement. "Cindy panicked, which cracked me up because she was twenty-one and usually did whatever she wanted. But like me, she didn't want to upset Mom. So she tried to throw everything in the trash."

Justice guessed, "Only the ash was still hot and the trash caught on fire?"

"It spread so fast." Fallon hated to relive it all. She saw again the flames licking out from beneath the cabinet, the way Cindy tried to drag out the can but ended up tipping it over. "Everything was so old and brittle, it seemed one moment I was laughing at her, and then suddenly the fire went everywhere. To the cabinets and walls." Her throat closed up. "On Cindy."

Justice crushed her close. "God, babe, I'm so sorry."

She fisted her hands against him. "I tried to help her, but I couldn't get the flames out and then she wasn't moving. I couldn't breathe. I couldn't breathe!"

Justice rocked her, his hold tight. "Shh. I'm so sorry. It's okay now."

"I got hurt. Cindy died and I got hurt."

He froze.

"I left her, Justice." Tears ran down her face and she choked with shame and remembered pain. "I left her."

"You escaped," he insisted.

If she'd kept her head, they both might have lived. But instead, she'd left her poor sister behind in a shack engulfed in flames.

Justice gave her a small shake. *"You survived."*

True, she had. And she didn't know if she could ever forgive herself. "I got as far as the porch before the overhang caved in on me." Memories flowed over her and she absently rubbed her shoulder. "I got pinned for a minute by burning wood."

Horrified, Justice stared down at her. In a tortured rasp, he asked, "Burned?"

She pushed back from him, one step and then two. Making herself look him in the eyes, she nodded. "My shoulder and part of my chest."

Breathing harshly, he listened, his gaze never leaving hers.

"In the car...when you touched me..." There was so much emotion in his face, but she didn't know how to read it. "I didn't want to take you by surprise."

Very slowly, he inhaled, then reached out a hand to her.

Uncertain, wary, she accepted, twining her fingers with his.

He tugged her in close, pressed his mouth to her forehead, her bruised cheek, then briefly to her mouth. "Will you show me?"

Her hand, so small in his, trembled just a little. The look on her face...so much devastation broke Justice's heart. He wished for a way to change the past, to make it easier for her, but she'd so obviously suffered, not only the physical pain but the emotional torture she'd put herself through since then.

His heart beat heavily as he led Fallon into his house. He didn't take her far, stopping just inside the closed front door. He'd given her a tour earlier, not that there was that much to see. But having her near his bedroom, even for those few minutes, had truly tested his resolve.

He sang a litany in his head: she wants to talk, she wants to talk.

If he'd known what she had to say, he'd have been better prepared. But he never would have guessed...

"Will the rest of the flowers be okay?" She shifted, crossed her arms and uncrossed them. "We should probably get them into the ground. Or at least set them in the shade. If you want, I could—"

By cupping her face and kissing her, Justice ended her nervous questions. It wasn't a hungry kiss, but one that, maybe, showed her how much he cared.

Against her lips, he rasped, "It's killing me, honey."

She tentatively flattened her hands to his bare chest. "What?"

"Thinking about you hurt." Closing his arms around her again, he pressed her head to his shoulder.

"Mother was hurt more." Her fingers, cool against his feverish skin, idly stroked him. "She had to make funeral preparations from the hospital."

When her voice broke, Justice damn near broke, too. He tangled a hand in her hair, squeezing her a bit more, needing the contact, wanting to get her as close to his heart as he could.

"She never left me. Every time I opened my eyes she was there. If she didn't know I'd awakened, I'd catch her crying very, very quietly. But…but as soon as she'd see me, she'd smile and touch me and tell me she…loved me."

Tears stung Justice's eyes and he fucking couldn't bear it. God, what her mother must have gone through. No one should ever have to be that strong. And her dad… Mr. Wade was so controlled, so dignified, but Justice knew the guy had to have broken down. How could he not?

As if she'd read his thoughts, Fallon whispered, "Dad was there a lot, too. He always looked so grim, so heartsick. But he, too, would smile at me—like somehow everything would be okay."

Her voice had faded until Justice could barely hear her. "I respect your parents a lot."

"They're amazing." She hesitated, drew a breath. "I was in the hospital for three weeks, so I missed the funeral. It was the only time I was there alone."

And it was probably the worst time to be alone. Not that it could have been helped. His heart ached for her and for her parents.

Justice didn't think about it. He just scooped her up and headed to the couch, then sat down with her in his lap.

Fallon didn't complain. She settled against him with a sigh. "I haven't talked about it much. Mom and Dad...it hurts them still. And not many other people know about it."

"When Leese and I did research, we didn't see anything about you being hurt."

She lifted her head to look at him. "Leese?"

"Yeah, remember we bodyguards do some background checking before taking a case." And going forward, Justice would remember how thorough that important step should be. "Leese is better at it than I am, but he didn't see anything about you being hurt. If he had, he would have told me."

"Money can buy a lot of privacy," Fallon said. "Hired guards stood watch outside my room while I was in the hospital so no one could come up to ask me questions without Dad knowing. There was already too much about Cindy...dying."

She had a hard time saying it, Justice noticed, as if the pain from the loss was still fresh.

"People speculated on how Mom and Dad might feel, and reporters constantly tried to get the inside scoop. Because of who he is and his financial influence, Dad had to make a statement, but he didn't mention me. He didn't want me put under the spotlight, too."

"It was a very personal matter," Justice agreed. "No one else had the right to prod any of you."

She nodded, waiting a moment or two, then whispered, "I wanted out of that hospital so badly, but they couldn't do the skin graft for seven days. Burns like mine require wound care first. Because of the damage...from the fire..."

Justice stroked her hair.

"The wounds can worsen for the first few days."

So even after she was safe in a hospital, her injuries didn't improve? As she talked, she seemed calmer about it and he wondered if she'd gotten to share with anyone. Getting things out in the open, his mom always said, was the best way to deal with them.

But if her involvement in the fire was kept secret, and her parents were so obviously grieving, had Fallon been given the chance to talk to *anyone*?

Somehow he didn't think so. "Will you tell me about it?"

"Why?"

"Because it happened to you, and I care."

She watched him, maybe gauging his sincerity, then nodded. "When they took the skin from the donor site, in a lot of ways that was more painful."

"Worse than the burns?"

She nodded. "They take that whole top layer of skin, down to the nerves. The nerves are alive and exposed—"

Jesus. He hugged her again.

Suddenly she skipped ahead, maybe sparing him some of the uglier details. "When I was finally able to go home, I still had a month of care, and I had to wear a compression vest and sleeve for what felt like forever."

"How long?"

She wrinkled her nose and admitted, "More than a year."

He whistled low.

Fallon surprised him with a half smile. "They weren't very comfortable, but they supposedly helped with scarring."

It wasn't the physical scarring that concerned him. "You're okay now?"

Her brows twitched, like maybe she thought he didn't understand. "Yes, I'm fine." Then she stressed, "But I'm *scarred*."

Though Justice didn't give a shit about any stupid scars, clearly Fallon did. "Where?"

She touched her shoulder and partially down her chest toward her breast. "Those are the worst ones." Glancing at him, she smoothed a hand over her thigh, too. "I've got another one here, but not from being burned. It's the donor site, where they took skin from my thigh to graft onto the burns."

His big hand settled over her thigh. "I hate that you had so much pain." Then, before she could say anything, he asked, "Will you show me?" To him, the best way to prove to her that it didn't matter was to get it out in the open. After that, they could move on.

Her gaze clashed with his. She looked horrified by the idea of baring herself to him. Horrified, but also resigned.

Eventually she nodded. "If you really want to see."

Oh, he wanted to see every single inch of her. And since the burn marks were such a problem for her, they'd start there. "I do."

She warned, "I won't drop my pants."

"Spoilsport," he teased, trying to lighten her fatalistic mood.

Her mouth opened, she paused, then closed it. It took her another second to say, "I can open my shirt."

Justice nodded. "Yeah." He had to be a heartless perv because even now, with such a sensitive concern for her, he felt himself stirring. Hell, he couldn't joke with her about dropping pants and opening blouses without getting a little turned on. He wouldn't do a damned thing about it, but it was happening all the same.

She sat up on his lap, half facing him, and her fingers went to the buttons on her shirt.

He held his breath.

Timidly, she opened one button, peeked at him, then opened another. He could see her upper chest now and just a hint of cleavage.

Keeping his hands to himself wasn't easy. He really wanted to help her hurry along. Being passive while a woman on his lap undressed was a new thing for him.

But then, a woman like Fallon was new, too, and he'd never dealt with an issue like hers.

Attempting to relax, he hooked one hand around her waist, leaving the other to rest on her thigh.

Sounding hoarse, he said, "You don't have to be shy with me."

"It's not that," she promised. "It's just…"

Heightened awareness had a stranglehold on him. "What?"

"They're ugly."

"They're just scars," he chided.

"Marcus thought that, too, until he saw them, then—"

"Fallon."

At his gentle rebuke, she lifted her brows.

"Don't compare me to that dick, okay?"

Nodding, she squared her shoulders, opened three more buttons and with a lot of palpable dread, pulled the loosened material down her right shoulder, taking her bra strap down at the same time.

Justice had difficulty getting his gaze off her face. She looked to be in an agony of suspense while she awaited judgment.

Silly woman. Finally he looked down.

He could only see a little of the mark, and as he'd suspected, it looked like what it was—scarring. He wasn't squeamish about it, and to prove it to her, he lightly traced the uppermost raised edges of her skin with a fingertip.

She would have recoiled, but he spread his fingers open on her back and kept her still.

Because he couldn't see much of it, Justice asked, "How big is it?"

Hesitantly, she opened three more buttons.

The puckered, damaged skin spread out in an arc over her shoulder, midway down her bicep on her arm, over to the bottom of her collarbone and feathered into the swelling of her breast. The skin was thicker, a darker pink, little tails reaching out in different directions.

Seeing the evidence of what she'd suffered made Justice swallow hard. Only the fact that she might misconstrue sympathy or concern kept him from reacting in any way.

"Anywhere else?" he asked.

Her confusion obvious, Fallon shook her head. She was so stiff that she looked ready to break. "Well, on my thigh. I told you that." Strain left her voice thready. "It's not as irregular."

He started to say more when he heard a car pull into his drive. He glanced through the window and saw Leese parking.

Before he ran out of time, Justice carefully pulled the material back together and closed the buttons.

"Justice?"

He drew her in for a soft kiss before explaining, "We have company."

She blinked fast. "We do?"

He smiled at her obvious confusion. She'd had herself all prepared for him to react a certain way, but he hadn't and now she didn't know what to say or do. No doubt she wondered what he thought, but she wasn't ready to hear the truth, and he needed time to figure out his next move.

"Leese is here." He lifted her to her feet just as the knock sounded on the front door. Stepping around her, Justice opened it.

"We have to talk," Leese said as he stepped in—then drew up short when he noticed Fallon. He stalled. "Sorry. I didn't realize you had company."

Fallon blurted, "We were planting flowers."

Biting off his grin, Justice nodded. "Yeah, that's exactly what we were doing."

Leese elbowed him. "Don't embarrass her, you ass." He turned to smile at Fallon. "Ms. Wade. How are you?"

"Fallon, please. And I'm well." She flashed a worried, uncertain look at Justice. "I'll just...go work on the flowers while you two talk."

"I'll only be a minute," Justice promised.

Once she'd politely pulled the door closed behind her, Leese slowly turned to stare at him.

"Shut up."

"I didn't say anything."

"But you're going to." Justice walked over to the window and saw Fallon standing there by the flowers, staring down at the grass, unmoving. Something inside him shifted, as if making room for unfamiliar emotions. It wasn't a comfortable feeling—but it wasn't bad either.

"She was in the fire," Leese said.

If he expected a big reaction, he'd be disappointed. "Just found that out for myself."

"She told you?"

"Yeah." Justice headed into the kitchen for a drink. "She has some scars and is really touchy about them."

"From what I read, it was pretty damned awful."

It was, but Justice felt the need to protect her privacy. "What'd you find?"

"One of the companies her father owns did a small report about it, mostly to let other employees know so they could share their condolences. Mr. Wade found out and squashed it, but you know how that goes. Digital trails are never completely erased."

"Her father didn't want her hassled. I don't blame him."

Leese leaned against the kitchen counter while Justice poured tea. "I wanted to talk to you about something else, too."

Determination rushed through Justice. He hated that Fallon had suffered, that she undervalued her physical appeal now, and he really wanted to go stomp on Marcus because he just knew the bastard had further damaged her delicate ego. Even more than that, he wanted to prove to her that the scars, no matter how harsh, in no way detracted from her appeal.

However, he didn't want Leese to know anything about it, so he shrugged and said, "Shoot. I'm all ears."

"I heard she took a fall down the steps last night."

"Yeah." And Justice really felt guilty about it. "I thought she was right behind me but—"

Leese interrupted to say, "Someone called the agency with an accusation."

Justice paused with the tea halfway to his mouth. "The hell you say. Who called?"

"Anonymous."

Very slowly, he set the tea aside. "To accuse me of *what*?"

Leese shook his head as he stepped away from the counter. "The guy who called claims he saw Tom with Fallon."

A smoldering anger softened Justice's tone when he asked, "Doing what?"

"Well…" Leese rubbed the back of his neck. "Supposedly he was giving her a shove—down the stairs."

Fallon tried to hide her hurt as Justice unexpectedly hustled her to the car and drove her home. He'd been in such a rush to get rid of her, he'd barely given her time to wash the dirt from her hands.

When she'd protested that there was one more flower to go in the ground, Leese offered to do it.

But damn it, *she* wanted to plant that flower.

And she wanted to know Justice's thoughts.

He'd looked at her, at the evidence of her burns and what she'd caused to happen five years ago…but he hadn't said a word. Was he repulsed?

No. Justice wasn't like that.

But had his interest turned to pity? That she could believe. Above all else, Justice was protective. He'd seemed as bothered by the retelling of the ordeal as she'd been.

So what had she expected to happen? For him to tell her it didn't matter? To say he would overlook the fact that he was her bodyguard and she was a scarred mess and that they'd…what?

Date?

Humiliation left her sick to her stomach. She was a complete fool to think—

"Thanks for planting the flowers." Reaching across the seat, Justice took her hand.

She badly wanted to hang on to him, to draw on his strength, but instead she squeezed his hand, said, "No problem. I enjoyed it," and pulled away.

He was so lost in thought, he barely seemed to notice. She wasn't used to him being this remote. Even that very first day, he'd been more...personal.

As soon as he pulled up in front of the house, she removed her seat belt. "You don't have to walk me in."

He scowled and put the car in Park. "Yeah, I do." He got out and crossed around to her even though she'd already left the car and was halfway up the steps.

When he reached her, he took her elbow. "Fallon—"

Oh, God no. She couldn't hear this, not yet. Not now. She turned to him and forced a bright smile. "Make sure you water those flowers when you get home. I'd hate for them to all die. Your mom wouldn't be happy."

He quirked a smile. "Can't have her unhappy."

She waited.

Suddenly his cell pinged. He pulled it from his pocket for a quick look, scowled some more and said, "I gotta run. Thanks again, honey." And with that, he turned and left.

He hadn't mentioned going to his friend's tonight. Did he plan to cancel? Given his rush in leaving, she should probably assume so.

Of course, she could ask... *No.*

It was all she could do to hold it together. If she started asking questions, she'd force him to make excuses.

She couldn't go through that again.

Glad that her parents weren't yet home, Fallon watched Justice drive away before going inside, doggedly climbing the stairs to her bedroom, then sitting down to cry.

CHAPTER ELEVEN

Justice strode into the rec center, his gaze scanning the interior as he looked for Tom. He didn't notice anyone else or anything else, so he was surprised when suddenly Armie stood in front of him. He almost plowed him over.

Mildly, Armie said, "Justice. What's up?"

"S'Tom here?" He continued to look past Armie—until his friend stepped closer. Backing up a step, Justice barked, "What the hell?"

Still casual, Armie asked, "Can I talk to you a minute?"

"I'm busy."

"Let's talk." He gave Justice a shove toward the front desk, away from the workout gear and padded mats crowded with fighters, both new and veteran.

Frustrated, Justice decided it'd be easier to deal with Armie than ignore him. He found an isolated corner and turned to say, "Make it quick."

Armie nodded. "Want to tell me what's going on?"

"No." Bristling with impatience, he asked, "S'that it?"

Shaking his head, Armie denied him. "Sorry, dude, but the thing is, you look ready to commit murder and I have a class of kids coming by in an hour. Don't want them to have to wade through blood and guts and shit like that, so take a breath, get a grip, and tell me what's going on."

The hell he would! "None of your business."

"It is if it involves the rec center."

Justice growled. Armie might be smaller than him, but that didn't make him small. He was the best fighter Justice had ever known. Lightning quick reflexes, unending endurance, deceptive strength and a twisted sense of loyalty to his friends.

Which meant he wanted to save Justice from himself.

Sighing, Justice gave up and explained what had transpired.

Armie listened, nodding occasionally, then asked, "Remember what I told you about facing off with a real asshole?"

"Yeah. Keep my cool."

"You are currently not cool, Justice."

Couldn't argue with that. Hell, from his toes to his ears, he was bunched up and ready for violence.

Didn't faze Armie though. "I'm not buying that Tom had anything to do with it, and until you have proof, you shouldn't buy it either. Anything anonymous pisses me off."

"Yeah, that part pissed me off, too."

"Looks to me like every part pissed you off. But my point is that you shouldn't put too much stock into an anonymous accusation."

"I didn't." Or had he? "I was just going to talk to him."

"Fine. Talk to him, hear what he has to say. But it's guaranteed he's going to blow up—same as you or I would over an accusation like that—so *you* have to keep it together to get the facts."

Justice hated to admit it, but Armie made sense.

"Can you really see Tom hurting a woman?"

Not really. But the bastard was awful pushy about a rematch. Justice drew a deep breath, let it out real slow and felt some of the tension seep from his muscles. "Got it. Now get out of my way."

"He's in the locker room." Grinning, Armie clapped him on

the shoulder and warned, "Know this, Justice—if any punches get thrown, I'm going to stomp both of you." And with that he returned to instructing some newer fighters.

Justice barked a short laugh. Now that he'd cooled down, he had to admit he appreciated Armie's interference. He didn't want to cause a scene, especially with kids coming in soon. It was a known fact that any dishonorable behavior at the rec center could get a guy kicked to the curb.

When Cannon had started the club, the primary use was for the guys to train. But because of Cannon and Armie, who were longtime best friends, it had soon become an integral part of the community. Now fighters at every level trained there, women took self-defense classes, at-risk kids had an outlet and positive influence, and it all appeared seamless because everyone took turns helping out by teaching, cleaning and training.

Though he was MMA's fastest rising star, Armie was still the one who usually organized everything. He had more energy than any three people combined and shared a special affinity for the rec center's origins and purpose.

With a new mindset, Justice started off again. He'd talk to Tom, gauge his reaction and then decide what to do.

Steam filled the locker room when he walked in. Fresh from a shower, Tom sat on a bench wearing only jeans while he pulled on shoes and socks. He glanced up, said, "Hey, Justice," and went back to dressing.

Same congenial greeting as always.

Folding his arms over his chest and leaning back against a set of lockers, Justice studied him.

Brows lifted, Tom sat up straighter and asked, "What?"

"You said Fallon was pushed down the steps."

"Elbowed. Some scruffy little dude who disappeared right after."

"You didn't bother to grab the guy?"

"With Fallon tumbling down the steps? I was more concerned with getting to her."

Justice slowly nodded. "You were there, looming over her, when I reached you both."

"I wasn't looming, you ass." Starting to sound irritated, Tom said, "Everyone knows she's with you."

Well, hell. "I'm her bodyguard."

"Yeah, keep spinning that tale if you want, but no one's buying it." Tom eyed him. "Gotta admit, she's different from the usual babes you like."

Since he didn't want to compare Fallon with the very casual relationships he'd had in the past, Justice bypassed the comment. "So why were you trailing her?"

"I wasn't." Tom sat straighter, his brows knit together. "Okay, so I was hoping to chew your ear a little more, try to talk some sense into you about the rematch. But then I saw Fallon veer off from you. Right after that, she started getting jostled and down she went. Hard as she fell, I didn't know if she'd broken anything or knocked herself out."

That all sounded plausible. "You think the guy elbowed her on purpose?"

"Sure looked like it to me."

"Seems like a hell of a coincidence that you were right there when it happened, but didn't grab the guy who supposedly caused her fall."

Slowly, Tom came to his feet. "If you're accusing me of something, get on with it."

Justice could see the anger starting to spark. Tom had never had great control. As to that, Justice often didn't either, but he was learning. From Leese, from Armie. And good thing, too, because a showdown between two pissed-off heavyweights didn't always end well. "Just asking."

"You know what?" Tom stepped closer, his stance combative.

"I *did* watch her once I saw she was alone and looking a little lost. Where the hell were you, Justice?"

He rolled a shoulder. "We got separated. Soon as I realized it, I backtracked to get her."

"Not in time."

Justice couldn't deny that.

Crowding closer still, Tom growled, "You should be thanking me for being there. She might've gotten trampled otherwise."

He was so obviously looking for a fight, Justice had to wonder if Tom would stoop that low just to get his attention, to maybe force a confrontation. Anything was possible, and when it came to Fallon's welfare, he planned to cover all his bases.

Without retreating, Justice relaxed his stance in a deceptive way.

If Tom lunged, he'd flatten him.

"Someone," he said casually, watching Tom's reaction, "called the agency where I work."

"Yeah, who?"

"Whoever it was didn't leave his name."

Bristling with impatience, Tom waited.

"The caller said you were with Fallon."

"You already knew that. I was..." Blank surprise wiped every other emotion off Tom's face, quickly replaced with indignation. "Wait a minute. You accusing me of something?"

Justice stared at him.

Clenching with outrage, Tom said, "If you think I had anything to do with her getting hurt—"

Justice relaxed. Tom suddenly looked apoplectic, and not with guilt but insult. "You didn't push her?"

"No, I didn't fucking push her! *I don't mistreat ladies!*"

"Take it easy."

"You take it easy!"

Justice laughed. Good thing Armie had forced that little talk on him or they'd be throwing punches right now. And where would that get him? He didn't really suspect Tom, not anymore, but he wouldn't entirely let him off the hook either, not until he found out what was going on.

"Relax," Justice said. "Given the information I have, I had to ask."

"I will not relax!" Tom practically heaved with fury. "How the hell would you feel if I accused you of doing something like that?"

"I'd be pissed." Because Justice knew for a fact he'd never hurt a woman.

Tom threw up his arms in an "exactly" pose. "Going after your lady would be chickenshit."

"Agreed."

"I'm not chickenshit."

Justice shrugged. Eventually Tom would understand that he wouldn't get a qualifying fight in the cage, so maybe he thought to rile Justice by using Fallon. Would he be content with an old-fashioned beat down in private, out of the limelight?

"I'll take you at your word," Justice said.

"Well, hallelujah, you prick."

"But stay away from Fallon."

Justice's attitude only infuriated Tom more.

Not that Justice cared. Because if it wasn't Tom, he'd need to figure out who *did* push her—and why someone wanted Tom blamed.

A few hours later, when her mother checked in on her, Fallon pretended to be napping. She didn't want her mother to see her swollen eyes. Tears were useless—she knew that, and she was now ashamed that she'd given in to them.

She had no intention of sharing her grief with her mother or father. It would only upset them. She'd learned years ago how badly they reacted to any show of sadness.

Keeping her eyes closed, Fallon expected her mother to turn

around and leave—instead, she sat on the side of the bed and shook her.

"Fallon, wake up!"

The urgency in her mother's tone startled her and she came up to an elbow before she thought better of it. "What? What's the matter?"

Her mother got one good look at her and sat back in horror. "You've been crying!" She looked more closely, then gasped. "And dear God, you're bruised!"

Rushing to reassure her, Fallon explained, "I fell, that's all. I'm fine."

Her mother scowled with accusation. "If you're fine, then why have you been crying?"

No immediate answer came to mind, so Fallon stalled. "Why did you wake me, Mom? What's wrong? Has something happened?"

As if only then remembering, her mother stood and said, "We'll talk about your fall later. Right now you have to hurry. Justice is downstairs and he's talking to your father." She added with emphasis, *"Alone."*

A dousing with ice water wouldn't have been as shocking. "Justice is here?"

"Yes. He wants to see you, as well, but first he said he needed a private word with your father."

No way. Fallon threw back the covers, stood, and then paused. Confusion warred with urgency. "Did he say what he wants?"

Her mother shook her head. "He didn't, but he looks different and very determined, and he was insistent that he had to talk to Clayton first before I came to get you."

Dejection made her chest tight. Justice was here to quit. Sinking back to sit on the side of the bed, Fallon folded her hands and concentrated on not looking lost. "I can't interrupt them."

"Why not?"

She sighed, searched for an out, but finally decided that she'd have to tell the truth. "I showed Justice my scars."

Her mother's eyes widened, then immediately softened. "And?"

"I don't know."

Her mother quickly sat beside her and took her hand. "Tell me everything that happened."

It was beyond embarrassing, but Fallon needed someone to talk to, so she shared it all without admitting that Marcus had seen them first, or his reaction.

"Justice was silent all the way home." Fallon drew a breath. "I think... I think he's probably quitting."

Her mother pushed to her feet. "Go down there and confront him. Tell him you deserve to know what he's doing."

"Mom! I can't do that."

"Oh, yes, you can, young lady!" She tugged Fallon to her feet, quickly smoothed her hair, straightened her now wrinkled clothing and stepped back. "There. Much better."

Fallon knew that was a lie. She looked horrible. "Mom—"

"You will get yourself downstairs this instant, young lady. Rebecca Rothschild Wade's daughter does not cower in her bedroom."

Hearing her mom reprimand her like a schoolgirl, Fallon half smiled. "I'm not a child any longer."

"Exactly. Now let's go."

Before Fallon could think of a way to dissuade her mother, she had the door open and was prodding Fallon into the hall. She was so emotionally distraught, it seemed easier to give in than to fight her mother.

In the end, what difference would it make if she heard from Justice face-to-face, or if her father had to explain things to her?

Halfway down the steps, raised voices caused Fallon and her mother both to pause. *Justice and her father were arguing!*

The men were in the dining room. Through the open archway, Fallon could see Justice's profile—and his appearance further shocked her.

He'd shaved! Gone was the sexy scruff she liked so much; his goatee was now neatly trimmed. And…and his hair was cut short to the same length all over, eliminating his messy fauxhawk!

She blinked twice trying to take it in.

In his usual jeans, but with a black polo shirt that hugged his massive shoulders, he still looked gorgeous, yet also very, very different.

What did it mean?

And then she heard him say, "Quitting is the only option."

Even though she'd expected it, the truth hit her so hard, she had to slap a hand to her mouth to keep from making a sound.

How had he come to mean so much to her in such a short time? *Why had she so stupidly let that happen?*

"I'm paying you," her father insisted.

Above her hurt, Fallon's pride rebelled. She would not let her father beg for Justice's service.

"This is pointless," Justice replied, just as irate. "Whether you pay me or not, I'm not budging. I'd be looking out for her anyway. It's personal now, not business."

Wait…*what?*

Trying to understand, Fallon gulped in air. How could he be her bodyguard if he quit? She glanced at her mother, and found her smiling. Even more confused now, Fallon turned back to stare at Justice.

"You say that like it's your decision," her father barked. "Fallon has some say in this, too, you know."

"I'll convince her." Justice folded his arms in what she now recognized as an arrogant and determined stance. "And since I'll be dating her, it'd be ludicrous for you to pay me as a bodyguard."

Dating her?

Before she fell down the steps in an ignominious heap, Fallon hurried down the rest of the way. "What's going on? Justice, what are you talking about? Why are the two of you shouting?"

Justice turned fast, saw her face and scowled. "What happened to you?"

Her father pushed rudely past him. "You've been crying."

"Crying?" Justice repeated. Then he glared at her father. "You made her cry?"

"Me?" He glowered right back. "I've only just gotten home!"

Her mother said, "I believe it was you, Justice, who did the damage."

"Mother!" Fallon knew a blush would add nothing to her ravaged appearance. She was such an ugly crier. With the very first tear her nose turned red, her eyes got puffy and blotches marred her cheeks.

"Dear God." Slowly, her father stepped closer, his gaze examining her face. With blood in his eyes, he pivoted to face Justice. "How did she get bruised?"

Fallon couldn't believe the level of accusation in her father's tone. "I fell down some steps, Dad, that's all."

"You *fell*?" he asked, incredulous.

"Yes, and it's absurd for you to act like Justice had anything to do with it."

"It is partially my fault," Justice said, willingly taking blame. "I should have had hold of her—"

Her father gaped at him, maybe because he didn't want Justice holding her.

Before this debacle could get any worse, Fallon redirected a frown at Justice. "We should talk privately."

He shook his head, refusing her, then wagged a finger from her to himself and back again. "Something's going on between us. You know it as well as I do. I'm trying to be upfront with your folks about it."

Furious, her father said to her, "He took advantage of you,

made you cry, allowed you to get hurt and now he wants to quit."

Her mother said, "Hush, Clayton. Let them talk."

"He wants to talk about *dating* her!"

"Yes, I know." Unlike her father, her mother sounded pleased.

"He is completely unsuitable—"

"That's enough!" Not about to let her dad interfere, Fallon huffed out a breath. "Justice did not take advantage of me, falling was my own fault and if he wants to quit, well—" It would break her heart, but she didn't want to guilt him into staying.

Justice took a step toward Fallon. "I know it shouldn't have happened, honey. On every level it was wrong. But I'm already more than a bodyguard and we both know it. I'm tired of being hampered by ethics."

"Of all the—"

"Clayton," her mother snapped, her voice shrill, "I told you to hush!"

He clamped his mouth shut and settled on an evil scowl.

Justice and Fallon both ignored her parents.

"I'll talk to my boss tomorrow, tell her how I screwed up and accept the consequences there. But understand, Fallon, regardless of anything else, you're stuck with me."

"Stuck with you?" She had a hard time taking it in.

"Yeah." He came closer still. "Whether Sahara blackballs me out of the industry, or your dad kicks my butt to the curb, even if you don't want to see me on a more personal level, there's no way in hell I'm going to let anything happen to you."

Her mother sighed happily.

"You can't just shadow her," her father barked. "It's absurd."

Justice touched her face, skimming his fingers over her bruise. "Why were you crying?"

No way would she explain it to him now, not with her parents both watching so avidly. "Would you step outside with me?"

He nodded. "After you tell me I can quit our business association and move on to a personal relationship."

Her teeth locked. She did not appreciate the forced confrontation.

"I want you protecting her," her mother said, smoothing over the moment. "Especially with that confusion the other night."

"Confusion?" Her dad jumped on that. "What confusion?"

"I'll explain in a minute," her mom said to soothe him before turning back to Justice. "However, I agree with Clayton. We must continue to pay."

Justice took a hard stance. "I'm not accepting your money."

"You," her father snapped, "signed a contract!" Then he stomped away.

"There, that's settled." Fallon's mother hugged her, and surprised Justice by hugging him, too. "I'm so pleased." She turned and went after her husband, already detailing the issue with the paint, the added camera on the driveway and Justice's concerns.

Justice cursed low, his demeanor rife with frustration. "Your parents are going to be really disappointed when things don't go their way."

Fallon's heart tripped with uncertainty and with...hope. "Meaning?"

"I won't take money to be with you. It wouldn't be right." He stared at her intently, his voice going gruff. "Ah, babe, I can't bear to see you cry."

"I'm not." Not anymore, though she knew she still looked hideous.

His fingers brushed over her cheek. "It hurts that much?"

"I'm not a wimp." Insulted, she attempted to explain. "It wasn't the fall. It's just that I thought...the way you brought me home, and you were so silent, I wasn't sure..." She sighed. How could she find out what was going on if she couldn't even finish a coherent sentence? Everything felt so awkward. She detested making a fool of herself. She detested the idea of not seeing Justice.

She detested being a coward.

As if it were the most natural thing in the world, Justice gathered her into his arms and pressed his warm mouth to hers, lingering for several seconds. His hand cradled the side of her face, his touch so incredibly gentle.

"I don't understand," she finally said, and to get to the point, she stated, "You saw my scars."

"Yeah, I saw them."

His matter-of-fact acknowledgment only bewildered her further. "I have more," she thought to remind him. "On my leg from the donor site and—"

"I know." His hands, so big and hot—*she loved his hands*—stroked up and down her back while his breathing went deeper. Against her lips, he murmured, "I want to see that one, too."

All but smothering in confusion, Fallon stared up at him. "Why?"

"They're a part of you, and every part of you fascinates me." He kissed her again, stroked her bottom lip with his tongue, then lightly tugged on it with his teeth.

"Justice…"

Almost in accusation, he said, "You opened your top and I got hard, babe. I *hate* that you were hurt. I wish I could take the memories from you. But damn, did you really think a scar or two would matter so much?"

Of course she did, because the scars had mattered to everyone else. They obviously repulsed Marcus, despite his current regret and assertions that they didn't. Seeing them still made her parents weepy. And the memories associated with them… She swallowed hard, nodded and said, "Yes."

He gave her a small, sexy smile. "I'm just a man, and anytime a gorgeous woman starts opening her top, I react." Voice even lower, he confessed, "If I hadn't gotten away from you, I'd have done things ass-backward, shaming the agency and myself."

"What do you mean?"

His hands went suggestively to her hips as he looked down her body. "If you'd dropped your pants…" His nostrils flared with a deep breath, then he half laughed as he let it out. "It's a fact I wouldn't be able to keep my hands off you."

So even after seeing the disfiguring marks on her, marks that spread out to one of her breasts, he still wanted her?

"I'm trying to be honorable and upfront," Justice asserted. "That's what you deserve."

Fallon really needed clarification. "You weren't…" How did she ask him? "That is…"

His mouth took hers again, a little hungrier, a little less restrained. When he pulled back, he rasped, "You're killing me here, honey."

She blurted, "You want me to believe the scars didn't bother you at all?"

"They almost leveled me." He closed his arms around her, hugging her in close to his broad chest. "If I could somehow go back in time and take the hurt for you, I swear to God I would." Levering her back again, he gave her a look so serious, so stern, she held her breath. "But in no way did they make me want you any less. Hell, I'm not sure anything could."

Fallon thought of the scars, of what he'd seen and how he'd reacted, and she badly wanted to believe him.

His dark eyes stared into hers. "Tell me you want me, too, and I promise I'll prove it to you."

She nodded in quick confirmation. "I do." As soon as the words left her mouth, heat filled her cheeks. That sounded far too much like an acceptance of marriage. "I mean—"

Smiling, Justice gave her a quick smooch. "Too late to take it back now." He smoothed a hand over her hair. "We need to get going if we want to make it to Cannon's on time. You about ready?"

Oh, good grief! "We're still going there?"

"You don't want to?"

"I do!" Damn it, she'd said it again. "I just thought—"

"A bunch of nonsense, that's what you thought." His gaze moved over her, but he didn't seem repulsed by the signs of her tears either.

Apparently, nothing bothered him.

"I'd like you to get to know the guys even better, and their wives will be there again. You like everyone, right?"

"Yes. They're all very nice."

"They're the best." Obviously relieved, he brushed a thumb over the corner of her mouth and asked, "You ready to go?"

Fallon loved how he kept touching her, like he couldn't resist. He made her feel pretty, when she knew she currently looked wretched in every way possible. "No, of course I'm not ready."

As if he really didn't see it, Justice asked, "Why not?"

She had to laugh. He was such an elemental male, so accepting, that he lightened her world just by being in it. "I'm a total wreck, Justice, that's why. I have to change my wrinkled clothes and repair my face and…"

"You're beautiful," he whispered.

Those words were so soft and earnest, she could have sworn her heart melted. "Justice—"

"Every part of you, Fallon." Looking and sounding utterly sincere, he teased her lips with a butterfly kiss. "I'm going to keep saying it until you believe it."

Hand to her mouth, she half cried, half laughed. "You're nuts."

He leaned closer to whisper, "Let's blame prolonged horniness, okay?" With a light swat on her butt, he added, "Now get a move on before your folks come back to grill me again."

"Five minutes," she promised, and ran up the steps, anxious to return to him.

Today, she decided, everything would be different.

Marcus checked his watch, then stared at his two companions. He grew impatient waiting for them to negotiate the lofty proposal for their participation. "I have to get going soon." He knew they would reject his first request, but he also assumed they'd give something, even if it was more meager than what he'd asked for. In business, Marcus had always found it beneficial to start high and gradually concede, rather than start out too low.

"Meeting up with your girlfriend?" Kern Arnold, the oldest of the two brothers, asked as he closed the file he'd been perusing. Kern turned to his brother, York. "What's her name again?"

"Fallon," York supplied with a sly grin. "And she's a cutie."

"She is," Kern agreed, resting his arms on the table. "Cute, apparently smart and obviously from a good family. She's a catch, Marcus."

Marcus detested these personal questions, but he wanted the contributions Kern and York would give to the literacy fundraiser. God knew the men could afford it.

At the MMA fights, they'd wagered twenty grand as if it were nothing, and when Kern lost to his younger brother for the third time in a row, he'd only laughed. Apparently York was on a winning streak, because he'd ribbed Kern mercilessly. Marcus was far from a pauper, but still it boggled his mind to see how easily the two men tossed around money.

With a benign smile, Marcus corrected the assumptions. "Actually, I'm meeting with Ms. Wade."

"Ah, the cutie's mom?" York asked.

"Yes." Marcus nodded to the file. "I'm working with her on the fund-raiser."

"Finding a way to edge back in, huh? Clever," Kern praised.

"If the mom approves of you, the daughter will be more inclined."

"Actually," Marcus said, his jaw tensing, "I sincerely wanted to help."

York slapped him on the shoulder and laughed. "What about that big bruiser with her?"

"I told you, he's her bodyguard."

"Uh-huh." York bobbed his brows at his brother. "Looked to me like he was guarding every inch of her body."

"Seemed to be loving his job, too," Kern added with a chuckle.

More irate by the moment, Marcus held silent.

"Who was that other fighter we met? Tomahawk, right?"

Something in the way York asked that, as if he held a private secret, put Marcus on edge. He replied with a clipped, "Yes."

"Tomahawk wants the bodyguard back in the cage. Just think, if he succeeds that'll leave sweet Fallon yours for the taking." Kern gave him a steely-eyed stare. "You could swoop in and be the little darling's protector."

"He could score big," York added, "especially if she's got real need of protection."

Marcus stared at the brothers while fighting the urge to react. Though he recognized there were subtleties afoot that he didn't entirely understand, he still detested hearing the two men discuss Fallon with so little respect. Never mind that he'd screwed up; he still cared for Fallon—for her whole family—but he also wanted the security that would come from such an alliance. One way or another he'd get her back. When she was his wife, spoiled rich boys like Kern and York wouldn't dare malign her.

He forced a smile. "Fallon and I have a history. It'll work out eventually. Now, about the fund-raiser—"

"Count us in," Kern said, sliding the folder back toward him.

Terrific. More than ready to wrap it up, Marcus segued straight into his sales pitch. "If you're ready to commit an amount—"

"The proposal works fine."

Incredulous, Marcus slowly withdrew while searching their faces. Wondering if this was more bullshit, he asked, "All of it?"

"Sure."

York added, "From each of us."

Stunned, Marcus gathered his thoughts. He couldn't keep staring like an idiot. "I see." But to be sure, he opened the file and turned the final figure toward the two men. "You understand—"

Kern gently closed it again and smiled. "We understand perfectly, and we're on board."

Marcus had no idea what to say. He'd have been happy with half as much from one of them, not the full amount from both. "I…" *Shut up and be grateful*, he warned himself. "Thank you. This is wonderful."

York shrugged. "It's a tax write-off."

"Well, whatever your motives for such generosity, I'm very grateful." They were right that getting on Mrs. Rothschild Wade's good side would aid his cause to win back Fallon. Since both ladies cared deeply about the less fortunate, this would be an amazing start.

As if he'd read Marcus's thoughts, Kern smiled. "Let me know when and where you'd like us to present the checks."

Easy, Marcus thought. Maybe *too* easy. Yes, the brothers threw around money, but usually with a wager attached. However, he wouldn't question his good fortune too much.

He didn't want them to renege.

After quickly discussing the arrangements and gaining their signed commitments, Marcus left the bar.

The brothers were spoiled, but he smiled because for once their money would go to very worthy causes—the fund-raiser… and his own.

CHAPTER TWELVE

Justice leaned against a deck post, a beer in hand, and watched while Leese, Catalina, Stack and Vanity chatted with Fallon. It warmed him, seeing his friends become hers.

She deserved more friends. Good friends—like his.

"Did you notice she's as far from the bonfire as she can get?" Armie sounded both curious and puzzled.

Yeah, he had noticed. Fallon had subtly nudged her lawn chair backward—farther and farther—until she was a good ten feet behind everyone else. Without questioning her, the others had gradually relocated, too.

They kept her surrounded and distracted and, in their own unique ways, protected—though they might not realize it.

Miles watched her intently. "Whenever the fire pops, so does she." Even as he said it, wood crackled and Fallon jumped.

But she didn't leave and the pride swelling inside Justice amplified every complicated feeling he had for her until he damn near shook with his need. He'd have to get her alone, and soon. He wanted her—more than he could ever recall wanting anyone or anything.

Armie and Miles stood with Justice, talking quietly while they took turns grilling hamburgers—and noticing Fallon.

They were each still looking at her when Justice explained, "She doesn't advertise it, but she was burned once."

Miles jerked around to stare at him, a frown in place. "Bad?"

Justice couldn't think about what she'd suffered without a resurgence of rage, empathy and an overwhelming desire to shelter her.

"Bad," he quietly confirmed. "Physically and emotionally." So others wouldn't overhear, he explained in a low voice what Fallon had gone through. "When I saw the setup for the party, I told her we didn't have to stay, but she wanted to, even insisted on joining the others around the fire."

"She has guts," Armie remarked with admiration. "I like her."

Miles nodded. "Me, too."

Justice didn't mind admitting it. "I more than like her."

Brows raised, Miles asked, "Is that allowed?"

"Because I'm her bodyguard? Probably not." Justice scrubbed a hand over his face. "For sure, Sahara is going to have a fit."

Armie grinned. "She doesn't know yet?"

"I told Fallon's parents today. They finally accepted it—I think." In fact, Rebecca had seemed to be on his side. Not that he needed their agreement or support, because he'd have gone after Fallon either way. "Tomorrow, first thing, I'll tell Sahara. I figured I should do it face-to-face."

"First Leese and now you," Miles laughingly complained. "I was thinking of checking out the whole bodyguard gig, too, but the boss lady isn't going to like her track record with fighters."

Justice assumed Miles was joking—hell, he still had a long fight career ahead of him. Sure, he'd taken some serious hits in his last fight, but he'd still won.

With concern shadowing his features, Armie stared toward the group around the fire. "It doesn't feel right, letting her do this. Look at her face. She's almost panicked."

True, and her panic put a vise around Justice's heart. More than anything he wanted to go to her, scoop her up and take her away from the source of her torment.

But he also wanted more than that.

"She needs to talk about it. She hasn't had much opportunity to do that. Even when she told me, I could tell it was new for her. For so long now she's kept everything bottled up and I think it's past time she let it out."

"It was a secret?" Miles asked.

"Of sorts," Justice admitted. "Her folks get upset if she mentions it." Before either man could get too riled about that, he added, "They're off-the-charts protective now after losing their other daughter and seeing Fallon so hurt. I'm not sure any of them have really recovered."

"It'd be tough," Armie admitted.

"Her dad was trying to shield Fallon when he kept all mention of her out of the news. He was dealing with his older daughter's funeral and with Fallon in the hospital and his wife's grief...he wanted to spare Fallon from reporters, and in doing that, only a few people even knew she'd been hurt. She couldn't talk about it with anyone even if she'd wanted to."

"Jesus," Armie whispered. "Her poor folks."

"Yeah."

"Good intentions," Miles noted. "I can't even imagine what they were suffering."

"Pure hell." Justice stepped away from his friends and loaded up two hamburgers. "Don't say anything to her yet, but if she gives you an opening—"

"We'll be all ears," Armie promised.

"Make sure you don't show her any pity. She'd hate that."

"Have you told the others?" Miles asked.

"No, but feel free. Just be discreet. I want her to feel accepted, not like the center of gossip." Justice headed off with a plate of food for both of them, drinks in his other hand, and on his way he announced to the collective group, "Food's ready."

That got the desired effect. Everyone headed for the grill, giving Justice a few moments alone with Fallon.

She'd just stood up when he reached her and, hands full, he bent down and settled his mouth over hers with new possessiveness. Knowing others might witness the kiss didn't bother Justice.

He wanted everyone to know about this new facet of their relationship.

As a couple, Fallon would have all the acceptance, backup and loyalty that he had from his friends. She deserved that, and more.

At first she was stiff with surprise, but she quickly melted against him, her hands sliding up his chest and around his neck.

Feeling her small, warm body pressed to his, Justice almost dropped the food, then he caught himself and lifted away. "Hi."

Still leaning against him, her eyes heavy, she smiled. "Hi."

"I missed you." He kissed her again, briefly this time, and then handed her the drinks.

She looked at them a moment before catching up. From the light of the bonfire, Justice watched the blush tinge her cheeks. She took the beers from him.

"If you don't mind sitting here, I'll join you."

"It's fine."

No, it wasn't. Now that he'd reminded her of the fire, the wariness came back into her gaze. "We don't have to stay."

"I want to." She sat down in her lawn chair and took the plate from him so he could pull a chair closer to her. "Could I ask you something, Justice?"

He settled himself beside her. "You can ask me anything."

She surprised him by reaching over and stroking a hand over his smoothly shaven jaw. "Why did you change so much?"

"Change?"

Her smile was gentle and curious. "The haircut, the close shave, the shirt?"

"Well now, honey, I wasn't just wooing you, was I?" He picked up a loaded burger. "Had to win over your folks, too."

"So you did it for them?"

"For you." He took a big bite while watching her, encouraging her to do the same.

She nibbled—and waited for an explanation.

After he'd swallowed, Justice opened a beer for each of them. "Just one for me—I'll be driving, and only one for you 'cuz now I know you can't hold your liquor." He leaned closer to whisper, "And I want you clearheaded for later."

Immediately diverted, she whispered, "Later?"

"When I plan to kiss you head to toes."

She flushed...with interest. Swallowing, she looked around to ensure no one had overheard, then jumped back to her original question which, honestly, Justice had hoped to avoid.

"So you changed everything—"

"Not everything. Not how much I want you. Not who I am." He scratched his chin. "I just figured it might be easier for your folks to swallow the idea of you and me together if they knew I wasn't totally irredeemable. I mean, a shave and haircut isn't much, but it shows compromise, right?"

"I don't want you to change at all."

He smiled, inside and out. "No?"

"Everything about you is appealing. The scruff you wore before, and the way you're shaved now. The messy fauxhawk and the shorter hair. Whatever you wear—" she slanted him a look "—or don't wear, I already like you." She took a shaky breath, her attention on her burger. "I just thought you should know that."

The smile spread into a satisfied grin. Damn, but she pleased him. "So if I don't shave every day, or my hair gets shaggy again, you won't mind?"

There was a load of emotion in her eyes when she looked up at him. She started to say something—

And others joined them.

Justice assumed Miles and Armie had filled them in on Fallon's background, but it didn't show. They didn't treat her any differently. But he noticed that a few of the women mentioned their own backgrounds, the difficulties they'd faced—and how they'd gotten beyond them.

Armie, too, talked about his dad, a subject that had once been very taboo but seemed to come easier to him these days now that he was a father, too. All in all, they created an atmosphere of camaraderie that felt both safe and accepting.

Fallon listened to each person with genuine concern and caring. She didn't shy away from their confessions, but she also didn't get too nosy with her questions.

Justice wasn't disappointed that Fallon hadn't yet chimed in; she needed time, he understood that.

But tonight, he felt, was a good start.

Tomahawk showed up an hour or so later, along with a few of the newer fighters. Everyone who joined them brought along beer or snacks and soon everyone was mellow from food, drink and friendship.

A million stars hung in the dark sky. A gentle breeze teased the air. All around them crickets sang.

And Justice was so horny, he could barely breathe.

It was nearing midnight when he decided he couldn't wait any longer.

The bonfire had died down and no one seemed interested in keeping it blazing. Some people had already left with the designated drivers, and the remaining couples were cuddled up together, talking quietly. Occasionally a soft laugh filled the air.

Justice lifted Fallon into his lap and nuzzled her neck with damp kisses. "You ready to go?"

The question, along with the intimate familiarity, left her muddled. "I… That is…"

Deliberately, he'd put his mouth near her burn scars. He needed her to know that he found every inch of her sexy.

Cupping a hand to her cheek, he encouraged, "Say yes."

She let out a shaky breath and nodded. "Yes."

Justice had to grin. Her reply had sounded like an answer to a lot more than what he'd asked. "I have a few things to say, but it'll wait until we're alone in the car."

Their goodbyes to the others took them a few minutes more. As usual, all the guys had to hug her, most of the ladies, too. This time, though, Fallon seemed more at ease with it.

Soon as that was done, she eased close to his side again. He put an arm around her shoulders and together they walked to the side yard.

It was as soon as they rounded the house to the front that Justice saw the dark Corvette parked on the street.

The same car that had tailed them days before.

After taking quick inventory of the other vehicles and assigning each to the people he knew, he jerked around to stare at the backyard—and realized Tom had arrived last. So was it his car?

Was it Tom who'd been following them? Was he possibly the one who'd...

But why? What was his end game?

Justice remembered that Tom was with Fallon when she fell— or was *pushed*—and his fury expanded.

"Justice?" Fallon peered up at him, her skin pale in the wash of moonlight, her eyes huge and luminous. "Is something wrong?"

The moment she spoke, he realized that he'd tightened his hold on her. Immediately, he let up, saying, "Everything's fine." He needed to corral his rioting thoughts and temper his automatic anger until he could talk with Tom.

It wouldn't be tonight. In fact, he thought, maybe he shouldn't say anything at all. He'd keep Fallon safe, so he knew no harm would come to her. And maybe if he gave Tom enough rope, he'd either hang himself, or prove his innocence.

Justice decided he liked that plan. Tomorrow, after he fessed up to Sahara, he'd discuss this new twist with Leese. Maybe Armie and Cannon, too, since they'd be around Tom more often.

"Come on." He walked with Fallon across the dew-wet grass to the curb where he'd parked. Keeping watch up and down the street, he unlocked the door and waited while she got settled inside, then went around to the driver's side.

Justice waited until he'd pulled away from the curb and driven two blocks before speaking. "I don't want you to be nervous."

She folded her arms around herself and, after glancing at him, looked out the windshield. "I'm not."

"Fibber," he teased. His heart pounded, he was already half-hard, but he didn't want her to be uncertain with him. "You know I want you, Fallon. So damned much. But that doesn't obligate you in any way. If you'd rather take this slow, I understand. It's your show, and if you want some time to think about things—"

"Things?"

Thinking about it stirred him. "Hot, sweaty, naked sex. With me."

When she drew in a sharp breath and blinked fast, Justice realized he shouldn't have been so blunt.

He smiled crookedly. "Sorry, honey, but no one's ever accused me of being smooth. You already know I want you. But I want you to want me, too. And until you do—"

"I do!" Then she frowned. And laughed. "Why do I keep saying that?" She didn't give him time to answer. "I want you just as much."

Justice blew out a relieved breath. "Best news I've heard in a really long time."

"It's just…" She waffled, cleared her throat. "The thing is, I've never… I mean, I almost did with Marcus, but then—"

"Yeah, let's don't go there, okay? If I hear the history of you and Marcus, I might get the urge to stomp on him a little, and I'd rather talk about you wanting me." He considered what she'd said. Curiosity and need sharpened to an acute ache softened only by tenderness. "You're telling me you're a virgin?"

She rushed into defensive explanation. "I was young, and then I got burned, and—"

"And you'll have to trust me that any guy would have been thrilled to get you horizontal."

She bit her lip and fell silent.

Sooner or later, Justice knew he'd get her to believe him. For now, though, she needed to know he understood. "But yeah, I get it. You've been reserved for a while." He shifted, wishing he could ease the restriction in his jeans because now he had a full-blown boner. "I get to be your first?" To himself he thought, *your only.* "Gotta say, that's pretty freaking awesome."

With a jittery laugh, she pressed her hands to her cheeks. After a moment or two, she asked around a relieved grin, "You really think so?"

Almost too turned-on to talk, Justice rolled one shoulder. "I mean, if you weren't, I'd be okay with that, too. God knows I'm as far from a virgin as a guy can get."

A scowl overshadowed her grin.

That made him chuckle. "I'm thirty years old, honey. I hope you weren't expecting a monk."

She put up her chin. "I'm not dumb. Of course I expected you to...have experience."

Done with that topic before he ruined her agreeable mood, Justice said, "So what do you think? My house?"

"Okay."

That squeaky voice got to him and he glanced at her. "In case you're wondering, I'm not going to rush you right to bed." No, he'd do a lot of kissing and touching first.

"Okay."

Still squeaky. He almost grinned, but instead shifted the sub-

ject to give her a different focus. "How weird will it be for your
folks if you don't come home tonight?"

That stumped her. "I don't know. I've never done that."

Amazing. He knew she was twenty-four, almost twenty-five,
but her life had been on hold for so long. Softly, Justice suggested, "You wanna call them and let them know?"

Watching him, she asked just as quietly, "Will I be spending the night?"

Hell, yeah. "I'd like for you to."

"You're sure?"

Justice gave it some thought. He hadn't made a habit of
sleepovers. Whenever he did spend the whole night with a
woman, it was out of convenience, and never with a woman
like Fallon. More often than not, he leaned toward female fans
who just wanted a notch on their bedpost. Like him, they wanted
a little fun, a little relief and nothing more.

For so long, his focus had been on training. But not anymore.
Now he could look at other things, like the future.

"Yup, I'm sure. Even if you aren't ready for everything I
want—" *and he wanted a lot* "—I'd still enjoy keeping you close."

"You want me to sleep with you even if we don't..."

When she trailed off, Justice nodded. "Even if we don't have
sex. What do you think?"

Reaching out, she lightly touched his shoulder. Her voice was
as gentle as her touch. "I think I want everything, and yes, I'd
love to stay over." She withdrew her hand and pulled her phone
from her purse, then hesitated. "What should I say?"

Hell, he had no idea, not with parents like hers. "When I
was nineteen and still living at home, and I knew I'd be out
all night, I'd call my mom so she wouldn't worry." He glanced
at Fallon. "I already told you she's an award-winning worrier,
right? Anyway, I'd just hedge all her warnings by promising
upfront that I'd be safe, I'd use protection and I'd be home for
breakfast. That was her cue not to wait up for me."

"Would she do that?" Fallon asked with a smile. "Wait up?"

"Nah, but there were a few occasions when I forgot to call. I'd get home in the morning and she'd be passed out on the couch, snoring real loud, then she'd jerk awake with a start and almost fall on the floor. She'd start right in giving me hell and swearing she hadn't slept a wink all night." He laughed remembering it. "No matter how big I got, she claimed she could still give me a whoopin' if I needed it." The laughter faded to a slight smile. "So I tried to remember."

Fallon sighed. "My parents are nothing like your mother. They really might stay up and they'd be thinking every terrible thing you could imagine."

"Yeah, and I guess the same reassurances wouldn't work for them, right?" When she looked puzzled, Justice said, "You'll be safe, I'll use protection and I can have you home in time for breakfast if you want."

Fallon laughed and blushed, and in the process turned him on even more.

"You are so pretty."

She ducked her face, but he could see her mouth curling over the compliment. "Thank you." She touched in a number and put the phone to her ear. After a moment, she said quietly, "Hi, Mom. I'm sorry if I woke you. Yes, everything is fine. I just wanted to let you know that I'll be out the rest of the night." She listened, gave a slight nod. "Yes, I'm still with Justice. He thought I should let you know so you wouldn't worry." She glanced at him, her gaze playful. "Yes, he is very sweet."

Justice felt awkward as hell listening in. It was a first, hearing a girl call her mom to make her excuses. Hell, not since high school had he dated anyone who still lived at home.

Fallon glanced at him. "Okay, yes, I'll tell him. Love you, too. Good night."

"You woke her up?" he asked as he made the turn onto the street where he lived.

"I think so. But she wanted you to know that she appreciated your consideration."

No recriminations? Rebecca was astute, so she had to know how the evening would roll out. She couldn't be happy that Fallon would be with a man like him—that is, unless she preferred him because she knew he'd protect Fallon.

It was something to think about—but later. Right now, as he reached his driveway, the last thing he wanted to think about was Fallon's parents.

Using a remote, he opened the garage door and drove in.

Fallon was remarkably silent.

Wooing was not his strong suit, Justice knew. Before now, it had never been necessary.

After he turned off the car, he paused with his hands on the steering wheel, his grip tight as he tried to find the right words.

Fallon's seat belt clicked as she released it, and the light flashed on when she opened her door and stepped out.

Well hell. She was moving faster than he was!

Justice quit worrying about rushing her as he hurried from the car.

Fallon didn't want to acknowledge her own uncertainty. After all, Justice was definitely different from Marcus. The two men didn't have a single thing in common, so it stood to reason that Justice's reaction to her scars would be different.

But fears weren't rational.

He'd already seen the worst, she reminded herself, and hadn't in any way appeared repulsed. Encouraged by her internal pep talk, she promised herself it would be okay—if she could just get her erratic heartbeat to slow down a little.

The garage opened into a short hall between the dining and living room, leading into the kitchen.

"Want a drink?"

She shook her head. "No."

His boyish smile took her by surprise. "How about a kiss, then?"

"Yes." When he kissed her, she couldn't think enough to worry.

Slowly, right there in the hallway, he pinned her to the wall. With excruciating buildup, he settled his hot mouth to hers in a damp, firm kiss. At first, he indulged a gentle exploration, his lips teasing over hers, his tongue touching her bottom lip, lightly dipping inside.

The way his hard chest pressed to her breasts made her nipples grow tight. Somehow, in some subtle way, he insinuated one thick thigh between hers—then pressed against her. Fallon ached, already wanting, needing, more.

Coasting her hands over his bulging shoulders, she thrilled at his strength and the flex of firm muscles. He crowded in closer until she felt surrounded by him and the press of his big body curled her toes.

His mouth opened hers with ease and his tongue stroked deeper, hotter.

God, he tasted good and smelled even better. She deeply inhaled his wonderful, stirring scent, then arched up against him, asking for more.

With a hungry sound, Justice held her face in both of his hands and ravaged her mouth. His tongue thrust in to play with her own. She couldn't think and didn't want to. Loving how out of control he seemed, Fallon wrapped her arms around his neck and held on.

Long minutes later when he took his mouth to her throat, he whispered, "God, you're hot." He drew her skin in against his teeth, making her inhale sharply at the pleasure.

Justice had it wrong. It was his mouth, his damp tongue and his hard frame that was hot.

Near her ear he breathed, "I want to fuck you, Fallon."

No one had ever spoken to her like that, and hearing it now, in such a gravelly voice, thrilled her.

He grazed the edge of his teeth down the side of her neck to a sensitive spot where it met her shoulder, then gave her a sizzling love bite.

In reaction, her nails bit into his shoulders.

He lifted away to look at her and her knees almost buckled.

Justice had the most beautiful, sinfully compelling eyes, currently filled with raw hunger.

His gaze moved over her face, repeatedly lingering on her mouth until he touched it with gentle fingertips. "I also want to treat you carefully, love you slowly and kiss you everywhere."

Her heart went into double-time.

Locking his gaze with hers, he whispered, "I want to make this so good for you, Fallon."

Holding on to him, trying to catch her breath, Fallon knew what she wanted: for him to not stop. She tried a smile to reassure him, but breathing was tough enough. "Honestly, I'm good with either way."

That heart-melting smile of his made him almost too gorgeous. "Beautiful, sexy and a real sweet-talker. Damn, Fallon, could you be more perfect?"

That sobered her mood. "I'm not perfect," she whispered. "You know that."

"Close enough to level me." Leaning down slowly this time, Justice nibbled along her jaw, her throat, and as he pulled the neckline of her shirt aside, he licked her neck. She felt the rasp of his tongue and his hot breath.

She hadn't realized her neck would be so sensitive. The way he drew on her skin kept her heart slamming in her chest. When his teeth tugged on her earlobe, she groaned softly.

She felt one of his big hands going down her spine all the way to her backside. He cuddled her, made another rough sound and came back to her mouth, but not for long.

Grabbing her hand, he started for his bedroom in a long, hurried stride.

Breathing hard in anticipation, Fallon laughed and rushed to keep up.

CHAPTER THIRTEEN

Justice knew he was about to lose it. Damn it, she deserved better than a wham-bam quickie, but it was all he could do to keep from having her there in the hallway. He wanted her naked, him naked, skin on skin.

He wanted to slide into her, feel her squeezing him tight.

And he wanted it *now*.

The bedroom, he decided. He at least had to make it to the bedroom—even though it felt too damned far away.

He got her into the room, closed the door and very deliberately put a little space between them. He couldn't touch her. Not yet. If he felt her softness, he'd cave again and be all over her.

Even amid the raging lust, he knew getting her clothes off was important. She had to know—had to *see*—that he wouldn't be put off by her burns.

Hell, at the moment, a tornado might not dampen his need.

Had he ever wanted a woman with this much desperate, clawing need? Maybe his first, but he doubted it. He knew what blind lust felt like, but this, with Fallon, was hotter, stronger, deeper.

It almost overwhelmed him.

As if she needed the support, Fallon leaned back against the wall, her chest billowing with her fast, deep breaths. Her heavy lidded eyes watched him closely, her expression sultry.

Justice held her gaze as he peeled off his shirt and tossed it aside. Sitting on the bed, he removed his shoes and socks. His attention never left her.

If she got skittish, he needed to know.

As she stared at his naked chest and shoulders, her lips parted and she breathed faster. She put a hand to her throat, her cheeks flushing. He stood again, and her concentrated gaze dropped down to his abs.

God almighty, he loved the way Fallon looked at him, with so much innocent, curious fascination. He was so hard that he strained his jeans. Knowing what would happen, what he'd do, that he'd soon be over her, sliding into her, made his muscles clench.

When he just stood there, letting her look her fill and trying to regain some control, she encouraged, "Go on."

Justice tried and failed to hold back his grin. "Jeans gotta stay on for now, babe. At least until you catch up." Once his pants were gone, he'd be gone, too.

In every way, Fallon was a priority—even over his own pleasure. He wanted her to enjoy every second of what they'd do.

She stared at his crotch and Justice felt himself twitch. Much more of that and he'd lose the battle.

"Okay." Lifting a hand, she touched the buttons at the top of her blouse.

"No." Anxious to fulfill a private fantasy, he stepped toward her. "Let me." He'd been dreaming about stripping Fallon bare since the day they'd first met, and by God, he'd savor every second of it.

She went still, a little wary.

"Keep breathing," he instructed, wanting her as into it as he was.

She nodded, and tensed up even more.

Instead of making a beeline for the buttons, which would quickly leave her exposed, Justice held her face in his hands and spent some time plying her soft, damp mouth with heated kisses. Not a chore at all; the lady had an *amazing* mouth, and the taste of her...

Thinking of her taste made him throb. He couldn't wait to lick, suck and nibble on every inch of her fragrant skin, and he would; her breasts, her belly...between her soft, tender thighs.

He held back the groan the visual caused.

Fallon's skin was warm and silky and he wanted to rub himself all over her.

Lazily, as if he wasn't on the verge of exploding, he cupped a hand over her left breast—for the moment, steering clear of her scars. Even through her bra and shirt, he found her stiffened nipple with his thumb and strummed over it, drawing it tighter.

She ended the kiss with a sharp breath.

Intent on devastating her, Justice took her mouth again. With a tilt of his head he deepened the kiss, eating at her soft mouth until she melted against him. Carefully, reining in the lust so he could go slowly, he slipped his hand under the hem of her shirt. He forced himself to go slow, to be content stroking his fingers over her narrow waist, absorbing the warmth of her skin before sliding his palm up her side, feeling her through her bra, teasing his fingertips over the upper swell—and then, with only the barest hesitation, he tucked his palm inside to hold her bare flesh.

She quickly ended the kiss again to stare at him with dark, dazed eyes, hazy with need.

Forcing the sturdy bra cup lower, Justice cuddled her breast in his hand. "You little faker," he murmured, loving the fullness of her, the weight of her heavy breast. "How come your bra hides this?"

"This?" she rasped as her eyes sank shut.

"How large you are." God, she was stacked and he hadn't

even realized it. "Don't get me wrong, it's a nice surprise, but you must squish these poor babies down."

"Minimizer bra," she gasped, distracted by how he touched her.

"What woman wants to minimize her rack? You should be showing it off."

She dropped her head back with a strained sound of pleasure. "I didn't want attention…ah, Justice."

Tugging her hands away from his neck, he held them both in one of his and pressed them to the wall above her head. His heart drummed furiously as he found the front closure to her bra and with a practiced flick of his fingers, released it. "Ah, that's better." Putting a tiny bit of space between them, he inched up her shirt until he could see her.

Breathing became a struggle.

Her utilitarian white bra had done a hell of a job restraining her lush breasts, now snugly framed by the cotton cups. *Could a woman be more beautiful?* He didn't think so.

With the shirt tucked up high, her scars remained hidden. Hopefully, that would keep her confidence in place, at least for now.

Holding her wrists over her head, Justice studied her. She had a rockin' body, more so than anyone would guess.

He stroked the backs of his knuckles over her midriff. "You look like this, and no one knows except me." His gaze came up to meet hers. "It's going to make me extra nuts every time I see you in your casual clothes."

She shifted, but didn't pull her hands free. Sultry need darkened her gaze. "You're embarrassing me."

"Nah, I'm turning you on." Lightly, he tugged at one nipple. "But just you wait." He leaned down and, after dampening the nipple with his tongue, drew it into his mouth to suck hungrily.

Her high, vibrating moan felt like a stroke to his dick.

She pulled her hands away from his, but only to press him closer. "Oh, God," she whispered.

He loved how she curled into him, and how she gasped for air.

Moving to her other breast, he gently nuzzled while using his fingers to play with the nipple he'd left wet and tight. He was now close to her scars, but she didn't seem to notice.

"Justice, please…"

Intent on keeping her thoughts scattered, he pressed one thigh between her legs, his hand clasping her bottom and rocking her while he leisurely enjoyed her breasts.

When her breathing turned ragged, broken only by small, desperate moans, Justice gave in to the urge to know more of her. Murmuring to her, he coasted a hand over her smooth belly down to her pelvis, then over the crotch of her pants.

Her fingertips dug into his shoulders.

"Easy now." Holding her, letting her get used to his hand between her thighs, he kissed a path back up her chest, her throat and to her mouth.

This time it was her kissing him with demanding intensity, and when she moved against his palm, sharing her need without words, he knew she was getting closer.

Not quite there, but maybe—

"My legs are shaking," she whispered breathlessly. "I need to sit down."

He scooped her up and took her to the bed, lowering her to her back, and as he straightened, he took her shirt with him, stripping it off over her head in one smooth movement.

She gasped and quickly covered her upper body. Shock widened her eyes, but he wouldn't let her dwell on anything but the need.

"My hands are bigger." Slowly, one by one, Justice caught each wrist and pressed her arms up to either side of her head. "Let me."

She closed her eyes, turned her head away.

Sitting beside her, he brushed the bra cups away and just looked at her. She was such a slender woman, her rib cage narrow, her stomach showing only the slightest, sexy curve. With each fast breath, her lush breasts rose and fell. A pulse beat frantically in her throat. Her nipples were flushed dark, stiff and still damp from his mouth.

Using care, he covered her with his palms, cupping his fingers around each breast.

Firm, full and so damned soft. Her nipples were stiff against his palms. He closed his eyes at the sensation, but only for a moment. He didn't want to miss a thing.

"Justice?"

She sounded as affected as him but also anxious to know his thoughts.

Of course he saw the scars, and he didn't shy away from looking at them. Fallon wasn't a dummy; she'd catch on real quick if he tried to pretend they weren't there. She watched him so closely, he didn't bother hiding anything he thought or felt.

"Say something," she whispered.

"I don't know what to say. I'm struggling to go slow here, babe. But you're everything I imagined and a hell of a lot more." He gave her body quick scrutiny and admitted, "Your boobs are so much bigger than I expected."

Blinking at him in surprise, Fallon's mouth twitched. "My... boobs?"

"Should I have said *breasts*? I should have, right?" He continued to caress her as he spoke. "You're a classy lady and probably don't hear things like—"

Fallon touched his mouth. "I want you to be you, Justice. You don't have to say anything differently. You just took me by surprise."

In a growl, he said, "I want you so bad, I'm starting to sweat."

Relief filled her eyes and her smile widened. "That's so romantic."

"Are you teasing me?" he asked, pleased to see her tension visibly ebbing away.

She nodded. "You're making me nuts, too. I've never felt like this."

"'Cuz no man's ever done this to you before." He had to keep reminding himself of that. She was a virgin, and her one attempt at sex had been botched, thanks to Marcus—the prick.

"Yes, but I promise, you don't have to treat me with kid gloves. I just want to be like every other woman."

Only she wasn't, not to him. "The way you react to me…" He got his attention off her body long enough to look into her beautiful eyes. He saw the same heat and need reflected in her expression that he suffered. Even as he held her breasts, he felt her trembling. "God, Fallon, that's such a turn-on. I'm on a hair trigger here, but this is your first time so I wanna go slow. This is special."

She bit her lip, then asked, "Because I'm a virgin?"

"Because you're you," he said with grave seriousness. "Because you're special."

She pressed a hand to his jaw. "So…not because I'm scarred?"

Frowning, Justice lightly touched the roughened skin on her shoulder, part of her chest and the top of her breast. She resisted, trying to stop him, but he did as he pleased anyway.

Even when she went stiff, he didn't let that sway him.

"They're just marks, honey. Emotionally, they're huge, I know. But physically, they aren't a big deal at all." He glanced at her face, saw her eyes were squeezed shut and asked, "Does it bother you that my ears are thicker?"

Her eyes popped open. "What?"

"From fighting. I have some cauliflower ear goin' on. Not as bad as some I've seen, but I notice it. My right ear is worse than the left. Doesn't mean enough to me to want to do surgery or anything—"

"You're gorgeous!"

A grin tugged at his mouth. No woman had ever angrily shouted that at him before. "My nose has been broken a few times, too. No way could you have missed the kink there. It's crooked as hell."

"Maybe a little, but it just adds to your appeal."

Did her blindness to his flaws mean she, too, cared beyond the sexual attraction? He hoped so, but with Fallon it was tough to tell. She'd lived such a sheltered life, and because he refused to count Marcus, Justice was, in effect, her first adult boyfriend. He was the first to be sexual with her. He was the lucky bastard who happened to show up when she decided to spread her wings.

While he had her talking again, he reached down to open her slacks. "See, that's how it is for me, too. I look at you and you're so hot, so sexy, who cares about a few scars? I sure as hell don't."

"Marcus did."

Scowling, he stripped the pants off her, taking her panties, too. She gasped, but didn't object. Looking her over, Justice fought for control. "Let's don't ever say his name again, okay? Definitely not at times like this." He drew her upright, untangled the bra straps from her arms and tossed it with her pants.

"But—"

He levered her back down on the bed. "He's an idiot not worth your breath." Because he couldn't resist, he briefly trailed his fingers down her body, ending at the neat triangle of dark pubic hair. She kept her legs together, but he didn't let it bother him as he stroked her, then on impulse, he bent to kiss her hip bone.

Her breath hitched and she blurted, "I told you I had a scar on my leg, too—"

He stood and stripped off his jeans.

That got her quiet. And alert.

While he looked at her naked body, she visually explored his. Justice didn't mind. She could look all she wanted.

He sure planned to.

Fallon cleared her throat. "You're...impressive."

"My dick?"

She half laughed, half coughed. "I meant all of you. You're so hard all over."

"Especially my dick."

This time the sound she made was all humor. "Are you trying to amuse me?"

"Trying to get you to relax." Standing close to the bed, he again trailed his fingertips over her body, starting with her breasts, down to her stomach, over a hip bone and to her outer thigh where he touched the other scar, the one where they'd taken skin to treat her burns. A donor site, she'd told him.

This scar was flatter, a neat rectangle with a grid-like pattern to it.

Though she didn't fight him, Justice chose not to linger there. He had the rest of her to play with, too.

He went back to caressing the taut muscles of her thighs. "Ease up, honey."

"I don't want to ease up," she said. "I want to touch you like you're touching me."

"Yeah," he growled, thinking about her small hands on him. "I'd like that, too." *Control*, he reminded himself. "If you relax, I can touch you more."

Reaching for him, she said, "I'll relax more if you kiss me."

"Is that so?" Justice willingly came down beside her, pulling her close against him. She automatically lifted a leg over his, and when he felt the heat of her against him, he damn near lost it. Tangling a hand in her silky hair, he drew her face up to his and kissed her hard, sinking his tongue into her mouth, stealing her small groan.

With his free hand, he touched her everywhere, sweeping over her body, wanting to learn all of her, her every secret. He loved the softness of her skin, disrupted only by the scars.

"Shh," he murmured, when she shied away from his touch.

Deliberately, he cupped her breast, letting his long fingers stretch up to the scar. He lifted his head to look into her eyes, saying just as quietly, "No secrets between us, okay?"

After several heartbeats, she cautiously nodded.

"I like touching you, Fallon. I don't want any hang-ups in the way."

She nodded again, then whispered, "Okay."

"You're beautiful and sexy. Believe me?"

Her mouth twitched even as her eyes grew damp. On a choked laugh, she agreed. "Okay."

Damn, she was special. He took her mouth again, voracious in his need, while he cuddled her plump backside, stroked her slender thighs and her downy soft stomach. With each caress, Fallon squirmed against him, into him, her hands on his shoulders holding him tight.

Justice couldn't get enough, fast enough.

Urging her to her back, he bent to one nipple, sucking strongly, insistently, and at the same time worked his fingers between her legs.

This time she was pliant, willingly giving him access, even arching up to him. He took his time exploring her, growing bolder with each touch.

Shifting restlessly, she groaned.

With one finger he stroked over the sleek, swollen folds until they parted, then he pressed in to the second knuckle. She was creamy wet, so damned hot and *tight*.

Her inner muscles clamped down on him, and he felt a surge of lust so strong, he almost came.

After taking a moment to regain his control, he levered up to his elbow and watched her expressions while he slowly worked his finger deeper inside her.

Her thick lashes were lowered, her eyes glazed with sultry need. A rosy flush colored her cheeks.

"Damn," he rasped, before looking down her body. The sight

of his rough hand between her tender, parted thighs gained all his attention.

He added a second finger and her thighs spread wider, her hips lifting into the touch.

Such a natural, carnal reaction; Justice liked that a lot.

He liked having her all stretched out, shivering with pleasure, waiting for him to continue...yeah, as hot as it got.

He brought his thumb up to her clit and watched her slender body tense. He forgot that he was trying to take it easy with her, that he wanted her to feel cherished.

He went blind to everything but having her.

On a path down her heated body, he licked, kissed, taunted with his teeth, until finally he settled himself between her spread thighs. In a voice gravelly with lust, he asked, "You want this, don't you?" He needed to hear her say it.

Taut with expectation, Fallon dropped an arm over her eyes and kept quiet—except for her harsh, unsteady breathing.

Justice lifted her thighs over his shoulders, pressed his face close and inhaled the scent of sweet, aroused woman. Heady stuff. Using just his fingertips, he parted her sex, drew his tongue along the glistening pink flesh, up and over the little stiffened clitoris.

The taste of her here only made him greedier for more.

As he ate at her, Fallon cried out over the sharp sensations.

"Tell me, Fallon," he growled, licking over her again, pressing his tongue into her heat to gather every drop of her excitement.

She whimpered, *"Yes."*

Keeping her still with one hand flattened on her stomach, he closed his mouth around her, using his tongue to mimic the sex act, then curling it around her clit and tugging rhythmically.

She almost came undone—and he *loved* it. His erection pressed into the mattress; he was so damned hard, throbbing with his need, he knew he'd lose it the minute he got inside her. Before that, he had to guarantee her climax.

He would not leave her with regrets.

When her hips began to move in time to her small gasping breaths, he knew she was close. Again he pressed two long fingers into her, stretching up inside her as far as he could go.

She was drenched, bathing his fingers, her body ripe and ready, trembling on the cusp of release.

Knowing it'd make this first time easier for her, he thrust in and out, twisting his hand each time, stretching her. She coiled tighter and tighter—and suddenly the climax hit her.

Wet heat accompanied her raw cries and the urgent, uncontrolled movements of her body. Pleasure contorted her expression, her release real and honest.

It was the hottest, most exciting thing ever, and it set him off.

The second she began to ease, her legs going lax, Justice stood. He damn near pulled the drawer out of the nightstand in his rush to find a condom. He jerked the packet open with his teeth and looked at Fallon with a burning gaze while he rolled on the protection.

Her thighs were sprawled, her long lashes resting on her cheeks damp with perspiration, her breasts heaving as she continued to gulp deep breaths.

Coming down over her, Justice kissed her parted lips and kneed her thighs wider. "I'm in a bad way here, honey, or I'd give you more time to recoup."

With a visible effort, her slumberous eyes opened. "I don't need time," she breathed. "I just need you."

She knew how to level him.

Justice put a forearm under her, raising her hips and instructed, "Put your legs around me."

Languidly, she did as ordered.

His vision narrowed until he saw only her. "Hold on tight."

"Yes, sir." Smiling, she looped her limp arms around his neck.

He promised, "Next time I'll be easier." He adjusted the head

of his erection against her, nudged forward and, without warning, drove his full length into her.

Well, that took care of her smile.

She gasped hard, her fingertips digging into his shoulders.

Growling with the pleasure of it, Justice did his best to hold
still when every fiber of his being told him to move. "You're
so tight."

She tried to shift and he groaned. Immediately, she went still
again.

"It'll be fine in a second." At least he hoped that was true.
He couldn't think of any other virgins he'd had. Not even back
in high school.

"I'm... I'm okay."

"I know it." His voice was rough, but he couldn't help it.
Caught in an unfamiliar maelstrom of physical need and incredible emotion, he nuzzled her lips. "You sure you know it, too?"

"Yes. Sorry. You just surprised me."

Even now, in a haze of lust, he couldn't resist teasing her.
"You thought we'd be doing something else?" Talking was
pretty damned tough. The hot, sleek grip of her body squeezing around his cock in little aftershocks left him rigid from head
to toes. Her lush breasts cushioned his chest, and her nipples
were still drawn tight. Her breath fanned his collarbone, adding to his fever.

It was like very sweet torture, but he was determined not to
hurt her.

"Justice?"

"Hmm?"

"Will you kiss me again?"

On a vibrating groan, he took her mouth. Hell, he could lose
himself in kissing her. He ruthlessly held himself in check until
she finally unclenched. The second she did, he drew back, only
to slide in deeply again. She freed her mouth on a soft, high-
pitched cry.

"Yeah, that's what I want." This time she gripped him with need instead of discomfort. Keeping his thrusts measured, he concentrated on her reactions, taking much of his pleasure from hers.

When she whispered, *"Harder,"* he gave up on all restraint and began driving into her, rushing them both toward completion.

Head arching back, slender body bowed, Fallon cried out another release. Her beautiful response triggered his own, and he put his face in her neck, crushing her close until the nearly painful pleasure finally began to fade.

While regaining her breath, Fallon idly smoothed her fingers over Justice's shoulders and back, and down the deep groove of his spine to a very tight behind.

Lord help her, the man was rock solid all over.

She didn't need experience to know that a man like Justice was rare. So earthy, so considerate and so incredibly hot. For now, he was hers, and she intended to make the most of it.

Nerve endings all over her body still pulsed with new awareness. His body covering hers was a delicious sensation, his hips holding her legs open, his breath on her throat, his chest hair tickling her breasts.

Unable to contain her happiness, she lightly hugged him.

"Mmm," he grumbled, with a faint, "G'me a minute."

Satisfaction curved her mouth in a secret smile. She'd gladly give him a lifetime if he wanted it.

Odds were he didn't. They hadn't known each other long enough for her to be thinking such things, much less for him to be thinking it.

However, she had here and now, and she wouldn't ruin it by reaching for more. "I'm good." She stroked back up to those broad shoulders, now damp with a light sheen of sweat that amplified his scent.

How could a man smell so incredibly good?

She breathed a little deeper and felt those still-tingly places flutter anew.

She'd never before noticed anything like it. She'd enjoyed the scents of aftershave and expensive cologne, sure. But this fresh, masculine, toe-curling scent, like earth and man and sex, made her want to eat him up. It was unique to Justice and everything female in her reacted to it.

She ran a hand over his short cropped hair. She'd liked his cut before and already missed it, but the new trim didn't detract at all from his sex appeal.

Feeling daring, she trailed her toes up the back of one hairy calf.

Suddenly Justice leaned up to see her.

His gaze was intent, a little curious, a lot triumphant.

She felt ridiculously shy, especially since he was still inside her, not as much now, but she felt him there teasing her sensitized flesh.

Without a word he leaned down and treated her to a warm, lingering kiss.

God, she loved his kisses.

When she thought of what he'd done with that mouth, how crazy he'd made her, the explosion of pleasure, she moaned softly.

Justice stole the sound from her, taking advantage and deepening the kiss with a stroke of his tongue.

Fallon didn't recall doing it, but when he finally let up, she had her legs wrapped around his waist, her arms locked around his neck.

He switched to her throat. "You tasted so fucking good, Fallon."

She hadn't expected him to talk about it! A little flushed, she whispered, "Thank you?"

His laugh teased her skin. "You're welcome." Then he shifted away. "I don't want to crush you." Leaving her body, he moved to his side and pulled her into his embrace.

She could have told him how much she'd enjoyed his weight over her, but this position was nice, too.

He touched her mouth. "You okay?"

"Very." Better than she'd ever been.

"Not sore?"

Though she was just a little, she shook her head. "Thank you for asking me to stay over. We're going to do this again, right?"

His eyes warmed, and his grin came slowly. "That would be my preference."

"Good." Feeling more free than she had in years, Fallon turned to her back and stretched. She was as aware of her scars as ever, but not in a tragic way. Their existence seemed more bearable, less...shameful.

Justice rested a big hand on her stomach, then leaned forward and brushed his mouth over the burn marks on her shoulder. It surprised her, until he casually remarked, "You left me weak. I'll need a few minutes, and maybe I can talk you into showering with me. Hopefully our next time I can keep it together and show you some of my better moves."

Fallon laughed at his hilarious comment and the easy way he treated her scars. She was honestly starting to believe that they didn't bother him, and somehow that made them bother her less, too.

"*Better* moves?" She turned her head to smile at him. "I can't imagine anything better than what you already did."

"Good." Feigning a serious attitude, he said, "Low expectations will make it easier on me." He pressed his hand down, insinuating it between her legs.

Her heart thumped at his easy familiarity with her body.

"Before long," he murmured, "you'll know all my moves. I want you to promise to tell me what you like the most, okay?"

Easy enough to do. Hoping she wouldn't overstep, she whispered, "I like you."

Her concerns disappeared when he said, "That's a fine start."

So not only could she freely show her body, she could also speak her mind? The urge to laugh, maybe even dance, swelled inside her. Justice's acceptance worked toward liberating her from the chains of the past five years.

Her thoughts buzzed about her future, and in rapid order she made several decisions, all thanks to Justice.

"I like you plenty too," he said. "You know that, right?"

Actually, she did. Sure, she was an easy conquest, but Justice wasn't a user. He wasn't the type of man to take advantage of anyone, much less a woman. Knowing her parents wouldn't approve, knowing it went against the agency protocol and could damage his career, he'd still come after her. If he'd only wanted sex, she had no doubt he could have had his choice of women. And if he'd wanted her specifically, well, he could have had her without anyone ever knowing.

His openness, the way he'd approached things, meant he cared. How much, she didn't know. Heck, she didn't even know how much *she* cared.

But she looked forward to finding out.

With a growing frown, Justice muttered, "You're taking a mighty long time to answer me."

"Just thinking—and yes, I know you like me."

His gaze warmed. "Good." Sitting up, he stretched his arms high, making those bulging biceps roll and the muscles in his back flex and pull. He twisted to see her. "Stay put and I'll play the gentleman."

Not understanding, she quirked a brow.

He whistled as he left the bed, returning a moment later with the condom gone and a damp washcloth in hand.

Until he went to bathe her between the legs, she didn't understand his intent. As usual, he didn't let her shy away and once he'd finished, he crawled back into bed and drew her close.

She couldn't remember ever feeling so content.

CHAPTER FOURTEEN

It was late morning, the sun slowly crawling into the sky and lightening the shadows in the bedroom, when Justice began to stir again. Fallon watched him with fascination. She should have been exhausted, but instead she fairly burst with energy.

They'd had sex three times throughout the night before taking a shower together and finally sleeping.

She rather liked his insatiable appetites because they indulged her own.

An hour or so ago she'd awakened, immediately aware of Justice beside her. His heavy arm had draped her body, one big rough hand opened over her breast.

His fingertips had touched the worst of her scar, but that had had little relevance against the reality of being naked in bed with him, filled with the memory of all they'd done and all they could yet do.

By slow degrees she'd freed herself of his hold and now rested on an elbow, just looking at him.

Even with the beard shadow darkening his jaw, he didn't appear as intimidating, not with his face so utterly relaxed. Visually she traced his well-defined lips and the slight kink in his strong nose.

Grumbling something in his sleep, he shifted and the sheet went lower, barely maintaining his modesty.

Not that he had much.

Justice Wallington was an extremely carnal man, and very unapologetic about it. In fact, last night he'd blamed her, saying she made him that way. Fallon smiled remembering it.

It was one of the nicest compliments she'd ever gotten.

Shifting again, he lowered one hand to his abdomen to scratch.

She breathed deeper. *His abs were stupendous.* "Justice?"

One eye opened, he looked at her, then stretched more deeply and turned toward her. "Come here, you."

Straight-arming him, she laughed. "Hold up."

He pulled her in anyway and his warm lips brushed her temple. "What's up—besides me?" To emphasize that, he nudged his morning erection against her belly.

"Yes, you are," she murmured, smoothing her hand over his crisp chest hair. "Before you take over, you should know that I want to touch you, too."

"Yeah," he growled with that now familiar edgy arousal in his tone.

Tucking her nose into his neck, she breathed deeply while moving her palm over his shoulder and biceps. She could spend a day just touching Justice, and still not get her fill.

"Is all this cuddling going to add up to morning sex?" he asked while dragging her pelvis into closer contact with his. "If so, I should warn you that I have to be at the office in two hours to talk to Sahara, and it's going to take me an hour to get you home and backtrack."

Thinking to save time, she asked, "Would it help if I took a cab home?"

"Hell, no. It'd help if we hurried things along, though."

"Yeah?" Smiling, she brought her hand down past his ribs,

those solid abs she'd just been admiring, across his hip…and then to his erection.

Justice went still, but only for a moment. "Now we're talkin'." With a groan, he turned to his back, inviting her to touch all she wanted.

"Talking first is just what I had in mind." Keeping her fingers firmly curled around him, she sat up to ensure she didn't miss anything. Now able to look him over as much as she wanted, she whispered, "You are such a stud."

When he said nothing, she glanced at his face. Smoldering heat burned in his dark eyes, giving her a taste of sexual power.

"You've got my full attention, babe."

Yes, she did. Though he didn't touch her, a man couldn't be more attuned to a woman. Not just now, but from the day she'd first met him.

Before she got carried away, she needed to explain something. "Yesterday, when I was stupidly crying—"

"Nothing stupid about it." More softly, he added, "I'm sorry I hurt you."

"You didn't. It was my own insecurity that did it. I know that. I promise I don't usually weep like a baby. In fact, I rarely cry." Crying had always felt so self-indulgent.

When his erection flexed in her hand, she decided to finish her talk in haste. After all, he was being incredibly patient with her.

So how did she explain? Since Justice was always so plainspoken, she decided to follow his lead. "The scar on my leg doesn't bother me as much because it's not in such an…intimate place. No one sees it either. I mean, I can easily wear longer shorts and it's hidden."

"You don't need to hide."

She loved that he thought that. "But these—" She shrugged her shoulder forward to indicate the uglier scar. "That's such a female part of me. A sexual part."

"I guess. But you're more than a stacked body, honey. A lot more. Any asshole who doesn't see that isn't worth your time."

Humor curled her mouth. "I thought we weren't going to talk about Marcus."

"No, we're not." Smug, he pointed out, "But you knew exactly who I meant."

"I want to thank you."

"For letting you hold my junk and not complaining that you're *only* holding it?"

Justice was so damned funny, even at the most awkward of times, that she had to laugh. "For that, too, yes. But I meant for reinforcing that the scars aren't what define me."

"Not even close."

"I don't want to be shy anymore."

"You still were? Because damn, honey, you've got a grip on my dick and—"

She halted his jokes by gently squeezing him.

"Go ahead," he rasped, his hands knotting in the sheet. "Be shy or bold or whatever. Long as you keep touching me."

"I plan to." The feel of him, smooth velvet over rigid steel, amazed her. Curious about every inch of him, she briefly cupped his testicles, now drawn tight, then trailed her fingertips up his length before clasping him again. He was thick enough that her fingers didn't quite meet her thumb, but while entering her, she felt only indescribable pleasure.

Fascinated by the drop of fluid beading the tip, she brushed her thumb over it.

As if pained, he briefly closed his eyes, locked his jaw and his body tensed.

"You liked that."

His eyes slowly opened. "Yeah."

"I'm not entirely sure where this is going—and no, I don't mean this," she said, giving his erection a slow pump.

The harsh groan interrupted whatever quip he'd planned to make.

"I mean you and me, in a bed. You said you wanted to date. I'm not so naive that I don't understand *dating* as a euphemism for sex." Lying to him and herself, she said, "I want you to know, if sex is all you want, I can be content with that."

"Goody for you, but I sure as hell can't."

She quickly continued past his denial, needing to get it all said. "I've been starving for this." She got more comfortable, straddling his thick thighs and coasting a hand down his big, gorgeous body. "So many nights I thought about being with a man, kissing and touching and doing all the things most women do." With a soft laugh, she admitted, "I never envisioned a man like you." With his size, his muscles and his body hair, he was pure male perfection. She'd been too realistic to ever hope for anyone like him. "But I have you now and I want to take advantage of every second we have together."

He caught both her wrists and carefully dragged her down to rest atop him, then folded his long arms around her. "You can get back to torturing me in a minute. There's something I want to say to you first, though, and I can't think clearly with you doing that."

She smiled. "Okay."

Beneath her cheek, his chest billowed on a long, slow breath. "First, hell yeah, I wanted to have sex with you. Still do. And I know I will tomorrow and the day after."

He didn't offer forever, and after knowing him such a short time, that made sense—to her head. Her heart, however, wanted to grab for it all.

Her head reminded her heart that she had to be reasonable.

Pressuring him wouldn't gain her anything, and who knew if they'd even suit for the long haul. Scarred or not, she deserved happiness. For right now, that meant Justice.

She turned her face to kiss his throat. "Okay."

"You know what I noticed about you right off? Your eyes. So big and soft and dark. Those eyes got to me from the start. Then your honesty. The way you react to everything." His fingers tunneled into her hair, close to her scalp. "And this baby-fine hair, all sleek and sexy."

Her hair? She levered up to see his eyes. "Seriously?" Her hair was…plain. She could grow it longer, could wear it more stylish, but she'd spent so much of her life trying to avoid notice as a woman…

"Okay, so maybe I noticed your ass, too." Justice kissed her forehead. "But your hair got my attention, too. So did your skin." His lips brushed her ear. "And the things you say and do." He moved to her throat, and she felt the hot brush of his tongue. "The way you smile." Growling softly, he added, "How good you smell, so good I could just eat you up."

He *had* eaten her up, and her entire body flushed anew with the memory.

When his hands coasted down her body and he began to rock her against his erection, she knew she had to regain control.

She pushed free of his hold to sit on his abs. "So," she began, only to gasp when he cupped her breasts. *Talk about making it hard to think.*

"You want to know what we're doing? We're dating. Exclusively."

Since he waited—while toying with her nipples—she quickly nodded agreement.

"Good."

"We're dating," she repeated, "and taking it one day at a time."

"Sure." He didn't sound enthusiastic about that part, but she took heart that he didn't deny her either.

"I won't pressure you," she promised. "And you won't hold back if there's anything you want to say to me."

"Know what, Fallon?"

"What?"

"You talk too much." He reached for her.

Laughing, she swatted his hands away. "One more thing."

His long groan was too amusing.

"You know how you wanted me to tell you what I like?"

That sharpened his interest. "Yeah? Got specifics for me?"

She shook her head. "The same goes for you." Leaning forward, she kissed his sexy mouth and whispered, "Let me know if I do anything wrong."

He inhaled sharply, especially when she kissed a damp path down his now-tensed body. His fingers tunneled into her hair, and when she reached his groin, he groaned in an agony of suspense.

Fallon loved his taut anticipation, the way he kept himself so still, almost as if he feared deterring her somehow.

"You like this?" she asked, and held him in her hand.

"Yeah." Strained, he added, "Tighter."

She squeezed, and got rewarded with his low growl.

"And this?" She feathered kisses all along his length.

"Yup."

Above her fingers where she held him, she slowly licked, up and over the tip of him. "And how about—"

He gasped for breath. *"Hell, yeah."*

Filling her head with the musky scent of him, Fallon drew him into her mouth, sucking as she took him deeper.

She'd expected a reaction, but got even more than she'd counted on. Justice held her head, his breaths laboring, his muscles shifting. After only a few minutes, he roughly drew her up and under him, taking her mouth hard. She felt him fumbling on the nightstand, then he rolled to his back, donned protection, and a second later, joined their bodies in one hard, smooth thrust.

As he began rocking into her, he growled against her lips, "Hope you're into a quickie, 'cuz I won't last."

She was into *him*, and given the sharp pleasure already coiling tight, it wouldn't be a problem. Putting her legs around him, hugging him close, she breathed, "Ah, God, don't wait," as the climax hit her.

Holding her hips, he moved harder, faster—and ground out his own release.

When he finished, he sank against her, kissed her brow and whispered, "Damn, Fallon, you make me wild."

For a brand-new relationship, she figured that was a pretty good start.

Making it to the Body Armor Agency with two minutes to spare, Justice strode through the foyer and headed for the elevator. Right before he stepped inside the car, Miles joined him.

"Hey, Justice." Miles did a double-take and asked, "What'd you do to yourself?"

"Nothing." Self-conscious, Justice ran a hand over his clean-shaven jaw. "What are you doing here?"

"Got an appointment with Ms. Silver."

"No shit."

Miles grinned. "No shit."

"Huh." The doors closed and belatedly, Justice remembered to push the button for the right floor. "So, what's up?"

"Don't make a big deal of it, Justice. I'm just checking it out."

Slowly, Justice grinned. "You're joining us, aren't you?"

"I don't know yet."

At first, the idea of Miles getting on board seemed great. Then he rethought it. "You're on a winning streak. Why would you want to leave—"

The doors opened a floor early and Leese stepped in. Like Miles, he showed his surprise at Justice's spiffed-up appearance. "Is this Fallon's doing?"

"It's a shave, all right? No big deal."

"And a haircut. When was the last time I saw you without the shitty hair?"

"Go screw yourself."

Grinning, Leese shifted his gaze to Miles. "What's up?"

"He's joining us," Justice offered.

"I didn't say that," Miles corrected, looking harassed. "Only that I'm checking it out."

Leese frowned. "But you're on a winning streak."

"That's what I told him." Justice was relieved to have their attention diverted. "Now that I think about it, though, he mentioned last night at Cannon's that he was interested. I thought he was joking."

Leese gave him a speculative gaze.

"I've been considering it, that's all." Miles shrugged. "Ms. Silver has a terrific pitch."

"She does," Leese agreed. "And I'd be the first to say it's a good gig. But it's not fighting."

Pinching the air, Justice said, "Maybe just a little fighting."

The elevator dinged as they reached the floor for Sahara's office. Probably to escape the inquisition, Miles quickly stepped out.

Bounding after him, Justice said, "Hey, I have to talk to her first." He had no idea how Sahara might react, if she'd raise hell with him or whether or not he might even be out of a job. The unknown sucked, so he wanted to get it over with.

"I have an appointment," Miles countered. "So get in line."

"I work here, damn it!"

Grinning, Leese followed them. "I think I'll just go along to watch."

Both Miles and Justice scowled at him.

Sahara's door stood open, which, when it came to his classy boss, was as good as an invitation. Justice slid in front of Miles and, after a perfunctory knock on the frame, sauntered in.

Miles crowded in behind him.

Leese leaned in the doorway, arms folded.

Justice did *not* want an audience for what he had to do. "Sahara—"

At the same time, Miles said, "Ms. Silver—"

With one finger raised in the air, Sahara quieted them both.

She sat behind her massive desk listening to her agenda from her personal assistant, Enoch, while making notes on her calendar. As usual, Enoch had already delivered coffee and pastries.

Sahara took her time, changing a few appointments, adding in a few others and organizing the calls she had to make. All in all she did a fine job of ignoring the men, not even looking up at them.

After she'd finished and Enoch headed out for his own office, she glanced up—and her eyes flared. "Justice!"

Grousing, he said, "It's just a shave and a haircut. I was past due, that's all."

"Well, my word." Looking from one of them to the other, Sahara clasped a manicured hand to her heart. "You gentlemen make a nice visual first thing in the morning. It's like an advertisement for testosterone." She fanned her face. "I must think about a billboard with the three of you on it to represent the agency."

"I don't work here," Miles said.

"Yet. But I'll win you over."

With a shake of his head, Leese said, "You're bordering on sexual harassment."

Sahara laughed and left her seat to circle to the front of her desk. Per her usual preference, she hoisted her rump onto the edge and got comfortable. "I'm serious. We could bring in all sorts of new clientele."

"Too expensive," Leese said. "Most people seeing the billboard wouldn't be able to afford your exorbitant pricing."

She shrugged a delicate shoulder. "You get what you pay for."

Bristling, Justice took a step forward. "Enough nonsense, already. I have to talk to you."

Very slowly, she turned her head and skewered him with her

blue-eyed gaze. "Oh, I'm not sure that you do, Justice. You see, Rebecca Rothschild Wade called me bright and early this morning."

Justice tucked in his chin. "It isn't even nine o'clock yet."

"She said she wanted to beat you to any self-castigation."

He had no idea what she meant. With suspicion, he said, "That sounds nasty."

"You know what's nasty? Being awakened at 6:00 a.m. by a client."

Justice wasn't sure what to say about that. He tried, "Sorry?" and knew by Sahara's withering look that it hadn't helped.

Turning back to Miles, she smiled. "I like order, you all know that. So, Justice, take a seat while I talk with your friend."

"What?" He knew Sahara could be unpredictable. A great boss, but he didn't understand this current mood of hers. "Why does he go first?"

Her eyes narrowed. "Because I said so."

Well, hell. He could feel Miles and Leese staring at him and he felt like a kid being sent to the corner. "Fine, no biggie." Refusing to look cowed, he folded his arms and planted his feet. "At least tell me if I'm fired."

A mean smile curled her glossy lips. "Now Justice, do you honestly think I'd let you off that easy?"

"Um…"

"Not a chance."

Huh. Okay, so at least he still had his job. Holding up his hands in a conciliatory gesture, he moved to the sofa and sat down to wait. Already he felt better. If Sahara had to vent, fine. He'd take it. He didn't mind being bitched out. He did like the job, though, and really didn't want to have to start over somewhere else.

For Fallon, he would have. But staying at Body Armor suited him.

After a deep, calming breath, Sahara released him from her stare. "Leese, this involves you, so please come inside."

Now Leese and Miles both looked uneasy, too. Good. Misery loved company. Justice smirked at them when they edged farther inside.

"Please, gentlemen, get comfortable."

"What's up with the gentlemen stuff?" Leese asked.

She rolled her eyes. "I'm wooing Miles so I'm trying to be more solicitous."

Justice grunted. She hadn't been solicitous to him.

"Wooing me?" Miles asked. "I'm just here—"

"He's only *curious*," Leese said, mocking their friend.

Sahara pretended to cast a line toward Miles, then slowly reeled it in. "I've got you hooked and we both know it. Don't fight me too hard, okay? Justice has taken all my patience for the day."

Appearing more uncomfortable by the moment, Miles rolled a shoulder. "Honestly, the way he's over there quaking in his boots, I'm thinking about running the other way."

"I'm not quaking!"

Laughing, Sahara said, "No, he's not. The big lug knows I value his role in the agency."

She did? Justice tried to hide his surprise. Sure, Sahara always made him feel important, and he knew she trusted him. But he also understood how important the agency was to her. She'd inherited it from her brother after his murder and she'd do just about anything to keep it as successful as possible.

That meant keeping the reputation golden.

Him hooking up with a client could cause real damage, so he'd have understood if she'd raged at him.

Under the circumstances, a few killing looks weren't so bad.

For the next twenty minutes, Justice had to sit there while Sahara extolled Body Armor, doing her best to win over Miles. He still didn't understand why Miles would even be interested, but he saw for himself how his friend asked enough questions to cover all the bases.

Sahara elaborated on the necessary requirements, the training regimen, the possible scenarios and the perks of working for the agency.

When she wound down, Leese asked, "Why am I here?"

"I want you to show Miles around the building. Not just the places he's seen while visiting one of you, but everything shut off to the general public, like where he could exercise and practice shooting and—"

"Got it," Leese said.

"If he takes the job, you'll be training him." She cast another dark look at Justice. "This one is going to be busy for a while."

Miles started laughing. "I get the feeling this is like a big family instead of a boss and employees."

"Don't," Justice said. "She can be very boss-like when it suits her."

"Yes," Sahara agreed. "I can." She crossed her legs and studied Miles. "But it's also true that a certain familiarity is necessary given the nature of the job. There could be times when, depending on what the client wants, you work around the clock."

Justice opened his mouth and she snapped, "Hush it!"

He clamped his lips together.

Scowling at him, she added, "Around the clock does not, in the usual course of things, include intimate involvement with the client."

Justice wasn't the only one to flush. Leese did his own fair share of looking chastised, and with good reason. His wife, Catalina, had started out as a client.

"Right," Miles said, clearing his throat. "I get that. But for the sake of clarity, I'm curious what's happening, too, so if you want to deal with Justice, I'm happy to stick around."

"Dick," Justice muttered.

"You may as well," Sahara agreed. Sighing, she shifted to face Justice.

As the silence stretched out, he said, "Well?"

"Rebecca is thrilled with how things are progressing."

Huh. Hadn't seen that one coming. "She is?"

"Very."

For reasons that had nothing to do with the job, Justice smiled. "Well...that's good, then, right?"

"If it's all fine," Leese interjected, "what's the problem?"

"The problem is that if Justice breaks her heart, I'm going to have some seriously irate clients on my hands."

Justice pushed to his feet. "I told them they weren't clients anymore."

Brows up, Sahara immediately understood. "You're that serious about her?"

"I am."

"You haven't known her that long."

Justice waved that away. "Have you met her?"

"Not personally, no."

"Well, they have," he said, nodding at his friends. "There was no way to resist her."

Miles said, "I resisted her just fine."

"Ha! Because you knew I'd flatten you if you didn't."

"I resisted her, too," Leese pointed out.

"You're disgustingly in love with your wife, so it doesn't count. And if you recall, you didn't resist Catalina worth a damn."

Leese smiled. "True."

"Boys," Sahara warned...but then she laughed. "Ah, this is starting to be a trend. At least I know Leese is now off the market, so he can henceforth perform his protection details without intimate involvement."

"Absolutely," Leese said.

"Same here," Justice assured her. "If Fallon hadn't been so... different, I'd have done fine with her, too. Hell, I worked for that movie star with chicks throwing themselves at both of us nonstop and I wasn't once tempted to be inappropriate. But Fallon got to me."

"You were different with her," Miles said, offering up some defense. "We all noticed that right off."

He sighed. "Yeah."

Sahara pointed at Justice. "I won't ask for details—"

"Good." He wouldn't have shared anything private anyway.

"But Rebecca insists that they continue to pay, so they're still clients—and no, don't argue about it. It's not your decision to make." Leaving her desk, she muttered, "I'm running an agency, not a dating service."

"Yes, ma'am."

She shot him a look so mean, he had to bite back a smile.

"Do not screw this up, Justice."

"Won't."

In a silent command for everyone to go, Sahara opened her office door. "Miles, let me know if you have any questions. If you decide to join us, we can meet again and go over any unanswered questions you might have."

"I'll be in touch," he promised.

Leese said, "I have time to give him a tour before I head out."

As Justice passed her, she touched his arm to get him to pause. To Leese, she said, "You're meeting with the lottery winner this morning?"

"Him and his wife. Seems like a real nice guy."

"Good, keep me posted." Pitching her voice low so the others wouldn't hear, she said to Justice, "At this point I'm starting to feel like a pimp but...keep up the good work."

She closed the door on his look of surprise.

Slowly, the grin spread over his face. Working for Body Armor was a hell of a good decision.

And thinking of the job... He jogged to catch up with Leese and Miles. "I'm joining you on your tour so I can talk to you about something."

"Something like Fallon Wade?" Leese asked.

He shook his head. "Something like... Tomahawk Nelson."

CHAPTER FIFTEEN

Justice parked in front of the Wade household and bounded up the steps. Anytime he was away from Fallon, he looked forward to seeing her again.

Every time he had her, he wanted her more.

He'd managed to cool his jets enough to actually help her experience some of the things she'd missed out on. The woman was a true movie junkie and wallowed in any theater experience. Together they could go through an entire tub of popcorn, two colas and a box of candy.

Her favorite flicks were of the action variety, and man, he loved her for it. He could tolerate a sappy movie just barely, and had in the past done so just to appease a date.

With Fallon, it wasn't necessary.

Scary movies spooked her, but that just meant she cuddled closer, especially once he had her in bed. He couldn't get enough of that.

Two weeks had passed, and he'd tried to be considerate with her parents by only keeping her overnight on the weekends. Little by little, she was coming into her own and he couldn't have been happier about it.

The whole bodyguard thing, though…nothing else had happened. They dated, had sex, enjoyed each other, and there wasn't a single risk to be found. So how did he justify charging them when he didn't do anything differently because of the job? He would always protect her when she was with him, and he wanted her with him more.

He figured he'd talk to her dad about it today.

Before he could knock, Rebecca opened the door.

"Good morning, Justice. How are you today?"

"Terrific." He looked past her but didn't see Fallon. "How about you?"

She drew him inside. "I'm well, thank you. But I have a favor to ask."

With the way she looked at him, suspicions sparked. He said only, "Yeah?"

Glancing around, she tugged him toward the dining room. "If Fallon heard me ask you this, she'd overreact."

Yeah…he was getting a really bad vibe about things.

"However, I'm not only certain you'll understand, I'm positive you'll agree."

Having no idea what she wanted, he said, "Yes, ma'am."

"Clayton and I are going out of town together for ten days. We haven't done so in a very long time."

Given the way they hovered over her, he figured they probably hadn't left Fallon alone since she'd been burned. "Someplace special?"

"Clayton has business in New York. I used to always go along and shop, then join him for dinners. But…" She faltered, then looked away.

Justice gently patted her shoulder. "I understand." He really did. Losing one child, having another so badly hurt, it made sense that they hadn't wanted her out of their sight.

"I'll be better able to enjoy myself if Fallon stays with you." Flapping a hand, she said, "Oh, I realize there hasn't been any real danger, but I'm still very anxious about it. The two of you have spent some nights together, so I was hoping, if it wouldn't be an imposition—"

"Totally works for me," he rushed to tell her. Have Fallon all to himself for ten days? Hell, yeah. "Don't give it another thought."

"If Fallon knows I asked you—"

"Yeah, about that." He rubbed the back of his neck. "I don't want to keep secrets from her, so how about I make the suggestion that she stay with me, then later—like after it's a done deal—I can tell her that you explained things to me up front?"

The way Rebecca's eyes softened and her mouth curled, Justice wasn't surprised when she hugged him.

It did startle him when she said, "You're just too, *too* wonderful, Justice. Thank you."

Wonderful? He didn't know how she figured that just because he agreed to keep her daughter close. True, he didn't know much about long-term relationships, definitely didn't have much experience with them, but everyone knew lies, even lies of omission, weren't the way to go.

"Is something wrong, Mom?"

They both turned to Fallon, who watched them closely.

"I was just telling Justice how I plan to join your father on his trip to New York tomorrow."

"Oh." She dusted her hands over trim denim capris that hugged her thighs and ass. "You're leaving early, right?"

"Too early," Rebecca agreed with a laugh. "But Clayton's first meeting is at lunch tomorrow and he wanted me settled in the hotel first." To Justice, she said, "We'll use the suite in our own hotel. Since so many people greet us, it takes a few minutes to actually get to the rooms."

Keeping his attention glued to Fallon, Justice barely heard her mom. It pleased him a lot to see her wearing a top with a more open neckline. The peach colored, V-neck T-shirt was still

modest and her scar didn't show, but at least she hadn't bundled
her neck in a scarf. Her hair was a little more tousled, her eyes
bright and already he wanted her.

"You look nice," he told her in a voice gone deep. But damn,
now he knew what she looked like naked, and it wasn't like he'd
be forgetting anytime soon.

"Thank you."

He watched as she stepped into casual flip-flops, then tracked
her every step as she came to hug her mother.

She said, "I can be home earlier tonight to help you pack."

"I've already gotten it done," Rebecca assured her. "You go
and have fun." She flashed a conspiratorial glance at Justice.
"Stay out as late as you'd like. In fact, we can make this our
goodbye right now."

Justice drew Fallon to his side, then said to Rebecca, "Call if
you need anything."

"Thank you, I will. And you have my cell number, as well."

It got more awkward by the second, so Justice urged Fallon
from the house. Wasting no time at all, the second they pulled
out of the drive, he asked, "Why don't you stay with me while
your folks are out of town?" He bobbed his eyebrows. "We can
play house."

Her smile twitched. "And how, exactly, do we play that?"

"It could start with us getting naked."

She laughed. "And getting into bed?"

"Or the shower or the couch or, hell, the dining table works
for me." Once he thought it, he pictured it, and he started to
get hard. "I'd love to see you laid out there on the table, like
my own private dessert."

"*Justice.*"

"Well, I would."

After a steadying breath, Fallon nodded. "Okay, I like those
ideas, too."

His cock jumped up in joy.

"But first…"

First? He glanced over and saw her withdrawing a list from her purse. *Time to rein it in.*

He cleared his throat. "Got something else you wanted to do?" Fallon had lived such an inhibited life that now he wanted her to see and do and experience everything that interested her. If that meant putting his own wants on hold for a while, he didn't mind at all.

"These are listings for apartments that interested me."

Apartments? Whoa. He squeezed the steering wheel and hoped he misunderstood. "Apartments for who?"

"Me." She laughed. "I've enjoyed myself so much lately, I've decided it's time for the next step."

"Your own place?"

"Exactly."

God, he hated that idea. "Why? I mean, we've been getting out a lot, right? Having fun?"

"So much fun," she whispered. "But at twenty-four I'm old enough that I shouldn't have to explain to my parents anytime I'm out all night."

So it was her nights with him that had put the idea in her head? Well, hell.

True, there hadn't been any recent threats. That didn't mean he was convinced that her fall down the stairs was an accident. Someone *had* tromped his flowers and painted her driveway.

Also, he couldn't forget that anonymous call claiming Tomahawk had pushed her…

Both Miles and Leese were helping to keep an eye on Tom. If he was anywhere around, one of them knew it. Yet they hadn't seen anything suspicious. Other than being a major pain in his ass, Tom hadn't made any untoward moves.

Justice decided he needed to reason with Fallon, and what better way to do that than to point out her close relationship with her parents. "You know, I think Rebecca might be more understanding than you think. She knows you'll be staying with me while she's away, and she didn't mind at all."

Fallon's head snapped up from her perusal of her list. "What do you mean, she *knows*?"

Uh-oh. "She, ah..." How to word it? "She would assume we'll be spending more time together while she's away. You know, because the opportunity is there and everything."

Fallon seemed to accept that but shrugged it off. "I'm not spending two weeks with you."

Wow. Okay, that hurt. He didn't bother hiding his scowl. "Why not?"

"Because I'm not going to intrude on you like that." Before he could set her straight, she added, "And you've known from the jump that I wanted to get out on my own."

But...yeah. He had known. Fallon deserved to be "free"— her word, not his. If living on her own would do that for her, how could he selfishly ask her to move in with him instead?

Was moving in together even the right move? They'd known each other close to a month. Sure, they'd packed a lot of together time in there, being nearly inseparable for most of those days.

He'd loved every second of it—but had she?

Was he being too clingy? Grabbing for more than she wanted to give?

Could be.

After all, when it all boiled down, he was still her bodyguard. Her best interests had to be his priority.

Hating it, Justice nonetheless agreed with her. At a stoplight, he said, "Let me see the list."

She handed it over without argument. The first two places he automatically discounted. They weren't in the best parts of town and they were too damned far away from him.

The third...yeah, the third was *maybe* doable. He did a quick calculation in his head and figured it was no more than ten minutes from his house.

Aware of Fallon watching him closely, he folded the list to the third address and handed it back to her. "We can check out that one."

"Justice," she said calmly. "I wasn't asking."

"I know." The light changed and he pulled away. "But I'm your protection and my recommendation—" *a better word choice than what he wanted to use* "—is that the first two are in dangerous areas. Your folks would worry endlessly." Hoping that'd seal the deal for her, he glanced her way. "You don't want that, right?"

"No, I don't."

Stalling for time, he said, "You know we can't go today, right? I'll have to scope it out first."

"Now you're just being silly."

As he started to deny that, he got a call on his cell. He glanced at the Bluetooth screen in the car, saw it was his mom and answered with a push of a button.

"Hey, Mom. I've got you on speaker, okay? There's a girl with me—"

"There's a skunk in the shed! A raccoon I could deal with, but not a skunk. Mom's here and she's insisting she can handle it, but, Eugene, you know the woman can barely walk after her accident!"

He winced at the name, avoided eye contact with Fallon, and said, "Is she at least wearing her glasses? Maybe she doesn't know it's a skunk."

"Oh, she knows because I told her. She said I was being a wimp and that she'd handle it."

Justice bit back his grin. "I'll be right over, okay? Tell Granny I'll wash her in the creek if she gets sprayed by that skunk."

In the background, he and Fallon both heard her yell, "He's going to drop you in the creek, Mom! You know he will, too."

His granny's voice came through loud and clear when she barked, "I'd like to see him try!"

Oh, man.

"I'll be right there, Mom. Sit on her if you have to." He disconnected, wondering what to say.

Fallon snickered.

Taking that as a good sign, he asked, "Mind if we make a detour?"

"Of course not. I'm sort of anxious to meet your family."

He reached for her hand. "The other women in my life, you mean?" Being honest with her, he said, "They're nothing like your folks, but they're great. I think you'll like them."

"They raised you, so I already do."

Nice. Justice knew his mom would go nuts over Fallon. He only hoped she didn't chase her away with her enthusiasm.

Alone in the living room with the two women, Fallon tried not to blush. The way they both stared at her, fixed smiles on their faces, didn't make it easy.

"You have a lovely home." Avoiding their piercing gazes, Fallon glanced around at the cozy home done in a traditional style with upholstered furniture, an enormous television, and plenty of colorful throw pillows. Homemade curtains covered the windows and a variety of braided rugs covered the hardwood floors. It was clean but a little cluttered; photos of Justice at various ages filled the mantel, the walls and the side tables, with photos of his father beside them.

"Thank you." Iris, his mother, never looked away. "I like the privacy here."

"I would, too. It's beautiful." Large shade trees filled the spacious lot, which was bisected by a long gravel drive that led to the house set a good distance from the main road. Woods on one side and to the back probably caused the problems with skunks and other critters. To the other side was the long creek separating the property from a farmer's field.

As Justice had said, both women were very petite, but that was where the similarities ended.

Iris, his mother, had the same flair for "style" as her son. Her shoulder-length hair had turned to silver, but she'd enhanced it with a wide purple streak off to one side. Bold makeup played up her dark eyes, and close-fitting jeans with a tank top emphasized her trim, toned figure. She didn't look trashy in any way, but she would most definitely turn heads.

His granny was the opposite. She wore her silvery white hair in a long loose braid with little soft wisps framing her tanned, weathered face. She didn't wear a speck of makeup, but wore a loosely fitted, tea-length cotton dress made for comfort, not style. Regardless, Fallon could see that she, too, had maintained her figure.

"How long have you and Eugene been dating?"

"A few weeks." Fallon didn't mention that he'd been—still was—her bodyguard.

"He never mentioned you," Mona grumbled. "I'm going to kick his butt for that."

Both women were a delight, and very openly nosy. "He's been sweet, and I'm afraid I've kept him quite busy."

Dark eyes brightening, Mona said, "Do tell," with a lot of suggestion.

"Mom," Iris chastised, but she did so with a smile.

Realizing how that had sounded, Fallon quickly clarified. "That is, we've done a lot each day—"

Their smiles widened.

Worse and worse. "I mean—"

Mona barked a laugh and slapped her knee. "We've got her blushing, Iris. When was the last time Eugene brought around a girl who even knew how to blush?"

"He never brings around *any* girls," Iris pointed out. "I was never sure if that was because of the girls, or because of us."

"Oh, he's really proud of both of you," Fallon rushed to assure them. "It's easy to see how close you are whenever you've been mentioned."

"He's mentioned us?" Iris asked.

"Well, when he met my father——"

Hand to her throat, Iris said to Mona, "He's met her father!"

Fallon knew she was botching her first meeting but had no clue how to fix it.

Luckily, Justice stepped in then. Even better, he didn't stink of skunk. He took one look at how his granny and mother sat in chairs facing Fallon on the couch, and cocked a brow. "Are you two behaving?"

Mona said, "No. I was trying to get some details, but so far all I know is that you're proud of us."

He grinned, bent to kiss the top of her head and said, "Wonder if I was drunk when I gave that impression."

Iris laughed, not in the least insulted. "Got the skunk taken care of?"

"Yup. It was a young one and didn't give me too much trouble when I relocated him a good distance into the woods. I found where he was getting into the shed, too. A couple of rotted floorboards at the back behind the mower made it easy for him. I nailed down a temporary barrier, but I think the whole floor probably needs to be replaced."

"Should I call someone?" Iris asked.

"Nah. I'll get to it."

Iris's gaze shifted to Fallon. "I don't want to interrupt your romance."

"You won't," he said without a single twinge nor any denials about a romantic relationship. "I can bring Fallon along with me."

Everyone looked at her. Put on the spot, Fallon said, "That's fine by me, but I don't want to intrude——"

"You're not," said three voices at once.

Fascinated by these women who'd known Justice—or rather, Eugene—as a little boy, she grinned. "All right, *Eugene*. Thank you. I'd love to visit more."

Iris popped to her feet. "While you're here, mind if I show you a few other things that need work? You could fix it all on the same day."

"Sure, Mom."

Clearly wanting to get him alone, Iris said, "Fallon, you just relax. I won't keep him long, I promise."

Justice cast Fallon a look, then Mona. "No shenanigans, Granny, or you might end up in the creek yet."

Mona put her nose in the air. "I haven't skinny dipped in forever. Might be refreshing."

Making a horrified face, Justice followed his mother out.

"Now." Mona quickly moved to sit beside Fallon. "Tell me everything before he comes back in."

"Everything?" Fallon asked.

"How you met, how long you've been together, and how serious it is. Hurry. There's no way that boy will leave me alone with you for more than a few minutes."

Seeing no way around it, Fallon shrugged. "Actually, it's a pretty romantic story." She smiled. "Justice started out as my bodyguard."

The second they were alone, Justice took his mother by the shoulders. "Okay, Mom. First, quit calling me Eugene."

Her mouth twitched. "It's your name."

"I know, but you're doing it on purpose to tease me." Most of the time she called him *son* or *sweetie* or some other endearment. "Second, don't go grilling Fallon."

She smacked his shoulder. "I wouldn't have to if you'd told me about her."

"She's special," he said, catching her off guard. "There, now you've been told."

Her eyes widened and her smile turned huge. "Oh, sweetie, that's awesome!" She threw herself against him and squeezed him tight.

Used to her demonstrative shows of affection, Justice hugged her right off her feet. "Thanks, Mom, but don't go getting ahead of yourself. I haven't known her that long, and just because I'm half in love already—" *what an understatement* "—doesn't mean Fallon is, too."

Iris pushed back to scowl into his face. "Well, of course she is. Look at you, son. You're a catch. Any smart girl can see that."

He laughed. "It's fair to say, you're a little bit biased."

"A good son makes a good husband."

"Mom," he warned. "Now you're definitely getting ahead of yourself!"

Tamping down some of her enthusiasm, she patted his chest. "I'm just saying, she'd be lucky to have you."

Justice figured she might have that wrong. Knowing his mother would see it differently, he paced away to the corner of the deck where a few screws were loose. "She's wealthy."

Iris caught up to him. "What's that?"

"She and her family. They're big bucks." Only that didn't really describe Fallon at all, so he added, "She's really sweet, though, and down-to-earth."

"Seems to be," Iris agreed. "And pretty, too."

"Yeah." Justice worked his jaw, then gave up. "She was hurt once."

"Hurt?"

Leave it to his mother to focus more on that than money. Caring for Fallon as he did now, it pained him to talk about it, so he gave her the quick version of the story.

His mother didn't need the nitty-gritty to understand the emotional damage. "Oh, honey, I'm so sorry. That poor, sweet girl."

"She's touchy about the scars."

His mom leveled a look on him. "You made it clear that they don't matter?"

"Yes, ma'am." Because physically, they didn't. "Little by little, she's starting to believe me. But now she's got this new confidence, and she wants to live a little."

"She can live a little with you."

He smiled. "Yeah, she has." The smile waned. Fallon wanted to move out on her own. He'd rather ask her to move in with him, but he couldn't steal anything from her. She deserved to have everything she wanted.

"What?" his mom asked.

Justice shook his head. There were some things he wasn't yet ready to share. "You're always my biggest cheerleader."

"It's easy to cheer for a winner."

Damn, he loved her. His granny, too. They always had his back, always... *His granny.* "Oh, shit."

"Language," Iris cautioned.

"Sorry." Already striding toward the house, Justice said, "Granny's in there putting Fallon through a cross-examination right now, isn't she?"

"Probably." Jogging to keep up with his long-legged gait, Iris laughed. "Slow down! Your Fallon didn't strike me as the type to let a little curiosity offend her."

"Granny's curiosity is the equivalent of a runaway Mack truck." He burst through the door, but ground to a halt when he found the two ladies sitting close together on the couch, looking through a photo album. Heat burned his face. "Damn it, Granny—"

"Language," his mom and Granny snapped at the same time.

Eyes soft and smile wide, Fallon looked up at him. "You were so stinkin' adorable."

Justice hated to look but couldn't seem to stop himself. He peered over her shoulder and saw the god-awful photo of him as a naked infant...sucking his thumb.

Fallon touched the photo, as if she touched the baby him.

"He was a big newborn," his mom said, crowding onto the couch on Fallon's other side. "And he was always a sweet baby."

Seeing that the women would be occupied for a while—
which, okay, kept Fallon from looking at apartments, so ultimately worked in his favor—he grumbled, "I'm going to go over
the house and see what other repairs are needed. Might even go
get some supplies since I'm already here."

No one replied. They were too busy turning pages in the
album.

Marcus walked into the office where Kern and York waited
on him. Smiling at the brothers, he said, "Sorry I'm late."

"You're not," Kern told him, extending his hand. "We were
a few minutes early."

Right there on the tabletop rested the check written out for
the full amount.

"How've you been?" York asked. "Things going well with
your lady?"

For a moment, Marcus didn't know what he meant. "Who?"

"Ms. Wade. You win her over yet?"

Bristling, Marcus took time to pour himself a drink. It was
only three o'clock, but Kern and York already had drinks; no
reason he shouldn't join them. After taking a fortifying sip,
Marcus pulled out his chair opposite the brothers. "Ms. Wade
and I are friends."

"Ms. Wade?" York repeated. "You're that formal with her
still?"

He'd been trying, obviously without success, to move away
from an intimate topic. "Of course not. As I said, we're friends."

Kern snorted. "Being *friends* is not what you want."

No, it wasn't. However, by all appearances, he had lost his
opportunity. Fallon might not believe it, but what he wanted
most was for her to be happy.

Damn it all, she appeared to be very happy with the bodyguard.

York hit the tabletop. "What the hell, man? Where are your balls? You've given up, and I would have put odds on you."

Yes, he likely would have. God knew the brothers loved a bet. Well, let them deal with a little reality.

Studiously avoiding looking at the check, Marcus sat back in his seat. "Actually, I haven't seen Fallon in a while. Mrs. Rothschild Wade arranged the fund-raising meetings away from the home." He didn't mention that Mr. Wade had also told him to stay away.

"So?" Kern barked. "Her daughter hasn't been around her house much anyway."

Marcus went still. *How would Kern know that?* A dozen concerns tripped through his brain before he found the composure to hide his surprise and distrust. Trying for a note of mere curiosity, he murmured, "Oh?" as if he wasn't all that interested in the answer.

He even opened the folder to the paperwork that would finalize their donation.

York cast a worried look at Kern, then pasted on a smile. "I told my brother that I'd seen her out and about with the bodyguard. Quite a few times, in fact. It appears he, at least, is on game."

"Meaning?" Marcus stared at the papers as if searching for a necessary notation, when in reality, the text blurred together as the ramifications of anyone spying on Fallon slowly sank in.

"Meaning he's beating you, man." Kern pushed back his chair and stood. "I thought that nice donation would give you a fighting chance, but you haven't even tried to use it to your advantage."

Ah, and since he hadn't produced the results they wanted, Kern now might pull the donation? *Not if I can help it.* Collecting his thoughts, Marcus tapped his fingertips together. "It still could help. Once it's presented, there's no way Fallon won't notice." Because he would tell her—about the donation and about his concern. "I'm flattered that you're both taking such an interest in my personal life, but is there a reason why?" Pretending amusement, he half smiled. "Perhaps a bet as to who wins the girl?"

Kern looked struck, then turned to York. "Hell of an idea."

Great, so he'd just encouraged them. Yet, Marcus knew that wasn't the only bet.

"One at a time," York said with some sly meaning.

Interrupting their debate on the odds, he asked, "Why, specifically, does it matter to either of you?"

They held silent, but not for long. The brothers were too cocky, too arrogant concerning their own wealth and influence, to understand his suspicions. They considered themselves beyond the reach of social boundaries. "The bodyguard keeps dodging Tomahawk."

Marcus gave a short laugh. "I seriously doubt that he dodges anyone. If he doesn't take the fight, it's because he has no interest in it."

Wearing his most charming grin, York added, "Do your part and we'll figure out the rest."

"The rest of what?"

Pushing the check toward Marcus, Kern added, "But do it soon." His smile looked like a threat. "Honest to God, I don't give a shit about literacy." He stormed out, his laughing brother behind him.

That check began to look like a bribe, and finally, Marcus knew what he had to do.

CHAPTER SIXTEEN

Instead of looking at apartments as she'd intended, Fallon ended up visiting with Justice's mother and grandmother nearly every day.

The women were absolutely delightful, very different from her relatives...and oh-so-similar to Justice, like tinier, female versions of his humor, warmth, caring and integrity.

Never, not once, had Fallon ever doubted the love of her parents. In a million ways, they'd shown her the depth of their feelings for her. Their love was quiet and fierce, an unwavering comfort.

For Justice's family, the love was bold and in your face, hilariously demonstrative and heart-meltingly unashamed.

From the start, they included her in those tight hugs, outrageous jokes and happy welcomes.

During the times that Justice did routine repairs to Iris's property, Fallon learned to make bean soup and braid a rug. She got a tour of Justice's old room, saw his many sporting trophies, heard stories of past girlfriends and watched all the DVDs of his fight career.

In some ways, she felt like an insider with the women, especially when they ganged up to tease Justice.

"Eugene" never seemed to mind, though. In fact, he would smile in an indulgent way, as if pleased to see them growing closer.

On the eighth day after her parents left, Fallon and Justice were finally going to check out the only apartment that was still available. Later they'd take his mother and grandmother out to dinner and she already looked forward to it. She wanted to go by her house first to get a change of clothes, and when they were five minutes away, she got a call.

She pulled out her cell, glanced at the screen and saw it was Marcus.

Justice said, "Ignore it."

He'd been in a sullen mood ever since she'd insisted on seeing the apartment. It wasn't as if she wanted to give up staying with him. Now that he'd involved her in his life and his family, losing either would be like losing a piece of her heart.

But it wouldn't be fair to him. Being her bodyguard had pulled him into her problems, and now she feared he was as overprotective as her parents. She couldn't burden him.

He needed choices. He needed to know that she'd be fine on her own. If their relationship grew after that, then and only then could she entirely trust in his feelings, accepting them for what she wanted them to be rather than what they might be—worry, or worse, sympathy.

"Of course I have to answer," she said, and put the phone to her ear. He needed to understand that Marcus was not a threat. "Hello, Marcus."

"Fallon. I haven't seen you in a while."

She watched Justice's profile. "There's no reason that you would."

Genuine sadness came through his reply. "I'd like to think we're still friends."

He'd humiliated her so badly that, before Justice, seeing Marcus only reinforced her insecurity. Now, however, she felt more than capable of being around him without a single twinge. "Of course we are."

"I'm sorry, Fallon. You don't know how many times I've regretted my reaction—"

Unwilling to rehash what had been a most mortifying situation for them both, she cut him off. "I'm over it, Marcus, I promise." Just as quickly, she asked, "Is there a reason for your call?"

She heard his sigh before he said, "Yes. I need to see you. And no, it's not to rekindle anything. There's something you need to know."

What could Marcus possibly have to tell her? Whatever it was, she didn't care. "Just tell me now."

He suddenly growled, "Is your bodyguard with you?"

She looked again at Justice. "Yes."

"I assumed," he said with resigned annoyance. "Let me speak with him, please."

Fallon didn't like the sound of that at all.

"Why do you want to talk to Justice?"

Brows shooting up, Justice glanced at her.

"It's important. Since he's with you and I'm not, I'm sure he can explain better than me."

Annoyance rising, Fallon scowled. "I'd prefer that you explain."

Justice held out his hand. "Give over, Fallon."

"No." Then to Marcus, she demanded, "Tell me right now or I'll hang up."

"If you do, I'll just have to call the agency where he works and hunt him down that way. And honestly, Fallon, that might take too long. Now please, put him on."

Marcus said nothing else, damn him. She didn't know what to do.

Wiggling his fingers, Justice asked, "Do you trust the putz or not?"

"Fine." Fallon put the phone on speaker and then slapped it into his hand, unwilling to mask her irritation with manners.

"Marcus," Justice said with malicious humor. "How's it shaking?"

"Rather than be harassed, I'll get right to it."

"Yeah, why don't you?"

"We need to get together to talk, and before you turn obnoxious again, you should know, I think it's possible that Fallon is in danger."

Justice glanced at her, frowned, and said, "Yeah, let's meet."

"No," Fallon insisted, wanting to ensure that they both heard her loud and clear. "This concerns me and I want to know what's going on. *Right now*, Marcus."

After a heavy pause, Marcus muttered, "You didn't tell me I was on speaker."

Justice shrugged. "Didn't know you'd have anything worthwhile to say."

"This is difficult to explain, especially over the phone. I'm free now if we can meet."

"All of us," Fallon said.

"Of course."

They agreed to meet at her parents' house, in the driveway near the road.

Justice didn't want him any closer than that and Fallon didn't care enough to debate it.

For the rest of the short drive, her thoughts whirled. *What could Marcus possibly know about a threat?*

Justice reached over and squeezed her knee. "You know I won't let anyone hurt you, right?"

Snorting, she said, "No one is trying to. Marcus is up to something. It's ridiculous."

"I thought you trusted him."

Why did Justice have to decide now to defend her ex? "It infuriates me that he would attempt to bypass me to talk to you."

Justice pulled into the driveway, drove all the way up to the house, turned around, then went back to the entrance, now facing the street. "I think he's trying to be considerate."

She gaped at him.

"He could be really concerned about something and doesn't want to alarm you."

"I am a grown woman!"

He grinned. "I know. So we'll talk to him together and find out what's what. Okay? Just don't run him off until I've finished asking questions."

Fallon didn't point out that it was usually Justice who sent Marcus packing. "If this last apartment is gone before we get there—"

Rather than listen to her grumble, Justice got out of the car and leaned against the front bumper, his arms crossed. That made her grumble even more, especially since she assumed her mention of the apartment was what had him looking cross.

She joined him, her hands on her hips and her good mood deteriorating. How could she get Justice to see her as a completely independent woman with no need of a bodyguard if Marcus planned to introduce some trumped-up danger?

Even now, feeling irked, Fallon couldn't help but notice how impressive Justice looked with his biceps bulging and a light breeze blowing his T-shirt flat against his abs.

"Stop it," she snapped, giving him a light shove.

Startled, he dropped his arms and scowled at her. "Stop what?"

"Posturing," she accused. "Looking all macho and disgruntled. You're doing it on purpose, aren't you? Know what I call that, Justice?"

Cautiously, his frown fierce, he asked, "What?"

"Pouting."

"Pouting!" He straightened to his impressive height to stare down at her. "I do *not* pout." He stepped closer. "Actually, I was contemplating things."

"What things?"

"If Marcus is right and there is a problem, you can't be alone in an apartment."

Fallon threw up her hands. She'd known his thoughts would take that path and it infuriated her. "How come every single time I try to prove that I'm the same as other women, something stupid comes up?"

"For one thing, you're not like other women." He cooled her anger by saying, "You're a damned heiress or something. No idea what kind of money your family has, but any idiot can see that you're loaded. That makes you a target."

He had a slight point. "Justice—"

"And whether you want to accept it or not, someone is up to something." He stepped closer still, until she had to tip her head way back to maintain eye contact. "Remember the red paint? My trampled flowers?"

"I don't have a faulty memory and it wasn't that long ago."

"Well, smart-ass, that's a problem. Sure, we could write it off as vandalism, except that you were *pushed down stairs.*"

She tried not to waver under his conviction. Honestly, she didn't want to believe that someone planned to harm her. She'd never hurt anyone—except her sister. "Damn." Now was not the time to get maudlin. "I could have just stumbled."

Justice tipped up her chin. "Stop dodging reality. Let me do what I do, okay?" He bent to brush his mouth over hers. "I couldn't stand it if anything happened to you."

She wanted to say that nothing would, but suddenly she wasn't so sure. Justice's concern was affecting her. *Could I really have an enemy?* The idea chilled her.

They both looked up at the sound of Marcus's Mercedes pulling into the drive. He parked to the side of Justice's car and, without pause, got out to stride toward them.

The breeze, growing stronger, played with his blond hair and blew his tie to the side. He looked trim, stylish and, she could admit, handsome. His toned physique showed the designer suit to best advantage.

It didn't matter. Next to Justice, he seemed completely insubstantial.

Marcus took one look at Fallon and his brows went up while his jaw slackened.

She shifted uneasily under his stare. Yes, little by little she'd changed her look. Today she wore a casual spring dress, yellow with splashes of floral that complemented her figure. Rather than conceal, the fit of the dress showed off her bust. The scooped neckline was high enough to hide her scars, but showed much more skin than usual, even a hint of cleavage. A sash belt was tied at her waist and the full skirt skimmed just above her knees. She'd finished the outfit with strappy sandals and a yellow cardigan.

"Fallon," Marcus murmured, and it sounded like a verbal caress.

Justice put his arm around her shoulders and drew her into his side. "Keep it up," he warned, "and I'm going to flatten you."

Drawn back to reality, Marcus blinked. "You look so different. Nice, I mean. Very nice."

Justice growled.

Ignoring him, Marcus said softly, "I just… You took me by surprise. It's as if you've bloomed."

Flushing, Fallon nodded. "Justice and I have plans, so if you wouldn't mind.?" She loved it when Justice looked at her with so much appreciation. From Marcus, it left her cold.

He looked momentarily wounded, then shifted his gaze to Justice. "I wanted to speak in person. The entire thing is awkward, maybe even far-fetched, but it just doesn't feel right."

"Tell us what it is," Fallon insisted, and she got a squeeze from

Justice. Right, he wanted her to let him do the questioning. She leaned into him, which was as much approval as he'd get.

"I think it's best if we keep this between us. You'll understand why—I hope—when I've finished." Marcus looked at each of them, then settled on Fallon. "You remember the men I had with me at the MMA competition?"

She lifted a shoulder. "A little."

"I remember them," Justice said.

"I believe I explained to you then that Kern and York Arnold are very wealthy men and they enjoy spending their money in outrageous ways."

It came back to Fallon in a rush. "You said they even bet with women as the prizes."

"Willing women," Marcus made clear. "But yes, it's as if they try to outdo each other in their extreme gambles." He shoved his hands into his pants pockets, his gaze on the ground. "Frankly, I've seen shocking behavior from both of them."

"They spoke with Tomahawk at the event," Justice said. "He knows them?"

His gaze shooting up to meet Justice's, Marcus frowned. "I don't know. Or rather, I'm not sure how well he knows them." He paced away, turned back. "They gave me an astounding amount for the literacy fund-raiser. Their one check equals the total we had hoped to gather in donations."

Fallon didn't understand. "That's good, isn't it?"

Justice took a step forward, his posture and tone hard. "Not if they're trying to buy him."

Marcus surprised them both by nodding. "My concern exactly."

Tucking her slightly behind him, Justice said, "So what is it they want you to do, and what does it have to do with Fallon?"

Looking past Justice, Marcus locked his gaze with hers. Softly, he said, "They want me to win you back."

★ ★ ★

"Like hell." Justice wasn't about to let some wealthy dude in a fancy suit get in his way. Fallon was his and she'd damn well stay his. It didn't matter that Marcus, Kern and York fit better into Fallon's world. It didn't even matter that he, himself, made good money, first as a fighter and now as a bodyguard. Fallon wasn't a woman who cared about material wealth.

She cares about me.

He believed it, and soon she'd admit it—preferably before she plunked down first and last months' rent for an apartment she wouldn't be using.

Having her around his mom and granny had been a stroke of genius. Fallon flourished under their easy acceptance and lack of formality. In no time at all she'd become a cozy part of the family.

The problem was, she'd loosened up enough that other guys took more notice of her—Marcus included. That wouldn't do. The sooner he got this settled and got her away from her ex, the more he'd like it.

Jealousy was a bitch.

"Just so I'm clear here," Justice said in what he hoped was a mild tone, "you have about thirty seconds to get the point."

"I'm trying, but it's not easy. Most of my concern is just a feeling."

"Gut instinct," Justice said, willing to give him his due. "Never ignore it."

Nodding, he glanced at Fallon, but seemed to find it easier to speak directly to Justice. "The brothers were in my office today and they were more than curious as to whether or not Fallon and I were back together."

Justice's jaw tightened and his eyes narrowed. "I hope you set them straight."

"In fact, I did. I explained that we were only friends now."

Lower, he said, "I've never liked to hear them say her name or speak of her."

Fallon asked, "Why would they talk about me?"

"That's just it, I didn't know. They tried to be subtle about it playing it off like male camaraderie or something, but no matter what they said, it felt disrespectful." He drew in a breath. "Believe it or not, Fallon, I care for you. Beyond that, I respect you a great deal and I don't want anyone in any way to slander you."

Muscles tensing, Justice asked through his teeth, "Exactly what did they say?"

"Nothing specific, definitely not any direct insults. It's that they're—" he searched for the words "—irreverent. Spoiled. Obnoxious. Selfish." He glanced at Fallon. "All things I would never associate with you. It doesn't matter what money they have or how much power that money brings them. They aren't good enough to joke about you as if you're just another woman, a woman they would know or would use in a bet."

Justice didn't like the small understanding nod Fallon gave Marcus. "Why the hell didn't you shut them up?"

"I'm a businessman," he snapped. "I can't go around alienating every person who's a jerk. Because of my position, I'm forced to use diplomacy."

"We understand." Fallon tipped her head. "But I still don't hear a threat."

Hands on his hips, head dropped forward, Marcus muttered, "They know the two of you are dating."

"So?" Justice said. "We haven't made it a secret."

"Justice." Fallon touched his arm, and the quietness in her tone alarmed him. "They don't travel in the same circles. Seeing them at the fights, that was a fluke. Since then, we've been to low-key places, or at your mother's. If these men know we're dating, someone is telling them."

"Or they've been spying on you." Marcus lifted his head.

"They know she's been staying with you, that she hasn't been home." Quietly, Marcus repeated everything that had been said.

Gut instinct. Justice felt it now and he wanted to whisk Fallon away from any possible harm. First, though, he had to uncover the source of the danger.

Doing his best to stay clearheaded and keep the rage at bay, he asked, "Any ideas?"

Marcus gave a brief shake of head. "I don't know anything for sure, but I suspect they have a wager on a fight."

"They want to see a rematch with Tom and me." Grim, Justice cursed low, his hands curling into fists. "I still don't see how Fallon plays into this, or why they'd be keeping tabs on her. Is Tom somehow in on it?"

"I don't know that," Marcus said quickly. "But an idea occurred to me for how we could find out."

Justice stiffened. "No."

"What?" Fallon asked, looking from one of them to the other.

"No," he said again.

"Tell me," Fallon insisted.

Marcus folded his arms over his chest and stared at Justice. "We need to pretend to give them what they want."

Miles sat at a booth in Rowdy's bar, slowly nursing a beer. At another table with a few other fighters, Tom brooded. He didn't join in on the jokes and he wasn't drinking as much.

Suspicions sucked. He liked Tom all right, but he trusted Justice more. Leese felt the same. If Justice had reason to doubt Tom, that was good enough for them.

A slim, familiar figure wearing designer jeans and a body-hugging top walked through the front door of the bar. Maxi Nevar's dark blond hair trailed down her back, and her brown eyes searched the crowd.

For him.

Miles waited, deciding if he felt like giving in to Maxi to-

night. He had twice before and both times the sex had been…
well, incredible. Mind-blowing, even.

The lady wasn't shy, and she knew what she wanted.

Her gaze met his and she smiled, proving that tonight, *again*,
she wanted him.

As she made her way toward him, Miles finished off his beer.
He couldn't say what it was about Maxi that made him want to
stay detached. Possibly her own detachment. She enjoyed sex
with him, but wanted nothing else.

Other men in the bar tracked her progress as she maneuvered
her way across the floor. He should just be flattered, but God,
he'd suffered from a weird mood lately.

When she finally reached him, she asked, "Alone tonight?"
as if it didn't matter all that much, as if, if he had a date, she'd
be okay with it and would just mosey on.

"I'm alone," he said. "But sort of working." His gaze skipped
over to Tomahawk. Miles watched him smile at something
someone said, then turn distracted again.

"Working on getting drunk?" Maxi asked with a laugh as she
settled her sexy behind across from him in the booth.

"Only one beer," he said, then resented that he'd explained.
He never got drunk, but since they only had a very limited relationship—which was exactly how he wanted it—she didn't
need to know his habits.

"Just a cola for me," she said to the waitress who stopped by
their booth.

"Another for me," Miles added, handing over the empty bottle.

Maxi tipped her head, causing that dark golden hair to cascade
over her breast. "Would you rather be alone tonight?"

Not really. "Just weighing my options."

To his consternation, she laughed. "Another woman has
caught your eye? Should I vacate the booth before she gets the
wrong impression?"

Sitting back, he stared at her. It wasn't natural, damn it. "What's the lure, Maxi? That I'm a fighter?" Because he might not be for much longer.

"That's a joke, right? The first night I came in here, I noticed you right off. When I hit on you, I had no idea what you did—and I don't care."

"So if I decide to take up waiting tables?"

"I assume you'd still have an occasional night off and I'd see you here, right?"

For a booty call. Frowning, more at himself than her, Miles said, "I don't know."

For only a heartbeat, her dark eyes looked troubled, then she quickly brightened again. "Well, that would be a waste, but I'm sure I'd survive."

No, he hadn't imagined it. He'd seen something, maybe worry? "Actually, I'm thinking about being a bodyguard." *Why the hell did I just tell her that?* He waited, wondering how she'd react.

"To protect someone specific?" She crossed her arms on the tabletop and leaned forward enough that he could see her cleavage.

Maxi had a nice pair on her, full and soft with sensitive mauve nipples. Once, she'd damn near come from him sucking on her. He stirred remembering it.

But then, the second she'd walked in, his temperature had spiked.

Without giving him a chance to answer, she added, "Not being nosy, but if you're involved, then I'll definitely move on."

Knowing she would, Miles shook his head. "I meant as a career choice."

"Sounds exciting—and I go back to my original question. You'd have the occasional night off?"

The server brought their drinks, giving him a moment to think and time to check on Tom. He saw a woman leaning over

Tom, whispering in his ear. *Good*, he thought. *Go home with her so I can quit watching you.*

To Miles's surprise, Tom kissed her palm, whispered something back to her and sent her away. The others at his table heckled him, but Tom only shook his head.

What the hell was going on?

A small, warm hand covered his, drawing Miles back from his curiosity. He met Maxi's dark eyes, already heavy with interest. While they looked at each other, she toyed with him, trailing her fingertips down the seam between two of his.

"So," she whispered. "Are you going to be free for a few hours tonight or not?"

A few hours. Nothing more. She wouldn't ask him why he planned to leave fighting, or why he was sulking over his beers. She never pried. Never asked anything personal.

She just enjoyed his body for a few hours, the orgasms he'd give her, and then she'd leave his house and he wouldn't even know if he'd see her again or not.

"Depends," Miles said, watching her. "Your place tonight?"

Her smile never slipped. "No."

"I'm starting to wonder if you're a serial killer. Maybe an escaped convict? Do you have a husband and kids at home?"

Slowly, she sat back, her smile gone. She stared at her drink. She seemed somehow…hurt.

"Maxi—"

"I'm not married. No kids. I don't like cheaters."

Well, that was something at least.

"I've never broken a law in my life. Not even the speed limit."

"A paragon of virtue, huh?"

"Hardly that, but I'm a coward." Her dark gaze met his. "Much too much of a coward to ever be a serial killer."

Pushing her, Miles asked, "What do you do for a living?"

"I'm a personal shopper."

Huh. That fit, given her great style. "One more question."

"I won't be grilled. You're either into it or you're not."

"It" being meaningless sex. *And since when has that been a problem for you?* "Why me?"

Her arched brows twitched. "That's it? That's your question?"

"Yeah."

The smile returned and she leaned forward again. "Let's go
to your place, get naked and I'll show you."

Maybe his dissatisfaction was because the guys were all starting to settle down. Gage, Cannon, Denver, Stack, Armie and
Leese. Now even Justice appeared hooked. Like dominoes, once
the first one fell, the rest tumbled. But here he was, feeling...
fuck it. He felt a little lost, and admitting that, even to himself,
burned his ass big-time.

"I told you, I'm working."

She bit her lip and, resigned, sat back again. Miles watched
her play with her purse strap, tuck her hair behind her ears, look
out at the bar and at the front door where she'd entered.

"What are you thinking, Maxi?" It struck him and he asked,
"Your name *is* Maxi, right?" How far would she go to stay an
enigma?

"Yes, that's my name. Short for Maximara." After a few seconds, she looked up at him again. "May I ask you something?
Nothing personal, I promise."

Miles laughed. "I don't mind if you ask anything personal."
Of course, he knew why she didn't. If she asked something personal, he might reciprocate. For whatever reason, she didn't want
him getting too close.

"Are you really that busy tonight, or have you lost interest?"
She rushed on, "If you have, you can just tell me. I'm not a
stalker type. I won't bother you."

His gaze moved to her mouth, and he thought of the incredible things she did with it. "See the big guy two tables over?
Heavyweight fighter?"

She glanced around. "I can't really tell weight classes—oh."

Turning back to him and leaning forward, she asked, "What about him?"

"I have a friend who works for the Body Armor Agency. That's the bodyguard gig I'm thinking about taking. Well, my friend needs me to keep an eye on the big lug over there, so that's what I'm doing."

Accepting that, Maxi considered things, then asked, "For how long?"

"Until he leaves here."

"So you could be really late."

Gently, he asked, "Got somewhere you need to be?"

"Not really, no."

"So stay. Keep me company. Tell me where you got that name and what a personal shopper does. When it's time to go, you can follow me to my place."

Over the next half hour, between flirting, teasing and laughing, Miles managed to pry a little info from her. As a near stranger, she'd been hot.

Seeing her like this, less "on the make" and more relaxed, only gave her more substance. When Tom got a call and stepped toward the front door, away from the din of conversation, to talk, Miles said, "I'll be right back," and followed him.

People entered and exited the bar, so Tom paid no attention when Miles moved to stand behind him, close enough to overhear.

"Right now?" Tom asked, looking out at the passing traffic, oblivious to everything else. "Yeah, I mean sure. I can make it." He nodded, repeating the name of a ritzy neighborhood as if to memorize it. "I'm familiar, yeah. I'll leave now, but that's across town, so give me a little time." He nodded again. "Thanks, Kern. See you soon." He disconnected and turned so fast, he damn near plowed into Miles.

"Tomahawk," Miles said, after he'd backed him off a little.

"Damn, man, didn't see you there." Distracted and in a hurry, Tom shoved the phone back in his pocket. "What's up?"

"Nothing. Just grabbing some air." Feeling like a sleuth and liking it, Miles asked, "You?"

"Meeting with a few sponsors. Big spenders." Smiling now instead of looking glum, Tom whacked him on the shoulder.

Miles stopped him from rushing off. "Sponsors for what? Got an upcoming fight?"

"If I can get Justice on board, yeah."

"I don't think that's happening."

"Hey, these guys can be persuasive. So don't count me out yet."

Miles watched him go inside to let his friends know he was leaving, then rush back out again. Once he'd driven down the road, Miles put in a call to Justice.

While the phone rang, he thought about life changes, and he thought about Maxi.

He'd made up his mind. Tonight would be a celebration, and he couldn't think of a better way to spend it than with a woman who burned him up, kept him guessing and didn't demand much in return.

CHAPTER SEVENTEEN

The restaurant was loud, the conversation at their table rowdy. Anytime Justice got his mom and granny out together, they had a great time. He didn't like the way Fallon had withdrawn. When his mother noticed, Justice subtly shook his head, warning her not to mention it. Marcus had thrown a lot at Fallon today, not only the possible danger but also the way they'd most likely resolve it. She deserved time to think about it, and hopefully she'd come to the right conclusions.

Let me protect you.

He couldn't take his eyes off her—something else his mother noticed. He saw Fallon smile as his granny described the way she'd taught him to dance. Many a night before dinner, they'd crank up the music and glide around the kitchen floor in their socks. Fallon obviously loved the story, but her smile didn't quite sparkle in her eyes as it usually did.

When his cell rang Justice barely heard it, but he felt it buzzing in his pocket.

He glanced at the screen, saw it was Miles and pushed back his chair.

Feeling like something was about to break, Justice said to the table, "I have to take this," and stepped to the entry.

Miles got right to the point. "I was hanging at Rowdy's, keeping an eye on Tom as I promised. But a few minutes ago he got a call from someone named Kern and took off."

"Shit," Justice muttered, not wanting to believe Tom would be such a dick.

"He said it's about a sponsorship—for a fight against you."

Justice listened as Miles related the conversation. Like hell anyone would "convince" him. More like they meant to coerce him somehow, but that wouldn't happen either.

"You said he left?"

"Going to meet the guy."

Justice held the phone back to see the time. Nearing nine o'clock. Okay, not a crazy time for a meeting, but definitely not routine either. "Did he mention where?"

"Yeah, see that's the thing." Miles paused as if he dreaded sharing the rest. "Tom mentioned the same neighborhood where Fallon lives."

"That's too much coincidence for me."

"Maybe," Miles agreed. "But don't do anything stupid."

"Like?"

"Hit first and ask questions later. Be cool, okay? Just because he knows those dudes—"

"And is associating with them." *Maybe conspiring.*

"—doesn't mean he's guilty of anything. You've known Tom awhile. He deserves an opportunity to explain."

Justice indulged a deep, cleansing breath. It helped, but not enough. "Right." At the moment, the urge to destroy anyone who threatened Fallon burned hot. Unfortunately, he knew Miles had a point. "And pulverizing him won't get me the answers I need."

Moving past the idea of violence, Miles asked, "So what are you going to do?"

"I'm going to call Leese. Then I'm going to do my own conspiring."

★ ★ ★

Snickering, he watched from a safe distance away as Tom Nelson, aka Tomahawk, arrived at the destination. Like a sitting duck, Tom put his car in Park on the side of the road, ready and willing to wait.

As bait.

The big brute was far too gullible.

He had it all planned out, but several things had to align. Would Tom be patient enough? Given the prize, he'd wait as long as necessary.

Fortunately, only ten minutes passed before Justice Wallington's car came into view. Anticipation sizzling, he crouched beside the tree, the lighter in his hand.

Before anyone had arrived, he'd poured a generous amount of diesel across the road, followed by a trail over to where he hid. Once everything happened, it'd be easy for him to sink deeper into the lush landscaping. As always, he'd get away without a scrape—but the two fighters wouldn't be so lucky.

As a kid, he'd pulled this prank often. He'd found the panicked results of the startled drivers keenly satisfying.

With luck, the results this time would be even better.

As Justice's car drew nearer, he flicked the lighter, saw the flame dance, and at just the right moment, he put it to the trail.

In the darkness of the night, the red and yellow flame licked quickly across the road, flaring up just as Justice reached it. He watched the fighter hit his brakes hard, swerving sideways until the car slewed partially off the road and came to a shuddering halt.

Gleeful at that reaction, he hunkered down out of sight, listening for the woman's cries. Holding in his chuckles, he cocked an ear, waiting.

He heard only the hoot of an owl and the sound of the breeze playing with leaves overhead.

Nothing even remotely like female hysterics.

A second later the driver's door shoved open and the fighter emerged, one very pissed-off man.

In that brief moment while the overhead light glowed, he saw inside the car and knew the fighter was alone. *Where was Ms. Wade?* Her fear would have added nicely to this confrontation.

It didn't matter, he convinced himself. The results would be the same.

Predictably, Tom, who had parked only a short distance away, came jogging closer to help.

Fists would be flying in no time—he was sure of it.

As he faded back, he waited for the fun to begin.

Justice stared at the slowly dying flame. *What the hell?*

Diesel, he thought, given the scent. He scoured the area, but the ritzy houses on this stretch of road sat acres apart from one another. Thick trees and high, manicured hedges lined the road to offer privacy.

Thinking he heard something in the woods beyond, Justice's eyes narrowed. He saw a shadow move and took a step in that direction.

"Justice?"

He jerked around at the shout and—surprise, surprise—found Tom jogging toward him.

Bewildered, looking at the flames, Tom asked, "What happened, man?"

Refusing to blow it by being too calm, or too enraged, Justice locked his hands down at his sides. "What are you doing out here, Tom?"

"Had a meeting, but the guy's late." He glanced at the car, still idling, with the ass-end over the shoulder of the road, almost in the gully. "You hurt?"

"No." Justice thanked God he didn't have Fallon with him. She, along with his mother and granny, were on their way home with Leese. Hitching his chin, Justice asked with lethal menace, "Who has a meeting here, on a dark road, at this time of night?"

Brows coming down, Tom stared at him. "Is this another accusation?"

"You're quick today, huh?"

Tom bristled. "I let you get away with that once, man. I won't take it kindly a second time."

"Take it any fucking way you want." Justice pointed at him. "Twice now shit has happened, and both times you're on the scene."

For a second, Tom looked like he might lunge for him.

Justice was counting on him wanting the sanctioned fight in the cage, not a street brawl.

At the last second, Tom visibly gathered himself and glanced around the area instead.

They stood to the side of Justice's car. The headlights cut across the road and into a line of thick shrubbery and pruned trees.

Rubbing the back of his head, Tom asked, "Did I see fire in the road?"

Aware of possibilities, Justice replied, "You did. A line of diesel, deliberately set."

Tom's gaze shot up. "Someone wanted you to wreck?"

"And here you are," Justice smirked.

Tom inhaled. "Yeah, okay, I admit, it looks bad." He glanced back at the car. "Fallon's not with you?"

"No."

"Small blessing, I guess."

He eyed Tom, surprised that he was staying so composed. That in itself made his cynicism grow. "What meeting?" Wondering if Tom would tell the truth, Justice asked, "Who's late?"

"Rich dude named Kern Arnold. He was at Stack's last fight..." Tom paused, then gave a rough laugh. "This won't exactly exonerate me, but Kern and his brother want to sponsor me—that is, if I can convince you to give me a rematch."

There'd be no rematch, but all he said was, "Sponsor you how?"

"Lots of bucks. Full ride." He stared at Justice. "They're big fans."

Did some lackey set the fire for Kern? Or was the bastard sick enough to want to see the reaction himself? Was it possible that even now, he lurked there in the shadows, listening?

Damned coward.

Searching the area, Justice said, "I got the impression the brothers didn't know that much about MMA."

"Yeah, they're new to the sport. They like it. Stack's fight was their first live event, but they're really into the heavyweights now. They watched our last fight on the internet and they're hoping for a rematch."

Just as Marcus had said. But why spy on Fallon?

Almost as soon as he thought it, Tom gave him a credible answer. "I told them I didn't think you'd go for it, that you liked your new job and were hung up on Fallon." He quickly held up his hands. "Not that there's anything wrong with that. Just that it looks like you're going in a different direction now." He shrugged. "They said they could convince you."

Did they hope to get Fallon out of the picture, to force him to refocus? "I've told you at least a dozen times that it's not happening. I suggest you convince them, as well."

Tom scowled. "You're killing me, man. The girl is nice and all, but—"

"No buts." *Fallon was considerably more than nice.*

"The brothers said they could bring you around. God knows they have the money to do it. So at least hear them out."

Would they offer him money, Justice wondered, or did they plan another form of leverage? Maybe something involving Fallon?

He glanced up and down the road. "I think you got stood up."

Frustration deepened Tom's frown. "I'll call him and see what's up."

"Yeah, before you bother, we need to talk."

"That's what we've been doing, right? But you're still being a stubborn ass."

Justice walked over to the driver's door and got in.

"What are you doing?"

With a little effort, he got his car back onto the road. Tom stood there, hands on hips, watching until Justice backed up alongside him. With the push of a button, he lowered the passenger window and said, "Get in."

He could tell that Tom wanted to refuse, but then with a curse, he opened the door and slid into the seat.

"You're damned annoying, Justice, you know that?"

Calmly, Justice drove up the short distance to where Tom had parked, pulled in behind his Corvette and put the car in Park.

Half turning in his seat, he faced Tom. "I'm going to believe you're here for a meeting, but if I find out otherwise, I'll destroy you."

Rage growing, Tom barked, "To hell with it. We can settle this right now." He reached for the door handle—and the lock clicked into place. Incredulous, he glared at Justice. "Are you out of your fucking mind?"

Since he planned to tell all to Tom…maybe. But hell, he was willing to work with Marcus, and that had already put him over the edge of sanity. "Let me lay out some facts here for you, okay?"

"You've got about two seconds."

Justice decided to start with the most pressing issue. "Someone is deliberately placing you at the scene each time something happens."

The scowl lightened, and Tom scoffed. "What are you talking about?"

"You don't think it's a hell of a coincidence that Fallon would get elbowed down the steps when she's away from me, but close to you? Then someone calls the agency and labels *you* a threat. Now we're both on this road—a road where we normally wouldn't run into each other—and some asshole pulls a prank with diesel that could've gotten someone killed."

Tom glowered as he considered it then shook his head. "I told you, I'm here to meet Kern."

"But the bastard's not here, is he? It's just you and me. I don't mind telling you, with everything's that happened, if Fallon had been with me, there's a damn good chance I'd be even more pissed than I am. It wouldn't take much for one of us to lose our cool and end up—"

"Fighting," Tom agreed with thoughtful uneasiness. He rubbed his face. "So you think what? That someone wants us to battle it out? We're on a dark street with no one around."

Calmly, Justice pointed out the obvious. "If it's just us, who set that diesel on fire?"

Bewildered, Tom sat back in his seat. "That's a hell of a conspiracy you're spinning."

"Yeah."

"I have to admit, it does seem off."

"Big-time." Justice rested an arm over the steering wheel. "Without any bullshit, have you ever followed me?"

"What do you mean?"

Resting his wrist on the wheel, he gestured toward Tom's car. "In your Vette."

Knowing he was busted, Tom shifted. "Well, fuck, this is awkward."

Justice waited.

"It's not what you think."

"No? So what is it?"

"I was on that side of town to get my car serviced and I just happened to see you. Sure, I followed for a bit. I couldn't think of any reason for you to be over that way unless you were going to another gym to train, which would mean you weren't as out of the game as you claimed."

"Why would you give a shit?"

"Because I want a goddamned rematch!"

Justice studied him. "You didn't follow me to Fallon's?"

Slashing a hand through the air, Tom said, "No. Hell, I didn't know anything about her until I caught up with you at Rowdy's."

"No way you didn't see her with me in the car."

Coldly, Tom said, "For someone who doesn't want a fight, you sure like to sling out the insults."

"Well?" Again, Justice waited.

"I saw you had someone in the car, yeah, but not her specifically. I figured just a date, you know? I wasn't interested in following you anymore, but we kept going in the same direction until somehow I lost you. I ran a few other errands, then we both ended up at Rowdy's, so I guess we were headed in the same direction." He shrugged.

"What's the name of the place where you get your Vette serviced?"

Tom told him without hesitation, even naming the street. When Justice pulled it up on his cell, the route made sense. "Pure happenstance, huh?"

"Believe it or not. I don't care."

But Justice could tell that he did. Hell, no one wanted to be unjustly accused. "That's the only time you've ever followed me?"

"Swear to God, and I didn't exactly plan it that time."

Justice believed him. "Okay then. You want to know why I'm so skeptical?" By the time he finished explaining all his concerns with Fallon, the brothers and Marcus, Tom was outraged.

"What can I do?" he asked simply.

Justice told him.

★ ★ ★

Marcus sat in uncomfortable silence inside the conference room of his offices. Across from him, Tom Nelson maintained a deadly stare. He was enormous, layered in muscle and presently in a bad mood. Or maybe he had no other mood—although, thinking back, Marcus remembered when Tom had met Kern and York at the MMA event. He'd been all smiles and "good old boy" charm then.

What the hell did these fighters eat? How many hours did they spend training?

Unlike Justice, Tom's mocking smile felt like a knife blade to his ribs. Justice, at least, had a little humor to him.

It had taken some fancy maneuvering to arrange the meeting. Justice wanted Tom and the brothers together, in front of Marcus, so that the puzzle pieces fit together in an unmistakable pattern. There could be no doubt, no suspicion of secret intent.

In the end, Marcus had called Kern to say he must meet with him that morning, only minutes after Tom had also requested a morning meeting. When Kern mentioned the conflict, Marcus offered to call Tom and arrange them to meet together in his office's largest conference room.

A small security camera was set up in the corner, and more importantly, Justice wasn't far away.

Hell of a situation to find himself in, Marcus mused. He currently relied on Justice, the man who had replaced him with Fallon, to keep him safe from harm.

Untenable, but what choice did he have? That same fighter would also keep Fallon safe, and that's what mattered most.

Getting up to pace, Marcus tried to ignore Tom's penetrating stare as it tracked him around the room. He was just about to demand that he cease and desist with the intimidation tactics when the door opened and his assistant announced the brothers.

Wearing wide smiles, Kern and York strode in. They'd dressed in casual clothes; khaki slacks on Kern, shorts on York, both wearing open-necked shirts and watches that cost as much as some people's cars.

Before Marcus could greet them, Tom growled, "Wasn't sure you'd show this time."

Why was Tom so damned hostile? If he didn't let up, he just might blow everything.

Marcus at least wanted to keep it together until the check cleared. The more ethical thing to do, he thought, would be to tear it up and toss it into the brothers' faces.

He wouldn't do it.

He'd earned the damned donation and knowing it'd be put to good use was enough of an incentive for him. Still, he had to keep the brothers trusting him another two or three days until they'd settled everything.

Taking the seat at the head of the long table, Kern smiled toward Tom. "Yes, I'm sorry about that. I got held up."

York sat at the opposite head of the table, stealing Marcus's seat. "Did you wait around very long, Tomahawk?"

"Got here five minutes ago."

Nonplussed at that reply, York shook his head. "Ah, no. I meant last night."

Shrugging, Tom sipped his coffee.

Determined, Kern leaned forward. "Last night—I tried to call but my cell service was acting up."

Again, Tom shrugged, and Marcus could see that it exacerbated both brothers. Were they hoping to discover what had happened last night? Or did they already know and only wanted Tom's accounting of it?

Marcus wasn't at all sure about Tom. He seemed sullen and unpredictable. Marcus's own ruse was enough to make his palms sweat, but at least he recalled what to say. "While we waited this morning, Tom and I have gotten better acquainted. He mentioned that he had unexpected company last night, so it wasn't a total waste."

"Oh?" Kern lifted his brows with fervent interest.

Finally, Tom deigned to play his part. "Justice Wallington had a mishap on the road, not more than a few yards from where you asked me to wait."

"Mishap?" Kern asked.

"Yeah. Some juvenile bitch playing a high-school prank. No big deal." Tom smiled.

"Do tell."

"You can imagine, he wasn't happy." As if they'd asked, Tom said, "No one was hurt."

Showing marked disinterest in that, Kern said, "Good thing," then asked eagerly, "So you and Justice. How'd that go?"

"Got a fight lined up."

Excitement caused a second of utter stillness before Kern and York celebrated with loud whoops. Kern left his seat to slap Tom on the shoulder, full of congratulations.

"So tell me," York probed, his tone cagey, "what turned the tide?"

Now that Marcus was onto them, the brothers were nauseatingly transparent.

"Guess there's more people like you two," Tom said, "fans who want to see me fight."

"And that mattered to Wallington?" York asked.

Tom snorted. "Why the hell would he care?"

He's toying with them, Marcus realized, appalled by the risk. Good God, were they all insane?

"Well," Kern suggested, somewhat unsure of himself in the face of Tom's attitude, "Justice was so dead set against fighting you—"

"He still is."

The brothers looked at each other, sharing their confusion, until Kern exploded. "You just said you had a fight!"

"I do, just not against Justice."

"But…" Kern pulled out the nearest chair and dropped into it. "The plan was a rematch."

"I had to give up on that," Tom said. "I'm set to fight Denver instead. He's another mountain, and damned good, so I'll get lots of exposure for the fight."

When Kern and York just stared at him, Tom continued pricking them with inane details. "It'll be the main event, probably in Vegas, but we're still waiting for the calendar to be finalized. My manager will let me know as soon as—"

Slamming his hand down on the table, Kern shouted, "What do you mean, you gave up?"

Marcus jumped in surprise.

Tom never even flinched. His flinty gaze met Kern's, and his slight smile slapped like an insult. "Not much choice. Some asshole is trying to make it look like I'd use Justice's lady to get my way."

York and his brother shared a fast, covert glance, so maybe Marcus was the only one to notice the clenching of Tom's jaw.

Kern cleared his throat. "You could—"

"No. If I press Justice now," Tom continued, "he'll never believe I didn't push the little lady down the stairs, or stomp on some fucking flowers or something."

"Uh…flowers?" York asked.

"Doesn't matter." Tom finished off his coffee. "Some gutless punk is playing childish games, and because of that I have to change my plans."

"This fight was important to you," York insisted.

"Not as important as my rep. A real man would never use a woman to get what he wants, and I'll be damned if I'll let anyone think I would."

Flushing, Kern tried a different tact. "You explained to Justice that it wasn't you, and he believed you?"

"Hell, no. Justice wanted a piece of me, no doubt about that. Thing is, he refused an actual fight in the cage, and I told him

I wouldn't risk an injury without an audience. He told me to stay away from him, and I agreed. End of story."

"We offered to sponsor you!" York accused.

"You still can."

Fuming, Kern snapped, "We wanted the damned rematch!"

"Get in line."

Everyone seemed to have forgotten him, Marcus thought, sinking back in his seat and staying still, content to be a silent observer. Tom's open disdain of the brothers, as if they were no more than troublesome brats, fascinated him. Kern's red-faced rage was a sight to behold. And York, his air conniving... Yes, fascinating—if it wasn't so dangerous.

Kern shoved back his chair so fast it hit the floor. "You don't understand. It doesn't have to be a professional fight. We don't care about that."

Tom curled his lip. "I care."

Edging his testy brother aside, York righted the fallen chair and turned to straddle it. He faced Tom with an implacable smile. "Here's the deal. Kern and I want to see you fight Justice, not some other goon. We've got a little wager on it, you see, and as Kern is the current loser in a string of bets, he's anxious to try to even the score."

"I'm betting on you," Kern offered for encouragement.

When Tom narrowed his eyes, unimpressed, York said, "You will fight Justice Wallington, wherever he wants—even in a goddamned alley for all I care—and we'll be your very generous sponsors for two years."

Tom lazily considered York. "So you're betting against me, huh?"

"There must always be a winner and a loser."

"This time," Kern said, "you and I will win, Tom. I'm sure of it."

Tom appeared unmoved by the pep talk.

"We'll supply you with comfortable living quarters wherever

you train, cell phone, insurance, a food and entertainment al-
lowance, and we'll provide any equipment or supplements that
you might need."

Kern rushed to support his brother. "Two years, Tom. You
won't get a more generous deal anywhere."

In a perfectly timed act, a knock sounded on the door, saving Tom from having to answer.

As if she owned the place, Fallon breezed in, then paused at
the sight of the three extra men. "Oh, Marcus, I'm so sorry.
Your assistant didn't mention that you had guests."

"No matter." Smiling, he stood. "I wanted to see you as
soon as you arrived." God, she was pretty, always had been, but
now that Justice had given her more confidence, she positively
glowed. She'd changed her hairstyle a little, dressed in femi-
nine clothes that showed off her body and smiled with sincere
happiness.

Marcus wished it wasn't a farce, that her smile was for him,
but in the years he'd known her, he'd never been as good for
her as Justice had in such a short time.

Did the fighter really not mind those awful scars?

Seeing them had completely caught Marcus off guard. With
time, he could have grown accustomed to them, but he'd never
suspected, never considered… For the hundredth time, he cursed
himself for reacting as bluntly as he had.

Fallon hadn't said it, but Marcus assumed she loved Justice.
He saw it in the way she looked at the man, how different—
how *carefree*—she was around him. Justice appeared to feel the
same. There was a possessive look in the man's eyes that went
beyond the duties of a bodyguard and a familiarity in the way
Justice watched her. Intimate familiarity.

Fallon deserved happiness, so for her, Marcus would recite
his lines and, hopefully, assist in securing her safety.

She hesitated at the door. "I can wait—"

"It's okay, this is both a business meeting and personal, but I wanted you to meet the Arnolds anyway." As he held out a hand to Fallon, he glanced at the brothers. They appeared confused by all the sudden changes. "Honey, these are the gentlemen who were so extremely generous toward the literacy fund-raiser."

Fallon smiled at the men. "Thank you so much, both of you. I'm still stunned, and of course, so incredibly pleased."

York held out his hand. "York Arnold, ma'am."

"Fallon, please," she said, taking his hand in both of hers. "It's very nice to meet you personally, York."

"This is my brother, Kern."

Kern gently took her hand. "Obviously Marcus has excellent taste."

Surprising Marcus, Fallon leaned against his shoulder in an affectionate way. "Thank you."

"I saw you at the MMA venue," Kern said, as if he'd just remembered it. "Excuse me, but I thought you were with that fighter, Justice Wallington."

Giving a rueful grimace, Fallon nodded. "I found out that Justice isn't quite done with the sport. It's a commitment leaving little time for relationships."

"Surely no man would neglect you," York said.

"It doesn't really matter because Marcus won me back." In a teasing stage whisper, she confessed, "I made him work for it."

The brothers actually looked captivated.

"And I," Marcus said, "used your generous donation as a good excuse to get her to talk with me again."

"It worked," she said with a laugh.

Suddenly Tom shoved back his chair. "I need to get going."

Kern stepped toward him. "But—"

"I'll let you know this afternoon what I've decided." Tom paused. "Either way, thanks for the offer."

Nice way to leave them wondering. Marcus watched Tom go, only half listening as Fallon picked up the conversation, keeping Kern and York from following.

After adequate time, Marcus reclaimed the room. "York, Kern, the reason I asked you to stop by is because we're creating a plaque to honor you for your lavish financial gesture. The plaque will hang in a prominent location in the new library. Now, thanks to you, at-risk children will have easy access to books."

York grinned. "I'm glad we could help."

"Let's celebrate over lunch," Kern said. "We can talk MMA, and maybe, Fallon, you can share a few tips on how to get Justice Wallington back in the cage for a rematch."

"I would love to help out," Fallon said with a laugh. "Unfortunately I already have another appointment for today." With Leese, who would ensure she got home safely while Justice kept an eye on the brothers.

Marcus's heart raced as he stood and walked her to the door. He looked down at her, wondering if she'd kiss him goodbye to seal the deal—but no, she patted his cheek, waved to the brothers and left.

Chagrined, despite the fact none of it was real, Marcus turned back to York and Kern. "Now, what was all that with Tom?"

CHAPTER EIGHTEEN

In the storeroom of Rowdy's bar, away from prying eyes, Justice pulled Fallon close and kissed her, first the tip of her nose, then her chin, her cheek, and finally he settled his mouth on hers. Her soft lips parted and he felt the touch of her damp tongue.

Groaning, Justice crushed her closer, taking her mouth in uncontrolled need, stroking deeply with his tongue, wanting to consume her.

"Excuse me." Avery, Rowdy's wife, laughed as she bumped her way past them, jarring Justice back to reality.

He lifted his head and saw Avery's long red ponytail swish as she reached high on a shelf behind them for a massive jar of pickles.

Justice easily stretched past her. "Let me." He fetched it down for her.

"Thank you." Hugging the jar to her body, Avery said, "Carry on!" A second later, they were alone again.

Fallon, trying to stifle a laugh, covered her heated cheeks. "Busted," she whispered.

Justice gathered her close and touched a finger to her now swollen mouth. God, he loved the taste of her, the way she fit against him. He pressed his forehead to hers and groaned again. His need was a live thing, always pushing at him.

Fallon smoothed a hand over his chest, then curled her fingers against his shoulder. "I missed you."

"Love hearing that." For only a few days they'd been playing this stupid but necessary game, yet it felt like an eternity. Damn it, he liked sleeping with her at night, waking with her in the morning. He'd grown used to her small body snug against his during the night, just as he'd grown used to regular sex, the hottest sex he'd ever had.

"Marcus has been nice," she said. "I thought I would be more uncomfortable with him, maybe even bitter, you know? But I'm not."

"Should I be jealous?" Stupid question; he already was.

She tucked her face against his throat. "Before you, I saw Marcus only as the man who'd rejected me."

"He's regretting that, I'm sure." *The putz.*

"Since meeting you, Marcus is just someone I know, someone I can think of as a friend." She tipped her face up to look at him with those big, soulful eyes. "His reaction to my scars was an eye-opener, but also real. I can't fault him for how he feels, but I'm glad I found out before we got any more involved."

"My reaction is real too, honey." He put his lips to her ear and whispered, "Seeing any part of you makes me hard."

She laughed. "That's the main reason I can now accept Marcus as an acquaintance, a friend and nothing more."

Marcus was no longer the man who hurt her. Justice only hoped that made him more irrelevant. "You're saying I helped you get over the bad memory?"

"You obliterated the bad memory, and I love you for it."

Justice's heart plummeted to his knees, then shot up into his throat. *Love.* Jesus, he almost felt dizzy.

The urge to swing her up, twirl her in a circle and tell her that he loved her, too, surged through him.

He held back only because she hadn't said it in a romantic way. She hadn't said, *Justice, I love you.*

Words he wanted to hear.

She'd only expressed her gratitude for the way he'd gotten her past her insecurity. This was too important to misunderstand; he wouldn't embarrass her by pouncing on such a simple statement.

Her gaze stayed with his, her smile in place, and Justice knew he had to say something.

Straight from the heart, he decided. "You're the most special person I've ever known, Fallon. I love everything about you." Watching the confusion flit over her expression, he smiled to himself and kissed her again.

Soon she'd understand, but damn, the storeroom of Rowdy's bar was hardly the place for declarations.

Hardly the place for him to be getting a boner either, yet after hearing that four-letter word, *love*, thrown around, he knew he was almost there.

He broke off the kiss and cupped her face in his hands. "Everything should be settled today." Then he'd get her back where she belonged—with him.

"God, I hope so." Her smile teased. So did her fingers on his chest. "I miss your house, Justice."

A hint? She'd been staying with Leese and Catalina for the last few nights. No way did Justice want to risk her being home alone in her parents' mansion, and he sure as hell didn't want to tempt fate by pushing her at Marcus.

It amused Justice that his house could fit into the garage of her parents' mansion, but Fallon never looked at it that way. Even her dad had assured him how little she cared for the pampered life.

He had to taste her again. If Fallon was close, she drew him in, sharpening every physical need. "I miss having you there," he admitted against her lips. "A lot."

"That apartment I wanted to look at is gone."

Justice froze. *Good.* He didn't want her in an apartment.

Unsure why she'd mentioned it, he tried for a neutral tone. "Still determined to go that way, huh?"

"I'd like for each of us to have options."

He didn't want options; he wanted Fallon. This time, though, with him, her needs had to come first. He smoothed his thumb over her downy cheek, knowing he'd do damn near anything for her. "Soon as we get this settled, we'll talk about it more, okay?"

She nodded, her dark eyes staring up at him. "Are you sure you know what you're doing?"

"Hope so." Taking her hand, he led her over to a stack of boxes to sit. It sucked, having to sneak around to see her, but the alternative, not seeing her, would be far worse. "The bastard brothers now believe you're with Marcus, so hopefully you're not on their radar anymore." That had been his number-one goal. He'd hated thinking she might be a target used to twist him into lashing out.

"It's not me I'm worried about."

"Don't worry about me either. You know I can take care of myself."

"Yes, but those men—"

He shushed her, saying gently, "Tom talked with Kern and said he'd do his best to convince me to take the fight. They seemed to think that with you out of the picture, I'd have less reason to want to be a bodyguard, plus I'd have a lot of anger to unleash."

"It's all so idiotic."

"They accomplished one thing." Justice shared a grim smile. "I'm furious, but then, so is Tom. Only we're not directing it at each other."

Fallon leaned against him, her voice low. "Tom's still disap-pointed."

"Yeah, but he'll get over it." Tom had a nice future ahead of him; he didn't need a stupid rematch. "If things go off as planned, he'll be in the headlines a lot. That should guarantee

him a good fight. The powers that be never miss an opportunity."

"I'm glad."

Justice rubbed the back of his neck. "The problem is that I
don't want your name brought into it. Somehow I have to bust
them without you being mentioned."

"I think it's a little late for that."

"No." He refused to believe that. "Your dad would have my
head if, after everything he's done to save you from the press, I
put you smack dab in the spotlight."

Slowly, Fallon stood to face him, her gaze direct and her expression tight. "We've already agreed, numerous times, that my
parents are overprotective."

"No argument from me." He understood them, but he also
knew they hadn't done Fallon any favors by smothering her and,
unintentionally, filling her with guilt whenever they worried.

"Since I met you, I've wanted you to know I'm independent."

"And you are, except when two psychos are plotting against
you, willing to do whatever it takes to get their way."

She gave a sheepish grin. "Justice." Putting a small, warm
palm to his jaw, she said, "I've wanted to keep you around, but
not like this."

Keep him around? He wasn't going anywhere. "This," he
emphasized, "isn't your doing. How do you think I feel? I'm
supposed to protect you and instead you're being used because
of me and a career I've already given up."

Frustration stiffened her shoulders. "I need you to be different, Justice. I need you to see that I'm capable of—"

He snatched her onto his lap and kissed away her gasp. "Now,"
he whispered, when she fell silent, "let me explain, okay?"

Gaze fastened on his mouth, she nodded.

Damn, but it was nice being wanted by Fallon Wade. "I'm
not giving you special treatment, not like you think, anyway.
If this was happening to my mom or my granny or any of my

friends' wives, I'd be the exact same way." Did Fallon understand that for any woman he cared about—any woman he loved—he would do everything in his power to protect her?

"You would?"

"I'd be as bad as the brothers if I didn't."

After giving it some thought, she nodded. "All right. But you have to understand me, too. If busting those creeps lands my name in the press, I'm okay with that. I can handle it. It falls on me, Justice, not you."

He looped his hands around her waist. "You're pretty amazing. You know that, right?"

Laughing at his praise, she rolled her eyes.

"Hopefully it all goes off without a hitch." He glanced at his watch and knew Tom would be calling Kern right about now. This time, Kern and York would be the targets. "I've talked it over with Leese and my boss, Sahara. I've got Miles and even Brand on board to help." Thinking about Miles's willingness to jump in, he said, "Did I tell you Miles might be joining us at the agency? I don't understand why. He's at the top of his game."

"Maybe he just needs a change."

Justice shook his head. "The sport is in his blood. Something else is driving him, I just don't know what it is."

Fallon jumped when his cell rang. Justice knew she was nervous about everything and wouldn't be reassured until it was over. He spoke with Tom, got the confirmation and, stepping out of the storage room to snag a bustling waitress, asked for Miles.

Before his friend could join him, he cupped Fallon's face. "I need you again. Soon."

Nervously, she nodded. "Tonight?"

"One way or another." Seeing Marcus pretend to be with her had been hell. Still, Justice had to give the guy props for playing his role so convincingly. Any fool could see that Marcus still had strong feelings for her but he had set those aside to help.

Miles stuck his head into the cramped room. "Everything set?"

"Yeah. I'm meeting Tom there in a few minutes."

"Good. Best to get it over with." Miles glanced at Fallon while saying, "I'll let the others know and be right back."

"Thanks."

Hands clasped behind her, breath uneven, Fallon watched him. Justice could damn near feel her nervousness.

He couldn't take it. Without planning the words, with no conscious decision to share them, he heard himself say, "I'm in love with you."

Her eyes flared and her hands dropped to her sides. "What?"

She needed to hear it again? Yeah, he sort of did, too. "I'm in love with you. I don't mean to put you on the spot, and you're under no obligation—"

"Justice."

"I'd planned on talking to you about it—" *It.* What a stupid way to refer to something so overpowering, so all consuming. "After this was all settled. But, I dunno, I needed to share, I guess."

She put a trembling hand over her mouth.

Miles stepped back in. "Everyone's ready. I can take Fallon out the back after you're gone. Cannon and Armie are going to follow, not that they don't trust Marcus, and not that I can't handle it, but you know how they are."

Still watching Fallon, Justice smiled. "Yeah, I do." He cupped her chin. "I'll let you know as soon as I wrap it up."

She flung herself at him, her arms tight around his neck, her breath choppy. "Please be careful."

"Hey," Miles said. "He'll be all right, honey. Honestly. It's covered."

Justice laughed, saying close to Fallon's ear, "I'm encouraged." He gave her a squeeze, kissed her temple and stepped away to sneak out the back door of the bar.

He'd had many fights, but this would be the biggest fight of his life because this time, there was a lot more on the line than recognition in a sport he loved. Regardless of the risk, he couldn't stop smiling. Soon as he rid himself of York and Kern, he could get back to Fallon.

That was a bigger payoff than he'd ever imagined.

Leese drove the car, Brand beside him in the front seat. Fallon was in back with Miles. The silence left her throat tight; these men, badasses all of them, were every bit as worried as she was. Slumping against the door and fighting off the fear, she watched the scenery speed past.

Brand twisted to look over the seat at her. His gaze, so sinfully dark, pinned her in place. "Tell me about the bodyguards you've had."

Drawn from her maudlin thoughts, Fallon started in surprise. "What do you want to know?"

"I take it Justice isn't the norm."

In a tart voice, she replied, "If you're asking if I've had sleepovers with other bodyguards, the answer is no."

Brand grinned, and he looked so sexy she had to sigh.

"You've had bodyguards since you were young, right?"

"Yes." She really didn't feel like chatting. She wanted to wallow in her concern. But how fair was that to the poor men assigned to keep her company? They were Justice's friends. She should treat them better. "My parents often thought it necessary to ensure my safety, at least at big functions. Usually the bodyguards were remote, not friendly like Justice. For different reasons, they were noticeable."

"Clichés?" Brand asked.

"Dark suits, precisely trimmed hair…even their body language screamed 'professional for hire.'" She gave it quick thought, then smiled despite herself. "Justice is the total opposite. He stands out, no way he couldn't. But it's not because anyone thinks he's been hired. It's just that he's so big and muscular, so cocky and—" Seeing Brand's grin, she cut herself off in midsentence. "I'm sure you understand, since you stand out, too."

"Thank you."

Oh, this one could be dangerous, she thought. Talk about cocky!

Miles turned in the seat to face her. "Was there ever a time when your folks didn't have a bodyguard hovering over you?"

"Yes." And it had been tragic—because of her. "My sister and I convinced them we'd be fine at a lake property they'd purchased but hadn't yet remodeled. The cabin was secluded, so there weren't any other people nearby and no one knew we'd be there." Odd that she could talk about this now without a single shiver in her voice.

Because of Justice.

God, in so many ways he'd dragged her out of a troubled past and into a very bright future.

He said he loved her, and she didn't have a single doubt that it was true. She didn't need to prove anything to him.

And she no longer needed to prove anything to herself.

"My sister died at that cabin, and I was badly burned." No one interrupted as she told what had happened. Telling it the first time to Justice had been difficult. Now, it truly felt like a memory and nothing more.

Brand's gaze never left her. "I imagine that made your folks even more determined to protect you."

"Yes. That's why they hired Justice." She felt a small smile tug at her mouth. "My mother thought he might blend in better."

Miles snorted. "He blends in about as well as a longhorn bull in a herd of calves."

Fallon laughed. "Very true." She sighed, "I took one look at him and fell hard."

"Fell?" Leese asked, the first thing he'd said.

"In love. Or at least, in deep infatuation. It wasn't long before I knew I was lost, though. Justice is just so…exceptional."

"Yeah." Brand laughed. "Exactly how I'd describe him."

Maybe because she didn't have many friends, Fallon found herself confessing all. "I wanted to prove I didn't need a body-guard, that I was as self-sufficient as any other woman. I had planned to get my own apartment and live off my own funds."

"But?" Miles asked.

"Justice told me that he loves me."

"Duh," Brand said. "We all saw the clues the first time he brought you around."

She remembered how each of them had treated her as Jus-tice's girlfriend instead of his client. "Well, you guys are more perceptive than I am." *And I was afraid to hope.*

"So what are you going to do?" Leese asked.

Was he concerned for his friend, worried about her breaking Justice's heart? Not likely. "I'm not sure yet, but I love him, too. Right now, nothing else seems as important as that."

Her statement effectively lightened the mood and the rest of the drive was spent with the fighters asking her various ques-tions about bodyguards, assuring her Justice could handle him-self just fine, and telling her more about his past.

If so much weren't on the line, if she didn't have so many le-gitimate reasons to fret, she would have honestly enjoyed herself.

Even in gym shoes, the cavernous room of the abandoned warehouse echoed his every footfall. Dust motes danced in the stale air and damp mold blackened the walls. Without being too obvious, Justice searched the perimeter of the room.

Broken equipment, piled off to the sides, offered lots of con-cealment. Only gray light filtered through the grime-covered windows.

The setting was perfect.

He strode to the middle of the cleared floor to join Tom.

Leaning against a section of dusty conveyor belt, anticipation bright in their eyes, York and Kern watched.

"You brought backup?" Justice asked Tom.

"Those two?" Tom laughed with derision. "They're just here to watch."

"Witnesses to your confessions, huh? I didn't think it'd be that easy."

"I'm not confessing shit." Tom squared off.

Impatient and very, very stupid, Kern shouted, "Enough chit-chat, boys. Get on with it."

Justice stared at him with all the rage he felt. "Get on with what? You want to see us fight?" He curled his lip. "I wouldn't waste my time."

Tom bristled. "Then why the hell did you come?"

"To tell you to your face how pathetic you are." Justice pointed at him, his voice cold as ice. "And to warn you for the last time to stay away from Fallon."

Red faced, Tom shouted, "I told you, I never touched her!"

"You're a miserable liar."

Hands clenched in his hair, Tom strode away in mock frustration.

Smiling, Justice turned to go.

A hunk of metal sailed across the room and crashed into the wall with a clatter. "No," Kern shouted. "Hell, no, it's not stopping here! You two have to fight."

Justice flipped him off and kept going.

"Damn you, Tom, do something!"

That's it, Justice thought. *Take the bait.*

Tom asked, "What the hell do you expect me to do?"

"Throw a punch!"

More quietly, Tom said, "Then I'd be the coward he accuses me of being."

Justice paused to look at him.

"I didn't touch your lady," Tom swore.

"She's not his lady," York snapped. "She went back to Marcus."

"Doesn't matter." Justice folded his arms over his chest. "A real man never threatens a lady, any lady."

Throwing up his arms, Tom raged, "I agree with you!"

Wearing a mask of scorn, Justice moved closer. "Admit what you did. Admit you're a pussy that picks on women, and maybe then I'll annihilate you."

Through his teeth, looking far too sincere, Tom said, "I have never abused a woman in my life."

Maybe because Justice had once accused Tom of exactly that, Tom wore his insult with convincing umbrage.

"Then fuck it. No fight." He turned his back and strode away.

"Wait!" Kern threw something else, making a terrible racket.

A temper tantrum, Justice thought. The lack of control disgusted him.

"Tom didn't do it!"

At the sound of Kern's frantic voice, followed by the equally appalled rush of his brother's whispers, Justice paused.

"I did it."

Slowly, Justice turned. Pretending he didn't understand, he narrowed his eyes on Kern. "You did what?"

York gripped Kern's arm, trying to hold him back, but Kern had lost all sense. "I was coercing you."

"Coercing me?"

Unashamed, almost boasting, Kern explained, "I had her pushed down the stairs."

Icy anger filled Justice's veins, but he feigned only mild surprise. "And the flowers and the paint on the driveway?

"The call to the agency accusing me?" Tom asked.

"Yes, all of it."

York gaped at his brother. "Shut up, you idiot!"

"What does it matter? They can't do shit." Kern pulled out his wallet. "I'll pay for the flowers and the paint." He threw a thick wad of bills at them. The money separated midair, fluttering in individual bills to the dirty ground, ignored by both fighters. "I'll give you each an extra twenty grand, too."

Walking toward him, Justice said, "I don't think so, you gutless prick. How can you pay for terrorizing a woman?" Justice loomed over him, forcing him to back up a step. "How the hell do you pay for her bruises?"

Smug and unconcerned, Kern said, "By not bruising anyone else?"

Yet another threat? "What are you talking about?"

"Fight Tom," he said. "Right here, right now."

Resisting the urge to punch the smile off Kern's face, Justice shook his head. "I don't think so."

"Oh, you'll do it," Kern growled, throwing caution to the wind. "Think about your mother, your grandmother."

Justice kept his expression set and said nothing.

"I've had you watched, of course. I know where they live." Kern fished out his phone and shook it at Justice. "One call from me, and my man will find new ways to convince you, I promise you that."

To keep him talking, Justice asked, "You really think you can get away with that? You want the fight so badly that you'd risk everything?"

"There's no risk to me," Kern boasted. "There never is."

Never is? So Kern had done this before?

"I want the fight and by God, you'll give it to me."

The silent "or else" hung in the air. Doing his own bit of gambling, Justice smiled. "If what you say is true, then you should know that I anticipated it." Yes, he had. He'd covered all his bases. "My family is safe, you psycho."

Kern laughed. "No one is ever safe."

Again, York tried to silence him, but Kern was beyond reason, intent on bragging.

"You think tucking that little slut away with a friend somehow protects her?" He leaned closer. "You'll do exactly what I say, and you'll do it now."

Fallon was with Leese, and no way would Leese let anything happen to her. Knowing it and convincing himself of it were two very different things, especially with the signs of insanity right in front of him. "Or what?"

Kern examined a nail. "Or I'll have my man burn Leese Phelp's house to the ground with everyone in it. Ah, I see that got your attention."

York said, "Jesus, Kern, you have to shut—"

Kern didn't listen. "I have men there, you know. It'll look like a gas leak. There's been no alteration to any insurance they have, the two pet dogs are still present, and they're all in the house. It'll be so tragic, no one will suspect a thing."

Panic tried to take hold, but Justice held it back. "You're full of shit."

"Boom," Kern said, fluttering his fingers into the air. "There will be nothing left but splintered debris. No one will ever suspect foul play."

Justice couldn't breathe. "That's not possible." *Don't let it be possible.*

"His house has natural gas, so of course it's possible. I've done it before," Kern bragged, "and no one suspected. Even if they did, so what? They couldn't confirm it, and they sure as hell could never peg it on me."

It hasn't happened yet. Justice clenched his fists, knowing he'd do whatever was necessary to keep Fallon from being hurt— even if it meant killing the man in front of him.

As Kern studied Justice's face, he whispered with satisfaction, "Yes, now you understand, don't you?"

"I understand."

"So throw a goddamned punch, already!"

Justice let out a breath. "Gladly." With one big step, he closed the distance between them.

Belatedly, Kern realized his error. He tried to lurch back and tripped into his brother.

Catching him by the wrist, Justice brutally squeezed until the cell phone dropped to the cement floor. He crushed it with his heel and, smiling at Kern, twisted his arm until a bone popped.

Kern screamed.

Justice silenced him with one solid hit to the jaw, breaking that, too.

York started to run and plowed headlong into Tom. "I don't think so," Tom said.

Police swarmed into the area.

York turned at the sight of a photographer recording everything, and his mouth flapped like a fish out of water.

Sahara stepped out, making a beeline for Justice. "I called Leese with the phone on speaker so he could hear. I didn't dare say anything to him for fear these miscreants would hear me." She touched his arm. "The line is dead now. An officer is already on his way there."

Justice inhaled shakily.

"Go," she whispered, "before you get detained here. Tom and I can handle this. But Justice, be careful."

Without another word, Justice ran out.

CHAPTER NINETEEN

Fallon stood across the street, her arms wrapped around herself, taking in the scene with disbelief. It wasn't that cold, but she couldn't stop shivering.

Brand looked down at her, then slipped his arm around her shoulders. "Reaction," he said in explanation. "It's a son of a bitch."

Brand was big and warm...but he wasn't Justice. "They wanted to blow us up." She still couldn't believe it. "All of us."

"Yeah." Brand pulled her in against his chest, now with both arms around her while he briskly stroked her back. "But they didn't succeed and we're fine. All of us," he repeated.

She didn't feel fine. Tears threatened, but she ruthlessly blinked them away. Her stomach knotted and her legs didn't want to support her.

"Come on," Brand said, leading her over to his car.

Fear squeezed her throat and she croaked, "I don't want to be alone."

"You're not." He didn't put her in the car, but guided her to sit on the front bumper. It was better. At least her knees weren't knocking anymore.

Leese and Miles had two men corralled on the curb a few feet away. The men's faces were badly battered. So were Leese's and Miles's knuckles.

Brand had helped some with that, until he'd noticed her standing there, useless, scared…

"You're not a trained fighter," he said.

Fallon shook her head. No denying that. Until recently, until Justice, she'd barely been an adult. No, that wasn't true and she wouldn't insult herself. She'd been overly reserved, but she'd known all along what she wanted.

Justice had helped her to get it.

Where are you, Justice? "All I did was panic and get in the way."

"Not true. You were the first to hear the noise outside. Then we got that call from Sahara." He fell silent, his shoulders tensing, probably in memory.

For a second, they'd all been in indecision. The threats they'd heard… If they rushed outside, were there men waiting to cut them down? For a certainty, they couldn't stay in the house while being threatened with a gas explosion. After she'd heard the noise, Leese had made the decisions. He'd settled, uncomfortably, on going out first with Miles while Brand waited just inside the door with her.

Repeatedly, she had sniffed the air, but she hadn't smelled anything. That hadn't reassured her, though. How much of a gas leak was needed? How did a person go about causing a gas leak? The stove wasn't on—what else should she check?

Fortunately, Leese's wife, Catalina, along with their two dogs, was visiting Yvette. Leese hadn't wanted her to be anywhere near possible trouble.

She and Brand heard the scuffle outside, the sounds of thuds and grunts and…pain.

Shortly afterward, Miles had called them out.

Did Brand resent having to babysit her while the others…

engaged? Maybe. He'd gotten involved, only briefly, before returning to her side.

When Brand sat beside her on the bumper, Fallon leaned
against him, seeking and offering comfort.

Sirens sounded in the distance, and shortly there were both
police and firefighters on-site. Officers handcuffed the two battered thugs and dragged them away.

Miles, flexing his knuckles, came to stand before her. "You
okay?"

"Yes."

Leese stepped up next, his hands still fisted. He looked to
be in a killing mood but he said calmly, "Here comes Justice."

Heart leaping, she twisted around to see the car haphazardly
parked. Before the engine had died, Justice jumped out.

Fallon said, "Excuse me," and then ran to him.

Behind her, she heard Miles laugh.

Laugh! How could any of them—

Justice caught her up in his arms and held her tight. One
hand on the back of her head pressed her to his shoulder, the
other low on her spine supported her since her feet were off the
ground. He didn't say anything, just tucked his face to her neck
and breathed heavily.

"I'm okay," Fallon whispered, teasing her fingers over his
short-cropped hair, inhaling his hot scent and relishing the
strength in his embrace. "Justice? Let me look at you."

"No."

He sounded choked, and her heart swelled. She squeezed him
tighter and said, "I don't want an apartment."

That loosened his hold enough for him to search her face.
"You don't?"

Damn it, now she felt choked. Shaking her head, she swallowed the stupid tears and whispered brokenly, "I only want
you."

His gaze warmed. "You have me, babe. I promise." He smoothed back her hair. "Tell me you love me."

"I love you so much."

His breathing evened out and he smiled. Then he laughed. Lifting her in his arms, he strode over to the others. "Hell of a night."

Brand cocked his head at Leese and Miles. "Those two had all the fun."

"It *was* fun," Miles said. "I mean, now that everything is okay. Hell of an adrenaline rush."

"So you're really going to do it?" Leese asked. "You're going to join Body Armor?"

"I think so." Before anyone could ask him why, he walked off to talk to an officer.

Fallon rested her head against Justice's shoulder. She didn't need him to hold her, but she liked it. She especially liked that Justice was such a big, buff guy who could do so with ease.

Before long, though, things got too chaotic for cuddling.

It was hours later when they congregated inside Leese's house. Catalina had come home and her two dogs were ecstatic with the company. Fallon sat on the floor in front of Justice, letting the dogs shower her with love.

Catalina was in the kitchen making coffee, whistling as if nothing out of the ordinary had happened. She saw Leese leave the room, go to his wife and hug her from behind.

They had such a wonderful life—a life she wanted, as well.

With Justice.

Behind her, the men talked quietly. Fallon was tired, but she enjoyed listening in on their conversation, learning more about how they thought, how they reacted to everything. Notes of serious reflection interspersed the joking insults and occasional murmurs of disbelief over what had happened.

When Tom and a beautiful woman showed up, Fallon could only stare in wonder.

Justice leaned down to say, "My boss, Sahara Silver. She owns the agency." Then he warned, "Prepare to be amazed."

And amazed she was.

Exhaustion and frustration weighed on Tom, but Sahara looked as if she'd stepped into a party—polished, fresh and energetic. Fallon knew she'd been at the warehouse during the entire confrontation, that she'd just spent hours talking to police and high-level contacts, ensuring that the brothers wouldn't be able to buy their way out of legal consequences, but looking at her, no one would know it.

Smiling, her stylish high heels dangling from the fingers of one hand—Sahara's only concession to the long, troubled night—she said, "I already talked with Senator Loy, and the prosecutor, of course. The Arnolds will not wiggle free this time. And, Tom, you were beautiful. So brave, so selfless. Please know that you'll be rewarded. I have friends at the SBC—that's the acronym, yes, for the Supreme Battle Challenge? Anyway, I've praised you and they're thrilled. You'll get great coverage from this. Who doesn't want to see a homegrown hero compete? I already feel sorry for your challenger."

As if he'd been listening to similar plans for a while, Tom's dazed but exhausted expression never changed.

Still talking nonstop, Sahara breezed in behind a dragging Tom—but drew to a halt when she spotted Brand. She drew a shaky breath and murmured, "Well, well. What have we here?"

"Hello, Sahara."

"Mr. Berry, what a pleasant surprise to see you again."

Fallon swiveled to see Brand, who only smiled lazily.

The rest of the men stared first at Sahara, then their friend and then each other.

When Fallon's gaze met Justice's, he only raised his brows, slowly smiled, and hauled her up to sit in his lap. "Tom will be okay," he whispered into her ear. "Sahara will see to it."

They drank coffee and ate some supposedly healthy treats that

Leese had made. Catalina confided that Leese was an organized, neat-freak health nut, but in the very nicest ways. To Fallon, it sounded like bragging.

It was almost morning before Justice and Fallon headed home…to his house. They didn't speak much, but once inside, he led her straight to the bedroom.

"Tired?" he asked.

Seeing that look in his eyes, she nodded, but said, "Never too tired for that, though." Never too tired for him.

He gave her a crooked grin, and as he stripped, he said, "Tell me again."

"I love you."

"I'm never going to get tired of hearing it."

Justice sat with Fallon and her parents at his modest dining room table, using his inexpensive dishware and his stainless-steel utensils. Together, he and Fallon had prepared baked chicken, potatoes and carrots. Candles burned in the middle of the table.

He felt damned domestic—and liked it.

After finishing off seconds, Clayton Wade looked stiff and was mostly silent.

Rebecca, bless her heart, praised everything. His house, his yard, his food…

Suddenly Clayton laid his fork beside his plate and looked up. "You have good security here?"

An odd, out-of-the-blue question, but Justice didn't hesitate. "Yes, sir." He detailed the measures taken, doing what he could to reassure the man.

"I like what you did with my system. You're knowledgeable about it?"

Justice scratched his forehead, and realized that he was. Huh. So Leese was good with research, and he was good with security systems. "Yes, sir."

Clayton nodded, and drank more of his wine.

Fallon touched Justice's hand, then said, "I've been trying to look at apartments."

Rebecca's head snapped up.

Clayton froze. "Trying?"

"It seems every time we made plans, something came up."

Rebecca shared a knowing look with Justice, then smiled.

Justice kept silent.

"Apartments where?" Clayton asked.

"It doesn't matter now." Justice laced his fingers with hers. "She's going to move in with me."

Expression neutral, Clayton repeated, "Move in with…"

"Me." Justice held his gaze. Damn, this was awkward. It'd be a whole lot easier to say she'd be his wife. Her parents were old-fashioned, protective beyond belief, and Fallon was their only child. But what Fallon wanted mattered most to him. "I love her. I'll take good care of her."

Rebecca tipped her head to one side. "You're going to live together?"

"A first step, ma'am." Hopefully with a second step to follow, but Justice wanted to give Fallon the time she needed just to be, as she often put it, free. "You know Fallon has lived a reserved life."

"But no more," Fallon said.

"She deserves a long courtship." Justice grinned, knowing he'd marry her tomorrow, but… "She deserves romance. She deserves to be chased for a while."

Fallon fought a smile. "I do." Then she flushed. "I mean—"

Rebecca laughed.

Clayton shot his wife a quelling frown before turning his serious gaze on Justice. "Rebecca is correct. You have a very nice home. You may not know this, but Rebecca grew up in a house this size." His voice lowered, going thoughtful, then he covered his wife's hand with his own. "Her father was a welder and her mother a bus driver. My parents, second-generation hoteliers, were resistant to our marriage. None of it mattered to me, though, and none of it mattered to Rebecca."

With clear exasperation, Fallon said, "None of *what*, Dad? Those are both good jobs. Besides, it's not like Justice is a slug who refuses to hold a job. He's not into hotels, but he *is* a well-known, accomplished sports figure, and now he's a highly valued bodyguard at one of the most reputable, prestigious agencies. He's the most dedicated, motivated, sweet—"

With a one-arm hug and a quick laugh, Justice kept her from extolling him straight into sainthood. "I think your dad was giving his approval, honey."

"I was," Clayton assured him, "and I hope I didn't insult you."

"I'm not blind, sir. There's a huge difference in what I can offer her and what she has in store from you."

"Financially," Clayton said. "But then, Fallon has never been all that concerned with luxury."

"And there are other things," Rebecca added, "that are far more important."

Fallon beamed at them.

Giving them their due, Justice said, "You raised a wonderful daughter. She's beautiful inside and out."

Rebecca sighed. "He's also very romantic, Fallon. I like him a lot."

The next part, Justice knew, would be tricky. He hoped he didn't trip himself up. "Speaking of finances, I want you to know that I'm not a gold digger. If you and Rebecca were..." He used the same example Clayton had. "Well, a welder and a bus driver, it'd be all the same to me."

"Still," Clayton said, "you stand to inherit—"

"No, sir." Justice needed them to know that money didn't influence him. "I make my own way."

Clayton studied him. "Well, we can certainly discuss this further in the future."

Once we marry. That's what her dad was thinking, no doubt

expecting. Justice said only, "The future is up to Fallon. But I'm here for the long haul."

Justice didn't mean to pressure her, but her parents' gazes shifted to pin her with their undivided attention.

She flushed before giving in to a laugh. "I'm here for the long haul, too, but I'm having so much fun right now, I don't want to spend time planning the future. I'd rather just enjoy the present for a while."

He could work with that, Justice decided. "Whatever you want, honey."

She fiddled with her napkin, glanced at him then lifted her chin. "Justice will no longer be my bodyguard. It's not necessary and of course he'll be taking other assignments. I was thinking of getting more involved in my own work."

"Travel?" Clayton asked.

"Yes, eventually. If that's okay?"

While her parents assured her they'd love it, Justice grinned, so damned proud of her.

"I think Justice and I need to have a normal life for a while. Without any threats, with him doing his own work and me doing mine."

Rebecca said, "I see. Yes."

Clayton slowly nodded. "You want some normalcy. A regular routine."

"I do." She rolled her eyes and laughed. "I'm forever saying that."

"Like you're answering a proposal." Justice gave her a crooked grin. "I like hearing it."

Fallon drew a deep breath, then twisted to face him. "What would you think about planning a wedding, oh, a year or so from now?"

A rush of emotion filled his chest until Justice could barely catch his breath. Fallon glowed with confidence, rightfully so, and he loved it. He loved her. Now and forever.

She'll marry me in a year.

He accepted that she didn't put it off out of indecision, but because they were already so content.

Together.

He ignored her parents and, smiling, leaned forward to brush his mouth over hers. "I think I have a year to show you that it's only going to get better."

Her palm settled against his jaw and she said sweetly, "With you, Justice, I never had a doubt."

To the sounds of her mother's happy excitement and her father's chuckles of amusement, Justice stood. "Guess it's time for dessert."

His life had taken a one-eighty from that of a bachelor fighter. And as he'd said, with Fallon, it was only going to get better.

★ ★ ★ ★ ★